"Racial Matters"

"Racial Matters"

The FBI's Secret File on Black America, 1960–1972

Kenneth O'Reilly

THE FREE PRESS

New York   London   Toronto   Sydney   Tokyo   Singapore

The Free Press
A Division of Simon & Schuster Inc.
1230 Avenue of the Americas
New York, N.Y. 10020

First Free Press Paperback Edition 1991

Printed in the United States of America

printing number

    5 6 7 8 9 10

Library of Congress Cataloging-in-Publication Data
O'Reilly, Kenneth.
  Racial matters: the FBI's secret file on Black America, 1960-1972/
  Kenneth O'Reilly.
    p. cm.
  Bibliography; p.
  Includes index.
  ISBN 0-02-923682-7:
  1. Afro-Americans—Civil rights. 2. United States. Federal Bureau
of Investigation—History—20th Century. 3. Civil rights
movements—United States—History—20th century. 4. United
States—Politics and government—1961-1963. 5. United States—
Politics and government—1963-1969. 6. United States—Race
relations. I. Title.
E185.615.074 1989   89-1554
973'.0496073-dc19   CIP

The author is grateful to Broadside Press for permission
to quote from James A. Emanuel, "Panther Man,"
copyright 1970 by James A. Emanuel.

for
Eamon and Teddy
and Sam

Contents

INTRODUCTION

=======◇◇◇=======

Civil Rights, Civil Liberties

S he was a child of Sunflower County, Mississippi, the youngest of twenty children born to two delta sharecroppers, and she had lived all forty-five of her years in a world of white over black. A large woman with soft eyes and a limp in her walk from a bout with polio, she never dreamed Jim Crow could be knocked down until 1962 when three voter registration workers from the Student Nonviolent Coordinating Committee (SNCC— pronounced "snick") changed her sense of the possible. "When they asked for those to raise their hands who'd go down to the courthouse the next day, I raised mine. Had it up as high as I could get it," she said, describing her decision in the spirit of the Exodus. "Headin' your flock out of the chains and fetters of Egypt—taken' them yourself to register—tomorra—in Indianola." A lifelong fear of the white men who ran Sunflower County disappeared that day. "The only thing they could do to me was kill me," she reasoned, "and it seemed like they'd been trying to do that a little bit at a time ever since I could remember." During the months ahead, they would certainly try.

Her name was Fanny Lou Hamer and her first encounter with J. Edgar Hoover's Federal Bureau of Investigation occurred after she attempted to place her name on the voter rolls at the courthouse. Arrested by county police and evicted from a shack on a cotton plantation that had been her home for eighteen years, she fled the state when gunmen fired shots into the Ruleville house of the friend who had put her up. FBI agents told her they could do nothing about the arrest, the eviction, or the shooting. Gathering the courage that led her to Indianola in the first place, Hamer came home to Mississippi after a few weeks to become one of the most beloved movement leaders in the

1

state. She had a rousing singing voice, and few civil rights workers easily forgot the sight of her swaying, crying, and shouting
out the verses of "We Shall Overcome," the movement "anthem." "I'm going to stay in Mississippi," she announced, once
and for all, "and if they shoot me down, I'll be buried here."

Fanny Hamer's second encounter with the FBI occurred on
the second Sunday in June 1963, after she stepped off a bus in
Winona, Mississippi. Hamer and five companions were returning from a voter registration workshop in nearby South Carolina when their bus pulled in for a rest stop. June Johnson and
James West went to the lunch counter to sit with Annell Ponder.
Euvester Simpson and Rosie Mary Freeman went to the whites-
only restroom. What might have been an uneventful encounter—
perhaps ending with a white waitress mumbling about how she
"can't take no more" and white customers mumbling about Negroes using the wrong toilets—ended disastrously. Winona Police Chief Thomas Herod ordered the five blacks out and arrested them on the parking lot when Ponder began jotting down
the license plate number of his cruiser. "Get that one, too," the
chief told Montgomery County Sheriff Earl W. Patridge, after
Hamer left the bus to see if she could help.

The officers brutalized four members of the group at the
Montgomery County jail. They botched the first beating. June
Johnson, a fourteen-year-old girl in a pink dress, bled profusely.
So they used blackjacks on the others, interrogating Ponder
about her interest in the license plate while batting her head and
shoulders. "They wanted to know who we would make a report
to. I told him the federal government. They said: 'Who do you
mean, Bobby Kennedy?'" They forced two black prisoners to
pound Hamer, an assault that permanently damaged a kidney
and an eye. A few hours later, Chief Herod and his men locked
up a seventh voter registration worker, Lawrence Guyot, who
had come to the jail to see about charges and bail. Standing
Guyot up against a cell wall, they pummeled him with fists and
gun barrels. "They beat him just as bad as they did me," Hamer
said. "The only difference was they taken paper and tried to
burn his private off," and then turned him over to the private
sector for a terror-filled automobile ride and another beating in
the hills surrounding the town. Things ended as they had begun,
with blood.

Everyone knew the FBI would investigate the Winona incident
to determine whether the police had violated the civil rights of

Hamer and her companions. After returning Guyot to the jail, one of the officers flashed a phony federal badge and asked him to "tell me all about what happened." When four or five real FBI agents showed up it appeared to Ponder that "they were cooperating with the chief, in a way. . . . I gave them a statement and they wrote it down," she remembered. "[But] they didn't ask me to sign it." "I just don't *trust* 'em, you know?," Hamer said, after her jailhouse interview with the FBI. "He say, 'Well, we would like to talk to you,' and I said, 'Well, I just can't do it.' You see, I didn't know whether if I said what had happened to me then he could tell the jailer, and I just couldn't do it—I just *couldn't!* But we sho' wanted—if we could have just seen anybody . . . I reckon now God is the only refuge we have because there wasn't nobody there from the Justice Department, nobody there to say *nuthin'*—just the Negro out by theirself."[1]

For Fanny Hamer, the FBI was too intimidating, too friendly with the other side, and above all too late. She found herself alone in her cell, alone with her God, even with the FBI there to interview her and to write a report for the Justice Department. The Bureau's agents had been with Hamer in a more timely manner, though, on the day in Sunflower County when she joined SNCC as a field secretary. They were with her a year later in Atlantic City, New Jersey, too, when she served as vice-chair of the Mississippi Freedom Democratic party and told the Winona story before network television cameras and the credentials committee at the Democratic National Convention. And they were with her when she went to Washington, D.C., at the beginning of the new decade to speak for a national holiday in honor of Dr. Martin Luther King, Jr. Bureau agents filed information about Hamer under the "Racial Matters" caption and sometimes even under the "100" classification, the subversive classification. They followed her not to protect her but to spy on her.[2]

John Lewis, SNCC's chairman in 1963 and later a United States congressman from Georgia (elected in 1986), posed a simple question a few months after the Winona incident: "I want to know—which side is the federal government on?" Lewis's organization had recruited Mrs. Hamer as a nonviolent soldier for a peoples' army engaged in a protracted conflict with the formal racism that ruled in Mississippi and across the South. In fighting that larger war, SNCC activists saw an ambivalence in the United States government's apparent refusal to choose sides in a conflict where right and wrong were clearly marked. Good and evil were easy to see with Hamer on one side and Mississippi segregationists on the other, yet it remained unclear whether the only federal representatives sent to the scene sided with the police or their victims. FBI agents had done nothing of consequence in Indianola and Ruleville, when Hamer was arrested, evicted, and shot at, and as far as she could tell they had done nothing but file a perfunctory report with the Justice Department after her assault in Winona. If the FBI, "the most symbolic example of a federal presence," actually stood against black people, as Hamer's experiences led her to believe, where did the federal government stand? Wasn't "the party of Kennedy," Lewis asked, also the party of Senator James Eastland, the man SNCC called "the massa' of Sunflower County himself"?[3]

The FBI investigation of the Winona incident was typical of its civil rights work. Bureau agents investigated thousands of skirmishes between movement troops and the segregationist resistance, and to describe one of these investigations is to convey a sense of them all. Federal agents stood by, to all appearances allied through their own studied neutrality with the enemies of black people rather than with those who risked their lives to demand justice, dignity, and a fair share of the democracy that white America always seemed to be celebrating. Hamer concluded her story in Atlantic City by "askin' the American people, 'Is *this* the land of the free and the home of the brave?'"[4] That such a thing could happen in the United States was bad enough. It was even worse that federal policemen seemed to encourage such brutalities by their refusal to protect people like Hamer in the first place or pursue justice after the fact.

During the first half of the 1960s the struggle for black equality raged around a "states' rights" ideology and a single basic question: who would protect the constitutional rights of black Americans in the Jim Crow South, where segregation was written into county ordinances and state law, and enforced by sheriffs, Ku Klux Klansmen, and white-collar Klansmen from the Citizens Council? A reluctant federal government assumed the burden, with the Justice Department shouldering most civil rights responsibilities and funneling those responsibilities to one of its parts—the Civil Rights Division. Division lawyers, in turn, considered what sort of legal action was appropriate in any given case. The police officer or Klansman or Citizens Council patriot who enforced segregation with a nightstick or a rope or an eviction notice might be prosecuted under an old federal law from the Reconstruction Era. A southern county might be sued under the modest civil rights legislation of the Dwight D. Eisenhower years (the Civil Rights Acts of 1957 and 1960) for refusing to allow Negroes to vote. To make informed choices about who to prosecute or sue, Civil Rights Division lawyers relied on the part of the Justice Department that gathered evidence and performed investigative work for the Department as a whole—the FBI.

FBI Director J. Edgar Hoover had no desire to be at the center of the struggle for racial equality and justice, but at the center is where he and his agents found themselves—in Winona and in every other dusty southern town and cotton county where that struggle raged. Hoover's objections to his involvement in the civil rights movement centered on questions of law and constitutional tradition. He argued, with some justification, that federal statutes provided little authority for the FBI to act in Winona or anywhere else. Intent on separating questions of law and morality in the age of racism, he confronted the southern legal system without reference to the values underlying that system.[5] The irony is that the director adopted such a view only on matters of civil rights enforcement. In all other areas, he bound up law and morality as tightly as any man. Hoover also argued that the FBI had no constitutional right to usurp the responsibilities of state and local police to maintain law and order. The culpability of Mississippi lawmen in denying Fanny Hamer her civil rights was not the issue. The director did not condone white violence. He simply dismissed it as a local problem.

With the government and the people of the United States uncertain about how to respond to the black struggle in June 1963, Hoover had no difficulty in locating broad constituencies for his position. President John F. Kennedy and Attorney General Robert F. Kennedy respected and sometimes deferred to the director's strict interpretation of federalism, while many whites in the South and across middle America shared the director's belief that "the Constitution . . . does not deal in general with the relationships between one private individual and another." Hoover made that point early on, in 1947. Four years later, Walter White of the National Association for the Advancement of Colored People asked him to protest the refusal of the Stork Club in New York to serve Josephine Baker, the singer and actress, on the grounds that "such discrimination . . . anywhere in the

United States plays directly into the hands of communists and other enemies of democracy." Though once a regular patron of that nightclub, Hoover ordered his agents to ignore White's request, scribbling the following comment. "I don't consider this to be any of my business." A states' righter in 1947 and 1951, he remained one in 1963.[6]

Hoover justified his reluctance to investigate the Winona brutality aggressively by reference to the constraints of existing federal statutes, states' rights principles, and the lack of consensus on the question of whether the nation needed a Second Reconstruction. Caught up in a mass movement determined to close the gap between "the theory and the practice of the republic," he fully mobilized his Bureau only when conducting domestic intelligence investigations. Given the absence of specific federal laws on which to base these investigations, Hoover cited no states' rights principles to justify his policy of monitoring the civil rights movement. Speaking only in terms of the cold war necessity of rooting out communists and other subversives who would manipulate the black struggle for their own ends if left alone, he developed a constituency among states' rights southerners for this investigative mission nonetheless. The director preferred the familiar comforts of dossier collecting to the alien business of civil rights law enforcement, and he had a mandate to follow the trail of the Communist party wherever it led. So the FBI spied on anyone interested in the state of race relations in the United States, including Hamer and her Mississippi Freedom Democratic party, from the first sit-ins and voter registration campaigns to the historic march in Selma, Alabama, that led to the Voting Rights Act of 1965; and the FBI spied on blacks as a potentially dangerous class of activists thereafter, a period that spanned the years of urban riots and Vietnam war protests.

More than Hoover's preference and ability to function as a semiautonomous political entity determined the FBI's investigative priorities. Presidents, attorneys general, and other government officials ratified the Bureau mandate. Decent men, for the most part, they tried to use the FBI's investigative resources within the limits of the conventional theories of federalism that governed race relations at the time. In Winona, for example, they pushed for an FBI investigation and a federal civil rights law indictment of the police officers who beat Hamer and her companions.[7] But they accepted the idea that the specter of communist influence in the civil rights movement justified FBI spying. They were reassured that the director's domestic intelligence resources would provide advance warning of civil rights demonstrations and thereby increase the government's chances of heading off anti–civil rights violence.

The ways in which Hoover explained FBI behavior to the public and to the men in the Justice Department and the White House seemed eminently reasonable. Constrained by law, the Constitution, and public opinion, the director lacked the authority to act decisively against Fanny Hamer's tormentors or other enforcers of white supremacy. If the American people and their representatives in the Congress had not decided to rid their land of Jim Crow, why should the FBI be expected to take the lead in doing so? Hoover saw no great question of right and wrong in the Winona jail, only the question of states' rights. How does the federal government go about protecting Hamer's civil rights without disrupting the federal balance? Exactly where do the rights of minorities end? Exactly where does the power of the majority begin? Defending his surveillances, Hoover said he spied on civil rights workers for their own good, keeping track of communist infiltrators and purging them when possible, and using the data gathered on demonstration plans to construct an informal system of protection. If the law and the Constitution and even public opinion prevented him from protecting civil rights workers directly, the director would improvise and use his domestic intelligence resources to do so indirectly.

Hoover's explanations appeared convincing for two reasons. First, he claimed to have no political agenda. He had spent most of his adult life battling against the twentieth century's great movements of social change, and no greater engine of social change roared through the century than the civil rights movement. Though uniquely positioned to obstruct the movement in the 1960s, Hoover apparently spurned the temptation. He simply claimed to be following orders, doing his job under trying circumstances in a manner that pleased neither side entirely. For every Fanny Hamer or John Lewis who criticized the Bureau for standing with the white southern resistance, a segregationist could be found to criticize the Bureau for standing with the integrationists. Second, FBI investigations of specific cases suggest that Hamer and Lewis were wrong. The Winona law enforcement officials ultimately escaped punishment in federal court through no clear fault of the FBI. A case-by-case examination of the FBI record does in fact reveal a bewildering collage, with

Hoover and his men appearing to stand with the movement on one day and with the resistance the next.

To understand the FBI's behavior and the consequences of that behavior, it is less important to look at FBI actions in isolation, or to listen to the apolitical explanations Hoover offered to the public and his ostensible superiors in the government, than to examine the totality of the FBI response to the black struggle for freedom and justice for all. Such an examination raises questions of motivation and agenda that go beyond Hoover's stated reasons for acting as he did, eroding the legal, constitutional, and national security expediencies that purportedly underlay those reasons. An inclusive examination suggests that personal, bureaucratic, political, and ideological choices shaped FBI actions. Regardless of the positive contributions individual FBI agents made to the black struggle, Hoover's perceptions, values, and vision gave rise to a politics which cannot be held legitimate in either a legal or moral sense.

A further examination suggests that the FBI's performance cannot be considered apart from the decisions of responsible federal officials in the White House and the Justice Department. No matter how autonomous it seemed, Hoover's bureaucracy was part of a larger structure, the federal government's executive branch. In the final analysis, then, the story of the FBI and black America is part of the larger history of a government that has been at odds, more often than not over the past two hundred years, with its own nonwhite citizens and its own professed values.

"The shadows disappeared," Don Whitehead wrote, in his authorized, celebratory history, *The FBI Story.* "I found in the FBI story a stirring American adventure," a "struggle to achieve incorruptible enforcement of the law by professionals trained to protect civil rights."[8] Black America's FBI story does not confirm the conclusions of Whitehead's best-seller and the Jimmy Stewart movie inspired by the book. It confirms instead a troubling tale filled with unlikely heroes and villains, and with origins that push back past the days of Kennedys and Kings to the World War I era and the beginnings of Hoover's career as a federal policeman, a time before most of those heroes and villains had even been born.

1

The Negro Question
Origins of a Private War

For better or for worse, the history of the Federal Bureau of Investigation and the history of black America have been linked together almost from the Bureau's beginning in 1908, when Charles J. Bonaparte, nephew of Napoleon III and President Theodore Roosevelt's attorney general, established a "Bureau of Investigation." (The word "Federal" was added in 1935.) The Bureau's decision to avoid protecting civil rights and to spy on blacks were more in reaction to directives from the White House and the Justice Department than results of its own policy. In 1910, during the second year of William Howard Taft's presidency and in response to a series of particularly brutal lynchings, the Department claimed "no authority . . . to protect citizens of African descent in the enjoyment of civil rights generally."[1] In contrast, by 1919, the year J. Edgar Hoover began his association with the Bureau and the seventh year of Woodrow Wilson's presidency, the Department was citing wartime security needs to violate the civil liberties of those same citizens. Expected by the Wilson administration to confine itself to gathering political intelligence on the "Negro Question," the Bureau paid little attention to day-to-day violations of federal civil rights laws—let alone to the episodic blood rites committed by Ku Klux Klansmen and other white supremacists to enforce deference and submission.

By the time John F. Kennedy entered the White House in 1961, Hoover had located his own grievances against black people in the four decades since the World War I era, when he first brushed against their demand for justice and equality. The director had learned a great deal about racial matters since 1919, but little about racial justice. He had learned that the Negro's fight for equality threatened his personal racial preferences and his Bureau's institutional interests and political objectives. He had learned that blacks who struggled to make the nation live up to its democratic ideals represented a threat to his America that one day might rival the threat posed by his dreaded communists; and he had learned that nearly every administration from Wilson to Eisenhower condoned his all-embracing definitions of subversion. But he had also learned that there was no American consensus on how to deal with the gathering struggle for black equality. So after a fiery start in 1919, he rarely acted forcefully on his feelings about the Negro Question. He proceeded cautiously, nurturing his grievances and studying the battleground, and, like Machiavelli's prince, preparing for war in times of peace.

It would have been surprising if Hoover had reacted otherwise. The director, born in 1895, and his FBI, born in 1908, both grew up at a time when racism was respectable. Jim Crow came to Hoover's native Washington, D.C., in 1900, and by 1920 segregation had visited all public accommodations save the buses and trolleys, the libraries, and the grandstands at Griffith Stadium. Hoover lived in a white city and an even whiter neighborhood, Seward Square, where restrictive housing covenants insulated his family and the larger community of middle-class civil servants. Other than domestic servants, like the maid who came to help Hoover's mother, Annie, with the cooking and cleaning, no Negroes came to Seward Square. In young Edgar's world, a white family's employment of a colored servant constituted a visible sign of gentility, even if that servant worked for an hourly wage. Hoover's school, Central High, the District's oldest, most prestigious public school, and, of course, all-white, represented another confirmation of status. From Central High, Hoover moved on to a position at the Library of Congress while studying law at George Washington University's night school. In the summer of 1917 he joined the Justice Department, where he kept alive the vision of the white, Christian America he grew up with, until he died on the job, fifty-five years later.[2]

While segregation swept over Hoover's city and other southern towns, the judicial and executive branches of the federal government were dispensing what the historian of Jim Crow, C. Vann Woodward, called "permissions-to-hate." In *Plessy v. Ferguson* (1896), the Supreme Court held separate-but-equal facilities to be good enough for the black man. The Republican party's Reconstruction Era crusade to make all men free had died twenty years before William McKinley's new crusade to project American rule over the eight million people in the Caribbean and the Pacific recently liberated from the Spanish empire. Theodore Roosevelt offered blacks at home no economic or civil reforms, only gestures—most notably inviting Booker T. Washington to dine at the White House. William Howard Taft offered blacks even less. Woodrow Wilson, a Democrat and a native southerner who told "darky" stories to his cabinet, brought the separate-but-equal doctrine of the *Plessy* decision to the federal bureaucracy. What Woodward called "the liberal retreat on the race issue" became a self-imposed rout under the missionary president. Wilson promoted segregation as an enlightened and scientific response to racial divisions, a progressive solution, his postmaster general said, for the good of "the negro and the Service." While the nation prepared to fight a war to make the world safe for democracy, workmen in the capital tacked up "White Only" or "Colored" signs over every federal toilet.[3]

Within the culture at large, respectable racism flourished. The man in the street hummed such popular turn-of-the-century tunes as "If the Man in the Moon Were a Coon," while students at Yale and Columbia listened to their professors lecture on the black man's incorrigible morals. With reputable periodicals pondering the fate of the "varied assortment of inferior races" recently acquired from Spain, the *Atlantic Monthly* posed a rhetorical question. "If the stronger and cleverer race is free to impose its will upon 'new-caught, sullen peoples' on the other side of the globe, why not in South Carolina and Mississippi?" And the *Saturday Evening Post* offered its pages to Thomas Dixon, author of *The Clansman* and other racist tracts, "orgies of hatred" whose "Negro characters, when they were not clowns, all seemed to be either contemplating or swiftly fleeing after the rape of a white woman." In 1915 Dixon's novel inspired D. W. Griffith's *Birth of a Nation*, the first great motion-picture extravaganza and a film that portrayed deceitful, lustful, and dangerous blacks laying seige to a prostrate white South during Reconstruction times. "History written in lightning," President Wilson said, after a private screening of this eulogy to the Ku Klux Klan at the White House.[4]

FBI surveillance activities aimed at black Americans began in this climate of respectable racism two years after Griffith's film appeared and immediately after Congress declared war on Germany. At first, Bureau agents visited black communities to assess attitudes toward the draft and to investigate rumors of subversion. The controversy over the infamous Zimmermann telegram, in which Germany had offered to help Mexico regain territory lost seventy years before in the Mexican-American war, led to a particularly outrageous rumor of German agents organizing an army of Mexicans and black Americans to fight a rearguard action in the Southwest on Kaiser Wilhelm's behalf. In addition to the cultural racism of the time, the FBI's behavior in investigating such rumors reflected the widespread wartime belief that traitors, spies, and saboteurs had provoked the race riots that shook some two dozen cities in 1917 and the "Red summer" of 1919. The epic Red scare of the immediate postwar years included a black scare.[5]

Concluding that second-class citizens would have second-class loyalty, the FBI dismissed every black dissident as subversive, every criticism of American policy as un-American. While Woodrow Wilson defended national self-determination at the Versailles peace conference, his State Department solicited intelligence reports from the Bureau on any black American who complained about riots and lynchings. While the president promised to bring democracy to the world, black activists reminded him that he had not yet brought democracy to blacks in his own country or to the not-very-white peoples who lived in America's overseas possessions. When Monroe Trotter, editor of the *Boston Guardian* and head of the all-black National Equal Rights League, pressed Senator Henry Cabot Lodge (R., Mass.) to read the Thirteenth, Fourteenth, and Fifteenth Amendments of the U.S. Constitution into the Treaty of Versailles, Hoover, already adept at making himself useful to the incumbent administration, called upon the Bureau to monitor "Negro leaders" and their "political stand . . . toward the peace treaty and the league of nations."[6]

By the fall of 1919 the FBI had institutionalized surveillance programs aimed at blacks. Bureau field offices across the country covered "the Negro Question" systematically, recruiting "reliable Negroes" as informants in the "various negro lodges and associations" and having them report on "negro ministers" and anyone else who preached "social equality" and "equal rights." The informants infiltrated every racial advancement and black nationalist group, from the moderate National Association for the Advancement of Colored People to the immoderate African Blood Brotherhood, hoping to detect "ultra radical activities" or even "liberal activities" in the "race riots, etc." The field agents who controlled the informants organized the mass of data collected and forwarded highlights covering "the entire field of so called 'Liberalism'" to the Justice Department's General Intelligence Division (GID), then headed by the twenty-four-year-old Hoover.[7]

From his study of liberalism and radicalism and his previous experience with the Department's Alien Enemy Bureau, Hoover concluded that "the Reds have done a vast amount of evil damage by carrying doctrines of race revolt and the poison of Bolshevism to the Negroes." Black Americans, he suspected, were "seeing Red," snuggling up to "the Bolsheviki" and even the one-big-union doctrines of Bill Haywood and the Industrial Workers of the World. Along with the "contemptible and wicked deeds" of Reds and Wobblies among the subversively inclined colored people, Hoover emphasized Thomas Dixon's theme—namely, the threat oversexed black men posed to white women. The GID chief located the "direct cause" of the riot that visited Washington in "the numerous assaults committed by Negroes upon white women."[8]

The most ambitious of the thousands of FBI/GID investigations of the Negro Question in these early years targeted Marcus Garvey, the Jamaican-born founder of the Universal Negro Improvement Association (UNIA), arguably one of the twentieth century's most important black American leaders. Concluding that Garvey was "the foremost radical among his race," Hoover decided, "once and for all," to "put" him "where he can peruse his past activities behind the four walls of the Atlanta clime"— that is, behind the walls of the federal penitentiary in Atlanta. In his search for an appropriate crime, Hoover hired four black men to work the case, and he assigned one of those men, James W. Jones ("undercover agent '800'"), to infiltrate the UNIA and shadow Garvey in Harlem. Among other strategies, Hoover tried to prove Garvey was an operative of the British and Canadian governments. He even pursued a "white slavery" case—a fa-

vored approach that may have reflected his own sexual anxieties. The White Slave Traffic Act, also known as the Mann Act,
made it a federal crime to transport a woman across a state line
for immoral purposes. Finally, in 1923, Hoover secured an indictment against Garvey on a charge of using the mails to defraud in the course of raising money for his Black Star Steam-
ship Line. A federal court found Garvey guilty, and he served
nearly two years of a five-year prison sentence before President
Calvin Coolidge pardoned him in 1927—and ordered his depor-
tation as an undesirable alien.[9]

Hoover attacked Garvey because of the black leader's all-
around "pro-negroism," and Garvey's "doctrine of the negro for
the negro"—not because Hoover considered him a Wobbly or a
communist or a White Slaver or a British agent or even because
he used the Post Office to cheat "many old Negroes" out of their
hard-earned money, as then FBI Director William J. Burns
claimed. Burns said Garvey was "the most prominent Negro agitator in the world today and we have been 'on' him." A magnetic
black leader who rejected the accommodationist ideas of "the
conservative element" had to be watched closely and brought
down if possible, so Hoover's GID, along with Burns's FBI, destroyed "the Negro Moses."[10]

While pursuing Marcus Garvey, the FBI and the GID launched
a major investigation of "the colored press." Hoover's disap-
proval here centered on "a well-concerted movement" among
black newspaper and magazine editors to subvert "the established rule of law and order" by promoting "defiantly assertive"
ideas about "the Negro's fitness for self-government," "race consciousness," interest in "sex equality" (miscegenation), and hostility "to the white race." In a few cases, claimed the GID director, the black press even threatened "retaliatory measures in
connection with lynching." The FBI's agents considered the editors of the monthly *Messenger*, the young socialists Chandler
Owen and A. Philip Randolph, especially bothersome; they also
had problems with the editors of the "better-behaved" publications—among others, W. E. B. Du Bois of the NAACP's *Crisis*.
Hoover wanted "something . . . done" to black journalists on the
grounds that their comments had incited "the negro elements of
this country to riot and to the committing of outrages of all
sorts." Under the name of law and order, Hoover proposed the
repression of any black dissident who challenged second-class
citizenship.[11]

By focusing on subversion, broadly defined (race riots, miscegenation, and all black political activity), the FBI barely had time for civil rights investigations. Prior to the 1930s, the only type of civil rights case where the FBI formally recognized federal jurisdiction involved involuntary servitude. Local law enforcement officers and prison officials in many southern states tolerated peonage—the practice of holding persons in servitude or partial slavery to work off a debt. In some instances, state laws permitted employers to pay a prisoner's fine in return for a contract forcing the prisoner to work out a debt. The FBI opened its most spectacular peonage case in 1921 against a Georgia farmer, John S. Williams, who had been buying black prisoners from state and county road gangs and jails for years. Upon learning of the Bureau's interest, a panicked Williams eliminated as many potential prosecution witnesses as possible—killing ten or twelve of his "slaves." Williams's brutality "so aroused [public sentiment] against these practices," *FBI Story* author Don Whitehead concluded, "that peonage became a charge rarely heard in courts of law." Offered as proof that the FBI had destroyed peonage, Whitehead's point of fact actually represented a tacit admission that the FBI had decided to avoid peonage investigations.[12]

Having begun a review of such cases in the summer of 1922, about a year after his appointment as an assistant FBI director, Hoover discovered that the numbers did not add up. The Atlanta office investigated 115 peonage violations under federal law in 1921–1922, an effort that led to a single conviction. (The state of Georgia tried Williams on murder charges.) Hoover did not like to lose cases. Always the good bureaucrat, he wanted his agency to look successful and to use its time as effectively as possible. He concluded that the peonage conviction rate was so low because "the standing of a colored person, as a witness, against a white man, does not amount to a great deal, in this section of the country," as Lewis J. Baley, then head of the Atlanta office, put it. Later, after he became director of the FBI, Hoover wrote what Baley had to say into the field agents' bible, the *Manual of Instruction*, along with a comment that "the type of person usually held a peon" was not "particularly intelligent," making it necessary to secure corroborating testimony from "neighboring farmers, or planters." But he had nothing to say about his colleague's suggestion to pursue all peonage cases anyway on the grounds that even unsuccessful prosecution would deter those persons who violated federal peonage statutes. In contrast to Baley, Hoover mixed legitimate bureaucratic concerns with an illegitimate assumption that the Negro was not worth protecting.[13]

The Ku Klux Klan also attracted the FBI's attention during these years, and as in the peonage investigations, Hoover called attention to a single heroic case to hide a larger pattern of neglect. The FBI began its probe in September 1922, when Louisiana Governor John M. Parker requested federal assistance to break the Klan's stranglehold on state political and legal institutions. President Warren G. Harding ordered the Justice Department to investigate on the condition that the state "handle any prosecutions," a decision that Hoover would point to in the years to come to justify the states' rights attitudes that increasingly dominated his approach to civil rights work. Over the next few weeks undercover FBI agents gathered evidence linking the Louisiana Klan to a series of murders and other crimes, but Klan-dominated grand juries refused to indict. Rather than give up, Hoover turned to the handiest federal law, the Mann Act, and had his agents examine the sexual habits of Klan leaders. Eventually, in Houston, Texas, the Justice Department prosecuted Imperial Kleagle Edward Y. Clark and several other officers on white slavery charges. "The red faces which occurred at that time as a result of those convictions soon ended the Klan in the South," Hoover said, in a wildly exaggerated statement about his accomplishment. Though the Ku Klux Klan continued to function, four decades would pass before the director again sent his agents into battle against Klansmen, and to announce, once more, that his Bureau had destroyed their organization.[14]

While cases involving civil rights issues remained consistently rare throughout the New Era of Warren Harding, Calvin Coolidge, and Herbert Hoover, FBI surveillance responsibilities changed dramatically. With Bureau agents implicated in the Teapot Dome scandals (they had been caught breaking into the offices and tapping the telephones of congressmen investigating the Justice Department's role in the Harding administration corruption), the Coolidge administration targeted the FBI for reform. In March 1924 the president fired Attorney General Harry M. Daugherty, replacing him with Harlan Fiske Stone, former dean of Columbia Law School. Stone then fired William J. Burns as director of the FBI and appointed Hoover acting director, dissolved the Red-hunting GID, and ordered the Bureau to confine its investigations to violations of federal law. Technically, then, Stone had abolished the apparatus for the FBI's original mission—domestic political surveillance.[15]

Hoover began to transform the FBI from an agency riddled with corruption and rocked by scandal into an efficient and respected police agency by imposing strict professional standards on the agent corps. He weeded out the political hacks and ex-convicts scattered in Bureau offices from coast to coast and required new agents to hold a college degree—preferably in law or accounting. Perhaps for reasons of race (there is no evidence of political or personal corruption), the new director also weeded out all but two of the handful of black agents employed by the Bureau.[16] By the early 1930s, however, Hoover may have realized that the days of respectable racism had passed. He reprimanded Clyde Tolson, one of his few real friends, for informing a black applicant that "colored messengers" need not apply. Tolson went on to hire a black man, James E. Crawford, who worked out of his office for a few months as a messenger before becoming his chauffeur. When Hoover's own black chauffeur died, Crawford began to drive the director's bulletproof Pierce Arrow. Hoover had room in his car for a black, but no room in his agent corps. There would never be more than a token number of full-fledged black agents in the FBI until after the director's death.[17]

Hoover had no intention of complying fully with Harlan Stone's restrictions on Bureau activities. With regard to the domestic political surveillance mission, he counseled patience, advising Attorney General Stone on November 5, 1924, less than two months before his permanent appointment as director: "Some of these [Bureau] offices have spent considerable time upon investigation of radical matters and seem to be at a loss now as to how to curtail the same." Though sharply curtailed, Negro Question investigations continued, with the director sending reports on the NAACP and the separatist Moorish Science Temple of America to the Herbert Hoover White House. The most extensive of the reformed FBI's Negro Question investigations focused on nine black Alabama teenagers, the so-called Scottsboro boys, sentenced to death for the alleged rape of two white women. The Communist party was active in the Scottsboro boys' legal defense and the propaganda battle that dragged on throughout the 1930s, and Hoover viewed this involvement as a particularly ominous sign. The party represented the single most dangerous subversive force in the nation, and its proposed alliance with the black cause raised the specter of thirteen million colored people willing to follow communist leadership. Though there were few black communists in the United States, Hoover's upbringing, prejudices, and political assumptions led him to question the loyalty of an entire race.[18]

The director's focus on the communist aspects of the Scottsboro case proved to be a harbinger of things to come. More troubled by Communist party activities than Herbert Hoover, President Franklin D. Roosevelt encouraged the FBI, as part of a broad federal investigation of "subversive activities," to gather intelligence on radical efforts to influence black Americans. In 1934, with Hitler in power and a number of boisterous and explicitly racist American fascists active in the United States, Roosevelt ordered Hoover to investigate the American Nazi movement. The director concentrated on "anti-racial" and "anti-American" activities. With the president's approval, FBI responsibilities expanded two years later to include communist activities, a development that led to a rapid reconstruction of the Negro Question surveillance machine. Though Roosevelt had no knowledge of Hoover's agenda on matters of race, he would raise no objections upon discovering the director's expansive notions of black subversion.[19]

Hoover had his agents collect information under a special "Negroes" category as part of their regular investigations of domestic communist and native fascist infiltration, and he invariably included their wartime reports on "Negro Organizations" with reports on "Communism" and "German, Italian, and Japanese" fifth columnists.[20] By the early 1940s the director's surveillance of blacks and their "subversive tendencies" had led to the filing of weekly reports with government policymakers on such expansive subjects as "Negro trends." He sent additional reports directly to the White House on individuals and groups involved in civil rights activities, from the Southern Conference for Human Welfare to the March on Washington Movement organized in 1941 and again in 1942 and 1943 by A. Philip Randolph. Randolph's threat of "monster mass meetings" prompted FDR to issue the first presidential directive on race since Reconstruction: Executive Order 8802 establishing a Fair Employment Practice Commission (FEPC) and prohibiting discrimination in defense industries. (The president ignored Randolph's third demand to desegregate the armed forces.) Because Roosevelt had acted even though the Bureau had offered the opinion that communists had infiltrated the March on Washington Movement and that Randolph himself was bluffing in his threats, Hoover may have concluded that the president's FEPC directive represented a surrender to "a pressure group" willing to ante the national interest in pursuit of a special interest. All black activists and any white liberal who contributed to the black demand for justice and equality represented a potential subversive threat.[21]

In the summer of 1942 the FBI launched its most systematic Negro Question investigation, a nationwide survey of "foreign inspired agitation" in "colored areas and colored neighborhoods." Hoover wanted to know "why particular Negroes or groups of Negroes . . . have evidenced sentiments for other 'dark races' (mainly Japanese) or by what forces they . . . adopted in certain instances un-American ideologies." To answer these questions, Bureau agents investigated all black-owned newspapers, recruited paid black informants, and tapped the telephones and bugged the offices of racial advancement groups, ranging from the procommunist National Negro Congress to the anticommunist NAACP. Investigative fallout included a mail cover on Rev. Archibald J. Carey, Jr.'s, Woodlawn African Methodist Episcopal Church in Chicago, where the Congress of Racial Equality had an office; a file check on Olympic track and field champion Jesse Owens (an agent compared the date of Owens's marriage with the birthday of his first child); and the transmittal of derogatory information on the NAACP and the National Urban League to prospective financial contributors. The director emphasized that any leak should be handled "cautiously as we don't want [name deleted] to ever say he refused money to any organization upon the recommendation of the FBI." Any such revelation would embarrass the Bureau.[22]

Hoover expanded his mandate in accord with his own private agenda, not the government's, with a search for foreign-inspired agitation among Negroes that led to Franklin Roosevelt's wife. Acting on complaints that the cause of black unrest in Alabama and other southern states could be traced "to the encouragement given Negroes by Mrs. Roosevelt," who had visited Tuskegee Institute in 1941 and "was entertained throughout her visit by Negroes," the director made a number of inquiries. He seemed especially interested in rumors about black domestic servants who supposedly joined "Eleanor Clubs" at the urging of "a strange white man and a large Negro organizer traveling in an automobile." He was also sympathetic to those "white people who found difficulty in retaining their servants as a result of better opportunities offered by various Defense jobs." Hoover ordered his men to find out if female black domestics were really "demanding their own terms for working" and using the slogan, "A White Woman in the Kitchen by Christmas." With black servants of his own, he clearly took a personal interest.[23]

Bureau agents never found the ideas and deeds of subversion that the director thought they would find, not even in their full-scale probe of communist attempts to incite "the feelings of Negroes" during the 1943 riots in Detroit and other cities. The Bureau uncovered "no information," Hoover informed the White House, to substantiate the charge that "foreign elements" inspired the riots. But the director's agents kept looking and kept tracking "a definite change in the attitude of some negroes." "A number of them," as the head of the Richmond, Virginia, field office mused, "appear to have become more disrespectful, more assertive of their rights and more discontented with their station in life." The net result, in this view, paralleled the "Axis aim . . . to cause the negro to wonder whether he should support our war effort whole-heartedly."[24]

Within the Communist party itself, the FBI noted the efforts of such black comrades as Hosea Hudson of Birmingham to "conduct classes in cooperation with the NATIONAL NEGRO CONGRESS for the purpose of teaching negroes how to become qualified voters." The immediate goal of the party's voter registration drive, the FBI agent in Alabama emphasized, was to insure "the re-election of President ROOSEVELT." The Bureau's domestic intelligence sphere remained as broad as it had been on the day in 1919 when Hoover took command of the General Intelligence Division, encompassing "the entire field of so-called 'Liberalism.'"[25]

The FBI's formal civil rights enforcement responsibilities also changed during the Roosevelt years, but progress on this front came in slow and fitful increments. Though sympathetic to the black plight, the president refused to expend any political capital or to antagonize southern Democrats on the race issue. Civil rights reformers remained optimistic nonetheless, particularly during the first New Deal years, when Roosevelt promoted the growth of the FBI as part of his administration's broader effort to extend federal authority over crime control, once considered the exclusive prerogative of state and local government.[26] Civil rights reformers hoped that the New Deal "war on crime" would extend to lynching and other crimes directed most often at black people. Federal concern, however, extended only to such crimes as bank robbery, racketeering, and kidnapping, inspired by the apparent inability of the states to take decisive action against the gangsters of the early 1930s, who exploited the limited jurisdiction of local police by fleeing across city, county, and state lines. The public's fascination with the depression era's flamboyant criminals and the media's romanticization of their exploits also troubled President Roosevelt and Attorney General Homer S. Cummings.[27]

When Roosevelt and Cummings moved decisively to solve both problems in a typical New Deal manner, Hoover proved to be the chief beneficiary. "The strong arm of Government," relying on innovative legislation and working through the alphabet agencies, would solve the nation's problems. In May 1934 Congress approved six anticrime bills without even taking a record vote; in June three more bills passed. The New Deal crime-control package extended the FBI's criminal jurisdiction and budget, granting its agents full arrest power and authority to carry any kind of firearm. To counter public adulation of the John Dillingers and George "Machine Gun" Kellys, Cummings supplemented the new legislation with an ambitious public relations campaign "to publicize and make the G-Men heroes."[28] By the mid-1930s Hoover had developed into a celebrity and his heroic bureaucracy rivaled baseball in popularity. Even H. L. Mencken, the scourge of "the booboisie," sat in the director's cheering section. "In general, I am strongly in favor of Hoover," he told *Liberty* magazine editor Fulton Oursler. "He has done more to improve police work in this great Republic than any other twenty men."[29]

For many Americans, the war on crime, initiated by Roosevelt and Cummings and led by Hoover, looked to be a smashing success; but it disappointed NAACP executive secretary Walter White and others who had an interest in racial crimes. Before sending the FBI and its director off to investigate the new federal crimes, New Deal liberals had jettisoned an antilynching bill from their legislative package. Presidential adviser Louis Howe thought the lynching bill might "create hostility to [the] other crime bills" among southern congressmen.[30] The NAACP's White urged the Justice Department to use the newly amended federal kidnapping statute (the so-called Lindbergh Law) against members of lynch mobs in such cases as the Claude Neal murder. A mob had abducted Neal in October 1934 from the Brewton, Alabama, jail where local police held him on suspicion of murdering a young white woman; he was taken across the state line to Marianna, Florida, and hanged after ten hours of torture. Although the press advertised the lynching and thousands of spectators watched, the Justice Department refused to send the FBI to investigate. The Department took "the position," White charged, "that the amended Lindbergh law covered kidnapping for the purposes of gain [ransom], but not for purposes of murder."[31]

Though Hoover and Roosevelt ignored lynchings for different reasons, the two men found common ground in the aftermath of Neal's death, with the FBI director following the New Deal president's lead. When a reporter asked if he would recommend passage of a pending lynching bill, FDR ducked the question by requesting time "to check up and see what I did last year. I have forgotten." Roy Wilkins, White's talented young assistant, said Franklin Roosevelt suffered from "expedient cowardice." Later, when radio commentator, newspaper columnist and Bureau confidant Walter Winchell sent the director a letter about the Neal lynching that he had received from a private citizen (a letter that did not mention the victim by name), Hoover told Winchell he had no idea what case the letter writer had in mind. More interested in promoting the FBI crusade against kidnappers who held white people for ransom, the director sent Winchell the following item for publication in his gossip column:

> The colored boys in Washington who are prone to play hunches in the numbers game are reported to have made a killing recently when they combined the numbers in connection with the days of the month on which the G Men apprehended a number of notorious kidnappers. Alvin Karpis was apprehended on May 1st; William Mahan and Harry Campbell . . . on May 7th, and Thomas H. Robinson, Jr., . . . on May 11th. The colored boys combined the numbers 1-7-1 and are said to have cashed in on the hunch.

The nation's chief of police preferred to grin and wink at "colored boys" chasing their numbers rather than confront a black corpse at the end of a rope.[32]

FBI responsibilities to protect the civil rights of black Americans expanded in 1939 when Roosevelt administration priorities began to change. With the coming of World War II, native American fascists and Nazis in Germany were drawing parallels between the Third Reich's policy toward Jews and United States policy toward Negroes. The mobilization for war increased the pressure on the administration to protect black citizens from the effects of a states' rights monopoly on civil rights enforcement. Attorney General Frank Murphy responded to this pressure by establishing a Civil Liberties Unit (renamed the Civil Rights Section two years later) within the Justice Department's Criminal Division. Murphy was a former NAACP board member who considered racial intolerance "the most un-American . . . thing in our life today."[33]

The investigative arm of the Justice Department noticed little change in its work load at first. In 1939 the eight attorneys assigned to the Civil Rights Section asked the FBI to investigate a mere seven of the several thousand complaints submitted by the public alleging civil rights/civil liberties violations. "Only a few" of the complaints submitted actually rested "within the jurisdiction of the Federal Government," reasoned the Section's first chief, Henry A. Schweinhaut, and most of these had to do with the rights of labor, not the rights of black Americans.[34] Section attorneys based their authority to conduct investigations on the National Labor Relations Act (the Wagner Act), the New Deal law that guaranteed employees the right to form unions and bargain collectively, and Sections 241 and 242 of Title 18 of the Federal Criminal Code, remnants of two Reconstruction Era statutes (the Enforcement Act of 1870 and the Civil Rights Act of 1866).[35] The Wagner Act contained no criminal provision, but the Reconstruction statutes were intended to guarantee equality of rights and to control Ku Klux Klan terrorism. Section 241, a felony statute, provided specific criminal sanctions of up to ten years in jail and a $5,000 fine against two or more persons who conspired to deprive "any citizen" of their constitutional rights. Section 242, a misdemeanor statute commonly known as the "color-of-law statute," brought local government officials, including police officers, under the umbrella of federal jurisdiction if they abused the powers of their offices to deny citizens their civil rights.[36]

Because Section 241 required proof of conspiracy and Section 242 required specific intent, the statutes raised hard questions about enforcement strategies and sparked a legal debate that dragged on for decades. As a result, the Justice Department and the White House usually indulged the FBI's reluctance to investigate civil rights cases aggressively. Department attorneys never used Section 241 in the manner that one of Murphy's successors as attorney general, Francis Biddle, recommended—as a "criminal catch-all." Instead, they concluded that "the outbreak of ruffian, vigilante activity, not participated in by public officials, whether directed against reds, nazis, negroes, soap-box speakers, or religious groups," lay outside Section 241. Nevertheless, the government either had to rely on Sections 241 and 242 or withdraw from the protection of civil rights. The Reconstruction Era statutes constituted the only available weapon for the federal government to use in defense of black citizens, and they would provide the basic authority for the FBI's civil rights investigations for the next twenty-five years.[37]

Most of the early cases the FBI investigated under these statutes, whether the civil rights of black people or the civil liberties of labor organizers, involved the politically explosive question of police brutality. The brutality issue made Hoover especially uncomfortable, because Bureau success in solving most federal crimes and piling up conviction statistics depended on the assistance of police officers. It could be awkward for a special agent to ask a policeman for help on a stolen car case in the morning, and then to come back to investigate a brutality complaint against the same officer in the afternoon.

Between 1940 and 1943 Hoover engaged the Justice Department in a struggle to define the proper scope of police brutality investigations. The occasion was a case Civil Rights Section attorneys considered to be a perfect test for Section 242. *United States v. Sutherland* involved an Atlanta policeman who used a hot branding iron to extract a confession from a sixteen-year-old black burglary suspect. On appeal, with the defense attempting to establish the good character of the accused police officer, the Civil Rights Section asked the FBI to determine whether the Atlanta Police Department routinely abused prisoners when questioning them and if the said defendant had a history of such conduct. Given Sutherland's good-character defense, these requests seemed reasonable, and the case itself represented one of the few instances where the Department made a sustained effort to force the FBI to confront civil rights enforcement head on. The FBI balked nonetheless.[38]

"The Atlanta Police Department," Hoover complained to Criminal Division chief O. John Rogge, "is not under investigation in this matter." When Rogge failed to respond, Hoover appealed to Deputy Attorney General Matthew McGuire. The initial investigation, he wrote, had created "considerable ill will" between the Atlanta police and the Bureau. A series of conferences "had resolved this problem," but another confrontation would likely "rupture the friendly relationship which has been established." Siding with Hoover, McGuire offered the following opinion: "It is questionable whether a right not to be beaten is secured by any provision of the Constitution or any Federal Statute. It is secured by State laws. . . . Certainly, it is questionable whether a police officer who hits a prisoner in an effort to make him confess is acting under color of any law, because there is no State law that authorizes him to do so." It would be hard to imagine how any reading of the statute could have been more deferential to the director's desire to keep his bureaucracy focused on crime-busting to the exclusion of any civil rights responsibilities. McGuire had no intention of alienating Hoover, let alone the white southern Democrats who made the Roosevelt coalition whole.[39]

No other responsible Justice Department officials endorsed McGuire's argument, but they did make certain concessions to accommodate the FBI and appease the Democratic party's southern wing. Wendell Berge, Rogge's successor as chief of the Criminal Division, narrowed the scope of police brutality responsibilities by requiring full investigations only in the "quite rare" case where "the victim himself," and not "some friend of the alleged victim," filed charges. Berge also required the Civil Rights Section to take "one added precaution," before calling for a full-field FBI investigation, by first requesting "a preliminary investigation . . . in order to ascertain the criminal record of the victim." Less interested in black rights and questions of law than protecting "law enforcement officers from 'smears'" and speculating about the motives of the people who filed civil rights complaints (and the "shyster[s]" who represented them), Hoover welcomed the new policy because it sanctioned his private agenda. By conceding power of discretion, the directive also sanctioned his bureaucratic agenda because it allowed him to treat police brutality investigations as sideshows. Sutherland, in the meantime, came to trial twice before the U.S. attorney in Atlanta gave up and dropped the case.[40]

While FBI agents continued throughout the war years to do all of the investigative work that was done on police brutality cases and other civil rights matters for the Justice Department, their efforts, as in *Sutherland,* were unenthusiastic and invisible to the world outside the Department.[41] The Bureau's public relations corps rarely bothered to mention civil rights. Crime Records Division agents did help Hoover's principal ghostwriter, former Kansas City newspaperman Courtney Ryley Cooper, with an article on peonage and police use of "third-degree tactics," but the initiative came from Cooper. Released under his name and not the director's, the piece reflected the Bureau's distinctly low-key approach—in contrast to "Gun Crazy" and fifteen other Hoover by-line articles Cooper wrote for *American* magazine celebrating the shoot-em-up gangster wars with Dillinger and cohorts. If the director had been left alone, he would have ignored the problem of police brutality in its entirety.[42]

Hoover and his public relations people could not afford to ignore civil rights during the postwar period. The first indication that the FBI role in the federal enforcement effort would pose larger political and institutional problems for the director came on December 5, 1946—when Harry S. Truman established the President's Committee on Civil Rights "to inquire into and determine whether and in what respect current law-enforcement measures . . . may be strengthened and improved to safeguard the civil rights of the people." Hoover, instinctively recognizing the threat the President's Committee posed to his bureaucracy's power and autonomy, dismissed Truman's decision as a capitulation to communist pressure groups. "Certain elements active in the United States are capitalizing upon every alleged violation of civil rights . . . for the ultimate purpose of launching and perpetuating an organized attack against . . . law enforcement agencies." With their "ulterior and often veiled motives," Hoover reasoned, these "selfish and conniving elements" had geared-up for "a widespread 'smear' campaign."[43]

Expecting to be called before the President's Committee and anticipating that the Committee itself would criticize his bureaucracy's record, Hoover acted to contain any damage. He worked with Committee member Morris L. Ernst, for example, to insure a fair hearing for the FBI position. An American Civil Liberties Union official and longtime adviser to the NAACP, Ernst admired the FBI and generally served Hoover as both an informer on these organizations and a public relations man.[44]

When the summons to testify finally came, the director ordered name checks "setting forth all available information in the Bureau's files" on all sixteen Committee members—with the exception of Ernst. The FBI described Sadie T. Alexander, assistant solicitor for the city of Philadelphia and a board member of the National Urban League, as a "Negress" and "Active Fair Employment"; CIO secretary and International Union of Electrical Workers president James B. Carey as "*Now* Anti-Communist"; Frank P. Graham, president of the University of North Carolina, as "An Innocent"; Rev. Francis J. Haas, former chairman of the Fair Employment Practice Commission, as a "Catholic Bishop. Liberal"; Dorothy Tilly, a lay activist in the Methodist Church, as a "Southern Liberal"; and the moderate Channing H. Tobias of the Phelps-Stokes Fund and the YMCA as a "Negro" and an "ultra liberal." Only Committee chairman Charles E. Wilson received a neutral description: "Pres. General Electric." The others were all dissidents, people who made trouble for the director and his America with their reformist ideas and liberal causes.[45]

Preparation for Hoover's appearance before the President's Committee went beyond name checks and furtive meetings with Morris Ernst. The director constructed the details of the FBI position himself, scribbling out a pile of handwritten notes and outlines. He adopted a direct, if inherently contradictory strategy: take the offensive against the liberal and ultra-liberal members of the President's Committee. He began by calling for enactment of "a clear-cut over-all Civil Rights Statute," but then quickly qualified his support for a tougher law. The federal enforcement effort must operate "against a background of reserved States' rights," he cautioned. Civil rights violations usually involved "private relationships," and such relationships should "remain a matter of interest to the States." The director reportedly expressed the same sentiment, in cruder fashion and in a different context, after attorney Joseph Rauh asked Attorney General Tom Clark to have the Bureau investigate the attempted murder of United Automobile Workers chief Walter Reuther. Rauh remembered Clark's account of Hoover's irrelevant though certainly revealing reply. "Edgar says no. He's not going to send the FBI in every time some nigger woman says she's been raped."[46]

Hoover had no intention of publicly commiting his bureaucracy to either side of a fundamental political debate between states' rights advocates and federal interventionists, and his agenda here was overt and somewhat legitimate. At the same time, he acted to protect his right to determine the FBI's work-load, image, and investigative priorities, and his agenda here was covert and illegitimate. While spying on Orson Welles, Frank Sinatra, and other prominent supporters of antilynching legislation, he complained to Attorney General Clark about all the time his agents wasted on "murders, lynchings and assaults, particularly in the Southern states." To make matters worse, these investigations had created a public relations nightmare. Because "the public judges the efficiency of law enforcement . . . upon the basis of prosecutions," and because the "nebulous" Reconstruction Era statutes precluded successful prosecution (1,570 investigations and only 27 convictions in the past twenty years), Hoover felt aggrieved by the widespread "feeling and be-lief that the Bureau has failed to 'solve' many cases into which it has entered." This "completely ineffective" civil rights en-forcement effort, he said, had the unhappy side effect of en-abling state authorities to "slide out of these cases as soon as the Department and the Bureau enter them."[47]

To solve the problem, Hoover urged Clark to adopt a rigorous policy to prevent the Justice Department's liberal attorneys from "rushing pell-mell into cases in which there is no apparent violation of a Federal Statute." The attorney general agreed that "a large percentage of the investigations initiated in this field prove in the end to be fruitless," but the Department had no choice. "If we do not investigate we are placed in the position of having received a complaint . . . and of having failed to satisfy ourselves that it is or is not such a violation. I know of no way to avoid at least a preliminary inquiry." Besides, "as a matter of policy," the Civil Rights Section had "requested only limited investigations in almost every case."[48]

Hoover's public strategy for containing the President's Com-mittee on Civil Rights emphasized accommodation and not con-frontation. He protested on practical, bureaucratic grounds, not theoretical ones, though privately he saw no harm in the white southern way. Inside the FBI, the director and his men accepted segregation in restaurants in New York, let alone Mississippi, and believed "Negroes go to silly extremes at times to obtain social equality." When they wrote memos back and forth, they usually referred to "alleged" civil rights violations and "alleged" lynchings. One executive, the head of the San Fran-cisco office, even referred to the "alleged persecution of negroes in South Africa." When testifying before the President's Committee, however, Hoover immediately endorsed its basic premise. Racial violence "in free America," he agreed, occasionally compared to "the horrors of Nazism and Fascism." The problem was real enough. It simply was not realistic to expect the FBI to do much—if anything—to solve it. Too many obstacles and too many interests worked to frustrate the Bureau. And with the exception of the director's own agents, nearly everyone was to blame.[49]

When the President's Committee asked why the training programs at the FBI National Academy in Quantico, Virginia, had no room for black police officers, Hoover falsely explained that state and local police departments unilaterally selected all candidates. Organized during the New Deal years to train local police "in the latest crime-fighting techniques," the director thought of the Academy as "the West Point of law enforcement." "You'd seek out . . . the best guys possible," one former agent recalled. "They were going to become key local officials. You took these people to Washington and Quantico, and you inculcated the hell out of them. . . . You really tried to get corruption-proof, young, upwardly mobile officers—you got some awfully good people and then they became your buddies in the field." In every case, the FBI selected the final (all-white) candidates for admission.[50]

Hoover also dodged the President's Committee when asked to explain why he assigned no black FBI agents to civil rights cases. Emphasizing the "hazards of such an assignment" and the predictable "reaction of local juries in the South to testimony by colored Agents," he saw no need to point out that the FBI had only three black agents—his driver, James Crawford, and office retainer, W. Samuel Noisette, and the sixty-eight-year-old veteran of the Marcus Garvey case, James E. Amos.[51]

Of the three, only James Amos even remotely carried out the duties of a regular FBI agent. The son of a Washington policeman who ran a chain gang in Rock Creek Park, Amos's work experience included seven years with the Burns Detective Agency and twelve years service as Theodore Roosevelt's valet. His references on the Bureau employment application in 1921 included Henry Cabot Lodge and Elihu Root, and he received his shield from Hoover himself at the corner of Vermont Avenue and K Street. A reputed master of disguise who could "shadow a suspect for days" and decode "cypher messages," Amos rarely functioned in such a manner after the Garvey case closed. Beginning in the mid-1920s, he contributed to the Bureau by providing common-sense advice. "Whenever F.B.I. agents are stymied on a case and don't know what to do next," wrote Fulton Oursler, then a *Reader's Digest* editor and newspaper columnist, "they have a heart-to-heart talk with the 'Dean.' . . . Jim never fails them because he is an expert in techniques of crime detection." Amos remained with the Bureau's New York office, where he supervised the weapons inventory, until September 1953. He died two months later, on Christmas day.[52]

James Amos received an occasional field assignment. Sam Noisette simply hung up the hats and coats of the people who came in to see the director, and James Crawford did nothing more than wear a chauffeur's uniform, complete with cap, and drive the director around. Crawford received his shield in 1941, after Walter White asked Hoover "about the capacities in which Negroes are employed" and the NAACP launched an investigation of the FBI practice of keeping black college graduates in dead-end jobs while "hiring white girls just out of high school and giving them clerkships." Crawford took his training on the segregated course ("I stayed by myself") at the National Academy, and when he returned from Quantico he went back into his chauffeur's uniform. Noisette also attended the Academy on the segregated course, and upon his return he went back to his desk in the director's outer office. Hoover appointed both men special agents not only in response to NAACP criticisms, but to keep them from being drafted and to exempt them from civil service protections.[53]

Having been placed on the defensive by the NAACP, Hoover proceeded to find fault with the nation's most prominent civil rights group. Earlier, in August 1946, the director had tried to pacify the organization after Walter White complained, once again, about "anti-Negro" FBI agents "messing up" lynching and police brutality cases; Hoover gave him the names and telephone numbers of the special agents in charge of all Bureau field offices. The director hoped such a gesture of implied assistance to the NAACP's mission would "aid us in our relations with the Negro race." In fact, he had been attempting to soften NAACP criticism of the FBI's civil rights enforcement record since the war years, when he wrote a testimonial for White on his twenty-fifth anniversary with the NAACP. But when White kept pestering Hoover to hire more black agents and to investigate civil rights cases more aggressively, the director regretted the "blunder made in committing me to this outfit." White's colleague, NAACP special counsel Thurgood Marshall, was equally annoying. When Marshall complained to Attorney General Tom Clark about the FBI's notably "one-sided" policy of investigating segregationist terror, Hoover drafted a letter for Clark's signature that accused the NAACP of frustrating civil rights progress by refusing to cooperate with the FBI. Marshall saw the document as confirmation of his original point. "I have no faith in either Mr. Hoover or his investigators."[54]

After complaining about the NAACP, Hoover singled out the Justice Department for a share of the blame. When the President's Committee asked why the FBI did not investigate civil rights cases immediately upon receipt of a complaint, the director suggested that the Committee direct the question to Clark. Justice Department policy required the Bureau to refer all civil rights complaints to the Criminal Division of the Department for an opinion before launching an investigation. In practice, this meant that complaints received by FBI field offices not only went to FBI headquarters and then on to the Criminal Division, but back to the nearest United States attorney's office in the field for an opinion and then back again, step by step. This usually resulted in delays of two weeks, a long enough period for evidence to turn stale. The Department initiated that policy, Hoover said, not the FBI. The director did not advise the President's Committee that he absolutely supported this particular policy.[55]

The Justice Department, Hoover added, rarely acted on the information that the FBI did gather. As an example, he cited the case of the recent Democratic party primary in Georgia. The Criminal Division originally ordered an investigation to determine if "a conspiracy" existed "to deprive the negroes of their right to vote." After conducting interviews in ninety Georgia counties, the FBI concluded that gubernatorial candidate Herman Talmadge and "his various colleagues" had removed the names of thousands of black citizens from voter registration roles. But the Department declined to prosecute any of the conspirators.[56]

Besides the reluctant Justice Department and over-eager colored organizations, the director told the President's Committee that public opinion posed an even greater obstacle to law enforcement in civil rights cases. "White citizens . . . opposed to the very principle involved in the investigation" invariably blocked prosecution of civil rights cases in southern states. To document his point, Hoover discussed the July 1946 lynching of Roger Malcolm, his wife, and another black couple by a mob near Monroe, Georgia. One of the agents who worked on the case, Clement L. McGowan, Jr., a Peach State native and Notre Dame graduate, remembered the details forty years later. "The guy was taking them from the county seat, back to the farm where they worked . . . and as they came to this one bridge, they were met by a hooded group." It should have been an open and shut case, but "local white citizens" and "the local sheriff's office failed completely to cooperate," and the state police cooperated only "in a perfunctory fashion." After hearing the testimony of 106 witnesses, the grand jury returned no indictments.[57]

By discussing these problems and by casting blame on virtually everyone from the lowliest NAACP worker to the entire white South, Hoover deflected the criticisms of the President's Committee on Civil Rights. Staff director Robert K. Carr, for one, described Hoover's appearance as "magnificent," telling him that he found it "difficult . . . to restrain my enthusiasm." If Carr's staff privately raked the FBI's "superficial and unintelligent work," their public report avoided such direct language. Noting the lack of specialized training, the Committee maintained that Bureau agents simply lacked the background "to cope with the elusive and difficult aspects of a civil rights case." The Committee itself lacked the political courage to confront the Bureau head-on.[58]

"In view of the public consciousness of the problem and the delicacy of it," Hoover responded immediately to the qualified criticisms of the President's Committee. He ordered additional civil rights training for all new agents, the establishment of "a special training school" for "a selected group" of veteran agents ("so that when one of these cases arises we at least might send in several key men"), and an expansion of the civil rights curriculum for police officers at the National Academy.[59] The only other visible response came from the public relations division. Crime Records helped Fulton Oursler with his articles on Jim Amos and arranged another piece in a black-owned magazine, *Ebony*, on Amos and Sam Noisette.[60] In the meantime, Hoover refused to give the persistent Walter White a straight answer when he again inquired about "Negro FBI operators." Obfuscation still reigned.[61]

A few administrative reforms, publicity releases to the press,

and creative answers to tough questions deflected the threat to
Hoover posed by the President's Committee on Civil Rights. By
placing the burden on Congress "to plot our policy for the protection of civil rights," the Committee actually lessened the "terrific pressure" brought to bear on the Justice Department and
the FBI to take decisive action in the absence of new legislation,
larger appropriations, and more staff. In a sense, the President's
Committee itself had taken Hoover's advice to "the various minority groups"—"get after Congress, not the Department of Justice." By emphasizing the legal and practical barriers to the effective enforcement of civil rights law, the Committee concluded
that the nation needed better legislation from Congress, not a
more dedicated enforcement effort from the executive. The final
report eased pressure on the FBI. With so little incentive, other
than public relations, Hoover scarcely followed through on the
modest administrative reforms he had implemented. Having
survived the challenge, retrenchment, not reform, was in
order.[62]

Justice Department officials, in fact, tried to impose one single substantive reform, designed to reduce the investigative delays that accompanied the typical civil rights case. From 1939
to 1947 the FBI had accepted complaints alleging violations of
federal civil rights law but had launched formal investigations
only at the specific request of the head of the Criminal Division.
Department officials generally had reserved such a policy for
three or four sensitive categories of investigation (antitrust matters, for example) in which there was special need to manage
test cases carefully to create a useful legal precedent. In April
1947, Attorney General Clark changed this policy by authorizing
the Bureau "to conduct *preliminary investigations* of any civil
rights complaints or incidents upon its own motion [emphasis
added]."[63] Hoover saw no threat in Clark's order, although two
of his closest aides viewed it as an attempt "to 'unload' responsibility onto the Bureau." In the director's view, "the Attorney
General asks us merely to institute 'preliminary investigation'
and still leaves us free to then forward the basic allegation to
the Department for decision as to . . . whether a full investigation should be instituted." The directive, therefore, was "not to
be construed as changing the existing instructions." Hoover, not
the attorney general, remained in control.[64]

J. Howard McGrath, Clark's successor, continued on this tack.
"I wish to make it clear," he informed Hoover in December 1951,

"that the Bureau can in the first instance originate, initiate, and carry through to a conclusion any investigation within its jurisdiction." This meant "blanket authority to conduct full and complete investigations in [civil rights] cases." The director responded by ordering all field offices to proceed only with approval from headquarters in any case considered undesirable, overly broad, controversial, or potentially embarrassing. Less than a year later, in October 1952, he convinced McGrath's successor, James P. McGranery, to rescind the directive entirely.[65]

During the Eisenhower years Hoover made a series of unilateral assaults on what remained of Justice Department policy, all designed to reduce his Bureau's civil rights workload.[66] By mid-1958 he had completely revised existing policy pertaining to every type of civil rights case, from police brutality to peonage, simply by declaring previous departmental instructions "permissive rather than mandatory." Hereafter, the Bureau refused to launch even preliminary investigations unless the attorney general issued a specific directive on a case-by-case basis. Besides being insubordinate, this new policy created certain risks. It would no longer be easy "to shut off criticism by the . . . [NAACP] and other groups," FBI Assistant Director Alex Rosen emphasized. "[We will not be] able to say at the very outset that the matter is being inquired into and the facts will be presented to the Civil Rights Division"—a policy that immediately took "the heat off." The benefits, however, outweighed the risks. A continuation of the old policy would expose the Bureau to heat from the other side. Believing that the growing civil rights movement was too "controversial," politics in the South too "inflamed," and community feelings too "emotional," Hoover intended to keep the FBI on the sidelines.[67]

For the time being, the director's "reforms" accomplished their purpose. Before 1958 the FBI's public reports listed the total number of preliminary civil rights investigations *conducted* in any given year—a total of 1,269 in 1958, for example. Beginning in 1959, the FBI simply listed the number of civil rights violations *reported* during the year. Outright insubordination now joined obfuscation and public relations trickery to govern the Bureau's civil rights policy. To keep the FBI on the sidelines, Hoover proved willing to risk direct confrontation with the Justice Department.[68]

No amount of bureaucratic maneuvering could make the issues raised by the President's Committee on Civil Rights or the political problems facing the FBI fade completely away. On nearly every other issue, with the exception of civil rights, Hoover had been able to build bipartisan constituencies—relatively easy to do when the issue was crime control or anticommunism—but this was a nearly impossible task when the issue was civil rights. Hoover knew that the Negro Question threatened to divide his supporters, and that whatever he chose to do (or not to do) would be controversial. By refusing to launch a crusade against civil rights violators along the model of his earlier campaign against the 1930s' gangsters, or his ongoing campaign against communist subversives, he risked censure from "vociferous minority groups" and their liberal allies. At the same time, even the most unenthusiastic investigations of civil rights abuses alienated his conservative, states' rights constituency.

The most dramatic example of this occurred in 1953 when guards at the Pennhurst School for the Feebleminded in Spring City, Pennsylvania, beat a young black inmate named Robert Byers to death. After Byers's father viewed his son's bruised corpse, he demanded that something be done. The Justice Department ordered the FBI to investigate—on the grounds that the Pennhurst guards may have violated Byers's civil rights by killing him. An important case for the Bureau, it demonstrated that states' rights issues cut across regional lines on the problem of police brutality and other matters covered by Section 242, the color-of-law statute.[69]

FBI interest in Byers's death attracted national media attention during a press conference at the annual Governors' Conference in Seattle in August 1953. John S. Fine of Pennsylvania, Allan Shivers of Texas, John Battle of Virginia, and Thomas E. Dewey of New York, among others, criticized the Bureau "and indirectly the Eisenhower Administration for not curbing its activities." "The publicity," Hoover complained to Attorney General Herbert Brownell, left the "general impression" that the FBI had "engaged in an unrestrained program of invading State's rights." A few of the journalists who publicized the charges, the director added, had deliberately incited "ill will on the part of local, county and state law enforcement agencies against the FBI."[70]

One of the worst offenders, Hearst columnist Westbrook Pegler, had been drawn to the civil rights topic earlier in the year—after another newspaperman broke the story of a Justice Department official's agreement with the New York City Police

Department allowing the police to investigate brutality complaints filed against their own officers. Pegler and states' rights advocates in general saw nothing wrong with that policy—and neither did Hoover, at least in theory. When the attorney general rescinded the agreement, however, Pegler suspected that Hoover had leaked the information that broke the story in the first place. Louis B. Nichols, chief of the Crime Records Division, then met with Pegler in an attempt to straighten him out, telling the Hearst columnist "that for a period of time I frankly wondered whether [Max] Lowenthal had converted [you]." (Lowenthal, a friend of Harry Truman's, had written a scathing book on the FBI.) Conceding that the Bureau had "a duty to do," Pegler said he simply believed policemen should use their night sticks "a little more frequently . . . on 'pimps, fairies and labor racketeers.'"[71]

Pegler's carping, Hoover lamented, had contributed to "a rather bad reaction . . . in various sections of the country." The director tried to limit this damage by going directly to the media, reminding *New York Times* publisher Arthur Hayes Sulzberger that the "FBI is not a policy-making organization. It is a service agency," with a mission to enforce federal law. "It makes little difference whether the Act of Congress was passed in 1866 or 1953 so long as it is the law of the land," he continued, adding that persons opposed to Section 242, the color-of-law statute, should stop criticizing the FBI and seek its repeal. He made this same point again in a press release, quoting a long-dead president. "Theodore Roosevelt, I believe, said that the best way to have a bad law repealed was to enforce it."[72] Nichols, meanwhile, solicited positive press coverage from Raymond Moley of *Newsweek,* Hearst columnists George Sokolsky and Howard Rushmore, and Hearst executive Richard Berlin (who had his own troubles with the incorrigible Pegler). Other prominent Americans, including Joseph P. Kennedy and Morris Ernst, volunteered their services to the Bureau. All of this publicity made the point that FBI agents investigated police brutality because they had to and not because they wanted to or were in any way critical of local police practices.[73]

After the flap over Byers's death and the New York police affair finally quieted, Nichols drafted a directive, for Hoover's signature, requiring all field offices "to be alert for any disgruntled public official who may be misinformed as to the Bureau's position in civil rights."[74] By the time Hoover issued that order the

Byers case had been closed for two months. Nearly as tentative
in the face of criticism from states' righters as the FBI itself,
the Justice Department advised the director one week after the
governors' conference that no further investigation into the circumstances surrounding Robert Byers's death would be necessary.

Because the FBI could withdraw only from particular cases
and not from its general civil rights responsibilities, the political
problems facing Hoover continued to mount. This was especially true among his white constituents in the South after the
Supreme Court unanimously ruled racial segregation in public
schools unconstitutional in *Brown v. Board of Education* (1954).
Congressman Mendel Rivers (D., S.C.) told Nichols "that the Bureau is getting itself in a bad situation when it is forced to do
the work of the NAACP." During the school desegregation crisis
in Little Rock, militant whites appeared to be as upset with Director Hoover for sending in the FBI as they were with President
Eisenhower for sending in the 101st Airborne—though Hoover
sent the FBI in only because Eisenhower told him to do so. Little
Rock segregationists failed to recognize the distinction. They
identified the Bureau's agents as enemies of their race because
(among other reasons) the G-men always stopped by the Sky
Room at the Lafayette Hotel, where the Citizens Council cau-
cused, to obtain specimens from the segregation-forever documents that the resistance had stacked up on tables everywhere.[75]

Civil rights matters posed a threat to the FBI and to Hoover's
own directorship. "A lot of the southern folks never know what
a position the Director has been in," Nichols explained, in February 1957, to Senator James Eastland (D., Miss.). A year later
H. L. Edwards, an aide to Senator Olin Johnson (D., S.C.), told
Gordon A. Nease, Nichols's successor as head of Crime Records,
that "many of the Southern Senators," not understanding why
the FBI "must investigate civil rights matters," had already
taken "definite steps" to remove the director "from his job."
Those senators held a meeting on this subject recently "on the
Hill," though "the matter had gradually calmed down."[76] Edwards recommended that Hoover "pressure" the Eisenhower
administration "to set up an investigative staff for the Civil
Rights Division of the Department," thus enabling the FBI to
"keep away from such matters entirely." Edwards said this
"could be accomplished if sufficient interest was aroused in
Congress," in the process suggesting that the director "speak to

his close friends." Hoover dismissed Edwards's "completely un-
tenable" ideas. "It is amazing how utterly unobjective some individuals get," he complained. "We have a job to do and we will
do it."[77]

That comment indicated no change in attitude toward civil
rights work, only a measure of resignation and more than anything else territorial instinct. An institutional interest in preserving the FBI's function as *the* investigative arm of the Justice
Department counterbalanced Hoover's personal interest in preserving segregation within his own Bureau and political interest
in letting it alone in those areas of the country where it already
existed. No matter how unpleasant the investigation, Hoover refused to establish the precedent of farming out particular tasks.

The struggle to retain bureaucratic autonomy on civil rights
enforcement matters plagued Hoover throughout the cold war
years, in contrast to the parallel investigations of civil rights activists on the domestic intelligence front. Here, the FBI and its
director found the pursuit of bureaucratic autonomy considerably easier. The surveillance mission produced no splits in
Hoover's constituency, only files bulging with rumor, gossip,
and allegation, which the FBI collected but did not always
bother to verify, on a range of people interested in civil rights,
from mainstream politicians to Communist party functionaries
and fellow travelers. The FBI did not harass civil rights activists
and their friends as often during the 1940s and 1950s as they
would do during the 1960s, but neither did they leave the movement alone. They were always tracking the radical and not-so-
radical ideas of the people involved in the struggle for black
equality and following the Red menace in and out of movement
groups.

Much of the collected information represented evidence of
subversion only to the FBI. The Bureau overlooked the membership of Eliot Asinof, a blacklisted television writer, in several
left-wing groups on the attorney general's list of subversive organizations, but not his signature on an old petition urging the
New York Yankees to sign black ball players. In the case of Minneapolis Mayor Hubert H. Humphrey, who advocated civil
rights within the Americans for Democratic Action and led the
civil rights platform fight at the 1948 Democratic convention,
the FBI prepared a "blind" memo citing his appearance at an
NAACP-sponsored meeting and implying that he had once paid a
"political debt to the Communists." Typed "on plain white bond,

unwatermarked paper" to disguise the Bureau's authorship, this blind memo was one of thirty the FBI prepared on Humphrey and other members of the National Conference on Prevention and Control of Juvenile Delinquency for Hearst executive Edmond D. Coblentz, one of Hoover's most powerful media allies—though apparently Coblentz never bothered to pick them up.[78]

There were additional blind memos concerning black communists and fellow travelers, which Louis Nichols delivered to Robert E. Stripling, chief counsel for the House Committee on Un-American Activities. One concerned Benjamin J. Davis, Jr., one of the first-string communist leaders convicted in the 1949 Foley Square Smith Act trial of conspiring to teach or advocate the violent overthrow of the United States government. Nichols gave Stripling another memo (with a copy to Illinois Senator Everett Dirksen) on Paul Robeson, the black singer, actor, and friend of the Communist party. FBI agents tapped Robeson's phone, opened his mail, and tried to find out if he really was having a rumored affair with Lord Louis Mountbatten's wife. A report "that Lady Mountbatten has a huge naked statue of Paul Robeson in her home" attracted Hoover's personal attention.[79]

While leaking information from FBI files to HUAC and the Hearst press, the director methodically continued to forward his conclusions about the subversive aspects of the Negro Question to the White House—a practice that reflected his personal bias and not a legitimate political position. Almost every document sent to Truman administration officials blamed the Communist party for "agitating pressure campaigns" on behalf of racial justice. The director even tried to smear Mary McLeod Bethune, former director of Negro Affairs for the National Youth Administration, as a communist agent. He had Bureau researchers compare the Communist party line on lynching with the views of journals like *The Nation* and the *New Republic*. The implication of these reports seemed to be that only communists supported racial justice in America. This notion allowed Hoover to link a consensus opinion (that communists posed a serious threat to American institutions and values) with a more problematic one (that civil rights advocates posed an equally serious threat to those same institutions and values). Hoover may have been even more concerned with undermining the legitimacy of the civil rights movement than in investigating the Negro Question activities of Communist party functionaries. For the director, the advocacy of racial justice was itself a subversive act, and his reports on communism were simply to support this thesis. By equating civil rights activism with un-American activity, he clearly went beyond his internal security mandate.[80]

A surprisingly high number of documents the FBI sent to Truman and then Eisenhower administration officials concerned the NAACP. The FBI claimed that an NAACP resolution praising former Secretary of Commerce Henry Wallace's public statements about lynching had actually been drawn-up "under the direction of the Communist Party." (FBI agents had been monitoring Wallace's "Contacts with Negro Communist-Controlled Organizations and Individuals" at least since 1945, more than a year before Truman dismissed him from the cabinet for criticizing the hard-line policy toward the Soviet Union.)[81] The Bureau's most notable reports on the NAACP to the Eisenhower White House were a 1956 series of letters and memos on communist interest in plans by the Leadership Conference on Civil Rights, led by the NAACP, to send a delegation to meet with congressmen. The director alerted the administration to the meetings that the Leadership Conference held with the senators from Illinois, the Democrat Paul Douglas and the Republican Everett Dirksen, and also briefed the president's aides on the UAW's support for the Conference.[82]

That same year, President Eisenhower's attorney general, Herbert Brownell, urged Congress to give the Justice Department power to file civil suits in support of voting rights, to create a civil rights commission, and to upgrade the Civil Rights Section to full division status within the Justice Department. Hoover showed his antipathy toward Brownell's efforts by making sure he made no statement in his reports on the NAACP or in his conversations with administration officials that the Department might "seize [upon] . . . to support its position in seeking enactment of civil rights legislation." A year later, after Congress adopted Brownell's proposals, the FBI's New York office sent a 137-page report on the NAACP to the White House and the military intelligence agencies. Based on information supplied by 151 informants, "bag squads" (that is, Bureau burglars), wiretaps, and other confidential sources, the report concerned "communist activity" in NAACP chapters from Miami, Florida, to Fairbanks, Alaska.[83]

Whatever his agenda, however, Hoover remained, as ever, determined to ingratiate himself with whatever president was in the Oval Office. Dwight Eisenhower gave the director an unprecedented opportunity in March 1956 when he asked for an extended presentation on the general subject of "Racial Tension and Civil Rights," and offered Hoover a chance to make his report at a cabinet meeting. Hoover told the cabinet that the Supreme Court decision in *Brown* had set the country on a course toward racial crisis. "Delicate situations are aggravated by some overzealous but ill-advised leaders of the NAACP and by the Communist Party, which seeks to use incidents to further the so-called class struggle. . . . The area of danger lies in friction between extremists on both sides"—"both those who stand for and against segregation"—"ready with violence."[84]

Eisenhower expected Hoover to explain (not defend) the white South's point of view. For the most part that is what the director did, but his briefing paper indicated that he stood with the segregationists. "The specter of racial intermarriages" and "mixed education" that haunted the South also haunted the FBI. Black groups and individuals preaching "racial hatred" had spread across the South, Hoover claimed, in contrast to the "pretty much defunct" Ku Klux Klan. "The leading citizens of the South"—that is, "bankers, lawyers, doctors, state legislators and industrialists"—composed the membership of the white-collar (or "readin' and writin'") Klans, the Citizens Councils. One of the director's aides claimed the Citizens Councils posed less of a problem than the "Negro publications" that ran "inflamatory articles concerning these councils."[85]

Hoover emphasized the communist threat for the Eisenhower cabinet in a way that clearly showed how biased he was. In discussing "the alleged lynching" of a fourteen-year-old Chicago boy, Emmett Till, the director worried more about a "pressure campaign on government officials" than a brutal, racist murder. Till had gone to Money, Mississippi, to visit relatives, and made the mistake, one afternoon, of "whistling at a distaff white." The woman's husband and half brother kidnapped Till, murdered him, and dumped his body in the Tallahatchie River. Till was found seven days later, a .45 caliber bullet hole in his crushed skull and a seventy-four-pound cotton-gin fan tied around his neck. After a state court jury acquitted both suspects of murder charges, a federal grand jury refused to issue indictments. (Technically speaking, the FBI never "investigated" the case; the FBI launched a "preliminary" investigation, not a "full" investigation.) When Illinois communists, along with thousands of other people, demanded that President Eisenhower take action, Chicago Mayor Richard J. Daley wired the White House urging federal intervention. The director concluded his discussion of the case by reminding the cabinet "that Mayor Daley [was] not a Communist," only a dupe: "Pressures engineered by the Communists were brought to bear upon him."[86]

Hoover strayed from the Red menace briefly to discuss Elijah Muhammad's Nation of Islam, a separatist group that accepted the general tenets of Islam. He incorrectly described the Black Muslims as one of the "organizations presently advancing integration" and "figur[ing] in the rising tensions." FBI interest in Muhammad's group resulted from their "violently anti-white rhetoric" and occasional verbal support for the Mau Mau in Africa and the Vietminh in northern Vietnam. The Bureau tried to have the Nation of Islam placed on the attorney general's list of subversive organizations and to jail its leaders for conspiring to violate the Smith Act and the Selective Service Act, but the Justice Department refused. Brownell merely approved a wiretap in 1957 on Muhammad's home telephone in Chicago "or any address to which he may move in the future." Interpreting this directive broadly, the Bureau also tapped and bugged Muhammad's winter residence in Phoenix.[87]

What the cabinet did not learn from the director's report was that Hoover privately shared the convictions of die-hard southern segregationists. But despite Hoover's personal hostility toward the integration movement, he would not commit the Bureau fully to the other side. In the decades following the black scare of 1919 and the dismantling of the old General Intelligence Division in 1924, Hoover presided over a bureaucracy that acted, as often as not, ambivalently toward civil rights activists and their alleged ties to communists and other extremists. Bureaucratic expediencies on matters of race determined outcomes as often as ideological assumptions about civil rights activists who demanded justice and equality for all.

FBI officials continued to disseminate alarmist information on the black freedom struggle. They sent a report to the White House on Eleanor Roosevelt's plans to hold a reception for the Southern Conference Educational Fund, and they briefed Vice-President Richard Nixon and Supreme Court Chief Justice Earl Warren on communist plans to infiltrate the Prayer Pilgrimage for Freedom. This was a demonstration to commemorate the third anniversary of *Brown*, during which Martin Luther King,

Jr., delivered his first major address on the steps of the Lincoln Memorial. The FBI also sent radio commentator and newspaper columnist Fulton Lewis, Jr., information about the civil rights activities of G. Bromley Oxnam, liberal Methodist bishop of Washington and president of the World Council of Churches. Hoover always made sure that the White House and the media were aware of Bureau resources and interests.[88]

When dealing with the southern segregationists, however, FBI officials had to proceed cautiously. Hoover regularly supplied information to the Senate Internal Security Subcommittee and its chairman, James Eastland (D., Miss.), and the House Committee on Un-American Activities and its chairman, Francis Walter (D., Penn.). But as a general rule the Bureau left documenting communist infiltration of the civil rights movement to the congressional committees themselves.[89]

HUAC opened its voluminous files to segregationists to help them discredit the civil rights movement. During House debate on Attorney General Brownell's civil rights bill, E. C. Gathings (D., Ark.) read into the *Congressional Record* HUAC reports detailing the "subversive activities" of eighty-nine people connected with the NAACP. In 1957 HUAC staff director Richard Arens released reports on fourteen board members of the Southern Regional Council, the moderate Atlanta-based interracial group, to Congressman James C. Davis (D., GA.). Arens, who often received information directly from the FBI's supposedly classified files, lost his own job with the Committee in 1960 when the press learned he was a consultant for a foundation that tried to prove Negroes were genetically inferior.[90]

Hoover supported the political position of the Un-American Activities Committee. When Congressman Gathings inserted his dossiers on NAACP activists into the *Congressional Record*, FBI Associate Director Clyde Tolson ordered all eighty-nine names run through the Bureau's files. The FBI and HUAC both helped the state of Kentucky prosecute Carl Braden of the Southern Conference Educational Fund on a sedition charge (for selling a black family a house in a white Louisville neighborhood). The FBI also ran name checks on civil rights activists and others who accused HUAC of "manufacturing the impression that liberalism is tainted with communism," and budgeted some $30,000 a year to the task of checking Committee files. When the Un-American Activities Committee published a cumulative name and organization index in 1955, the FBI ordered thirty copies.[91]

Struggling to form an accurate picture of the Communist party's attempts to take over the civil rights movement, FBI agents had a difficult time collecting specific evidence of significant communist influence. One of their best cases was Carl Braden's real-estate maneuver, which they called "one of the few known instances in which *it appears* a racial situation was created by a communist, *but not* necessarily *by the CP* [emphasis added]." Even the Bureau's best case had two qualifications.[92] The FBI concluded that the Communist party never had much success in its campaign to "sway the Negro" despite an "inordinate" investment of "time, funds, propaganda and personnel," including Comintern subsidies as high as $300,000 and dating from 1922. The Bureau would not even credit the party with attracting a significant minority of black members. In 1928 the CPUSA claimed 50 Negro members, though some of the comrades, according to FBI sources, estimated the total number of black recruits could be counted "on the fingers of one's hand." If the party did better in the 1930s and 1940s, it probably never had more than 4,000 active, disciplined, dues-paying Negro members. By 1956 total black membership dropped to less than 1,400. Ironically, as recent scholarship on the history of the party has shown, the FBI consistently *underestimated* the number of black communists and their accomplishments, such as they were, in black communities.[93]

Hoover's aides identified "the opposition of responsible Negro leaders" as "one of the most influential factors in the failure of the Communist Party." Most prominent blacks, they said, including Willard S. Townsend of the United Transport Service Employees, George Schuyler of the *Pittsburgh Courier*, and the firebrand from the GID era and the World War II March on Washington Movement, A. Philip Randolph, then president of the Brotherhood of Sleeping Car Porters, recognized "the specious nature of [the communist] program."[94] Bureau officials singled out Roy Wilkins ("he has been strongly anti-communist, and has done everything possible to keep the NAACP clear of communist infiltration"), along with his predecessor, Walter White, who died in 1955, for particular praise. Thus, the director wrote his testimonial for White at the very time he approved the wiretap on the office telephone of the NAACP branch in Philadelphia. And he had Louis Nichols and New York special agent in charge Edward Scheidt give White (and Wilkins, too) information "regarding Communist activities directed at the NAACP" even while he ordered an escalation of the Bureau's investigation of their group. The FBI could find no more than 467 past or present communists (or suspected communists) active in the NAACP—out of a total NAACP membership of more than 300,000.[95]

Neither the Communist party's failure to recruit blacks nor Hoover's refusal to commit his resources fully to the segregationists had a discernible impact on FBI surveillance policy. Bureau agents continued to monitor communist efforts to infiltrate groups like the NAACP and the Brotherhood of Sleeping Car Porters, and they continued to report even the most far-fetched rumors—including an informant report of a power struggle between White and Wilkins that had Wilkins representing "the Trotskyite element in the NAACP." And FBI officials continued to worry about what they called communist agitation "among the Negroes on the same old themes . . . 'equal rights' and 'self-determination,'" despite the "obvious" fact (obvious to the Bureau) that "the condition of the American Negro has improved materially during the past generation." If they located few registered black comrades, Hoover's agents remained equally interested in "approximately 18,000 other Negroes who have some contact with the Party and its front groups, and who are, to a certain degree, influenced directly or indirectly by its program, propaganda and agitation."[96]

Surveillance of the civil rights movement would continue for reasons of politics, not internal security. Hoover equated the Negro Question with subversion, but as FBI director he rarely accepted the risks involved in acting on that belief. Consequently, he proved quite tolerant of the contradictory belief of the men around him that the Red menace among blacks should not be taken all that seriously.

By the last of the Eisenhower years, despite the ability of the FBI to intervene in the affairs of black Americans, and despite the existence of a long list of FBI grievances against black people, Hoover remained uncertain about how best to use his power to redress his grievances. The director's racial ideas had not changed much since 1919, but he knew that any attempt to link the civil rights movement to the Red menace would not be persuasive outside the white South, and he knew that explicitly racist policies no longer had national support. His 1931 reprimand of Clyde Tolson for refusing to hire a "colored messenger" indicates an early awareness of the delicacy of the Negro Question. Hoover was sensitive in appearance, though he encouraged the practice, of racism within his own bureaucracy. After *Brown v. Board of Education* he tried to eliminate any overt "bias or prejudice" on the part of his field agents in the South. He had Clement McGowan, then a supervisor on the civil rights desk at headquarters, "personally caution that the Supreme Court justices didn't ask anybody's opinion when they were passing on the case and they didn't need any dissenting opinions or concurring opinions when you're out conducting investigations." "Nothing can hurt you quicker," McGowan said, "than somebody opening his mouth. The biggest enemy most of the agents had was their own little mouths—or big mouths."[97] Hoover was a racist, but he always let his political and bureaucratic instincts control his feelings.

The civil rights movement may have been a faceless thing to much of white America, but Hoover knew that after *Brown* the movement was a gathering social and political force that was already beginning to develop its own political culture, its own leaders, and its own ideas. It was a force strong enough to challenge the director's personal notion of the black man's place in a white man's country, and his preference for an orderly national security state rather than one that lived up to its own democratic creed. Hoover's response to the Negro Question was based on his bureaucrat's instinct to avoid the sticky, divisive issue and his politician's understanding of the politically and morally ambiguous context of the government's response to the black struggle. The result was a position not much different from that of other federal officials (no one stood up for full equality), though Hoover's stance certainly differed in degree. The director went beyond the call of duty when fulfilling what he considered to be a states' rights responsibility to avoid civil rights enforcement and a national security responsibility to monitor communist activity among blacks.

While the civil rights battles were being fought, Hoover positioned his FBI and waited, hoping for a Negro Question policy that might somehow minimize "the terrible pressures coming from both sides," from the integrationists and the segregationists, and as well the more modest pressures that had been coming since 1939 from Civil Rights Section (Division, after 1957) lawyers in the Justice Department. His real hope was that the civil rights movement would disappear on its own, that he personally would not have to expose himself to the risk of openly opposing it.

Hoover kept this hope even as the civil rights movement went from the courtrooms into the streets, with the NAACP-preferred strategy of litigation giving way to a protest-oriented politics of mass direct action. When Mrs. Rosa Parks refused to give up her seat on a Montgomery, Alabama, bus to a white man, "somewhere in the universe," as the Black Panther party's Eldridge Cleaver would later write, "a gear in the machinery had shifted." But no gear shifted in Hoover's FBI during the subsequent bus boycott—or during the sit-ins that swept the South beginning in February 1960, when four black students from North Carolina A & T College ordered coffee at a lunch counter in a Greensboro Woolworth and refused to leave when a waitress denied them service. "If you are Hoover," surmised Nashville newspaperman John Seigenthaler, "you look at Greensboro and you think it's going to be a problem. But it's going to be somebody else's problem."[98] The FBI launched a communist infiltration investigation of the Montgomery Improvement Association only in the second year of the bus boycott, and when investigating the sit-ins found few communists at the lunch counters. If Hoover embellished (the CPUSA considered "these demonstrations . . . the next best thing to 'proletarian revolution'"), his ultimate conclusion reflected his agents' findings and his own caution. "The Communist Party took advantage of the [demonstrations]," he told a House Appropriations Subcommittee. "They did not originate them."[99]

Prudence told Hoover to keep a distance from the risky and unpleasant challenges posed by the Negro Question, to avoid the sort of engagement that might push his Bureau towards an open and inextirpable conflict with black America—or, for that matter, his own states' rights constituents. And that is exactly what he did over the course of the four decades since 1919. But he never stopped spying and he never stopped plotting how to avoid civil rights work. He never stopped sniping at the men and women involved in the black struggle for equality, and he never stopped cataloging grievances against civil rights activists and the everyday people who lived in black communities. He never stopped preparing for that day when his Bureau would no longer be able to dodge the Negro Question.

2

Paper Chains

The Kennedys and the Voting Litigation Campaign

For J. Edgar Hoover and his agents, the modern civil rights movement began in a surprising way. The FBI's inextirpable engagement with the movement began not with Mrs. Rosa Parks in December 1955 or the students at North Carolina A & T in February 1960, but in the last months of the Eisenhower presidency and the first year of the Kennedy presidency with a Justice Department litigation campaign designed to win southern Negroes the right to vote. For all the progress the black struggle had made on the Montgomery buses and among the businesses and public facilities visited by the sit-in activists, blacks across much of the South still lacked the most fundamental right of all. With the franchise, all other rights and privileges would follow, and the franchise had to be won in the courts and not the streets. This strategy was especially appealing to President John F. Kennedy, Attorney General Robert F. Kennedy, and the lawyers who served in the Department's Civil Rights Division. The Kennedys viewed voting litigation—a strategy of moderation, compromise, and confrontation avoidance—as the antithesis of direct action.[1]

John Kennedy's interest in civil rights dated from the early 1950s, and he took calculated risks from time to time on behalf of the black struggle—most notably during the 1960 campaign, telephoning a pregnant Coretta Scott King, while her husband sat in a Georgia jail. But the new president believed a legislative assault on segregation would founder before an unsympathetic Congress and that an executive order would alienate key southern committee chairmen. The voting litigation campaign risked the least political capital. Robert Kennedy had no civil rights program at the time. Though White House aide Kenneth O'Donnell would later say "Bobby was in [civil rights work] up to his eyeballs," that description did not apply in 1961. "I did not lie awake at night worrying about the problems of Negroes," Robert Kennedy said. Sleepless nights would come later. In the interim, a voting litigation campaign would suffice.[2]

John Kennedy's predictions about the risks involved in a more aggressive approach proved to be correct. "We had his whole program bottled up," boasted Senate Judiciary Committee Chairman James Eastland (D., Miss.). In the House, Rules Committee Chairman Howard Smith (D., Va.) handled such chores. Hoover considered both men "members of the [FBI] family." They were contacts of the director and his agents in the Crime Records Division, and FBI Assistant Director for Crime Records Cartha D. DeLoach sometimes had the more conservative members of Smith's Committee out to his house for dinner. Hoover and DeLoach actually gave more aid and comfort to Eastland and Smith than to the Kennedys.[3]

Expected by the Kennedy administration to gather the raw data needed to file and win cases against white southern registrars, FBI officials considered the voting litigation campaign immoderate, arbitrary, and contentious. While binding the FBI more tightly to the Negro Question in ways that the director found particularly unpleasant, however, the campaign also bound the FBI more tightly to the politics of the White House. The Kennedy administration balanced its attempts to force the FBI to act on behalf of the civil rights movement with an entirely understandable desire to protect its own political interests, a strategy that led on occasion to the contradictory position of White House and Justice Department support for the director's barely concealed hostility toward black people and their right to vote.

White House aide Lee C. White once described voter registration programs as "something like motherhood—nobody can be opposed to them."[4] Hoover proved him wrong. He shared the white southern fear that the black vote would destroy a way of life, and so he opposed the voting litigation campaign for reasons of race and politics as well as bureaucratic interest. In the director's world, white southern fears took precedence over the civil rights movement's faith that America would one day guard and protect the black voter, just as the FBI's rights as a bureaucracy took precedence over black people's rights as American citizens. Hoover tried on every front to impede the implementation of the voting litigation campaign, and his behavior represented more than a bureaucratic commitment to avoid civil rights work. Despite the obvious problems caused by Mrs. Parks, the sit-in activists, and other proponents of the new direct-action protest, Hoover's behavior during the course of the voting litigation campaign represented the initial engagement of the struggle that the director and his FBI would wage against black America throughout the 1960s.

By the time Robert Kennedy's Justice Department began its attempt in 1961 to guarantee the right to vote for all in the black-belt South, Hoover and his aides had some inkling of what to expect from such a project. Given their experience with voting rights cases since the 1940s, they foresaw "the potential publicity" involved in "any case of this type."[5] Determined to avoid any act that might alienate their southern white constituents, they investigated voting cases only when they had to and never in an aggressive manner. They were somewhat less restrained when snooping around after the National Committee to Abolish the Poll Tax, a group devoted to ridding the land of one of the oldest and most pervasive forms of disenfranchisement. "There were a few Communists around the poll tax committee," said Virginia Durr, a racial liberal from Montgomery and a friend of Rosa Parks. But "we were surrounded by the FBI."[6] Since the Justice Department rarely prosecuted voting cases during the Roosevelt and Truman eras, few conflicts developed. If the Department pursued its voting rights mission more aggressively during the 1950s, the Eisenhower administration still proceeded "with all deliberate lethargy"—especially after March 14, 1956, when nearly one hundred members of Congress from the South issued a manifesto pledging themselves to resist desegregation by every legal means. The president himself had promised, in a letter to South Carolina Governor James F. Byrnes, "to make haste slowly." For most of the Eisenhower years, then, responsible government officials rarely encouraged the FBI to intervene.[7]

On those occasions when an ostensible superior asked the FBI to do something, Hoover warned the Justice Department of undue pressure on the Civil Rights Division. He said the Division should pay less attention to the demands of people like Martin Luther King of the Southern Christian Leadership Conference and Clarence Mitchell of the NAACP, and more attention to "the feeling of the [white] officials and [white] people in the states targeted for voting drives." At the time, the tentative plans of the SCLC and NAACP to launch a Crusade for Citizenship across the South and a voter registration campaign in Mississippi greatly disturbed the director, as did a grand jury probe of six FBI agents in Louisiana who had investigated (and allegedly harassed) the Webster Parish voter registrar at the Civil Rights Division's request. Even the Bureau's minimal involvement in voting rights work led to bureaucratic and political headaches.[8]

Justice Department attorneys generally followed Hoover's go-slow advice until the last six months of the Eisenhower administration, when Harold R. Tyler, Jr., took over the Civil Rights Division. Tall and angular, the thirty-eight-year-old Tyler had served in World War II and Korea and for seven years as a federal prosecutor in New York. Far more aggressive than his predecessors, the first two assistant attorneys general for civil rights, W. Wilson White and Joseph Ryan, he pressed Hoover to enforce the Civil Rights Acts of 1957 and 1960 and used Division attorneys as investigators whenever the FBI appeared unwilling to perform. Both laws emerged from the post-*Brown* climate and Attorney General Herbert Brownell's advocacy of black civil rights. They provided for injunctive relief against any person, "acting under color of law or otherwise," involved in racial discrimination regarding the registration process or voting itself through threats, intimidation, or any other form of coercion. By July 1960, three months after Eisenhower signed the Civil Rights Act of 1960, which granted the "Attorney General or his representative" authority to inspect and photograph voter registration records, Tyler's attorneys and Hoover's agents had undertaken three voter discrimination suits in Georgia, Alabama, and Louisiana, and two economic intimidation cases in Tennessee.[9]

The most important of these early cases, and the one in which the FBI demonstrated most clearly its reluctance to get involved in civil rights enforcement, concerned the Haywood County (Tenn.) Civic and Welfare League, which had been formed to encourage black voter registration. When the white county elite threatened a number of sharecroppers who joined with eviction by their local landlords, the FBI balked at the Civil Rights Division's request for an investigation—arguing that coercion of local blacks merely resulted from League membership and not League members' attempts to place their names on the Haywood County voter lists. When Division attorneys told the FBI to do its job, the FBI filed reports that simply repeated the allegations of Haywood County blacks while ignoring a blacklist organized by county landlords, merchants, and bankers. Bureau agents in Tennessee, much like the director himself, remained more attuned to "the feeling of the [white] officials" who saw this as a local affair than to the black sharecroppers whose civil rights those officials had violated. It would have been surprising if the FBI had reacted otherwise. Several of the Bureau's domestic intelligence programs were intended to police the various Eisenhower-era blacklists of members of the Communist party and other unpopular groups.

The FBI executive responsible for voting rights cases, General Investigative Division chief Alex Rosen, "was very uncompromising," Tyler remembered. "He was stifling the lawyers in the Division, choking everybody with paper"—including lengthy memos detailing the political affiliations of movement people in Tennessee and elsewhere. On one occasion, when the Knoxville Human Relations Council complained about the Bureau's refusal to investigate civil rights cases in Tennessee, Hoover ordered name checks on the Council's board of directors and forwarded the results to Tyler. Several Council members had radical affiliations dating back to the 1930s and another had "unorthodox attitudes." (He once sent flowers and mash notes to a woman in his church.) "Rosen told me I should read all these FBI reports," Tyler said. "'There are subversives in these civil rights groups.' I said, 'Come on, Al. If these guys are subversives we're all in trouble.'" For Hoover, anyone who caused trouble for the Bureau was a subversive.[10]

By September 1960 the Civil Rights Division had gathered enough hard evidence, despite FBI foot-dragging, to file suit against twenty-nine persons in Haywood County. When Division attorneys went down to take depositions, the victims of the blacklist documented an "economic squeeze ... much worse than had been reflected in the Bureau reports." Written affidavits from fifty evicted sharecroppers, eviction notices from landlords, and interviews with white citizens opposed to the blacklist led the Division to name thirty-six more defendants, and to prevent a large-scale eviction of black sharecroppers scheduled for January 1, 1961. The Division's evidence underscored the Bureau's deliberate omissions.[11]

Tyler teased Hoover about how one of the Civil Rights Division's attorneys, John Doar, "obtained more evidence in West Tennessee with a $19 camera than the whole Bureau. That shamed the Bureau. Hoover called me and said, 'I'd never dreamed you'd do this on your own.' I said we had no choice." Actually, the Division had not acted alone. Tyler hired investigators like Doar with money from a special appropriation secured with the assistance of Senate majority leader Lyndon B. Johnson. With Johnson's help, Tyler established the precedents on which his own successors, former Exeter schoolmate Burke Marshall and Princeton classmate John Doar, would rely.[12]

With the change in administration in 1961 the Civil Rights Division's workload expanded dramatically. At the end of John Kennedy's second month in office, on March 19, the new assistant attorney general for civil rights, Burke Marshall, and a number of other Division attorneys met with the president's brother, Robert, to discuss their plans for extending the right-to-vote litigation drive. The attorney general wanted Hoover to sit in on the strategy session, but the director declined. He was busy on another matter: expediting Frank Wilkinson's one-year prison sentence for contempt of Congress, the result of an encounter with the House Committee on Un-American Activities in Atlanta where HUAC had gone to look for communists in the integration movement.[13] With the director otherwise engaged, Robert Kennedy settled for FBI Assistant Director Courtney Evans, who was a personal friend. Toward the end of the meeting, John Doar remembered Kennedy telling Evans "to be prepared for a large number of voter investigation requests." Evans forwarded the message to Hoover.[14]

With the Kennedys' support, Marshall and Doar planned "a gigantic enforcement assignment" in Alabama, Georgia, Mississippi, Louisiana, and South Carolina, and within three months a reluctant FBI completed voter registration investigations in thirty-four southern counties. By that time the attorney general's commitment to civil rights had taken hold. "[Bob] thought . . . voting rights was the most natural way to move," John Seigenthaler, then one of his aides, said. "If Negroes were voting in places like Mississippi . . . people like Jim Eastland wouldn't be so fresh." By the time Kennedy resigned the attorney generalship in September 1964, the Justice Department had filed fifty-seven voting suits—thirty of them in Mississippi, including one in Eastland's own Sunflower County.[15]

Doar described this litigation strategy as a war against Jim Crow, and he realized that the Civil Rights Division had drafted the FBI's agents ("unwitting soldiers") to take an exposed point position in a crusade unsupported by public backing or a politically strong administration. "What a situation for the Bureau!" Doar noted, some fifteen years later. "At the time *no one* was with the Division . . . and yet the FBI had been involuntarily enlisted." Given the director's assessment of the bureaucratic and political difficulties inherent in such an assignment, even in the best of times it would have been extremely difficult to enlist the FBI in a war *against* segregation in the South. "Mr. Hoover," Seigenthaler recalled, was a white man with white southern values, and he "was not easy to push."[16]

Robert Kennedy expected the director to resist on partisan and ideological grounds as well. "He's basically very conservative," the attorney general said. Whenever Hoover complained about John Doar "causing us headaches," accusing "the Bureau of unnecessary delays," and requesting "expeditious handling of matters," Kennedy reminded the director that the Republicans had hired Doar. (Doar considered himself "a Kennedy Republican.") Hoover's bureaucracy, moreover, reflected the director's conservatism. A week after the March 19 meeting in Kennedy's office, the FBI ran a file check on one of its most persistent media critics, the liberal *Christian Century*, and uncovered the following "derogatory" item: the magazine's condemnation of "the treatment of Negroes . . . during World War II." If FBI officials offered as evidence of *Christian Century* editors' latent subversive tendencies a mere complaint (twenty years old, at that), one wonders what they thought of the Justice Department lawyers who actually ordered their Bureau to do something about "the treatment of Negroes." Hoover continued to equate the Negro Question with subversion, and he found it especially irritating that the Kennedys expected him to defend racial agitators and oppose people who shared his own white, Christian vision of America.[17]

Hoover responded by launching a campaign of his own—a campaign of bureaucratic resistance that circumscribed his contribution to the voting drive. FBI agents in the field photographed registration records and, when requested to do so, conducted interviews of registrars and persons attempting to register to vote. But they did not analyze those records. "We didn't suspect the romance hidden in the records," Doar explained. "Occupied," as they were, "with other duties," Civil Rights Division attorneys failed to recognize that "the FBI was not being fully utilized in its interrogation assignments, and that its agents were utilized in an almost demeaning fashion in inspecting and photographing voter registration records." By accepting a clerical function and abdicating an investigative responsibility, Hoover outmaneuvered the Civil Rights Division. The Division, in effect, signed a treaty with the FBI, a treaty ratified and put into effect even before Marshall's attorneys fully understood how much detailed investigative work their litigation campaign required.[18]

When Marshall and Doar tried to renegotiate, Hoover resisted. "They thought we should . . . draw the conclusions for them," FBI civil rights section chief Clement McGowan remembered. "Photograph the records, go through all of them, and then present us, 'here, this is the whole story.' The analysis of the evidence is up to the Department. As an investigator," McGowan continued, comparing voting cases with stolen car cases to make his point, "you don't go in and check to see how many Cadillacs were stolen there in Georgia, for example. We're investigating the theft of a Cadillac. I'm not interested in how many other Cadillacs were stolen in that same county right at the outset." This approach, however, could not work on voting cases.[19]

Without access to FBI resources the Civil Rights Division was unable to pursue its litigation on the desired scale. Each case needed analysis of voting rolls, comparison of handwriting samples, interviews with registrars and witnesses, identification of the race of the successful and unsuccessful registrants, surveys of literacy tests and poll taxes, compilation of demographic statistics and background data on historical registration patterns. The tedious work taxed the limited capacity of the Division's fifty-three lawyers and fifty-three clerks, taking a heavy toll. Having "found themselves graduated into the view box rather than into the appellate courtroom," many of the Division's young attorneys, "top graduates of the prestigious law schools," began to look "elsewhere for employment." By placing limits on the uses to which his agents' investigative skills could be put, Hoover also placed limits on the uses to which the Division's legal skills could be put.[20]

With over six thousand agents and eight thousand clerical and technical employees, the FBI had the personnel to do the necessary analysis of voter registration records but not the necessary commitment from the director—or from many of the field agents who worked in the South. So the Bureau did as little as possible. "The FBI snaps the shutter on the camera," Marshall complained. "That is all they do." Even then, the FBI camera man needed a Civil Rights Division lawyer on hand to tell him what to photograph—and in some cases to make sure the agent did not sit in a bar for three hours at lunch break "talking football." One of Marshall's lawyers, Hugh Fleischer, who worked in Mississippi and Louisiana, observed Bureau agents "siding up with the people who were being investigated. I talked to the Bureau's agents all the time and a number of them were racists . . . there was one guy whose name was Robert E. Lee." Racism within the agent corps contributed to the success of Hoover's campaign of bureaucratic resistance.[21]

Racism at the top of the FBI pyramid, however, was far more important. "Not all of their agents in the South were antiblack, anti–civil rights, or anti-Kennedy. The real question," as Robert Kennedy's press secretary, Edwin Guthman, noted, "was what happened when the information got to Washington."[22] When responding to Civil Rights Division requests for assistance, FBI officials emphasized "the variety of circumstances which may attend" voting rights and all other civil rights cases. "The investigations themselves will likewise vary, and therefore, a complete list of investigative suggestions is not possible. Ordinarily the Department in its request will outline the type of information desired. . . . In such circumstances, the Field should confine itself strictly to these suggestions."[23]

The literalist policy dated from the 1940s, when FBI executives in Washington imposed it to force a work slow-down on their own field agents. This effectively limited the investigations and sometimes rendered them useless, even in cases where the agents conducting the investigations supported the right of blacks to vote. "We know," FBI Assistant Director Edward A. Tamm complained to Hoover in 1947, after President Truman's Committee on Civil Rights released its report, that agents investigating civil rights abuses often "ignored logical leads" simply because they "went beyond the investigation requested by the Department." Field agents should be allowed to do their job in a "thorough" and "adequate" manner, he argued. Although the

Bureau's public relations people, Louis Nichols and Gordon Nease, favored Tamm's proposal, Hoover and Clyde Tolson decided for the literalist policy because it required "a minimum of investigation." They preferred to live with the complaints of liberals and movement people rather than risk criticism of their Bureau for violating states' rights by engaging in "extensive [civil rights] inquiries." Back in 1947 Hoover told Truman's Committee that protection of civil rights generally should remain a matter of local concern. A states' righter then, so he remained in 1961.[24]

No longer the heroic bureaucracy that would engage machine-gun toting gangsters or search out every detail needed to make a case against a subversive or a car thief, the FBI became humble and hamstrung. The Civil Rights Division wanted G-men. Hoover sent over clock punchers, nine-to-five men who *apologized* before asking any white person a question in a voting rights or other civil rights case. This so-called "disclaimer policy" took the form of a standing directive to inform the public that the FBI investigated "these things" not "because they wanted to but because they were told to." Hoover considered the disclaimer absolutely necessary—"so there can be no misconception upon the part of anybody that it is being done at the whim of the FBI." Hoping to avoid "unfavorable criticism and publicity," particularly "in districts having a large Negro population," he deliberately rendered his agency ineffectual in the fight for civil rights, depriving black people of a resource that could have been an effective weapon in their struggle.[25]

Nearly as old as the Civil Rights Section that Attorney General Frank Murphy had created in 1939, the disclaimer policy went through a series of arcane revisions over the course of the 1960s. During the first two Kennedy years, FBI agents investigating civil rights matters advised interviewees that Robert Kennedy had requested the investigation. Beginning in December 1962 Hoover designated Burke Marshall as the instigator. After Marshall left the Department to take a job with IBM, the FBI selected John Doar and then Robert Kennedy's successor, Nicholas Katzenbach. FBI officials discontinued the disclaimer itself only in 1974—two years after the director's death—on the grounds that they conducted civil rights inquiries "because of a Federal statute . . . not because of a specific request in each instance by the Department." Beyond the veracity problem, field agents complained about having to "apologize at the outset of each and every interview." Many felt the same way in 1961, but in the director's day of authoritarian rule, few agents dared to complain about official Bureau policy.[26]

In practice, the FBI's jurisdictional humility meant that the Civil Rights Division, in Doar's words, "got exactly the information we asked for—no more, no less." The Division countered by issuing incredibly detailed instructions to Bureau agents to collect the data needed to make a voting rights case, a guaranteed performance technique referred to as "the box memo." Routine requests for readily accessible information often had to be typed out on pages that ran into the low three figures. Doar remembered one memo that "went on in the most minute detail for 174 pages, explaining, anticipating, cautioning and coaching the Bureau agents," telling them what to do and what not to do. ("Do not go to the sheriff.") Determined to control the FBI investigators in the field and to by-pass the FBI leadership in Washington, Marshall resorted to a bureaucratic solution (coercion) to combat a bureaucratic vice (inaction). Hoover viewed the box memo as an inefficient, ineffective method, and it suited him fine. The box memo allowed him to tell the integrationists that the FBI completed each and every task assigned by responsible government officials, and it allowed him (in the manner of the disclaimer policy) to tell the segregationists that the FBI scrupulously confined its actions to the specific orders of those same officials. By paying attention to the letter of the law, Hoover negated the intention of the law.[27]

While adapting the Civil Rights Division's box memo to meet its own needs, the FBI resisted Marshall's call for "special squads" of elite agents "who would travel from state to state . . . handling voting discrimination matters." Hoover had in fact ordered the creation of "specially trained squads to handle such investigations" many years before, in response to criticism from Truman's Committee on Civil Rights. But he mobilized these squads only for public relations purposes. The director quickly abandoned even the pretense of a voting rights strike force, and he had no intention of creating the real thing when the Kennedy-era Civil Rights Division asked him to do so. When Marshall brought up this "old routine" in a meeting with Alex Rosen and Clement McGowan, the two FBI men hit it "on the head and knocked it down hard."[28]

Marshall also responded to FBI intransigence, as had Harold Tyler, by relying on volunteers and Civil Rights Division attorneys to do the FBI's work. The Division often sent one of its own lawyers to a southern city or county to check on minor matters rather than work through the FBI. Andrew Young of the Southern Christian Leadership Conference suggested that Hoover had Marshall's men "all scared to death." Actually, the motive was convenience more than fear. "[It was] more expensive, but easier," one roving lawyer explained. "You don't fight the FBI. You work around them." John Doar considered it the natural thing to do. "I was a small-town lawyer and used to doing my own investigating," he said. Because the Civil Rights Division had few illusions about the director's views on voting rights, Marshall even segregated the investigations conducted in the South. FBI agents handled interviews with the white majority because Doar and his fellows had "no rapport" with white southerners. "They [wouldn't] talk to us." Division attorneys handled interviews with blacks. "[The FBI] did not have the resources to interview blacks," Marshall explained. "Their mode of operation was to inform the local police of what they were doing and this exposed blacks to economic and physical intimidation." Whenever the Bureau did interview a black man, one of Marshall's men added, "it was unbelievable." "They would . . . scare him out of his pants," and then write up a report giving no indication of the agent's actions. The Bureau kept its paper "clean," another attorney assigned to the U.S. Civil Rights Commission concluded. That attorney never read an FBI report revealing any bias—let alone "an FBI report saying, 'This guy's a nigger.'" Hoover always hid his personal feelings on race, along with the strain of racism that ran through his Bureau.[29]

Over time, John Doar did a fine job, as Anthony Lewis of the *New York Times* observed, "risking his life to gather the evidence that made his law suits irresistible." In the Macon County, Alabama, voter discrimination case, with Division attorneys scrambling to meet a trial date and lacking the time to spar with the FBI, Doar and another lawyer went into the field themselves. Relying on Tuskegee voting league volunteers to organize photostats of registration records, they came "upon a gold mine" when they began to interview black school teachers, professors, and professionals who had been denied the right to vote. Comparing the literacy tests of these well-educated black citizens with those of barely literate whites who had been allowed to register, Doar and his volunteers gathered the documentation needed to make their case.[30]

But a price had to be paid for writing-off the FBI's investigative resources, and the civil rights movement ended up paying
it. The policy spread Civil Rights Division attorneys too thin,
preventing the filing of voting suits that should have been filed
and the prosecution of southern lawmen who should have been
prosecuted under the color-of-law statute for harassing voter
registration workers. "We closed investigations which I just
knew if we had the time and the resources we might have developed into cases," Marshall affirmed. And the good and brave
work that Doar performed in the deep South came at a price
of inefficiency. "Administratively," Clement McGowan asserted,
"he was probably the worst. Apparently, no one [at the Civil
Rights Division] could make a closing decision until John approved it. Often, he was off travelling somewhere. Things really
got bogged down over there."[31] That was Hoover's idea in the
first place—to slow down the Division and its voting litigation
campaign.

Hoover's attitude about what the FBI could do and the Justice
Department's deference to that attitude also meant that southern sheriffs and Ku Klux Klansmen could beat voter registration
workers right under the FBI's nose. According to the Department's office of legal council, Bureau agents could make an arrest if they observed "a crowd of White citizens . . . pursuing and
beating a Negro student."[32] But the no-arrest policy ruled, with
Hoover finding allies for his position in Attorney General
Kennedy and Assistant Attorney General Marshall. They sided
with the director for the very reasons of politics that led to the
voting litigation strategy in the first place, reasoning that a more
aggressive stance might result in conservative southern congressional Democrats blocking even the administration's modest
civil rights initiatives. So the FBI stood, watched, and took
notes, and sometimes even snapped photos with "35mm cameras disguised in shaving kit, lunch pail, and necktie clasp con-
cealments," while the resistance beat up voter registration
workers and other movement people.[33]

Hoover's own analysis of the "technical and general consider-
ations" underlying the no-arrest policy would have complicated
matters even if the Kennedys had been more aggressive. For the
director, the relevant laws, Sections 241 and 242, provided no
authority for on-the-spot arrests. "Independent action by the
FBI would . . . only aggravate the problem," Bureau executives
concluded, since agents on the scene would probably be outnum-

bered and outgunned, and an arrest in such a circumstance would be an adventure. It wasn't quite the same thing as shooting it out with John Dillinger, since civil rights cases were "hurried," "often hazardous," and more than anything else "ambiguous." The director found it disturbing that he might have to protect people challenging the values and laws of the white South.[34]

Though Hoover blamed the voter registration workers for bringing the beatings on themselves, he realized that anti–civil rights violence mocked the authority and dignity of the United States. The FBI had always presented itself as a can-do bureaucracy, compiling an impressive and highly publicized record of the spectacular (combat with the gangsters of the 1930s) and the tedious (the millions of man-hours spent tracking spies and subversives during World War II and the McCarthy era). Led by its celebrity director, the FBI did not simply enforce federal law or cooly gather intelligence. It crusaded against evil. On civil rights, however, Hoover was being asked to go against his own sense of good and evil, so he ordered his agents to stay away. In his view, protecting civil rights was not their job, and technically, of course, he had a case. Under the federal system the maintenance of law and order has principally been the responsibility of state and local police officers, though they were the very people who had abdicated their responsibility in the American South of 1961. Those were extraordinary times and the FBI had built its reputation by doing extraordinary things during extraordinary times, but the director would fill no law-and-order vacuum here. In the end, his stance damaged the image and role of the FBI, just as it impeded the progress of the struggle for black equality.[35]

Although racism in the FBI was a serious problem, the director's noninterventionist policy probably perplexed two or three everyday G-men for every one who applauded it. Many of the agents who stood by and took notes on civil rights abuses fought in World War II and Korea, and as a group they were what Hoover said they were—brave men. "You had agents prepared to do anything they could get away with to help black people," Nicholas Katzenbach believed. Joseph Rauh, general counsel for the Leadership Conference on Civil Rights, described the field agents he encountered as "decent guys doing their job." These decent guys made up "a different level of people, the nonpolitical level," and they worked, or at least they thought they did, for "a different Bureau."[36]

On occasion, FBI agents acted decisively. When white by-standers attacked demonstrators in Bogalusa, Louisiana, John Doar said he would "never forget" Joseph A. Sullivan "moving in, dressing down the local police authorities for their failure to do their duty." Clement McGowan said "a number of your SACs [Special Agents in Charge] or assistants or resident agents were going around to the police departments and told them, 'Chief, you've got to put some men out there to [protect the demonstrators],' and talked to them just like a Dutch uncle. And that, basically, was what Sullivan was doing. Hollering at them to get out there and get on the job."[37]

FBI field agents, however, rarely acted in such a manner. Generally, they followed orders and remained on the sidelines. Calvin Williams, a voter registration volunteer for the Congress of Racial Equality, said "we never saw anybody walk up and say, 'I'm an FBI agent.' . . . Never actually saw one come out and throw his shield out and say, 'I'm protecting you.'" "When a case gets national attention, the FBI seems to be able to do an impressive job," C. T. Vivian of the Southern Christian Leadership Conference observed. "But the day-by-day violations don't make headlines. That's where we get disillusioned." "Our experience with the FBI," Vivian's SCLC colleague, Andrew Young, recalled, "was that no matter what kind of brutality [took place] . . . all the FBI agents did was stand over on the corner and take notes."[38]

Hoover and the bureaucrats around him ignored their own field agents who chafed under the noninterventionist policy as well as the voter registration activists in Mississippi or Civil Rights Division lawyers in Washington. "Most of the damage [the FBI hierarchy] did was a failure to do what they should have been doing," Katzenbach maintained. "There was no [commitment to civil rights work]. Hoover would have preferred to keep black people in their places," and in pursuit of that end he made certain that his own agents remained in their proper place.[39]

FBI policy on the issue of physically protecting civil rights workers encountered little resistance in the White House. "It was very important, as far as we were concerned," Robert Kennedy said, that Hoover "remained happy and that he remain in his position because he was a symbol and the President had won by such a narrow margin and it was a hell of an investigative body and he got a lot of things done and it was much better for what we wanted to do in the South, what we wanted to do in organized crime, and what we wanted to do in a lot of other areas, if we had him on our side." The Kennedys understood the limits of their own power and the formidable base of Hoover's power. They lacked the political strength to take an aggressive stand on the protection issue themselves or to force Hoover to do so. Political reality prevented them from making a total commitment to racial justice. Neither John Kennedy the president nor John Kennedy the candidate for reelection in 1964 would risk alienating the FBI director or southern Democrats in Congress.[40]

Hoover always cited a string of legitimate reasons for not protecting civil rights workers, and he based an additional argument here on a tortured version of civil libertarianism. Attempts to assign FBI agents the task of protecting the voting rights activists would lead to a national police force. "This was one of Hoover's favorite *ex cathedra* assertions repeated so often on social occasions," Victor Navasky wrote in *Kennedy Justice*, that the attorney general himself used this convenient formulation. The director found common ground with the administration once again, with the Kennedys willing to protect themselves from the political risks of an aggressive civil rights program and the voter registration workers from "the specter of a national police force *cum* Gestapo." But the Kennedys would not protect movement activists from segregationist terror.

"These kids were out there," John Seigenthaler remembered, referring to the young people who risked their lives to canvass the rural South. "They couldn't get the FBI to answer them." Rather than pressure the Bureau to do something, "Bob gave them my number. And Burke Marshall's number. 'Any hour of the day or night, you call.' God, they called," Seigenthaler continued. "Burke got the most of it. It's no way to tell how many late nights Burke Marshall would wake up out of a sound sleep—some kid in the county store in McComb, Mississippi, who was looking out the front door, at 10 or 15 young white punks who just wanted [him] to come out." McComb, Mississippi, was a long way from Washington, D.C., where Marshall and Seigenthaler lived. What could they do, beyond lending a sympathetic ear and giving advice? Call the FBI? The FBI would tell them the same thing they told the kids. "We are not a protection agency."[41]

The movement and its supporters could not understand the constraints under which the Kennedy administration operated. For them, according to Marshall, "the constitutional question was merely a technicality," especially since "the federal government had enormous power. The government had an army, a navy, an air force—as well as an FBI." For people "whose lives were on the line all the time," Marshall said, "the idea that the power wouldn't be used was incomprehensible. It was lawyers' piddling talk."[42] Over time, the fundamental difference in spirit between Hoover's investigators and Kennedy's lawyers blurred in the minds of "the kids who were out there." Roy Wilkins's nephew, Roger, then with the Agency for International Development and later director of the Community Relations Service, remembered "a lot of people in the civil rights division at the Justice Department [who] kept telling us how complicated matters were and developed to a high art the practice of splitting the difference between right and wrong. . . . But at least the Kennedy-era pragmatists asked the right questions and pressed in the right directions," at least they had a "moral compass." The men who made the decisions in Hoover's FBI had an entirely different sense of right and wrong.[43]

Burke Marshall complained about the FBI's "*pro forma*" civil rights work, saying it was "worth nothing." But his idea of federalism, with its elaborate systems of deference to state and local authority, resembled the director's own self-serving notions about the FBI's jurisdictional humility. When Marshall took those phone calls from voter registration workers in McComb and elsewhere, he proved, finally, no more comforting than Hoover. Marshall's view—that the government lacked the constitutional authority to protect civil rights workers—may have won him the position of assistant attorney general for civil rights in the first place. The Kennedys, according to former Deputy Attorney General Byron White, wanted "a first-class lawyer who would do the job in a technically proficient way that would be defensible in court—that Southerners would not think of as a vendetta, but as an even-handed application of the law." Robert Kennedy did not want a civil rights activist, noted John Seigenthaler, so "Whizzer White brought [in] Burke Marshall," a Yale Law graduate who came to his post from the prestigious firm of Covington and Burling with a background in corporation law.[44]

Marshall's respect for federalism and the Kennedys' respect for political reality, coupled with what one historian has described as the president's "simplistic . . . view of Reconstruction as a vindictive reign of terror and corruption which the North had visited upon the South," make it easy to see why Hoover could function without serious interference. These things also make it easy to see why the administration sided with voter registration workers only in spirit. Ultimately, white southerners would have to take responsibility for the restoration of southern order. "We ought to live through it," concluded Marshall. Robert Kennedy elaborated: "Now maybe it's going to take a decade; and maybe a lot of people are going to be killed in the meantime; and I think that's unfortunate. But in the long run I think it's for the health of the country and the stability of this system; and it's the best way to proceed." The decision to uphold federalism tormented Kennedy and Marshall—Marshall especially. The FBI director did not seem to be bothered in the least. On the contrary, this view best served his private agenda.[45]

Even if the Kennedy administration had succeeded in mobilizing Hoover's agents, the available manpower was inadequate to do the job. The logistics made no sense, Marshall argued. "The only effective protection would have been to give each [civil rights] worker a guard. And there are no civilians that could do that." A public alliance with the civil rights movement on the protection issue would have led to a false sense of security, a stronger backlash, and the mobilization of the only available "political force . . . the United States Army." Marshall said "it was a matter of prudence." If voter registration workers from the Student Nonviolent Coordinating Committee (SNCC) "thought they could push the Civil Rights Division around, they could force confrontation." One single concession in a hard-line state like Mississippi and there would be "no stopping point . . . [short] of military occupation"—Reconstruction II, in other words. Marshall saw no middle ground.[46]

Hoover understood the politics of the issue from the beginning; the voting rights activists who needed federal protection did not. After meeting with Robert Kennedy and Marshall in June 1961, SNCC workers thought they had struck a deal with the administration. The attorney general wanted the movement's action wing to redirect its energies, to move away from sit-ins and freedom rides and toward the Justice Department's more manageable and less confrontational voting litigation campaign. (Historian Vincent Harding called it an attempt "'to get the niggers off the street.'") Kennedy and Marshall suggested that financial support would be made available through private foundations—a promise that the Southern Regional Council (SRC) helped fulfill by administering the Voter Education Project.[47] But Kennedy and Marshall never promised to protect the students from segregationists who were just as prone to beat up voter registration workers as lunch-counter protestors or freedom riders.

Harold Fleming, former SRC executive director, described the price of political innocence. "Not protecting the kids was a moral shock, more than a cold-blooded, calculated reckoning. It was bruising and deeply emotional. To have the FBI looking out of the courthouse windows while you were being chased down the street by brick throwers deeply offends the sensibilities. So people wept and cursed Robert Kennedy and Burke Marshall more than the FBI, whom they never had any confidence in to begin with. . . . SNCC *et al.* thought Justice's bargain was protection in exchange for a shift from direct action protest to a voter registration drive. Because of the Kennedys' own view of reality they encouraged this belief. . . . Nobody would ever forgive the Kennedys for playing politics because they weren't supposed to on this front."[48] John Kennedy's civil rights adviser, Harris Wofford, a man deeply committed to the black struggle and the first white man to graduate from the Howard University Law School, underscored Fleming's point. "What Kennedy liked best in my role and what I liked least," Wofford confided, "was my function as a buffer between him and the civil rights forces pressing for presidential action. . . . I got tired of him accosting me with a grin and asking, 'Are your constituents happy?'"[49]

With Hoover and the administration, each for their own reasons, unwilling to provide the requested protection, the voter registration workers and the entire civil rights movement were bound to suffer. The FBI's investigation of five instances of violence aimed at SNCC in southwest Mississippi in the late summer and fall of 1961 helped dissipate the naiveté Fleming described. The first episode occurred on August 15, when the Mississippi Highway Patrol arrested Robert Moses, a SNCC worker who left Hamilton College and Harvard and a comfortable teaching job for the poverty and danger of the delta. Billy Caston, a cousin of the Amite County sheriff, beat Moses bloody a week later, after he went to the courthouse in Liberty with three local blacks who were trying to register. Two weeks later, a white mob attacked Travis Britt on the Amite courthouse lawn. On September 7, John Q. Woods, registrar of voters in the Walthall County seat of Tylertown, hit John Hardy in the back of the head with a gun barrel, and on September 25 state legislator

Eugene H. Hurst shot and killed Herbert Lee during a confrontation at a cotton gin.

Not only did the FBI refuse to protect these civil rights workers, it neglected its investigative duties in the aftermath of all five cases. Bureau reports sent to the Civil Rights Division failed to note the nine stitches in Moses's scalp and face, and contained little data on the Lee killing regarding powder burns, the angle of the bullet entering the head, and conflicting witness statements. After Moses sent his own report of events in southwest Mississippi to the Justice Department, John Doar compared it to the FBI report and ordered the Bureau's agents back into the field. One of those agents, the resident agent from Natchez, threatened Moses with bodily harm "for going behind his back, for calling him a liar." Doar also sent two Civil Rights Division attorneys, Bud Sather and Gerald Stein, into the field, and they gathered more documentation in four or five days regarding intimidation of blacks in Walthall and Amite counties than the FBI had in a month. "Whatever the shortcomings of the Justice Department, they certainly made a visible impact on the black population of Mississippi," Moses observed. "People like E. W. Steptoe, down in Amite County. His face lit up when John Doar and the Justice Department came out . . . so different from when a local resident FBI agent came."[50]

Moses charged that police officers murdered a black farmer named Louis Allen because he had trusted one of the FBI's resident agents assigned to investigate the Lee killing. Allen agreed to be a witness against Hurst, but he told county police "what they wanted to hear. . . . The FBI leaked this to the local authorities, and the Sheriff, and the Deputy Sheriff, came out, you know," Moses alleged. "And they had been picking on him ever since—that was in September '61. At one point a deputy sheriff broke his jaw—and then they killed him. With a shotgun." Allen's widow remembered "Louis walking through the house before he was killed, saying he didn't want to die, that he knew people who had been dead, died when he was a boy, that when you're dead you're dead a long time."[51]

"The Bureau performed its normal functions," Nicholas Katzenbach explained, "in a situation which was anything but normal."[52] Reluctance to protect voter registration workers before the fact was one thing; reluctance to investigate after the fact quite another. And this reluctance remained throughout the Kennedy years and beyond. In 1962 FBI agents investigated the shots that night riders fired into a Ruleville, Mississippi, home where Charles McLaurin and other SNCC workers stayed. "They asked the people if we did the shooting," McLaurin recalled. In 1963 segregationists attacked Moses and Randolph T. Blackwell of the Voter Education Project while driving near Greenwood, Mississippi, and shot a passenger, SNCC field secretary Jimmy Travis, in the head and neck. An FBI agent asked the victims, "Are you boys sure you didn't shoot up this car?" "[Like] talking to a member of the Ku Klux Klan," Blackwell said.[53] During James Meredith's 1966 march from Memphis, Tennessee, to Jackson, Mississippi, to encourage voter registration, Hoover refused to assign more than a token number of agents. "Just enough," as former FBI Assistant Director William Sullivan charged, "to avoid criticism." Birmingham police officers saw "only ten F.B.I. agents accompanying the marchers from the time they left Hernando, the place where Meredith was shot on the second day of the march, until the tear gas was dispersed in Canton on Thursday night." When Hoover sent in forty more agents after that, a number of them complained to the Birmingham policemen that John Doar used them as "errant [sic] boys." In the meantime, Hoover told Eastland that "67 Commie organizers" had entered Mississippi during the course of the march. The director always kept his priorities straight.[54]

FBI behavior led the American Civil Liberties Union to conclude that Hoover's bureaucracy lacked "a psychology of commitment" when "enforcing laws which guarantee Negroes equal rights." Movement people demanded "the kind of diligence the FBI shows in solving kidnapping and bank robberies." They settled for a bureaucracy that appeared more apathetic than heroic. Even Robert Kennedy began to wonder whether the FBI was more obstacle than resource in the war against the white southern way of black disenfranchisement.[55]

During the first of the Kennedy years the most serious challenge to the FBI's noninterventionist policy on voting rights and other civil rights enforcement came not from the ACLU, the NAACP, or even Burke Marshall's Civil Rights Division, but from the U.S. Civil Rights Commission. With the Civil Rights Act of 1957 authorizing the Commission to hold hearings on any prima facie denial of civil rights, the FBI concluded that publicity surrounding any such hearings would lead to increased pressure for federal intervention. Assistant Director Louis Nichols discussed this possibility with Senator Eastland even before the

Civil Rights Act became law. "I told Jim that one thing that some of the southern folks should think about is that if they get a President's Commission there is going to be an invasion of the South with all sorts of hearings."[56] In preparation for such hearings, the Commission would likely audit FBI investigations. To counter this move, Hoover denied the Commission access to investigative reports on voting rights matters. Ultimately, this policy forced Robert Kennedy to choose between the FBI's *de facto* authority to keep its secrets and the Civil Rights Commission's *de jure* authority to "investigate allegations . . . that certain citizens of the United States are being deprived of their right to vote."[57]

Initially, the FBI's insistence on keeping its secrets caused few problems. Under Eisenhower, the Civil Rights Commission had been "a cautious and rather technical body, compiling information and proposing modest remedies," and making few formal demands on the FBI for voting rights data—especially after the October 1957 resignation of Attorney General Herbert Brownell, the only civil rights advocate in President Eisenhower's cabinet. With the Commission's methods expected to change under the Kennedys, the FBI tried to delay the inevitable. Harris Wofford told President Kennedy that the Bureau's security check of Berl Bernhard, the administration's nominee for staff director and a holdover from the Eisenhower-era Commission, was "holding up staff reorganization."[58]

The FBI's opposition to Berl Bernhard began a few months before John Kennedy put his name up. "I was on a panel at Catholic University on civil rights and in the course of it I made a comment, which got front-page headlines in the *Washington Post*, that was critical of civil rights enforcement by the Bureau," Bernhard remembered. "I was hauled before the Senate Internal Security Subcommittee by Senators Eastland and [Thomas J.] Dodd," a Democrat from Connecticut and a former FBI agent, "and a director named Jay Sourwine, and received a visit from one of Mr. Hoover's people. It became a major issue when I had a meeting with Bob Kennedy about whether the president was going to nominate me. Mr. Hoover determined I was—there's a phrase for it—'not to be contacted.' Then Mr. Hoover did an evaluation of me. He came up with all kinds of stuff I never heard before." Upon completing its investigation in March 1961, moreover, the FBI turned over its report to the chairman of the Senate Judiciary Committee—James Eastland.

Eventually, Bernhard saw his FBI file. "Bob Kennedy showed it to me and said, 'How can I have my brother nominate you with this kind of material?'" Kennedy made that remark in jest, more or less, "because he was having his own problems with Mr. Hoover."

When the FBI finally cleared Bernhard and the Senate confirmed him, he began an ambitious investigation of FBI policy on voting rights, police brutality, and other civil rights enforcement responsibilities—an effort that led to another confrontation with the director. "I was summoned to Mr. Hoover's office," Bernhard continued, along with the chairman of the Civil Rights Commission and then-president of Michigan State University, John A. Hannah. "I called Senator Hart, Phil Hart, who was on the judiciary Committee, and told him about it—he was a friend of Dr. Hannah's from Michigan. He came with us. It was Hart, Hannah, and me. Mr. Hoover was, to say the least, irate. He didn't know what was wrong with us. He launched into a monologue about the irrationality of the civil rights movement and asserted that we had become dupes of the civil rights movement and the left wing of this and that." Although prepared for this outburst, Hannah, Hart, and Bernhard gave ground. "We said, 'Look, we will take another look at the report to be sure that whatever we say is factually accurate before it's published.'"[59]

The Civil Rights Commission did not tone down its report enough to please Hoover. Released as part of the Commission's annual report for 1961, the FBI section reviewed many of the issues Truman's Committee on Civil Rights originally raised in 1947 and in some ways extended that earlier critique. To document Bureau priorities, Commission staff searched back issues of the *FBI Law Enforcement Bulletin* and found dozens of articles on the apathy of the American people toward the Red menace, but only one item focusing on civil rights. The report's principal author, Arnold Trebach, a lawyer who also held a Princeton Ph.D., went into the field to review particular FBI investigations. He had seen hundreds of Bureau case files in the months preceeding the change of administration, courtesy of Civil Rights Division attorney Arthur B. Caldwell—who had the Bureau send over any file Trebach requested without alerting Hoover or any of his aides. Trebach's audit of these investigations provided the foundation for his conclusion that the FBI had a consistent history of avoiding civil rights work. Its record in 1961 was much the same (lethargic and ineffective) as it had been in 1941 or 1951. A packed press conference accompanied the report's release, and Trebach remembered two *Pravda* correspondents sitting in the second row.[60]

Robert Kennedy and Burke Marshall refused to side with the Civil Rights Commission, even though they agreed with nearly everything the Commission had to say about the FBI. Commission members also criticized the Justice Department voting litigation strategy and urged the Department to support a broader attack on inequality through legislation. One Commission member, Harvard Law School dean Erwin Griswold, considered the Marshall-Kennedy emphasis on litigation "a retail operation." The Civil Rights Commission favored a "wholesale operation," a broad attempt to change "the whole situation" by holding hearings and developing new legislation. In the process, Griswold identified Marshall—unfairly—as a particularly "negative influence," a "conservative" and "cautious" man who "had no broad vision of the whole thing at all."[61]

Ultimately, Marshall advised Bernhard not to pressure the FBI. Hoover needed time to cool off.[62] Robert Kennedy identified the Civil Rights Commission—and not Hoover's FBI—as the principal problem. "I didn't have any great feeling that they were accomplishing anything of a positive nature. . . . It was almost like the old House Un-American Activities Committee investigating Communism. . . . They were not objective investigations. . . . So I had no confidence in them," he said, in an ironic comment, as he had worked for Senator Joseph R. McCarthy's Permanent Subcommittee on Investigations during the 1950s and retained "a fondness for McCarthy." At the same time, the Civil Rights Commission had invaded the Justice Department's domain. "Doing what we were really doing," Kennedy complained. "Voting." Bernhard said he "had never seen anyone so angry at the Commission as Robert Kennedy, not even John Patterson or George Wallace." In his struggle with the Commission, the FBI director would find no more valuable ally than the attorney general.[63]

Hoover received Robert Kennedy's help when the Civil Rights Commission asked the FBI for the firsthand information it needed to do its job. Kennedy stopped Arthur Caldwell from giving any more voting rights and police brutality files to Arnold Trebach and other Commission staff. "We should have had access to FBI reports," Bernhard said. "When we'd get complaints my inclination was to defer to the Department because they could take remedial action. But then we'd want to get the factual basis from the Department and they wouldn't let us see the Bureau reports. . . . Justice would come in and we'd have a big meeting with Seigenthaler, Doar, Bob, Burke and me. There'd be lots of give and take. But in the end, we'd lose out because the Attorney General wasn't willing to take on the Bureau."[64]

Bernhard asked Doar and Marshall why segregationist congressmen received FBI data and not the Civil Rights Commission. "I knew that Mr. Eastland, Mr. Thurmond, and the rest of them did not have the investigating capacity to get the facts that they had. . . . I knew they got them from somewhere, from the Civil Rights Division or the Bureau." It did not do much good to raise this issue either. Doar and Marshall shrugged. "They were very chary," Bernhard thought. "They would say, 'We've got material from the FBI, we can't let you see it.'"[65]

Hoover did not leave the Civil Rights Commission entirely out in the cold. Wofford said the Commission accepted Hoover's offer to assign an FBI liaison officer to work with it daily, but this only led to "the FBI knowing everything about the commission's work, without the commission getting any more information from the FBI." Bernhard said "this fellow was at my office every morning. Full time. After I had been taken off the 'not-to-contact' list, he gave me specific documents. I got one or two direct from Mr. Hoover saying, 'You might be interested to see some of the activities of your friend, Dr. Martin Luther King.' That kind of thing. I got one on Roy Wilkins. I remember *very clearly* looking at it and saying, 'Why am I getting this?' The FBI fellow would say, 'Well, we thought it would be helpful.'"[66] The FBI provided "name checks on witnesses" to prevent "people who were just out-and-out communists from testifying," and security reports on applicants for Commission employment—all "throwbacks to the McCarthy era," said William L. Taylor, Jr., the Commission's liaison with the White House. It worried Bernhard that if he put someone on the payroll that the FBI did not approve of, he knew what the director "might do in terms of turning it over to Mr. Eastland. I could just see the McCarthy-like destruction. I've been there."[67]

None of these services lasted very long. J. Edgar Hoover—not Robert Kennedy—cut them off. FBI officials, as Bernhard suspected, were indeed leaking information to Senator Eastland's Internal Security Subcommittee and as well to the House Committee on Un-American Activities. Kennedy knew it, but he could not stop it.[68] The FBI leaked information that might hurt the voting litigation campaign and the civil rights movement to the Civil Rights Commission and the segregationists alike—while closely guarding information that might help blacks. Having reaffirmed its autonomy (winning the only bureaucratic battle that really mattered), the FBI concerned itself with cosmetic reforms to appease the Civil Rights Commission. Clyde Tolson prepared a what-is-to-be-done memo in December recommending civil rights articles for the *FBI Law Enforcement Bulletin* and additional civil rights material in Hoover's annual testimony before the House Appropriations Subcommittee. Tolson also suggested that Alex Rosen meet regularly with the Commission chairman. The FBI, he said, should make every effort "to indoctrinate Hannah in the manner in which . . . [we] function in Civil Rights matters."[69]

Robert Kennedy knew Hoover had no "great sympathy" for voting rights, but he believed the director gave ground and eventually made a positive contribution. "He . . . recognizes where the power is and what he has to do; and, once he reaches that decision, that is paramount. I think he reached the decision that we were going to do things in civil rights and that that's the way it was going to be. . . . So that either you'd have to do it or you'd have to get out." "When they did things," Kennedy added, "frequently they did them damned well." Burke Marshall's number two man in the Civil Rights Division, St. John Barrett, said the FBI's "investigations were vital. They simply happened to be the bureaucratic instrument that was in place and could do things nobody else could do." Barrett gave a backhanded compliment. The FBI was "not in the forefront of the legal implementation of civil rights by any means, but they nonetheless provided invaluable logistical help."[70]

In 1961, however, the FBI did not actively intervene in voting rights cases or other civil rights matters. Marshall considered the Bureau "absolutely useless." Wofford identified the Bureau as the principal "bottleneck." Katzenbach labeled the Bureau's ultimate contribution "marginal and somewhat grudging." Even Doar, while noting the paucity of "written documentation one way or the other" and recognizing the fallacy of transferring "our impatience with America itself, onto the FBI," considered the Bureau's agents "ill-prepared," their performance "lackluster," and their superiors at the "seat of government," as Hoover referred to FBI headquarters, ignorant "about the realities of life in the South."[71]

FBI executives reciprocated in their opinion of the civil rights people in the Justice Department and the White House. They considered Wofford a "security risk," Doar a "bellyacher," Marshall no "friend of the Bureau." Three years later, when Marshall accused the FBI of leaking derogatory "background information" to the press on the alleged subversive associations of Martin Luther King, he received a telephone call from Rosen, who said: "The Director wants you to know that you are a goddamned liar!" "Hoover wouldn't talk to me, basically," Marshall said. The director never spoke much to Doar either, and in fact Doar remembered (vaguely) only one inconsequential conversation. "I think I rode up with him in the elevator once." After John Kennedy's death, the director only spoke to Robert Kennedy when he had no choice.[72]

The FBI's public posture of studied neutrality was anything but neutral in its impact. If the Bureau did not completely torpedo the Civil Rights Commission's grand plans to change "the whole situation," Hoover's refusal to cooperate did not make the Commission's work any easier. The Bureau's resistance to the active advancement of civil rights law further constrained the voting litigation drive. The failure to protect SNCC and other voter registration workers represented the beginnings of a rupture between the movement's action arm and the government they assumed would support them. The defendants in the civil suit SNCC filed a year later, in 1962, to force the government to protect its citizens, were Kennedy and Hoover. Robert Moses himself believed that the Civil Rights Division never pursued a voting rights case down in Amite County, Mississippi, and the other places where blood flowed, "precisely because there was violence. They didn't want a case moving through the courts that opened up the issue of the federal government protecting voter registration workers and black people attempting to register."[73]

The spectacle of the federal government, usually in the form of an FBI agent, passively watching the brutalization of voter registration workers, helped spur "on the movement's determination to succeed," observed Bayard Rustin of the Southern Christian Leadership Conference. But it also led to "battle fatigue" among SNCC activists and other movement "shock troops." "In many ways these young civil rights workers are in a war and exposed to the stresses of warfare," Harvard psychiatrist Robert Coles wrote. "Clinical signs of depression," including "exhaustion, weariness, despair, frustration, and rage," would be visible by the end of the Kennedy years, leading some movement people to walk away and others to question the turn-the-other-cheek assumptions of nonviolent protest.[74]

Government officials' announcements about the inability of the FBI to protect civil rights workers may have encouraged the more primitive elements of the white southern resistance. "That led to injury and death," Roger Wilkins concluded. "And it deterred a lot of people who might have worked for civil rights. Not everyone who believed in civil rights was brave." Berl Bernhard said the FBI and its director had

> almost made civil rights leaders available to bounty hunters. In saying that, I accept the fact that it was a very difficult period because the people who were in control of the Congress by and large had very strong constituencies in the South. No one wanted to antagonize the McClellans and the Eastlands and the Thurmonds. But the result, for the bounty hunter, was that it was 'OK.' . . . The federal government wasn't there.

"The message coming out of Washington, from Mr. Hoover," SNCC's John Lewis reiterated, "was very clear."[75]

Who was responsible? "There's probably enough blame to spread around," conceded Civil Rights Commission attorney William Taylor. "Ultimately, the policy decisions were made at the very top of the government, by the attorney general and by the president, by the head of the Civil Rights Division. There was an excess of caution. Bobby Kennedy came to understand the nature of the problem that he was dealing with in far more depth than he had in the beginning. And when he understood the nature he was an extraordinarily effective and articulate person in dealing with the whole question of civil rights. But I don't think [he] understood it in the beginning." Years later, after Kennedy had moved on to the United States Senate and turned "to peace and populism," he remembered how mad he had been at Taylor and the other people who worked for the Civil Rights Commission, and how willing he had been to take Hoover's side, and he shook his head, laughing bitterly at himself.[76]

Would things have been much different if Robert Kennedy had understood "in the beginning" the things that William Taylor wanted him to understand? If he had tried to force the FBI to plunge headfirst into voting rights work, to protect "the kids," to cooperate with the Civil Rights Commission, to worry less about Bureau rights and more about black people's rights? The FBI director's refusal to enforce the law represented more than bureaucratic politics and bureaucratic arrogance. It was the first systematic and sustained attempt to impede the people of color who were causing so many problems for the Bureau in the first place. Hoover had not asked the Kennedys to put the FBI in the path of the onrushing civil rights movement. But once there and upon discovering that he could not leave, he developed strategies for countering the movement and exploiting the political constraints that the Kennedy administration faced. The director even found common ground with the administration from time to time, forming alliances that caused ruptures between the movement and the government and among those government agencies committed to the struggle for black equality.

Having engaged the civil rights movement during the voting litigation campaign of 1961 largely on his own terms, Hoover would spend the next two years skirmishing with the movement on every imaginable front and expanding the only Negro Question responsibility that he felt comfortable with—domestic political surveillance of anyone, black or white, who undermined the peace and quiet of his Bureau and the internal security of his America by struggling for racial justice.

3

===========〜〜〜===========

Unbecoming Deeds

From FREEBUS to BAPBOMB and the Albany Movement

J Edgar Hoover stopped speaking to Burke Marshall shortly after the first skirmishes of 1961–1963, about a week after Mother's Day in May 1961 when Ku Klux Klan mobs attacked two groups of Freedom Riders at bus station terminals in the Alabama cities of Birmingham and Montgomery. Marshall had criticized the Bureau for its failure to provide adequate intelligence about the plans of the Freedom Riders or the Klan's plans (with its allies in the Alabama law enforcement community) to greet the riders. "When the bus arrived in Montgomery and the local police . . . were purposely not there to meet it," Marshall said, "I realized for the first time that we didn't have any spy system, we didn't have any information."[1] His words reflected an emerging Kennedy administration consensus on the need to collect intelligence about civil rights protest.

Having rejected a protective role, and negligently fulfilled an investigative role, Hoover's FBI now succeeded in turning a surveillance role to its own purposes. If the civil rights movement was active in a particular southern city or county, the Civil Rights Division came to expect police brutality and Ku Klux Klan violence. Division lawyers wanted to know what would happen ahead of time, and they asked the FBI to provide the answers—even though they knew that the intelligence they would receive from the FBI would reflect the director's personal and political assumptions about the Negro Question and his bureaucratic preference for maintaining a smooth working relationship with southern lawmen. Hoover believed all civil rights activists were troublemakers, that many of them were communists or had communist associations. So the intelligence he provided minimized the collusion between the Klan and local police, and exaggerated the political associations of the people who organized the demonstrations and voter registration drives in the first place. No matter how much they objected to these priorities, Kennedy administration officials accommodated themselves to them. Things had changed a great deal since the days of Woodrow Wilson and the black scare of 1919, but the government still viewed surveillance as something far more convenient and far less controversial than an aggressive, all-out effort to enforce federal civil rights law or to protect civil rights workers. Once again, Hoover's private bias and the administration's political expediency led in the same direction.

Under the pressure of events that began with the Freedom Rides and continued over the next two years, Hoover escalated FBI intelligence gathering activities. Earlier, in the mid-1950s, the Bureau conducted investigations of racial disturbances, particularly demonstrations and clashes arising out of school desegregation, but generally did not file reports with the Civil Rights Division. Instead, the Bureau sent its reports to the Department's Internal Security Division, where the Division bumped them back over to Civil Rights after five or ten days. By organizing information from the FBI "around the requirements of internal security surveillance rather than civil rights protection," this procedure focused the Civil Rights Division's attention on the activities of the Communist party and not disenfranchisement, segregated schools and transportation, and other obstacles to black equality.[2]

By Hoover's reckoning, the FBI had no "investigative jurisdiction over . . . general racial matters." His Bureau had an "intelligence function" based on "U.S. Army regulations [which] place responsibility upon the Army to keep advised of any developments of a civil disturbance nature which may require the . . . intervention of Federal troops." On the eve of the Freedom Rides, then, FBI policy required investigation of all "proposed or actual activities of individuals, officials, committees, legislatures, organizations, etc., in the racial field." Between March 1959 and January 1960 Bureau executives disseminated 892 reports on racial matters to the Justice Department. By that time they sent copies directly to Civil Rights Division attorneys, forwarding additional copies to the military intelligence agencies and state and local police departments whenever they detected a rumor of violence.[3]

Compared to what would follow, FBI surveillance activities were minimal and the spy gap that Burke Marshall had complained about would not close until the Freedom Rides ended in mid-summer 1961. To remind Marshall of this fact, the Bureau began calling him at home, at 3:00 A.M., with reports of racial unrest in a Shreveport, Louisiana, diner and other minutia usually gleaned from the daily press. This petty harassment came in the form of middle-of-the-night phone calls from G-men who read Marshall newspaper stories. If the Civil Rights Division wanted intelligence, the FBI would provide it. The problems Marshall and the Kennedys encountered in Birmingham, Montgomery, and the other cities where the Freedom Riders stopped, however, were less the result of inadequate intelligence than the decisions made by FBI officials about how to respond to what was known. For all of his complaints during the Freedom Rides about not having sufficient notice of impending civil rights demonstrations and anti–civil rights violence, Marshall simply misunderstood the FBI "spy system's" hidden agenda: to damage the struggle for black equality.

The idea that led to the Freedom Ride of 1961 actually dated from 1947, when a group of pacifists and socialists from the Congress of Racial Equality (CORE) and the Fellowship of Reconciliation tested a Supreme Court ruling (*Morgan v. Virginia*) against segregation in interstate transportation. They organized a Journey of Reconciliation and traveled on buses and trains through the upper South, attracting only the passing interest of Hoover's FBI. Thirteen years later, when the Supreme Court extended its earlier prohibition against segregation to include all terminal accommodations (*Boynton v. Virginia*), CORE planned a more adventuresome Freedom Ride. James Farmer, the organization's national director and founder, said the riders would tour the Deep South, hoping to "provoke the southern authorities into arresting us and thereby prod the Justice Department into enforcing the law of the land." Roy Wilkins thought it "a desperately brave, reckless strategy, one that made those touch-football games played by the Kennedys look like macho patty-cake."[4]

Farmer saw himself as an "action man" who had pioneered nonviolent direct action against racial injustice for twenty years, since the day in 1941 when he and a pacifist friend, Jimmy Robinson, participated in what may have been the first sit-in at the Jack Spratt Coffee House in Chicago. When more sit-ins followed during the war years, the FBI opened a communist infiltration investigation of CORE—some four years before the first Freedom Ride and eighteen years before the second.[5] Farmer believed a new Freedom Ride might provoke "a crisis"—"an international crisis." He intended to bring a fundamental contradiction of cold war America to the world's attention: the United States' presentation of itself to Third World peoples as freedom's hope while consigning its own nonwhite peoples to an unequal status.

"We were counting on the bigots in the South to do our work for us," Farmer said, promising that the Freedom Riders would "fill up the jails, as Gandhi did in India," with a jail-no-bail strategy designed to move the struggle onto the high moral ground of global politics. To inform everyone of CORE's plans to commit civil disobedience, Farmer "wrote to the Justice Department, to the FBI, and to the President, and wrote to Greyhound . . . Trailways." But the response was always the same. "We got no reply from Justice. Bobby Kennedy, no reply. We got no reply from the FBI. We got no reply from the White House, from President Kennedy. We got no reply from Greyhound or Trailways. *We got no replies.*" The Freedom Riders were on their own.[6]

Afterward, the Justice Department's public information director, Edwin Guthman, explained why things did not filter through: someone routed the CORE press release "to Marshall's desk. Marshall did not bring it to the attention of Bob or Byron White. Then Marshall came down with the mumps . . . " More interested in planning for his June 3 meeting with Khrushchev in Vienna, John Kennedy regarded the timing of the Freedom Ride as particularly inappropriate. With the Soviet Union still exploiting Little Rock and the sit-ins for propaganda purposes in the Third World, the president wanted to avoid another racial incident at all costs. He tried to have the Freedom Ride canceled at the very moment he found out about it, telephoning civil rights advisor Harris Wofford with a direct order: "Tell them to call if off!" "I don't think anybody's going to stop them right now," Wofford responded. In the days to come, the Kennedy administration would make several more attempts to abort the riders' journey south.[7]

The FBI probably knew more about the Freedom Riders' itinerary than either the White House or the Justice Department. Assistant Director Cartha DeLoach reported a telephone call at 12:30 A.M. on May 3, only a few hours before the riders boarded their buses, from Simeon Booker, an *Ebony* reporter who would travel with the riders. DeLoach noted that Booker wanted "to tip us off." The assistant director worked with Booker and his employer, Johnson Publishing Company, from time to time, and one Crime Records Division agent remembered that accord. "*Ebony*, Johnson. Yeah, Johnson Publishing. . . . We had a great, we had a good relationship with *Ebony, Jet*. We used the black publications for stories. . . . We gave material to anybody that came to us," the agent claimed, adding that "Simeon Booker was in with Lou Nichols" and then "Mr. DeLoach."[8] Booker's role, nevertheless, is unclear. Farmer had already sent the FBI a copy of the Freedom Riders' schedule in the form of a press release. Booker may have been trying to manipulate the FBI with his middle-of-the-night phone call on the matter of protecting the riders (and himself) from the violent resistance they expected.

The Freedom Riders left Washington, D.C., on May 4, seven blacks and six whites riding South in two interracial groups on a Greyhound and a Trailways. A southerly flow of FBI teletypes from one field office to the next accompanied them. Bureau interest, nonetheless, was casual and in no way related to the issue of protecting the riders—or the *Ebony* reporter who rode with them. With the notable exceptions of arrests in Charlotte, North Carolina, and Winnsboro, South Carolina, and an assault at the bus station in Rock Hill, South Carolina, few serious incidents occurred during the first part of the trip.[9] The FBI began to pay closer attention to the Freedom Riders only on Mother's Day, May 14, when the Greyhound arrived in Anniston, Alabama, sixty miles from Birmingham.

Local FBI agents expected trouble. Alabama Klansmen planned a baseball-bat greeting for the riders, and the FBI forwarded this information on May 13 to the Anniston police.[10] When the Greyhound parked for its scheduled fifteen-minute rest stop, an angry mob surrounded it and began smashing windows and slashing tires. Police officers diverted the mob and the bus pulled out, but Ku Kluxers pursued in cars, catching up to the bus six miles out of town, when the tires either went flat from the earlier slashing or were shot out. A homemade bomb came through one of the windows. The bus quickly filled with smoke. The passengers tried to flee, but the mob held the door shut. The realization that the bus might explode finally convinced them to back up, and they beat the riders as they left the bus. With flames and smoke gutting the inside of the Greyhound, the beating continued until E. L. Cowling, a representative of Alabama Governor John Patterson and of Public Safety Director Floyd Mann, "drew his pistol" and "backed the crowd away," telling "them that if anybody touched anybody he'd kill them." One man's courage brought the first major incident of the Freedom Ride under control.[11]

The FBI watched as the second bus, the Trailways, pulled into Anniston within an hour. Eight toughs boarded, demanded that the black riders move to the rear, and then beat two of the white riders, Dr. Walter Bergman and James Peck, who had been on the Journey of Reconciliation. The sixty-one-year-old Bergman, a retired Detroit school administrator, suffered permanent brain damage. When the bus arrived at its terminal in Birmingham fifty minutes later, a mob of about forty Klansmen and members of the National States Rights party greeted the Freedom Riders. Most carried baseball bats or chains. A few had lead pipes. One of the Klansmen knocked down the unfortunate Peck once more. "Before you get my brothers, you will have to kill me," Gary Thomas Rowe, an FBI informer who had infiltrated the Klan, heard Peck say before he hit the floor.[12]

While the Freedom Riders not in need of overnight hospitalization gathered at the Birmingham home of Rev. Fred L. Shuttlesworth, the FBI launched a civil rights investigation that included interviews with all of the injured riders but only two or three of the uninjured ones. Though Simeon Booker received a telephone call from Robert Kennedy at Shuttlesworth's house, no Bureau agent contacted him or the photographer he had with him. Thereafter, the FBI claimed to have lost track of the Freedom Ride group, making contact only upon discovering that they were on their way out of town.

In Washington, Hoover demonstrated little sympathy for the Freedom Riders' plight. The riders had tried to move on to their next stop in Montgomery before accepting the advice of both Governor Patterson and the United States Department of Justice to get out of Alabama. They tried to arrange a bus to New Or-

leans, but could not find a driver. A bomb threat prevented them
from boarding a special flight on Eastern Airlines (the FBI and
the Birmingham police refused to search the plane), so they tried
to make arrangements with another airline. The pilot refused to
fly.[13] They finally boarded an Eastern flight to New Orleans, and
when they arrived Louisiana segregationists heckled them and
organized a rally that evening in the Municipal Auditorium. The
crowd listened to speakers warn of NAACP plans "to mongrelize
the people," Communist party attempts to aid and abet the ongoing "racial revolution," and CORE sponsorship of a mysterious
"training school" in Miami. When Hoover received a report on
the rally from the New Orleans field office, he asked: "Do we
know anything about this school?" That question revealed a
great deal about his priorities in the midst of the Freedom Ride
crisis.[14]

Clearly, FBI surveillance had not served to protect the Freedom Riders. Back in Alabama, the director's men opened a case
file on the Anniston bus burning, captioned FREEBUS, under
Title 18, Section 33, of the U.S. Code ("destruction of aircraft or
motor vehicle"). Burke Marshall told Hoover he "appreciated
the promptness with which we went into this matter," and Robert Kennedy described the FBI's efforts as "magnificent" following the arrest of four members of the mob. The director's private
response—Kennedy "should tell off 'bellyachers' like [John]
Doar"—was predictable. Doar constantly complained about the
FBI's civil rights performance, and he had just requested a
sweeping investigation of the Anniston and Birmingham violence, including an FBI survey "of all assaults and violent activities engaged in by the Klan or Klan members in this general area
within the last five years." Hoover had no complaint when Ed
Guthman put in a request for name checks on the Freedom Riders themselves. The attorney general's office wanted to know if
any of the civil rights activists had a criminal record.[15]

FBI agents in Alabama helped federal prosecutors secure indictments against nine people for their role in the bus burning.
(No one was indicted in connection with the Birmingham riot.)
After the first trial ended in a hung jury, Doar told FBI Assistant
Director Alex Rosen "that some of the jurors wouldn't have
voted guilty" unless the indictments had included a tenth
name—Bobby Kennedy. According to a Bureau informant, moreover, one of the jurors had attended a Klan meeting and had lied
about it during the jury selection process. Hoover's men

launched a perjury investigation. Ultimately, six defendants changed their pleas from not guilty to nolo contendere. The court placed five on probation, on the condition that they sever their connections with the Klan. One went to prison.[16]

Led by Kenneth N. Raby, assistant special agent in charge of the Birmingham office, and the Anniston resident agent, Clay Slate, a squad of FBI agents spent over 4,800 man hours on the case by June 6, logging some 14,000 miles in Bureau cars. "It seemed like we interviewed everybody in the state of Alabama at least twice," one FBI man recalled. For such trouble, J. B. Stoner and his National States Rights party hung Slate, two other agents, Farmer, Kennedy, and Hoover in effigy. When Slate came to Washington a year later, Doar pulled him out of an in-service training class and took him over to shake hands with Robert Kennedy.[17]

Clay Slate and the other FBI agents assigned to the FREEBUS case had done a fine job; but the bus burning as well as the Birmingham assault might have been prevented in the first place if FBI officials had chosen to act in a timely and judicious manner on the extraordinary intelligence that they held on the collusion between the Ku Klux Klan and the city's law enforcement community. Aware of the planned violence weeks in advance, the FBI did nothing to stop it and had actually given the Birmingham police details regarding the Freedom Riders' schedule, knowing full well that at least one law enforcement officer relayed everything to the Klan.

Local FBI agents had suspected close ties between the Klan and the Birmingham Police Department since September 1960, when their prize informer in the city Klavern, Gary Rowe, first raised the issue. The FBI knew "that Commissioner [of Public Safety] EUGENE (BULL) CONNOR and the great majority of the officers of the Birmingham Police Department [were] strong segregationists." When three young black men visited the mayor's office and started "yapping around about the lunch counters in the department stores," Connor gave one of the officers suspected of helping the Klan, Sergeant Thomas H. Cook, a typical assignment. "I want you to get all the information you possibly can on these three Negroes, and watch them closely from now on." Thomas Jenkins, the special agent in charge (SAC) of the Birmingham FBI office, was also aware that Cook ("one of CONNOR's boys") took "most of his orders directly from CONNOR and not from Chief [of Police Jamie] MOORE," a graduate of the

FBI National Academy and a considerably less extreme segregationist than the commissioner.[18]

Sergeant Cook exercised little restraint when forwarding material to the Klan. Gary Rowe, the FBI informant who would remain in the Klan for four more years and who would play a central role in the history of the civil rights movement on two other occasions, described his access to police files as complete. Cook once opened two file drawers in his office and told Rowe to help himself, "for the use of the KLAN, in general." Material leaked to Rowe and other Klansmen, Jenkins advised headquarters, included "information concerning potential violence given [Cook] by the Birmingham FBI Office." The Klan, in turn, supplied ad hoc personnel for the police department's surveillance squad. Klansmen covered black churches and movement meetings, jotted down license plate numbers, and sometimes rode around on patrol in squad cars.[19]

The FBI considered Rowe one of its best Klan informants and a number of agents had an interest in his cover and credibility, including Thomas Jenkins. "I think Gary Thomas Rowe made him," John Seigenthaler speculated about Jenkins, who advanced rapidly after he left Birmingham. Thus, to protect Rowe's cover, the Bureau restricted dissemination of certain types of information to the police. Official policy allowed the dissemination of "information relating to racial matters . . . only to reliable law enforcement officials and agencies." But the Bureau made a slight modification here because the most unreliable lawman, Tom Cook, furnished information on Edward R. Fields, the Birmingham chiropractor who headed the local branch of the National States Rights party. The doctor carried a gun and had threatened to shoot any FBI agent he caught snooping around.[20]

FBI officials adjusted their dissemination policy to protect Rowe's informant status and their absolute control over the information Rowe and other Klan informants gathered. They would not change this policy in order to protect the Freedom Riders—even though the Kennedy administration wanted a "spy system" that could be used to head off segregationist terror. Hoover had no sympathy for violent resistance to civil rights protest, and his agents had investigated the Klan intermittently since 1919. But he would not allow his "spy system" to be used on behalf of those who struggled for racial justice. In Birmingham, local FBI agents understood the director's position on groups like the Klan and the National States Rights party. These groups were viewed as minor irritants, at worst, and their violent acts were the concern of local law enforcement and not the FBI. In other words, Klansmen created problems from time to time, but they never created serious problems for the FBI. The FBI always went ahead with its investigations. Not even Sergeant Cook, the gun-toting Dr. Fields, nor Commissioner Connor himself created problems for the FBI in Birmingham. Besides, in the FBI view, the Klan and its friends generally did more talking than anything else.[21]

Such claims to the contrary, the segregationists did cause real problems for the FBI. Rowe's reports on the Klan's plans for the Freedom Riders dated from mid-April, three weeks before their scheduled Mother's Day arrival. The FBI knew all along that Klan leaders would divide into two groups, with half their number stationed in the vicinity of the bus terminal and the other half on call at a nearby hotel. The FBI also knew about the police commissioner's encouragement ("By God, if you are going to do this thing, do it right"), his promise to keep all policemen away "until the Klan had time to act." Connor had guaranteed the mob twenty minutes to beat the riders until "it looked like a bulldog got hold of them." In one way, the FBI "spy system" had worked perfectly.[22]

The "spy system" broke down only when FBI agents on the scene asked the executives in Washington how to use their intelligence about Connor, Cook, and the Klan. After conferring with Alex Rosen, civil rights section chief Clement McGowan phoned Kenneth Raby in Birmingham and said to "go ahead," to "tell Chief of Police JAMIE MOORE . . . that apparently several groups are interested in the arrival of the CORE party . . . and there could be some violence." McGowan said the information should be furnished in "general terms," mentioning neither the Klan by name nor the bus station where the Klan would gather. He said no "information concerning Commissioner CONNOR" should be furnished, on the grounds that "we have to be careful to protect our informant and be alert to any possible 'trap.'"[23] With these instructions in mind, Birmingham field office agents had warned Jamie Moore on at least five separate occasions "that groups hostile to integration were contemplating violence." In Moore's absence, they passed on information to Tom Cook, including details about CORE's itinerary taken directly from their own files. None of this did the Freedom Riders any

good, and when the bus station riot ended someone asked Bull
Connor why the police had not been present. He said his men
were all home with their mothers.

The FBI made no such flippant response, but Hoover admitted
no mistake. When advising Robert Kennedy that his men had
notified the police "that the Congress of Racial Equality would
arrive in Birmingham on May 14," he refused to tell the attorney
general how many agents were on the scene. When Kennedy
buzzed Hoover on the intercom with this simple request, a non-
commital answer ("we have enough") followed a vintage fillibus-
ter—a "torrent of words," one of Kennedy's aides recalled. In
Hoover's mind, the FBI had done all it could have done and all
it should have done by alerting the Birmingham Police Department. After things had settled down, a headquarters directive
reminded the field of the new facts of life regarding dissemination policy to police departments suspected of having been infiltrated by the Klan. "It is immaterial whether the law enforcement agency is trustworthy and also whether it will properly
fulfill its responsibility." Hoover adjusted policy under the pressure of the Freedom Ride, but in a way that made it even less
likely that Bureau resources could be used to prevent anti–civil
rights violence.[24]

Aware of the Connor-Cook-Klan connection and the Birmingham police boycott of the bus station riot, the FBI also knew
that Cook was the first officer to arrive on the scene. Hoover
informed Kennedy of this fact as well.[25] And Kennedy knew that
what happened in Birmingham was only the most dramatic example of the consequences of FBI policy. The Bureau routinely
forwarded intelligence regarding movement strategies to police
departments across the Jim Crow South. As often as not, the
people who received Bureau information opposed the civil
rights movement and were willing to use it to their own advantage. They may have passed on information from FBI teletypes
to Klan groups in other cities.

The FBI argued that it was up to the Department of Justice to
issue special instructions in Birmingham and that the Department failed to do so.[26] Although the FBI provided the Department with few details ahead of time regarding Cook's and Connor's connections with the Ku Klux Klan and its strategy for
discouraging the Freedom Riders, it is clear that Kennedy did
not press for details. The attorney general accepted the Bureau's
assurances, and the director neglected to tell him about Con-

nor's promise to give the Klan twenty free minutes. If Kennedy learned a lesson in Birmingham, he never did challenge the FBI's dissemination policies to police departments that had been infiltrated by violence-prone segregationists. Kennedy never did tell Hoover what to do.

With the Student Nonviolent Coordinating Committee determined to keep the Freedom Ride moving, Hoover continued to act freely on his own assumptions. Two of the original riders, John Lewis and Henry Thomas, returned from New Orleans to Nashville to help Fisk student Diane Nash's group of ten sit-in veterans begin a journey of their own to Birmingham. Connor arrested all ten just outside the city limits, releasing three almost immediately and driving the other seven to the Tennessee-Alabama line. When they returned to Birmingham by car, additional volunteers joined them at the Greyhound terminal, where a more cautious police commissioner confronted them—thanks to Robert Kennedy's apparent threat to bring Connor up on federal charges. When Greyhound could not locate a driver, moreover, Kennedy phoned a company superintendent to suggest he get in touch "with Mr. Greyhound" and find one. Kennedy also convinced Governor Patterson to intervene, prompting Rev. Shuttlesworth to remark with surprise and delight: "Man, what this state's coming to! An armed escort to take a bunch of niggers to a bus station so they can break these silly old laws." Robert Kennedy, not Hoover, protected these riders.[27]

On May 20 the FBI watched twenty-one well-guarded Freedom Riders board a bus for the two-hour trip to Montgomery. Once the bus left the highway and entered the Montgomery city limits, the police car and helicopter escort promised by Governor Patterson disappeared. "We stepped off the bus" at the station, John Lewis remembered, and "people just started pouring out of the station, out of buildings, from all over the place. White people." John Doar phoned in a report to Washington from across the street. "The passengers are coming off. . . . There are no cops. It's terrible." Lewis was soon lying in a pool of his own blood.[28] John Seigenthaler, who had been sent south, as Alex Rosen noted, "because the Attorney General felt his presence might prevent violence," was pulled from a rented car, dragged, and beaten after he tried to help two white Freedom Riders, Sue Harmann and Susan Wilbur. Seigenthaler lay unconscious and bleeding profusely for twenty-five minutes before an ambulance arrived. Commissioner of Public Safety Lester B. Sullivan, who had been alerted to the scheduled arrival of the bus by the FBI, explained the delay. "Every white ambulance in town reported their vehicles had broken down." While the police and ambulance drivers boycotted and the mob attacked the Freedom Riders, the FBI stood across the street, taking notes, "for the specific purpose of observing and reporting the facts to the Department of Justice in order that the Department will have the benefit of objective observations."[29]

FBI policy prevented the agent across the street from coming to Seigenthaler's aid: "If the agent should become personally involved in the action, he would be deserting his assigned task and would be unable to fulfill his primary responsibility of making objective observations." "They had agents all over the place," Seigenthaler complained, but they never fulfilled any of their responsibilities. "When I got out of the hospital and got back to my office, there was a letterhead memo on my desk, from Hoover to the attorney general, indicating who the assailants were," he said. "It galls me to think that the FBI stood there and watched me get clubbed." Remembering Seigenthaler in the years to come as someone who had embarrassed their Bureau, FBI officials eventually opened a file on him—a file that included allegations about "relations with young girls."[30]

Enraged by the Montgomery riot, Robert Kennedy at first planned to write to the governor of Alabama demanding an explanation. "We took the additional precautionary step," he wrote on May 20, "of having the FBI notify the police department that these students were coming and asked the police to take all necessary steps for their protection. . . . The F.B.I. was informed and in turn notified us that all necessary steps had been taken and that no action on our part was necessary," yet "no police were present," only "an armed mob." To prevent any repetition of these sad events, Kennedy said he would have the FBI "send in an extra team to intensify its investigations." The attorney general retained his hope that Hoover could be persuaded to act.[31]

Robert Kennedy never did send that letter to Governor Patterson; instead, on Sunday, May 21, his brother ordered five hundred U.S. marshals into Montgomery with Byron White in command. Reinforced by Floyd Mann's state troopers and finally the Alabama National Guard, the marshals held off another mob that evening at Ralph Abernathy's First Baptist Church, where Martin Luther King, the Freedom Riders, and some fifteen hundred blacks had gathered for a rally. John Lewis called the battle of the First Baptist Church "a real testing moment . . . without the support of the federal government at that time and a commitment, I think it could have been real bad." But when Doar met Lewis in the backyard of Abernathy's Montgomery home, he told him not "to talk to the FBI" before talking with the Civil Rights Division. "From that in itself," Lewis concluded, "I got the feeling . . . that even people within the Department of Justice had somewhat of a mistrust, distrust of their own FBI agents." The commitment from the federal government that Lewis spoke of had nothing to do with the FBI.[32]

Repeating his familiar refrain ("I can't guarantee the safety of fools") in the aftermath, Governor Patterson ordered Public Safety Director Floyd Mann to terminate his department's "working relationship with the FBI." Montgomery city officials hoped at the same time to convince the FBI to investigate the Freedom Riders on the grounds that they had placed an undue burden on interstate commerce—and life in general. City attorney Calvin M. Whitesell used the same argument when he asked Judge Frank Johnson to impose a permanent injunction banning the Freedom Ride. "They put a burden on our police department. They put a burden on our highway patrol. And they put a burden on the FBI. All because they insist upon a right to ride a bus," Whitesell said. Johnson's reply: the police, the patrol, and the FBI had a duty "to maintain law and order." Hoover disagreed.[33]

Thirty years earlier, during the time of John Dillinger, the director and his bureaucracy had grown in power and influence precisely because state and local police could not cope with the depression era's mobile gangsters. Now, the director was unwilling to fill this new vacuum left by the usual guardians of law and order. He dispatched Alex Rosen to Montgomery, but only because Byron White complained about difficulties in securing timely information. Before Rosen arrived, White had to file a request with the local FBI man, Richard Held, and then wait until the request filtered up to Hoover's aides at the seat of government and then back again. When the Freedom Riders moved on from Alabama and Louisiana to Mississippi, Kennedy, as promised, had the FBI send additional agents to Jackson, Meridian, and Hattiesburg. But these agents concentrated on the gathering of political intelligence about the riders almost to the exclusion of any law-enforcement responsibilities.

Because Robert Kennedy never forcefully challenged this priority, Hoover continued to act in a vacuum. The attorney general first suggested a "cooling-off period," prompting James Farmer to remark: "We had been cooling off for 100 years." He then asked the director to have his "Special Agents drive buses loaded with Freedom Riders through Alabama to Mississippi." Hoover "emphatically refused" this attempt "to use the FBI for improper undertakings." In interviews with *U.S. News and World Report* publisher David Lawrence and *FBI Story* author Don Whitehead, he summarized what he told Kennedy. "I stated that as long as I am Director of this Bureau I do not intend to allow it to be misused by pressure groups." "[If] Mr. Kennedy . . . did not like it," Hoover threatened, he could "get himself another Director." Ironically, Bureau agents had curried favor with prominent Americans since the 1930s and they had chauffered Kennedy's father around on several occasions during his travels outside the Boston area. Unwilling to confront the legal and practical merits of Hoover's argument, let alone the uproar that would follow Hoover's resignation (no matter how unlikely that prospect), the attorney general backed off.[34]

FBI policy remained frozen—as if the violence in Anniston, Birmingham, and Montgomery had not occurred. After CORE's James McCain advised the Bureau of the Freedom Riders' schedule on the Illinois Central Railroad from New Orleans to Jackson, Hoover's men alerted railroad security, the Mississippi Highway Patrol, the Hinds County sheriff, and the Jackson Police Department.[35] With their law-enforcement responsibilities fulfilled, they turned to their intelligence responsibilities. When Martin Luther King demonstrated an interest in the Freedom Riders, the FBI ran his name through the files.[36] As Jackson police locked up the Freedom Riders *en masse,* moreover, the director sent the attorney general a *Reader's Digest* article, "I Was a 'Student' at Moscow State," about Soviet-bloc discrimination against visiting African students. The piece had "tremendous counterpropaganda value," Hoover told Kennedy.[37] At other times, FBI officials went to their constituents in the media and Congress with derogatory information on the Freedom Riders, hoping to bring public and congressional opinion around to their view that civil rights advocacy was un-American.

FBI agents assigned to the Crime Records Division helped radio commentator and newspaper columnist Fulton Lewis, Jr., with a Reds-move-in-on-riders story, and Senator Strom Thurmond of South Carolina with a speech after a wiretap revealed the plans of two reputed communists to form a CORE chapter in San Francisco.[38] It was no coincidence that the FBI selected a segregationist to help publicize Communist party interest in CORE. "Thurmond was probably one of our strongest bulwarks in the Congress on law-enforcement problems," one of De-Loach's Crime Records agents reasoned. "We wanted somebody to know that CORE was being infiltrated. And if you would give it to Joe Blow down the street . . . it wouldn't do any good. But if you give it to Strom Thurmond, a powerful senator . . . [CORE] should have done something about getting those people out of there. . . . You can't have everything. You can't have it both ways."[39] CORE had to act in an acceptable manner or accept the consequences. In this case, however, there is no evidence that the Bureau alerted the organization to the Communist party's interest. Hoover had DeLoach go straight to Thurmond.

The FBI could have it both ways, criticizing "the caliber of the people engaged in the freedom rides" as well as their political associations. The abysmal treatment of the riders in the Jackson city jail and the state penitentiary at Parchman led the Civil Rights Division to order an investigation, but Hoover did not object to "the thumps and whacks" of the jailers. Instead, when a rider complained about being held in solitary confinement in a cell kept completely dark during the day and illuminated by a glaring light at night, Hoover told Robert Kennedy that this fellow had "a private cell" with "a window and a street light shines through the window at night." The director then dismissed a hunger strike in the Jackson jail as a hoax, advising Burke Marshall that the conspirators threatened one of the prisoners who had refused to cooperate. In his reports to the White House and the Civil Rights Division, and in his leaks to his contacts in the media and the Congress, Hoover suggested that the riders brought all their troubles on themselves, that they deserved worse than they got.[40]

While the Freedom Riders made their way home from Mississippi at the end of the summer, a number of them accepted an invitation from a former NAACP leader, Robert F. Williams, to stop in Monroe, North Carolina, a Klan stronghold and the scene of numerous civil rights demonstrations.[41] One of the earliest and most militant advocates of armed self-resistance against segregationist violence, Williams began a week-long picket at the Monroe courthouse that provoked violent reactions. He telephoned the FBI office in Charlotte "each time the Freedom Riders would get ready to go on the picket line . . . The FBI would say, 'We're on the way.' But they would never be there when anything happened." After several days of tension, a mob of at least two thousand whites attacked the line—"a moment of death," thought James Forman, who would soon become SNCC's executive secretary—and the police arrested the Freedom Riders. In the aftermath, with Monroe on the verge of a riot, a car carrying a middle-aged white couple happened to wander into Monroe's black neighborhood. The occupants, Williams claimed, stayed at his home for their own protection.[42]

To the FBI and the state of North Carolina it looked like a kidnapping. Edward Scheidt, commissioner of motor vehicles and public safety, and a former FBI executive who had testified against the civil rights bill of 1957 before the House Judiciary Committee, sent in fifty-two highway patrolmen. Two FBI agents on the scene helped out and Governor Terry Sanford's office kept the White House posted.[43] While the state filed charges against Williams and four others, including one of the Freedom Riders, the FBI ran a name check on Forman that included a quick (and apparently routine) search of the files of the Anti-Defamation League. In Cleveland, the Bureau arrested Mae Mallory, a member of Williams's Crusader Family, who claimed "about 25 members of the F.B.I. came into the house with guns drawn and everything." Williams himself fled the country, imagining "500 FBI men . . . setting up a dragnet." While waiting for the rest of the defendants to stand trial for kidnapping, the FBI focused on the Trotskyite Socialist Workers party's attempt to organize a "Committee to Aid the Monroe Defendants." Hoover tried to smash the group for its work on "integration problems arising in the South."[44]

Ultimately, as in the voting litigation campaign, the FBI record during the crusade to desegregate the buses improved. Despite its failures in Birmingham and Montgomery and interest in the politics and integrity of the Freedom Riders themselves, within two years the Bureau claimed that its investigations played a decisive role in victories over Jim Crow. This was an exaggerated claim, to be sure. By 1963 even the Republican National Committee claimed credit for abolishing segregation "in bus and train interstate travel," a preposterous boast based on the coincidence that the Supreme Court had decided *Boynton* (which prohibited segregation in all terminal accommodations) during the last year of the Eisenhower presidency.[45] The FBI, on the other hand, made a contribution, even though the dissemination of derogatory information on the riders suggests that this may have been the last thing that Hoover wanted to do. While some Bureau agents spied on the Freedom Riders, others, at the insistence of Kennedy's Justice Department, conducted surveys of bus, railroad, ferry boat, and airport terminals, surveys that the Department used in the courts and elsewhere to end segregation on the highways, rails, and inland waterways, and in the skies.[46]

Most of the credit belongs to the Freedom Riders themselves and Robert Kennedy. Kennedy prevented the tragedies of Anniston, Birmingham, and Montgomery from escalating into major catastrophes. He also managed to ram through the historic Interstate Commerce Commission order of June 21, 1961, banning segregation in interstate bus facilities. Though far more willing to protect civil rights workers from segregationist violence than Hoover, Kennedy operated within the confines of his own theory of federalism. Even Seigenthaler understood the attorney general's deference, in practice, to the director's position on the matter of protection. "I thought there were some days—one, for sure—when they should have kept [Hoover] in a cage," he said. "It does make you wonder about the milk of human kindness ... [but] there were legitimate jurisdictional policies ... I accepted his official explanation." The protection issue remained complex, and within the government nearly everyone with an interest in civil rights responded ambiguously.[47]

On the surveillance front, no complexities or ambiguities existed. No theory of federalism applied. In the months after the Freedom Rides ended, Burke Marshall complained no more about a spy gap. Instead, he expressed "his deep appreciation" to the FBI "for having kept him so fully informed in connection with the current racial disturbances (walk-ins, sit-ins, etc.). He said this was of inestimable value." Eventually, Marshall began filing "Monday and Wednesday" reports with Robert Kennedy regarding "matters of significance in the Division." These reports, all part of "an advanced warning system," invariably contained intelligence data submitted by the FBI.[48]

No complexities or ambiguities clouded Hoover's view of the FBI's mission. "We are an intelligence agency and as such we are expected to know what is going on," he once said. And he announced hundreds of times that his FBI "was not a protection agency." A case could be made for Hoover's position that the FBI had no authority to protect civil rights activists and full authority to spy on those activists. A case could also be made that "legitimate jurisdictional policies" determined the FBI's reluctance to get involved in civil rights enforcement. In fact, however, the director resisted everything the Kennedys asked him to do on behalf of the black struggle, not just the demand that he act more aggressively to protect civil rights activists.

When the attorney general asked the director to assign agents to drive Freedom Riders into Mississippi, Kennedy understood the irony of Hoover's response. At the time, the FBI employed only a handful of black agents (all of them chauffeurs, according to Washington legend), and the attorney general had his staff recruit blacks for the FBI as part of the administration's broader affirmative action plan for all executive agencies and departments.[49] One of the people Ed Guthman brought in, William Lucas, a Fordham Law School graduate and a Catholic, made it through the FBI National Academy and went on to become sheriff of Wayne County, Michigan. Many years later, in 1986, Lucas ran for governor of the state on the Republican party ticket with an "anti-affirmative action, pro-life, tax-cutting" campaign that won praise from President Ronald Reagan. But during his FBI days not even a conservative black could win the director's favor. The *National Review* quoted *Detroit News* columnist Pete Waldmeir that to impress Hoover "a black dude had better talk better than Harry Belafonte and dance better than Sammy Davis."[50]

FBI officials responded to the Kennedy recruiters with cynicism and flim-flam, and a few agents parodied JFK by warning one another to "work with vigah" or "be replaced with a niggah." Hoover responded to Robert Kennedy's requests for the number of black agents employed by the Bureau with a standard answer: the FBI catalogued no employee by race, creed, or color. A commendable sentiment, the attorney general replied, before repeating his request.[51] Hoover finally told Kennedy that the FBI had five black agents on its 5,500-man roster. He did not indicate that at least one (and possibly three) of these agents were in fact drivers, and two others, Sam Noisette and Worthington Smith, as Guthman observed, "took your hat and coat when you went in." In Washington, James Crawford carried a gun and doubled as a bodyguard and handyman. He kept Hoover's house and garden in good shape for thirty-seven years; looked after the dogs,

Cindy and G-boy; and did the cooking and cleaning when Annie Fields, the director's live-in black servant, had to be away. "James worked fifteen hours a day, seven days a week. Holidays, too," wife Dorothea said. The identities of the other two black agents remain a mystery. They were probably among the handful of black Bureau employees who reportedly received field assignments from time to time—Carl V. Mason in Chicago and Kansas City; Jesse S. Strider, Jr., and his son Robert in Los Angeles; Harold A. Carr and James T. Young in New York; and Leo J. McCairen in Miami.[52]

When "leaning on [Hoover]" to hire black agents, Robert Kennedy used an argument he thought the director would understand. "We saw a problem coming in civil rights," former White House aide Kenneth O'Donnell remembered, "and we saw also the possibility that the Communists might attempt to infiltrate the black movement, and a lot of other people might too, and how do you police Harlem with a white guy who is a spy? They send an FBI guy down in a Brooks Brothers suit and a snap brim hat. He couldn't catch cold in Harlem." That policy, in an area so near Hoover's heart, was simply "ridiculous." The director would have to agree.[53]

Affirmative action was one of the issues that lay at the heart of Hoover's intense dislike of Robert Kennedy. The two men "didn't agree on everything," one Crime Records Division agent recalled, with considerable understatement. "Mainly, they didn't agree on black agents. Kennedy wanted us to lower the standards. Hoover said, 'Bring me all the black agents that meet these standards and I'll take them.' Bobby Kennedy said, 'No, you can't get them at Bureau standards, you've got to come down to here.' And Hoover says, 'Forget it.'"[54] Beyond a college degree (preferably in law or accounting), no one could define the director's "terribly high" standards. Harold P. Leinbaugh, another former Crime Records agent and soldier who landed at Omaha Beach, said Hoover had a "concept of the FBI as an absolutely, totally elite [force]—you know, rangers, commandos . . . paramilitary. His defense in all of this was that he was trying to find qualified men . . . a guy hopefully with a Harvard law degree that was black and had an IQ of 147 and had all the physical and other qualifications . . . which is a pretty good argument . . . Hoover demanded a holier-than-thou attitude. You could always find some excuse for not hiring anybody. . . . They could say, 'Well, you had an uncle who signed a Communist party nominating petition in 1939.'" No excuse satisfied Robert Kennedy however.[55]

Hoover believed blacks were inferior, intellectually and otherwise. He even complained, privately, and as late as 1969, about police departments "lowering the physical qualifications so they could get more Negro officers." He also believed blacks could not be easily integrated into his homogenous agent corps, which hardly represented a broad sampling of the white American male. So the FBI hired few black agents, the attorney general's complaints notwithstanding. By the end of 1962 the Bureau had only ten. Hugh Fleischer, a Civil Rights Division lawyer for six years, said he never saw a black FBI agent. "All we heard [was] that there was a chauffeur or somebody who drove J. Edgar around." When the director died in 1972, blacks made up less than .5 percent of the agent corps, and it would be two more years before headquarters permanently assigned a black agent to the Jackson, Mississippi, field office. What one Bureau executive described as "our posture on blacks" had scarcely improved even twenty years after Kennedy resigned the attorney generalship.[56]

During the Kennedy years affirmative action remained what it had always been for Hoover—a public relations problem to be solved by helping place yet another *Ebony* article. The Bureau had done this most recently in 1958, with a photo of a chauffeur assigned to the Los Angeles field office and his son, Jesse and Robert Strider, peering down the sights of Thompson submachine-guns. The latest article, prepared by Simeon Booker, praised the Bureau's past ("the FBI's history . . . sparkles with seldom told exploits of courageous Negro special agents") and again mentioned Sam Noisette as one of Hoover's most valuable employees. "The relationship between the two men virtually sets the race relations pattern for the huge agency," Booker wrote, with no irony in mind. Rather, he hoped to encourage blacks to join the FBI.[57]

Booker's piece focused on the first two legitimate black agent trainees: James W. Barrow, a Brooklyn College graduate from Amityville, New York, and a former Bureau clerk; and especially Aubrey C. Lewis, a twenty-seven-year-old former Notre Dame football star brought in by a Bureau official active in the Notre Dame Alumni Association. The first black candidates to make it through the FBI academy in Quantico on the unsegregated course, both men went on to serve with distinction—though

Lewis did not remain with the FBI for long. Some civil rights people and even a few of his fellow G-men saw him as a token, an honorary Irishman from Notre Dame among Hoover's heavily Catholic agent corps. Such pressures made the opportunities for other employment tempting.[58]

While Hoover and Kennedy battled over questions of affirmative action during the Freedom Rides and beyond, surveillance remained the FBI's primary function in 1962. "They certainly cooperated fully in passing intelligence, but not in other respects," Nicholas Katzenbach recalled. "The Bureau refused to take any kind of responsibility for the maintenance of law and order"—"and they weren't asked to."[59] Katzenbach referred to the Ole Miss crisis in Oxford, where Governor Ross Barnett blocked the door to prevent James Meredith from attending classes at the University of Mississippi; the resulting riot left two people dead and 375 injured. Eventually, President Kennedy sent in Army troops and federalized the state national guard to support the federal marshals already on the scene. The FBI moved in only after the smoke had cleared, to conduct lab tests on the marshals' pistols. There had been little federal gunfire as it turned out, and not a single casualty could be traced to the marshals.[60]

Expected only to collect intelligence at Ole Miss, FBI agents relied on their many sources in and around Oxford, including Hugh H. Clegg, formerly an assistant director for Hoover, and at that time an assistant to university chancellor John D. Williams. From these sources, however, Hoover often received biased information. A graduate of the George Washington University law school and a Kappa Alpha, like Hoover and Tolson, Clegg was also a Mississippi native. He had been the first Bureau agent assigned to coordinate civil rights training for police officers at the National Academy back in the 1940s. From his new post in Williams's office, he forwarded information to the FBI from the moment Meredith's application for admission arrived. He told the Bureau the university rejected Meredith not because of his race, but because he failed to "name five alumni . . . with whom he was acquainted which is a requirement for admission." Clegg described the Citizens Council ("composed of many of the leading citizens of Mississippi") in words nearly identical to those used by the director six years earlier when briefing the Eisenhower cabinet on racial matters.[61]

The Civil Rights Division called upon FBI surveillance services once again a few months later. Alabama Governor George Wallace had pledged to stand in his schoolhouse door, and Burke Marshall encouraged the Bureau to tape-record the governor's speeches. Fortunately, when Wallace tried to prevent the admission of two black students, Vivian Malone and James A. Hood, to the University of Alabama, events were less chaotic than in Mississippi. Katzenbach handed Wallace a proclamation from the president commanding him to cease and desist his unlawful obstructions of a federal court order; the governor did not budge at first, but withdrew after a second confrontation. The students registered. As the drama unfolded, the FBI remained on the periphery, phoning in developments to the Justice Department, photographing the happenings, and trying to remain inconspicuous.[62]

Hoover intended to spy on the civil rights movement, and Robert Kennedy's Justice Department encouraged him to do exactly that. By the spring of 1963 the Civil Rights Division routinely filed specific requests with the FBI for such services as "photographic coverage" of activities planned for the one hundreth anniversary of the Emancipation Proclamation. More often, the FBI reported directly to Marshall's office. One agent discussed forty-two separate racial incidents during a single telephone call. The reports themselves ranged from the Alabama Highway Patrol's use of electric cattle prods on would-be black voters to a report from Paris that "William Marshall, Negro actor, James Baldwin, Anthony Quinn and Gregory Peck . . . plan to present petitions against racial discrimination to American Embassies throughout Europe." Civil Rights Division staff found it difficult to keep pace with both the sheer number of demonstrations (1,580 in thirty-eight states plus the District of Columbia during the summer of 1963) and the volume of FBI intelligence. Bureau officials supplemented their telephone calls with 8,114 letterhead memos (eight copies each) regarding racial matters for dissemination to the Justice Department, Military Intelligence, and other interested government agencies.[63]

Hoover responded ambivalently to the demand for intelligence, sometimes resisting the requests of Robert Kennedy and Burke Marshall, and sometimes volunteering information. In May, Kennedy wired all U.S. attorneys asking them to make surveys of "segregated business facilities" and to list all places where racial demonstrations could be expected in the next thirty days. The attorney general also "asked" the FBI "to cooperate."

Hoover responded to the second request simply by increasing the volume of his reports to the Department. The other request presented problems. Because of his own racial bias, Hoover wanted to investigate civil rights activists, not white southern businessmen; but he had to respond to Kennedy's directive, so he instructed his agents to advise the U.S. attorneys orally, based on their "personal knowledge and views." The Bureau actually conducted no investigation for the purpose of identifying segregated businesses.[64]

That same month, Robert Kennedy met in New York with Jerome Smith, a CORE field worker and Freedom Rider who had been repeatedly beaten and jailed, and a number of friends of novelist James Baldwin—including playwright Lorraine Hansberry, psychologist Kenneth Clark, singers Harry Belafonte and Lena Horne, and actor Rip Torn. Smith set the tone of the meeting when he said that being in the same room with the attorney general made him feel like throwing up. "Bobby took it personally," Baldwin remembered. "And he turned away from him. That was a mistake because he turned toward us. We were the reasonable, responsible, mature representatives of the black community. Lorraine Hansberry said, 'You've got a great many very, very accomplished people in this room, Mr. Attorney General. But the only man who should be listened to is that man over there.'" The group then criticized the FBI. Kennedy passed this issue to Burke Marshall, who said the Justice Department sent in "special men" from the Civil Rights Division whenever the Bureau refused to do its job. The reply "produced almost hysterical laughter."[65]

After accounts of the meeting appeared in the press, Hoover sent unsolicited dossiers on all those present to Kennedy, who sent them to Marshall with a note. "What nice friends you have." The director had spent the past forty-four years linking protest with disloyalty and impugning the integrity of the protesters. It would have been unusual if he had treated Baldwin's group otherwise. Unfortunately, the Kennedy administration tolerated this behavior and even credited it with some validity. The attorney general read the dossiers, as did the assistant attorney general for civil rights and the Civil Rights Division's "special men." Earlier, when Stokely Carmichael and five other anonymous civil rights activists staged a brief sit-in in the attorney general's office, Kennedy had specifically asked for memos on all six. Marshall's number two man, St. John Barrett, said the director "[was always] telling us between the lines that we were accepting uncritically the assertions of people who really weren't as credible as we thought they were."[66]

Neither Robert Kennedy nor the attorneys in the Civil Rights Division were struck by the contradiction between the FBI's strict-constructionist posture on civil rights enforcement and its anything-goes activities in surveillance. "I took the world as I found it," said Marshall. "We got a lot of what you might call letterhead memos," Doar explained. "To tell you the truth, I didn't react too much one way or the other." "We didn't get into any intellectual debate," Barrett conceded. "You kind of shrug and say, 'What are these guys spending their time on this for?' But you never ask them or raise it with them."[67] Kennedy himself encouraged some of this pervasive name checking. He had learned how the FBI worked and how to use its intelligence gathering resources even before his appointment as attorney general. As chief counsel of the Senate Rackets Committee in the 1950s, he received dozens of blind memos on union organizers and mobsters from FBI agent Courtney Evans. Later, when Kennedy was running the Department, Evans was running the Bureau's Special Investigative Division and serving as Hoover's liaison with the administration.[68]

Evans's Division ran the names of hundreds of individuals and groups through the files at the request of Kennedy administration officials.[69] The subjects of these searches ranged from the National Negro Congress, a communist front that had been dead for fourteen years, to James Baldwin, William Faulkner, and fifty other Nobel Prize laureates whose names graced a White House dinner invitation list—part of John and Jacqueline Kennedy's program to encourage and honor cultural and intellectual achievement. In Faulkner's case, the Bureau noted his statement to the Civil Rights Congress, another communist front and successor to the National Negro Congress, on behalf of Willie McGhee, convicted of raping a white woman in Laurel, Mississippi, in 1945. (McGhee exhausted all possible appeals by March 1951, when the Supreme Court refused to hear his case, and to the day the state executed him the FBI seemed most interested in exploring the "Communistic connections" of one of his noncommunist lawyers, Bella Abzug.)[70] W. Mark Felt, former head of the FBI's Inspection Division, said "Attorney General Kennedy thought of the FBI as a kind of private police department, with Hoover as its desk sergeant."[71] Felt was referring less to the name checks and other surveillance services than to Kennedy's attempts to have the FBI assume more responsibilities in the areas of civil rights and organized crime. The Bureau had been running name checks for the White House since the 1920s.[72]

FBI surveillance activities received implicit if limited approval not only from the Kennedy administration, but from some sections of the civil rights movement itself. Civil rights leaders cooperated with the FBI for two basic reasons. The first had to do with the lingering effects of the domestic communist issue. When HUAC investigator W. Jackson Jones visited the Southern Regional Council (SRC) in 1956, he asked executive director George S. Mitchell about "communist[s] climbing aboard." Mitchell told him the SRC had been "set up by an entirely different stripe of people than those that had established the Southern Conference for Human Welfare"—a group that did indeed have communists among its membership—and gave him a "two-minute lecture on the utter Americanism of the NAACP." Mitchell's willingness to deflect HUAC's criticism onto the nearest available group on the left represented a fairly typical attitude within the established civil rights groups.[73]

This attitude represented a concession to the segregationists who Red-baited the movement well into the 1960s. Long before the cold war settled in, a good many people on the left had been driven into the anticommunist camp by the damage they thought the Stalinists in America were doing. Some civil rights groups, like the NAACP, responded to the pressures of the cold war and the stiffening climate by embracing more conservative politics. Uncomfortable with the mass black activism of the New Deal and World War II years, NAACP leadership retreated to the more familiar and cautious turf of litigation and lobbying. At the same time, the NAACP instituted loyalty oaths and created committees to investigate the political histories of prospective members.[74] "We do not want a witch hunt," Roy Wilkins advised Walter White, "but we do want to clean out our organization." To escape the real McCarthyites, the NAACP purged itself.[75]

By the early 1960s the FBI extended name-check services to several civil rights groups in an informal and usually indirect manner as part of its COMINFIL (communist infiltration) and COINTELPRO (counterintelligence program) efforts to purge Communist party members and others from "legitimate mass organizations." The method began with the compilation of "public source or similar material identifying . . . [the targeted] individual with the communist movement," followed by a discreet effort to "ascertain the most logical officer or prominent person in the organization on whom there is no derogatory information." If this person "could be expected to take . . . action to remove the communist from the organization," he would receive an anonymous letter or phone call or perhaps a blind memo delivered in person by an FBI agent.[76]

In practice, this meant FBI mailings about communists or former communists associated with his group to A. Philip Randolph, then president of the Negro American Labor Council. There were FBI briefings for the NAACP's Thurgood Marshall, and anonymous letters, telephone calls, and blind memos for other "anticommunist officers" at NAACP offices in New York. In the case of the Southern Regional Council, FBI agents questioned the politics of specific activists. "Field men would come in to talk to us," former SRC executive director Leslie Dunbar remembered, and ask, "'What do you know about him?' 'What do you know about her?'" The FBI sent letters to "reliable, intelligent" CORE officials who had "expressed concern over possible 'radical' influences."[77] FBI agents from the Atlanta and Washington field offices may have provided name-check services to the Southern Christian Leadership Conference at Rev. Ralph Abernathy's request.[78]

Leaking information on communist infiltration to "responsible leaders" of civil rights groups was only one aspect of what FBI officials described as a broadly based "liaison program." By identifying people who would move against communist infiltration of particular movement groups, Hoover's agents were able to solicit "a constant flow of intelligence-type information" on "the planned activities of . . . the most active groups . . . staging racial demonstrations." "Our liaison program," Hoover told Robert Kennedy, two years after the attack on the Freedom Riders in Birmingham, "has also enabled us to alert local law enforcement agencies in advance in order that these . . . agencies may take appropriate action to maintain peace and order and to prevent unwarranted situations from developing." FBI surveillance could be used to protect civil rights workers, Hoover seemed to be saying, but actually he remained interested only in rooting out communists from civil rights groups and maintaining friendly relations with segregationist southern lawmen.[79]

Robert Kennedy's aide, John Seigenthaler, said the FBI had

excellent sources "within the civil rights movement." Hoover aide Alex Rosen cited Julius Hobson, who was president of CORE's Washington, D.C., chapter until his dismissal in 1964 for being too militant, as one of the Bureau's more effective contacts. Cartha DeLoach met with Freedom Ride organizer James Farmer in 1963 to discuss "the possibilities of the FBI advising him on a confidential basis whenever members of the Communist Party sought to infiltrate and take advantage of CORE." The FBI also claimed to have an "agreement" requiring Farmer to consult with DeLoach before issuing statements regarding the Bureau's civil rights work. Because Farmer had recently criticized an FBI agent in Birmingham who "had not been very helpful to CORE members," DeLoach believed Farmer was not keeping his word and thus tried to arrange another meeting to straighten him out. He had a hard time contacting him; like so many movement people, "Farmer was either in jail or constantly in travel status." Nearly ten years later, Farmer confirmed the existence of a liaison arrangement by noting one occasion where an FBI agent briefed him on a part-time CORE staff member and alleged "card-carrying member of the Communist party."[80]

The FBI rarely helped the black activists who cooperated. Field agents solicited information from members of state NAACP affiliates about local movement strategies—information that they sometimes passed on to local police officers and sometimes used to exacerbate rivalries between the NAACP and other civil rights groups. On the national level, the FBI favored executive director Roy Wilkins, occasionally sending him derogatory personal and political information on other civil rights leaders—most notably Martin Luther King. Crime Records agent Lawrence Heim described the FBI's relationship with Wilkins as excellent, and the NAACP chief even met with DeLoach once to discuss how the Bureau might brighten its image in the civil rights field.[81] The FBI also established liaison with National Urban League executive director Whitney Young, who tried to turn the liaison program around to meet Urban League needs and not Bureau needs. Young told the special agent in charge of the FBI's New York office that he was interested in this program because it might facilitate the recruitment of black applicants for the position of FBI special agent—"inasmuch as one of the functions of the URBAN LEAGUE is to place Negroes in desirable positions." Young's deftness, in Hoover's view, marked him as "a very expedient person," though the director still rated him "one stripe above [Dr. King]."[82]

Few of the movement people who shared information with the FBI thought it was wrong. If the Bureau identified Farmer, Hobson, and Wilkins, as "sources," those men should not be considered "scabs to the movement."[83] They did not resemble people like Julia Brown, a black woman from Cleveland and a longtime FBI operative who surfaced in the early 1960s to testify before HUAC and the Subversive Activities Control Board.[84] Hobson, for example, met regularly with FBI agent Elmer Lee Todd, reported on civil rights demonstration plans at the 1964 Democratic National Convention in Atlantic City, and received $300 from the Bureau for services rendered at the Convention. But Hobson's widow claimed he joked openly about his relationship with the FBI and actually used his stipend to bring more demonstrators to Atlantic City. The Bureau finally "discontinued" Hobson "as a liaison source . . . when he advised the press of his relationship with us"—an admission that prompted Hoover to complain "that Hobson talks from both sides of his mouth." Shortly thereafter, the Bureau tried to interfere with Hobson's campaign for a seat on the District of Columbia School Board by spreading a rumor that he was an "Uncle Tom."[85]

Even when sharing information with the FBI, most movement people believed they were informing on themselves ("us") and not their enemies ("them"). There were exceptions—notably Farmer's dismissal of that CORE staff worker and the willingness of a surprising number of NAACP activists to discuss the activities of rival civil rights groups with the Bureau. But the FBI's so-called liaison sources did not always "name names." Former agent Arthur Murtagh, who operated a number of formal black informants who monitored the Southern Christian Leadership Conference, claimed nearly all of the information they provided could have been acquired simply by picking up the phone and calling SCLC or asking a representative to stop by the Atlanta field office.[86] Similarly, John Lewis said the FBI often called Julian Bond at the SNCC office in Atlanta "to find out what was going on or should they be notified, that sort of thing." North Carolina attorney Floyd McKissick remembered "FBI agents who needed information coming into CORE offices in New York to get it." Medgar Evers, the NAACP leader in Mississippi, kept the FBI posted on events in Jackson from time to time. Andrew Young, James Farmer, and A. Philip Randolph occasionally alerted the FBI to their travel itineraries. "I agreed to keep in touch with DeLoach," Young said, with some exaggeration, "when we were moving anywhere."[87] Farmer kept in touch with the FBI at the suggestion of DeLoach and John Malone, the FBI executive who ran the New York office. Malone asked Farmer to have his "secretary give me a call whenever you're going south."[88]

The goal of obtaining FBI protection, even more than communist infiltration or factionalism within the civil rights movement, was what made some movement people willing to cooperate. "When you were down South and something happened, you'd call the FBI," SNCC's H. Rap Brown later wrote. "They represented the federal government, and you didn't want to face the fact that the federal government wasn't on your side." "They were a problem almost from the beginning as they sat around taking notes while people were getting beat up," Andrew Young said. "But we always felt their presence was welcome and that they did serve as a restraint on Southern law enforcement . . . which would have been far more violent without the FBI. So in spite of the fact that we knew they were somewhat antagonistic to our goals, we always cooperated with them—all the way through. . . . For instance, when we were going into Birmingham for a demonstration, we would call the FBI, call the Justice Department . . . just to make sure that everybody understood exactly what we were there for." "It's hard to remember back then," Young concluded, "but when you were anxious about your life, civil liberties seemed a tertiary consideration."[89]

Movement leaders may have been "compulsive about freedom," maybe even paranoid, in Young's view, but those feelings did not stop the movement from cooperating, in a limited sense, in its own surveillance. Dr. King himself told Hoover that "it was vitally necessary to keep a working relationship with the FBI." Another SCLC colleague, Bayard Rustin, said "we had to call upon them." Mary King, who handled communications for SNCC with Julian Bond, said "we believed that we should lay the groundwork by providing the agency with a steady flow of information," and that was a mainstream movement view.[90]

Not everyone shared that view however. SNCC's Jim Forman also wanted protection, but he concluded that it was an impossible task—because the FBI ran the liaison program to gather derogatory information on civil rights activists that could be used to divide and otherwise discredit the civil rights movement. The liaison program was never intended to protect those who risked their lives for racial justice. The FBI, "a part of the governmental structure," served as a barrier between power and "the people," Forman wrote. In effect, the FBI was "the enemy of black people. . . . We did not say it that way in 1963, but we did know that the FBI was a farce. It wasn't going to arrest any local racists who violated any and all laws on the statute books. Instead, it would play a game of taking notes and pictures. The files in Washington must have been growing thick even then with documents from the civil rights movement and with photographs of us all—doing everything but screwing, and maybe even that."[91]

On June 12, 1963, three weeks after Hoover told Robert Kennedy that the liaison program's principal purpose was "to prevent unwarranted situations from developing," a gunman shot and killed Medgar Evers, the Jackson-based NAACP field representative in Mississippi. (He was one of the movement leaders who sometimes kept the Bureau posted on demonstration plans in his area.) FBI agents entered the case under civil rights law, on the grounds that the murderer or murderers had conspired to deprive Evers of his civil rights; and in the face of the usual criticism. James Wechsler of the *New York Post* said Evers "went to a lonely death, as he had feared he would, while the G-men slept."[92] The FBI's after-the-fact investigation, however, was thorough and generally impressive, involving agents from forty-eight field offices.[93] They developed ballistic and fingerprint evidence, and identified a new Golden Hawk telescopic site found in a vacant lot near the thicket where the sniper and his 30.06 had waited for Evers. The scope was traced to a fertilizer salesman from nearby Greenwood who wondered "why the world was in the hands of the Communists." Arrested by the FBI on June 22 and turned over to the Jackson police, he faced two murder trials. Both ended in hung juries.[94]

Not all of the FBI agents on the case looked for Evers's killer, however; other agents covered the funeral in anticipation of a riot.[95] Jackson police officers and troopers from the Mississippi Highway Patrol, also expecting trouble, armed themselves with shotguns, carbines, tear gas, and nightsticks. There was a corps of German shepherds and their handlers nearby. Evers's brother, Charles, said he "came back to Mississippi to kill every white man I saw." Roy Wilkins, who spoke at the funeral, condemned "the Southern political system" for putting that crazed white man "behind the rifle." Rocks, bottles, and chants of "we want the killer" filled the air as the mourners moved toward the business district. Only John Doar's courage prevented a bloody confrontation. Stepping out between the two sides, with the FBI on the edges taking notes and pictures, he turned to the blacks, and said, "You can't win this way. . . . Don't throw bottles, that's what they want you to do." When Doar spoke, the mourners, and the cops with their clubs and dogs, all drifted home.[96]

Evers's death had little impact on the FBI in Jackson. The decision to cover the demonstrations after the shooting and to send the photographers and note takers to the funeral was routine. Bureau agents had been sending memos to the Jackson Police Department on the efforts of movement people to organize boycotts of Capital Street stores from the day the first picket appeared. And they had demonstrated a remarkable tolerance for police brutality for just as long a time, making only a perfunctory investigation of the city policemen who beat John R. Salter, Jr., a half-blooded Micmac/Penobscot Indian and a professor at Tougaloo College just outside Jackson, during a march. Salter gave this account of a follow-up interview with two special agents:

> There was now, they said, considerable doubt that the police who had struck me and who had struck the others could be conclusively identified. I pointed out that every major television network had carried film sequences of my beating, at least, if not the other incidents, and that the faces of the police involved were clearly seen. They shrugged and indicated that there would still be difficulty.

The FBI described Salter as "a chronic complainant," a "determined, belligerent, and confused young man . . . [who] obviously does not like the FBI, having without a doubt been influenced by the writings of LOWENTHAL"—referring to the only critical book on the FBI written during the depths of the domestic cold war.[97]

"The FBI," maverick journalist I. F. Stone charged at the time of Medgar Evers's death, "lives in cordial fraternity with the cops that enforce white supremacy." To a degree, this charge was also true in Birmingham during the mass demonstrations of April and May organized by the Southern Christian Leadership Conference.[98] Hoover's men telephoned reports to the police, including details about the planned march and the distribution of leaflets in the Birmingham schools.[99] Bureau officials in Washington kept the White House posted. As the FBI disseminated intelligence, Commissioner Connor hooked up fire hoses and uncaged police dogs—a brutal repression of the schoolchildren that Dr. King had put on the front line. It proved to be a strategic blunder for Connor however. "There were times," Bayard Rustin remembered, "when we didn't have to be supreme strategists. Bull Connor helped us."[100]

With the September 15 bombing of Birmingham's Sixteenth Street Baptist Church, the FBI had the opportunity to do much more than observe demonstrations and send memos off to the local police or to the White House. This was the twenty-first bombing attack against blacks in Birmingham (Bombingham, as it came to be called) during the previous eight years, and it left four girls—Carole Robertson, Denise McNair, Addie Mae Collins, and Cynthia Wesley, ages eleven to fourteen—dead. The first twenty bombing incidents had gone unsolved, and the FBI admitted (privately) that its record "in bombing cases is not good."[101] The city established a reward fund to help solve the twenty-first crime, but one person sent in a few green stamps and a facsimile of an old $100 confederate bond as a contribution to the fund.[102]

FBI agents immediately opened a full-scale investigation captioned BAPBOMB. "It is one thing to explode dynamite outside a house or in an empty building, with the aim of scaring Negroes and integrationists," as one Bureau executive noted, "but it is quite another thing to take the lives of innocent children."[103] The investigation, nonetheless, included questionable decision making by the director. The Bureau wasted time pursuing a wild and completely unfounded rumor about a liaison between a police detective and a female Klan informant; supposedly this had prevented the police from learning about the bomb in time to clear the church. There was an even wilder rumor "as to the possible involvement of members of the Nation of Islam (NOI) in the bombings." The Bureau looked into "all angles," including what Georgia Senator Richard Russell described in a conversation with Cartha DeLoach as the "possibility . . . that Negroes might have perpetrated this incident . . . to keep emotions at a fever pitch."[104]

Hoover's refusal to disrupt his surveillance network in Alabama or to subject his bureaucracy to any possibility of "embarrassment" also hindred the pursuit of justice in the BAPBOMB case. Some of the informant reports Hoover ignored, for example, involved Gary Rowe, the FBI veteran from the Freedom Ride episode at the Birmingham bus station and still the Bureau's number-one informant in Eastview Klavern 13. Another informant, John Wesley Hall, named Rowe as a member of a three-man Klan security committee that held veto power over all proposed acts of violence; this raised the possibility that Rowe might have been involved in the Baptist Church bombing. In fact, the Birmingham police considered Rowe a prime suspect. But the FBI did not investigate. Hall, who went by the nickname of "Nigger," went on the Bureau payroll two months *after* the explosion despite a polygraph test that convinced FBI agents in Alabama that he had been involved in the crime. Hall also admitted having moved some dynamite for the principal BAPBOMB suspect, Robert E. ("Dynamite Bob") Chambliss, a fifty-nine-year-old truck driver for an auto parts company who had joined the Ku Klux Klan in 1924. Two weeks after the bomb exploded on Sixteenth Street, the Birmingham Recorder's Court sentenced Chambliss, Hall, and another suspect, Charles Arnie Cagle, on a misdemeanor charge—possession of an explosive without a permit.[105]

FBI officials devoted substantial resources to the BAPBOMB investigation. They sent Little Rock SAC Roy K. Moore and other top troubleshooters to Birmingham, and assigned as many as 231 agents to the case at a single time—including two men from the FBI lab who flew down on board a military jet from Andrews Air Force Base, accompanied by Burke Marshall. (When the director found out how his lab men got to the scene so quickly, he penned the following order: "hereafter commercial aircraft should be used if available.") Because no indictments followed, it looked like the Bureau had failed, and John Kennedy and then Lyndon Johnson constantly pressured Hoover to do more.[106] With Johnson still reminding him some seven months after the tragedy to leave no stone unturned, the director told the president that everything that could be done had been done, and every known investigative technique (polygraphs, "constant harassment," and at least seventeen microphone surveillances) had been employed.[107]

Hoover was not as enthusiastic about the case as he seemed when speaking with John Kennedy or Lyndon Johnson. He would not proceed until his agents had built an airtight case,

and he would not allow Justice Department access to the potentially embarrassing informant files. On more than one occasion
he rebuffed the agents in Birmingham who told him they had a
good but not conclusive case. They said the government had to
move against the principal suspects anyway, playing off their
fears until one of them cracked and talked. Hoover would say
no, don't present this or that piece of evidence, don't meet with
the lawyers, don't give Justice any "details." "We must not give
a 'blow-by-blow' account" to the Civil Rights Division, he reasoned, "because it will appear in the Star or Sat. Evening Post."
Ironically, Bureau officials limited their own contacts with the
media about **BAPBOMB** to the argument "that primary jurisdiction" in all bombing cases should remain "at the local level."
DeLoach claimed to have arranged stories making this point
through his high-level contacts at the Copley and Hearst newspaper chains, and through his "sources on the working level at the
Washington Post and . . . the [New York] 'Daily News.'"[108]

Hoover's reading of white Alabaman public opinion shaped
his course in Birmingham. Believing the chance of conviction
remote, he refused to listen to his own agents who saw a "climate of public opinion favoring prosecution." More interested
in assigning blame than taking a tough case to court, the director tried to explain why **BAPBOMB** had not been cracked even
though the FBI knew who was responsible—a small group of
ambitious Klansmen and ex-Klansmen who broke away from
Birmingham's Eastview 13 Klavern to form a tight cell known
as the Cahaba River Group. When the Alabama Highway Patrol
arrested three suspects from this group on September 30, including Chambliss and Hall, Hoover told Robert Kennedy that
the troopers had acted prematurely. "They have certainly
'flushed' the case and I doubt that they will be able to hold these
two men."[109] He was particularly upset with the state police because Robert Shelton and two other Klan leaders had been riding around in a patrol car, helping the troopers finger the renegade "Chambliss crowd" and thus scoop the Bureau. "We had
been putting tremendous pressure on," one of the director's
aides noted, and "obviously the word got back to Shelton's
crowd and they apparently felt they had to jump in." Indeed,
immediately after the arrests Governor Wallace announced:
"We certainly beat the Kennedy crowd to the punch!"[110]

Nevertheless, Hoover wrote to Robert Kennedy that the "Negro elements" were the real villains. Their constant carping

about the cozy relationship between the G-men and segregationist law enforcement officers in the South had forced the FBI, "over the last year," to refrain "from close contacts or connection with the local authorities." Now "a gulf" had emerged that prevented the cracking of BAPBOMB and the "Negro elements" were to blame. Courtney Evans delivered the document containing this explanation to Kennedy personally, going over every line and adding one additional comment: "If we sent our Negro Agents to the South, the situation would be even worse." Having battled with Hoover over civil rights matters for two and a half years, Kennedy lacked the stomach for another fight. He listened to every word Evans spoke and "only remarked 'Yeah.'"[111]

The state of Alabama finally indicted Chambliss twelve years later. President Jimmy Carter's Justice Department concluded that the trial jury that convicted the seventy-three-year-old Chambliss for the murder of eleven-year-old Denise McNair "heard less direct evidence than was available to Mr. Hoover in 1964, when the Director ruled against prosecution." State Attorney General Bill Baxley considered this assessment too harsh, and his chief investigator, Bob Eddy, agreed—even though the director refused to make the BAPBOMB file available in 1971 when the state first started pushing for an indictment. "I wouldn't say Hoover blocked it," Eddy reasoned. "He did turn down the FBI Birmingham request to pursue the case with an indictment. But he pursued the case. He was looking for more evidence and it turned out they never did get any more."[112] Through it all, Hoover focused on his bureaucratic and political interests, and he appeared more interested in indicting the "Negro elements" than convicting Chambliss and the other white men who killed the four little girls.

By pursuing justice in its own way, whether in the Medgar Evers murder or the Sixteenth Street Baptist Church bombing, the FBI contributed to the growing polarization between civil rights activists and the federal government. The movement continued to perceive the Bureau as indifferent to everyday civil rights violations in the South and strangely incompetent even when investigating the big cases—the kind that "so shock the conscience."[113] No single event turned the movement's young people against their most potentially valuable ally, the federal government. Rather, it was a series of events and consequences shaped in part by FBI actions and value preferences from the first days of the voter registration campaign to the Birmingham horror. But those young activists largely directed their rage toward Hoover's boss. There were people in the civil rights movement, Arthur Schlesinger wrote, "who regarded the Attorney General as the devil incarnate."[114]

Jack Newfield, who had grown up in Bedford-Stuyvesant, helped organize SDS, joined SNCC, and went to Mississippi, where he had been jailed twice in civil rights demonstrations, explained this sentiment. "As civil rights activists in 1963 we liked Kennedy as little as the Southern Governors did. We saw him recommend Harold Cox, James Eastland's college roommate, to be a judge in the Fifth District Court [sic], where he was to call Negro defendants 'chimpanzees' from the bench. . . . We saw Negroes trying to register to vote in Greenwood, Mississippi, urinated upon by a white farmer, while lawyers from the Justice Department calmly took notes destined to be filed and forgotten. We agreed with James Baldwin, who pronounced Kennedy, after their stormy confrontation, 'insensitive and unresponsive to the Negro's torment.'"[115] All of Newfield's examples involved the FBI. The Bureau never made on-the-spot arrests of men like the Greenwood farmer, never investigated the charges of a James Baldwin when Baldwin himself could be more easily investigated, and never paid much attention to the segregationist history of any nominee to the federal bench.[116]

If one single event made things clear to the movement, it was Robert Kennedy's decision, and the FBI's enthusiastic response, to prosecute a group of civil rights activists while continuing to uphold the Bureau's noninterventionist policy with regard to the people terrorizing those activists.[117] That August 9, 1963, action grew out of the so-called Albany Movement. In October 1961 SNCC's Charles Sherrod and Cordell Reagon opened an office in Albany, Georgia, a black-belt city in the southwestern part of the state not far from Plains, and tried, with mixed success, to forge alliances with CORE, SCLC, and the NAACP. They also recruited students from Albany State College and area high schools, including Albany High—where Hamilton Jordan, the future chief of staff of the Carter White House, presided over the student body. In December 1961 SNCC sent eight Freedom Riders from Atlanta (among them future SDS activist Tom Hayden) to test the ICC order that had desegregated train facilities and the waiting room at the terminal. When they moved onto Roosevelt Avenue to demonstrate, the police arrested all eight, plus SNCC worker Charles Jones and two city residents who had come to greet them. Civil disobedience in Albany then became as common as peanuts. This began the Albany Movement, the first city-wide campaign of civil disobedience to force enfranchisement and the integration of all public facilities.

The Albany Movement was unpopular among white city residents for the usual reasons, and it did not become any more popular when SNCC began bringing in "white girls" to help. Marion Cheek, the FBI's resident agent, remembered a scene in a nearby town. "Huggin' and kissin' in Americus' court house lobby, black boys and white girls . . . that went over like a lead balloon." This also made the white people of Albany and environs more tolerant of the city's mass arrest tactics. On December 12, the police locked up 265 demonstrators. By December 16 they booked and transported to neighboring city and county jails a total of 735 people. By October 1962 the police made another 600 arrests, including Albany Movement organizers William G. Anderson and Slater King and SCLC leaders Martin Luther King and Ralph Abernathy. The cash and security bond approached $400,000.[118]

The initial focus of attention in southwest Georgia was not on the FBI and its director but on Albany Police Chief Laurie Pritchett, who responded to the nonviolent civil rights movement with a "nonviolent movement by the Albany Police Department"—on the grounds that the city "can't tolerate the N.A.A.C.P. . . . or any other nigger organization to take over this town with mass demonstrations." To find out what the Albany Movement was up to, Pritchett stationed his officers inside the black churches that served as meeting places and solicited tape recordings from newsmen who attended the meetings. He had other sources as well, mostly black adults who passed on what they had heard from their teenage children. At least two of his contacts, NAACP member E. D. Hamilton and Albany Movement secretary Marion Page, also kept in touch with the FBI. With Albany jails filled beyond capacity, however, Pritchett had to ship hundreds of demonstrators to neighboring jails where the police had more faith in night sticks than a "nonviolent movement" of informants and undercover cops.[119]

Not even the most disturbing incidents of brutality unduly troubled the FBI. Perhaps the worst single incident involved Slater King's wife, Marion. When she took food and clothing to a group of demonstrators held in the Mitchell County Jail in nearby Camilla, the sheriff and his deputy greeted her, seven months pregnant with a one-year-old in her arms, a three-year-old held by the hand, and her third child looking on, by knocking her to the ground and kicking her. Later, when investigating the officer to determine whether he had violated Mrs. King's civil rights by assaulting her, the FBI said Slater King "abused" the agent assigned to the case "and 'damned' [the] Federal government." A month later, Mrs. King suffered a stillbirth.[120]

There were other incidents—Dougherty County Sheriff Cull Campbell caned Slater King's brother, the attorney C. B. King— but Laurie Pritchett outmaneuvered the Albany Movement activists. "We were naive," SNCC worker Bill Hansen concluded. "[We thought] we could fill up the jails . . . we ran out of people before [the chief] ran out of jails." Unlike Birmingham and Montgomery, there were no roving bands of Klansmen carrying baseball bats, and most of the overt police brutality took place beyond the Albany city limits. President Kennedy saw no need to send marshals or troops to counter the "Nazi-like forces" about which the SNCC people were complaining. Besides, "SNCC has got an investment in violence. They're sons of bitches," the president said. Pritchett, in contrast, had his men under control, and his relationship with the FBI was good. "They cooperated with us one hundred percent." Claude Sitton of the *New York Times*, an Atlanta native and one of the most knowledgeable reporters assigned to the movement beat, said FBI agents needed the cooperation of Pritchett's men to solve stolen car cases and apprehend fugitives, so "they worked hand in glove with the local police and the local police were trying to destroy the civil rights movement."[121]

Albany Movement activists reported the assaults on Marion King and C. B. King to the FBI and the Justice Department. The FBI investigated. Nothing happened. There was simply not enough evidence, the Department said, to prove a federal case. When Vincent Harding, a deeply religious activist, led a group to city hall to pray for Slater King's wife, Pritchett told the group to move on. Harding and his people said they had a right to be there. They kept coming back, until the police arrested them just before midnight and charged them with refusing to obey an officer and blocking the sidewalk. The Albany Movement again reported the details of these arrests, along with dozens of other cases and signed statements by the people who claimed their civil rights had been violated. Again, nothing happened. The complaints always filtered through the Bureau's res-

ident agent, Marion Cheek. The Albany FBI office always described its relationship with the local police as excellent.
Responsible Bureau executives always said they were investigating. The Department always said there was not enough evidence
to file under the civil rights statutes.

Albany Movement activists never had any confidence in the
FBI; but they did have hope that the Justice Department would
finally intervene. C. B. King remembered his attempt to convince Burke Marshall to do something. "I had worn his patience
a little bit. And he said, 'Mr. King, you talk like these people are
communists or affirmed criminals.' . . . I reminded him that it
wouldn't make a damn bit of difference to me in terms of the
bludgeoning quality of the blow that struck me on my head,
whether it was a damn communist or whether it was a damn
good sheriff." The meeting itself "was a rather tragic comment-
ary," King thought, reflecting the Albany Movement's gradual
erosion of confidence in the Justice Department. Marshall had
adopted a "kind of milk-toast position . . . and it was quite dis-
tressing." All the federal government had to offer was the FBI,
King concluded, an agency most proficient at demonstrating
"empathy for . . . the white, hostile community."[122]

FBI agents who worked in Albany in those times had a different perspective, arguing that the broader problem of public
opinion among whites in southwest Georgia prevented law enforcement in civil rights cases. "We solved every church burning, every house shooting, every attempt to interfere with voting
rights," Marion Cheek claimed. "I didn't work a single criminal
case for eighteen months. I worked 7 A.M. to midnight seven days
a week . . . I was on the phone to Washington four times a day
and I rolled out of bed many a morning to investigate a civil
rights case. We brought in stenos, clerks, and everything else—
we took over a motel, we handled the whole thing as a special.
But we couldn't get a grand jury indictment even with a signed
confession. We lost every case over a two and a half year period."[123] There was some truth in what Cheek said, but such efforts remained invisible to the black community, civil rights
leaders like Martin Luther King, and newsmen like Claude Sitton. Those who came to Albany with sympathy for the black
struggle carried away no memory of the things Cheek spoke of.
Instead, they formed a clear image of the close relationship between Hoover's agents and Pritchett's officers.

One of the lost cases Cheek mentioned led directly to the indictment of the Albany Nine. The case, which involved the FBI only briefly, concerned L. Warren ("Gator") Johnson, sheriff of Baker County. Johnson had pistol-whipped the pregnant wife of a black man, Charley Ware, then beat Ware, handcuffed him, and shot him three times in the neck. Miraculously, Ware lived. "Gator walked scot free," Cheek recalled. A powerful man in southwest Georgia, "he was strong enough to keep the state patrol out of his county. . . . They were afraid of him. Johnson was crazy. He'd kill you and get away with it down there." Later, Johnson walked free from a subsequent civil action in federal court. In the aftermath, one of his jurors, Carl Smith, the owner of a foodmarket in the Harlem section of Albany, claimed the Albany Movement picketed his store as punishment for his vote. Smith was "a cool, clever individual who got rich selling to blacks" (Cheek's description), and the movement had put similar pressure on other Albany business owners to force them to change their hiring and promotion practices. No picket sign made reference to Johnson's trial, and the picketing itself lasted about an hour on the morning of April 20, 1963. Pritchett's men arrested several pickets; the line broke up and never reorganized. On April 22 Smith announced that he would close his store permanently. "The last day Carl Smith was in business he took in $9," said Cheek.[124]

Albany Mayor Asa D. Kelley, Jr., a racial moderate by southwest Georgia standards, called for a federal investigation, and J. Edgar Hoover and Robert Kennedy responded. A grand jury convened in Macon and summoned fifty-eight blacks to testify. "Marion Cheek issued everybody in the neighborhood a subpoena," recalled Robert Thomas, who had only passed by the pickets and waved on his way to work at the Harlem Barbershop. At first, almost everyone assumed the FBI had finally gathered enough information to seek the indictments of the officers who beat Marion King and C. B. King and deprived hundreds of others of their constitutional rights. Instead, the grand jury indicted three movement people for conspiring to obstruct justice (that is, for conspiring to injure a juror) and six for perjury, including Robert Thomas, Slater King, and Joni Rabinowitz. A student doing voter registration work in Albany in partial fulfillment of an Antioch College work-study assignment, Rabinowitz denied she was at the store, denied she saw the picketing, denied she knew about the picketing. The result: a three-count perjury indictment. "Marion was the one who got on the stand and lied about Joni," C. B. King charged. "A vicious guy, really vicious." Robert Kennedy, however, said the grand jury's proceedings were "fair and reasonable throughout . . . a completely nonpreferential exercise of Federal responsibility."[125]

Not surprisingly, Albany Movement activists, city police, and Hoover's agents all saw things clearly, each in their own way. A police officer told one Albany veteran, "Now that the federal government is going to put the Movement's ass in jail, we will put your ass in too, if you don't stay off the street." C. B. King remembered "a rather elderly Negro woman" telling him, "You know what, lawyer, the Federal government ain't nothing but a white man." Attorney William M. Kunstler called the Albany prosecutions "a bone thrown" by the Kennedys "to the segregationists," and the National Committee for the Albany Defendants published an aptly titled pamphlet, *Upside-Down Justice*. Martin Luther King served as honorary chairman of this Committee and two reputed communist sympathizers, Carl and Anne Braden, helped write the pamphlet. In response, the FBI dusted off HUAC's old characterization of the Bradens' group, the Southern Conference Educational Fund, and dismissed the Albany Movement's concerns out of hand. "Criticism of the F.B.I. is typical of communist propaganda attacks." Cartha DeLoach attempted to contact Dr. King in order to tell him "the true facts," but never could arrange a meeting. So he did the next best thing. He contacted the publishers of the *Chicago Defender* and other black-owned newspapers that carried "King's lies," and told Hoover he had "set [them] straight."[126]

Movement people in Albany and beyond criticized the FBI's law enforcement priorities. "At least thirty-eight" FBI agents worked on the Albany Nine prosecutions, according to U. S. Attorney Floyd Buford's estimate. C. B. King's estimate was considerably higher. "The Justice Department sent eighty-six FBI agents in here to investigate that case. They were thick as hogs." When the police knocked down Marion King, in contrast, the only Bureau agent in sight melted "right in with the total whiteness of the community." One of the few other arrests the FBI made was when a white man attacked an agent near the site of a burned-out church.[127]

The Albany Movement did not know that the FBI intercepted two telephone calls placed by New York attorney Victor Rabinowitz to C. B. King one week after the grand jury handed down the indictments. Rabinowitz wanted to discuss strategies for having the charges against his daughter and the others withdrawn by the Justice Department.[128] Movement activists suspected that the government engaged in electronic snooping, a suspicion seemingly confirmed by their own "informants" within the telephone companies—that is, sympathetic phone company workers. But at the time the charge sounded like so much conspiracy fodder. "I hate this about Robert Kennedy," Slater King said. "We knew our phones were tapped by the Federal government, that he was a pretty vindictive guy and he damn sure meant to get even with us. . . . It also happened that Victor Rabinowitz's daughter [was indicted]. . . . Victor represents Cuba, Algeria. I think that [Victor] had beat [Robert] on several cases. . . . I think that [Kennedy] wanted to tie us all together."[129]

Attorney General Kennedy was probably aware of the wiretap, and he was almost certainly aware of the FBI effort to extend the Albany Nine prosecutions. "They tried to get me too," Charles Sherrod recalled. "Once I was sick in my bed and old Cheek came in there, in the house there, and told me I had to get up because I was impeding justice." Harvard Law student Elizabeth Holtzman, later United States representative from New York and Brooklyn district attorney, was nearly the eleventh person indicted, according to Cheek. "She sat in C. B. King's office and told them what to tell the grand jury," he claimed. "We tried to indict her for subornation of perjury. We weren't allowed to. The Justice Department wouldn't allow it. The reins were pulled in."[130]

Hoover acted in Albany as an enemy of the civil rights movement; Robert Kennedy acted as a lawyer and as a politician—as the attorney general of the United States and as a member of his brother's administration. Robert and John Kennedy did not believe they could ignore political reality as they saw it. Early in Robert's tenure, as biographer Arthur Schlesinger wrote, "he saw civil rights . . . as an issue in the middle distance, morally invincible but filled for the moment with operational difficulty." That operational difficulty never quite faded, even in the summer of 1963, so the attorney general continued to speak the language of federalism whenever it was convenient. The last thing the Kennedy brothers wanted to do was alienate the white South. "The Justice Department," to quote Roger Wilkins, "wasn't trusted in the civil-rights community. It had too often seemed an impartial arbiter between two equally valid competing views in the South when the basic civil-rights assumption was that we were right and the Southern bigots were wrong."[131]

Hoover contributed to the Kennedys' mixed record. The Kennedy brothers stood with the movement. They made substantive contributions to the struggle for black equality, and on the whole John Kennedy's presidency was an activist one in civil rights matters. Caution and inaction on protecting activists must be balanced by the record of executive actions, the introduction of the civil rights bill of 1963, and the voting litigation suits.[132] But the Kennedys were active on another civil rights front, spying on the movement through the FBI. They accepted Hoover's domestic intelligence services as an inevitable part of the governing process, and they tried to sweep away operational difficulties in civil rights by turning to the FBI director, by selecting his intelligence services as the best available means of "protecting" civil rights workers.

Robert Kennedy and the people who worked in his Justice Department, from John Doar to Burke Marshall, agreed with Hoover on one point: namely, the need to limit somehow or direct the struggle for black equality. They viewed the FBI's domestic intelligence services as inherently useful, something that might help with the complex task of managing the civil rights movement. "When you say John and Burke did it for the noblest of reasons, I don't agree with that," Wilkins added. "They wanted to know ahead of time so they could do the things the government wanted to do . . . Burke and Bobby and those guys didn't want the movement to be as aggressive as it was in the early days. John and those guys, Burke and those guys, they were for civil rights . . . but they wanted it on their terms, on their timetable, to their end, their agenda." "The Kennedys were tough people," affirmed former Civil Rights Commission attorney Arnold Trebach. "They wanted to do it their way."[133]

The Kennedy way included tolerance of the FBI's ways. Responsible government officials went along with Hoover's notion that the Bureau did not have the necessary authority to protect civil rights workers, while encouraging the director to conduct widespread surveillance (which he was disposed to do). The New Frontier reformers who debated the constitutionality of federal protection never considered the constitutionality of federal surveillance. In retrospect, it seems surprising that movement people did not forcefully challenge these assumptions and priorities at the time. The idea of civil liberties, to quote Andrew

Young once more, "seemed a tertiary consideration." The movement itself, along with the movement's friends in the White House and the Justice Department, made it easier for FBI officials to operate on their own terms, on their own timetable, to their own end, their own agenda—even before Hoover's bureaucracy moved beyond the skirmishes of the first two Kennedy years to destroy the movement's most charismatic leader, before the movement itself turned left and the government right during the Vietnam peace demonstrations and the riots of the late 1960s.

CHAPTER
4

———————⋈⋈⋈———————

Black Dream, Red Menace
The Pursuit of Martin Luther King, Jr.

Nineteen days after the grand jury handed down the Albany indictments, on August 28, 1963, J. Edgar Hoover and the Kennedys turned their attention to Martin Luther King, Jr., and the 200,000 Americans, black and white, who had gathered around the Lincoln Memorial on the mall in the nation's capital. The civil rights movement came to participate in the March on Washington, the largest of the civil rights demonstrations of the summer of 1963. They came to demand justice, to hold hands and sing freedom songs, to pressure Congress on the Kennedy administration's civil rights bill, and to listen to Dr. King talk about a dream "deeply rooted in the American dream."

> I have a dream that one day, down in Alabama, with its vicious racists, with its governor having his lips dripping with the words of interposition and nullification, one day, right there in Alabama, little black boys and black girls will be able to join hands with little white boys and white girls as sisters and brothers. . . .
> When we allow freedom to ring, when we let it ring from every village and every hamlet, from every state and every city, we will be able to speed up that day when all of God's children—black men and white men, Jews and Gentiles, Protestants and Catholics—will be able to join hands and sing in the words of the old Negro spiritual, "Free at last, free at last; thank God Almighty, we are free at last."

FBI agents and informants were on hand to observe the great majority of the civil rights movement seize the moment to dream King's dream, but even within the movement there was more than a little ambivalence. The radicals wondered if the Kennedys had co-opted the "Farce on Washington," as Malcolm X called the March. Based on "a body of experience" that "definitely" included encounters with Hoover's FBI during the past two years, SNCC chairman John Lewis wanted to tell the crowd wading among the lily pads in the Washington Monument reflection pool not to "support the Administration's civil rights bill. . . . There's not one thing in the bill that will protect our people from police brutality." But Burke Marshall talked to UAW chief Walter Reuther, and Reuther, among others, including Washington's Archbishop Patrick O'Boyle, and King himself, convinced Lewis to tone it down. "Two Kennedy aides stood ready to pull the plug on the public address system in case anything went amiss," and Lee White said the administration "had troops all over," stationed in "places where they could get here" quickly in the event more serious problems developed. Some of the people on the mall that day would have preferred the original version of Lewis's text. As King delivered his own speech, one black man kept shouting, "Fuck that dream, Martin. Now, goddamit, NOW!" Even at its most optimistic moment the movement still wondered, to use Lewis's unspoken words, "which side is the federal government on?"[1]

The March on Washington convinced Hoover that the civil rights movement would not wither away on its own, that he would have to smash it before it irreparably damaged his America. Before the summer of 1963 ended, the FBI began to transform what had been a holding action against black demands for justice and equality into a frontal assault on Dr. King and the movement he helped lead. By FBI standards, it was a conventional war. "The director fell back on the cry that had never failed him in the past," Arthur Schlesinger wrote: "The ineluctable threat, evidently undiminished despite all his effort, of Communist infiltration into American institutions." After the March on Washington, FBI officials devoted as much time and energy to the communists-in-the-civil-rights-movement issue as they had once devoted to "the cause"—that is, the McCarthy-era purge of communists and other dissidents from the government and the professions.[2] The director had spent his life destroying communists and their causes, and now he would try to destroy King and his cause.

Hoover's decision in August 1963 caught even his closest aides by surprise. The director saw communism as "secularism on the march," but few of his executives could detect this secularist advance, since Martin Luther King and other black Baptist churchmen were among the primary organizers of the civil rights movement. Ever since the sit-ins began in February 1960, the FBI had been predicting a revival of communist activity in the southern black belt.[3] But it never came. When Bull Connor and King faced off in Birmingham, the local FBI office informed the seat of government that no "CP activity" could be found "in connection with these demonstrations and no Communists are known to be participating." Even Hoover's public pronouncements lacked their old ring of conviction: all he could say was that the party merely attempted to infiltrate "the legitimate Negro organizations for the purpose of stepping up racial prejudice and hatred."[4]

The dearth of communists simply encouraged FBI officials to look harder. On the eve of the March on Washington, a headquarters directive advised twenty-seven field offices to "be extremely alert to data indicating interest, plans, or actual involvement of the [Communist] Party in the current Negro movement." And the FBI devoted its entire Current Intelligence Analysis of August 21 "to the communist plans for the Negro March," distributing at least 149 copies to forty-four government agencies.[5] Other agents searched the files for "subversive data" on March leadership and filed reports with the Civil Rights Division. In one case, a wiretap revealed "extensive contact" between black Communist party functionary Ben Davis and Bayard Rustin, the organizing genius behind the March and longtime associate of A. Philip Randolph. The New York office proposed to mark Davis as an informant. Educated at Amherst and Harvard Law School, Davis had worked for the party since the 1930s, when he served as an attorney in the Angelo Herndon case; in the summer of 1963 he was dying of cancer.[6] While headquarters considered Rustin's associations and the New York proposal, other field offices forwarded reports on more obscure March participants. San Francisco reported that Vivian Hallinan, the wife of the Progressive party's presidential candidate in 1952, Vincent Hallinan, planned to bring her six sons to Washington. "All of the

Hallinans," Burke Marshall learned, "have been active in communist party front and civil rights affairs." The FBI opened a new file, captioned Communist Influence Racial Matters (CIRM), for all the inbound information.[7]

While the field filed its reports, Hoover requested a general summary of communist attempts to infiltrate the civil rights movement, assigning the task to the Domestic Intelligence Division (Division Five). On August 23, five days before the March on Washington, the Division submitted a sixty-eight page brief that minimized the Red menace. Communist efforts to infiltrate such groups as the NAACP and SCLC had been "limited," at best, while most "other legitimate . . . organizations in the Negro, civil rights and integration fields," including CORE, SNCC, and the National Urban League, merely provided inviting, "ready-made targets" for communist infiltrators. According to FBI informants in New York, however, many party members did not even try to infiltrate CORE. They did not want "to harm CORE's work." If they stayed away, perhaps the Red-baiters and spies would leave CORE alone. In those few cases where the party had succeeded in its infiltration schemes, Division Five concluded, the civil rights groups generally policed themselves.[8]

The closest thing to a Communist party front in the civil rights field, the Southern Conference Educational Fund (SCEF), was active, by the Division Five estimate, in "raising bail funds for those arrested in connection with integration activities, sending food and other relief shipments to depressed southern Negro areas and holding conferences." Of the eleven SCEF officers, the FBI *suspected* only three "of being CP members." An informant identified Carl and Anne Braden as communists back in 1954, and another "source reported that in the past he has considered James Dombrowski . . . to be a communist, if not actually a CP member, because he followed communist principles." The standard Bureau description of the Bradens' and Dombrowski's group was just as thin. "The source stated SCEF is a progressive, liberal organization which he considers a CP front . . . because it has gone along with the CP on certain issues, particularly the racial issue." Division Five was not even sure about its own best case.[9]

Neither the Communist party's efforts nor its record of failure surprised Hoover's aides in Division Five. "Control of the Negro population in this country" simply represented a logical goal "tied to the dictates of the Soviet Union and not . . . any benevo-

lent or altruistic principles." No matter how troubling in a theoretical sense, in the real world communist ideology guaranteed
the party's inability "to appreciably infiltrate, influence or control large numbers of American Negroes." "The CP does not
seem to understand," Division Five concluded, "that its failure
can be attributed to its adherence to Marxism-Leninism. The
Party views the struggle for equal rights as part of the Marxist
concept of the never-ending class struggle and not, as most Negroes see it, an attempt to solve a racial issue. Thus, the Party
would involve the Negro in a much broader struggle than the
already titanic one in which he is now engaged." Perhaps if America's Reds had stopped being Reds, Division Five seemed to be
saying, they would have had a better chance.[10]

Although Division Five qualified the report before sending it
on to Hoover, its conclusion was unambiguous—given the FBI's
unwritten rule that it was far more important not to be wrong
than it was to be right. "We are right now in this Nation involved
in a form of racial revolution," FBI executive Fred J. Baumgardner advised the assistant director in charge of the Domestic
Intelligence Division, William C. Sullivan, "and the time has
never been so right for exploitation of the Negroes by communist propagandists. The Communist Party in the next five years
may fail dismally with the American Negro as it has in the past.
On the other hand, it may make prodigious strides and great
successes with the American Negroes, to the serious detriment
of our national security. Time alone will tell." In the meantime,
the communist menace merited little attention.[11]

When Hoover read the report of August 23 he rejected its
premise (that communist influence was "infinitesimal") and lectured Division Five chief William Sullivan. "This memo reminds
me vividly of those I received when Castro took over Cuba. You
contended then that Castro and his cohorts were not Communists and not influenced by Communists. Time alone proved you
wrong." The report, Sullivan remembered, "set me at odds with
Hoover. . . . A few months went by before he would speak to me.
Everything was conducted by exchange of written communications. It was evident that we had to change our ways or we
would all be out on the street." When the director began scribbling sarcastic notes on routine Division Five memos, Sullivan's
agents "discussed how to get out of trouble. To be in trouble
with Mr. Hoover was a serious matter. These men were trying
to buy homes, mortgages on homes, children in school. They

lived in fear of getting transferred." The Division had to give Hoover what he wanted, or risk the consequences.[12]

William Sullivan had the most to lose. It had taken him twenty years in the FBI to rise to the rank of assistant director for Domestic Intelligence, an appointment he received in 1961, a mere two years before the March on Washington. An odd creature in Hoover's FBI, Sullivan was certainly the oddest of "the Gandy dancers," as field agents referred to the director's immediate circle of aides in honor of Helen Gandy—"a wraithlike, grim-faced spinster from New Jersey who . . . was Hoover's secretary and administrative assistant from the day of his appointment until the day of his death." A farm boy from New England and a former school teacher whose management style matched the wrinkled suits and spotted ties he wore, Sullivan was always misplacing things, whether a pen or a classified file or his own train of thought, and always losing control of his terrible temper. When not berating his colleagues, he liked to describe himself as "a lifelong Democrat," probably the only FBI executive who voted for John Kennedy and not Richard Nixon. Known inside the Bureau as the house intellectual, Sullivan buried his nose in a book at every opportunity, reading most everything from Marx's *Kapital* to Schlesinger's *Age of Jackson*. He rubbed elbows at cocktail parties with Henry Kissinger, then a Harvard professor, and lectured three years running at the Harvard Graduate School of Business Administration. Whenever he wanted to flatter Hoover, he compared him to German Chancellor Konrad Adenauer or French President Charles de Gaulle.[13]

In no position to challenge the director, Sullivan submitted Division Five's apology on August 30: "The Director is correct. We were completely wrong . . . the Communist Party, USA, does wield substantial influence over Negroes which one day could become decisive." He discussed King's "I Have a Dream" speech, labeling it "demagogic," and marked King "as the most dangerous Negro leader of the future in this Nation from the standpoint of communism, the Negro and national security." To meet the threat, the FBI must concentrate on "the many Negroes who are fellow-travellers, sympathizers or who aid the Party, knowingly or unknowingly, but do not qualify as members." It would "be unrealistic to limit ourselves as we have been doing to legalistic proofs or definitely conclusive evidence that would stand up in court or before Congressional Committees."[14]

A few weeks after the March on Washington, on September

16, Division Five again recommended "increased coverage of communist influence on the Negro," stressing the "urgent need" to use "all possible investigative techniques." Hoover responded with more sarcasm. "No. I can't understand how you can so agilely switch your thinking and evaluation. Just a few weeks ago you contended that the Communist influence in the racial movement was ineffective. . . . Now you want to load the Field down with more coverage." Sullivan thought the director was "egging us on." After returning from a brief vacation, he made another attempt to repair the breach. "As we know, facts by themselves are not too meaningful. . . . It is obvious that we did not put the proper interpretation upon the facts." Division Five had always been "in complete agreement with the Director," particularly with regard to Dr. King, "the most dangerous and effective Negro leader in the country." Sullivan resubmitted his proposal for an escalation of "our coverage of communist influence on the Negro," the CPUSA's "favorite target."[15] Explaining this reversal years later as "a lot of nonsense which we ourselves did not believe in," he said he instructed his aides to "state the facts just as they are and then let the storm break," knowing full well that Hoover believed the civil rights movement was riddled with Reds and thus would be enraged by the Division Five conclusions.[16]

In Hoover's FBI orthodoxy on matters of policy was sacred. If Sullivan understood this simple fact better than most of the men who became special agents, he did not realize, at the time Division Five prepared the August 23 report, that Hoover was reevaluating previous policy, and that the March on Washington itself would convince him to make the change.[17] "The FBI saw the march, in a sense, as far more important than we did," said Bayard Rustin. "The March terrified them. People in the Congress and the White House were beginning to change their attitude toward us."[18] The movement's explosive growth convinced Hoover that he could no longer contain it through a noninterventionist policy on the law-enforcement front or a relatively passive surveillance policy on the intelligence front. The tactic now would be all-out surveillance (that is, counterintelligence) based on the ongoing operations aimed at the Communist party—specifically, the COMINFIL (communist infiltration) and COINTELPRO (counterintelligence) programs designed to "expose, disrupt, or otherwise neutralize" party members.

The original Division Five report and accompanying memo of

August 23 represented a rational attempt to explain the CPUSA's utter irrelevance to the civil rights movement. That position had been FBI policy, more or less, since the Second World War, and the Division had stated it in similar language on numerous occasions during the 1950s and early 1960s, notably in two monographs on "the Communist party and the Negro" and in a counterintelligence program "idea book." The latter, entitled "Current Weaknesses of the Communist Party, USA," included three sections on the party's *incompetence* in the racial field and recommended counterintelligence actions designed to exploit the party's *"self-defeating policies relative to the Negroes* [emphasis added]." If Hoover never agreed with Division Five conclusions on a personal level, he accepted them as policy. He even approved the writing and publication of a pamphlet comparing the positive results achieved by the NAACP with the CPUSA's dismal failures. Sullivan, then an inspector in the central research section, received the assignment—but he gave up after six months, citing a lack of pertinent material.[19]

By the standards of the mid- and late 1960s, FBI surveillance of black political activists prior to the summer of 1963 was limited and cautious because Hoover deemed the political risks of more aggressive involvement to be too great. But beginning in the summer of 1963 there was a fundamental change in Hoover's willingness to assume the risks of more aggressive involvement, a change that can be explained by his belief that blacks had gone too far with their protests and now posed an imminent threat to the established order. Bureau documents immediately before, during, and after the March on Washington are filled with references to an impending "social revolution." Sullivan himself saw it in those terms. "It was a classic confrontation: Hoover vs. Communism, blacks, and social change, and Hoover gave it everything he had, which in his case was considerable."[20] It was no coincidence that President Kennedy and the FBI director concluded at roughly the same time that a strategy of limited intervention in the civil rights movement was neither prudent nor politically feasible. It was a reflection of Hoover's arrogance that he thought he had just as good a chance to influence the nature and direction of the coming revolution as the president of the United States. It was a reflection of Hoover's power that he was probably right.

Hoover based his case for a more aggressive intervention in the civil rights movement on the contention that communists were manipulating Martin Luther King. Neither the director nor any of his aides considered King an actual member of the Communist party, a charge widely circulated in the white South and among right-wing circles in the Southwest and in California. In the FBI view, King was merely a "security risk," to use one of William Sullivan's more restrained descriptions, because of his associations. At least eight persons, according to the FBI's count, who had helped King and SCLC, particularly during early movement days, were Reds of one sort or another—either former communists or the spiritual, never-had-a-card kind. Stanley Levison, Clarence Jones, and Hunter Pitts (Jack) O'Dell headed the list, followed by Harry Wachtel, C. T. Vivian, Randolph Blackwell, Lawrence Reddick, and Bayard Rustin. The charges were soft, products of a utilitarian definition of communism. FBI officials knew they had little to work with. How much mileage could they obtain from King's signature on petitions demanding abolition of the old House Committee on Un-American Activities?[21]

The FBI had explored Dr. King's communist associations prior to the summer of 1963, but Hoover did not act forcefully. Even the case of Stanley Levison, one of King's closest advisers and a man who had been named by prize informants during the early 1950s as a Soviet courier, failed to stir the FBI at first. By the late 1950s Bureau officials knew that Levison had "been closely associated with Reverend Martin Luther King" and at least a few other civil rights leaders, including A. Philip Randolph. But they collected "public source information" only on King's Southern Christian Leadership Conference and did not open a COMINFIL file until October 1962.[22] Sullivan himself was not quite sure what to make of Levison. He contacted Donald E. Roney, the assistant special agent in charge of the New York office, the office of origin in the Levison investigation, and asked (according to Roney's summary of their conversation): "Exactly what is LEVISON's status within the CP?; is he or is he not a member of the Party?; is he subject to Party discipline, or not?; has he actually broken with GUS HALL and other CP leaders?" The FBI moved against King and used his association with Levison as a pretext for doing so, but the decision to destroy King was not made until the March on Washington demonstrated that the civil rights movement had finally muscled its way onto the nation's political agenda.[23]

Bureau surveillance of Levison produced a tremendous

amount of information on the civil rights movement and little information on communist attempts to infiltrate the movement. Some of the information picked up through wiretaps on Levison's telephone was actually supportive of the FBI's work and critical of King. Levison reportedly "commented that King is a poorly read man who probably has not looked at a book in 20 years." On another occasion, after the Bureau arrested thirteen Ku Klux Klansmen in Mississippi, the wireman heard Levison say the director's men had done a "terrific" job. Most of the intelligence gathered through electronic surveillance on Levison and sent on to Burke Marshall and the Kennedys was political, highlighting Levison's contacts with King, Clarence Jones, and Jack O'Dell—his advice on fund-raising and speech-writing, his recommendations that King hire O'Dell as an administrative assistant and support the Negro judge William Henry Hastie in the event the president nominated him for a seat on the Supreme Court.[24]

With Burke Marshall and the Kennedy brothers genuinely troubled by the communists and communist sympathizers who, in Marshall's words, were "always hanging around" the movement, Hoover's steady stream of memos on Levison and O'Dell served to reinforce their fears. By the summer of 1963, with the administration "staking its future on the integrity of the civil rights movement," John Kennedy decided to explain the facts of life to King. The president met him at the White House and took him outside—"I guess Hoover must be bugging him too," King later speculated—for a walk in the Rose Garden. "They're Communists," Kennedy said. "You've got to get rid of them." Public exposure would harm the movement and jeopardize the administration's civil rights bill. "If they shoot *you* down, they'll shoot *us* down too—so we're asking that you be careful." Hoover had already told the president's brother that King would "hurt his own cause" if he did not cut his ties to Levison and O'Dell. "There are more and more communists trying to take advantage of the hate movement," the director advised, in words that he used interchangeably to describe both the civil rights movement and the violence-prone wing of the white resistance. "And bigots down South who are against integration are beginning to charge King is tied in with communists."[25]

The FBI had already compiled an intermittent record of Red baiting. When Hoover, or perhaps one of his aides, mentioned

Bureau interest in Stanley Levison and communist infiltration of the civil rights movement to James Eastland, the Senate Internal Security Subcommittee promptly subpoenaed Levison, who took the Fifth Amendment. The FBI obtained the transcript of Levison's executive session testimony and sent copies to Kennedy and Marshall at the Justice Department and Kenneth O'Donnell at the White House.[26] Other incidents also predated the March on Washington, notably the New York field office's suggestion that an anonymous mailing be sent "to appropriate southern newspapers to expose the communist background of Hunter Pitts O'Dell." After a slight modification at headquarters, Division Five gave a blind memo to Crime Records chief Cartha DeLoach "for his consideration and possible use by his contacts in the news media field." DeLoach alerted the *Augusta* (Georgia) *Chronicle* and a number of other papers "in such southern states as Alabama where King has announced that the next targets for integration of universities are located." FBI officials may have been interested in putting optimum pressure on King to fire O'Dell, but their method represented a direct form of assistance to the segregationists.[27]

In reality, there were few ties between the Communist party and the civil rights movement and only one dusty connection (Stanley Levison) serious enough to give reasonable men pause. Though the cry of communist infiltration remained a false (or at least greatly exaggerated) issue, it was impossible to prove or disprove the validity of the FBI's communist-search justification for spying on civil rights groups. There might not be any hard proof one way or the other. In the case of Bayard Rustin, the FBI conceded the absence of "direct evidence placing him in the Communist party," and then argued that evidentiary voids cut both ways. "While there may not be any direct evidence that [Rustin] is a Communist neither is there any substantial evidence that he is anticommunist."[28] The director's proposition justified a request to Robert Kennedy for a wiretap on Rustin's home telephone. (The attorney general approved the tap.) On an informal level, John Lewis suspected, it also led the FBI to leak derogatory information on Rustin to Whitney Young and Roy Wilkins in an attempt to exacerbate divisions among the so-called Big Six (King, Lewis, Young, Wilkins, Farmer, and Randolph) during the planning stages of the March on Washington. "It was over this whole thing of being too close to . . . subversive elements in the larger society," Lewis said. Wilkins was especially upset about Rustin's prominent role in organizing the march.[29]

For Hoover, the Red menace was a commodity as well as a threat, something to be possessed and used, something to justify the surveillance of any group because "the CPUSA views every noncommunist organization as a target for infiltration."[30] Many years later counsel for a House committee asked former FBI executive Charles D. Brennan, one of the principal authors of the Division Five report of August 23, why the FBI tried to "neutralize" Dr. King if he was the victim of communist infiltration? Why didn't the Bureau spend more time under the counterintelligence and communist infiltration programs targeting the alleged perpetrators, Levison and the Communist party, for "disruption" and "neutralization"?[31] Brennan had no good answer to that question, but it seems clear that Hoover wanted to destroy more than the CPUSA. The director intended to smash the equally serious (and certainly more imminent) threat to the existing social and political order posed by the civil rights movement and its most charismatic leader.

In late September, Hoover finally approved the Division Five request to use "all possible investigative techniques" in its "coverage of communist influence on the Negro."[32] In October, Robert Kennedy approved the director's request to wiretap the phones in King's home in Atlanta and SCLC offices in New York and Atlanta. Two months later, on December 23, representatives from the Atlanta field office and Division Five met at headquarters for nine hours to discuss how best to expose "King for the clerical fraud and Marxist he is." Constrained only by a desire to avoid "embarrassment to the Bureau," Sullivan's group proposed to infiltrate "King's office" with "colored" agents or perhaps "a good looking female plant," and to utilize "specialized investigative techniques [break-ins, in other words] at the SCLC office." Six days after the Division Five gathering, when *Time* magazine named King its "Man of the Year," Hoover responded: "They had to dig deep in the garbage for this one." Nearly a month later, he described King as "a 'tom cat' with obsessive degenerate sexual urges." The director clearly supported the Division Five proposals.[33]

Hoover scribbled this last comment on a document about a microphone that Division Five had installed in King's room at the Shroeder Hotel in Milwaukee. This bug, as well as the other fourteen microphone surveillances the Bureau employed against King (without bothering to obtain Robert Kennedy's authorization for a single one), presented a minor managerial problem. Hoover had to find the money and personnel necessary to transcribe hundreds of reels of tape. Given such a pervasive and intrusive surveillance, SCLC leaders knew they were being tapped and bugged, and they often moved from one lodge to the next in the hope of staying a step ahead of the inevitable FBI wireman. The parking lot of virtually every hotel and motel used by King's group, Andrew Young remembered, had one or two of "these little plain green Plymouths with two-way radios in them," a sure sign the Bureau had already checked in.[34]

By expanding its surveillance of the civil rights movement in the wake of the March on Washington, the FBI moved beyond peripheral operations in civil rights areas where the Communist party was thought to be active. From the fall of 1963 onward, FBI officials used counterintelligence tactics to "expose, disrupt, discredit, or otherwise neutralize" the civil rights movement itself. A few field offices had difficulty finding their targets. Describing the Communist party's southern California district as dormant in "the Negro field," the head of the Los Angeles office said there was nothing to "counter." In Chicago, the special agent in charge advised headquarters that the only current Negro Question counterintelligence operations concerned Claude Lightfoot, a black communist and longtime party functionary. There were "no incidents of misuse of the Negro or the Negro civil rights movement . . . available to us [to exploit]," he continued. Nor were there "any Negro communists," besides Lightfoot, worth targeting. None of the black party members in Chicago, Lightfoot included, were "influential professionally and in the civil rights movement."[35]

Both field offices missed the point; FBI officials wanted their agents in Los Angeles and Chicago and elsewhere to focus on Dr. King and the civil rights movement, not obscure activists like Lightfoot. By targeting King rather than the Communist party, the FBI broadened its assault. King himself, not Levison or some controller in faraway Moscow, was the explicit threat to law and order, and so he was the target of dozens of counterintelligence operations carried out by William Sullivan's Division Five with the cooperation of Cartha DeLoach's Crime Records Division. Crime Records disseminated the embarrassing personal and political information collected through the taps and all those hotel-room bugs not only to the media and King's own wife, but to virtually any individual or organization courted by the movement.[36] The FBI bombarded the White House with data on King, along with select members of Congress—Congressman John Rooney (D., N.Y.), Speaker of the House John McCormack (D., Mass.), and Senator Leverett Saltonstall (R., Mass.), among others. Vice-President Hubert Humphrey, U.S. Information Agency director Edward R. Murrow, Community Relations Service director LeRoy Collins, United Nations representative Adlai Stevenson, and dozens of other government officials, moreover, received oral or written briefings. A leak to the office of the National Science Foundation (NSF) was typical. The Foundation received a Bureau monograph on King as part of a general effort to convince the agency to purge the Southern Christian Leadership Conference from "the NSF program to obtain qualified Negro students from southern schools."[37]

In the private sector, FBI officials tried to discredit Dr. King and the movement through leaks to various university administrators, foundation trustees, and labor leaders. In some cases, the Bureau targeted those persons who promised support for the movement. When King aborted a meeting with Teamster boss Jimmy Hoffa after Crime Records alerted reporters for the *Washington Daily News*, the *Washington Star*, and the *New York Daily News*, the FBI tried to exploit "the white backlash within [Hoffa's] own union ranks." (King had thought the Teamsters might be a possible source of funds.) While King was concluding negotiations for a $3 million grant from the Ford Foundation, DeLoach arranged for an ex-agent and current Ford Motor Company employee, John Bugas, to brief Foundation president McGeorge Bundy. In this case the approach failed. When Bundy asked if the FBI was the source of the allegations, DeLoach told Clyde Tolson it was useless. "Bundy is of the pseudo-intellectual, Ivy League group that has little respect for the FBI." Bundy, however, was the exception. Most of the people who greeted Bureau agents bearing dirt on King were considerably more gracious.[38]

The FBI quickly expanded its intelligence and counterintelligence operations beyond King and SCLC. Many of the COMINFIL reports on such groups as the American Friends Service Committee, for example, bore the Racial Matters caption and were directed at the civil rights movement as well. (The Bureau even ran a name check on George Fox, the founding Quaker who died in 1691.) Bayard Rustin, who went on from the March on Washington to organize the New York City school boycott in 1964, was the target of a press leak that had the FBI salivating over the prospects for dissension within the movement. A long-time pacifist and former member of the Young Communist League, Rustin had gone with a group of fellow pacifists to the headquarters of the Soviet delegation to the United Nations in the hope that they might somehow keep dialogue between the two superpowers open in a nuclear age. FBI agents pointed him out to newspaper photographers, a story appeared the next day in the *New York Daily News* implying that he had a close relationship with Soviet leaders, and a number of "embarrassing" articles followed—including an item in *Time* magazine.[39]

Most COINTELPRO schemes attempted to influence public opinion on the un-American nature of the civil rights movement and its leaders in a similar manner. Cartha DeLoach helped arrange an interview in the August 19, 1963, issue of *U.S. News and World Report* featuring S. B. Fuller, a wealthy black businessman and publisher from Chicago, who claimed, as quoted by the FBI, "the current civil rights demonstrations (which are being supported by the Communist Party) do not encourage the Negro to work harder or become more self-reliant." With his advocacy of self-help and modest sixth-grade education, Fuller symbolized black mobility and the efficacy of the American dream. Because "his success gives the lie to the communist contention that the Negro is downtrodden," Hoover ordered De-Loach to circulate the article widely, "particularly with the Negro press," in the wake of the March on Washington.[40]

The Martin Luther King investigation was the most sustained and adventuresome because King was the most influential civil rights leader; but the FBI counterintelligence campaign against the whole civil rights movement, as Sullivan later explained, was in accord with "Mr. Hoover's policy" and FBI practices dating back to the early cold war years. Since 1946 Bureau officials had pursued counterintelligence actions designed to develop an informed public opinion about "the basically Russian nature of the Communist Party in this country"—an ambitious program that they described as "a campaign of education directed to the proposition that Communism is dangerous." In linking King to the Communist party, they hoped to make a public case about the basically un-American nature of the civil rights movement. They devoted themselves to a campaign of education directed to the proposition that racial justice was dangerous, and their action in so doing was "not an isolated phenomenon." Sullivan said it was "a practice of the Bureau down through the years."[41]

By the summer of 1964 the FBI had focused its attention not only on Dr. King but on all civil rights leaders and all race-related events, including the riots in New York, the Mississippi Summer Project, the national conventions of the Democratic and Republican parties, and, more generally, the emergence of civil rights as "the primary domestic issue on the political front today." With "both sides" in the Senate debate on the civil rights bill bombarding the Bureau with requests for information on "communist penetration with the racial movement," internal security section chief Fred Baumgardner said Division Five had to be in a position to make "a proper presentation of the facts." The Inspection Division concurred, advising Hoover of the "urgency" in the Bureau's attempt to "stay ahead" of civil rights debate and of "complex political situations in an election year where civil rights and social disturbances will play a key role in campaign efforts and possibly election results." Political concerns, not internal security concerns, were in the forefront.[42]

Granted the necessary resources to stay ahead, Division Five executives set up a special desk in the internal security section to coordinate its Communist Influence Racial Matters investigation (a CIRM unit manned by two supervisors) and reminded every agent assigned to a CIRM case to interpret the term "communist" in the "broadest sense." If they directed field agents to "separate ... the bona fide communist from the mere 'do-gooder'" and to avoid the inclusion of "information concerning legitimate efforts in the racial movement where there is no communist taint," they required the filing of detailed reports on "communist infiltration in various organizations, such as the Congress of Racial Equality, Student Non-Violent Coordinating Committee, and the like; ... subversive individuals active in the racial movements; ... communist fronts and other miscellaneous organizations; and racial disturbances and other racial matters."[43] The apparent restriction—"if a particular event had no communist involvement, it should, of course, not be included in the report"—was intended to direct general "Racial Matters" intelligence into the proper file and not the CIRM file. When the FBI ran its first name check on King's young and ambitious SCLC colleague, Jesse Jackson, the Chicago field office, having failed to develop an appropriate "subversive characterization," provided "descriptive data" instead. Division Five sent out instructions requiring the field to file "matters which do not fit into any other specific category" under "the character of 'Racial Matters.'"[44]

No matter how sweeping, the FBI's domestic political intelligence activities clearly centered on Dr. King. "King is no good," as Hoover put it back in February 1962.[45] The ferocity of the Bureau's pursuit does suggest a vendetta, an overreaction to a new and potent social force. But King's targeting was quite rational. He was the available man, the most well-known, effective, and charismatic civil rights leader. After the March on Washington, King and the movement were inseparable in the public mind. If King could be damaged, the movement could be damaged. King was vulnerable to a subversion charge, FBI officials reasoned, because of his associations with Levison, O'Dell, and others. Beyond that, as the FBI discovered first through the wiretapping of Clarence Jones's telephone, King's personal life made him vulnerable on another front. The ease with which the FBI slid from the communist issue to the morality issue indicates that the director and his aides were looking for something—anything—that might work to discredit King. It also paralleled the typical racist belief in the sexual prowess of the black male and the threat to white society that posed. Hoover's fears were deeply personal.

No matter how promising, the FBI drew a blank on the Levison-Moscow connection—despite "electronic surveillances on Levison dating back to 1954" and forward to the first of the Nixon years, and at least twenty-nine entries (burglaries) into Levison's business office in New York between 1954 and 1964.[46] The Jones tap and then the bugs in King's hotel and motel rooms, however, provided another connection to exploit. If King could not be ruined by publicity charging him with subversion, perhaps he could be ruined with publicity charging him with adultery. "Hoover was a strict Presbyterian–brought up individual," Crime Records Division agent Lawrence Heim said. "If the Ten Commandments said 'Thou Shalt Not Covet Thy Neighbor's Wife,' that meant [exactly that]." Years later, after the tragedy in Memphis, the director initially suspected that King's assassin had been a vengeful husband.[47]

Hoover dreamed of destroying Dr. King and replacing him with "a manageable black leader," another former Crime Records agent, Harold Leinbaugh, said. And a few of the more confident FBI officials, William Sullivan included, tried to find one. In January 1964, when Sullivan proposed to remove King from his pedestal, he suggested that the Bureau replace King with the "right kind" of black leader. John F. Malone, the FBI's man in New York, nominated Roy Wilkins. Division Five agents also favored Wilkins ("a man of character"), but in this instance Sullivan overruled his men—offering instead Samuel R. Pierce, Jr., a talented, conservative attorney who joined the Ronald Reagan cabinet seventeen years later as secretary of housing and urban development. Both men, Wilkins and Pierce, were unaware of the plans of their Bureau cheerleaders.[48]

The FBI campaign to take King off his pedestal went on and on, finally cresting in the late fall and early winter of 1964. Upon learning on October 14 that King would receive the Nobel Peace Prize, Hoover sent a flood of reports to the White House, the Department of Justice, the State Department, the U.S. Information Agency, and American embassies across Europe concerning King's character. Then, during a November 18 meeting with a group of women reporters, the director labeled King "the most notorious liar in the country." DeLoach passed Hoover three notes asking him to retract the statement or at least request the reporters to consider it off-the-record, but the director threw each note in the trash and finally told the assistant director to mind his own business. Needless to say, the notorious-liar quote was the one item that stuck out during Hoover's three-hour oration. "The girls," DeLoach noticed, "could hardly wait to leave to get to the telephone." King learned of the remark while vacationing in Bimini, and he responded in kind, labeling his sixty-nine-year-old adversary senile and expressing his "sympathy for this man who served his country so well."[49]

Hoover's specific reference in calling Dr. King a liar was a year-old statement the civil rights leader had made to the *New York Times*. A reporter asked King if he agreed with a report on the Albany, Georgia, protests prepared by the historian Howard Zinn for the Southern Regional Council. One of the statements in the report charged FBI agents assigned to civil rights cases in the South with racism, and King said he agreed with Zinn. Too many agents were "white Southerners who have been influenced by the mores of the community." Southern agents were "friendly with the local police and people who are promoting segregation," he added. "Every time I saw FBI men in Albany, they were with the local police force."[50]

This was a serious charge. It could not be answered with a file check on Howard Zinn or explanations about how blacks considered black agents "finks" because they worked in law enforcement. Hoover ignored the racism issue, concentrating instead on the accuracy of King's statement—specifically, the notion that all agents assigned to the Albany office were southerners. Only one was a native southerner. The other four were from New York, Indiana, Minnesota, and Massachusetts.[51] If wrong on the specific question, King was quite correct on the larger issue. Calling him a liar was not "simply a matter of calling a spade a spade," as DeLoach, in an incredible choice of words, told CORE's Val Coleman. Any FBI agent assigned to the Deep South would have to confront his own "psychological needs," Albany movement attorney C. B. King said. "He wants social approbation. He wants his wife to be accepted as the wife of a regular fellow in this community. He wants her to have friends to be invited to dinner. And the only people who are relevant to him are white people." In the end, the agent would likely be a reformed Yankee, just another "local redneck with an FBI tag."[52]

Many of the FBI's agents supported civil rights, Bayard Rustin said, but the executives in Washington did not send in "flaming liberals. By and large they did what they could to send in people who were not going to be helpful." The one native southerner assigned to the Albany FBI office, Marion Cheek, whose family had once owned a large piece of land in DeKalb County, just north of Atlanta, land that Sherman's troopers had once camped on and tore up, found himself at the center of the entire controversy. Arthur Murtagh, the Atlanta agent who sometimes worked out of the Albany office and whose waistline exceeded Hoover's notion of what the proper girth of a G-man should be, said he considered Cheek "a friend, but on the question of race I could not discern much difference between his view and the view of the Ku Klux Klansmen that I would have occasion to interview from time to time." Hoover spoke to Cheek only once in Cheek's twenty-six-year Bureau career, to advise him that Martin Luther King was trying to "get you transferred out of there."[53]

Division Five responded aggressively as Hoover's mostly one-sided feud with King moved into the public realm after the March on Washington. The Division had the FBI lab make a composite tape of the "highlights" of the various microphone surveillances (mostly "dirty jokes and bawdy remarks . . . plus the sounds of people engaging in sex" in King's room at Washington's Willard Hotel), and in November 1964 William Sullivan himself drafted a ghastly note recommending suicide as a way out:

> King, look into your heart. You know you are a complete fraud and a great liability to all of us Negroes. . . . King, like all frauds your end is approaching. You could have been our greatest leader. . . . But you are done. . . . No person can overcome facts. . . . The American public, the church organizations that have been helping—Protestant, Catholic and Jews will know you for what you are . . . So will others who have backed you. You are done . . . there is only one thing left for you to do. You know what this is. You have just 34 days in which to do (this exact number has been selected for a specific reason, it has definite practical significant [sic]). You are done. There is but one way out for you. You better take it before your filthy, abnormal fraudulent self is bared to the nation.

On November 21, thirty-four days before Christmas, Sullivan put the tape and letter in an unmarked package, gave the package to one of his agents, Lish Whitson, and instructed him to fly to Miami. Once in Miami, Whitson called headquarters, and Sullivan (or one of his men) told him to address and mail the package to the SCLC office in Atlanta.[54]

Three days later, on November 24, Hoover again went public with his attack on King, with an indirect reference in a speech at Loyola University in Chicago to "pressure groups" headed by "Communists and moral degenerates." In the meantime, DeLoach offered a copy of a King microphone surveillance transcript to Benjamin Bradlee, *Newsweek* Washington bureau chief. When Burke Marshall and Nicholas Katzenbach learned of this, they asked President Johnson to look into the matter. Johnson did so by warning the FBI about Bradlee. He was unreliable, the president said, and was telling the story all over Washington.[55]

These and other FBI efforts to smear Martin Luther King led to a series of meetings between Bureau officials and various civil rights leaders intent on making peace. Roy Wilkins approached Cartha DeLoach first, shortly after the director's Loyola speech. According to the assistant director, however, Wilkins was on the Bureau's side and willing to assist in the planned removal of "King from the national picture."

> I told [Wilkins] that the Director, of course, did not have in mind the destruction of the civil rights movement as a whole . . . [but] if King wanted war we certainly would give it to him. Wilkins shook his head and stated there was no doubt in his mind as to which side would lose if the FBI really came out with all its ammunition against King. I told him the ammunition was plentiful and that while we were not responsible for the many rumors being initiated against King, we had heard of these rumors and were certainly in a position to substantiate them.

"The monkey was on his back and that of the other Negro leaders," DeLoach reiterated. Wilkins promised to "tell King that he can't win in a battle with the FBI," that "the best thing for him to do is to retire from public life." With that comment, the meeting concluded. Not surprisingly, Wilkins described DeLoach's account of what was said at their meeting as "self-serving and filled with inaccuracies." Hoover passed along that account, nonetheless, to President Johnson.[56]

Wilkins's assessment of what actually transpired in his meeting with DeLoach is no doubt closer to the truth. Indeed, Hoover abruptly (if briefly) cut off Wilkins a few months later. "I don't want anything given to [him] . . . in view of [his] visit to the President demanding my dismissal because of what I had to say re King." Edwin Guthman, who went back to his office and typed up a memo for the files after every one of his meetings with De-Loach, had the opportunity to compare his recollections with the assistant director's several years later. "It was like we were at two different meetings," he said. Even within the Bureau, neither field agents nor his fellow executives completely trusted DeLoach. "Many FBI colleagues observed that [he] seemed to fulfill the role of a son to Hoover," Sanford Ungar wrote. "Others thought it was more like a hatchet man." In either case, Hoover trusted DeLoach absolutely.[57] Born poor in Claxton, Georgia, De-Loach had been with the FBI since 1942, when he dropped out of the Stetson College School of Law in Florida to sign up, and since 1951 he had been under the director's wing at headquarters. In meeting with Wilkins, DeLoach did exactly what Hoover wanted him to do.[58]

Another Big Six civil rights leader who had a close relationship with the FBI, James Farmer, met with DeLoach on December 1, in the back seat of a limousine while driving around Washington. According to DeLoach, the two men discussed "warfare" between Hoover and King. "I told him that if this war continued that we, out of necessity, must defend ourselves. . . . Farmer got the point without any difficulty whatsoever. He immediately assured me that there would be no further criticism from him. He stated he felt certain there would be no further criticism from King." Farmer also disputed DeLoach's recollection. He did not remember DeLoach saying anything about "warfare," and he did not make any commitment to stop sniping at the FBI. Farmer said he knew what DeLoach and Hoover were up to. "They wanted to isolate King."[59]

Later in the day, Martin Luther King himself, accompanied by Ralph Abernathy, Andrew Young, and Walter Fauntroy, met with Hoover and the ever-present DeLoach. The civil rights leaders discovered what everyone who had ever been in the same room with the director already knew—as Robert Kennedy once put it, "You know, he talks a hell of a lot, J. Edgar Hoover." When King did say something, the director maintained, it was generally "laudatory about the Bureau's work." DeLoach described the meeting as "a love feast," and for once the civil rights leaders agreed with him. "You would have thought you were watching a mutual admiration society," Young said, calling it "a completely nonfunctional meeting."[60]

While Hoover and DeLoach met with King and the other civil rights leaders, William Sullivan planned the secret convening of a group of prominent black leaders—Roy Wilkins and two or three other movement leaders (Farmer and Randolph), "top Negro judges" (James B. Parsons and William Henry Hastie), "top reputable ministers" (Robert Johnson of the Washington City Presbytery), and "other selected Negro officials from public life such as the Negro Attorney General from one of the New England states." Division Five intended to enlist these men in the campaign to topple King and to promote "the stature of Roy Wilkins." The group could learn "the facts" about the FBI's many civil rights accomplishments, the truth about King's sexual and political transgressions. While trying to make the necessary arrangements, Division Five blackballed Carl Rowan, director of the U.S. Information Agency, and Ralph Bunche, undersecretary-general of the United Nations, on the grounds that "they might feel a duty to advise the White House of such a contemplated meeting." In this case, the proposal was simply too incredible. The meeting with "reputable Negroes" never happened.[61]

William Sullivan's Division Five and Cartha DeLoach's Crime Records Division remained active on other fronts and they sometimes acted in concert. They wanted to be certain King's rivals in the civil rights movement had the facts, so DeLoach offered the microphone recordings that Sullivan's agents had compiled to various civil rights leaders. C. Sumner Stone, Jr., editor of the *Chicago Defender* and later in the year a special assistant to New York Congressman Adam Clayton Powell, Jr., said a fair number of movement people "claimed to have heard the tapes. Whitney Young heard them. Roy Wilkins heard them." And of course King himself heard them. The Division Five package mailed on November 24 had sat in the SCLC office in Atlanta until January 5, when Coretta King stumbled over it. She listened to a brief portion ("just a lot of mumbo jumbo"), read the accompanying letter, and then called her husband, who had returned from Oslo only the week before. A Nobel laureate to the world, to the FBI, in Sullivan's words, King was "a dissolute, abnormal moral imbecile," "an evil, abnormal beast."[62]

FBI interest in Martin Luther King's private life was not unprecedented. Some of the older movement people had a clear sense of *déjà vu*. What Jesse Jackson called the director's "Peeping Tomism," his "sick interest of the white male in black sexuality," was arguably present in his predecessors as well. (Heavyweight boxing champion Jack Johnson had his troubles with the FBI and "the Mann" in 1912.) In December 1964, only a few days after he met with King, Hoover told *U.S. News and World Report* publisher David Lawrence that the White Slave Traffic Act was "supposed to protect the virtue of womanhood."[63] His interest in interracial sex and the morality of individual black activists was nothing if not consistent.[64] The old General Intelligence Division of 1919 focused on the specter of miscegenation, but so did the Domestic Intelligence Division of 1953. "It is interesting to note that one of [the Communist party's] 'concrete demands' . . . advocated 'the removal of all legal restrictions and social censorship of intermarriage in the Southern States.'"[65] For the director, interracial sex, extramarital sex, premarital sex, homosexuality, bisexuality, and sexual deviancy was all something that could be used to discredit political adversaries. And it was something to which Martin Luther King—and in a broader sense the civil rights movement as a whole during the 1960s—appeared to be particularly vulnerable.[66]

FBI interest in Dr. King as "the 'top alley cat'" accompanied a parallel interest in the sex lives of virtually anyone interested in the subject of racial justice. New York agents tried to find out who the Communist party's top black functionaries were "carrying on" with, while Washington agents worked up a memo on a Civil Rights Division attorney who had gone off on an interracial date. Division Five investigated "the moral character" of Andrew Young and Jesse Jackson and looked into a rumor about Stanley Levison "having a paramour." In the meantime, Hoover discussed the "immoral conditions" within the black family with the ubiquitous David Lawrence, told the House Appropriations Subcommittee that Bayard Rustin (who was in fact homosexual) had once been "convicted for sodomy," and flooded the White House with memos concerning the "personal behavior" of Community Relations Service workers. "He spread garbage about us," Roger Wilkins charged, "and he spread garbage about everybody in the civil rights movement."[67]

Having documented "the depraved nature and moral looseness" of Dr. King and other black activists, FBI officials' attempts to use the information uncovered met with little success. Sumner Stone said "Hoover was a real prude—he misjudged the morality of the average American." When DeLoach offered transcripts based on the King buggings to a variety of newspaper reporters, columnists, and editors, nobody accepted the offer. Jim Bishop of the Hearst chain even claimed to have seen photographs, snapped by the FBI "through a one-way mirror," of King chasing "White women . . . in motel rooms." "The old man," Bishop concluded, "saw the preacher as a buffoon" and "could barely mention the name without bubbling at the lips."[68]

Hoover could not even convince the Catholics to do anything. The Chicago archdiocese published a pamphlet describing King as being "like Jesus," and Marquette University, a Jesuit school, invited him to receive an honorary degree. (Since World War II the FBI recruited heavily at Jesuit schools, and by the 1960s Protestant agents considered themselves a distinct minority, members of a "PU"—a Protestant underground.) In this last case the FBI claimed to have convinced a source at Marquette that King was unworthy, and King did not receive the degree—but the excuse was that he was unable to attend the ceremonies and Marquette had a policy against awarding honorary degrees in absentia. The FBI agent who approached University officials, nonetheless, received a monetary award from his superiors. All this was quite minor compared to King's plans to meet with the Pope. That audience had to be "nipped in the bud," so the director sent New York SAC John Malone off to brief Francis Cardinal Spellman and to have Spellman alert the Vatican. "Hoover always . . . kept a Cardinal in the background," Harold Leinbaugh remembered, and Malone said the King matter had been handled. But it did not do any good. "I am amazed that the Pope gave an audience to such a degenerate," Hoover responded, upon discovering that Malone and Spellman had failed.[69]

Hoover's obsession with the sexual habits of Martin Luther King and other civil rights activists posed an irony. The suspicion that the director himself was homosexual followed him for most of his career. Not even the FBI's own agents were quite sure about Hoover, a result of his "strange relationship" with Clyde Tolson, his second in command, with whom he took all his meals and vacationed over a period of thirty years. "I don't think anybody really knows," Leinbaugh concluded.[70]

Whatever the nature of Hoover's own sexuality, his concern with and condemnation of other people's sexuality was severe, and he was determined to use anything, including sexual inferences, to damage Dr. King and other black activists. "The Negro community," however, was not much troubled by "a conventional standard of morality," in the FBI view, and programs designed to discredit movement people by emphasizing "alleged immoral or un-American political inclinations" simply were not working. If anything, the "moral turpitude" label enhanced "the status of these individuals among their peers." Promiscuity, much like "a criminal record or associations with radical groups," was less "a thing of shame to be hidden from public view" than "a badge of honor," sometimes even "a prerequisite to leadership."[71] "Can you imagine anything sillier than somebody starting a rumor that Martin liked women?," asked Charles Evers, the NAACP leader in Mississippi and brother of the slain Medgar Evers. "Now, if he had a hankering for men, that's something else. That's my argument with J. Edgar Hoover. I mean, who's talking about whom? I'd say this to Hoover: You don't have any women anywhere. We might go and check *you* out."[72]

The FBI kept trying to use sexual rumor and innuendo nonetheless, usually in the form of anonymous telephone calls or letters to the spouse of a key activist. Typically, the FBI phone caller—"a Negro agent," if one could be found, or, more likely, "a Negro . . . male clerk"—would "attempt to leave the impression that he is the current lover of the wife." Letter writers concentrated on similar themes, with a Bureau "soul sister" addressing the following to the husband of a white woman active in ACTION: "Look man, I guess your old lady don't get enough at home. . . . Like all she wants to integrate is the bed room and us Black Sisters ain't gonna take no second best from our men. So lay it on her."[73]

Despite the FBI's all-out attempt to destroy Dr. King, whether as a communist dupe or an adulterer (in order to smear and thereby slow down the black struggle which King helped lead), neither the director nor the men who ran Division Five found themselves completely free from constraints. In standing against the civil rights movement, Hoover's Bureau had to distance itself from other groups that opposed the movement. The FBI could not stand with the Ku Klux Klan, or even such nonviolent resistance groups as the American Flag Committee and its preposterous claim that all civil rights law could be traced to a modest Communist party civil rights initiative known as the Lincoln Project. The FBI investigated the obscure Flag Committee, as well as those southern newspapermen who spread its ideas, on the grounds that they were plotting "to defraud the public." Hoover opposed the black struggle by upbringing, temperament, politics, and bureaucratic instinct, but he would not allow extremists to control or even influence the nature and form of his resistance.[74]

Perhaps the best example of the FBI's refusal to join the lunatic fringe involved the charge raised by Mississippi Governor Ross Barnett in July 1963 at Senate hearings on the civil rights bill. Barnett displayed a poster-sized reproduction of a photograph, snapped by an agent of the Georgia Commission on Education, showing Martin Luther King attending a "communist training school." The photo depicted "the 'four horsemen' of racial agitation"—King, former *Daily Worker* writer Abner Berry, Aubrey Williams of the Southern Conference Educational Fund, and their host, Myles Horton—at the twenty-fifth anniversary celebration of the Highlander Folk School just outside of Monteagle, Tennessee. Highlander had provided training for labor organizers and civil rights activists since the Work War II years, and right wingers in the South and elsewhere took the "communist training school" claim seriously; but the FBI did not. The

Georgia Commission distributed over 100,000 copies of the Highlander photo, and it graced hundreds of billboards along the highways in the Deep South. After Governor Barnett displayed his copy, Clyde Tolson recommended a file check and Robert Kennedy requested "a brief squib on" the three men in the photo with King.[75]

FBI officials knew all about Horton's Highlander Folk School and King's appearance there six years earlier. They had gathered and occasionally leaked information on the school since the early 1950s, sending Senator James Eastland and other more respectable segregationists blind memos on Horton. In the 1960s, moreover, someone from Cartha DeLoach's office briefed Congressman Roman C. Pucinski (D., Ill.) on "the background" of the Highlander Folk School. When King explained his appearance there on *Meet the Press*, the Atlanta and Knoxville FBI offices ran name checks on all officers, teachers, and students.[76] After Governor Barnett waved his copy of the Highlander photo and Senators Mike Monroney (D., Ok.) and Warren G. Magnuson (D., Wash.) wrote Hoover to ask about the authenticity of the photo, however, the director simply forwarded the letters to Attorney General Kennedy—along with a memo summarizing the extent of communist influence in the Southern Christian Leadership Conference. John Kennedy responded to Barnett by dismissing the Red menace at a news conference. Robert Kennedy responded to the Monroney and Magnuson letters with a similar disclaimer. "Based on all available evidence from the FBI and other sources, we have no evidence that any of the top leaders of the major civil rights groups are Communists, or Communist controlled."[77]

Rather than risk the uncertainties of involvement in the public debate over the Highlander photo, Hoover pursued his opposition to the civil rights movement on safer ground. He sought the safety of a formal alliance not with Governor Barnett and other extreme segregationists, but with the Kennedys, pressing Robert Kennedy to approve an FBI wiretap on King's home phone and SCLC office phones in New York and Atlanta. The attorney general was considering that request at the time he responded to the Monroney and Magnuson letters. That fall, as noted earlier, he approved another FBI request for electronic surveillance on King and SCLC.

FBI agents installed the wiretaps while President Kennedy considered a response to yet another query from a member of

Congress, Richard Russell, chairman of the Senate Armed Services Committee, whose interest in King's association with Jack O'Dell presented particular problems. An ardent segregationist who had worked tirelessly on behalf of Jim Crow America since the 1940s, Russell was also one of the most powerful men in the Senate.[78] After Burke Marshall wrote the first draft of the reply, he sent it to the Bureau. He wanted to know, as FBI executive Alan Belmont said, "whether it would jeopardize our informant or otherwise interfere with our investigation." The Bureau had a number of objections, most of which concerned a reference to sensitive sources. But when Marshall eliminated this reference, Tolson complained once more: "[It] still 'clears' King." Marshall and Kennedy ended up writing three drafts, each of which they read to John Kennedy over the phone, before the president decided that Marshall and Courtney Evans should deliver "an innocuous letter" to Russell personally. On November 1, Evans and Nicholas Katzenbach (substituting for Marshall) took the Bureau's file on O'Dell to Russell's office.[79]

This would not be the last time Senator Russell's interest in Martin Luther King led to a conference with an FBI agent, dossier in hand. Nearly two years later to the day, Cartha DeLoach, who served the Johnson White House as Courtney Evans had served the Kennedy White House, met with Russell and brought along files on King and someone else. Russell, nevertheless, proved to be less of a problem than Hoover. During the floor fight against the administration's civil rights bill, he did not use the information about King that he had received from the FBI. Evans said Russell "did not believe Martin Luther King himself was a communist," only "that obviously the Negro Movement was ready for exploitation by the Communist Party." Katzenbach remembered the senator as being "a pretty good fellow on [not] hitting below the belt."[80]

Less restrained than Russell, Hoover sent a "highly explosive" document on Dr. King, entitled "Communism and the Negro Movement," to the White House, the attorney general, the secretaries of state and defense, the CIA director, and the military intelligence agencies. Alan Belmont had pointed out that the eleven-page document would likely "be regarded as a personal attack on Martin Luther King" and "may startle the Attorney General," who "may resent" the decision to circulate such information outside the Justice Department. Beyond that, if one of the recipients were to leak all or part of the Bureau's analysis, it would "add fuel to a matter which may already be in the cards as a political issue during the forthcoming Presidential campaign." Hoover made his decision ("we must do our duty") despite the guarded advice of his number-two man.[81]

Alan Belmont's predictions were astute. When Robert Kennedy found out that the Army had received a copy of "Communism and the Negro Movement," he called Courtney Evans to ask "what responsibilities" the Army had "in relation to the communist background of Martin Luther King"? "He was obviously irritated," Evans said. Since the FBI's "explanation seemed to serve no purpose" and he believed the "information would leak out as the military didn't like the Negroes," Kennedy ordered the report recalled. In off-the-record testimony before John Rooney's House Appropriations Subcommittee on January 29, 1964, Hoover said "both of us had feared a leak might get out from the Departments which had copies of the monograph; and if it happened during a sensitive time of negotiations going on with the Negro leaders, it would have caused a ruckus." Actually, only Kennedy had such a fear. The director was merely trying to cover himself before the Democratic members of the Rooney Subcommittee. He had approved the distribution of the report, after all, in the face of Belmont's pointed warning.[82]

Blaming "someone on Rooney's Committee" for betraying the confidence of his off-the-record remarks, Hoover reverted, for a time, to a more cautious policy. This new tack was in evidence when Edwin Willis (D., La.), chairman of the House Committee on Un-American Activities, tried to arrange a meeting between Cartha DeLoach and Howard Smith (D., Va.), chairman of the House Rules Committee and progenitor of the rider to the Alien Registration Act of 1940 that bears his name. At this particular time, Smith was sitting on the administration's civil rights bill. When DeLoach met Smith on March 13, the congressman "asked if he could receive information concerning King," stating "that he would be glad to make a speech on the Floor of the House at any time" and pointing "out that this would offer immunity to him and to newspapers who might desire to quote his remarks." Afterward, DeLoach submitted his recommendation. "Judge Smith is an honorable reputable Congressman. His word carries great weight on the Hill. It may be that after a period of time the Director might desire to have me furnish Judge Smith with information concerning King [deleted] so that he can make a speech. . . . Undoubtedly newspapers all over the Nation would pick this story up." Given his recent conflict with Robert Kennedy over the Rooney Subcommittee briefing, Hoover put the project on hold. "I do *not* want anything on King given to Smith nor anyone else at this time."[83]

Hoover's reluctance to help Howard Smith represented only a pause in the campaign to discredit Martin Luther King and the civil rights movement. The director sent eleven letters about King to Walter Jenkins at the White House between early February and late April. And he had DeLoach orchestrate a HUAC hearing a month after he met with Smith for the purpose of having a friendly witness "publicly expose . . . [name deleted] communist background and thus have a neutralizing effect on his activities and influence in the legitimate Negro freedom movement."[84] When the House Appropriations Subcommittee released the on-the-record portion of the director's testimony that same month, it became clear that the FBI was the principal source of allegations about Reds in the civil rights movement. "Communist influence does exist in the Negro movement," Hoover said, "and it is this influence which is vitally important. It can be the means through which large masses . . . lose perspective" and "succumb to the party's propaganda lures." Communists, he added, had "magnified and dramatized" every "racial incident" to date "in an effort to generate racial tensions"—part of a sinister campaign to "control . . . the Negro population" and embarrass the United States "in the eyes of the rest of the world, particularly among the African and Asian peoples."[85]

With his warnings about subversives on the loose in Georgia or Mississippi, Hoover performed a valuable service for the white southern resistance. The press widely reported his testimony, with the *New York Times* running the story under the caption "Hoover Says Reds Exploit Negroes," and movement activists regarded his remarks as an attempt to influence debate over the 1964 civil rights bill. John Lewis said FBI agents should spend less time worrying about phantom Reds and more time tracking down "the bombers, midnight assassins, and brutal racists who daily make a mockery of the United States Constitution." Dr. King was equally direct. He wanted to hit the director "hard—he made me hot and I wanted to get him"—and his statement read, in part: "Mr. J. Edgar Hoover . . . has allowed himself to aid and abet the salacious claims of southern racists. . . . It would be encouraging to us if Mr. Hoover and the FBI would be as diligent in apprehending those responsible for bombing churches and killing little children as they are in seeking out alleged communist infiltration in the civil rights movement."[86]

The civil rights movement's strategy had always been to force the FBI to choose sides, to turn toward civil rights law and away from the segregationists and the Red menace. "We were not so stupid as not to understand that other Americans who were opposed to what we were doing were also pressuring them," Bayard Rustin said.[87] The FBI's strategy had usually been to avoid a clear-cut choice, a rather predictable strategy regardless of Hoover's own conservatism and fundamental assumptions about the Negro Question. Since the twilight of Reconstruction nearly every American politician with dreams of forging a national constituency had tried to dodge the race issue. The March on Washington, nonetheless, demonstrated that the movement was finally strong enough to force the FBI, and the rest of the federal government as well, to choose sides.

"It was all taking sides," recalled Harold Leinbaugh, the former agent whose Crime Records Division served as the "carrier" of FBI information to Senator Eastland and other segregationists on the Hill. "If Hoover could be disembalmed, he'd probably say, 'I'm taking the side of America.'"[88] Obviously, Martin Luther King did not see it that way at the time. And when he said the director had chosen to move his bureaucracy alongside the cause of the southern racists, he was right.

CHAPTER

5

===========××××===========

Mississippi Burning
Freedom Summer 1964

While the Johnson administration's civil rights bill moved through Congress and into the federal statute books during the summer of 1964, the FBI was wrestling with the civil rights movement in Mississippi. The battleground was not the choice of J. Edgar Hoover and his Bureau or Martin Luther King and the Southern Christian Leadership Conference, but of Robert Moses and the Student Nonviolent Coordinating Committee. Earlier, when returning to Mississippi after the March on Washington, SNCC activists mobilized the Council of Federated Organizations (COFO), a nearly dormant umbrella organization of racial-advancement groups estabished in 1961 to assist the jailed Freedom Riders in Jackson, and organized a Freedom Vote Campaign. Assisted by CORE's David Dennis, Moses served as program director. Aaron Henry, the respected Clarksville druggist and head of the state NAACP, was named president. Volunteers from all the major civil rights groups participated, but COFO was primarily a SNCC operation, and Moses as one civil rights worker noted, was "more or less the Jesus of the whole project."

Hoover's FBI watched events in Mississippi closely as the Freedom Vote Campaign in the fall of 1963 led to Freedom Summer in 1964. In November nearly 80,000 disenfranchised Mississippi blacks participated in a mock election, casting ballots for Aaron Henry for governor and Rev. Edwin King, the white chaplain of Tougaloo College, for lieutenant governor. A week later in Greenville, forty-five COFO representatives (forty from SNCC and five from CORE) organized a massive voter registration drive for the summer months and invited white college students from the North to participate. Such an effort, Moses and Dennis reasoned, would incite unprecedented segregationist violence and thus force the federal government to protect the lives of civil rights workers and the voting rights of Mississippi's 916,000 blacks.

Allard Lowenstein, a thirty-four-year-old activist in the National Student Association who taught at the University of North Carolina, had recruited nearly a hundred college students, mostly from Yale and Stanford, to help with the earlier Freedom Vote Campaign; and the FBI director had seemed to demonstrate a token interest in their safety. When a handful of Yale students had visited the SNCC office in Hattiesburg, Lawrence Guyot recalled, "it was really a problem to count the number of FBI agents who were there to protect the students. It was just that gross." It seemed the Bureau might guard northern college students in Mississippi once again during Freedom Summer. "While these people are here national attention is here," Stokely Carmichael promised. "The FBI isn't going to let anything happen to them." If Carmichael believed the first part of that prediction, it is doubtful that he or any other civil rights worker in Mississippi believed the second. "It simply made good copy," Robert Moses admitted. Hoover may have understood power, but everyone understood the director's lack of sympathy for student activists ("young punks") of any color.[1]

No one expected white Mississippi to respond to Freedom Summer peacefully, and no one expected Hoover's FBI to do much about it unless forced to. "The question," as Moses remembered, "was this: Were we gonna be able to force the rest of the country to take a look at Mississippi. The white students brought the rest of the country down with them for a look and we knew Mississippi couldn't stand a hard look." "We all understood that whites could be used as a force," Marion Barry, SNCC's first chairman, said. "Whenever you had blacks who were killed who cared about that? They die everyday. Blacks were jailed by the hundreds, who cared? When you've got a Congressman's son or you've got some white professor's son or you've got some white students who are jailed or killed, then the whole focus comes. You know, 'Boom.' " A few COFO people even considered how the death of a student volunteer might benefit the movement.[2]

Hoover actually expected more trouble during the summer of 1964 from Dr. King's Alabama Project. Robert Moses and his co-workers knew better, and they prepared for a violent confrontation with the white resistance. On June 15 the first three hundred Summer Project volunteers gathered in Oxford, Ohio, for a week-long training session. They listened to the administration's representative, John Doar, lecture on civil rights law, and they heard him say the government would do "nothing" to provide protection. "There is no federal police force." They listened to Moses's prediction of guerilla war "not much different from that in Vietnam," and they heard him outline COFO's modest goals: to go, to register black voters, to "come back alive." One of the students, Stephen M. Bingham, remembered being "told that people *would* not return, not that they *might* not return." Moses also told the volunteers about the attempt to arrange a meeting with Lyndon Johnson. "His secretary said that Vietnam was popping up all over his calendar and he hadn't time to talk to us." White House special counsel Lee White found it "nearly incredible that these people who are voluntarily sticking their head [sic] into the lion's mouth would ask for somebody to come down and shoot the lion." In one way, the administration view paralleled the FBI view. The COFO activists were a nuisance, with their unreasonable demands for protection and a federal war on the Klan.[3]

While Hoover and Johnson hesitated, white Mississippi made time for the summer volunteers. Expecting an "invasion" of "mixers" and "outside agitators," the city of Jackson doubled the size of its police force, modified its garbage-truck fleet to double as paddy wagons, and bought what Guyot called "a damn armored truck—satirically referred to as [Mayor] Thompson's tank." The two hundred troopers added to the Highway Patrol helped intercept the SNCC activists who had begun to trickle into Mississippi by late spring, seizing their property and sometimes leaking such things as address books and copies of Communist party historian Herbert Aptheker's study of slave revolts to the press and the FBI. Sam Bowers, Jr., founder and imperial wizard of the White Knights of the Ku Klux Klan, developed the most explicit strategy for dealing with "COFO's nigger-communist invasion." "Catch them outside the law," he advised his fellows, according to an FBI informant report, "then under Mississippi law you have a right to kill them."[4]

According to the FBI's uniform crime reports, however, Mississippi was a picture of tranquillity. The state had the lowest crime rate in the nation. But for blacks it was, as Moses said, "the middle of the iceberg." The state had a seige mentality. Automobile bumper stickers advised motorists to "Drive Carefully: You Are Now In Occupied Mississippi," while the Citizens Council listed the FBI as subversive—along with the Elks, the Red Cross, the YMCA, and even the United States Air Force. In a few counties it was actually a status symbol among segregationists to have been under investigation by the FBI.[5] John Doar said Mississippi "didn't have to intimidate via violence," at least "until December of 1963," when COFO began to organize Freedom Summer, "because the legal structure was impervious. That was the Maginot line." When it "began to crack . . . Mississippi turned to violence." And that was the precise time, "as the curve started up," that "Bob Moses and his guys decided the way to confront that curve was to bring a lot of white kids down and get some white kids hurt and the country would be up in arms."[6]

COFO activists from SNCC and CORE called the voter registration drive Freedom Summer, but it was really the summer of the Ku Klux Klan. By the FBI's conservative count, "SNCC and its supporters endured at least 1,000 arrests, 35 shooting incidents, eight beatings, and six murders."[7] With the Bureau continuing to speak the language of federalism, and responsible officials in the Justice Department and the White House continuing to do the same whenever the protection issue forced itself upon them, the Klan rode strong in Mississippi during the summer of 1964. The people on the front line registering black voters wanted to know which side the federal government was on. By the time Freedom Summer ended, the movement had an answer to their question, and a few thought they saw blood on the FBI's hands. The director investigated the Klan and the horrors committed by its members during that summer, but his performance reflected his belief that those who challenged white rule had committed a crime worse than murder.

While the movement and the resistance prepared for Freedom Summer, Robert Kennedy and Burke Marshall pressed the FBI to expand its coverage of Ku Klux Klan violence. They tried to convince the Bureau "to come down and shoot the lion." On one night, April 21, Klansmen burned sixty-one crosses in southwest

Mississippi. Between April 1 and July 1, they firebombed three black homes and a barbershop in Pike County. In Adams County, they chased and shot at two civil rights workers, and killed two local blacks. In Madison County, they bombed the Freedom House and a church. In the rest of Mississippi, they damaged or destroyed at least seven churches and bombed or shot up eight homes. The FBI submitted memos to the Civil Rights Division on every incident, but did not appear to be interested, as Marshall complained, in taking the necessary steps to combat "terrorism in Mississippi."[8]

Kennedy and Marshall hoped to pressure the FBI into launching a counterterrorism program. First, the attorney general dispatched ex-FBI and National Security Agency man Walter Sheridan, along with six or seven members of his "Terrible Twenty" (the "get Hoffa squad"), a crack team of Criminal Division investigators, "to get something on the Klan." "We were sent," Sheridan recalled, "because the Bureau wasn't doing anything. There were twenty FBI guys in the state . . . but they weren't doing anything unless they had to. Talk to John Doar. He would do whatever was done. The Bureau would say it didn't have jurisdiction." Marshall and Kennedy understood Hoover's territorial instincts. When Sheridan's squad arrived in Jackson, the director began sending memos to Marshall about "a man in Mississippi named Walter Sheridan who claims to be doing investigative work for the Department of Justice. This is to inform you that he is not a member of the FBI." The director also dispatched an agent to read the riot act to Doar: "Either the Bureau is going to be *the* investigative agency of the Department or it's not. Either it's going to do all of it or none of it." The irony is that Hoover wanted no other federal investigators in Mississippi, but neither did he want to do the civil rights work that the Department demanded. Caught between his bureaucratic interests and his personal and political preferences, for the time being, as Marshall remembered, the director "sealed off the Bureau from the Civil Rights Division," throwing up a wall of institutional resistance.[9]

Anticipating Hoover's reaction, Kennedy and Marshall next launched a Pennsylvania Avenue end run. Marshall drafted a memo to President Johnson in which he tried "to avoid . . . any appearance of criticism. . . . The problem is not one that can be cured by reprimands to particular agents on particular incidents, even if the Bureau could be persuaded that the agents did not perform their investigative function well." Hoover had to be stroked, not criticized. Above all, the director should not be told how to do things in Mississippi once the commitment had been made, Marshall wrote. "The problem is rather to describe what is happening in such a way as to permit the Bureau to develop its own new procedures for the collection of intelligence." When investigating "fundamentally lawless activities" in Mississippi "which have the sanction of local law enforcement agencies, political officials, and a substantial segment of the white population," Kennedy and Marshall offered, as a model, "the information gathering techniques used by the Bureau on Communist or Communist related organizations." Describing these techniques as "spectacularly efficient," the attorney general recommended that President Johnson "take up with the Bureau the possibility of developing a similar effort to meet this new problem."[10]

Robert Kennedy was in an awkward position. Despised by Johnson and Hoover, and embroiled in feuds with both men, he was, in effect, immobilized during the summer of the Klan. President Johnson had long hated the Ku Klux Klan. When he was thirteen, Klansmen had threatened to kill his father, and young Lyndon had spent a night in the cellar of the family home with the women and children while his father and uncles stood watch on the porch with shotguns.[11] But in 1964 LBJ seemed more worried about RFK than the KKK. He saw in Kennedy a rival who could challenge his claim to legitimacy and to party and national leadership; the president used the FBI to investigate "Bobby Kennedy's boy[s]"—that is, members of the administration who "had more loyalty to the Attorney General than . . . the President"—while getting "ready to take Bobby on." Hoover probably hated Kennedy even more that he hated Martin Luther King. His objections ranged from the trivial—the attorney general let Brumus the dog run up and down the halls of the Justice Department building and let his children run back and forth in the director's office—to the substantive. Kennedy turned up at field offices to ask hard questions. He did not want a public relations visit; he wanted to know how the Bureau did things. And he made Hoover do civil rights work. "Why would he like it?," Kennedy asked. "He hadn't made any changes himself in twenty years."[12]

Hoover refused to launch the kind of operation against the Mississippi Klan that Marshall and Kennedy wanted, and Johnson saw no reason to pressure him to reconsider his decision.

The attorney general believed the FBI lacked "civilian control," that its director was "rather a psycho," a "senile" and "frightening" head of "a very dangerous organization," who realized "after November 22, 1963, [that] he no longer had to hide his feelings. . . . He no longer had to pay attention to me; and it was in the interest, evidently of . . . President Johnson to have that kind of arrangement and relationship." When a Justice Department attorney summarized the view from Kennedy's office, Cartha DeLoach passed the information on to Hoover: "A number of individuals close to the Attorney General felt that the President's body had not even become cold before you started circumventing the Attorney General and dealing directly with [President Johnson]."[13] LBJ began to pressure the director to act in Mississippi only on June 21, when COFO reported three civil rights workers missing in Neshoba County.

The FBI held files on two of the three, and Michael Schwerner was of particular interest. A native New Yorker, Schwerner had joined New York's downtown CORE the previous summer and went to Mississippi with his wife, Rita, to run the COFO community center in Meridian—a particularly dangerous assignment. In early June 1964 they received a letter from Richard Haley, assistant to CORE's national director, indicating a concern for their safety. "Obviously the tension is gradually rising as your activities probe more deeply into direct action. I am pushing very hard for the national office to set up a high level Justice Department conference to discuss specific protective measures."[14] A few days later, the Schwerners and James Chaney, a twenty-one-year-old black high-school drop out and CORE field worker who had also attracted the FBI's attention, drove up to Oxford to help prepare the summer volunteers. They came back almost immediately, accompanied by one of the volunteers, Andrew Goodman, a student at Queens College in New York, to investigate the beating of three blacks following a meeting at the Mt. Zion Church in Longdale and the burning of the church.

On Sunday morning, June 21, unknown to the FBI or anyone else outside the Mississippi civil rights network, the three young men drove a CORE station wagon from Meridian to Longview. On the return trip Neshoba County Deputy Sheriff Cecil Price arrested them for speeding, jailed them in Philadelphia, and finally released them a little after 10:00 P.M. and told them to leave town. A few miles outside of Philadelphia, the deputy stopped their car again—this time after a wild chase—and turned them over to a group of Neshoba County Klansmen. One of the Ku Kluxers, with one hand on Schwerner's shoulder and a gun in the other, asked, "Are you a nigger lover?" Schwerner, "the Jew-boy with the beard" and the bright blue New York Mets baseball cap, was the Klan's principal target during the evening's "missionary work." When he started to say, "Sir, I know how you feel," the night riders shot him dead. The Klan then murdered Goodman and Chaney, set fire to the CORE station wagon in a sweetgum thicket deep in the Bogue Chitto Swamp, and carted the three bodies off for burial at a dam construction project.[15]

The FBI learned almost immediately that Schwerner, Chaney, and Goodman had failed to return to Meridian on time Sunday evening. Hoping to convince someone to investigate, SNCC workers called everybody on their "hot list"—starting with the authorities in every town along the Longview to Meridian route. Using the name of "Margaret Fuller," a "reporter" for the *Atlanta Constitution*, Mary King spoke to Deputy Sheriff Price himself, who denied knowing the whereabouts of the three young men. At 10:00 P.M., only minutes before Price released his prisoners from the Philadelphia jail, Sherwin Kaplan, a law student, spoke to Hunter E. Helgeson, one of the FBI's resident agents in Jackson. Helgeson asked to be kept informed. Thirty minutes later the COFO office in Meridian contacted Frank Schwelb, a Justice Department lawyer who was staying in town. More phone calls followed at 11:00 P.M.. At midnight, Schwelb "stated that the FBI was not a police force." When Robert Weil of the Jackson COFO office phoned Helgeson once more, the FBI agent "took in the information curtly and did not allow a chance for further conversation." Aaron Henry had a similar experience when he called the FBI.[16]

SNCC kept pressure on the FBI and other government agencies throughout the early morning hours and into the next day. At 1:00 A.M. the Atlanta office telephoned John Doar, and following more phone calls at 3:00 A.M. and 6:00 A.M. Doar said the FBI would "look into the matter." At 7:30 A.M. and again at 8:30 A.M. SNCC contacted Helgeson, who said he could do nothing until he heard from the FBI field office in New Orleans. Another phone call to Doar followed at 9:15 A.M. At 11:00 A.M. Helgeson said the Bureau would now "take the necessary action." Because Schwerner, Chaney, and Goodman may have been beaten after their arrest and before their release from the Philadelphia jail, the civil rights statute may have been violated. This "threw new light on the FBI's role in the case." At noon, however, Helgeson said the New Orleans office still had not ordered an investigation. Fifteen minutes later, an agent from the field office told a SNCC volunteer that no instructions had been received from the seat of government. At 1:40 P.M., and again an hour later, SNCC tried to get through to Doar. At 5:20 P.M., Doar called back with news that the FBI resident agent in Meridian, John Proctor, was coordinating a search. Proctor had in fact interviewed Cecil Price—an interview that concluded with the deputy slapping Proctor on the back and saying, "Hell, John, let's have a drink." The two men then imbibed from a cache of contraband liquor in the trunk of Price's cruiser.

Meanwhile, the movement continued to press the FBI and the Justice Department to intervene. The first clear sign of progress, other than Proctor's casual inquiries, occurred around 6:30 P.M., when Robert Kennedy instructed the FBI to treat the disappearance as a kidnapping. But when Bill Light of the SNCC office in Jackson asked the Bureau to confirm the investigation, the agent he spoke to told him to direct "all inquiries . . . to the Justice Department." At 8:45 P.M. SNCC placed a collect call to Doar at his home. He refused to accept charges. Later in the evening the movement finally learned, from the newspaper reporters who had converged on Philadelphia, that the FBI was indeed organizing a search. New Orleans SAC Harry Maynor sent five agents and an inspector to Meridian on June 23. "We're going to see if we can find those guys," Maynor told Proctor. Agents from other field offices, including the Bureau's major case inspector, Joseph A. Sullivan, soon joined the New Orleans squad. On the night of June 24, FBI Assitant Director Alex Rosen arrived on the scene, having flown down from Washington aboard one of President Johnson's jets.[17]

By then, the movement had assumed the worst. "The kids are dead," Robert Moses told the summer volunteers back at their training site in Ohio. "No privileged group in history has ever given up anything without some kind of blood sacrifice." COFO wanted the FBI to mobilize and find Schwerner, Chaney, and Goodman, but there was more to their concern that that: they intended to force the protection issue. Moses urged the parents of the summer volunteers "to use their influence" to pressure President Johnson and Attorney General Kennedy into a commitment to protect workers *before* violence occurs." The chronology of the SNCC/COFO attempt to force an FBI investigation,

Moses added, "shows that it took 24 hours—undoubtedly the critical 24 hours—to get the Federal Government to act." Bureau officials found the chronology especially troubling. They suspected movement people had tape recorded phone conversations with field agents, and they took the time to see if any wiretapping statutes had been violated.[18]

Eventually, COFO had more success in forcing Lyndon Johnson to act than J. Edgar Hoover. Pressure on LBJ built slowly, and in a distinctly political mode. "Congressman Bill Ryan [D., N.Y.] called me," Lee White recalled, "so I go to the president and say, 'Mr. President, Bill Ryan's calling on behalf of the parents . . . they really want to see you.' " "*What for?*," Johnson asked. "Well, they just want the world to know and they want to be reassured that you're doing everything you can to find those kids." "This is June," Johnson told White. "Every goddamn time somebody's going to be missing, I got to meet with all those parents." "He sort of said, 'No,' " White continued. "I said, 'Well, it's not a case of whether we're gonna invite them. I have to go back and tell Ryan no. . . . The *Herald-Tribune* is going to have an article saying the president refuses to see the parents of the missing civil rights workers.' Now he's really getting mad. . . . In any event, the president saw 'em"—Schwerner's and Goodman's parents, anyway—and "while they were all there, Hoover called and said we found the station wagon." Actually, several Choctaw Indians had come across the car by chance.[19]

To Michael Schwerner's wife, a slight, pale woman with black hair, it looked like nobody cared. A secret service agent took her late-night telephone call to the White House, declining to wake the sleeping president. "Mrs. Schwerner sounded quite upset," the agent concluded. "She wished to know how many agents of the FBI were working on the case and where they were working" and "could possibly cause embarrassment."[20] Two days later, on June 25, Rita Schwerner tried to see Mississippi Governor Paul Johnson in Jackson. Accompanied by Edwin King and Bob Zellner, SNCC's first white field secretary, she was kept out of the governor's waiting room by "a fat man" who "zoomed ahead . . . and slammed the door." After a few knocks, the group spoke briefly to one of the governor's assistants and a receptionist—who "started telling Rita what a beautiful state Mississippi was." They caught a glimpse of Governor Johnson later that day at his mansion, escorting Alabama Governor George Wallace and Jackson Mayor Allen Thompson up the steps. When Gover-

nor Johnson saw who they were he "started walking," leaving
Michael Schwerner's wife facing another closed door. From Governor Johnson to President Johnson, and from Mayor Thompson
to FBI Director Hoover, everyone hoped Rita would simply go
away.[21]

Mrs. Schwerner and her companions had better luck seeing
President Johnson's special emissary, former CIA Director Allen
Dulles, over at the Federal Building. Dulles granted the group
an audience of two minutes. The government was doing all that
it could, he said. When Rita said the government was not doing
much of anything, an FBI agent sitting in the room told her the
remark "was a poor joke in poor taste." The two minutes were
up. When Dulles offered his hand, she refused to shake it. She
"didn't want sympathy," she "wanted her husband back." She
headed out the door and toward Philadelphia to confront Neshoba County Sheriff Lawrence Rainey. Dulles moved on to his
next appointment, receiving Henry, Moses, Dennis, and Guyot.
When he told them "we want this mess cleaned up," Henry
asked what he meant. "Well," Dulles said, according to Henry's
recollection, "these civil rights demonstrations are causing this
kind of friction, and we're just not gonna have it, even if we have
to bring troops in here." The COFO delegation was incredulous.
"You talkin' to the wrong people," Henry told the president's
emissary.[22]

On the evening of June 25, the same day that Rita Schwerner
saw Paul Johnson and Allen Dulles, television newsman Walter
Cronkite described the search for the three civil rights workers
as "the focus of the whole country's concern."[23] Lyndon Johnson
finally met with Mrs. Schwerner on June 29, and with Chaney's
mother in early July, and he had more on his mind than public
relations. Burke Marshall described the apparently "silly idea"
of sending an aging ex-CIA chief to Mississippi as a "pretty effective" strategy in the long run. "There's three sovereignties involved," Marshall explained. "There's the United States and
there's the State of Mississippi and there's J. Edgar Hoover."
The president "dealt with them separately, and he used Allen
Dulles to do that, and it worked." When Dulles returned to
Washington he advised Johnson to send more FBI agents to Mississippi, and further noted that the agents already there were
too close to segregationist politicians. Having been "maneuvered" (Marshall's word) by Johnson, Hoover decided to open "a
new big office in Jackson"—a bit of presidential persuasion that

an amazed Ramsey Clark described as "one of the great positive feats of contemporary American history."

It was also an Oval Office end run around Robert Kennedy. Nobody bothered to tell the attorney general. When Kennedy asked about the new Jackson office after reading about it in the newspapers, Hoover told him to "direct his inquiries to President Johnson." That comment best reflected the director's reasons for succumbing to White House pressure. He would act in Mississippi in exchange for more independence from the Justice Department.[24]

Roy K. Moore, the new special agent in charge, arrived in Jackson on July 5, giving him only five days to have an office ready for opening. Hoover was due to arrive on July 10. The FBI had not had a field office in Jackson since the Second World War. Bureau agents in northern Mississippi operated out of six resident agencies and reported to the Memphis field office. The seven resident agencies in the southern portion of the state reported to New Orleans and Jackson was the largest of the resident agencies, with six agents quartered in a few rooms in the Federal Building. So Moore looked up an old friend from Charlotte, who was then president of a Jackson bank, and talked him into leasing the top three floors of the bank's new office building. More contractor and carpenter than G-man for the next four days, Moore beat his deadline with "a dummy office—a sort of false-front Potemkin village—just opposite the elevators on the top floor."[25]

FBI Assistant Director Cartha DeLoach arrived on July 9 to handle arrangements for Hoover's security. In most ways, as syndicated newspaper columnist Nicholas Von Hoffman commented, the director was the rarest of human beings in Mississippi—"a popular Federal official." Even the July edition of the White Knight's *Klan Ledger* had something good to say about him. Dismissing the Schwerner-Chaney-Goodman "disappearance" as "a communist hoax," the Klan recommended that any person who did not understand the ways of America's subversives "do a little reading in J. Edgar Hoover's primer on communism, MASTERS OF DECEIT." The director had powerful friends in Mississippi, too. He included the names of both United States senators, James Eastland and John Stennis, on his Special Correspondents List. But neither DeLoach nor Hoover took any chances. Among other services, DeLoach screened all phone calls to the Sun 'n' Sand Motel where the director had reservations, including at least one anonymous, threatening call.[26]

When Hoover and his associate director and constant companion Clyde Tolson arrived on the morning of July 10, they were greeted at the airport by Mayor Thompson, State Commissioner of Public Safety T. B. Birdsong, Jackson Police Chief W. D. Rayfield, "and other city and state dignitaries"—the very people the civil rights workers said they needed protection from. After meeting briefly with Moore, Rosen, and Sullivan, and accepting their recommendation that he not visit Philadelphia, Hoover went to the governor's mansion for his first appointment. He promised to help professionalize the Highway Patrol by reserving space in the FBI National Academy for additional Mississippi applicants and by lobbying in Washington for money to upgrade the state police academy. He also gave Governor Johnson and Commissioner Birdsong the names of those highway patrolmen who had joined the Klan. The meeting lasted about an hour. Hoover's group moved on to their second appointment at the capitol building with Mississippi Attorney General Joe T. Patterson, who introduced his entire staff, most of his family, and "a large number of state employees." Hoover found everyone "friendly" and "warm."[27]

The ceremonies opening the new FBI field office began at 1:00 P.M. At the press conference that followed, Hoover made it clear that he had not sent 153 agents into Mississippi to protect civil rights activists. Earlier, he offered COFO workers the opportunity to leave their fingerprints at the nearest FBI field office and that was about as far as he would go. The director went on to describe Governor Johnson, who had called NAACP activists "Niggers, Alligators, Apes, Coons and Possums" during a recent campaign, as "a man I have long admired from a distance." Neil Welch, the assistant special agent in charge of the Jackson office, said Hoover "had declared war, but, unlike the Justice Department, he had carefully avoided making Mississippi the enemy." "The FBI comes in here everyday and we have coffee everyday," the sheriff of nearby Clarksville told reporters after the press conference. "We're good friends." Though SNCC workers had named this particular law man in dozens of affidavits charging brutality, his faith in the FBI was well put. "A few Civil Rights Division attorneys," Welch claimed, "actually manufactured" a good many of the police brutality complaints in Mississippi.[28]

Hoover's last appointment was with Charles Evers of the Mississippi NAACP. "Evers was difficult to reach," Joseph Sullivan remembered. "He appeared to feel he had no need for liaison with the FBI." But Evers talked to Hoover. When he mentioned the burden of constantly living under the threat of violent death, the director "suggested he carry on in the tradition of his late brother. . . . I told him that while I could understand his feelings, he must expect some degree of personal danger—particularly in view of his position of leadership during an era of turbulent social upheaval. I mentioned the numerous threats to my life over the years, mostly from the lunatic fringe." Before moving on, Hoover lectured Evers on the criticism leveled by "a number of [his] followers" in the wake of the FBI's investigation of Medgar's assassination. Evers himself remembered Hoover as "a racist. . . . He didn't have time, he didn't want to sit down. . . . I kept pressuring him about why there were no Negroes in the FBI," but all he wanted to do was look "for a bugger bear behind every stump."[29]

Having spent twenty-four hours and five minutes in Mississippi, Hoover returned to Washington the next morning, where he found a grateful Lyndon Johnson. "I find it a great solace to lean on an old friend, such as you in handling such delicate assignments," the president wrote. "You left behind you in Mississippi a feeling of good will." With Martin Luther King scheduled to speak in Greenwood ten days later, Johnson asked Hoover for one more favor. He wanted the FBI to protect King, to station agents "in front and back of him when he goes in; that at least there ought to be an FBI man in front and behind to observe and see what happens." The director agreed to do so.[30]

Hoover's largess set no precedent. His FBI provided protection for one civil rights leader during one speech—and only after a phone call from the president. Johnson placed that phone call six minutes after Robert Kennedy told Hoover to protect King. The director said no. "I told the Attorney General that once we start protecting [one of] them, we are going to have to do it for all of them. The Attorney General stated he had raised the point with the President so perhaps I would want to discuss it with the President. I told the Attorney General that I will do whatever he thought should be done . . . but I had taken a firm stand on it. The Attorney General stated he had never asked me to do it." When refusing Kennedy's request, Hoover created a paper record denying his own insubordination.[31]

Afterward, the FBI received letters from two suspects in the Philadelphia murders, Sheriff Rainey and a Neshoba County judge, complaining about the twenty or twenty-four agents who protected Dr. King "at all times." Both men argued, as Hoover had countless times in the past and would continue to do so once King had left Greenwood, that state and local police should have handled the assignment. The SNCC people also noted the Bureau presence when King arrived in Mississippi, and a few responded with sarcastic comments. When four car loads of FBI agents showed up with King in Jackson, summer volunteer Sally Belfrage said no one knew why they were there—"since they were not, of course, a police force and could not, of course, protect anyone."[32]

Both the civil rights community and the white resistance adopted a skeptical, wait-and-see attitude toward the new FBI presence in Mississippi. During an interview for the Walter Cronkite broadcast on CBS, King referred to the publicity regarding the Jack Gilbert Graham case that had accompanied Roy Moore to Jackson. Graham had detonated a bomb aboard a commercial airplane, and the case was one of the toughest in the FBI's history. Moore broke it nonetheless. King wondered how "a plane can be bombed and its pieces scattered for miles and the crime can be solved, but they can't find out who bombed a church." Dick Gregory, the black comedian and activist, dismissed the Bureau as "a joke . . . a second Ku Klux Klan." "If these Mississippi white Klansmen, who do not know how to plan crimes, who are ignorant, illiterate bastards, can completely baffle our FBI," Gregory asked, "what are those brilliant Communist spies doing to us?" Three days after the murders, a group of SNCC workers "went into the county (Neshoba)," but "didn't see any police cars or FBI and we went over lots of portions of the county. The only thing we saw was a marine helicopter flying above us . . . we didn't see any FBI."[33]

The reason for the skepticism about the FBI presence was obvious. The violence had not abated. By COFO's estimate 450 incidents marked the three months beginning June 15. Segregationists assaulted three voter registration workers in Hattiesburg as Hoover made his speech in Jackson. In Canton, when police officers beat another voter registration worker, McKinley Hamilton, Minnie Lou Chinn described the reaction of two FBI agents. "[They] saw it all just as we did, and them bastards had the nerve to ask what happened." When assistant SAC Neil Welch arrived in early July, he saw fresh blood on the sidewalk outside the bank building that housed the new FBI field office, evidence of the axe-handle beating three black COFO activists had received on Jackson's main street. The victims of this assault, still bleeding, were inside waiting in Welch's office, and they told Welch their story while another FBI agent crawled around on the floor, spreading newspapers to keep the blood from staining the carpet. Even the reporters who helped make 1964 "a banner year for the Mississippi motel and car-rental business" invariably checked in at The Embassy—their name for the Jackson field office. "People coming in from outside, that is, from anywhere except Mississippi," Roy Moore said, "were afraid for their lives. And with good reason . . . we had about ten murders altogether."[34]

COFO workers never received adequate protection from the FBI, but they did notice a few encouraging signs. Moore launched a speech-making campaign to alert the public to the danger posed by terrorism, and the FBI arrested three white men in Itta Bena for threatening two summer volunteers who were canvassing with SNCC staff member Willie McGhee. Over time, Moore and his men accomplished most of their goals. They identified all of the Klan officers in Mississippi, escalated their Klan infiltration investigations of city, county, and state police, and notified "the head of the law enforcement agency involved," along with the governor of the state, if "any member of his organization . . . [had] been sworn into the Ku Klux Klan." This was not done in every southern state—Hoover said his men could not deal with the Alabama Highway Patrol because of Governor George Wallace's "psychoneurotic tendencies." In Mississippi, though, things worked smoothly. Governor Johnson "summarily fired" five troopers identified in this manner, and ordered uniformed members of the Highway Patrol to interrogate every known Klansman "out in the rural." All this was accomplished, Nicholas Katzenbach later advised President Johnson, "at the urging of the FBI."[35]

A few FBI agents resigned rather than go to Mississippi with Roy Moore. For a time, Jackson became a "voluntary office." The hours were too long, community pressures too intense, the danger too imminent. A few young, aggressive agents, however, leapt at the chance to go South and work the tough cases in a tough environment. It was glamorous, or at least exciting, to crawl under a black grocery store or a COFO Freedom House to look for a bomb on your first night on the job. "The breakdown in local law and order" appalled most of the agents who did volunteer, John Doar concluded. "They were ashamed of the Bureau's prior performance," its deference to the rule of white over black and its indifference to the rule of law.[36]

FBI Inspector Joseph Sullivan led the effort in the field to solve the Philadelphia murders. Robert Wick, a Bureau executive who had worked on the Mack Charles Parker lynching in Poplarville, Mississippi, back in 1959, said Sullivan was "absolutely the best there is. If I ever did anything wrong, the last man in the world I'd want after me would be Joe Sullivan." The people who buried Schwerner, Chaney, and Goodman learned that first hand. Sullivan headed a massive investigation, captioned MIBURN (a reference to the burning of the church in Longdale), that involved 258 agents. They interviewed over 1,000 Mississippi residents, including 480 Klansmen—"just to let them know we know who they are," Hoover said; spent $815,000; and "worked in swamps infested with rattlesnakes and water moccasins." The dredging process turned up several black corpses and parts thereof—including a torso clad in a CORE t-shirt. Many agents missed vacation time, and "only a few got home for Christmas." They overlooked nothing, missed no angle. "We also have a long line of individual Negro women with whom the Sheriff has had sexual relations," the director told the president. "We are digging into that more for persuasive evidence on him when we bring him in," so "[we can] put pressure on him."[37]

The pressures on the FBI were enormous. "You got questions everyday," civil rights section chief Clement McGowan recalled. "Have you found the bodies, have you found the bodies, what are we doing? We got just an awful lot of heat from Mr. Hoover. . . . That was a rough one to handle." "You know, they went like a pack," McGowan continued, describing the subjects of the investigation. "Everybody knows everybody else and they could see, say, that Agent A and Agent B were interviewing suspect No. 5 here. . . . As soon as the agents left they moved in on him to see what was going on and what he told him. That made conducting interviews extremely difficult." Joseph Sullivan said nobody would talk "save for a few brave ladies"—Florence Mars, Ellen Spendrup, and a few of their friends. Mrs. Mars and her friends did what they could, but they did not really know very much and no one else in the Philadelphia area would talk. "Fear of the Klan overlay the uncooperative attitude of some," Sullivan noted. "Others perceived that the civil rights workers were outside troublemakers who had received their just dues."[38]

Things were so tough that Hoover nearly brought in the marines to help—after the White House garbled a message about sailors from a nearby naval air station participating in the search for the bodies. When President Johnson told Hoover to "get two hundred marines down there right away," the director delegated the task to William Sullivan, who phoned Secretary of Defense Robert McNamara and Undersecretary of Defense Joseph A. Califano, Jr. After Califano called back with a progress report—the corps supposedly had one helicopter carrying twenty or thirty marines in the air and was lining up the rest at Fort Bragg and Paris Island—Hoover phoned the White House once again. In the interim, with Governor Johnson and Senator Eastland threatening to go to the press ("Marines Invade Mississippi!"), the commander in chief aborted the mission, with the chain of command flowing, as ever, through Sullivan's Division Five desk to the Pentagon. The marines never landed.[39] The whole thing was more unusual than most of the requests for FBI assistance that emanated from President Johnson's Oval Office, but Hoover knew that he had to respond—that it was part of the price he had to pay for the greater independence he gained from the Justice Department. The president concluded that the director's promptness in handling such requests indicated an absolute loyalty. He was mistaken, and he would ultimately pay a price for misreading Hoover.

The FBI forced the first real break in the Neshoba County case by paying an informant $30,000. "We bought the informant," one agent said. "Cheap. We'd have paid a lot more if we'd had to. We'd have paid anything." On August 4 the informant's tip led Joseph Sullivan's men to a dam construction project on the Ollen Burrage farm. Working with a Link-Belt dragline and a Caterpillar bulldozer with a ten-foot blade, the digging went on for nearly six hours in 106-degree heat before the blow-flies began gathering, "numerous vultures or buzzards were observed reconnoitering," and Michael Schwerner's body appeared, face down in the Mississippi clay. The three civil rights workers had not "gone to Cuba," as the Klan kept telling everyone. When the FBI telephoned the White House to say that two "WBs" (white bodies) and one "BB" (black body) had been found, the president interrupted a National Security Council meeting to take the call.[40]

By early September the FBI had sent the Justice Department thousands of pages of investigative reports and other documents on the murders, the beating of the three blacks at Longdale, the burning of the Mt. Zion Church, and dozens of other civil rights complaints against Neshoba County law enforcement officers. By the end of the month, in the wake of a state grand jury's refusal to return a single indictment (and the FBI's understandable refusal to share information with segregationist state prosecutors), Department attorneys began their presentation of evidence to a federal grand jury in Biloxi. Acting Attorney General Katzenbach, nonetheless, cautioned President Johnson not to expect too much. The FBI had not "solved the murder case" and thus its reports contained "no evidence which can form the basis of an indictment for these murders."[41] Instead, the Bureau and the Department pushed for a Section 241 indictment against Rainey, Price, and others, on the grounds that they had conspired to deprive the victims of their constitutional right to do voter registration work in Mississippi. State authorities charged no one with murder or conspiracy to commit murder.

Indictments and convictions on federal civil rights charges were difficult to obtain even after the FBI obtained the confessions that broke the case wide open. On December 1, after Martin Luther King met with the director and told the press immediately thereafter that arrests were imminent, Roy Moore told Hoover that it appeared to white Mississippians "that King was calling the shots." Hoover sent Moore's message to the White House. Three days later, on December 4, the Bureau arrested the sheriff, his deputy, and seventeen other men on the conspiracy charge. Six days later, United States Commissioner Esther Carter dismissed all charges at a preliminary hearing.

The FBI and the Civil Rights Division persisted, however, and in January 1965 secured indictments against all nineteen suspects. When Judge Harold Cox threw out the substantive part of the indictments (that is, the Section 241 counts), the Division appealed to the Supreme Court. In March 1966 the Court overruled Judge Cox, reinstating the original indictments. Nearly a year later, in February 1967, a new federal grand jury convened (defense counsel had argued that the original grand jury pool of potential jurors had not included a sufficient number of blacks, Indians, and women), and handed down indictments against seventeen conspirators. Finally, on October 20, 1967, based in part on the testimony of two paid FBI informants, an all-white jury found seven of the defendants guilty of violating Section 241. They found Rainey not guilty. Klan leader Sam Bowers received the maximum ten-year sentence; the others, including Price, received three to ten years. "They killed one nigger, one Jew, and a white man," Judge Cox explained, years later. "I gave them what I thought they deserved."[42]

At one time, there appeared to be a consensus that the FBI had done a good job. Hugh Fleischer, a Civil Rights Division attorney who worked in Mississippi, said the FBI acted throughout "as if it were a real investigation." Martin Luther King said the FBI's work "renews again my faith in democracy," while Whitney Young praised the FBI's "outstanding effort" and Roy Wilkins noted simply, "the FBI has done its job." After Cartha DeLoach briefed the black-owned *Chicago Defender*, Sumner Stone raved over the G-men in his "Orchid for the Day" column: "To the FBI for its usual relentlessly brilliant and painstaking police work," the same "kind of magnificent detective work that traced the bullet which killed Medgar Evers." Stone urged his readers to write the Bureau to say thanks. Hoover sent a copy of the column to the White House. Later, when Joseph Sullivan left the Bureau, about four hundred agents and two former Civil Rights Division lawyers attended his retirement party. The two lawyers were John Doar and D. Robert Owen, the man who presented the Neshoba County case to the federal jury.[43]

Not everyone was appeased. "It's a shame," John Lewis said, "that national concern is aroused only after two white boys are missing." SNCC placed "the full responsibility for these deaths directly in the hands of the United States Justice Department and the Federal Bureau of Investigation." That statement reflected, more accurately than the words of praise from King, Young, and Wilkins, or the comments of Sumner Stone's "Orchid for the Day," the view of the people who had organized Freedom Summer in the first place.[44] Joseph Sullivan and the other FBI agents in Mississippi had done a good job, but SNCC activists still believed they had enemies within the hierarchies of the FBI and the Justice Department. Other FBI actions during the course of Freedom Summer would show that the SNCC people were right about Hoover and his men, and nearly right about the Department.

In Mississippi and elsewhere, SNCC and the larger civil rights movement were always in a state of flux. The pace of change, however, quickened after the tragedy in Neshoba County. Berl Bernhard, the former staff director of the Civil Rights Commission, said the government's conservatism on the protection issue "broke down a trust on the part of people who were on the front lines of what was nothing less than a battle. . . . It had a detrimental effect on respect for the authority and the dignity of the United States of America," and contributed to "a further severing of the possibility of resolution. . . . The streets became the battleground and violence enveloped the movement." The movement began to split, moderates versus radicals, moderates moving to the left and a few radicals beginning a slide towards nihilism.[45]

There was a break in the movement and some abandoned the longtime commitment to nonviolence. The fracture was there for the FBI to exploit. Hoover ordered Roy Moore to set up a special squad to exacerbate the growing divisions within the movement, and the "civil rights desk" in the Jackson field office handled the counterintelligence responsibilities. One of the agents on the special squad, James O. Ingram, had originally requested a transfer to Mississippi because he wanted to work on civil rights cases. The chief counsel for the Jackson office of the National Lawyers Committee for Civil Rights Under Law, Lawrence Aschenbrenner, remembered him as "a good guy . . . the head of the Klan detail." But Ingram ended up on the Black Nationalist Unit-West of Division Five's Racial Intelligence Section, where he worked under another former Jackson agent, Hunter E. Helgeson, and he was sued, along with Moore and yet another Jackson agent, for violating the civil liberties of a black man. Bureau agents went after the Klan in Mississippi, but they also went after black nationalists and even moderate advocates of racial justice.[46]

FBI priorities did not change much during Freedom Summer. The Philadelphia horror and the pressure of events had combined to get the Bureau moving in Mississippi. But the bureaucratic priorities of Hoover and his men continued to prevail. In one way, Robert Kennedy and Burke Marshall received what they had hoped for on the eve of Freedom Summer. "The problem," to quote Marshall again, was "rather to describe what is happening in such a way as to permit the Bureau to develop its own procedures for the collection of intelligence." Hoover ended up with a brand new field office (and another one in Columbia, South Carolina, the next year), larger budgets, more agents, and control over his bureaucracy's destiny.

A few weeks before his agents arrested Price, Rainey, and the rest, Hoover described himself at a press conference as a "states' righter" who believed civil rights enforcement should remain the responsibility of local police officers. He praised the Mississippi Highway Patrol and "rapped," in an oblique reference to Robert Kennedy's attorney generalship, "the harsh approach toward Mississippi taken by the Justice Department during the past three years." He made a few references to "water moccasins, rattlesnakes, and red-necked sheriffs," then repeated the familiar refrain: "We don't guard anybody. We are fact-finders. The FBI can't wet-nurse everybody who goes down and tries to reform or educate the Negroes in the South." A few weeks later, in an interview with David Lawrence, Hoover again chose those code words for racism to describe himself. "I had spoken of being a states' righter . . . I was a states' righter." President Johnson had forced the director to send a positive signal to the civil rights community by opening a new FBI office in Jackson, and the director was determined to send a signal of his own to his white southern constitutents.[47]

Hoover knew what he was (a states' righter) and what his white constituency in the South demanded (surveillance of civil rights workers). Even during the most desperate days of Freedom Summer, when his agents scrambled to find the bodies, he did not neglect the Red menace. He briefed Burke Marshall on the "subversive activities" of Michael Schwerner's father back in New York, and his agents investigated anyone who had any connection with Freedom Summer whatsoever. In the case of Allard Lowenstein, who had visited South Africa and written on what he saw there, the Bureau noted his opposition to apartheid. The Bureau also clipped a newspaper article about Lowenstein's appearance at a dinner party given by Arkansas Senator J. William Fulbright. Other guests included Robert McNamara, Adlai Stevenson, and Lyndon and Lady Bird Johnson.[48]

Meanwhile, at FBI headquarters, Division Five directed the field to identify the college students who signed on as summer volunteers and to run their names through the files.[49] This type of trolling was not very useful. Few twenty-year-olds possessed old-left pedigrees. Bureau agents carried on nonetheless. They followed the students home through the late summer and early fall, visiting anyone who had criticized their organization's work in Mississippi and characterizing them in the files as "immature, unreliable and obnoxious." And they opened files on every resident of every COFO Freedom House—including one house whose residents included a Catholic nun, a former FBI agent, the son-in-law of a newspaper publisher, the daughter of a Communist party member, a newspaper reporter, and "an oversexed Vassar girl." "Of course there were associations," Roy Moore said. "There were quite a few hard-core communists, but they weren't any more important than any other group." The most extreme example of communist infiltration involved a new-lywed couple in southwest Mississippi—"the son and daughter of two of the leading Communist party leaders in Wisconsin and Illinois" who came down "on their honeymoon" to handle "communications out of a COFO house."[50]

The FBI investigated another COFO house resident, Larry Rubin, a summer volunteer from Pennsylvania who had been assaulted in Holly Springs, Mississippi, after receiving a phone call from Senator James Eastland. Because he had been co-chair, along with Joni Rabinowitz, of the Fair Play for Cuba Committee back at Antioch College, the Bureau lumped Rubin with its uncounted group of "individuals with communist backgrounds [who] are known to have assisted in SNCC's 1964 'Mississippi Project.' " Moore may have been low key about the Red menace in the Magnolia state; Hoover was not. Three weeks after the call from Senator Eastland, he briefed New York Governor Nelson Rockefeller on the "communist problem" in connection with "the racial situation in Mississippi."[51] The FBI disseminated information to interested politicians like Rockefeller, "cooperative news media sources, educational officials and other sources in an effort to expose the background and activities of these communists."[52]

FBI officials also pursued their anticommunist goals by cooperating with the law enforcement community in Mississippi, sharing information with the intelligence units of the Jackson Police Department and the Highway Patrol. This last agency claimed to have files on "all known radical agitators in the State." The FBI received additional information from the Mississippi State Sovereignty Commission, one of the more primitive public-sector agencies formed in the wake of *Brown v. Board of Education* to "resist the usurpation" of states' rights. The Commission channeled tax dollars to the Citizens Council, hired informants, organized mass mailings, and, according to director Erle Johnson, Jr., "turned over information on subversives to the FBI." For a time during the late 1950s and early 1960s, chief investigator Zak Van Landingham—an FBI agent for twenty-seven years—coordinated these activities.[53]

The FBI's relationship with groups like the Sovereignty Commission and far-rightists like Erle Johnson and Zak Van Landingham was ambiguous. Hoover had only contempt for the methods of the Ku Klux Klan, but he recognized his constituency on the radical right. When Senator Karl E. Mundt (R., S.D.), a former member of HUAC and the McCarthy Committee, wanted a speaker for a Sioux Falls television station, he asked Bureau officials what they thought of Fred C. Schwarz of the Christian Anti-Communist Crusade. "The FBI reports Schwarz's material is intelligent, high level, and helpfully informative," Mundt advised the station manager. "They also told me that if you can't get Schwarz you might get an equally high level discussion on the Communist menace by Paul Harvey."[54] FBI officials even tried to manipulate far-right groups that they clearly identified as threats to the peace and stability of their America, sending information on black activists to J. B. Stoner's National States Rights party. They also sent Klan publications or "any other literature that can be obtained from organizations having an extreme hatred for black people" to black activists in Mississippi.[55]

Hoover never ignored the right, but he always focused on the left, and in Mississippi that focus led to the Medical Committee for Human Rights and especially the National Lawyers Guild (NLG), whose members had volunteered their respective medical and legal services. The FBI characterization of the NLG ("the foremost legal bulwark of the Communist Party") had been released under the name of the House Committee on Un-American Activities back in the 1950s, a time when Louis Nichols briefed a variety of groups and individuals on the Guild—from the American Bar Association to Senator Eastland's Senate Internal Security Subcommitee (SISS) and even Walter White and the NAACP. The damage was extensive. The Guild shrank to about 500 attorneys, with only a handful of members at large in the South and only four active chapters.[56]

The FBI had been monitoring the National Lawyers Guild's interest in the civil rights movement since 1959, when two attorneys from New Orleans, Benjamin Smith and Bruce Waltzer, tried to convince the Guild to become more involved in the black struggle. Not much happened until 1962 when two black attorneys from Norfolk, Virginia, Len Holt and E. A. Dawley, made an emotional plea for assistance at the NLG's national convention in Detroit. After extensive debate, the Guild decided to organize a Committee for Legal Assistance in the South (CLAS), selecting as co-chairmen two Detroit attorneys—one black, George Crockett, Jr., and one white, Ernest Goodman—and naming Holt and Smith field secretaries. In the months that followed, NLG members watched events in the South closely, particularly an October 1963 raid on the law offices of Smith and Waltzer, the two attorneys who had originally solicited their assistance.[57]

FBI officials also monitored these events closely. Louisiana police officers, acting on behalf of Jack Rogers, counsel for the Joint Legislative Committee on Un-American Activities, arrested Smith, Waltzer, and Southern Conference Educational Fund (SCEF) board member James A. Dombrowski, charging them with failing to register with the Department of Public Safety as agents of the Communist party. They confiscated all SCEF records—including a copy of Thoreau's *Journal* and a photograph inscribed for Dombrowski by Eleanor Roosevelt.[58] Rogers told the press that he had not coordinated the raid with local FBI agents because "they would have to tell Bobby Kennedy. We cannot trust him and expect he would tell his friend Martin Luther King." When King himself sent a telegram to the Civil Rights Division protesting the raid and requesting federal intervention, Burke Marshall said there was nothing the Department or the Bureau could do. The FBI had more freedom to act on the day after the raid, when SISS Chairman James Eastland sent Jay Sourwine, staff director of the Subcommittee, to New Orleans. Sourwine subpoenaed all 30,000 items seized in the raid and brought them back to Washington, where several FBI agents reviewed them. In March 1964, while the FBI indexed the names listed in the SCEF files, the Guild accepted an invitation from Bob Moses and SNCC to open an office in Jackson.[59]

The SNCC alliance with the National Lawyers Guild troubled nearly everyone. Senator Eastland told Cartha DeLoach that he was conducting "extensive" research "into House and Senate hearing records to build up a case against . . . [NLG] attorneys." He wanted "to show communist influence in the civil rights movement in the South," and planned "to make a talk very soon in the Senate on this matter."[60] Guild involvement even troubled the movement and its friends. SNCC said that Jack Greenberg and the NAACP Legal Defense and Education Fund had threatened to cancel plans to provide legal aid to the Summer Project unless Guild lawyers were purged. "We didn't want a lot of people barreling in here, spending thirty-six hours in Jackson, and then going home and telling people what great civil rights lawyers they were," Greenberg explained.[61] Others, including Carl Rachlin, CORE's chief counsel; Edwin J. Lukas, general counsel for the American Jewish Committee; and Leo Pfeffer, general counsel for the American Jewish Congress, met with De-Loach to discuss the "plans of the National Lawyers Guild . . . to encroach on the role of CORE lawyers." All three groups were "perturbed," Rachlin said. "Many of the younger attorneys in their own organizations had not had any experience in opposing the communists such as Messrs. Pfeffer, Lucas, and he had encountered during the 1930s."[62]

After giving DeLoach a list containing the names of lawyers who had volunteered to work in Mississippi, the Rachlin delegation left to meet with Burke Marshall. Hoover ordered a memo sent to Walter Jenkins at the White House—Marshall having already received a memo characterizing the National Lawyers Guild as a communist front. From there, the FBI ran additional name checks, disseminated follow-up memos on the Guild's civil rights strategies to Jenkins, Kennedy, and Marshall, and placed George Crockett and Ernest Goodman on the counterintelligence program target list. In one operation, a John Birch Society official who was "very close to the Bureau" obtained a Birch booklet (*It's Very Simple—The True Story of Civil Rights*) for the FBI, and the FBI sent it, along with an anonymous letter, "to numerous ministers, priests and rabbis in Detroit." The Bureau hoped to discredit Crockett and his work in Mississippi, and eventually tried to sabotage his campaigns for seats on the Detroit City Council and the Recorder's Court by working with an extremist group called Breakthrough. The Detroit FBI office fantasized about taking over Breakthrough and directing its "right-wing conservative" activities. Hoover approved any "justifiable expenditure of funds to further this operation at any appropriate time."[63]

Besides Crockett and Goodman, the FBI focused on Guild members Henry Wolf and Martin Popper. Both men happened to represent Andrew Goodman's family, and Popper had been part of the Hollywood Ten defense team back in the late 1940s. (Goodman's parents were in fact part of leftist circles in New York; their dinner parties were attended by Zero Mostel, Alger Hiss, and others.) Popper and Wolf had accompanied Goodman's parents, Schwerner's parents, and Congressman William Fitz Ryan, among others, to the Justice Department, where they met with Nicholas Katzenbach and, briefly, with Robert Kennedy.

Hoover responded, once again, by sending memos to Walter Jenkins—with copies to Kennedy and Marshall and presumably Katzenbach as well. Describing the Lawyers Guild as a communist front, the director noted Popper's own conviction (later reversed) for contempt of Congress following his appearance in 1959 before the House Committee on Un-American Activities.[64] Turning from the Goodman family lawyer to Schwerner's parents, Hoover approved a wiretap (NY 4539-C*) on the home telephone of Michael Schwerner's father. Mostly, the tap uncovered information regarding "contacts of NAT SCHWERNER, in his activities to raise money for COFO."[65]

The FBI had also focused on Popper in early July, when he phoned Katzenbach to complain "that the Goodmans, as parents of one of the victims, have in effect been told nothing about the investigation to locate their son; that the parents want to know more; and are entitled to be told more than that the FBI is doing everything that can be done." "It appears," Courtney Evans wrote, after Katzenbach briefed the FBI, "that the Goodmans have been reading . . . highly speculative . . . newspaper items"—stories inferring "that possibly the local county sheriff at Philadelphia, Mississippi, has been involved." That was "an understatement," Hoover said. The director did not "care what the Goodmans nor Popper say or do. They are not going to intimidate me with their threats and innuendos. We have nothing to say and we will stick to 'no comment.' " If the FBI did tell the family anything, the director added, in a revealing comment, they would simply run "to the press—probably N.Y. Post or Worker."[66]

The FBI's pounding took a toll. By mid-summer, James Forman said "pressure on SNCC" to drop the National Lawyers Guild was coming "from the heartland of the administration itself." "[SNCC] workers are also involved in the COFO plans for the summer," Robert Kennedy told Lyndon Johnson. "They are seeking assistance from [the] National Lawyers' Guild . . . and some of them are more interested in forcing federal action in connection with street demonstrations than anything else."[67] (By relying on FBI reports for his understanding of the situation, Kennedy did not seem to realize that Freedom Summer was largely a Student Nonviolent Coordinating Committee project.) Forman's reference had its roots in a mid-summer meeting with Justice Department officials arranged by Alfred M. Bingham, who had left his Connecticut home for Jackson to see his son,

Stephen M., a summer volunteer from Yale. Bingham "almost had a fit" when he saw "the Lawyers Guild in operation there." Upon returning North, the senior Bingham, Burke Marshall, John Doar, and Arthur Schlesinger, whose own son Stephen planned to go to Mississippi, met with Steve Bingham, Forman, Moses, and Guyot. The ostensible purpose of the gathering, to discuss the situation in "the hill country of McComb and Natchez where the Klan rode strong," seemed secondary. "The Lawyers Guild," Forman said, "seemed to be the main subject on the minds of our hosts."[68]

From Forman's perspective, the civil rights workers might just as well have met with J. Edgar Hoover and his top aides. When they pressed the protection issue, Marshall "pleaded with us to go slow." When they said "all the United States Government had to do . . . was throw one of the racist sheriffs in jail," there was no reply. Only silence. After Marshall finally said something about the threat of "a guerrilla war in Mississippi" if the government locked up even one sheriff, Schlesinger brought up the Guild's tolerance of communists in its ranks. He made a point about the fight against communism in the 1930s and 1940s and then, "out of the blue," told the activists straight out, according to Forman's recollection: "We find it unpardonable that you would work with them." (Schlesinger does not remember using that particular locution.) The group emphasized "freedom of association" and "the unwillingness of the Justice Department and the NAACP Legal Defense and Education Fund to take aggressive action," but it did not do any good. Moses and Marshall "had a hot exchange on this point."[69]

Neither Bingham nor Schlesinger shared Hoover's alarmist assumptions about subversion, but in this particular case they believed communists in the National Lawyers Guild intended to send the sons of well-known people into dangerous areas. They called the meeting "out of a perhaps excessive but not unnatural concern for the lives of [their] sons." Nevertheless, as Forman later wrote in *The Making of Black Revolutionaries*, "the rupture with the government was complete and the issues absolutely clear. The words of Schlesinger echoed in my head, 'We find it unpardonable . . . ' What blindness and arrogance, I thought. He knew nothing of our struggle in the South." Forman and the others had gone into the meeting with the idea that they might finally convince the federal government to act in Mississippi. They walked out convinced that the government was the enemy of black people.[70]

Both Stephen Bingham and Stephen Schlesinger lived through Freedom Summer, and one of them went on to attract the FBI's interest. Schlesinger remained a liberal, eventually writing a book about the CIA overthrow of the Arbenz government in Guatemala and serving as special assistant to New York Governor Mario Cuomo. Bingham slid over to the far left. Grandson of Hiram Bingham (archeologist, governor of Connecticut, United States senator, chairman of the Loyalty Review Board), and great- and great-great grandson of two more famous Hirams (the Hawaiian missionaries), he moved on to law school at Berkeley, the Peace Corps, and Cesar Chavez's farm workers. He ran into trouble with the FBI and the law in California, after allegedly slipping a gun to the Soledad brother, George Jackson, at San Quentin Prison. Three white guards, two white trustees, and three black inmates, including Jackson, died in the violence that followed. (Bingham escaped and went underground for thirteen years before surrendering himself to authorities; in 1986 he won acquittal on two counts of murder and one count of conspiracy to commit murder.)[71]

Had Doar or Marshall told Hoover about the drift of their Freedom Summer conversation with Forman, Moses, Guyot, and Bingham, the FBI director probably would have been pleased. With three of their own buried under thirty feet of Mississippi mud, the movement asked for protection. The listened instead to a lawyer speak the director's language, the language of federalism, and a professor lecture on the director's issue, the communist issue.[72] The movement was told the truth—told to look for shades of gray because "the constitutional issues" were complex. The movement saw right and wrong, black and white, the corpses of summer volunteers and grinning sheriffs and deputy sheriffs with cheeks full of Redman. Jim Forman recognized "a pattern. If government agents take a position that, 'well, we don't care,' or 'it's complex, and so therefore we won't do anything, and so you can continue to beat people, you can continue to lynch people,' and so forth, then people will know that they're encouraged," he said. "I mean, you can encourage the Klan or you can discourage them."[73]

For the FBI, during the third month of Freedom Summer, spying remained the preferred task. This was especially true when

President Johnson asked Hoover to cover the Democratic National Convention in Atlantic City, New Jersey. Two events planned for the convention troubled the president. The first was a tribute to John Kennedy to be delivered by his brother, who had just announced his candidacy for his party's nomination for United States senator from New York.[74] The second was the Mississippi Freedom Democratic party (MFDP) challenge to the seating of the regular, all-white Mississippi delegation. Formed and staffed by native Mississippians from SNCC and other veterans of the Freedom Vote Campaigns and the Summer Project, the MFDP threatened LBJ's dream of convention harmony. White House interest dated from late July when Walter Jenkins submitted the inevitable name-check request to the FBI. John Doar followed this request with another on August 19, submitting the names of forty party leaders, delegates, and alternate delegates—including Fanny Lou Hamer.[75]

At the same time, and at the president's specific request, Hoover sent what Arthur Schlesinger described as a special squad of "snoops and wiretappers" to Atlantic City to spy on Robert Kennedy and the Mississippi activists.[76] Not surprisingly, the director selected Cartha DeLoach to run the operation. (The president called for assistance so often and on so many fronts that he ordered a direct telephone line installed in the assistant director's bedroom.)[77] DeLoach organized a squad of twenty-seven agents, one radio maintenance technician, and two stenographers. He also received an agent from New York who had accompanied Robert and a pregnant Ethel from the Kennedys' Manhattan apartment to LaGuardia Airport and then on to Atlantic City on the family plane. DeLoach's team set up a command post in the Post Office Building, averaged eight hours of overtime a day, and "approached each assignment as a challenge and with enthusiasm." They completed one assignment while Dr. King testified on the MFDP's behalf before the credentials committee—by tapping the telephone in his room at the Claridge House Hotel. They tried to install a bug, too, but "had to get out before they could get mike coverage." From there, they tapped the phone in Bayard Rustin's room, and planted a microphone in the storefront serving as the SNCC–CORE headquarters. CORE was an incidental target. The real targets, DeLoach said, were the "sixty members of the SNCC from Jackson, Mississippi, [who] plan to . . . assist in seating the Mississippi Freedom Democratic Party delegation."[78]

FBI agents monitored every tap and bug from their own room in the Claridge House, and the two-way radios used by the Freedom Democratic party and several of the other civil rights groups from "one of the rooms in the Post Office Building." Whenever they intercepted an interesting bit of conversation on MFDP strategy, they telephoned it to Robert Wick at Crime Records offices in Washington, and Wick dictated the information to stenographers (who typed it up on "plain bond paper") and then rushed the document to the White House by special messenger. President Johnson, as one commentator later put it, "had the convention wired—literally."[79]

To keep track of the Mississippi activists in Atlantic City, the FBI also secured press credentials, with "the cooperation of management of NBC news," for two or three agents who went out onto the convention floor, posing as newsmen. One agent "was so successful," DeLoach bragged, "that [name deleted] was giving him 'off the record information' for background purposes, which he requested our 'reporter' not to print." Another agent, Lloyd Nelson, posed as a news photographer, and yet another, Ben Hale, interviewed "key persons in various groups, using walkie-talkie equipment" and broadcasting not to NBC but to the Bureau control center in the Post Office. Other agents operated an informant who "penetrated" MFDP headquarters in the Gem Motel and the place where the delegation held strategy sessions, the basement of the Union Temple Baptist Church. Most of the remaining agents watched the demonstrations out on the Atlantic City boardwalk. Michael Schwerner's widow, older brother, and mother and father were there, along with about 120 SNCC and CORE activists. DeLoach's squad ended up with "separate files" on the MFDP, King, and SCLC; several far-left and far-right groups; local hoodlums; and what seemed like every single movement group—CORE, SNCC, COFO, ACT, and the NAACP; among others.[80]

The Johnson White House had other sources of information on the Freedom Democratic party besides the FBI. One of Bill Moyer's friends, Robert Spike of the National Council of Churches ("one of these quiet, anonymous, little guys who devotes his life to causes like this"), had "the confidence of the Negro groups working in Mississippi" and relayed what he had learned. Martin Luther King himself kept in contact with Lee White, though he no doubt sought leverage of his own. He told White to expect "demonstrations and riots . . . unless some sort of satisfactory adjustment of the 'Freedom Party' issue is found."[81] Attorney Joseph Rauh, who represented the MFDP, also kept in touch with Johnson administration officials and responded, in the manner of Dr. King, with his own form of pressure. After the president had Walter Reuther and Hubert Humphrey ask him to drop his efforts on the party's behalf, Rauh told Humphrey "if I get out, the National Lawyers Guild fellows are going to take this fight over and they're going to be really wild. You guys just don't know. At least you've got a sensible guy here."[82]

Nearly all of the information gathered by DeLoach's squad on the Mississippi activists and their strategies and allies, much like the information gathered by the administration's other sources, had a political slant. The FBI supplied the type of information President Johnson craved. What would King and Rauh do if the president met with them? What did the movement think about the possible vice-presidential nominees? Would the MFDP accept the compromise engineered by Oregon Congresswoman Edith Green? Was New York Congressman Adam Clayton Powell, Jr., carrying a revolver on the boardwalk? What was the NAACP up to? Why was CORE planning to picket the office of Charles Diggs, the black congressman from Detroit? Although they were not always right, DeLoach and his team always had an answer.[83]

Among other services, DeLoach convinced White House aides Bill Moyers and Walter Jenkins, through "counseling," to support changes in procedures for granting admission to the convention floor. This enabled the FBI to "preclude infiltration of the illegal Mississippi Freedom Democratic Party (MFDP) delegates in large numbers into the space reserved for the regular [all- white] Mississippi delegates." Through other "counterintelligence efforts, Jenkins, et al., were able to advise the President in advance regarding major plans of the MFDP delegates." Because the FBI overheard a number of congressmen, state governors, and other prominent political figures on the various taps and bugs in use during the convention, DeLoach furnished intelligence that ranged far beyond MFDP strategies.[84]

"It was obvious that DeLoach wanted to impress Jenkins and Moyers with the Bureau's ability to develop information which would be of interest to them," special agent Bill D. Williams conceded. On one occasion, during a lengthy telephone conversation with Jenkins, DeLoach "appeared to be discussing the President's 'image.' At the end of the conversation [the assistant direc-

tor] told us something to the effect, 'that may have sounded a little political to you but this doesn't do the Bureau any harm.' "
"[I was merely keeping] Jenkins and Moyers constantly advised by telephone of minute by minute developments," DeLoach explained. "This enabled them to make spot decisions and . . . adjust Convention plans to meet potential problems before serious trouble developed."[85]

When DeLoach returned to the seat of government on August 28, Jenkins called Hoover to let him know the president "thought the job the Bureau had done in Atlantic City was one of the finest [he] had ever seen," that "there were a lot of bad elements up there and because of the work some of the Bureau people did [the administration] knew exactly where they were and what they were doing." Upon hearing this, the director recommended DeLoach for "a meritorious award." A few days later, on September 10, DeLoach thanked Moyers for his "very thoughtful and generous note concerning our operation. . . . It was a pleasure and a privilege. . . . All the boys that were with me felt honored in being selected for the assignment. . . . I'm certainly glad that we were able to come through with vital tidbits from time to time which were of assistance to you and Walter."[86]

The FBI continued to monitor the Mississippi Freedom Democratic party in the aftermath, even as party activists returned home to prepare for the elections and to suffer continuing harassment at the hands of the white resistance. October 21 was a typical day in the town of Marks: "Campaign worker forced off highway, beaten by 4 whites and urinated upon: suffered concussion." Things had not changed much since June 21. The Klan still rode strong. Johnson administration officials, for their part, ignored the defection of most of the Mississippi delegates recognized by the credentials committee in Atlantic City to Barry Goldwater in the November elections. The administration continued to view the MFDP as part of the "leftist elements of the civil rights movement," and the FBI continued to feed that view by sending alarmist reports on the party to the White House. "There was a fear in this country of ordinary people havin' power," Freedom Democractic party chairman Lawrence Guyot said. "And there was no better illustration of that in American history than sharecroppers, and day laborers, and beauticians, and barbers, and preachers, sittin' and sayin' to the president and everybody else in the Democratic party, 'NO.' "[87]

Hoover helped Johnson achieve his goals in Atlantic City, but the president paid a price for his success. Joe Rauh said the civil rights movement never quite trusted LBJ after August 1964. Theodore H. White had once described LBJ as the man who made "the matter of race relations again a subject for discussion and legislation in Washington." And Johnson helped bring the country the Civil Rights Act of 1964 in the middle of Freedom Summer. "Lincoln struck the shackles off the slaves," Virginia Durr contended with a rhetorical flourish that nonetheless contained a kernel of truth. "Lyndon struck the shackles off the South." But Atlantic City was not forgotten. Fifteen years later, Edwin King said the spying was "led by Lyndon Johnson, endorsed by some of the most respectable people like John Doar," and not much different from "the kind of things for which we impeached [sic] Richard Nixon." Roy Wilkins noted the "lasting sense of grievance" that followed Atlantic City, the "terrible damage to relations between white liberals and black organizers in the South."[88]

On the eve of the next Democratic National Convention in 1968, William Connell, an aide to Hubert Humphrey, asked Hoover to assemble another Atlantic City-type team and "do the same thing for the Vice President out in Chicago." The director said it was already in the works. The assistance actually provided was neither so pervasive (in part because Attorney General Ramsey Clark refused to authorize wiretaps in Chicago) nor political (in part because "Hoover was friendly with Nixon and supported his candidacy"). The Jackson field office, however, did send seven informants to cover the Chicago convention—assigning five of them to the Loyal Democrats of Mississippi, a coalition group whose members included MFDP representatives. This time, the Loyal Democrats successfully challenged Mississippi's segregated delegation after a stormy convention floor fight, thus enabling three of the FBI informers to sit in the convention hall and vote as delegates or alternate delegates.[89]

Back in Mississippi during the summer of 1964, the FBI hung a picture of the director in its new Jackson field office. In their own office nearby, SNCC hung a sign that read:

> There is a place in Mississippi called Liberty
> There is a department in Washington called Justice.

The disillusioned SNCC people hung that sign and wondered whether they should carry guns. After Klansmen firebombed the home of one of the black farmers who worked with SNCC to

register voters in Holmes County, the farmer said "I got a automatic shotgun, Remington, twelve gauge, them high-velocity
buckshot. So I jumped up and run out and turn it loose a time
or two." Julian Bond remembered the farmer, who served as a
Freedom party delegate in Atlantic City, and the debate in SNCC
about carrying guns. "This old guy, Hartman Turnbow . . . He
used to carry an army automatic in a briefcase and it's funny to
see a man who looks like a farmer and is dressed like a farmer
in coveralls and boots and, let's say, an old hat, with a briefcase.
And he opens the briefcase and nothing's in it but an automatic."
By the time Freedom Summer was half over, most SNCC field
workers were carrying guns of their own.[90]

One week after the FBI found the bodies of Michael
Schwerner, James Chaney, and Andrew Goodman, Cartha De-
Loach met with Roy Wilkins to discuss SNCC and Forman. According to the Crime Records Division account of that meeting,
"Wilkins advised . . . that James Forman, whom other Negroes
refer to as 'the Commissar,' was actually the man who was in
control of SNCC and that John Lewis was merely a front man.
. . . Wilkins also felt that Forman had brought Lewis instructions from the CP."[91] Nearly a year to the day after the Philadelphia murders, on June 15, 1965, Attorney General Katzenbach
finally acted on such reports, approving Hoover's request for a
wiretap on SNCC—because the FBI had identified the group as
"the principal target for Communist Party infiltration among
the various civil rights organizations." Eventually, Katzenbach
would call for the creation of "a militant but peaceful organization of young [black] people which could successfully compete
with SNCC."[92]

While the FBI wiretap request made its way back through
channels, Neshoba County Deputy Sheriff Cecil Price arrested a
volunteer attorney for the Lawyers Constitutional Defense Committee (LCDC), Dennis Seinfield; a law student, J. V. Henry; and
a young black man, Richard Tinsley, who had just been bailed
out of the Philadelphia jail. When Price released all three men
in the early evening, they telephoned Alvin Bronstein,· director
of the Jackson LCDC office, who asked the FBI to alert the Highway Patrol and to call the sheriff in Philadelphia. When the
agent who took the call refused his request, Bronstein asked,
"Do I need three more corpses to prove jurisdiction?," hung up
the phone, and called John Doar. "It's a shame that Doar yields
to such hysterical calls from obviously biased *sources* in these

situations," Hoover wrote, upon learning about the incident and the belated mobilization of his Bureau. "I do not intend that our Agts. waste time and money following out unfounded calls."[93]

That same summer, when responding to Civil Rights Division requests to send more men to Mississippi, the FBI assigned at least a few agents with no civil rights experience but plenty of experience in communist infiltration matters. Hugh Fleischer, who was working on a segregation case in Greenwood at the time, remembered "guys who spent most of their careers watching the Lawyers Guild in Chicago or wherever. That's all they did. This one guy said, 'That's what I do. I watch the Lawyers Guild.' "[94]

Hoover was sending a message to civil rights workers and his own white southern constituents alike: The young people who came to protest the ways of white Mississippi had committed the crime of subversion, a crime worse than the crimes of the Klan on the night when Cecil Price stopped that CORE station wagon. Hoover's message exacerbated the dilemmas created by the Justice Department's own civil rights enforcement strategies. Two months before Schwerner, Chaney, and Goodman died, Burke Marshall noted "the loss of faith in law . . . among Negro and white civil rights workers. The consequences in the future cannot be foreseen."[95] The consequences were easier to see after Freedom Summer. The great majority of SNCC workers never really had that much direct contact with the FBI before Freedom Summer. In the aftermath, they did not remember the job Hoover's agents did in solving the Philadelphia murders or in breaking the back of the Neshoba County Klan. They remembered the Bureau's coldness during those first twenty-four hours after three of their fellows disappeared. They remembered the Bureau as a symbol of the federal government's caution, its interest in splitting the difference between right and wrong.

Seven years after Michael Schwerner, James Chaney, and Andrew Goodman had been buried, Charles Evers asked the FBI field office in Jackson to come to the aid of two Georgetown University students trapped in a barn in Scott County by Klansmen who were throwing a rope over a tree branch. Mayor of Fayette and candidate for governor of Mississippi, Evers telephoned "one of the top brass" and told him "to get some men over there." He stopped talking for a minute before frowning and shouting into the phone: "Listen! I don't give a damn *what* FBI policy is! You can observe and take notes all you want. But if I don't hear about those kids gettin' out safe in ten minutes, I'm goin' down there myself, *with* my bodyguard, *in* my campaign cars! I got forty reporters from all over creation sittin' right out here in the lobby who're gonna go with me. An' they'll tell the whole world how y'all never saved those kids after you were tipped off. Now that'll make one damn fool outa J. Edgar Hoover!" In some ways, white Mississippi changed faster than the director and his FBI.[96]

6

Klan Wars

The Ku Klux Klan and the Good Name of White America

On September 2, 1964, one month after the retrieval of the three civil rights workers' bodies in Neshoba County and five days after Cartha DeLoach and his team returned from Atlantic City, the FBI declared war on the Ku Klux Klan. Eventually, the Bureau would fight that war directly on two fronts, an extralegal front of COINTELPRO (counterintelligence program) dirty tricks and a legal front of investigation of Klansmen suspected of violating the old Reconstruction Era statutes; and indirectly on a public relations front of newspaper stories, magazine articles, books, and television specials designed to tell the story of its battles with the Klan on the other two fronts. For the first six months of this war, however, not much happened. It was a time of phony war, and it ended only on March 25, 1965, in Selma, Alabama, a former slave market town on the Alabama River, with a Klan murder of another white civil rights worker, Viola Liuzzo, a red-haired Detroit housewife and mother of five.[1]

For differing reasons, the movement, the FBI, and the Johnson administration expected trouble in Alabama. J. Edgar Hoover told Martin Luther King "that FBI Agents would be in Selma, not for the purpose of protecting anyone, but for the purpose of observing and reporting to the Department of Justice."[2] The director warned President Lyndon Johnson and Vice President Hubert Humphrey that communists and other radicals might provide confrontations.

But when Andrew Young and Ralph Abernathy asked Cartha De-Loach to identify the communists in the civil rights movement and to describe their influence, the assistant director referred the two civil rights leaders to HUAC and the American Legion. "The very racists we've been fighting," in Young's view. Nicholas Katzenbach centered on SNCC participation in the Selma demonstrations and James Forman's alleged threat "to send some of the toughest SNCC members to Washington with a view of demonstrating here." The attorney general was depending on the FBI for "intelligence."[3]

Under Hoover's watchful eye, the movement had been in Alabama since January for the Selma voting drive, and by early February state and local police had arrested Dr. King and three thousand others.[4] On March 9 segregationists beat Rev. James Reeb, a Boston Unitarian, and when he died two days later the movement had its first white martyr in Selma. Reeb's death attracted national attention, in contrast to the earlier killing of a young black man, Jimmy Lee Jackson, by a state trooper. On March 12 Katzenbach told Hoover he was "trying his best to keep troops out of there, and wondered whether an operation like [the FBI] ran in Neshoba County, with a special detail and a fellow like [Joseph] Sullivan [in charge]" might "keep the situation from getting too far out of hand." Hoover said Sullivan and a nine-man squad had already left to join the twenty-six agents on the scene—although he complained to his senior staff about "a situation where almost everyone is having hallucinations." On March 13 President Johnson asked Congress to act on the pending voting rights bill. On March 21 King began the Selma-Montgomery march, after the police had turned back two earlier attempts, including the attempt that led to the Bloody Sunday spectacle of March 7—the single most brutal repression of any civil rights demonstration. Katzenbach spoke to Hoover again on March 23 to thank him "for the help Bureau people have been on the march in Alabama, particularly the way they are getting information to the Army and to Ramsey Clark."[5]

The FBI had seventy agents in and around Selma by March 25, a day Viola Liuzzo spent on Highway 80 shuttling marchers back to the city in her car. On the last trip of the day, near Big Bear Swamp in Lowndes County, twenty-five miles from the Edmund Pettus Bridge, another car carrying four Klansmen drove past and one of the passengers shot Mrs. Liuzzo in the head. The bullet cut her spinal cord in two at the base of the brain, sending blood spurting from her temple, and she died instantly, crashing her car into the ditch. The man who reportedly pulled the trigger, Collie Leroy Wilkins, said to one of his companions as the Klan sped away, "Baby brother, I don't miss. That bitch is dead and in hell." The only passenger in the victim's car, Leroy Moton, a nineteen-year-old black barber and sometime SCLC volunteer, hitchhiked into Selma for help.

President Johnson ordered the FBI to "find the perpetrators of this heinous crime," to "do everything possible around the clock." He telephoned FBI headquarters twice and Hoover himself two or three times in the middle of the night, and again at 6:00 A.M. He followed this last telephone call with a call to Katzenbach at 8:00 A.M. By that time, the president learned, the Bureau had already solved the case. Most of the conversations that followed concerned White House strategies for maximizing press coverage of the forthcoming announcement that FBI agents had arrested four Klansmen. Johnson suggested that Hoover and Katzenbach "come over to the White House; that maybe we could get there before the statements and let television cover us as we come in; that we don't need to have any appointment, to just call [press secretary] George Reedy and tell him I'm coming over to see the President, then tell the Attorney General and just get in the car and come over." The only problem, Hoover reasoned, "is the astronauts get there at eleven o'clock and we can't complete matters by that time." It would be better to wait until "right after" the forty-five minute ceremony for the spacemen.[6]

A few minutes after noon, on live, nationwide television, flanked by his FBI director and attorney general, President Johnson announced the arrests. Hoover understood Johnson's interest in orchestrating this publicity, the use of the occasion to denounce the Klan and to pressure Congress to enact the voting rights bill the administration had submitted on St. Patrick's Day. The publicity helped LBJ and the movement obtain one of the things they wanted—the Voting Rights Act of 1965. "I don't know what they would have done if it hadn't been for Selma," Burke Marshall said. "But President Johnson at that time, at least, was very responsive and pretty smart about public opinion. When the Selma march took place, he saw that as an opportunity."[7]

Hoover understood that Selma could also help him achieve one of his own goals. Unlike the president, the director had no interest in "the colored people" and their right to vote. "Many who have the right to register very seldom do register," he said. But Hoover and Johnson were alike in one way, as a Crime Records Division agent noted. They were both "totally consummate, skilled politician[s]."[8] The FBI's public relations people accelerated their activities in the wake of Liuzzo's murder in order to change the Bureau's image as a silent ally of the white southern resistance and its brutalities. After Selma, as every consummate politician recognized, Jim Crow America was doomed. The new consensus would no longer tolerate the visible, on-the-books discrimination that had ruled in the South for so long, let alone the horrors and idiocy of the Ku Klux Klan.

Hoover made no concession to protect movement activists. He continued to oppose them even in the midst of his Bureau's battles with the Klan. From beginning to end, the Klan wars remained a sideshow to the real war against the black struggle for racial justice. Hoover saw the Ku Klux Klan as another subversive threat to the peace and stability of middle America, but he also saw the Klan as a threat to the good name of the anti-civil rights movement. Klansmen were discrediting all forms of resistance, including the FBI's preferred forms, and for that, the director decided, they had to be stopped.

The Klan wars began with the launching of a formal FBI counterintelligence program against "white hate groups." This was the third COINTELPRO, the first two having been launched in 1956 against the Communist party and in 1961 against the Socialist Workers party; and like its predecessors the Bureau designed the new program "to expose, disrupt, discredit or otherwise neutralize" the targeted group. Individual counterintelligence operations (dirty tricks) often violated federal criminal statutes relating to mail fraud and incited violence, and sometimes involved the sending of obscene material through the mail and extortion. But neither the COINTELPRO against the Klan nor any of the other programs had the solitary goal of invoking sanctions against dissidents. They had an explicitly "educational purpose" of bringing Klansmen or communists or Trotskyites "into disrepute before the American public." While William Sullivan's Division Five supervised the COINTELPROs, Cartha DeLoach's Crime Records Division had counterintelligence responsibilities of its own—including the recruitment of over three hundred newspaper reporters, radio commentators, and television news investigators. These sources could be counted on to publicize the FBI's position on virtually any issue and to discredit the KKK and the CPUSA and even "the liberal press and the bleeding hearts."[9]

The roots of the White Hate Group counterintelligence program lay in Philadelphia, Mississippi. During a White House meeting in June 1964, President Johnson said, "Edgar, I want you to put people after the Klan and study it from one county to the next. I want the FBI to have the best intelligence system possible to check on the activities of these people." The question was not whether a counterintelligence program should be launched, but which FBI division should handle it. Division Five had responsibility for Klan matters, including informant and intelligence functions, until 1958, when Bureau executives transferred those responsibilities to the organized crime section of the General Intelligence Division. "One of the prime factors" in this original transfer was "the almost complete absence of Communist Party activity in the racial area." Since the Bureau did not consider the Klan subversive and the communists were nowhere in sight, the experts in Division Five were not needed. Alex Rosen's General Investigative Division handled the Philadelphia murders, not William Sullivan's Domestic Intelligence Division.[10]

By mid-summer 1964 the FBI found "the KKK and supporting groups" to be "essentially subversive" after all. "They hold principles and recommend courses of action that are [as] inimical to the Constitution as are the viewpoints of the Communist Party." The Bureau used the Red menace to justify the recommended transfer of Klan matters back to the Domestic Intelligence Division. The party's more recent focus on "the racial problem" indicated a "definite need for an intelligence type penetration of these racial and hate groups," and only one FBI unit could handle such a responsibility. Division Five agents had spied on "subversive organizations through informants, anonymous sources, sophisticated microphone and technical surveillances, interview programs of highly specialized nature, etc.," for years, and they "could put this experience to excellent use in penetrating the Klan." If prosecution of individual Klansmen for violating the Reconstruction Era statutes and other federal civil rights law remained "an ultimate objective," the Bureau now deemed "intelligence" and "informant" needs to be more pressing.[11]

Though hardly routine, the transfer was not unusual. FBI officials' notions of exactly what type of word or deed constituted subversion were constantly in flux. They not only debated whether the Klan was subversive, but many other groups as well—including CORE and SNCC and even SDS. As late as June 1965, the Chicago field office advised headquarters flatly and without fear of reprisal: "These are not subversive organizations." This sort of debate, however, had little, if any, impact on surveillance priorities. Katzenbach approved the Bureau request to tap SNCC's office telephone during the same month that the Chicago field office filed its report. The attorney general had approved a tap of the SDS telephone the previous month.[12]

Division Five proposed a counterintelligence program against the Ku Klux Klan at the end of August. Hoover quickly approved a directive targeting seventeen Klan groups and nine far-right hate groups, ranging from the American Nazi party to the National States Rights party. The names of several unaffiliated racists, people who referred to the G-men as "Nigger babysitters," were also included on the target list. Division Five intended "to expose, disrupt and otherwise neutralize the activities of the various Klan and hate organizations," to continue "the policy of aggressively seeking out persons addicted to violence even though they have not violated a Federal law as yet." Sullivan expected the results to rival "our accomplishments in similar-type programs directed against [communist] subversives."[13]

Even though Hoover disliked the Klan for making white supremacy disreputable, he would not have attacked it as he did on his own. Of all the FBI's counterintelligence programs—against the CPUSA and the Socialist Workers and eventually black nationalists, Puerto Rican nationalists, New Left activists, and Chicanos and Mexicans on both sides of the border—only the Klan effort resulted from outside pressure. The pressure came from the press and the White House, from Robert Kennedy and then from Nicholas Katzenbach, and from the civil rights movement itself. The proof can be found in the contrast between the FBI preference for the intelligence investigation and the counterintelligence action over the criminal investigation and courtroom prosecution.

When asked to protect civil rights workers, Hoover's FBI claimed limited jurisdiction, warned about the constitutional dangers of a national police force, and posed as a disinterested, apolitical, fact-gathering investigative agency. Yet, during the counterintelligence period, it swallowed "an intelligence offensive completely outside the forms of the law." The goal in both cases was not so much prosecution as intimidation. Only the means differed. (Hoover once told Martin Luther King "that the FBI had put the 'fear of God' in the Ku Klux Klan.") In the manner of its investigations of civil rights violations and more ambitious investigations of civil rights activists, the Bureau thus entrenched its intelligence and counterintelligence mission as an alternative to its law enforcement mission "in connection with activities unrelated to internal security."[14]

In the process, Hoover largely avoided a public clash with the police in the South, so the FBI's "buddy system" remained intact. By relying on extralegal action, he avoided the headaches of bringing routine cases of Klan harassment before white juries in the South. By pursuing the Klan wars outside the legal system and in a secretive way, he increased his authority to act without interference from the Justice Department's dreaded liberal lawyers. Movement people demanded protection and asked the government to enforce the civil rights conspiracy statutes, Sections 241 and 242. The Johnson administration prescribed a heavier dose of FBI surveillance. The movement sought the rule of law and received a lawless counterintelligence program.

Hoover closely proscribed the Klan wars nonetheless. During the life of the White Hate Group program (1964–1971), the FBI authorized 287 operations, or roughly 40 per year compared to the 100 plus of the Communist party program. Few disruptive actions, moreover, were undertaken against individuals who did not belong to the various Klan organizations. Nothing rivaled the open-ended COMINFIL (communist infiltration) investigations, where the Bureau targeted "legitimate mass organizations in the integration field." There were no KLANINFIL or KLUX-INFIL investigations, no effort to determine whether the Klan had infiltrated "legitimate mass organizations in the segregation field." As a general rule, the Bureau did not bring the Citizens Councils under conventional passive surveillance operations. "We have never had any formal investigation of the Mississippi Council," Burke Marshall complained. "We have also had no results from suggestions that the Bureau should keep itself informed in the same way it does with the Klan."[15]

Once Division Five began to implement COINTELPRO–White Hate Group in the months that followed Viola Liuzzo's murder, Hoover briefed Katzenbach on the FBI's accomplishments. The attorney general thanked the director for the "detailed information," but he kept pressuring him to do more. Hoover said

his men were "getting on the Klan—that this was well begun in
Alabama but had not been developed as far in Mississippi." He
promised to "pass on the order to intensify our efforts," and to
seize "every opportunity to disrupt the activities of Klan organizations." Over time, Katzenbach thought the FBI had done its
job, investigating, penetrating, and disrupting "activities of the
Ku Klux Klan . . . vigorously, actively, overtly and with outstanding success." But he made no effort to find out exactly how the
Bureau got on the Klan. How many "black bag jobs" (burglaries)
of Klan members' offices and homes did FBI agents carry out?
How many taps and bugs did they plant? The attorney general
never asked.[16]

The operations against the Klan legitimized the FBI's preferred response to all forms of dissent, since they paralleled the
more ambitious operations implemented first against Martin
Luther King and later against broad sectors of the black movement. Division Five, the driving force behind the Klan wars (just
as it had been in the campaign against King), exerted constant
pressure on the field to pursue the new mission. The field reacted ambivalently however. Roy Moore dismissed William Sullivan's plan to "embarrass" the Klan by placing a bogus order
for twelve cases of embalming fluid in the name of the
Mississippi-based Americans for the Preservation of the White
Race. Yet he reportedly authorized a number of operations too
extreme even for the COINTELPRO file. Rumors flourished concerning the kidnapping of a Klansman to help solve the firebombing of a black family's home. On another occasion, after
the Klan had threatened to kill any FBI man seen in Natchez,
Paul Cummings "organized a squad of G-men and headed for the
Klansmen's favorite bar." The KKKs did not come into the street
when called out, so Cummings shot the windows out of the bar.
"We were at war and we used some muscle," he said. The macho
appealed to Hoover. While a few fist fights broke out between
Klansmen and G-men, on the whole, the director bragged, the
Kukkers were "yellow," "afraid to 'mix' with our Agents." The
FBI could "outshoot and outfight" anybody, from Mafia soldiers
to Klan missionaries.[17]

In Charlotte, North Carolina, FBI agents experienced the same
ambivalence, sometimes resisting pressure from Division Five
and sometimes submitting proposals as controversial as William Sullivan's ideas. After the special agent in charge filed a
report about Klansmen donning dresses, padded bras, and wigs,

and strolling through black neighborhoods, Division Five ordered "a critical cartoon" prepared for release to a Crime Records source in the media. The SAC protested because it would "make 'heroes' of the Klan." A group of white men "willing and able to take steps to prevent the molestation of white women by Negroes would be heartily endorsed by most of the white population." The KKKs, hardly "shrinking violets," "homosexuals or transvestites," "did not indicate a 'desire' to wear female clothing." On the contrary, they were "eager to, and feel capable of, engaging Negroes in physical combat." On another occasion, the Charlotte office proposed to arrange for "this country's leading evangelist," a person whose name (Billy Graham?) was included on the FBI's Special Correspondents List, to preach a sermon on the Klan. Division Five liked the idea. Hoover vetoed it.[18]

Most counterintelligence operations involved physical, economic, and emotional harassment. When the Alabama Klan met for its national Konvocations, the Birmingham field office sent anonymous letters and placed last-minute phone calls canceling motel reservations. If a Klansman was a veteran and receiving benefits of any kind, Hoover sent his name to the Veterans Administration. Division Five published a joke book, *United Klowns of America* ("light in presentation," but "a serious effort at counterintelligence"), and established "a Bureau-approved vehicle for attacking Klan policies and disputes from a low-key, common sense, and patriotic position." Named the National Committee for Domestic Tranquillity, this organization had "chapters" in eleven states and published a regular bulletin "under the signature of Harmon Blennerhasset, an obscure figure in American history who gave financial support to Aaron Burr." The Bureau advised readers of the bulletin to quit the Klan and support "our boys" in Vietnam.[19]

The FBI pursued the two most notable Ku Klux Klan leaders, Sam Bowers of Mississippi's White Knights and Robert Shelton of the Alabama-based United Klans of America, with special zeal—but with nowhere near the ferocity that characterized the pursuit of Martin Luther King. Roy Moore called several meetings with his field agents to discuss how they might harass Bowers, and at headquarters Division Five had the IRS send over his tax returns. In Shelton's case, Division Five asked field agents in Alabama and Georgia for "a summary of information concerning [his] close associates, likes and dislikes, drinking habits, and social habits . . . his relationship with his wife, any other females or males." Bureau executives already knew Shelton did not like grits. They wanted to know more—facts, rumors, whatever. The information compiled did not have to be "accurate. . . . If [American Nazi party chief George Lincoln] Rockwell printed a report that Shelton had some Negro ancestors, it would [only] be necessary for us to know the names of certain ancestors who could, perhaps, have been an illegitimate child related to Shelton."[20]

Shelton had enough problems with the House Committee on Un-American Activities; a Division Five agent wrote those words about "Negro ancestors" two days after HUAC chairman Edwin Willis (D., La.) asked the House to cite the imperial wizard for contempt of Congress. Shelton had refused to cooperate with the Committee's investigation of the Klan—an investigation supported by the Johnson administration and the FBI and opposed by the civil rights movement on the grounds that HUAC's real interests lay elsewhere. While the Bureau directed the Committee to an ex-agent who Willis hired to head up a fact-gathering team, the movement wondered whether the Klan hearings would be followed by hearings on their own organizations. SNCC's Charles Cobb remembered a visit to Washington and a side trip to the Hill, where he wandered into HUAC's offices. "They had charts right on the wall. I mean, our names and photographs graphed out and where we were in SNCC or CORE or SCLC." After a wiretap revealed Southern Christian Leadership Conference concern, Hoover ordered the Un-American Activities Committee alerted "as a matter of cooperation."[21]

The FBI helped HUAC with its investigation after Willis met with DeLoach in March 1965, the same month Viola Liuzzo died, and admitted his Committee had "no information currently concerning Klans." DeLoach gave Willis a Division Five document, entitled "The Klan Today," and worked out a more ambitious delimitations agreement two months later—principally because the staff investigators HUAC had sent into Alabama and Mississippi were interfering with the Bureau's work. When Willis agreed to keep his people out of the South, the FBI agreed to provide information on Klan members "so that the Committee can intelligently question the individuals when they are on the witness stand." In Hoover's view, the HUAC investigation raised only one substantive problem: "We will be doing all of the digging and staff of House committee will take the bows." Both the Committee and the FBI wanted the credit for destroying the un-

Americanism of the Ku Klux Klan. Neither sought credit for protecting the equally un-American civil rights movement from Klan violence.[22]

While pursuing its counterintelligence assaults against the Ku Klux Klan, the FBI played a role in several civil suits and criminal prosecutions. One of the most important cases, outside of the Philadelphia murders, involved the shooting of Lemuel A. Penn, director of adult and vocational education for Washington's public schools and a lieutenant colonel in the Army Reserve, who died in rural Georgia while driving with two other black officers. Penn was on his way home after a two week tour at Fort Benning when a Klansman noticed the District of Columbia tags. "Must be some of President Johnson's boys," he said. "Out of town niggers." Hoover learned of the incident while returning to Washington himself, having just opened the new FBI office in Jackson. Calling it "cold-blooded murder," he assigned eighty-three agents to the case under Assistant Director Joseph J. Casper's direction. Those agents quickly arrested a small group of Ku Klux Klansmen, and Georgia authorities tried two of them in state court for murder. With defense counsel attacking a "carpet-bagging administration of justice" headed up by a horde of FBI agents "infiltrating our land" in search of "white meat," an all-white jury found both Klansmen not guilty.

That decision, Hoover suggested, privately, was in part the FBI's fault. The agents assigned to the Penn case "made it known" that the Bureau would trade cash for information, an offer that "created suspicion upon part of jury against FBI." "I didn't know that FBI had become an arm of the 'poverty campaign,'" the director complained, in a revealing comment, upon learning of his agents' actions in Georgia. He intended to smash the Klan in a way that would not align his Bureau in the mind of the white South with the cause of the civil rights movement— or the larger cause of liberalism. Eventually, in two trials in federal court, two Klansmen were convicted and four other acquitted of violating the Reconstruction Era statute for their actions on the day Lemuel Penn died.[23]

Hoover's men had other successes. In Bogalusa, Louisiana, an area where the FBI had been collecting intelligence on the Ku Klux Klan since the mid-1920s, a federal judge issued an injunction against segregationist violence ("an act of the Nation against a klan") based primarily on the results of a massive FBI investigation.[24] Roy Moore set up a field post in nearby Hattiesburg, Mississippi, to investigate the murder of Vernon Dahmer, a black farmer and leader in the state NAACP who died when terrorists firebombed his home. FBI agents arrested fourteen Klansmen in connection with that murder. They made additional arrests when investigating bombing incidents in Mc-Comb, Mississippi, and New Bern, North Carolina.[25] Because the prospect of convicting a segregationist in any southern court, state or federal, remained problematic, the FBI escalated its intelligence and counterintelligence functions while pursuing indictments against specific Klansmen. The Bureau fully mobilized its law enforcement function only in those cases, such as the Penn and Dahmer murders and especially the Liuzzo murder, that attracted major media coverage.

The media itself represented the third battleground in the Klan wars. A media campaign enabled the FBI to publicize its accomplishments on the other fronts, and for Hoover it was a natural direction to move. Few Americans paid more attention to public opinion. Even fewer had tried to influence national politics over such a long period of time. Back in the 1940s, Senator George Norris (R., Neb.) called Hoover "the greatest publicity hound on the American continent." In the 1960s, John Kennedy described him as one of "the three masters of public relations in the last half century," along with financier Bernard Baruch and CIA Director Allen Dulles.[26] Hoover knew his task would be difficult. In the wake of Selma, the nation would not only take pride in destroying the Ku Klux Klan, but the entire segregationist apparatus. The new consensus had no patience for the Jim Crow sign let alone the Klansman's rope, and yet the FBI director, with his record of lethargic civil rights enforcement, charges of communist influence in the civil rights movement, and feud with Martin Luther King, was firmly allied in the minds of civil rights activists—and many other Americans as well—with the old and now thoroughly discredited order. Hoover would continue his opposition to the black cause, but for the time being his principal task was to improve the FBI's image.

Hoover used all the media skills he had acquired over the years. He had worked tirelessly to promote his Bureau's politics and reputation since his tenure as General Intelligence Division czar. In 1927 Franklin Dodge, a former agent, helped Senator Thomas J. Walsh (D., Mont.) document Hoover's history of granting "writers, who wrote articles that met with the Bureau's approval," "desk space" and access to "the radical files."[27] Hoover moved into radio in the early 1930s with *The Lucky Strike Hour*, a program that recounted Bureau exploits. During the New Deal years, he established the FBI building as one of the principal tourist attractions in the capital. Bureau displays treated the public to such sights as a plastic replica of Dillinger's death mask and the fingerprints of prominent Americans. The director kept everything up to date. When his favored ghostwriter, Courtney Ryley Cooper, committed suicide in 1940, the Bureau pulled his prints from the exhibit room and replaced them with Walt Disney's. The fingerprints were symbolic. Hoover cultivated support from prominent Americans systematically. People as diverse as Bruce Barton, America's first advertising and sales guru, and William Allen White, the Republican editor of the *Emporia* (Ka.) *Gazette*, sat in his "cheering section."[28]

FBI agents assigned to the Crime Records Division, under Louis Nichols and then Cartha DeLoach and Thomas Bishop, supervised these efforts to enhance the FBI's image and to promote the menace of crime and communism. Special agents in charge of the various field offices established ties with the media, and as well business leaders, law enforcement officers, mayors, and other prominent public officials in their respective cities. Following the establishment of the first counterintelligence program against the Communist party in 1956, Crime Records developed its Mass Media Program, a program that Bureau executive James B. Adams described as a modest effort "to get the truth out, to get a proper picture of the FBI's jurisdiction, its activities."[29]

By the early 1960s Crime Records had arranged extensive media coverage of the FBI's accomplishments, such as they were, as an equal-opportunity employer. On occasion, the Division had unexpected allies in publicizing the Bureau's record in the civil rights field. Hoping to manipulate Hoover with praise, Robert Kennedy urged his brother to mention the FBI in his 1962 state of the union address. "It would make a big difference for us," the attorney general said. More often, Crime Records mobilized its own allies. All special agents in charge received ten copies of Hoover's article in the August 1963 edition of *Yale Political* magazine, "The FBI's Role in the Field of Civil Rights," for distribution to "civil rights leaders." DeLoach had already sent copies to all "SAC contacts" and "other special friends of the Bureau." At the same time, said *St. Louis Globe-Democrat* reporter Patrick J. Buchanan, who would go on to serve the Nixon White

House during Watergate and the Reagan White House during the Iran-Contra scandal: "The FBI channeled up constant information on local Communists, radicals, and even national civil-rights leaders." The director never forgot his real enemies.[30]

As the movement criticized the FBI's civil rights record more effectively, Crime Records became more aggressive. Cartha De-Loach had lunch in February 1964 with Drew Pearson and Jack Anderson, the investigative columnists who at one time received preferential treatment but were by then on the Bureau's not-to-contact list. When they asked about civil rights, they heard De-Loach mention Hoover's recent interview with "a cub reporter from the 'Afro-American,'" and then sat and listened to a monologue:

> I told Pearson of the Director's insistence that there be no discrimination in the FBI and of the rapid progress made by a number of Negro Agents in our organization. I told him . . . of my association with Negroes in The American Legion, of the FBI's sponsorship of a boy scout troop at the Juvenile Training Center where 90% of the membership is Negroes, and of the fact that our Civil Rights investigations have always been very clear-cut and incisive.

"Jack Anderson spoke up at this point," according to DeLoach's account of the conversation, and said "he felt the Director would go down in history for the protection of civil rights. Pearson agreed and stated the Director's record in this regard was very clear."[31]

DeLoach also tried to cultivate contact with the black press. The case of C. Sumner Stone, Jr., of the *Chicago Defender* provides an example. Describing Stone in 1963–1964 as a "reliable contact," DeLoach gave him a scoop on the arrest of Medgar Evers's assassin, arranged an exclusive interview with Hoover, and provided other services. Whenever Stone needed something he would telephone DeLoach ("a very likable guy"). After the *Defender* fired him in 1964, for jeopardizing the paper's advertising revenue by criticizing Chicago Mayor Richard Daley, Stone went to work for Congressman Adam Clayton Powell and continued to receive services from the FBI—with DeLoach once running a name check on one of the persons invited to attend the First Black Power Conference. Stone wanted the FBI to check for any "communist connections," and that was the last time he remembered hearing from DeLoach.[32]

In the wake of the Philadelphia and Selma murders, Crime Records again escalated its public relations. Concentrating on conservative white newspapermen and not blacks like Sumner Stone, DeLoach sent Walter Winchell twelve blind memos regarding "the outstanding work the FBI has done under Mr. Hoover's leadership." With Hoover's feud with Dr. King spinning out of control, Winchell reciprocated by sending the director information on the civil rights leader. (Winchell had been doing this sort of thing since the 1940s, when he sent in dirt on Paul Robeson.) From there, Hoover granted David Lawrence an exclusive interview, giving him the FBI version of what he and King had said during their much-publicized meeting. The director hoped to counter a critical story in *Newsweek* magazine with a piece in Lawrence's *U.S. News and World Report*. Lawrence, like Winchell, was one of Hoover's favorites. His syndicated column had run in the *Washington Star* since 1918, and in 1919 he received an advance copy of a lengthy General Intelligence Division memo that questioned the loyalty of Negro newspaper and magazine editors. In the 1960s he received an edited version of Division Five's Current Intelligence Analysis.[33]

Other Crime Records activities included assistance with the preparation and publication of an article, "The FBI's Secret War Against the Ku Klux Klan," for *Reader's Digest*. DeLoach then had Senator Karl Mundt (R., S.D.) insert the piece into the *Congressional Record*. "People are amazed," Hoover told Katzenbach, "when I begin to tell them of the things that have been done."[34] The director contributed an article of his own, "The Resurgent Klan," for the *American Bar Association Journal*. Besides arranging for publicity and distribution of this piece, Crime Records found time to help prepare a children's book—*Kids' Letters to the FBI*—and to help David Sentner, Andrew Tully, and Harry and Bonaro Overstreet with more serious books on the Bureau and its achievements in the civil rights and other fields. Tully concluded a section on "Civil Rights and Civil Wrongs" with a chapter entitled "A Look at the Record." Chapter twenty ("That Bitch Is Dead . . . ") focused on the Liuzzo murder and the Klan wars.[35]

Most Crime Records projects were covert. FBI publicists camouflaged their activities with great care under DeLoach's mentor, Louis Nichols. He was the "master," Lawrence Heim said. "Nobody can track Nichols." Nichols recorded his contacts with newsmen in memos marked FOR ADMINISTRATIVE

PURPOSES TO BE DESTROYED AFTER ACTION IS TAKEN AND NOT SENT TO FILES, and he also tried to control the paper record outside the Bureau. When *Reader's Digest* editor Fulton Oursler died, Nichols asked Oursler's widow to purge her husband's papers, before donating them to a college library, of the "numerous [FBI] memoranda" that had been furnished "over the years." DeLoach, more flamboyant than Nichols, left tracks everywhere. His leaks to journalists include the following greeting to *Chicago Tribune* Washington bureau chief Walter Trohan in a letter about a minister at the St. Luke African Methodist Episcopal Church in East Chicago, Indiana: "Hi Comrade: This is certainly a person who should be exposed."[36]

One of DeLoach's most ambitious projects involved a publicity drive as Hoover's feud with King moved into the public arena. After receiving his orders—"the Director has instructed that we have friendly news sources use an approved blind memorandum which sets forth the FBI's numerous accomplishments in the civil rights field"—DeLoach went to work. He convinced some of the nation's most prestigious conservative newsmen to come to bat for the Bureau—among others, Jeremiah O'Leary of the *Washington Star*, Ed O'Brien of Newhouse Newspapers, Ray McHugh of the Copley chain, Warren Rogers of the *New York Journal-American*, David Lawrence of *U.S. News and World Report*, and Hearst columnist Fulton Lewis, Jr. Lewis's column alone appeared in "approximately 318 newspapers." Clyde Tolson had read an advance copy and was quite pleased. Lewis also used the FBI-prepared material on his national radio program.[37]

For DeLoach, this was routine. He did it again during the summer of 1965 in response to Joseph Rauh's criticisms in a speech before the National Student Association. Rauh said Hoover was the wrong man for the job of enforcing federal civil rights law. When Tolson read the speech, he told DeLoach to do his job. The first reporter contacted, Miriam Ottenberg of the *Washington Star*, had supported the director on a number of previous occasions, most recently in a February 23, 1965, *Look* magazine article, "What's Ahead for the FBI." Crime Records promised to "prevail on her" once again. Tolson wanted an article by the weekend. In the meantime, DeLoach "sent material . . . to a number of columnists including . . . Paul Harvey, Bob Allen of the *Hall Syndicate*, Ray Cromley of Newspaper Enterprise Association, [and] Ed Mow[e]ry of General Features and the Newhouse chain." "That was the system we had," Crime Records agent

Lawrence Heim remembered. "If somebody came out with something erroneous about the Bureau, we were going to correct it. . . . We would put out the correction to as many people as we could.[38]

With or without Cartha DeLoach, Crime Records always corrected people like Joe Rauh. Rauh recalled his review of Max Lowenthal's book on the FBI in the *Washington Post* back in 1950, a review that had noted Hoover's attempt to ingratiate himself with southern congressmen by playing up his own segregationist credentials. "The first thing that happens is Justice [Felix] Frankfurter calls me up and says, 'Honestly, Joe'—that's the way he talked—'Honestly, Joe, that's the best thing that could have happened. Somebody had to say all that. I think you're absolutely great.' I'm feeling top of the world. I go to the football game, the Redskin game, and over the loudspeaker its says, 'This is a great afternoon for the Redskins—J. Edgar Hoover is attending the game.' I went home and told my wife. I said 'We're in. Hoover didn't even think enough to spend the afternoon smearing me.' How wrong I was. At 12:00 the next afternoon, Senator Bourke Hickenlooper [R., Iowa] takes the floor, my whole FBI file is spilled all over it. What I forgot when he was at the game, was that there were fifty assistants doing the work."[39]

The FBI kept coming back to Rauh—in 1965 after the National Student Association speech and again eight years after that. In anticipation of Rauh's testimony at the Senate confirmation hearings on Hoover's proposed successor, L. Patrick Gray III, Bureau executives prepared a seven-page blind memo for another group of friendly reporters because they expected Rauh to raise the civil rights specter once again.[40] By that time DeLoach had been out of the Bureau for three years, and Crime Records had been renamed the External Affairs Division.

The public relations machine ran before DeLoach came to the FBI and it ran after he left; but DeLoach served at a time when the FBI had more things to sell than ever before, and Hoover greatly appreciated his efforts. Promoted in December 1965 to the rank of assistant to the director, DeLoach's responsibilities broadened to include supervision of Division Five. Opinions concerning DeLoach vary, but all agreed that he represented power. Hearst reporter Jim Bishop described him as the "abbot" of the FBI "monastery" and "the coolest man under stress I had ever seen." Edwin Guthman said he never trusted DeLoach. "I was fully warned about him" by "other people in the Bureau, field agents who were friends of mine." Andrew Young said he had "almost a kind of fascist mentality." Joe Rauh said if you were a liberal and you met him (or any of his Crime Records agents), so was he. "These guys, when they saw you, you were really a fine fellow. 'Hail and well met' type of stuff. . . . A lot of people were fooled." When DeLoach received his promotion, Martin Luther King, who was not fooled, sent an ingratiating telegram nonetheless. "It makes me doubly proud," King wrote, in his own hand, "to know that a fellow Georgian has been elevated to such a key position in the federal government."[41]

To counter the adverse publicity regarding civil rights cases in the South, the Crime Records Division commissioned its most notable 1960s' project, the ABC television show *The FBI*. "We finally decided," DeLoach explained, "to clarify for the public what the FBI does. We're simply an investigative agency. We can't protect people—like civil rights workers, for instance. There's some confusion about what we do and I hope this program will show people how we really work." Crime Records routinely rejected scripts on police brutality or any other phase of civil rights responsibilities. David W. Rintels, who went on to chair a Writers Guild committee on censorship, chose a plot based on the bombing of Birmingham's Sixteenth Street Baptist Church when asked to write an episode for the series. After checking with the FBI, the producers told him "they would be delighted to have me write about a church bombing subject only to these stipulations: The church must be in the North, there could be no Negroes involved, and the bombing could have nothing at all to do with civil rights."[42]

Hoover and DeLoach worked out the arrangement for the television series with James Hagerty, ABC's president and Dwight Eisenhower's former press secretary; Jack Warner of Warner Brothers; and Quinn Martin, producer of *The Untouchables*. (The director considered *The Untouchables* "rotten from every view point.") They struck the deal in December 1964, two weeks after Hoover met with King, when Warner Brothers and ABC purchased motion picture and television rights to Hoover's book on the communist menace, *Masters of Deceit*, for $75,000, plus $500 for each television episode during the second and each subsequent year of production. Thanks to the promotional efforts of DeLoach and Nichols, *Masters of Deceit* was a best-seller. Among other efforts, Crime Records worked with the anticommunist

Operation Alert in the early fall of 1961 to distribute 5,500 copies to freshmen entering South Carolina colleges and universities.[43] But neither the book's subject matter nor format lent itself to television or the big screen. No network or motion picture company every filmed under the *Masters of Deceit* rubric. Warner and Hagerty, nonetheless, had ingratiated themselves with Hoover by guaranteeing him a profit. *The FBI* began its nine-year, Ford Motor Company-sponsored run on ABC television in September 1965, with Crime Records maintaining control over scripts, personnel, and sponsorship.[44]

Another major Crime Records project involved a book on the Philadelphia murders by Don Whitehead, a writer with a history of telling the story of Hoover's bureaucracy. Louis Nichols first brought him in for "a special project" in the mid-1950s, after investigating his "character, reputation and loyalty." The Crime Records chief needed someone to write a history of the FBI, and Whitehead seemed to be the best candidate. He received a United States Army Medal of Freedom for his combat reporting in North Africa and Europe during World War II, and his work as a feature writer after the war won two Pulitzer prizes. In March 1956, upon winding up his special FBI project, he joined the *New York Herald Tribune* as its Washington bureau chief. Whitehead's *FBI Story,* published later in the year by Random House, remained on the best-seller list for thirty-eight weeks, and at least 170 newspapers ran excerpts. When Whitehead sold the books' movie rights to Warner Brothers, Hoover and Nichols accompanied him to the closing. James Stewart ("Special Agent Chip Hardesty"—starred in the movie.

Whitehead began his next Crime Records project in 1964, a series of articles for the Associated Press on the FBI's handling of civil rights matters. Crime Records set him up with desk space at the seat of government and asked Hoover to grant an interview. "Don is anxious to do a good story in order to assist the Director and the FBI," DeLoach advised. Hoover granted the interview on December 1, only a few minutes after meeting with King. The director talked for fifty minutes about his weight and having to give up chocolate cream pie, his "long and close friendship" with Lyndon Johnson, his "strained" relationship with Robert Kennedy, his trip to Jackson, Mississippi ("without the knowledge of Robert Kennedy"), his "thoroughly" enjoyable statement labeling King "the most notorious liar in the country," and his assessment of the "tricky decisions" of the Warren

Court—"the type that interferes capriciously with efficient law enforcement."[45]

From there, Whitehead, DeLoach, and "officials of 'Reader's Digest'" began planning the book on the Philadelphia murders. *Reader's Digest* intended to publish a condensed version of *Attack on Terror* and have a subsidiary company, Funk and Wagnalls, publish the hardback. Crime Records agents set Whitehead up with desk space once again, pulled files, reviewed chapter drafts and galley proofs. Hoover complained about Joseph Sullivan and the other agents who worked on the case receiving too many accolades ("the Bureau is a 'We' organization not an 'I' organization"); but the book had redeeming features. Whitehead, as Crime Records agent Milton Jones pointed out, "deals briefly with the antics of the Mississippi Freedom Democratic Party at the August, 1964, Democratic National Convention in Atlantic City." The FBI Recreation Association bought 2,000 copies, and Whitehead remained close to the director. Whenever he traveled, an FBI agent from the nearest field office met him at the airport with a car. When he checked into Emory University Hospital in 1972 for surgery, Hoover sent flowers.[46] Years later, after Hoover died, FBI Director Clarence Kelley struck a deal with Quinn Martin for a full-length feature film based on Whitehead's book for the CBS television *Thursday Night at the Movies. Attack on Terror* premiered on February 21–22, 1975, and enraged Michael Schwerner's father, who responded with a one-page article ("Mississippi: Whitewashing the FBI") in a civil liberties magazine with a tiny circulation; and former Neshoba County Sheriff Lawrence Rainey, who filed (and lost) a lawsuit.[47]

DeLoach resigned from the FBI the same year Whitehead's book appeared. He went to work for Richard Nixon's friend, Donald Kendall, at Pepsico, and Paul Harvey said the stock market jumped thirteen points on his first day in the world of free enterprise. Pontificating in his usual style, Harvey was trying to make a point about DeLoach's remarkable skills. In the civil rights field, however, even such Bureau friends as Harvey realized that DeLoach had failed to accomplish his purpose. While Crime Records worked to establish a heroic image, events reinforced the lingering image of FBI agents standing off to the side, notebooks and pencils in hand, while movement people suffered harassments and beatings and much worse. These problems of image emerged from the tragic events of Selma.

Hoover's men had solved the Viola Liuzzo murder so quickly because they had a paid informant among the Klansmen in the murder car. The questions arising from that fact, questions about the Bureau's ability to control its own operatives and possible use of *agents provocateur*, cut across the ideological lines that separated the civil rights movement from its more civilized enemies, and remained to haunt the FBI for the next twenty years. Even such staunch allies as Fulton Lewis, Jr., an active participant in DeLoach's Mass Media Program who had defended the Bureau regularly since the school desegregation crisis at Little Rock Central, wondered why the FBI man in the car had not tried to prevent Liuzzo's murder. Didn't he have a moral obligation to do something, Lewis asked?[48]

The movement's friends in the government expected no such problems. If they had, Lyndon Johnson might not have arranged his dramatic announcement on national television and Ramsey Clark might not have applauded the FBI for doing an "incredible job" in breaking the Liuzzo case. There was even praise from within the movement. "The Agents assigned to Alabama," Dr. King told Hoover, "have done an outstanding job." Although his comments came before the government announced the informant's presence, King had spoken on an earlier occasion about the need to work "within secret groups" to find out "what is going on in conspiratorial racist circles." Similarly, James Wechsler of the *New York Post* called for the FBI to infiltrate the Ku Klux Klan and its fronts. "If only a fraction of the FBI manpower dedicated to the care and feeding of the Communist treasury had been allocated to undercover work in the rightist network," he wrote, "perhaps at least a few of the more deadly Southern explosions might have been forestalled."[49]

John Doar knew better. "You take informants as they come. You and I might have saved Mrs. Liuzzo's life, but you or I could never become FBI informants." That comment was right on the mark. It was difficult to recruit Ku Klux Klan informants in the rural areas where the Klan flourished, and the FBI took them as they came. A Laurel, Mississippi, agent compared the recruiting process to hunting quail. "Once the covey has scattered, you look for the singles." Hoover's men compensated by loosening standards. "The Bureau is willing," Assistant Director Fred J. Baumgardner noted, "to pay an informant to give you negative information, that nothing is going to happen or that nothing is going on." Informants would be dismissed if they drank too much or if they engaged in "sex perversion," and headquarters would not put "a screwball" on the payroll. "Most of them," Crime Records agent Harold Leinbaugh said, "were unguided missiles. You can't tell a criminal informant too much. You hope and pray a lot. He's probably not too bright, he's certainly unreliable, but you've got to . . . hook him somewhere." Baumgardner was more direct: Informants "did not have to be lily white."[50]

Gary Thomas Rowe, the FBI informer who rode with Collie Leroy Wilkins, Eugene Thomas, and William O. Eaton the day they murdered Viola Liuzzo, was not lily white. "He couldn't be an angel and be a good informant," one of the FBI handlers explained. Rowe grew up in Savannah, Georgia, married a nurse at sixteen, and moved to Birmingham where he joined the Eastview Klavern of the Alabama Knights and was recruited as an informant by special agent Barrett Kemp. A big man who suffered bouts of macho fantasy, Rowe liked to fight and sit on bar stools. When he began collecting his stipend, a little over $400 per month, plus expenses, an agent told him "the FBI took no position on the question of segregation or integration." The Bureau only wanted intelligence, particularly information regarding violence. It was not "our policy," Division Five agent Fred Woodcock reiterated, "to ask the informant to engage in any forms of violence." On the other hand, the FBI knew that only a tiny "inner group" of Klansmen in any given Klavern engaged in violent acts. If the informant failed to "get selected for the inner group . . . he may never know what is actually going on."[51]

In Rowe's case, that was not a problem. The FBI's principal source of information on the Klan in the Birmingham area from 1960–1965, Rowe attained a position in the Klan's own Bureau of Investigation, and he said the FBI instructed him to be "where the action was." He led a Klan attack squad when the Freedom Riders arrived in Birmingham and accompanied the two Klansmen who smashed radio newsman and "SAC contact" Clancy Lake's car window. The first person to put in a call to the police that Mother's Day, Lake was broadcasting on the car radio when Rowe and the others approached, tore his microphone out of the dashboard, pulled him out of the car, and nearly beaned him with a lead pipe. After things had quieted down around the bus station, Rowe returned in search of black people to beat up, this time receiving all he could handle—including a knife slash on the throat. For the day's work Rowe received a $125 bonus from the FBI, plus medical expenses. The cut took eight stitches.[52]

Rowe went out regularly for missionary work—boarding buses and kicking people, raiding the home of a white family raising a black child, entering integrated restaurants and even an amusement park and beating blacks "severely . . . with black jacks, chains, pistols." There were rumors of Rowe's involvement in the firebombing of the home of a wealthy black Birmingham resident, A. G. Gaston, the detonating of shrapnel bombs in black neighborhoods, and the murder of a black man in 1963 during the spring demonstrations. There was even some speculation that FBI agents in Birmingham helped cover up Rowe's involvment in segregationist terror because he was such a good informant. Rowe reported on all the violence, as well as the regular stuff—the cross-burning rallies, the conversations about "Jews and Dagos" and fluoridated water and movie stars changing their names, and his Klavern's showing of *Birth of a Nation*, D. W. Griffith's eulogy to the Klan. The projector kept breaking down, he said. Rowe also alerted the FBI to a Klan plot to assassinate Fred Shuttlesworth, a tip that may have saved Rev. Shuttlesworth's life. The segregationist who allegedly volunteered to kill Shuttlesworth, John Wesley Hall, later joined Gary Thomas Rowe as an FBI informant.[53]

Within six months of the Liuzzo murder, the FBI operated nearly 2,000 informants, 20 percent of overall Klan and other white hate group membership, including a grand dragon in one southern state. Bureau agents set up and financed one Klavern, with an exclusive, charter membership of informants, to siphon recruits from regular Klan groups. Eventually, the Klavern grew to 250 members. (FBI officials were only slightly less enthusiastic in their quest for a substitute and acceptable Klan leadership as they were in their quest for a substitute and acceptable black leadership.) When Hoover told Katzenbach and White House aide Marvin Watson that his men had been developing two "informants and sources" per day, the attorney general said he hoped it might be possible "at some point . . . to place these achievements on the public record, so that the Bureau can receive its due credit."[54]

Crime Records was taking care of that; but it was a sensitive business because dozens of Klan informants rivaled the controversial Gary Rowe. One informant, when addressing a Klan rally attended by thousands, predicted "peace and order in America" even "if we have to kill every Negro." Another informant, a key witness in the Neshoba County case, Delmar Dennis of Meridian, was a bona fide member of the John Birch Society. When the House Committee on Un-American Activities requested his presence during its Klan investigation, he worked with Roy Moore's men to avoid the subpoena. The FBI thought HUAC might jeopardize the trial of Bowers, Price, and the others, so agents from the Jackson field office reportedly pushed Dennis's empty car down a thirty-five foot slope and into a creek, helped Dennis get back in, and then waited for someone to spot the wreck and call an ambulance. After Dennis wired HUAC from a hospital bed, Committee staff said they would get back to him. They never did.[55]

A number of other informants posed a threat after they broke cover and discovered they could no longer count on the FBI. One bitter ex-informant, who said his reputation as "a 'Nigger Lover'" cost him his home and job in Georgia, asked Robert Kennedy for help in finding "a more democratic environment." He even offered to "take a civilian job in Viet Nam." The man turned to Kennedy because he considered it "useless to ask the F.B.I. to assist," complaining that "they use a person then desert them when they are through regardless of the predicament it leaves you in."[56]

FBI officials did not desert Gary Rowe. Their initial reaction to the murder on Highway 80 had less to do with Rowe, a live informer with a history of involvement in violence against civil rights workers, than whether there was something in the history of Mrs. Liuzzo, a movement martyr, that might be considered derogatory. Upon completing name checks on Viola Liuzzo and her husband, Anthony, Hoover's phone started ringing. Katzenbach called first, a few hours before President Johnson planned to announce the arrests. He wanted to know if there was anything in the files that might prove embarrassing to the president once the television people turned off their klieg lights.

What had the FBI found out? "The man doesn't have too good a background"—he was a Teamster business agent—"and the woman had indications of needle marks in her arms." "[She] was sitting very, very close to the Negro in the car," Hoover added. "It had the appearance of a necking party." The president called a few minutes later and the director elaborated. "I don't say the man has a bad character but he is well known as a Teamster strongarm man." Mrs. Liuzzo may have "been taking dope although we can't say that definitely because she is dead."[57] The autopsy said nothing about needle tracking anywhere on the body, and that fact slowed Hoover. When sending additional information to the White House and the Civil Rights Division, he left out most—but not all—of the voyeuristic speculation that revealed more about himself and his Bureau than the victim and her husband. "They didn't like Mrs. Liuzzo," Lee White remembered. "In their description of her she didn't come off looking like a virtuous woman."[58]

Where Hoover's reports were not absurd, they were soft, and so President Johnson ignored them. Viola Liuzzo had been arrested once, in June 1964, for refusing to send her children to school. She was protesting a Michigan law allowing children to drop out of school at age sixteen. The court's probation department described her as "emotionally disturbed," and she had received psychiatric treatment at one point. Letters found in her car after the shooting also indicated an emotional involvement in the movement.[59] FBI officials' interest in Anthony Liuzzo led to a check with the Detroit Police Department regarding the funeral—because they expected various labor leaders (Hoffa and Reuther) and movement people (King and Wilkins) to attend. Later, when Liuzzo complained about the refusal of Alabama authorities to release the family car, which he had to make payments on, or his wife's wedding ring, Hoover said he "seems more interested in cash . . . than in grief."[60] Nothing in any of the FBI's reports imperiled the dramatic announcement the president had planned. The director kept digging, but even he expected to find nothing. Viola Liuzzo was neither promiscuous nor a drug user. The worst anyone could say was that she left her husband and children behind (temporarily) for duty on the movement's front line in Selma.

The FBI apparently did not leak much on the Liuzzos beyond a few items to Klan informants and one or two newspaper reporters. But on March 31, six days after Mrs. Liuzzo's death, Crime Records did brief Douglas Smith, an aide to Congressman George W. Andrews (D., Ala.), on James Farmer of CORE, John Lewis of SNCC, and Hosea Williams of SCLC. "An urgent request from Governor George Wallace," Smith said, had "precipitated" his visit to the Bureau in search of "information indicat-

ing communist connections on the part of civil rights leaders."
The public-source data supplied by the FBI, he added, "would
not satisfy the Governor."[61]

The segregationists, in contrast to the FBI, remained anxious
to use anything to discredit the civil rights movement. Another
Alabama politician, Sheriff Jim Clark of Dallas County, a man
who often greeted would-be black voters in Selma with electric
cattle prods and organized the brutal police assault on Bloody
Sunday, received more detailed help from his fellow policemen
in Michigan. The FBI collected most of its information on the
Liuzzos from the Detroit police, and one officer, the head of the
criminal intelligence bureau, sent copies of the reports to Marvin G. Lane, police commissioner of suburban Warren and former captain of detectives in the Detroit Police Department. Commissioner Lane sent the reports to Sheriff Clark,who told a UPI
reporter that Liuzzo's murder might have been averted if the
FBI had alerted his office. "They had a carload of Ku Klux
Klansmen under surveillance" and did not tell anybody, he said.
The Bureau issued a rebuttal, but quickly dropped the matter to
avoid a feud with the sheriff. When the Detroit police reports
ended up in Clark's hands, Hoover quietly blackballed all members of Lane's department from the FBI National Academy.[62]

Clark's comment about the carload of Ku Kluxers was revealing; because the FBI's man was in the murder car, even the segregationists suggested the FBI was somehow responsible for Liuzzo's death. For Hoover, this represented the beginning of a
major public relations problem, but he had no idea how to respond—beyond his wild swing at Warren police officers, men
who had nothing to do with Sheriff Clark or Commissioner
Lane's indiscretion. DeLoach and his Crime Records agents
were not necessarily of much use here.

The prosecution of Collie Leroy Wilkins and the other Klansmen who killed Viola Liuzzo also created public relations problems for the FBI. On the matter of legal representation, Gary
Rowe's attorney of record, Matt Murphy, was a Klan attorney,
an "Imperial Klonsel." Once the Bureau and the Justice Department removed the client from that attorney-client relationship,
Murphy sued Rowe to recover fees of $6,000 for professional ser-
vices allegedly rendered. The FBI's Mobile field office responded by proposing a leak to HUAC to publicize "the role of
the subversive lawyer in promulgating the aims of the KKK."[63]
Next, Rowe faced indictment for murder. Eventually, in the fall

of 1978, a Lowndes County grand jury acted against Rowe, contending that he had fired the murder weapon. Finally, the prospects of convicting the three other KKKs in state court were remote. With the prestige of the FBI and the Justice Department at stake, Hoover and Katzenbach "both felt that if we only got disagreement" among the members of the jury "it would be a victory."[64]

FBI agents in Alabama checked jury panels, defense attorneys, and state prosecutors, looking for ties to the Citizens Council or the Klan. Civil Rights Division attorney St. John Barrett put in the request for a check on Arthur Gamble, the Lowndes County circuit solicitor. Barrett wanted "to know what kind of prosecutor Gamble is; whether or not he is or has been affiliated with organizations such as Klan groups; and any information concerning his background which might indicate what kind of a job he will do."[65] The FBI expected Gamble to do a good job, and he did; but the three Klansmen, Wilkins, Thomas, and Eaton, escaped conviction. "Do you know those big black niggers were driven by the woman?" Matt Murphy asked the jurors, in a manner reminiscent of Hoover's necking party innuendo. "One white woman and these niggers. Right there. Riding right through your county." When the first trial ended in a hung jury in May 1965, the FBI tried to identify the two jurors who had voted for acquittal.[66] At the second trial in October, another jury acquitted Wilkins. The FBI encountered embarrassment during this trial in the form of defense attorney Arthur J. Hanes, former mayor of Birmingham and FBI agent who replaced Murphy, who died in a car crash, after the first trial.

"I was hired by these boys," Hanes said, "but as far as I know the Klan had nothing to do with paying me." FBI executives in Washington weren't so sure. Hanes was a pallbearer at Murphy's funeral, as the Crime Record Division painfully noted, and he went on to represent Martin Luther King's assassin, James Earl Ray, for a short time. Hoover said Hanes was "no good," "a very strong supporter" of Bull Connor "in the use of police dogs," "a fellow who has certainly a strong smell of the Klan about him." Hanes never noticed any animosity on the part of local FBI agents. He always found "the Bureau boys" in Alabama "very friendly."[67]

The best hope for a conviction in the Liuzzo case rested in federal court where the charge would be violation of the Reconstruction Era statutes and not murder. There were problems

here, too. The FBI had a terrified Rowe hidden in the San Francisco area. He was "torn to pieces" and needed to be "toned
down a bit," Hoover concluded. "I thought the Attorneys who
are going to try the case should see Rowe and size him up and
see if he is going to explode on the witness stand." But Rowe had
"no confidence in the attorneys of the Department." The Justice
Department's "leverage," Hoover told Katzenbach, could be
found in Rowe's "confidence in the FBI." Fearing leaks and Klan
vengeance, Bureau officials refused to "furnish information to
the Department in writing concerning [Rowe's] status." They
briefed John Doar orally. Division Five, nonetheless, screened
the cash offers from reporters seeking an interview and more
ambitious writers attempting to purchase rights to Rowe's
story.[68]

Rowe held up through the trial in Birmingham, and none of
the FBI's taps or bugs proved to be an embarrassment. Apparently, the only technical surveillance relevant to the Liuzzo case
was a microphone (BH 325-R) planted in Rowe's car, with
Rowe's consent.[69] In December 1965 Justice Department prosecutors succeeded where the Lowndes County circuit solicitor
had failed. Thomas, Wilkins, and Eaton received the maximum
ten-year prison term under Section 241. While free on appeal
bond, Eaton dropped dead of a heart attack.[70] The FBI held open
its file on Thomas, a suspect in the Sixeenth Street Baptist
Church bombing as well. At the end of the month, Hoover informed Katzenbach that the Bureau would "no longer accept responsibility" for the temperamental Rowe, "either financially
or security wise."[71]

While the director washed his hands of Gary Rowe, President
Johnson's advisers debated the question of how to address the
lingering protection issue, with Katzenbach noting the continuing pressure from "civil rights groups . . . for legislation which
would greatly expand federal jurisdiction with respect to crimes
affecting civil rights workers." The administration recognized
the need for "modest legislation," but was not willing to go as
far as the civil rights organizations or to trust the House Judiciary Committee. Committee members might give movement
people everything they wanted. "Pressures from the left" and
the prospect of "a run-away House Committee" would make
"the Administration the target of civil right criticism without
any compensating political advantage."[72]

Convictions in the Liuzzo case took some of the pressure off the FBI and the White House. Hoover was pleased that things had worked out. "This case [was] being viewed rather as a 'symbol' case," but the convictions marked a "turning point." The "Mississippi thing," he told Katzenbach, referring to the anticipated federal court trial of the suspects in the Schwerner-Chaney-Goodman murders, still needed watching, but "there was a different attitude today and the Governor had helped materially." The attorney general agreed, according to Hoover's account. The corner had been turned in Alabama. "The Bureau did a terrific job not only originally but in the way the testimony went and the way they conducted themselves and it was really a victory for the Bureau." "The Bureau was itself on trial in a sense," Katzenbach said. "The Bureau was held back . . . in the state court trials," but Department prosecutors obtained convictions in federal court because they "relied on the reputation of the Bureau . . . that is what won it."[73]

Three months after this victory, on March 24, 1966, William Sullivan recommended an escalation of intelligence and counterintelligence actions against the Klan. He told an executives' conference that the FBI was "not adequately coping with the problem created by the Ku Klux Klan." Policy required investigation of all "Klan members who are violence prone," but Division Five did not have "sufficient manpower" to do so. Of the 152 Klaverns, Sullivan said, the FBI desperately needed informant coverage of 81. Of the 14,000 Klan members in the United States, Division Five had the resources to investigate a mere "300 violence prone" members, "of whom there are many more," and "only 1,500" officers.[74]

Although Hoover rejected Sullivan's call for "a special squad directed against the Ku Klux Klan," Division Five gradually escalated its counterintelligence program and general intelligence gathering efforts. It was, perhaps, another example of the empire-building that has often been raised to explain Sullivan's actions in particular, and the FBI's accelerated racial matters activities in general. On the other hand, it took the FBI more than a few months to gear up. Division Five implemented most of its COINTELPRO operations against the Klan after the executives' conference met to discuss the new proposals. It also took the FBI time to wear down the Klan. In Mississippi alone from 1964–1970, Roy Moore remembered, "we averaged 250 acts of violence per annum. After 1970, practically nil. It took us that long to put the fire out."[75]

By the late 1960s, FBI surveillance of white hate groups had moved beyond coverage of Klan "rallies and demonstrations" to include the investigation of all segregationists regardless of their "potential for violence." This did not mean a parallel expansion of COINTELPRO—White Hate Group. It increased the number of intelligence targets, as opposed to counterintelligence targets, leading to more "informant coverage of the Klan, White Hate groups, and *white ghetto areas* [emphasis added]." The FBI opened files on "unaffiliated white racial extremists" and "neighborhood groups" in the suburbs ("white ghetto areas of the large cities which border on minority group living areas"), particularly if "these groups are known to sponsor demonstrations against integration and against the bussing of Negro students to white schools." Because "many of these organizations" were founded "on principles of fear rather than hate" and thus could not "be classified as hate groups," all Bureau investigations were "discreet." Whenever a white neighborhood group formed, the FBI sent in informers and "established sources" to gather "background data" and to document "the aims and purposes of the organization."[76]

Hoover brought the FBI to the ghettoes of black America as he reached out to the suburbs—though with a difference in scope and intensity and intent. As a general rule, in the director's view, fear motivated white Americans and hate motivated black Americans. "White citizens are primarily decent, but frightened for their lives," he told a group of newspaper editors in April 1965, less than three weeks after Mrs. Liuzzo died out by Big Bear Swamp. "The colored people are quite ignorant, mostly uneducated."[77]

Hoover's FBI waged war on the Klan, but it was a limited war, a sideshow to the real war. In 1967 the Miami field office helped an NBC television affiliate prepare documentaries on the National States Rights party and the Florida Klan. In 1968 the same office and its "friendly and reliable" media contacts began work on a far more ambitious series of documentaries on the Nation of Islam and other black groups. Hoover's heart was with the frightened people in the "white ghettoes" and their racist nightmares about an American Mau Mau or declining property values or black schoolchildren enrolling in *their* schools. The director may have ordered his agents to spy on the frightened people along with the frightening Klan, but he was on their side. He waged war on the Klan because the Klan had discredited the good name of white America.

Johnson administration officials knew as much as they wanted to know about the FBI's activities. They were neither shocked nor outraged. Instead, they encouraged the FBI to do more, to gather more intelligence on the civil rights movement, to do a better job disrupting the Klan. The surveillance went as far as it did not only because Hoover wanted it that way, but because he was allowed to have his way. His politics and genius, his bureaucratic priorities and maneuverings enabled him to pursue a private agenda. Along with the men around him, men who invariably shared his conservative values, and the deference of the men in the White House and the Justice Department, men who certainly did not share those conservative values, he fought a private war against black people at the very time he was destroying the Ku Klux Klan.

Exactly what did the FBI accomplish during the Klan wars? "In five years we blew them all to hell," a former Division Five agent concluded. "We never got any credit for that." "By the time I left the South in 1966," Joseph Sullivan said, "an entire society had resolved to suppress outlawry in racial matters. This goal was achieved through a team effort by Lyndon Johnson, J. Edgar Hoover, and the prosecutors representing the Justice Department. Hoover did his job well, and much credit must go to the president for providng the sources and support the FBI needed for this task."[78] But to Hoover and the men in Crime Records, it was not the hour of the FBI's greatest triumph. They could not escape the embarrassing details of the Liuzzo case, from the informant's presence in the murder car all the way down to the sight of a former agent helping to carry a Klan attorney's coffin.[79] Charles Morgan, Jr., the Birmingham lawyer who opened the ACLU's first southern office a few months before the Selma march, recognized the irony. "Years before those miserable, ignorant white men killed Mrs. Liuzzo, FBI agents surreptitiously peddled the lies which those killers believed and which lawyer Matt Murphy openly argued"—namely, that "Communists dominate them niggers."[80]

While Nicholas Katzenbach, John Doar, Burke Marshall, and a few other Civil Rights Division lawyers stood by the FBI when the revelations of intelligence and counterintelligence abuses poured out a decade later, they struck a defensive posture. When

asked what type of "civil rights work" the FBI did best, Marshall
said "the only thing they were good at" was waging war on the
Klan. The FBI won the Klan wars by doing what had to be done:

> It was done . . . by bribery, by payments to informers, by
> whatever eavesdropping was then permitted under the
> bureau's rules, by the sowing of suspicion among Klan
> members so that none knew who was an informer and who
> was not, by infiltration and deception, and in at least one
> incident by the participation of a bureau informer in the
> planning and attempted execution of a murder.
>
> It did not appear to those involved at the time, and it does
> not appear to me now, that the criminal conspiracy of
> violence that existed in the State of Mississippi then could
> have been handled by less drastic measures.[81]

The Klan moved outside the law, so the FBI moved outside the
law. For every counterintelligence trick, the FBI had a story
about Klansmen putting rattlesnakes in an agent's car or leaving
a coffin on the porch of an agent's home, ringing the bell, telling
the wife that her husband's body was inside. "The Bureau was
up against it," one agent said, "up against the wall."

In the end, the FBI pleased only the men in the middle, the
men in the Justice Department and the White House. Hoover
and his agents pleased neither the Klan (obviously) nor the
movement. The Klan has always been resilient. If Klansmen are
no longer as prone to leave civil rights people for dead along
Alabama highways or buried under thirty feet of Mississippi
mud, they are likely nowadays to engage in voter registration
drives ("If you are a White American you owe it to your wife and
children to register and vote"); campaigns to gain access to cable
television channels ("And now, a word from the Klan"); and the
filing of at least a few civil suits against the FBI.[82]

The victims of Klan violence have also taken FBI agents to
court, with two major suits filed by movement people or their
families emerging from the Klan wars. Walter and Frances
Bergman, two of the Freedom Riders beaten in Anniston and
Birmingham, filed after learning about Gary Rowe's participation and warnings to the FBI to expect a Klan riot.[83] Viola
Liuzzo's husband and five children put in the other suit. Mrs.
Liuzzo's family did not win their suit; the issues, after all, are
complex, especially if one accepts the assumptions of the surveillance consensus. And it is difficult to sue the government in

the government's courts. The FBI won, but not convincingly. The FBI had to open its files and provide fodder for newspaper headlines and clips on the evening news and even a *Playboy* article entitled, "Did the FBI Kill Viola Liuzzo?"[84]

That was not the kind of publicity Lyndon Johnson wanted back on March 26, 1965, when he stepped in front of the klieg lights. It certainly was not the kind of publicity Hoover and his Crime Records agents wanted. Even Gary Thomas Rowe, a troubled man in search of a separate peace was telling anybody who would listen that he was just as perplexed as the next fellow. "I inquired several times as to, 'Jesus, why wasn't something done after those acts were carried out'; and I was told that the FBI was not a police body, that the FBI was simply an investigating body and that their function was to gather information. That's all they needed."[85]

White Backlash

LBJ and the Politics of the Urban Riots

Viola Liuzzo's tragic murder presented a public relations dilemma for J. Edgar Hoover and a public relations opportunity for Lyndon Johnson. The riots that began in New York in the summer of 1964 and swept through the urban North in the years thereafter were tragic, too, but they presented opportunities only for the FBI director, not the president. The ghetto eruptions in Watts in 1965 and especially Newark and Detroit in 1967 seemingly confirmed Hoover's lifelong assumptions that subversion and not racism lay at the heart of the Negro Question, that the fires in the cities could be explained by the deeds of communist conspirators and not by the forces of poverty and despair. Yet the new rhetoric of "law and order" and not the archaic rhetoric of the domestic cold war structured the nation's response to the riots. The riots led to a search for communists in the ghetto, but that search was secondary to a national and increasingly partisan debate over the causes of the riots that placed liberalism and not communism at the center of controversy.

Initially, Hoover merely observed while the Johnson administration argued for its war on poverty and other Great Society initiatives as a solution to the great American dilemma, and the president's adversaries in the Republican party and the conservative wing of his own party blamed the permissiveness of liberal reform for causing the chaos and crime of the cities in the first place. For Johnson, the words "law and order" were "code words for racism."[1] For Hoover, law and order meant more money and agents, and therefore a more powerful base from which he could march against the black demand for justice on new fronts in the urban North. By reorienting American politics, the riots eventually provided Hoover the opportunity to abandon his alliance with the segregationists and their doomed cause, and to form new alliances with the administration's adversaries and their efforts to mobilize the "white backlash vote."

On the surface, Hoover's conduct during the course of the riots appears bewildering. The director moved from one riot to the next, sometimes in the same direction as the president, at other times in conflicting directions. His domestic intelligence reports often blamed subversives for instigating the riots, but at other times he provided a voice of reason in a White House increasingly dominated by a president's "incursions of paranoia."[2] Hoover's fundamental beliefs about race, nonetheless, remained unchanged. Black America represented a subversive threat, with or without communists, to the peace and stability of middle America, and the FBI had a responsibility to counter that threat. Hoover formed and pursued his agenda accordingly, building up a surveillance empire capable of intruding into every corner of black America and obtaining authorization for that empire from the Johnson administration—even as he gradually moved the FBI out from under the president's thumb and formed new alliances with the president's law-and-order adversaries.

By the time the riots had run their course, Lyndon Johnson was back on the ranch in Texas, Richard Nixon was president of the United States, and J. Edgar Hoover was in absolute command of an FBI with an ever-expanding "Racial Matters" mandate. Johnson's decision not to seek his party's nomination in 1968 can be best understood by reference to a failing policy in Vietnam and particularly the North Vietnamese army's Tet offensive of January 1968. But his decision was also influenced by the law-and-order politics of the riots, and Hoover's success in influencing those politics against the president's interests and in favor of those who chased the "white backlash vote." Johnson was the thirty-sixth president of the United States; Hoover was merely the sixth director of the FBI. Yet, when they clashed over ways to respond to the civil disorders, the director won, and the president, surely one of the most adept politicians ever to occupy the Oval Office, lost.

The riots themselves took the Great Society by surprise. Few people in the White House, the Department of Justice, or the FBI for that matter expected the "racial problem" to jump the Mason-Dixon Line. "When we thought of the North we didn't think of civil rights," Ramsey Clark remembered.[3] Things changed on July 18, sixteen days after President Johnson signed the Civil Rights Act of 1964. The riots began in New York after an off-duty police officer shot a fifteen-year-old Negro boy, James Powell ("a young colored hoodlum," in the FBI view), and CORE organized a rally and march on a police station to demand the officer's ouster. Rioting broke out in Brooklyn the next day, and yet another riot followed in Rochester upstate five days later. In August rioting swept through cities in New Jersey, Illinois, and Pennsylvania.

The riots posed a threat to President Johnson's Great Society programs, to his administration's attempt to promote consensus and achieve racial and economic justice.[4] A political threat, it took the form of Barry Goldwater, the Republican party's presidential candidate in 1964.[5] Aware of (and perhaps encouraged by) the strong showing of an unabashed racist, Alabama Governor George Wallace, in Democratic presidential primaries in Wisconsin and Indiana, Goldwater conservatives argued that liberal reform in general, and LBJ's war on poverty and civil rights legislation in particular, would encourage civil disobedience and a new permissiveness. Black Americans, who stood most to gain from the Great Society, would have no incentive to work. They would simply be granted money, food, jobs, scholarships, affirmative action promises, even their own special law. The work ethic would die. Disrespect for law, laziness, and criminality would emerge as the new values. The Republican right pointed to the riots ("Goldwater rallies," as they were sometimes called in Democratic circles) as proof of their predictions about Great Society permissiveness and the lax law enforcement policies of elite reformers who saw the roots of crime in poverty.[6]

The conservative critique fed a resentment that first surfaced among blue-collar whites in the South and quickly spread into the North, as Wallace's success in the primaries attested. William F. Buckley, Jr.'s, *National Review* published a symposium on the opportunities for a new political alignment made possible by this embryonic white backlash, with one writer predicting "Suburbia May Explode." On a far cruder level, the Ku Klux Klan issued constant reminders that Great Society reform was for blacks only. While watching FBI agents drag the Pearl River in search of the bodies of Michael Schwerner, Andrew Goodman, and James Chaney, a Neshoba County farmer called out: "Hey, why don't you hold a welfare check over the water. That'll get that nigger to the surface." Another Klansman, a grand dragon in North Carolina, said "the only contact" poor white trash had "with the federal government is the FBI bug."[7]

The Democratic party had worried about a Republican "southern strategy" even before the riots and Goldwater's candidacy. By 1960, Theodore H. White, the chronicler of the campaign trail, pointed out that millions of southerners had begun to recognize Republicans as "natural allies in preserving state sovereignty in race relations." By 1963 Andrew Young and other movement people interpreted federal recalcitrance on civil rights issues by reference to the Kennedys' attempt to undercut the GOP's southern strategy. John and Robert Kennedy, Young said, were trying "to assure the nation that they are still 'white.'" Less than a year later—and two months before the riots began—in an appearance on *Face the Nation*, Martin Luther King said the Republican party might become a "white man's party."[8]

The Goldwater-Republican attempt to capitalize on the breakdown of law and order threatened to cost President Johnson votes in the November 1964 elections. In a meeting with Cartha DeLoach after the summer rioting had run its course, White House aide Walter Jenkins described the political impact of the riots as the administration's "Achilles' heel." Hoover's agenda had little in common with Johnson's. The two men, as Arthur Schlesinger noted, "had been Washington neighbors and friends for many years. They understood each other."[9] Johnson turned to the FBI for assistance in managing the politics of the riots because he thought the FBI could be controlled. He wanted his FBI director, the most respected policeman in the nation, out front, in the public eye, and on his side. If Hoover said Johnson was tough enough, who could criticize the administration for being soft on law and order? The president was "toying with many possibilities," DeLoach told Hoover after his meeting with Jenkins, "which will give him favorable publicity inasmuch as he considers the various riots to have lost him many votes."[10]

The most ambitious plan involved the solicitation of an FBI report intended to counter Goldwater's law-and-order politicking and to recapture those lost votes. Johnson coaxed from the very conservative Hoover an endorsement (of sorts) for the war on poverty, and brought in a prominent if decidedly anti-Goldwater Republican, Thomas E. Dewey, to put all the memos the FBI had submitted on the riots into a final draft.[11] In late September the media received a report surveying nine cities where rioting had occurred. The report had Hoover's name on it, but Dewey, who ran for president in 1944 and 1948 on the Republican party ticket, wrote it. (Johnson held Dewey's authorship in reserve, just in case Hoover's name alone had failed to do the job.)[12] The episode deserves further attention because it demonstrates just how seriously the president took the threat posed by the new politics of race, and the reasons why he assumed that Hoover would stand with the administration during the more serious rioting and law-and-order politicking in the years to come.

Dewey's name first surfaced in the White House in mid-July, when he spoke to Max Kampelman, the lawyer, businessman, sometime diplomat, and former legislative counsel to Senator Hubert H. Humphrey (D., Minn.). Dewey would not "bolt with fanfare," a White House aide concluded, but he was "fed up with the GOP. . . . Should the President call him after the convention Max is certain that Dewey will promise his support and quiet help during the campaign." The idea intrigued Johnson, Nicholas Katzenbach remembered. "The president was always a big fan. . . . He liked Dewey's image, the image he had as the district attorney, as the special prosecutor in New York." With Dewey's offer in mind, Johnson met with Hoover on July 22 to discuss the Goldwater candidacy and how the administration might counter any attempts to exploit the riots. The president wanted the FBI "to get in there and see about the communist groups and the right wingers." Hoover promised to "dig into it at once." When the White House finally contacted Dewey a few weeks later, he agreed to help.[13]

Dewey came to the FBI riot project with ghost-writing experience (having received data from the FBI during the 1948 campaign), and with a desire to find a middle ground between Johnson's welfare state and Goldwater's warfare state.[14] When speculating with Hoover on "the new permissiveness," he asked about the salacious novel *Fanny Hill.* The director sent a memo. When the two men talked about the "timidity of prosecutors and judges," Dewey told Hoover about his recent conversation with the New York district attorney on the subject of Michael Schwerner, who had been arrested back in the summer of 1963 during CORE demonstrations against building trades discrimination in Manhattan. "[Frank] Hogan had said that one of the civil rights workers killed in Mississippi had been convicted in New York and was out on appeal and had the Judge affirmed the appeal [sic], he would have been in jail and it would have saved his life, that this was the fellow with the communist parents."[15]

Johnson expected Dewey to be the more moderate half of the partnership. He expected Dewey to control Hoover, to keep Hoover's crusty anticommunism out of the report. As it turned out, the director was on occasion the more moderate of the two men. When Dewey mentioned the culpability of "the responsible Negro organizations" and the "more violent" actions (as he designated the nonviolent "sit-ins, et cetera") of the past three years, Hoover counseled caution. "All of those actions" have contributed to "a breakdown of law and order and respect for the administration of justice," the director agreed. But "it was a delicate situation," and it might be best to avoid any reference to this in the report "because Roy Wilkins of the NAACP and [Whitney Young of] the Urban League" were "trying to be the restraining influence." When Dewey said "they started it and now want to put out the fire," Hoover pointed out that "they are being called by the younger generation 'Uncle Toms' and are being disregarded and people of more violent disposition are taking over and that is the thing I would hesitate about and think over very carefully about attaching blame to them."[16] In the meantime, the director sent Dewey memos (with copies to the White House) on the involvement of any CORE, NAACP, SCLC, or SNCC member in the riots.[17]

Hoover and Dewey agreed on the big question—whether communists or other radicals sparked the riots. Because the riots "caught" them "by surprise," Communist party members "moved in" only "after the riots started." The violence that followed, the director admitted, was merely "communist encouraged," "not communist inspired." At the same time, neither man intended to ignore the radicals, whether they were card-carrying Reds or not.[18] When Hoover telephoned Nelson Rockefeller at Jackson Hole, Wyoming, on the second day of the riots, the governor complimented the director on the work of the New York State police superintendent, former FBI agent Arthur Cornelius, Jr., and then complained about the "left-wing groups." "[Wasn't] anyone at the Federal level going to say anything about the kind of encouragement this is getting from radical groups," he wanted to know? Hoover told Rockefeller not to worry. "I have been keeping the President advised. . . . I send him a summary each day on the racial situation in Mississippi and Georgia, where there is the same communist problem, and also New York."[19]

Because the riot report, released to the press on September 26, identified poverty and discrimination as the principal causes of unrest, the FBI implied that Johnson administration programs designed to address those problems represented the best possible response. Not surprisingly, many conservatives worried about Hoover's apparent defection from right-wing orthodoxy.[20] The report emphasized social and economic factors, not subversive conspirators, and "cleared the civil rights movement completely," Roy Wilkins wrote. "After the F.B.I. report there was no excuse for race to be drawn into the campaign." When William Buckley objected, the liberal Catholic magazine *Commonweal* conceded a "twinge of sympathy," pointing out that "there is nothing wrong with coming out in favor of the Johnson war on poverty, but it is not for Mr. Hoover to do so in a report on civil rights disturbances."[21]

Johnson achieved a significant success. He had covertly maneuvered a prominent Republican and overtly maneuvered his anticommunist FBI director into issuing a report that endorsed the war on poverty, helped blunt the Goldwater challenge, and played down every sort of conspiracy theory. There was no evidence, the report concluded, that any group or person organized the riots on a national basis or that any of the disturbances were a "direct outgrowth of conventional civil rights protest." And there was little black-white violence—the only interracial clash of note involved blacks and Puerto Ricans in Brooklyn. In the Hoover-Dewey view, the incidents in New York, Illinois, Pennsylvania, and elsewhere were not even "race riots." That was a comforting thought, exactly the sort of message Johnson had hoped to propagate when he first called on his FBI director and a disaffected Republican. Because Hoover had evidently abandoned his traditional focus on communism, it is easy to see why the president concluded that he had the FBI under contol.[22]

Hoover and Dewey raised the radical specter, but in a calm manner. They explained the government's interest in the politics and everyday doings of the people who inhabited America's black ghettoes in the language of federalism *and* of federal surveillance: "Keeping the peace in this country is essentially the responsibility of the state government. Where lawless conditions arise, however, with similar characteristics from coast to coast, the matter is one of national concern even though there is no direct connection between the events and even though no federal law is violated."[23]

Johnson commissioned the report for reasons of politics, not policy. The report's value was therapeutic, its usefulness confined to public relations. Hoover, however, managed to tell the president what he wanted to hear, much to Buckley's chagrin, and to expand his bureaucracy's surveillance mission. He did so, not by promoting the Red menace but by downplaying it. "In certain instances," a headquarters directive of August 20 reminded all Bureau field offices, the evidence "clearly indicated that such [racial] disturbances were sustained and nurtured, if not actually initiated by, subversive elements and/or other organizations." FBI officials could not even define who they wanted to spy on. The "subversive, criminal, or other elements" who interested them were not connected in any way with "socalled civil rights groups." These elements were simply people who "may initiate and fan such smoldering racial resentments into violence solely to serve their own purposes."[24]

In the aftermath, while Dewey returned to the business of his law firm, Johnson asked Hoover to expand the riot control curriculum at the FBI National Academy.[25] The FBI also published a manual on urban violence, "Prevention and Control of Riots," with the assistance of the U.S. Army and the approval of the Civil Rights Division. According to an agent in the Training Division, John Doar reviewed every word of the manual, which included instructions for state and local police officers in baton techniques, among other things. All strokes, including the "smash," should be "short and snappy," the FBI advised.[26] The president's decision to expand FBI riot control responsibilities after the summer's violence cut across the grain of his political instincts. Always the good politician, he hedged his bet. But he did not expect the riots to continue. When they did, he sounded, at times, like former president Herbert Hoover, who implied that blacks had no reason to riot because "our 19 million Negroes probably own more automobiles than all the 220 million Russians and the 200 million African Negroes put together." "How is it possible," LBJ asked, "after all we've accomplished? How could it be? Is the world topsy-turvy?" Johnson had matured politically under the patronage of the New Deal, and in his experience the disadvantaged did not respond to federal largess in such a manner.[27]

Hoover expected the riots to continue; but not a single policeman trained by the FBI's riot control instructors was on hand when the Watts ghetto exploded in August 1965. The chief of the Los Angeles Police Department, William H. Parker, was a fiercely independent man often at odds with Hoover, and as punishment the director denied Parker's officers entry to the FBI National Academy. In any event, Los Angeles police needed no introduction to "the smash." Roger Wilkins, then an assistant director of the Justice Department's Community Relations Service and a member of a federal team sent to Watts, identified police brutality as one of the fundamental causes of the riot. The LAPD "was not fond of Negroes," he concluded. "Its members had killed about thirty looters and many of them called their nightsticks 'nigger sticks.'" With the exception of Ramsey Clark, however, no one listened to Wilkins. The Johnson administration seemed more concerned with subversives than with brutal police officers or Director Hoover's feud with Chief Parker.[28] With the law-and-order issue building all over again, the president—unable to comprehend the visible rage of Watts—turned to the FBI once more. This time, he used the Bureau's agents as the professional countersubversives they were and not as amateur sociologists.

On August 17 Hoover submitted a long memo on the Watts riot to Nicholas Katzenbach, who forwarded it to the president. If there was little "in the way of evidence as to subversive involvement," Katzenbach advised Johnson, the FBI would keep looking and investigate "this aspect" more "directly." But there would be no "general investigation through the FBI of other aspects of the riot." That remained the responsibility of city and state police. After reading the FBI memo and Katzenbach's proposals, the president approved a "limited investigation."[29]

The Johnson administration expected Hoover to help control

the political damage. Earlier, in a June 4 speech at Howard University, the president had called for a White House conference to propose strategies for moving black Americans "beyond opportunity to achievement." Preparations for the conference on civil rights, however, took on a different character after Watts. Berl Bernhard, who was then organizing a planning session for the conference, told Cartha DeLoach that the real purpose of the affair was "to prevent 'rioting' in major metropolitan cities . . . to let the participants freely 'sound off' and to let off steam."[30] The administration then requested name checks on every person the president intended to invite, and briefings for Democratic National Committee (DNC) officials on the alleged plans of certain "elements . . . to disrupt the White House Conference on Civil Rights." Louis Martin, one of the president's black advisers and the DNC deputy chairman for minorities, asked the Bureau to identify "the sources of revenue which enable these bomb throwers to carry out their programs." He found Hoover "very warm and cordial," anxious to cooperate. The director promised to prepare a report "for the chief."[31]

After more summer rioting in 1966, Hoover began preparing semimonthly summaries of possible racial violence in major urban areas. The director anticipated a long, hot summer for 1967, predicting "trouble" in "8 or 9 cities"—an overly optimistic forecast, as it turned out.[32] In all, black neighborhoods in nearly 150 cities experienced disorders—from minor disturbances to widespread looting, arson, and sniping in Newark and Detroit.

Republicans and conservative Democrats blamed the permissiveness of the Great Society once more. In Congress, the Johnson administration's adversaries favored an investigation of the urban disorders, but fortunately for the White House they had no idea "how to handle [it]." There seemed to be a "vacuum of Leadership," as Chalmers Roberts of the *Washington Post* described it to White House aide Douglass Cater. "The Leadership doesn't seem to have any policy." The administration was particularly worried about Senator James Eastland, who wanted to "carry the ball" on the proposed riot investigation, and Senator Everett Dirksen, who had set "out to make hay on the issue." Outside of Washington, the FBI described the riots and the decision to commit paratroopers in Detroit as "a political football between the President and the [Republican] Governor of Michigan," George Romney. In Maryland, another Republican governor, Spiro T. Agnew, claimed the riots had been "thoroughly planned beforehand" by subversive conspirators. Even Dwight Eisenhower discerned "a pattern" to the riots. Implying that Johnson had Hoover on a short leash, the former president called on Congress to pass whatever legislation was necessary to "empower the FBI to move into the situation."[33]

Administration officials controlled the damage as best they could, with Johnson himself asking Hoover to confront Agnew and Eisenhower. In the former case, when two FBI agents buttonholed the governor, he admitted "he had no firsthand information." "He is now backwatering completely," the director said. In the latter case, Johnson told Hoover to contact General Andrew Goodpaster, Eisenhower's aide, and to let him know the FBI had "full authority to spend anything to get the facts." The director summarized LBJ's order:

> Tell Eisenhower we don't want to put it on full page
> headlines the FBI is going to 'eat you up' and scare
> everybody and put them on notice what we are doing, but I
> have the authority and the President is on top of it and
> called me weeks ago when in Newark and insisted I get
> anybody, including their wife if she contributed. The
> President then stated he noticed this Rap (Brown) outfit said
> he was going to get a gun and shoot Lady Bird.

Before hanging up, Johnson told Hoover once again to "call General Goodpaster and say I have all the approval and authority and money and if I don't he, the President, will go to Texas and get it, and to tell Goodpaster to get Eisenhower fully briefed." Hoover responded, "I told the President I would do this." Goodpaster said "he would talk to General Eisenhower and straighten him out."[34]

Johnson faced a dilemma. While the Republican law-and-order strategy was growing in appeal, the Great Society faced criticism from an unexpected source. Radical black nationalists said the war on poverty and the civil rights reforms confirmed the elitism of liberal politicians. The movement's left wing demanded power, not paternalism, and offered a critique of the Great Society that undermined the president's constituency. From the skewed perspective of the radical left, the movement's principal enemy was not the red-necked southern sheriff or the reactionary senator from Mississippi or the nihilistic rioters or even the reluctant FBI director. Liberal reform was the enemy; LBJ was the enemy. The radicals' exaggerated focus on liberalism as an enemy of black people fractured the movement and put one more crack in Johnson's constituency.

To compound things, many black groups, from the moderate SCLC to the immoderate SNCC, were emerging as critics of the Vietnam war.[35] The radicals thought they had more in common with the world's colonial peoples and former colonial peoples, including the North Vietnamese, than their erstwhile benefactors, the liberal reformers of the Great Society. The United States raised a lower-class and disproportionately black army to fight a white man's war against a nonwhite people, a war to eradicate communism in a far-off country that made it increasingly difficult to eradicate poverty and racial injustice at home. "Johnson did make a brave—and in the end tragic—effort to resolve that visceral contradiction in the imperial way of life," wrote historian William Appleman Williams. "He tried to make major improvements in the quality of life for the poor and disadvantaged of all colors . . . and at the same time secure the frontier in Indochina. That proved to be impossible . . . [he] was trying to swim in the sky. But at least he tried."[36]

So the radicals turned their backs on Johnson and the reformers. They went off to confer with LBJ's enemies (Marxist-Leninists in Cuba, Algiers, China, and North Vietnam), threatened to shoot his wife, and insulted his family. "War," Stokely Carmichael said, was "for the birds, Lynda Bird and Lady Bird." This new black radicalism, in turn, alienated the administration's constituency in the Congress. After "approximately 300 Negroes brought in by CORE" confronted Congressman Lionel Van Deerlin (D., Cal.) and accused him of being a racist during a speech before a youth leadership training program in San Diego, Van Deerlin complained to Office of Economic Opportunity head Sargent Shriver. "Was [it] OEO's function to finance Black Power rioters?"[37]

Desperately trying to hold their voting block together, Johnson and his White House staff tried to discredit their leftist adversaries as followers of Trotsky or Marx or Mao.[38] They did so while trying to contain the growing conservative critique of the administration's lax law-and-order policies. Edwin Willis, the Louisiana Democrat who chaired the House Committee on Un-American Activities, reminded the president of how effective such Republican party tactics might turn out to be. "Just like some years ago the Republicans made a dent in the Democratic column on the false issue that Democrats were 'soft' on Communism, so I regret to say that in my opinion they will try to portray the Democrats in general, and you in particular, as being 'soft' on law enforcement and respect for law and order."[39] Johnson had even less luck in countering such charges than Harry Truman had had twenty years earlier; at least Truman won his election. LBJ claimed the left-wing critics of the Great Society and the Vietnam war were all radicals or revolutionaries or plain criminals. Richard Nixon, who had experience with this sort of thing (Alger Hiss and the New Deal), said the radicals and revolutionaries and criminals were all children of the Great Society. The radicals and Nixon had one thing in common: they were all critics of liberal reform.

Concerned about the continuing implications of the law-and-order issue in the midst of the Detroit riots, Johnson called upon Hoover once again on July 25, summoning him to a White House meeting with Secretary of Defense Robert McNamara, Attorney General Ramsey Clark, Supreme Court Justice Abe Fortas, Secretary of the Army Stanley R. Resor, and Army Chief of Staff Harold K. Johnson. Cyrus Vance called in every half hour with a report from Detroit. Obsessed with "intelligence," according to Hoover's account of the meeting, the president said "there was a concerted action and a pattern about all of these riots . . . [and] that members of the Poverty Corps had been participants." He told the director to keep his "men busy to find a central character to it, to watch and see and we will find some central theme."[40]

Hoover said he "would dig into that thoroughly," but advised Johnson not to expect much. Standing with the advocates of law and order who traced the causes of the riots to liberal permissiveness and not communist conspiracy, Hoover actually minimized the Red menace. In a notable irony, the liberal president rambled about subversives while the conservative director calmly advised him that "outsiders" did not initiate any of the riots. "Carloads of individuals," including communists, merely arrived after the riots were "in full force." With regard to the poverty workers, Hoover did single out Julius Hobson, then an HEW economist and local chairman of the civil rights group ACT who was "making militant speeches throughout [the District of Columbia]." (Hobson had filed a suit against the Washington school board that had resulted, the previous month, in a federal court ruling against de facto segregation in the District's schools.) Hoover also mentioned Marion Barry, SNCC's first chairman and then director of the group's Washington office and a $50-a-day consultant for a community relations program that received federal funds. Johnson asked for memos on both men and a general summary of subversive influences in the riots.[41]

Hoover submitted a Division Five report that summarized rioting in twenty-nine cities. The basic conclusion was restrained and accurate. In almost every case "a single incident generally following an arrest of a Negro by local police for some minor infraction" sparked the disturbance. From that modest conclusion, however, Division Five credited "the exhortations of 'Black Power' advocates Stokely Carmichael and H. Rap Brown" with triggering "volatile situations . . . into violent outbreaks" in specific cities; condemned "the involvement of other violent, criminal, subversive and extremist elements" for fanning the flames of "spontaneous outbursts of mob violence"; and suggested that the principal blame for the riots could be traced to the civil rights movement. "Certain individuals who have been prominent in civil rights activities must bear a major burden of the guilt and responsibility for the turmoil created by the riots," Division Five concluded. "Hypocritical individuals" and "false prophets," movement people "who have openly professed abhorrence for violence," had worked "the civil rights field," sowing "seeds of confusion and disorder. . . . The Nation is [now] reaping the harvest of their handiworks."[42]

The Division Five report also included a section on the connection between the antiwar and civil rights movements. Hoover's conclusions here more closely reflected the traditional FBI view that communist subversion lay at the heart of the problem.[43] The director had been delivering reports to the White House about Martin Luther King's position on the Vietnam war since the summer of the Watts riot, when Nicholas Katzenbach ordered the preparation of a memo ("The Position of Martin Luther King, Jr. and the Communist Party, USA, on Vietnam") for Secretary of State Dean Rusk. Katzenbach wanted Hoover to pay particular attention to "any hard Communist Party line tying together Vietnam and the civil rights movement." And that is exactly what the director did, here and especially in the Division Five report prepared in the midst of the Detroit riot, by fusing Vietnam protests and urban rioting with the communist line. The CPUSA's "massive effort to create a united front in opposition to United States military presence in Vietnam" supplemented a parallel effort "to exploit racial issues." The ultimate goal, the Bureau concluded, was to create "the chaos upon which communism flourishes"—an entirely "predictable" Communist party policy. Though Hoover developed little hard information to support such conclusions, he advised the Justice Department on perhaps a dozen occasions that electronic surveillance in the King investigation had produced general intelligence on "the Vietnam situation." The director did not indicate that his ubiquitous wiremen even listened in on one of King's telephone conversations with President Johnson himself.[44]

Hoover had DeLoach brief Speaker of the House John McCormack (D., Mass.) and other members of Congress, including former FBI agent and then Senator Thomas J. Dodd (D., Conn.), on the link between civil rights leaders and antiwar sentiment. When Dodd criticized Dr. King's call for negotiations with the Vietcong, DeLoach told Dodd about King's relationship with Stanley Levison. Dodd had been on the movement's side, more or less, during the early 1960s, commending SCLC for its "excellent work" during the Albany demonstrations. (Nine of the people arrested in southwest Georgia were from his home state.) But King's brief comments on Vietnam ended all that. When Dodd questioned his "competence to speak out about complex matters of foreign policy," King dismissed the senator as a "supporter of the FBI and its invasion of privacy."[45] Meanwhile, King praised Robert Kennedy's position on Vietnam and, more broadly, "contemporary colonial revolutions." SCLC also debated a resolution condemning "the immorality and tragic absurdity of our position" in Vietnam, and a few antiwar activists fantasized about a Kennedy-King ticket in the 1968 presidential elections—a prospect, no matter how unlikely, that alarmed both Johnson and Hoover. "What a pair!," the director wrote.[46]

By breaking with the administration over the war, SNCC's John Lewis said, Dr. King was no longer LBJ's "head nigger when they come to the White House." "It is clear that he is an instrument in the hands of subversive forces seeking to undermine our nation," one of Hoover's agents in Division Five concluded, with far more crudity: "A traitor to his country and his race."[47] Condemning American involvement in Vietnam as an attempt "to perpetuate white colonialism," King called on young black and white men to boycott the war. It appeared, for a time, that the civil rights movement and the antiwar movement might indeed unite under the leadership of a single individual. Hoover responded by increasing the flow of letters and phone calls to the White House, the attorney general's office, and the Civil Rights Division, and most of these communications described King's ideas as identical to "the communist line." Not surprisingly, the White House was receptive. Johnson aide Harry McPherson described King as "the crown prince of the Vietniks."[48]

Hoover and Johnson found common ground on the question of communist influence of the antiwar movement. The modern civil rights movement started out in an uneasy alliance with the liberal reform state, engaging Jim Crow in limited moral skirmishes under conditions that pleased neither the government nor the movement itself. The government never controlled the movement and the movement never convinced the government to intervene on anything but its own terms. The campaign to force the FBI to protect civil rights workers was only the most dramatic element in that larger struggle. By the time the long, hot summer of 1967 began, some civil rights leaders had moved beyond a limited moral struggle to raise questions about power and national policy from Watts to Saigon. It was one thing to challenge Bull Connor and the city of Birmingham or J. Edgar Hoover and the Federal Bureau of Investigation; quite another to challenge Lyndon Johnson and the United States.

With black activists challenging the policies of the reform state at home and abroad, emphasizing the connections between racism, poverty, and militarism, Hoover's assessment of the seriousness of the threat posed by these activists grew exponentially. The antiwar rhetoric of the militants scarcely differed from Dr. King's. Black people, Black Panther Eldridge Cleaver said, "are asked to die for the system in Vietnam. In Watts they are killed by it." Calling for "a radical redistribution of economic and political power," King said "we are not interested in being integrated into *this* value structure." No longer content merely to change the segregated South, many black leaders once considered "responsible" now proposed to remake America. From segregated buses and swimming pools and voting booths, the movement moved on to battle the less visible racism in the North and the far reaches of the Third World where "God's military agent on earth" was doing so much damage.[49]

The call to remake America looked dangerous to Hoover, and the critique of the liberal reform state offered by men like King and the more disjointed critiques offered by men like Carmichael and Cleaver looked dangerous to LBJ. "The war engulfed the poor man," Roger Wilkins remembered, "and then Martin came out against the war. Johnson was distracted and angry, and his cities were burning. His soul hardened against us then ... and he liked very few of us."[50] Fully committed to discrediting the civil rights movement by the time Detroit exploded in July 1967, the president relied on the FBI to provide the evidence he needed to make his case. Bureau officials flooded the White House with intelligence on the radicals and the moderates, and the sheer volume of information overwhelmed Johnson's staff. When asked to hold the "more or less minor" stuff and send over "the major information" only, Hoover refused. "If they don't want to use it after they get it, it is their responsibility." Even when pursuing an assigned agenda, the director stuck to the myth that his Bureau never evaluated the intelligence gathered.[51]

The White House wanted Hoover to supply "correct information" showing that all the riots and demonstrations were "well-planned" and "in very many cases" organized by "the same people"—the sort of information, secretary to the cabinet Robert Kintner suggested, that could be "authentically prepared" and disseminated in "a speech by someone who cannot be criticized as a McCarthyite." The FBI's reports, however, were short on hard evidence and long on rhetoric. Rather than conclude that they were searching for something that did not exist, administration officials responded by asking Hoover to dig deeper. They also assigned foreign policy adviser Walt W. Rostow the task of collecting "such evidence as there is on external involvement in the violent radical fringe of the Negro community in the U.S." Rostow mobilized the entire intelligence community, but his people realized that "the hard evidence will have to come from inside the U.S. via the FBI." Once again, however, Hoover and his agents could not get the job done. "[They] came up with a blank."[52]

Hoover had no intention of deflecting the law-and-order focus away from liberal permissiveness. In mid-September 1967 the Justice Department received a tip from Walter Sheridan, the former FBI agent and troubleshooter for Robert Kennedy's Justice Department, that his employer, NBC News, had interviewed a number of black citizens who claimed the riots were thoroughly organized. The network planned to use those interviews, along with photographs of several Soviet-made AK-47 assault rifles confiscated in Detroit, during a special television documentary on urban violence. Attorney General Clark responded by order-ing the FBI to "use the maximum available resources, investiga-tive and intelligence, to collect and report all facts bearing upon the question as to whether there has been or is a scheme or con-spiracy by any group of whatever size, effectiveness or affilia-tion, to plan, promote or aggravate riot activity." The FBI nearly balked at Clark's order and at Doar's attempts to follow up. "Up to now," one Division Five executive complained, "we have run out any logical leads indicating possibility of a conspiracy. . . . The attached [memo] appears to be an attempt on the part of John Doar to involve the Bureau in a fishing expedition of the rankest type."[53]

FBI surveillance responsibilities would expand, and along with that expansion would come more money and more agents. But Hoover was never interested in trading autonomy for a larger taxpayer subsidy. If the FBI was to move into community surveillance, Hoover would do so on his own terms and not the terms imposed by the Johnson administration. FBI Inspector Jo-seph Sullivan, who was assigned to the Cleveland field office at the time, questioned the desirability of a greatly expanded do-mestic intelligence mission by asking, "Where do we go from here?" "The primary troublemakers throughout the riots were not organized groups in the sense that they represented some subversive forces in some civil rights or racist collectives. They were, rather, the street-corner hoodlum gangs," he concluded. "Do we now program ourselves into coverage, into the develop-ment of sources, in these teen-age, street-corner gangs?" The Bu-reau must define its "interests" before committing major re-sources to this "whole new field of racial operations" where questions of law and order would take precedence over ques-tions of subversion. When Sullivan proposed a conference of field agents to discuss the possibilities, Hoover said no. If the senior staff at the seat of government hadn't made up their minds yet and didn't have "the answer," the director wrote, "cer-tainly no field group would be of aid."[54]

In the interim, Hoover advised the field of the facts of life. "There exists in high Government circles a tremendous interest in all information regarding the racial situation throughout the United States."[55] In Chicago, that meant a leak to Mayor Richard J. Daley regarding Dr. King's (alleged) assessment of the riots. "They don't plan to burn down the West side. They are planning to get the loop." In Detroit, where the violence was much worse, it meant surveillance of a citizens action committee and its plans to hold a "people's tribunal," a mock prosecution of Detroit policemen for the crime of murder. On the national level, it meant the dissemination of a Bureau monograph on SNCC to fifty-one government officials and agencies. The INS received fifty copies and the marines thirty-one. Hoover sent a more modest number of copies (two) to West Point.[56]

This "tremendous interest in . . . the racial situation" also led to an escalation of the FBI's investigation of Office of Economic Opportunity personnel who might have been involved in the riots. Law-and-order advocates and other opponents of liberal reform "were trying to put us out of business," OEO inspector general Edgar May recalled. "They were going to use the riots to do it," by charging subversive infiltration of the poverty corps and poverty worker responsibility for creating a climate ripe for rioting. The White House was interested in damage control, once again, and had more confidence in an FBI probe than in OEO chief Sargent Shriver's in-house investigation. The president himself had mixed feelings on the whole question of poverty worker involvement in the riots. "Johnson was genuine in his concern for the poor and the blacks," OEO general counsel Donald M. Baker said. "He understood as well as anyone how the old fogies over in the Senate can take advantage of bad publicity and do a lot of damage to programs. At the same time, he never quite approved of community action and never really approved the participation of the poor. He talked to Sarge about it. He was never sure we were doing the right thing." So Johnson pushed the FBI investigation.[57]

Officials at the OEO were always bothering Hoover with requests to investigate harassment of poverty workers. Baker recalled one incident where Klansmen shot up a car carrying "do-gooder liberals" from the Child Development Group of Mississippi. "We called the FBI . . . their report came back about three months later and it was sort of typical. Random hunter's shots! That was their opinion! They put it in writing, for God's sake! Just absolutely ridiculous." FBI officials routinely sent reports on organizations that received war-on-poverty funding, in contrast, to OEO through Robert Emond, Edgar May's deputy and a former Bureau agent. One report described a tutorial program for children in Memphis as a fraud, with an emphasis on teaching the "black thing" and not "constructive black history."[58]

Concerned about the potential political impact of poverty worker involvement in the riots, the White House took the FBI's reports seriously. When one of the first reports came in on August 12, 1967, President Johnson met with Marvin Watson to discuss Leander Scott, a black activist and a member of the board of directors of the Kane County (Ill.) Council. The Council received OEO funds and the Bureau linked Scott to the racial disturbances in Elgin, Illinois. More reports followed. In Harlem, the FBI said, OEO funded a "hate school" and antipoverty organization, Haryou (Harlem Youth Opportunities Unlimited)-Act, Inc., whose employees included two members of a gun club formed by the Revolutionary Action Movement. Student Nonviolent Coordinating Committee firebrand Rap Brown, moreover, had used a car leased to the Haryou-Act employment center. These and other FBI reports prompted Sargent Shriver to fire or suspend a number of persons connected to OEO, including a consultant to a Harlem youth group and a Peace Corps trainee who also happened to be an antiwar activist. But no wholesale purge took place. "We never got a marching order from the FBI," Edgar May said.[59]

Instead, the FBI sent "around reports saying this Community Action guy or that Community Action guy was a communist"— a measured charge of communist infiltration of a Great Society program as opposed to the wild charge that communists had instigated the riots. "What did they expect me to do with this stuff?" Donald Baker remembered asking himself. "There were people in the White House from time to time who used to get antsy about some of this crap. Joe Califano once crawled all over us for not [firing] LeRoi Jones [Amiri Baraka]," the poet and playwright then with Haryou. Shriver himself had once complained to Hoover, according to Cartha DeLoach, about "the difficulty encountered in being able to summarily dismiss an individual who had subversive, homosexual or a bad criminal record."[60] There were radicals in OEO, mostly people described by one of Shriver's executives, Hyman Bookbinder, as "ultra left-wing elements in the program who saw this as an opportunity to give hell to both major political parties." There was some corruption, too, in terms of misuse of funds or unaccounted funds.[61] FBI officials showed some interest in this type of corruption, but they showed more interest whenever a countersubversive angle surfaced—like the Rap Brown connection with Haryou-Act. Hoover understood how the white middle class would react to news that the Harlem group received at least some money from OEO, from their war-on-poverty taxes. One way or another, the largess of LBJ's Great Society had provided a rental car for Rap Brown.

Hoover remained less than enthusiastic about President Johnson's OEO probe nonetheless. He would monitor OEO personnel, but not for the purpose of helping the president contain political fallout. After Marvin Watson requested an escalated investigation, the director informed the White House that the FBI had already given the National Commission on Civil Disorders (the Kerner Commission) everything in the files. Armed with a brief prepared by Division Five and "a summary of available information concerning each Commission member," Hoover had just finished detailed testimony on OEO before the Kerner Commission. His briefing papers were divided into seven sections, with the sixth section devoted entirely to the "conduct of anti-poverty workers."[62]

The Kerner Commission itself settled nothing for either the director or the president. Johnson had appointed the Commission on July 28, 1967, to investigate the origins of the riots and to make recommendations "to prevent or contain such disorders in the future," an exercise similar in intent, though certainly not in scope, to the effort to use Hoover and Dewey in 1964.[63] He brought in prominent people, Governor Otto Kerner of Illinois to serve as chairman and New York Mayor John Lindsay as vice-chairman, among others, and ordered the director to cooperate. Hoover supplemented his testimony on OEO before the Commission with a general discussion of the causes of the riots and his bureaucracy's responsibilities, though he qualified his call for stronger antiriot legislation. FBI agents photographed rioters and took notes, he testified, but arrested no sniper or fire bomber because looting and arson were local crimes outside the Bureau's jurisdiction. On the intelligence side, Hoover described for the Commission the "catalytic effect of extremists," focusing on the "vicious rhetoric" of SNCC (Rap Brown and Stokely Carmichael) and SCLC (Martin Luther King), and finding time to mention the Communist party, the pro-Chicom (Chinese communist) Progressive Labor party, Students for a Democratic Society, and various teenage gangs.

On the whole, the Kerner Commission rejected Hoover's conclusions. Its final report, submitted in February 1968, dealt less with the "catalytic effect" of the Browns and Carmichaels than with the social problems facing the United States. America was "moving toward two societies, one black, one white—separate and unequal." To reverse the "deepening racial trend," the Commission called for a massive and sustained "commitment to national action," recommending sweeping reforms in the areas of employment, education, welfare, housing reform, news reporting, and law enforcement. "Discrimination and segregation have long permeated much of American life," the report concluded. "They now threaten the future of every American." Dr. King compared the report to "a physician's warning of approaching death (of American society) with a prescription to life."

The Johnson administration rejected most of the Kerner Commission proposals on budgetary grounds. "That was the problem," LBJ later wrote, "—money." Because the money simply was not there, the Commission, as one of the president's most thoughtful advisers, Harry McPherson, noted in his memoirs, created more problems for the administration than it solved. "It intensified arguments about the war, raised impossible demands, and implicitly diminished the significance of what was already being done."[64] Hoping to break the conservative monopoly of the law-and-order issue at the very least, the administration seized upon one of the Kerner Commission's less costly recommendations—namely, its unintentional embrace of the surveillance mission that Hoover had advocated. A minor recommendation, buried in the appendix, called for the creation of police intelligence units "staffed with full-time personnel," including "undercover police personnel and informants."[65]

Not bothering to wait for publication of the Kerner Commission's findings, the administration encouraged local police departments to establish intelligence units and to funnel any information collected to the Justice Department through the FBI. As a result, the domestic intelligence apparatus became bigger, harder to control, more intrusive—and more incompetent. A Cook County grand jury investigation of the Chicago Police Department's security section concluded that its "inherently inaccurate and distortive" data contaminated federal intelligence. The security section forwarded to the FBI the name of "any person" who attended two "public meetings" of any group under surveillance. The Bureau then passed along the "*fact*" of membership in a subversive organization when conducting background checks on persons seeking federal employment or grants. "Since federal agencies accepted data from the Security

Section without questioning the procedures followed, or methods used to gain information," the grand jury noted, "the federal government cannot escape responsibility for the harm done to untold numbers of innocent persons."[66]

Hoover felt the Kerner Commission paid too much attention to the sociological side of urban violence and not enough to the law-and-order side. When Johnson appointed yet another study group, the National Commission on the Causes and Prevention of Violence, and selected Dwight Eisenhower's brother Milton to chair it, the director told Ramsey Clark that there was too much "emphasis today in the press that society is sick. . . . I said I hoped the new Commission . . . will keep a balanced viewpoint as to that because the other Commission went far astray in regard to white racism. I said there is racism but not as predominantly as the Kerner Commission found it to be."[67] When testifying before the Eisenhower Commission in September 1968, Hoover stressed the "Mau Mau–type tactics" of SNCC and other militant black groups. (The FBI could not decide whether SNCC was a Mau Mau–type New Left group or "a Ku Klux Klan in reverse—a black Klan.") On the issue of police brutality in the ghetto, the director returned to first principles, linking Moscow-directed revolutionaries with "vicious, hate-filled . . . black extremists." The "communist policy to charge and protest 'police brutality' . . . in racial situations" was part of an "immensely successful" and "continuing smear campaign," he said. "The net effect . . . is to provoke and encourage mob action and violence by developing contempt for constituted authority."[68]

An Eisenhower Commission study group headed by Jerome Skolnick saw things differently, placing Hoover, not communists, at the center of the problem. The director's propaganda about subversives "who misdirect otherwise contented people" was particularly effective among police officers. How many radical squads resembled the Nashville Police Department's intelligence division, with its subscriptions "to all known communist publications," its filing system patterned after the Bureau's, its exclusive focus on "subversive organizations," and its "almost daily" contacts with G-men? The FBI, according to Skolnick's group, had helped politicize the police and was at least partly responsible for the "police violence" that so often preceded a riot or accompanied a civil rights demonstration.[69]

The Kerner Commission and the Eisenhower Commission prompted the FBI to take "counterintelligence action" to negate the impact of their findings. One Bureau field office responded to the Kerner Commission's tendency "to absolve the Negro rioters from any large blame" by suggesting that the Crime Records Division publish a public-opinion poll, "either a true poll or a false poll," that would indicate the public's tendency to place all blame on "the Negro rioters."[70] Although Hoover rejected the proposal, he moved quickly to support a law-and-order alternative to the presidential commissions by working with Senator John L. McClellan (D., Ark.), chairman of the Permanent Subcommittee on Investigations (PERM) and a longtime, hard-line foe of the civil rights movement.

McClellan's Subcommittee, the same Subcommittee that Joseph McCarthy had once chaired, was actually the third and last of the old cold war–era investigating committees to probe the origins of the riots. The Senate Internal Security Subcommittee had begun such hearings, but the House Committee on Un-American Activities did not expect much on that front. HUAC Chairman Edwin Willis told Cartha DeLoach "the Senate hearings would amount to only a lot of 'socialistic crap,'" in that the Senate would . . . demand better housing, better jobs, et cetera." Willis wanted to know whether the FBI would provide "guidance" for his Committee's law-and-order hearings. Although the Bureau helped with other hearings, including the SDS investigation, and would continue to help in the coming years with reports on such things as the stockpiling of weapons by radical black groups, HUAC's position on the riots was too extreme. To say "that subversive influences had triggered the riots," DeLoach told Willis, was irresponsible and "bad . . . for the country."[71]

The FBI preferred to work with Senator McClellan. He was far more powerful than any HUAC member, and his PERM staff were far more reliable (and therefore far less likely to compromise their relationship with Bureau agents) than the HUAC people. In their political responses to the riots there was little difference between Willis and McClellan, DeLoach's comment to the contrary notwithstanding. Before the Senate had even voted to fund his inquiry, McClellan said he would emphasize "law enforcement rather than the social causes underlying the disorders." When the authorization came through in August 1967, the McClellan Committee began work on a twenty-five part, three-year investigation into the causes of the urban riots. Sixty-three policemen from local Red squads testified, including a sergeant from the Chicago intelligence unit who assured the Committee that "the Communist threat . . . does exist."[72]

Senator McClellan explained the origins of the riots with the sort of logic favored by the late Senator McCarthy. In September 1967, following a state police raid on the home of two poverty workers in Pike County, Kentucky, Margaret and Alan McSurely, a local prosecutor gave the papers seized in the raid to one of the Committee's investigators. The state charged the McSurelys, organizers for the Southern Conference Educational Fund, with violating a sedition statute. The defendants attracted PERM's interest, McClellan said, because Stokely Carmichael had addressed a SCEF staff meeting and had spoken at Vanderbilt University a few days before the Nashville riots. There was a thread connecting everything back to SCEF, and back through that organization to the Communist party. (McClellan, Hoover, and even a few civil rights leaders believed SCEF to be "communist controlled.") Since the McSurelys were poverty workers, the thread could be traced all the way back to the Great Society. The Pike County prosecutor, however, was not a disinterested Red hunter. He had political ambitions and economic interests. As a candidate for lieutenant governor on the Republican ticket and owner of property leased to coal mine operators, he intended to drive the McSurelys and all other poverty workers out of Kentucky.[73]

These facts slowed the FBI, but not the McClellan Committee. A federal judge ordered the McSurelys' papers sequestered, but a member of McClellan's staff took them to Washington anyway. The senator centered on love letters that newspaper columnist Drew Pearson had sent Margaret McSurely, with whom he had once had a brief affair. A persistent critic of McClellan, Pearson had most recently discussed the senator's activities in a column dated August 10—the day before the Pike County raid. It was indeed a small world. Ultimately, PERM summoned the McSurelys and had them indicted for contempt of Congress. Now facing prosecution on a second front, the McSurelys sued the Committee and the Bluegrass prosecutor. Meanwhile, terrorists (literally) bombed them out of their Kentucky home, and the FBI gave everything it had on the McSurelys and Joseph Mulloy, a worker with an antipoverty group (Appalachian Volunteers) who was also arrested, to the Kentucky State Police. Admittedly, it was not much, and in Mulloy's case there was absolutely nothing in the files. But it was "a matter of police cooperation." Back in

Washington, an FBI agent reviewed the records seized in the raid, and Hoover sent a memo to the White House.[74]

The whole thing was part of what the White House called a "nationwide investigation of the OEO involvement in the riots," an effort that confirmed the president's concern about the vulnerability of the Office of Economic Opportunity and the whole war on poverty.[75] The White House, however, did not realize that the FBI had entered that nationwide investigation on John McClellan's side, not Lyndon Johnson's. If FBI officials kept a reasonable distance from the McSurelys' civil suit and the "political fight" down in Kentucky, they helped with other aspects of the McClellan Committee investigation. In September 1967, when McClellan asked for "the cooperation of the FBI in checking names," Hoover assured him "we would give . . . every assistance we could." The director ordered Crime Records executive Thomas Bishop to handle all requests from the Committee's chief counsel, Donald O'Donnell, "promptly."[76]

A typical PERM request called for the FBI to list all "the militant organizations" in a given area and to provide identifications "of the individual members." Blind memos followed. This was done in about two dozen cities. In Boston, the FBI provided dossiers on such groups as Mothers for Adequate Welfare and such individuals as a Roxbury housewife and sit-in veteran—"a Negress . . . married to . . . a white male" and an antiwar activist to boot, the Bureau said. Other FBI offices kept PERM posted on the activities of their rivals. Whenever something interesting turned up, Hoover issued the appropriate order. "Let our contact on McClellan's Com. know." Since Kerner Commission investigators often focused on police brutality, Hoover countered by sending McClellan data on "bombings" and other "attacks on police."[77]

McClellan was always asking Hoover for help. A week after working out the terms of assistance for the riot hearings, on September 13, 1967, DeLoach met McClellan over lunch to discuss the agenda of another appendage to the Senate Government Operations Committee, the Subcommittee on Criminal Laws and Procedures. Their conversation centered on a provision in "the pending legislation involving the Crime Control Act" that authorized an expansion of the FBI National Academy. McClellan asked DeLoach to write a speech for him on law and order and to provide backup information on the Bureau's desires in the area of police training. Crime Records agents wrote the speech and prepared blind memos, though DeLoach did not believe this latter service was necessary. "Senator McClellan apparently was not aware of the tremendous amount of information we had already furnished his Staff Director, James Calloway."[78]

McClellan also offered the FBI help. He gave DeLoach a copy of his omnibus crime control bill, and "asked that the FBI study this bill very carefully and actually prepare language which could be inserted into the bill for his usage." "This would be done," DeLoach said, "on a confidential basis." When Calloway finished work on a new version of the bill, he handed Bishop a copy of another bill, the law enforcement assistance bill (which would be added to the omnibus bill), and requested, "on an informal basis," the FBI's "views with regard to it. This would include not only the portions dealing with the FBI, but all other portions of the Bill."[79]

A few weeks later, in November 1967, Deputy Attorney General Warren Christopher phoned DeLoach to discuss an amendment to one of the pending crime control bills concerning law enforcement training. "Our conversation," as DeLoach summarized it for Tolson and Hoover, "was not a pleasant one." "[The Deputy Attorney General] and the Attorney General both felt that perhaps the FBI did not want to be saddled with the tremendous responsibilities it was being given." DeLoach told Christopher that was not the case. "To the contrary, we insisted upon such responsibilities . . . we would have no part of recommending legislation which would establish useless substructures or a waste of the taxpayer's funds." Senators McClellan and Eastland, he added, sided with the FBI. While acknowledging the FBI's "powerful allies," Christopher said the attorney general thought "another agency," a national office on law enforcement, should at least "*share* the responsibilities with the FBI." The director favored McClellan's version. "We will not agree to *sharing* any part of this." If Christopher tried to do something about it, "he would meet considerable resistance on the Hill."[80]

The skirmishes here were part of a larger battle between Justice Department attorneys who believed crime would disappear if poverty disappeared and FBI officials who believed crime would disappear if the permissivists in the Department (Ramsey Clark) and on the Supreme Court (Earl Warren) would disappear. Having failed to persuade DeLoach and Hoover to modify the crime control bill, the Department turned to Senator Robert Kennedy for assistance—hoping "to knock out the FBI provision." The Johnson administration experienced some success in attaining a "consensus between hard-line demands for crackdown and constitutional solicitude for civil liberties and due process."[81] When the Omnibus Crime Control and Safe Streets Act became law in 1968, it included a provision creating the inhouse bureaucracy Clark and Christopher wanted, the Law Enforcement Assistance Administration, and another provision increasing the number of police officers authorized to attend the FBI National Academy from 200 to 2,000. Title I appropriated $5,110,000 to the Bureau in fiscal year 1969 for training programs at the Academy.[82]

While the FBI expanded the National Academy, published pamphlets and instructed local police in the "fundamentals" (DeLoach's word) of riot control, Hoover sought an exemption from the Justice Department policy requiring an automatic preliminary investigation upon the receipt of a police brutality complaint. The number of police brutality cases was expanding at an alarming rate by 1968, and movement radicals were publishing pamphlets of their own—for example, a *Black Survival Guide* subtitled *How to Live Through a Police Riot*. But the FBI had no time for investigating police brutality. The FBI had plenty of time for the people who raised the issue, however. The special agent in charge of the Pittsburgh field office tried to "neutralize" a National Urban League grant proposal on the grounds that it called for the creation of a citywide civilian police review board. The Bureau furnished "documentation opposing such civilian review boards" to a "source at the Mellon Foundation."[83]

Even the Orangeburg, South Carolina, "riot" of February 8, 1968, was little more than a minor irritant for the FBI. Highway patrolmen fired on 400 students from State College and other young people protesting a segregated bowling alley near the campus, killing three and wounding nearly thirty. Twenty-eight people were shot in the side or back. A few were hit in the soles of their feet. The FBI agent assigned to supervise the subsequent civil rights probe shared a motel room with one of the subjects of the investigation, and two of the agents on the scene at the time of the shooting told the Civil Rights Division that they had not been there. Hugh Fleischer, who worked on the case when it came to trial during the Nixon years, said they "falsified the information to protect the [nine indicted] troopers. . . . I happened to get the call from Dick Kleindienst," then deputy attorney general, "to not crossexamine the Bureau agents because it would be detrimental to the relationship between the Department and the Bureau." Under pressure from Division lawyers who threatened to resign and go to the press, "[we] got the department to back off," Fleischer continued. "Sadly, it didn't help. The jury was out for twenty minutes and acquitted," having concluded that the troopers had not imposed summary punishment "under color of law" by firing into the crowd.[84]

That decision pleased the director. He sympathized with law enforcement officers caught in "an intense demoralizing situation where [black people] cry 'police brutality' on the slightest provocation" and insist on being addressed "in courteous language"—"particularly in the case of Negroes as instead of saying, 'Boy, come here,' they want to be address[ed] as 'Mr.'" Hoover's sympathies, as ever, were with the "officers above" and their nightsticks and guns, not the "Negro on the ground."[85] In South Carolina, the director also stood with state officials. While the civil rights case worked its way through the federal courts, state prosecutors blamed the Orangeburg violence on one of the wounded protestors—SNCC's Cleveland Sellers. "The biggest nigger in the crowd," the governor's representative said. Sellers was locked up "in a tiny cell on death row," where he said he found it hard not to think about Schwerner, Chaney, and Goodman. Seven weeks after the massacre, moreover, he went to trial on a federal charge of violating the Selective Service Act. The court found him guilty, though that action was complicated when the FBI admitted reviewing Sellers's file at his draft board and monitoring his telephone conversations. In the fall of 1970 the state finally convicted him of participating in a riot *two nights before the shootings*. The events in Orangeburg, Tom Wicker of the *New York Times* wrote, suggests "how casual is this country's sense of justice for black people, how careless it is of its own humanity."[86]

Things had changed since the spring of 1964. The FBI had provided "civil rights training" for law enforcement officers, but it was a token effort, in effect a public-relations gimmick. Riot training for these same policemen, in contrast, was a serious business. It may have been public relations, too, but it was a way for the FBI to expand in size, and to spread its ideology about racial matters and subversives and what Ramsey Clark described as its "hostile view of the life of poor blacks in America." The same thing could be said about the FBI's commitment to affirmative action within its ranks. If black agents were still hard to find in Hoover's FBI, the few the director had hired were easy to see. When the Bureau arrested Rap Brown in late July 1967, Hoover immediately called the White House. "I took the occasion," he told Marvin Watson, "to have a Negro Agent participate in the arrest."[87]

FBI riot training for policemen, arrests of people like Rap Brown, and covert assistance to Senator McClellan provided a law-and-order alternative to the social, cultural, and economic prescriptions of the Kerner Commission. It was no coincidence that John McClellan had turned to the FBI for help with the PERM hearings and the Omnibus Crime Control and Safe Streets Act. Hoover knew the Kerner Commission and McClellan's projects symbolized a division in the nation. With the war and the riots, the United States was coming apart. Richard Nixon, with his slogan of "bring us together again," updated version of Goldwater's southern strategy, and politics of resentment, best understood the depth of the division. "The whole secret of politics . . . [is] knowing who hates who," said Kevin Phillips, aide to John Mitchell and the Nixon campaign expert on ethnic voting patterns. "The Republicans have the political freedom to disregard [Negroes]," to "build a winning coalition" by exploiting "Negro-Democratic mutual identification."[88]

Alone in the White House, with his three-screen television console, Lyndon Johnson watched his own tragedy unfold each evening on the network news. He knew what was happening, but did not know what to do about it. He never really made the choice, never really decided on a political strategy, never really gave up his dream of consensus for a more cold-blooded politics of "positive-polarization" (Spiro Agnew's words). Perhaps he was too decent a man, after all. He kept drifting from the world of the Great Society and the Kerner Commission's sociology to the segmented world of Hoover and McClellan and the Nixon campaign.[89] "It is time to rip away the rhetoric and to divide on authentic lines," Vice-President Agnew said without apology after the election. "When the President said 'bring us together' he meant the functioning, contributing portions of the American citizenry." The FBI director agreed. "To Hoover," as one of his biographers noted, protesters of every stripe, whether ghetto rioters or college students marching against the war, "were not part of the real America, 'the hard-working, tax-paying, law-abiding people of this country.'"[90]

President Johnson never gave up completely on the citizens the new vice-president and the old FBI director held in contempt. If he could explain the riots by reference to "a few hoodlums sparked by outside agitators who moved around from city to city making trouble. Spoiling all the progress I've made," in the next breath he could say, "God knows how little we've really moved on this issue despite all the fanfare. As I see it, I've moved the Negro from D+ to C−. He's still nowhere. He knows it. And that's why he's out in the streets. Hell, I'd be there too."[91]

When the riots began, Lyndon Johnson was not sure he could trust Hoover. Ironically, by the time the riots had run their course, he was certain of Hoover's loyalty—and that certainty may have been his grandest delusion. "Dick, you will come to depend on Edgar," LBJ told the new president-elect. "He is a pillar of strength in a city of weak men. You will rely on him time and time again to maintain security. He's the only one you can put your complete trust in."[92] The director, nonetheless, had been working for the McClellans and Nixons all along. In the end, Hoover made things harder for Johnson and the social reformers of the Great Society, and he made things easier for Nixon and Nixon's heirs. He helped make the Republican party the white man's party Martin Luther King had feared it might become, back in the spring of 1964, a few months before the fires started burning.

The FBI director's maneuverings during the riot years suggest that he was no shrill anticommunist ideologue or practitioner of what Richard Hofstadter once called the paranoid style of American politics. Rather, he was a sophisticated politician who understood power and public opinion. He ingratiated himself with the president and with the president's domestic political adversaries while pursuing his own personal, bureaucratic, and political interests. Johnson tried to use Hoover to help him manage the politics of the riots, but he had no more success in controlling the director than had any of his Oval Office predecessors dating back to Franklin D. Roosevelt. He used the FBI to help him manage particular problems and to help him govern, and Hoover damaged Johnson's interests on both fronts. In the end, the director's bureaucracy, the FBI, and the director's mode of operation, federal surveillance, became further entrenched in the governing process.

One of Hoover's aides said "he handled the presidents as well or better than any bureaucrat in the city of Washington ever has."[93] It would be hard to argue with that assessment, and harder still to overstate the consequences for black Americans. Throughout the riot years Hoover's pronouncements on the menace of subversion oscillated wildly, with the director sometimes exaggerating the communist role in the riots and sometimes minimizing it depending on the particular audience to be addressed and the bureaucratic imperatives of the moment. That inconsistency of word, however, should not obscure the fundamental fact about the FBI agenda in those times, whether the director spoke the language of anticommunism or the new language of law and order—or even on occasion the language of social scientists who saw poverty and despair at the center of the riots and not Reds or liberal permissivists. Hoover worked every day to build up a surveillance system that reflected his belief that all of black America, not just Brown and Carmichael and the always troublesome King, posed a subversive threat to the real America—the hard-working, tax-paying, law-abiding white people of this country. He worked every day to spread the white backlash that had infected American politics during the riot years.

8

Black Hate

Community Surveillance and Counterintelligence

J Edgar Hoover focused on the black menace and not the Red menace during the last of the Great Society years, and he framed the FBI response to the chaos and crime of the cities accordingly. With black activists sowing seeds of discontent and militant protest in the ghettoes, and with the Johnson administration giving him free reign to march against the new black menace in any way he saw fit, the director constructed a pervasive two-track surveillance system. Hoover mobilized the FBI to smash the vanguard (black political activists of liberal and radical views) and to keep track of the masses (the everyday people who lived in black communities). In August 1967, with the Great Society consensus crumbling amidst burning cities and war in Southeast Asia, the FBI launched a new counterintelligence program, patterned after the Communist party and Ku Klux Klan operations, that targeted civil rights movement leaders and black power advocates alike under a "Black Hate Group" caption. At the same time, the FBI targeted all of black America under a series of community surveillance programs.

Lyndon Johnson might have been ignorant about the details surrounding the "black hate" disruption effort, and it is possible, perhaps likely, that he was not even aware of its existence. Yet Hoover and his principal aides interpreted the president's obsession with militants and nationalists, and as well with those

civil rights leaders who opposed the Vietnam war, as an Oval
Office grant of authority to do whatever was necessary to neutralize them. On the other hand, community surveillance clearly
resulted from White House pressure. Though structured more
by the conservative politics and values of internal security bureaucrats than the liberal politics and values of LBJ's social reformers, FBI counterintelligence programs aimed at black leadership and community surveillance programs aimed at blacks
as a group were as much a Great Society legacy as the Civil
Rights Act of 1964 or the Voting Rights Act of 1965. By giving
the FBI carte blanche, the Johnson administration contributed
to the emergence of surveillance as the principal element in the
federal government's relationship with its black citizens during
the president's last two years in office.

The FBI director found the Great Society tolerant of surveillance even before the riots and the antiwar movement led President Johnson to imagine dissent as a gigantic conspiracy led by
his enemies.[1] Washington legend credits Johnson for remarking
how he would rather have Hoover inside the tent pissing out
than outside the tent pissing in. Perhaps the best proof of that
LBJism lies in the volume of names submitted to the FBI for
clearance during the Great Society years. Even the president's
grandson received a check. At his first birthday party, his grand-
mother joked with the press corps about the White House pass
around the toddler's neck. The clearance had included "a letter
from J. Edgar Hoover himself, saying that 'nothing derogatory
was found in the files of the FBI against Patrick Lyndon Nugent!'"[2] Johnson's people so often sent Hoover's people into the
files for more serious work that Mildred Stegall, who served as
the designated White House recipient of the FBI's reports,
thought the administration abused the service.[3] A low-profile,
tight-lipped employee known as "the sphinx," Stegall reportedly
went on the FBI payroll for a time. The real name-check person
on the staff was Marvin Watson, one of the president's closest
aides and a man who had much faith in the integrity of the FBI.[4]

When submitting requests for reports on "matters of extreme
secrecy," Waston asked the FBI not to "respond in writing by
formal memoranda." "The President actually wanted," as Cartha DeLoach advised Clyde Tolson, "blind-type" memos bearing
"no government watermarks or letterhead." Neither DeLoach
nor Tolson needed detailed instructions. The Bureau had been
preparing blind memos for decades and marking documents

PERSONAL AND CONFIDENTIAL AND NOT FOR FILES since 1920, if not earlier. And the Bureau had been handling "delicate" matters, matters, as Hoover said, "that we don't want any publicity on" because they "would just be terribly embarrassing to the big boss," at least since the Franklin Roosevelt years. The FBI knew how "to put a special on" whenever the chief executive requested assistance, and how to ingratiate itself with the White House when doing so.[5]

Mildred Stegall's "special files" include sixty-two boxes of FBI reports on "individuals other than staff." The FBI even dug up "derogatory information" on Joe Louis and Jesse Owens. "Owens ... sent greetings to the National Negro Congress on October 15, 16, 1937," the FBI said. On one January 1967 day Stegall submitted the names of thirty black Democrats—elected officeholders and party organizers. The FBI uncovered "no pertinent derogatory information" on Harold Washington, then a member of the Illinois State Senate and later mayor of Chicago, and sixteen others. The FBI did uncover some on two future members of the U.S. House of Representatives, George Crockett (D., Mich.) and Mervyn M. Dymally (D., Cal.), and eleven others.[6] Another nineteen boxes in Stegall's files concern subjects ranging from the Harlem Freedom Forum to South African Affairs and Vice President Humphrey's Files on FBI Investigations. From 1964 to 1968 Stegall received 738 Bureau reports, most of which were not specifically solicited, under a single category, Race Relations and Related Matters.[7]

A broad FBI community surveillance program on Race Relations and Related Matters had begun in 1966, when the Justice Department assigned a handful of law students to a so-called Summer Project and told them to organize newspaper clippings, data from United States attorneys, and "some Bureau material." The Department wanted to find out "what's going on in the black community." A year later, in the wake of the Newark and Detroit riots and President Johnson's "standing instructions," Department attorneys pursued the law students' effort on a more systematic basis. What Joseph Califano described, many years later, as an appalling "lack of intelligence ... for us in the White House," however, was actually a lack of analysis. The real need was to coordinate the already "heavy flow of FBI reports."[8] Califano believed the White House pressured Justice to produce the wrong type of intelligence. The emphasis should have been on "physical intelligence" (basic urban geography) and "social intelligence" (socioeconomic data) in cities racked by rioting. It was more important to know the location of the hospitals and power stations and schools and the unemployment and high school dropout rates than what the local SNCC contingent or the Revolutionary Action Movement people were up to.[9] But no one even thought of that at the time. The president's men seemed interested only in compiling "advance intelligence about dissident groups."[10]

FBI officials continued to dodge Attorney General Ramsey Clark and Assistant Attorney General for Civil Rights John Doar when they issued directives regarding police brutality or voting rights matters. They were receptive, however, when Clark and Doar spoke of expanding surveillance. At Clark's request, Doar studied the Justice Department's "facilities for keeping abreast" of the racial intelligence the Bureau kept sending over, recommending the establishment of "a single intelligence unit to analyze the FBI information we receive." He also suggested the solicitation of data from the Great Society bureaucracies—"the poverty programs, the Labor Department programs, and the Neighborhood Legal Services." "This is a sensitive area," Doar conceded, but the administration could maintain its "credibility with people in the ghetto" by keeping the unit's existence secret. He recommended no limitation on FBI coverage, arguing that the past surveillance consensus, with its relatively narrow focus on "a limited number of traditional subversive groups" and "individuals" suspected "of a specific statutory violation," was part of the problem. "A broad spectrum approach" was essential—at least until the proposed intelligence "unit became knowledgeable and sophisticated and could make reasonable judgements and . . . [narrow] its spectrum to a more limited target." In the interim, Doar saw no alternative to community surveillance.[11]

Clark created an Interdivisional Intelligence Unit (IDIU) in December 1967, assigning supervisory responsibility to Doar, Assistant Attorneys General Fred Vinson (Criminal) and J. Walter Yeagley (Internal Security), and Community Relations Service Director Roger Wilkins.[12] The IDIU proposed to use FBI reports to compile "a master index," organized on a city-by-city basis, "on individuals, or organizations." Clark based his authorization on executive discretion and criminal statutes regarding rebellion and insurrection that dated from the Civil War era. He also cited the Smith Act, the World War II–era law that made it a crime to conspire to teach or advocate the violent overthrow of the government. Clark thus emerged as one of the founding fathers of community surveillance. Complaining about the limits of "existing intelligence sources," he championed instead a "broad investigation," one that would monitor all possible riot conspirators in "the urban ghetto." He ordered the FBI to "use the maximum available resources, investigative and intelligence, to collect and report all facts" regarding any "scheme or conspiracy by any group." This included the development and expansion of "sources or informants in black nationalist organizations," from SNCC to "other less publicized groups."[13]

Roger Wilkins, then the highest ranking black man in the Justice Department, said "Johnson despised us ... because we wouldn't put Stokely Carmichael in jail." Fred Vinson said the Department averaged "fifty letters a week from Congress" demanding that "people like Carmichael be jailed." In this view, the IDIU and the other community surveillance programs that followed were a product of "the atmosphere of the time." Vinson remembered one congressman saying "to hell with the First Amendment." So the Department kept trying to put Carmichael behind bars; only Clark's men never could figure out which, if any, federal law he had violated. "The only thing you could get Stokely on was speech," Wilkins said. The administration intended to collect advance intelligence about possible disorders in the ghetto and at the same time focus the blame for the riots on subversive conspirators. This last goal came directly from the Oval Office, and Clark and Doar grudgingly acceded to it even as they dismissed the president's obsessions.[14]

"The Department made a judgment that you could [gather intelligence] for a good purpose," Doar said, reflecting on the origins of the IDIU and the decision to rely so heavily on FBI data. "We didn't think it through, I didn't think it through—that if you could do it for a good purpose, there was concern that some people might be able to do it for a bad purpose.... If I'd been smarter I'd probably have figured out that's what's going to happen." Doar based his original recommendations on his experiences in the South during the voting litigation campaign of the early 1960s. To change society for the better, he said, "you had to be on the scene, you had to know the territory." But by relying on the FBI to provide information about the black community in the urban North, the IDIU functioned in the manner of a "crazy counterintelligence program"—a "lunatic operation," in White House aide John Roche's words. "Clark was in charge of it," Roche added. Years later, "[he] tried to pretend he never heard of it." Clark said he was only aware of about 10 percent of what the FBI was doing, and while that may have been true overall, he was certainly aware of the IDIU and the birth of community surveillance.[15]

The irony is that the Republican party singled out Clark, along with Supreme Court Chief Justice Earl Warren, as the main target of its law-and-order politicking during the 1968 presidential campaign. Even a few members of Johnson's White House staff referred to Clark as "Ramsey the marshmallow," and Hoover himself labeled him a coddler of crooks and black terrorists and an enemy of the law-and-order values of Richard Nixon's silent majority. The attorney general's record, in his own words, of denying "a good many" FBI requests "to wiretap or bug people that worked in this [civil rights] area," was especially irritating.[16]

Attorney General Clark may have encouraged the FBI director to recruit informants and spy, but Hoover, as ever, did so on his own terms, considering primarily the needs of the FBI, not the needs of the Great Society reformers who ran the IDIU. While reminding field agents to take advantage of opportunities whenever "an entree to develop sources in the Negro community" presented itself, the director had supervisors at headquarters review "the informant situation in all areas for each field division" and submit recommendations for new informant programs that ranged far beyond the typical communist or communist infiltration investigations.[17] Recruitment of black informants to cover the Communist party had always been a priority, in part because the CPUSA's lingering obsession with white chauvinism protected black members from suspicion. White communists who accused Negro comrades of working for the FBI often found themselves accused of racism and drummed out of the party. As a result, the Bureau recruited a disproportionately high number of black informants. In some local communist units during the early 1960s, all of the FBI's informants were black. By the mid- and late 1960s, however, black informant coverage of the CPUSA gave way to new priorities—in the words of FBI Assistant Director W. Mark Felt, "live coverage of (1) black nationalist groups, (2) ghetto areas, and (3) groups expected to capitalize on racial disorder and civil disobedience."[18]

The CPUSA fit the third category, but even here party members were not the focus of attention. The FBI centered on black activists and black people in general, emphasizing a black menace almost to the exclusion of the communist menace. The major FBI operation in the first and last categories mentioned by Felt was the TOPLEV (Top Level) Informant Program, later known by the more appropriate acronym, BLACPRO. By the fall of 1967 each field office assigned at least one (and often as many as four) agents to work exclusively on the development of "quality non-organizational sources ... for the purpose of expeditiously infiltrating militant black nationalist organizations." A more convoluted BLACPRO objective required the placement of informants in "new groups" that *might* "spring from the mass Black Nationalist movement." These informants reported on "obscure community activists" who *might* "become agitators for violent protest," and they allowed the Bureau "to position" itself "ahead of the growth of these groups and leaders and to record their development and demise." The striking thing about such programs is the dearth of references to communism—the traditional subversive bogey.[19]

Under BLACPRO and various other informant programs, the FBI covered the entire spectrum. Division Five, the Bureau unit responsible for the great majority of the "Racial Matters" investigations, operated informants within the Southern Christian Leadership Conference national office in Atlanta and among Stokely Carmichael's entourage. The FBI man in the SCLC was comptroller James A. Harrison. William Sullivan described the informant assigned to Carmichael, a bodyguard named Peter Cardoza, as a "tough customer" and "a real discipline problem for the bureau."[20] Most informants were not positioned as well as Harrison and Cardoza. They operated out of cities like Minneapolis, where FBI agents asked "criminal informants in the Negro community" to "furnish information on racial matters." As in the parallel Ku Klux Klan informant program, black informants also operated out of remote regions like southwest Texas, where the FBI had seventeen "Negro informants and sources" in El Paso, four in Midland, nine in Odessa, and two in Pecos.[21]

In October 1967 FBI officials launched an even more pervasive informant program—a "Ghetto Listening Post" or a "Ghetto Informant Program." Their definition of a "listening post" embraced "any individual who resides in a ghetto-type area" or "who frequent[s] ghetto areas on a regular basis." Prospective recruits for the Bureau's "grass-roots network" included employees and owners of taverns and liquor stores, drugstores and pawnshops, candy stores and barbershops, and other ghetto businesses; honorably discharged veterans and especially members of veterans organizations; janitors of apartment buildings; newspaper and food and beverage distributors; taxi drivers; salesmen; and bill collectors. Bureau agents steered these sources toward "Afro-American type book stores" and asked them to identify their "owners, operators and clientele." The informants also reported on persons with criminal records or teen-age gang members "operating in the ghetto," "changes in the attitude of the Negro community towards the white community," and "the sentiments and feelings of individuals" who reside in black neighborhoods. By the summer of 1968 FBI agents had recruited a 3,248-person army to carry out these tasks.[22]

Why would a black person in those times knowingly inform to the FBI? There is no single answer to this question. In the great majority of cases, fiscal and ideological motives were secondary. Ghetto informants, as a general rule, only received modest, sporadic payments "on a c.o.d. basis," with local special agents in charge having the authority to dispense up to $400. Informant recruiters, moreover, did not look for hostility toward a particular black nationalist group. The recruiters sought persons who owned property in the ghetto or had an interest in protecting ghetto property. In fact, age may have been the key factor in ghetto informant recruiting—with the FBI trying to establish contacts with the parents and grandparents of the militants. Amiri Baraka remembered one time, in Newark, when the FBI came "snooping around," and "my father told the FBI where I was, not knowing he didn't have to say shit to them." Most of the informants probably cooperated with the FBI in a similar manner. The initial decision to talk to the Bureau was an unthinking one.[23]

Because Hoover deemed the 1968 number (3,248) inadequate, Division Five developed "a kind of quota system" that required all field agents to develop ghetto informants. It was part of their job. If an agent's territory included no predominantly black communities, he had to "so specify by memorandum"—"so that he will not be charged with failure to perform." The special agents in charge of Bureau field offices never knew how many informants were enough, only that they had to recruit "a large number of additional racial informants." FBI Assistant Director

Felt told the men who ran the New York office to be grateful for all the ghettoes in their territory. "Opportunities to engage in racial informant development," he said, were boundless.

A few FBI field offices met their big-number quotas by reclassifying criminal informants as ghetto informants, and a few agents simply invented ghetto informants. A small though perhaps not insignificant percentage of informants existed only on paper. This type of fudging could not satisfy Hoover's concomitant demand to improve the quality of the information provided. To meet the director's goals, the field "converted . . . exceptionally intelligent and knowledgeable" ghetto sources to "regular racial informants" (as opposed to "probationary racial informants"); gave them "specific assignments where appropriate"; and encouraged them to speculate "on the general mood of the Negro community concerning susceptibility to foreign influences"—"whether this be from African nations in the form of Pan-Africanism, from the Soviet or Chinese communist bloc nations, or from other nations." The New York office even assigned informants to report on "Subversive and/or Communist Links Between Harlem and Africa."[24]

FBI officials forwarded much of the information gathered by their ghetto and BLACPRO informants directly to the IDIU, where Justice Department attorneys processed 3,500 incoming intelligence reports a month. By the time Nixon took his oath of office, Department attorneys had reviewed 32,000 FBI documents "concerning individuals and organizations involved primarily in the area of racial agitation." Hoover disseminated a more modest amount of cable traffic regarding "selected racial developments" to the White House.[25] In either case, the FBI reviewed the intelligence collected from over 3,000 ghetto informants and an unknown number of BLACPRO informants, passing on the worst of the black-scare stories and feeding President Johnson's fears. Were "black nationalist organizations, as well as independent Negro extremists," really planning to dynamite the Empire State Building? Were the radicals plotting to assassinate "white political candidates" in retaliation "for the killing of Martin Luther King"? Were a handful of black men in Santa Barbara scheming "to 'get' Governor Ronald Reagan"?[26] FBI headquarters required the field to prove or disprove all these rumors and the countless others that showed up in informant reports.[27]

The Johnson administration provided a context for the FBI to proceed on an intrusive and provocative course. The IDIU itself did not extend community surveillance fast enough or far enough to please either the administration or the FBI. The Unit had been functioning for less than a month when Attorney General Clark, Deputy Attorney General Warren Christopher, presidential assistants Joseph Califano and Matthew Nimetz, Deputy Secretary of Defense Paul Nitze, and Acting Army General Counsel Robert Jordan attended a White House strategy session on the riots expected for the summer of 1968. When briefing the group on the new "secret intelligence unit" and its study of "Black Nationalist groups," Clark complained about "the lack of intelligence these groups have received in the past." He stressed "the difficulty of the intelligence effort," pointing out that the FBI's continuing refusal to hire black agents complicated the government's surveillance mission. At the time, the FBI had some forty black agents.[28]

The purpose of this White House meeting had not been to moan about FBI employment practices. The president's men intended to mobilize the Army's intelligence resouces, thereby requiring better coordination between the Justice Department and the Pentagon, for drawing up "contingency plans for troop movements, landing sites, facilities, etc.," for rating "various cities as to their riot potential." According to former Army Chief of Staff Harold K. Johnson, this was only one of several meetings where the administration urged the military to accept a greater responsibility in the civil disturbance collection effort. Clark asked the Defense Department to "screen'" all "incoming intelligence," and to forward "key items" to the Justice Department and the IDIU. Because FBI officials based their own authority to collect "racial matters intelligence" on "Army regulations," they proved willing to assist a more aggressive military surveillance program and did not exhibit undue concerns about the intrusion of Army agents into their internal security domain.[29]

The FBI also began to solicit "racial matters intelligence" systematically from another intelligence bureaucracy, the Central Intelligence Agency, and one of its mail-opening operations, Project Hunter. CIA agents read the mail of thousands of Americans, black and white, from Richard Nixon to Mrs. Martin Luther King, and FBI agents themselves opened and photographed at least 130,000 first-class letters. The most ambitious of the CIA's domestic intelligence gathering projects, CHAOS, concentrated on foreign links to the peace and black movements and even the Nation of Islam. The Agency tried to prove that the Black Muslims received funding from Libya, and that "U.S. Negro Militants" received training "in guerrilla warfare" from Cuba. A third CIA program, RESISTANCE, concentrated on "the influence of Communists and Revolutionaries on the [black] movement" and the "brown [Mexican-American] movement." Another CIA source, the Weekly Situation Report, covered such topics as the 1968 Democratic National Convention. Of all the groups planning to demonstrate, the Agency said, the black groups were "the most dangerous."[30]

Despite an intense jurisdictional rivalry, intelligence on black militants and antiwar activists flowed freely between the FBI and the CIA. The collection of information bearing upon "foreign influences in the Black Nationalist movement" emerged as a priority for both the Bureau and the Agency in 1967, and FBI officials solicited data from the sophisticated CIA sources in Langley, Virginia, just as they had solicited the opinions of the best and the brightest of the ghetto informants in Watts and Detroit.[31]

Investigation of "foreign influences" was only one of the FBI's priorities. Hoover required "immediate and priority handling" of all racial matters investigations—particularly coverage of "those groups which appeal to the young militant Negro." His agents identified one of these groups, the Congress of Racial Equality, as a formerly "legitimate civil rights organization" that had recently adopted a "black nationalist posture." Because CORE leaders Floyd McKissick and then Roy Innis condoned "violence as a means of obtaining Negro rights," and because communist infiltration remained "negligible," the FBI shifted its CORE file from the COMINFIL category to the Racial Matters category and escalated the entire investigation. This was only one of many adjustments made in the late 1960s, and it reflected Hoover's view that blacks represented a greater threat to white America than did the communists.[32]

By this time FBI interest in communist infiltration was secondary even in the case of Martin Luther King and the Southern Christian Leadership Conference. When King went to Memphis in 1968 to help with the garbage collectors strike, the FBI was already there. The Bureau interjected itself into the politics of a labor dispute between the city and 1,300 garbage workers, nearly all of whom were black, by monitoring at least a few of the negotiating sessions organized by the city council and Local 1733 of the American Federation of State, County and Municipal Employees. The Bureau also monitored the principal black power group in Memphis, the Invaders, describing its members not as communists per se, but as a "conniving," "criminal-minded," "monkey-like," "sullen," "loud-mouth" collection of teen-age "dope-head[s]," "movement pimps," and "Beale Street bums" who were also "serious reader[s] of Afro-American literature."[33]

At the same time, FBI officials considered how best to respond to the Poor People's Campaign that King and SCLC planned for May and June 1968 in Washington, D.C. In the past, according to a Division Five analysis, the presence of "a large, well-established, responsible Negro middle class" had combined with the city's physical geography ("its Negro ghettos are spread out and interspaced with pleasant neighborhoods") to prevent the outbreak of large-scale racial disturbances. The Poor People's Campaign, however, threatened the capital's stability. "King's spring project could easily get out of control, degenerate into violence, and thus endanger peace and order." To compound things, Stokely Carmichael had recently formed a Washington-based Black United Front. If King's project represented "the immediate threat to Washington," Division Five reasoned, Carmichael represented "the long-range peril."[34]

When Poor People's Campaign participants began arriving after King's assassination on April 4 and after major rioting in the District, the FBI ran the names of as many people as possible through the files—including those who "appeared to be of the 'hippie variety'" and various "black power sympathizers." William Sullivan even donned some old clothes and went for a stroll through Resurrection City, the plywood and canvas encampment built near the Lincoln Memorial to house some 3,000 campaign participants, where he tried to strike up a conversation with Carmichael. The Division Five chief's presence supplemented the work of regular racial informants in Resurrection City. The informants tracked no Communist party member however. Instead, they gathered "valuable information about the personality traits, weaknesses, and strengths of these people." Division Five told the informants "to document such things as immorality, dishonesty, and hypocrisy."[35]

Hoover sent copies of his reports on the Poor People's Campaign to the Army and the CIA, with sanitized versions going to newspaper reporters, "responsible Negroes," and congressional leaders. Speaker of the House John McCormack (D., Mass.), Senate Majority Leader Mike Mansfield (D., Montana), and PERM Chairman John McClellan (D., Ark.) all received oral briefings, write-ups, and photographs showing "the militant, aggressive appearance" of the young black men and women who came to Resurrection City.[36] The director sent additional reports on the campaign and its aftermath and related topics to the IDIU and the White House. Dr. King had been dead for only a few weeks when Hoover wrote Mildred Stegall with news that Nelson Rockefeller had contacted Coretta Scott King to ask if SCLC or her family needed money. The FBI picked the information up from the Stanley Levison wiretap. Bureau agents followed Levison himself to King's funeral and later Robert Kennedy's funeral, where he was observed talking with Detroit Congressman John Conyers and Gary, Indiana, Mayor Richard Hatcher. By offering to raise funds for the National Committee of Inquiry, a group formed to evaluate candidates for the presidency and other national offices and how they might "respond to the needs of America's black community," Levison inspired the director to send yet another letter to Mrs. Stegall.[37]

Concerned about their own response to the Poor People's Campaign, Johnson administration officials proceeded cautiously. Matthew Nimetz urged Joseph Califano to read what Arthur Schlesinger had to say about Herbert Hoover and the Bonus Expeditionary Force (BEF) in his book, *The Crisis of the Old Order*. The Johnson White House simply had to "deal with the Poor People's Campaign in a more civilized manner" than the Hoover White House had dealt with the BEF, Nimetz wrote, implying that FBI dossiers were more civilized than Army bayonets.[38] Given the scope of the intelligence programs and the counterintelligence programs to come, the FBI was certainly not part of a measured, civilized response to the dissent of the Poor People's Campaign.

FBI officials continued to downplay the communist menace even as they watched their surveillance empire grow day by day. They defined the problem posed by "the black movement" by reference to "militant racial agitators" who "go about the land inciting riots and preaching and instigating anarchy and revolt." This "new type of . . . agitator," Mark Felt concluded, when reviewing the New York field office's coverage, "evolved from unsettled racial and social conditions" and posed a completely new set of problems "which parallel the dangers presented by the pure communist elements." Thus, Felt attributed "most racial disturbances" to "semi-professional hate-mongers and rabble rousers who spend much of their time" waging war on "the status quo" and "teaching the ghetto's . . . receptive elements doctrines of hate."[39] Labels had changed, with the communist menace now becoming the black menace, but the threat stayed the same. Viewing all black citizens as potential threats to his America, Hoover had his justification for violating their rights.

To meet its responsibilities in New York, the FBI assigned twenty-five special agents to the racial squad (Division Four, Section 43) and supplemented that number with at least twenty-five more agents during the summer months. The squad spent its time supervising and recruiting informants for the Ghetto and BLACPRO programs, locating forty-two "ghetto areas" in the city's five boroughs, opening case files on individuals, and occasionally tailing black militants. Squad members used this last tactic rarely—three physical surveillances on Rap Brown by the fall of 1967, two on Stokely Carmichael, three on Revolutionary Action Movement members, and two on Black Muslims—because "surveillances in Negro areas are not generally practical without Negro agents."

In all, the FBI had between 5,000 and 10,000 active cases on matters of race at any given time nationwide. In 1967 some 1,246 FBI agents received civil rights enforcement or racial intelligence assignments each month. By President Johnson's last year in the White House, that number jumped to 1,678 with the vast majority of those agents undertaking intelligence responsibilities and not civil rights responsibilities.[40]

To keep track of the most prominent "racial agitators," the FBI relied on the so-called Security Index (formerly the Custodial Detention Program)—a listing of dissidents ranked according to their "degree of dangerousness" that dated from 1939 and remained an integral part of "Bureau War Plans" until the Watergate era. Intended to facilitate mass arrests in the event of a national emergency, the Security Index contained the names of 15,000 Americans by the early cold war years and included a special section, a Prominent Individuals Subdivision, listing persons whose "apprehensions might be attended by considerable publicity tending to make martyrs of them and thereby [embarrass] the Bureau." FBI officials rarely included black radicals in this section. Not even Paul Robeson rated a "prominent Negro" listing.[41]

Though the Security Index shrank to less than 10,000 names by the early 1960s, the main listing included the names of Martin Luther King and 1,497 other black Americans. The FBI added the names of an additional 400 blacks during the Kennedy and Johnson years. The largest category listed 673 Black Muslims, followed by 476 communists (or former communists or suspected fellow travelers), 66 SNCC activists, 60 Revolutionary Action Movement members, and 222 persons in a general black nationalists' category. Beginning in the late 1950s and continuing throughout the 1960s, the Security Index facilitated target selection for the COINTELs and the Mass Media programs. For a six-month period beginning in April 1961, the time when the Civil Rights Division made its most serious effort to enlist the Bureau in the voter registration campaign, the FBI leaked blind memos detailing the communist associations of 91 Security Index subjects to the press, and sometimes sent clippings from the resulting newspaper stories to the children of the subjects.[42]

The percentage of communists listed on the Security Index declined steadily throughout the decade—from 83.8 percent in 1961, to 55.9 percent by the time LBJ left the White House. According to the FBI's count as of November 1968, party membership stood at 3,198, and that number included a great many who could hardly be considered part of a Leninist vanguard. Others, perhaps as many as one-third, were informants. An FBI executives' conference considered these facts and unanimously recommended a six-month suspension of "investigations, and particularly report writing, in routine Security Matter–Communist cases throughout the field." "It got to be nothing more than a statistical burden," one Division Five executive said. Communist matters now absorbed too much manpower. The "anarchistic tendencies" of New Left and racial militants needed greater attention.[43]

Hoover himself seemed more concerned about noncommunist racial militants than card-carrying communists. Earlier, when testifying before the Kerner Commission, he discussed the impact of "rabble-rousers who initiate action and then disappear," mentioning King, McKissick, Brown, and Carmichael. "Any law that allowed law enforcement the opportunity to arrest . . . vicious rabble-rousers," he said, "would be healthy to have on the books." One Commission member, New York Mayor John Lindsay, asked "if it would be possible to total up and fully identify the number of militant Negroes and whites who were in the same category as Carmichael and Brown." He wanted to know "just exactly what the hard core in this country amounted to." Hoover responded by ordering Division Five to compile a more refined listing of "vociferous rabble-rousers" than provided by the Security Index.[44]

Hoover hoped the first edition of the new Rabble Rouser Index of "individuals who have demonstrated a potential for fomenting racial discord" would facilitate target selection for the new black nationalist counterintelligence program, launched on August 25, 1967. Initially, FBI officials defined a rabble-rouser "as a person who tries to arouse people to violent action by appealing to their emotions, prejudices, et cetera; a demagogue." They quickly broadened these standards to include persons with a "propensity for fomenting" any type of disorder affecting the nation's "internal security." New Rabble Rouser Index categories included "black nationalists, white supremacists, Puerto Rican nationalists, anti-Vietnam demonstration leaders, and other extremists." Subcategories pertaining to black dissidents included CORE, SNCC, SCLC, Revolutionary Action Movement, Nation of Islam, Black Panther party, and a black nationalist catchall. Everything was computerized.

In March 1968 the Rabble Rouser Index received a new name, the Agitator Index, and headquarters directed the field to submit "visual material relating to violence by black extremists." Division Five wanted "clear, glossy, 8″ by 10″ photographs." Sullivan's men also requested a photograph of each of the one hundred or so persons listed on the Agitator Index. Upon receiving and pasting the photos in the Black Nationalist Photograph Album, Division Five sent copies of this mug book to the field, along with a Racial Calendar highlighting "the dates of . . . racial events." To make sure that his agents could track any "militant black nationalist" who might "turn up" in another country, Hoover approved distribution of the Black Nationalist Photograph Album to the CIA and the Royal Canadian Mounted Police.[45]

The original edition of the Rabble Rouser Index was a disappointment. Bureau field offices had submitted a mere one hundred names.[46] Consequently, the agents assigned to select targets for the new counterintelligence program (COINTELPRO–Black

Hate Group or –Black Nationalist) had little to do. The entire program floundered despite Williams Sullivan's best efforts. Hoover approved the transfer of black nationalist intelligence and counterintelligence responsibilities to Division Five following the summer riots, and Sullivan immediately organized a racial intelligence section to manage the new work. George C. Moore moved over from the nationalities intelligence section to supervise racial intelligence and Theron D. Rushing ran the new COINTELPRO.

Deeming the initial Rabble Rouser/Agitator Index inadequate, Division Five sent another directive to the field in March 1968 requesting an "estimate" of the "propensity for violence" within specific black groups. Interested in "target evaluation," not "record purposes," Division Five told the field to concentrate on "the most violent and radical groups and their leaders"—among others, Martin Luther King of the Southern Christian Leadership Conference, Stokely Carmichael and Rap Brown of the Student Nonviolent Coordinating Committee, Maxwell Stanford of the Revolutionary Action Movement, and Elijah Muhammad of the Nation of Islam.[47]

FBI field agents searched their files and sent their target evaluations back to the seat of government. The new listings, however, were hardly more encouraging than the first edition of the Rabble Rouser Index. The Omaha office reported no "organized Black Nationalist Movement" in Nebraska, and ten other field offices reported no black nationalists beyond the membership of the Nation of Islam (NOI). And nearly every special agent in charge believed Black Muslims merited little attention. In Milwaukee, the FBI man said NOI members were not involved in civil disturbances or civil rights activity of any kind. "A counterintelligence program," he added, "may change the present situation." In Kansas City, two racial informants covered the local mosque, but their reports never indicated any involvement in situations "conducive to tension or violence." Given the Nation of Islam's "present indicated ineffectuality," the SAC wrote, COINTELPRO targeting would not be "suggestible as practicable at this time." This last assessment applied to black nationalist activity in general, he added, advising Division Five not to waste its time with target lists. The FBI man in Kansas City thought it more valuable, when preparing "for future contingencies," to encourage "public and private expressions of favorable Negro leader-figure contacts," to work with "trustworthy liberals," and to "delicately utilize, where practicable, Negro school and church teachers and persons influential with Negro youth."[48]

Division Five subjected Black Muslims to dozens of counterintelligence actions nonetheless. George Moore, the racial intelligence chief, conceded that Muhammad kept his followers "under control, and . . . did not have them on the streets at all during any of the riots." Moore could only emphasize the NOI's "paramilitary . . . potential." The special agent in charge of the Jackson office, Roy Moore, claimed that Muhammad operated a "hit group"—a vague reference, apparently, to the renegade Muslims who had murdered Malcolm X in Harlem's Audubon Ballroom.[49] Thus, Bureau officials had all the justification they needed. They approved the mailing of cartoon leaflets intended to ridicule Muslim life-styles and beliefs to the media in nearly a dozen states, and in Texas they had local agents investigate a mosque in search of a White Slave Traffic Act violation. In Washington, D.C., they attempted to close a Muslim grade school by unleashing the local zoning, tax, and health and safety bureaucracy, and by opening files on the parents of each of the approximately 150 children enrolled in the school.[50]

Every FBI field office experienced difficulty in locating targets for the counterintelligence program beyond the membership of the Nation of Islam. Pittsburgh identified a grand total of two potential targets: the Afro-American Institute, "a study group whose purpose is to promote an interest in black culture," and the Organizers, a teenage group active in issuing "public letters protesting . . . the solicitation of Negro girls in ghetto areas by white males." In Newark, most black groups (SNCC, SCLC, RAM) had "not been factors thus far." The field office merely suggested the targeting of the general membership of the United Afro-American Association and LeRoi Jones (Amiri Baraka). New York identified fewer than one hundred prospective targets, and even that number included members of groups with the sole mission of spreading African culture in Harlem.[51]

The Detroit FBI office identified few potential targets beyond members of the Malcolm X Society, the SNCC contingent (mostly teenagers from city high schools), and the City-Wide Citizens Action Committee. This last group, the SAC noted, continually harassed "the Detroit Police Department, accusing the department of police brutality." Marlin Johnson, head of the Chicago office, listed nine groups, but one of those was inactive and another was "a one man operation." The most likely candidates for the counterintelligence program in Cleveland were New Libya and the Afro American Sect. Members of the first group met at an astrology shop, spending their time "drinking wine, smoking 'pot,' . . . playing cards, and engaging in various forms of criminal activity" and "sexual promiscuity." These "heavy drinking" black nationalists, the local FBI man concluded, possessed a "great potential for violence." The members of the second group spent their time taking "instructions in Karate" and planning "the takeover of Cleveland and the entire country by black revolution." In California, a growing Black Panther party and about forty-five or fifty "hard core" members of Maulana Ron Karenga's US (as opposed to "THEM") attracted some concern, along with various student associations and at least one group whose membership studied "the Swahili language and Karate."[52]

Black nationalists with a propensity for violence were particularly hard to find in the South. In all of South Carolina, the FBI could find only two SNCC representatives and two black student organizations. In Mississippi, Roy Moore located a Political Action Committee at Tougaloo College. Miami described CORE and SCLC as "relatively inactive." The Bogalusa Voters League was the only viable target in Louisiana. The Mobile and Birmingham special agents in charge noted the presence of various SCLC and SNCC representatives, but said they expected no violence in Alabama.[53] The Jacksonville office had seven or eight sources (students, faculty, staff) at Florida A&M University, and "constantly" worked "to increase . . . informant coverage." But to what purpose? In Tennessee, the Bureau ran file checks on faculty at Tennessee A&I University and other predominantly black colleges where students supported SNCC and opposed "the school administration," and sent the names of "black militants . . . enrolled at the various universities [in the state] . . . to trusted and reliable sources at these . . . universities."[54]

On balance, few of these targets posed a danger, and thus required little attention. Still, the FBI ended up harassing, as one COINTELPRO supervisor admitted, "a great number of organizations that you might not today characterize as black nationalist but which were in fact primarily black."[55] The breadth of targeting resembled the pattern under the Communist party counterintelligence program, where the FBI used a loosely defined notion of "communist association" to focus on broad noncommunist sectors. COINTELPRO–Black Nationalist was unique in that the FBI defined "black nationalist" loosely enough to include, in theory, at least, every member of a particular race who happened to be a member of any organization whatsoever.

The target evaluation request sent to the FBI field offices in March 1968 was part of a broad expansion of the black hate group operation. The original directive establishing the program emphasized the immediate goals in a straightforward manner: "to expose, disrupt, misdirect, discredit, or otherwise neutralize the activities of black nationalist, hate-type organizations and groupings, their leadership, spokesmen, membership, and supporters." Long-range goals followed: to prevent militant black groups from forming coalitions, building up their membership, gaining respectability, and developing a charismatic leader. Twenty-three field offices participated, with the various special agents in charge assigning "experienced and imaginative" agents as "counterintelligence coordinators."[56]

The FBI had been engaged in "felonious" harassment of Dr. King and other black activists long before the summer of 1967. All of this harassment, a Justice Department task force later concluded, was "very probably" in violation of the old Reconstruction Era statutes, Sections 241 and 242, that provided for criminal penalties against any person, acting "under color of law" or otherwise, who denied any other person their civil rights.[57] Some of it was carried out informally. Other actions were part of other formal, structured COINTELPROs—against the Communist party, the Socialist Workers party, and, inexplicably, the Ku Klux Klan. One of the Cleveland field office's most ambitious operations, against the Jomo Freedom Kenyatta House, arose from the white hate group program even though no segregationists were involved. FBI activities increased in the first few weeks and months following the launching of COINTELPRO–Black Nationalist, but not dramatically. To cite a rather typical case: the Bureau failed to prove that Herbert Aptheker, the historian and Communist party functionary, provided bail money for Rap Brown, and thus had nothing to leak to its "cooperative and reliable" newspaper sources.[58]

One of the few early efforts deemed successful, an effort that actually began several months before the birth of the black nationalist program, involved Revolutionary Action Movement members in Philadelphia, Pennsylvania. While arguing, as ever,

that police brutality was a false issue, the FBI arranged for Philadelphia police officers to arrest RAM members "on every possible charge until they could no longer make bail." On one occasion, after the police had been sent around for still another
nuisance arrest, a RAM leader lay down in frustration and rage,
and began to beat the floor of his apartment with his fists.[59]

In anticipation of the approach of summer, Division Five proposed an expansion of counterintelligence activity to disrupt
and discredit civil rights activists and black nationalists. In
March 1968 representatives from forty-one field offices met at
the seat of government for a racial conference, and on the second day of that conference they agreed upon the new request for
target evaluation. They also developed the original long-range
goals of COINTELPRO–Black Hate Group in considerable detail. When seeking "to provent the . . . *growth* of militant black
nationalist organizations," the field was told to implement "specific tactics to prevent these groups from converting young
people." This goal was closely related to another basic investigative mission—to prevent violence by "pinpoint[ing] potential
troublemakers and neutraliz[ing] them before they exercise
their potential for violence." "Obviously," one COINTELPRO supervisor reasoned, "you are going to prevent violence or a
greater amount of violence if you have smaller groups." In other
words, "the programs were to prevent violence indirectly, rather
than directly, by preventing possibly violent citizens from joining or continuing to associate with possibly violent groups."[60]

The remaining long-term COINTELPRO goals demonstrate
FBI officials' more explicitly political and elitist assumptions
about their duty to smash any perceived threat to the existing
social order. These counterintelligence goals were also representative of the social and cultural conservatism that permeated
Hoover's FBI, a conservatism that sometimes expressed itself in
a cartoon view of the changes occurring in American society.
Division Five mused over an old truism, "in unity there is
strength," and considered it "no less valid for all its triteness."
Sullivan's men found justification here for a fundamental objective: to "prevent the *coalition* of militant black nationalist
groups." "An effective coalition," Division Five concluded, in a
wild assessment of one highly unlikely outcome, "might be the
first step toward a real 'Mau Mau' in America, the beginning of
a true black revolution." While waiting for the real thing to arrive, the Division placed the fifteen or twenty members of

Charles 37X Kenyatta's Harlem Mau Mau on the COINTELPRO target list. Kenyatta's group armed itself with bayonets and machetes, but nonetheless cooperated with John Lindsay and Nelson Rockefeller to keep peace in the ghetto following King's assassination.

Division Five also worked to "prevent the *rise of a 'messiah'*— someone "who could unify, and electrify, the militant black nationalist movement." Malcolm X had been the most likely candidate, but his assassination removed that threat. Malcolm was simply "the martyr of the movement today." Muhammad was hardly a more viable threat "because of his age." In the final analysis, Division Five said, Carmichael and King were the only serious candidates. They both dreamed of becoming a messiah and had "the necessary charisma." Not even Sullivan considered King to be a militant, but that was beside the point. "King could be a very real contender for this position should he abandon his supposed 'obedience' to 'white, liberal doctrines' (nonviolence) and embrace black nationalism."[61]

This particular counterintelligence goal represented one of the few areas where current FBI policy proved less ambitious than previous policy. Its fears of an American Mau Mau aside, Division Five demonstrated a more rational view of the black movement here than it had in 1963–1964, when it assumed that King was already a messiah, someone who needed to be "taken off his pedestal." At the time, Sullivan believed King would be destroyed, and that the subsequent "confusion . . . among the Negro people" and "the emotional reaction that will set in" would provide opportunities for the FBI. King's collapse would be followed by "ridiculous developments similar to the Old Father Devine and Daddy Grace organizations," leaving "the Negroes . . . without a national leader of sufficiently compelling personality to steer them in the proper direction."[62] The apparent unity of the civil rights movement at the time of the March on Washington had disappeared by 1968, with the new militants deriding King as an "Uncle Tom" and much of white America no longer considering King a wholesome, respectable Negro—given his comments on Vietnam and his increasingly strident call for an economic restructuring of American society. Division Five intended to keep black activists bickering among themselves and to focus white America's attention on the inherently un-American nature of black protest.

While subverting the efforts of black activists to build bridges between their mostly tiny organizations and plotting to quash the rise of a black messiah, Division Five directed the field to prevent those activists and groups "from gaining respectability." Sullivan hoped to discredit black nationalists in the eyes of "three separate segments of the community"—"the responsible Negro community," "the white community," and the black "followers of the movement." Division Five broke down the white community into a responsible element and an irresponsible element, with the latter consisting of "'liberals' who have vestiges of sympathy for militant black nationalist[s] simply because they are Negroes."

Field office response to this last goal was mixed. What was the point, Chicago SAC Marlin Johnson asked? "There remain very few hard core white liberals who continue to attempt to work with and aid the militant black nationalists as opposed to the more legitimate civil rights groups." Other FBI men, particularly those who lived and worked in the South, were more enthusiastic about this part of the counterintelligence program. The special agent in charge of the Charlotte office saw nothing wrong with a campaign "to eliminate the facade of civil rights," a campaign to "show the American public the true revolutionary plans and spirit of the Black Nationalist movement and its leaders." Hoover's man in North Carolina also saw nothing wrong with giving the campaign a boost by "counterfeiting literature damaging to the [movement]."[63]

The FBI effort to discredit black dissidents before "the responsible Negro elements" and "the followers of the movement" was more complex. It required "entirely different tactics," Division Five reasoned, because "publicity about violent tendencies and radical statements merely enhance" the prestige of black nationalist leaders in the eyes of the rank and file. "It adds 'respectability' in a different way." Bureau officials hoped to accomplish their goal here by developing "news media" contacts from coast to coast "that cater to the Negro community." If the special agent in charge of a particular office did not have any "established, reliable, contacts among Negro news media," he was told to develop such contacts—an order that led to some fudging in the field.[64]

Both the New York and San Francisco offices claimed columnist Carl Rowan as "a responsible Negro" media contact, but Rowan's assessment of that claim, in these years, at least, is probably correct. "J. Edgar Hoover hated my guts; nobody from the F.B.I. ever fed me any information." In 1964, as director of the U.S. Information Agency, Rowan did receive a two-page document from the FBI entitled "Martin Luther King, Jr., His Personal Conduct." In the late 1960s, however, the director dismissed Rowan as a "racist columnist." The FBI had only a handful of black media contacts, and no evidence indicates that Rowan was one of them. Mostly, the Bureau relied on anonymous mailings to Rowan and other black newspapermen, with Crime Records sending clippings from mainstream newspapers or the NAACP's *Crisis* that were critical of the new militants.[65]

FBI agents also disseminated "anti-violent statements" issued by such prominent black citizens as former boxing champion Archic Moore, and arranged for another boxer, Olympic gold medalist George Foreman, to receive an award from the Freedoms Foundation. Foreman, as Division Five noted, "gave every American an emotional lift" by beating "a Soviet fighter in the finals," by showing "the world . . . he was proud to be an American by waving a small American flag," and by singing "the national anthem at the award ceremonies." This conspicuous patriotism stood in "sharp contrast with the earlier despicable black power-black gloved demonstration of Tommie Smith and John Carlos on the Olympic victory stand and the anti-Vietnam stand of Cassius Clay." The Freedoms Foundation was a logical choice. Headquartered in Valley Forge, Pennsylvania, and closely connected to the J. Edgar Hoover Foundation, the Freedoms Foundation had at one time or another been associated with a number of right-wing personalities and segregationists, from Billy Hargis to Howard "Bo" Callaway. When Foreman finally received his award in February 1969, Cartha DeLoach arranged appropriate media coverage.[66]

With regard to white-owned newspapers widely read in black neighborhoods, the FBI faced something of a dilemma. To circulate Bureau propaganda, as the Boston office reminded Division Five, it was necessary to work with such relatively liberal newspapers as the *Boston Globe*. If the *Globe* was basically "anti-Bureau in tone," "a much larger percentage of Negroes in the Roxbury area" read it "than any other Boston paper." The *Globe* covered "Negro complaints against discrimination, segregation, and poor housing," and "was a vigorous supporter of the Negro complaint of 'de facto' segregation in the Boston Public School system," the SAC pointed out. FBI officials at the seat of government did not care for the *Boston Globe*'s politics or its implied criticisms of their bureaucracy. They denied the request to work with the paper.[67]

A month after the counterintelligence program expanded in March 1968, Division Five sent the COINTELPRO file to a special room at FBI headquarters. Sullivan controlled access even within the Bureau to the "sensitive" and "highly confidential" paperwork generated by the black hate program.[68] From there, Division Five ordered the field to consider "the entire racial field" for potential counterintelligence action, and to "use every possible technique" in pursuit of the program's immediate and long-range goals. At least one field office positioned itself by breaking into a SNCC office and filming "all the SNCC records." Another field office kept itself up to date by monitoring the credit-card purchases of prospective targets.[69]

The FBI supplemented the black nationalist counterintelligence program with yet another program intended "to expose, disrupt and otherwise neutralize" the antiwar movement—the so-called COINTELPRO–New Left. Hoover sent Bureau data on the antiwar and civil rights linkage to virtually anyone with an interest, from Vice President Humphrey to the commandant of the Marine Corps. And specific COINTELPRO operations included blatantly racist and obscene mailings filled with casual references to niggers, sexual deviancy, and even the diet of black antiwar activists. "Let them eat bananas," one FBI-authored communication read, in a thinly veiled allusion. The FBI also launched a news media campaign to counter coverage of the police riot at the 1968 Democratic National Convention. New Left activists, along with "the liberal press and the bleeding hearts," Division Five complained, "continually and falsely" charged police brutality and "on many occasions viciously and scurrilously attacked the Director and the Bureau in an attempt to hamper our investigation" and "drive us off the college campuses." In one way, not much had changed since the early 1960s. The FBI investigated Chicago's club-swinging policemen at the Civil Rights Division's request, but FBI headquarters assigned the local field office a conclusion: to "develop all possible evidence . . . to refute these false allegations [of police brutality]."[70]

To gather data for the New Left disruption efforts, FBI agents submitted quarterly reports and opened subfiles under RACE RELATIONS and seventeen other headings. In June 1968 the Bureau embarked on a campaign to expose the membership of various "'pacifist' type organizations" as de facto segregationist.

New Left groups, the FBI said, were invariably composed "almost 100 per cent of Caucasians." By the end of the year, Bureau efforts expanded to include "the use of informants to encourage, within the Negro community," the idea that SDS, the principal antiwar group, was "a racist organization." "They are just like the commies and all the other white radical groups that suck up to the blacks," read one of Division Five's anonymous communications. FBI officials pursued this line of attack even though they knew that a sweeping charge of racism was not true. The special agent in charge of the Newark office nominated Tom Hayden for the Rabble Rouser Index precisely because the SDS leader had "worked with and supported the Negro people in their program."[71]

Even though Hoover and his men in Division Five had free rein when implementing both the Black Hate Group and the New Left programs, the COINTELPROs did not develop in a vacuum. Various White House aides and the president himself had encouraged Hoover to do more than simply gather intelligence on black and white antiwar activists since mid-1966, one full year before the Bureau launched COINTELPRO–Black Hate and two years before COINTELPRO–New Left. President Johnson noticed little difference between antiwar demonstrators and ghetto rioters. He saw every dissident as a personal enemy, and he saw all of his enemies united and plotting against him. The civil rights movement and the peace movement never fully embraced each other, but in Johnson's mind they did.

President Johnson's assumptions about the nature of dissent led to some strange alliances. Earlier, when watching televised HUAC hearings in August 1966 on a series of bills to criminalize "assistance to enemies of U.S. in time of undeclared war," the president ordered Marvin Watson to arrange Hoover's appearance "before this group." He wanted his FBI director to name "rioting participants as members of various subversive groups." He told Watson to call DeLoach and have him make the necessary arrangements. Watson told DeLoach not to do anything unless he called back. He never did.[72] Nearly a year later, Johnson summoned DeLoach again and filed a similar request. "[He] asked if the FBI knew anything regarding the activities of King, Carmichael and McKissick. . . . He asked if the FBI could have Chairman Ed Willis of the House Committee on Un-American Activities hold hearings." "[HUAC had] little reputation at the present time," DeLoach responded, adding that "hearings on

McKissick and Carmichael might react to their advantage rather than hurting them. The President then asked how much information could get out."[73]

Turning away from the proposed HUAC alliance, DeLoach fed Johnson's fears without agreeing to any of Johnson's suggested plans of action. He told the president that Carmichael, McKissick, and King "had realized that there was more financial gain and more publicity in being in anti-Vietnam activities than in heading up civil rights drives. . . . The general public is gradually beginning to realize that the civil rights activities of these men have been phoney since the start." Since the president wanted to know "who was behind these people," DeLoach mentioned Stanley Levison, again—falsely identifying him as a "prominent member of the National Committee of the Communist Party." The assistant director dismissed Carmichael and McKissick as "self-styled civil rights leaders who were seeking only to get as much money out of a troubled situation as possible."[74]

If DeLoach thought little of the president's suggestion regarding the Un-American Activities Committee, he found nothing unusual about the general drift of the conversation. The president also announced his intent to mobilize the American Legion in the Vietnam propaganda wars, and he expected the FBI to help on this front as well. A national vice-commander in the Legion, DeLoach's Crime Records Division more or less ran the Americanism Committee. Walter Trohan, Washington bureau chief of the *Chicago Tribune* and a recipient of the American Legion's fourth estate award, described the Legion as "an adjunct of the FBI with FBI men writing speeches for prominent orators, drafting resolutions and sparking the show generally." If Trohan exaggerated (only the Americanism Committee and to some extent the national office were adjuncts of the FBI), his point was well taken. He thought the FBI was doing a wonderful job. Johnson, in contrast, wanted the FBI and the Legion to do more. He did not want Legionnaires running around "placing flowers on black coffins when dead servicemen were returned." He wanted them out "meeting troop ships, having parades, giving presents to returning servicemen and generally stirring up great publicity."[75]

With Hoover's help, the Johnson administration tried to mobilize the old McCarthy-era internal-security machinery. HUAC worked with the Pentagon to run the names of news correspondents in Vietnam through its files, and held hearings on "subversive influences in the riots." Johnson himself helped the Committee get the money it needed to do its job. With civil rights people still complaining about the Justice Department's failure to enforce existing civil rights law, the Department attempted to register the communist-controlled W. E. B. Du Bois Clubs, among other groups, with the Subversive Activities Control Board (SACB). (SNCC activists said the president had a greater interest in registering his Vietnam war critics than in registering Negro voters in the South.) These efforts, nonetheless, frustrated both Hoover and Johnson. The FBI kept sending over files on individuals and organizations (all "good cases," the director declared), but Ramsey Clark kept complaining about tainted evidence. Almost everyone the White House and the FBI wanted to haul before the SACB had been the specific target of electronic surveillance or had been overheard on other taps and bugs.[76]

With the SACB case against the Du Bois Clubs fizzling, Crime Records wrote and disseminated, under the name of the Pennsylvania department of the Catholic War Veterans, some 30,000 copies of a leaflet on the group. DeLoach then worked with the national office of the Junior Chamber of Commerce to discredit the Du Bois Clubs, and arranged for the Catholic War Veterans to publish yet another item. Walter Winchell announced the release of this last document, an FBI-authored pamphlet, in his column.[77]

A few White House aides rivaled DeLoach in his aggresiveness. In April 1967 press secretary George Christian contacted Carl Rowan to discuss Dr. King's antiwar statements—particularly his speech at New York's Riverside Church. Christian told Johnson that Rowan was "exploring the . . . King matter. He said everyone in the Civil Rights movement has known that King has been getting advice from a communist, and he (Rowan) is trying to firm up in his own mind whether King is still doing this. He wants to take out after King, because he thinks he has hurt the Civil Rights movement with his statements."[78]

Another White House aide, John Roche, a political scientist and former head of Americans for Democratic Action, told Johnson that he would try to find out who had written King's Riverside Drive speech. Roche described the speech, in an eyes-only memo for LBJ, as "quite an item," a clear indication "that King—in desperate search of a constituency—has thrown in with the commies" and their "ideological valet service." The civil rights movement was "shot—disorganized and broke," led by an "inordinately ambitious and quite stupid" man who was being "played," along with "his driving wife," "like trout," by "the Communist-oriented 'peace' types." "The president was deeply committed to civil rights," Roche explained, "and upset at the thought that real leaders such as Whitney Young, Roy Wilkins, Clarence Mitchell would be displaced by opportunistic loudmouths using Martin as their front man." Ironically, Roche admired Bayard Rustin—"Martin's original guru on nonviolence and close adviser until he was defenestrated by the 'Abernathys.'"

Roche later advised Watson of his wry plan to neutralize Carmichael: "I have planted a rumor that Stokely is really *white*." In yet another, more serious eyes-only memo, Roche outlined a strategy to discredit the Senate's most persistent dove, J. William Fulbright, the Arkansas Democrat whose segregationist voting record marred his liberal credentials. "I have 'encouraged' my old friend Sidney Hook to take up the franchise," Roche wrote. "He has written a blistering piece for the *Los Angeles Times*. . . . He is also willing to testify before the Senate Foreign Relations Committee 'as an expert witness on Communism and Democracy' to indicate the damage Fulbright's views on civil rights have done to the cause of freedom." "This would be an *event*," Roche told Johnson. "Could it be arranged?"[79]

At the same time Roche was sending his proposals to the Oval Office, the FBI was dreaming up its own ideas—though it is important to note, once more, that the Bureau saw no need to launch a formal counterintelligence program against the New Left until the summer of 1968.[80] Indeed, FBI officials were relatively passive until well after the Tet offensive of January 1968 in Vietnam—that is, until they fully understood the disastrous political implications for the president and his party.[81] Roche's proposals, moreover, were not out of place in the Johnson White House. Other presidential aides also searched for political fodder in the murky world of the subversive.

On one occasion Joseph Califano telephoned Hoover to find out what he thought about King. The director said he was "under active and tight control of the communists," a comment that reflected the habits of rhetoric more than the actual FBI focus at the time, a focus "grounded purely in political-intelligence concerns."[82] From there, Hoover told Califano what he thought about newspaper reaction to General William C. Westmoreland's recent speech on the war. "The Administration came out aces high," he said, adding that Westmoreland should be more active on the speaking circuit. "The man knows what he was talking about as he was just in from Viet Nam." Califano passed on a rumor of his own about the influence Herbert Aptheker, of all people, supposedly had with King and other civil rights leaders who had spoken out on Vietnam. The director knew all about Aptheker, the historian of American Negro slave revolts who had been to Hanoi and the man the Bureau described, quite accurately, as "the principal link between the Communist party and the Nation's campuses." FBI agents kept track of Aptheker by wiretapping his phone and consulting with a source within the Organization of American Historians. At one point Division Five planned to commission a scholarly book-length critique of his work in the field of black history, but Hoover blocked the project. Too expensive. Division Five settled for a pamphlet. All this was routine, and in no way the result of Califano's farfetched rumor of a relationship between Aptheker and King.[83]

Despite the general enthusiasm for counterintelligence action within the White House and within Cartha DeLoach's Crime Records Division and William Sullivan's Domestic Intelligence Division, as often as not the FBI's own field agents remained indifferent to the new COINTELPROs. Bureau executives chastized several offices, including the largest, New York, for not submitting a sufficient quantity of counterintelligence proposals.[84] It is significant that even New York, with its sizeable ghettoes and great numbers of black activists, failed to identify enough targets or to launch an appropriate number of dirty tricks. If the Black Panther party for Self Defense had not emerged in the director's mind by the fall of 1968 as "the greatest threat to the internal security of the Country," the new counterintelligence program might have remained a sideshow— something roughly comparable to the COINTELPRO against the tiny Socialist Workers party. Members of this Trotskyite group, all "home grown tomatoes," the Bureau conceded, had been initially targeted because they supported "such causes as . . . integration problems arising in the South."[85]

The Black Panthers had not even made the initial FBI counterintelligence target lists of August 1967 and March 1968—even though they had received their first major wave of publicity in 1966, when twenty party members, wearing black leather jackets and black berets and toting rifles and shotguns, walked into the California capitol building to protest a bill outlawing the carrying of loaded weapons within incorporated areas. But the FBI's San Francisco field office was not sufficiently impressed, and Division Five somehow neglected to list the Black Panther party. Hoover and Sullivan would not make up for that oversight until Lyndon Johnson's last few months in the White House. Ultimately, Division Five subjected the Panthers to 233 of the total 295 formal counterintelligence actions carried out against black nationalists.

Counterintelligence was far more pervasive than the readily available record indicates. It is impossible to say how many COINTELPRO actions the FBI implemented against the Panthers and other targets simply by counting the incidents listed in the COINTELPRO–Black Hate Group file. The Bureau recorded COINTELPRO-type actions in thousands of other files. Most of the operations to discredit Martin Luther King, for example, were not part of the black nationalist counterintelligence program. The FBI often filed documents recording these actions under King's name or, to a lesser degree, under the name of his organization—and not in the central COINTELPRO file. Still other written records repose in the files of King's associates and advisers, and there are even documents regarding COINTELPRO-type tactics in the files of the newspaper reporters who received derogatory personal or political information leaked by Crime Records. (One FBI executive described the COINTELPRO caption as simply an "administrative device to channel the mail to the Bureau.") To cite another example, the counterintelligence program against the Socialist Workers party consisted of a mere forty-five actions. But, in the more recent past, the FBI implemented a much greater number of informal operations, including some two hundred incidents that occurred after April 1971 when Hoover terminated all the COINTELPROs for security reasons.[86]

The same point could be made about the pervasiveness of the FBI community surveillance programs, from the Ghetto Informant Program to the Rabble Rouser Index and all those other indices. No matter how intrusive and institutionalized these programs may have been, they represented only the tip of the proverbial iceberg. At times, Hoover himself complained about his staff simply throwing money at the problem of black nationalism. Where were the resources needed to run all the new community surveillance and counterintelligence programs going to come from, he wondered?[87] With black activists sowing seeds of discontent and militant protest in the ghettoes, and with the Johnson administration encouraging him to react to the black scare in any way he saw fit, Hoover constructed an unprecedented surveillance system—a system that reflected his belief that any movement for social change was dangerous, and that black demands for social change represented the single most dangerous subversive threat facing the nation.

CHAPTER

9

────────────◇◇◇────────────

The Only Good Panther

The Pursuit of the Black Panther Party for Self-Defense

By word, and sometimes by deed, the Black Panther party came to occupy a special place in the history of black radicalism at a time when the outrageous was commonplace, and to incite FBI actions as outrageous as anything the Panthers did. Of the thousands of domestic intelligence and counterintelligence investigations launched against black activists, only the Martin Luther King case rivaled the Panther case in its ferocity, with FBI officials pursuing the most prominent proponents of violent resistance to white racism with the same zeal that had characterized their pursuit of the most prominent proponent of nonviolence. Just as King had been a symbol to so many Americans, black and white, of all that was good and wholesome about the struggle for racial justice, the Panthers were a symbol of all that was bad and frightening about that struggle. While King was in the mainstream of the civil rights movement, Panther leadership never moved off the fringes of a quite different black liberation movement.

Huey Newton, Bobby Seale, and Eldridge Cleaver were all peripheral characters who relied on the rhetoric of revolutionary prophets and not the rhetoric of Christian prophets. They preferred Fanon's *Wretched of the Earth* and Mao's *Little Red Book* to the Bible, armed self-defense to passive resistance, power to morality. The Panthers never built a black army and never attained mass support even among the most frustrated and bitter young men and women who lived in the ghettoes. They did learn how to use the media however. With their manifestos and predictions of race war, and their poster of Newton, the supreme commander, sitting in a wicker chair, in black leathers, holding a shotgun in one hand and a spear in the other against a background of African shields and a pelt, the Black Panther party made good copy. "Shoot-outs, revolutions, pictures in *Life* magazine of policemen grabbing Black Panthers like they were Vietcong," journalist Tom Wolfe wrote. While the media and the Panthers engaged in a form of mutual exploitation, other Americans romanticized Newton and his comrades. The Panthers inspired awe among white antiwar activists in SDS, who called them "the vanguard of an anticapitalist revolution involving the whole of American society," and they acquired what Wolfe called "radical chic" among some affluent urban liberals.[1]

The Black Panthers attracted the nation's attention, so J. Edgar Hoover decided that they had to be destroyed. Launched in the last lame-duck months of Lyndon Johnson's presidency, the Panther campaigns had entered their most repressive phase before the Nixon administration began to pressure the FBI to do more. Hoover's pursuit of the Black Panther party was unique only in its total disregard for human rights and life itself. The 1960s had begun with FBI agents standing by while southern lawmen beat black activists, and ended with FBI agents inciting police violence against black activists in the urban North. Just as the Bureau's policies of the earlier period represented official government policy, its interventionist law-and-order policies of the later period also received an implicit authorization.

During the Nixon years the FBI's covert counterintelligence campaign accompanied an overt Justice Department assault against the Panthers, all part of a broader attempt to exploit the new white backlash. While Hoover and his superiors in the Justice Department marched against Black Panthers, the Nixon administration urged Congress to impose a moratorium on court-ordered school busing, and to defeat a fair-housing enforcement program and the extension of the Voting Rights Act of 1965. The president also had the Civil Rights Division plead before the Court for a postponement in the desegregation of public schools in Mississippi. And Vice President Spiro Agnew traveled the country, stoking the racial anxieties of Richard Nixon's silent majority wherever he stopped. "It is clear that for the bulk of our (nominal) countrymen," James Baldwin concluded about those times, "we are all expendable. And Messrs. Nixon, Agnew, Mitchell, and Hoover . . . will not hesitate for an instant to carry out what they insist is the will of the people."[2]

Though the Black Panthers would not make the FBI's initial counterintelligence target lists, Hoover's agents gathered intelligence on the party's gun-carrying cadres from the day in 1965 when they began following police cruisers through the streets of the Oakland ghetto, pledging to intervene whenever they felt "the man" had stepped out of line. Confrontations and arrests occurred almost daily, until October 1967, when a shootout left Newton wounded and Oakland police officer John Frey dead. Following Newton's indictment in November on a charge of involuntary manslaughter, the Panthers began a national recruiting drive. In April 1968 another confrontation resulted in the wounding of two Oakland policemen and the death of the Panther's minister of finance, Bobby Hutton. In September, Newton was convicted on the manslaughter charge, receiving a sentence of two to fifteen years imprisonment. By that time the Panthers had established themselves nationally, building a modest following in the streets and on the campuses, and among print and broadcast newspeople eager to write about Negroes predicting race war, the overthrow of capitalism, and a North American liberation front to help the yellow people of Vietnam. Eldridge Cleaver even went to Hanoi in October 1969, where he made a radio broadcast urging black GIs to desert and otherwise sabotage the American war effort.

With their rhetoric and what Yippie-founder Jerry Rubin called their "far-out guerrilla theater," the Black Panther party invited the sort of FBI repression that typified Lyndon Johnson's last two years in the White House and Richard Nixon's first four.[3] Cleaver's threat to torch the White House ("I'll burn the mother fucker down") and to beat California Governor Ronald Reagan ("the punk") to death with a marshmallow attracted Hoover's attention, as did an off-the-pig Christmas card, a coloring book depicting black children challenging white law and order in the ghetto, and a call for black terrorists to infiltrate the law-enforcement and intelligence communities. "We need Black FBI agents," as one anonymous Panther put it, "to assassinate J. Edgar Hoover, John Mitchell and Richard Nixon, and Black Boss agents in New York City to do the same to Mayor Lindsay and Police Commissioner Murphy. Nigger CIA agents are obliged to kidnap the Rockefellers . . . and the Kennedy's [sic] and hold them for ransom."[4]

Black Panther party rhetoric was anything but crazy to the FBI or the Panthers themselves. For many of the young men and women who joined the party, all social ills could be traced back to the police who patrolled the ghettoes and the larger law enforcement establishment. "Off the Pig!" became the Black Panther slogan, and it suggested to some, Hoover included, that the party had assumed the right to liberate black people from a police army of occupation by murdering anyone who wore a badge. The Panthers saw the image of lawmen who enforced Jim Crow with nightsticks and arrangements with the Ku Klux Klan on the face of every cop and G-man in the ghettoes of the North. When Bobby Seale first heard about Malcolm X's assassination, his mind filled with thoughts of "Bull Connor" and "white-ass cops," along with "the mother fucking white racist president and the FBI." "The FBI killed him," Seale charged, so "let's talk about shooting the God damn FBI." That Malcolm died at the hands of black men was beside the point.[5]

FBI officials also saw connections between the black civil rights workers of the early 1960s and the angry young black men and women of the late 1960s. Whether working to register voters in the Jim Crow South or riding around with the Panthers on community patrol, black activists were challenging the existing social order. It made no difference to the FBI that most of white America supported wholesome civil rights goals like voter registration and opposed the Black Panther party's revolutionary goals. The director's form of resistance might vary in scope, intensity, and intent from case to case, depending on his assessment of the imminence of the threat and his reading of public opinion, but Hoover always stood against leftist demands for social change.

The rhetoric of the ghetto made the Black Panthers an especially safe target. Panther pronouncements on matters of war and revolution allowed FBI officials a degree of credibility when presenting their war with the Panthers as a simple matter of self-defense. Hoover told a House Appropriations Subcommittee that the Communist party might "unite" with the Black Panther party. He told Nixon's attorney general, John Mitchell, that the Panthers intended to stage "an armed black revolution against the Government of the United States." He told the field that the Panthers were "armed and extremely dangerous," and "reportedly attempting . . . to kidnap and kill FBI agents"—a prelude of sorts to their "'Third World' idea which envisions the eventual destruction of the white race." Ironically, given the temper of the times, these outbursts, and especially the grand charge labeling the party as "the greatest threat to the internal security of the country," may have made "J. Edgar Hoover . . . the nation's greatest Panther recruiter."[6]

Hoover and the men around him had an interest in blurring the distinction between verbal violence and frustration and hard-core revolutionary activity. In Andrew Young's view, "their intelligence into the black community was so far fetched they really couldn't understand the information they were getting. They didn't understand minorities." Roger Wilkins elaborated. "A bunch of black guys sitting around drinking in the middle of the night, yelling about how mean white folks are and what they'd like to do to them, is part of the catharsis. But the Bureau was not equipped to deal with black hyperbole. So, if some black guy said, 'I'm going to kill that so-and-so,' the Bureau took it fairly literally." In either case, as Wilkins knew from firsthand experience, the FBI passed the information up to responsible federal officials "who were unsettled themselves and frightened about what was going on in the ghettos. They took the Bureau's information seriously," and "the information . . . provided did not illuminate the stream, it polluted it."[7]

There was more to the Black Panther party than preening ghetto generals spouting off-the-pig rhetoric and sporting black leathers, Cuban shades, and unkempt Afros. Counting the Newton and Hutton incidents, party members engaged police officers in more than a dozen firefights from October 1967 to December 1969, and at least two policemen and as many as ten Panthers died in that two-year period.[8] In 1969 alone law enforcement officers arrested 348 Panthers on murder, armed robbery, rape, bank robbery, drug trafficking, burglary, and dozens of other charges. The shootouts and arrests overshadowed the Panthers' main interests. By the time Nixon moved into the White House, the party was trying to rid itself of criminal elements and to move away from direct confrontations with police officers and toward a program of community control of the police and the schools, tenant strikes, free breakfasts for ghetto children, clothing drives, community day care, and health clinics. The Panthers mixed the rhetoric of revolution with a legitimate social agenda. Every Black Panther who broke the law should have been investigated and called to account in a court of law. But no Panther should have been subjected to any kind of extrajudicial punishment, let alone the illegal and immoral punishments imposed by the FBI, for what they said.

Jerris Leonard, the head of the Nixon-era Civil Rights Division, admitted that he could support many things in the Black Panther party's "serve the people" program. But on the whole the Panthers were "nothing but hoodlums," he said. "We've got to get them." The Justice Department set up a Panther task force in 1969 "to develop a prosecutive theory against the BPP [Black Panther party]," and dispatched five line lawyers to the Bay area to run a special grand jury investigation. "Whatever they say they're doing," the United States attorney in San Francisco charged, "they're out to get the Panthers." Other federal grand juries convened in other cities. In Philadelphia, Pennsylvania, the Department subpoenaed Nathan Schwerner, the father of one of the three young men murdered outside of Philadelphia, Mississippi, and then an official of the International Committee to Defend Eldridge Cleaver. In Seattle, Mayor Wes Uhlman refused a federal request to have city police roust Panther offices by announcing, "We are not going to have any 1932 Gestapo-type raids against anyone."[9]

The FBI responded to the flurry of departmental activity by compiling hundreds of prosecutive summary reports on the Panthers under a "Racial Matters–Smith Act" caption. By June 1969 the Bureau was investigating all forty-two Panther chapters and approximately 1,200 members and sympathizers in order "to obtain evidence of possible violations of Federal and local laws." This effort included the examination of every aspect of Panther affairs, from financial records to the Free Huey posters. The FBI even conducted a survey to determine "how many members are on welfare."[10]

There were limits to this assault nonetheless. In April 1969, when Hoover told Nixon he had "been trying to get the [Justice] Department to move against the Black Panthers," "the President said he would put a word in on this himself" and then asked the director if he "had put it up to the Department." When Hoover said he had and the Department's attorneys were considering it, Nixon "said they should do more than that." Three months later, in July 1969, Hoover discussed the matter again with Mitchell. The attorney general wanted to know if the director thought "their recommendations [for prosecution] are going to be too onerous." He intended to seek the indictment of Panther leaders and wanted "to hang" the "Chicago rioting business" on Bobby Seale, even though Seale had little to do with the demonstrations during the Democratic National Convention in August 1968. At the same time, Mitchell deferred to Hoover. Not wanting to expose sensitive Bureau sources in open court, he asked for the director's clearance and reminded him that "we always have the ultimate action of dropping prosecutions . . . if it too materially affects internal security."[11]

The FBI pressured the Justice Department to get on with the conspiracy prosecutions, and the Department asked the Bureau how far it was willing to go. Neither the Department nor the Bureau were willing to disclose the electronic surveillance records that facilitated the covert war against the Panthers but greatly complicated any overt action in federal court. Thus, the Department dropped a number of prosecutions, including actions against Seale and against Panther functionary David Hilliard, who had threatened Nixon's life in the course of a speech. "The Department," William Sullivan wrote, "needs to be . . . educated to some of the ugly realities of the Black Panthers" and "pushed into getting some prosecutive action underway. People around the country are beginning to wonder why something isn't being done." Hoover and his second-in-command, Clyde Tolson, doubting "the wisdom" of a conspiracy prosecution under the Smith Act, rejected Sullivan's recommendations on the grounds that Supreme Court decisions dating from 1957 had rendered the Smith Act "technically unenforceable." Law enforcement had failed, one counterintelligence supervisor explained. "There were [no] adequate statutes" on which to proceed against any subversive or extremist organization.[12]

Division Five also encountered resistance from the San Francisco field office, the office of origin in the Black Panther party investigation and the office responsible for implementing counterintelligence proposals against national Panther headquarters in Oakland. Most of the resistance came from Charles W. Bates, the special agent in charge who considered William Sullivan ("Crazy Billy") a "kind of wild man" who "had a lot of ideas" but lacked "street sense" and skill as an administrator. Favored by Hoover and popular with the agents who worked under him, Bates was an uncommon Bureau executive. Field agents liked him because he was a "stand-up guy," a man who refused to search for scapegoats among the underlings and resisted unreasonable requests from headquarters. When he thought a directive was foolish, he said so.[13]

With regard to the counterintelligence program, Bates and his Panther squad, particularly thirty-year veteran agent William Cohendet, questioned how serious was the Black Panther threat to the nation's security, and the appropriateness of the Division Five response. "It did not mean that we didn't feel it had some merit. We just felt it wasn't the way to go. . . . There were parts of COINTELPRO we didn't agree with," Bates said. "We can pat ourselves on the backs when we harass a [Nation of Islam] grade school and have local police arrest [Revolutionary Action Movement] leaders on every possible charge," Cohendet told Division Five, "but this is not solving any problems. It is only buying time and building up greater resentment among persons who already hate the system. Shall we continue to have all black nationalists locked up all summer, every summer, or perhaps all year long?" The FBI was wasting too much "talent, time and money" on "what amounts to harassment techniques, often euphemistically called counterintelligence. . . . The likelihood is that it will be too little too late and we will win a few battles and lose the war. . . . The Bureau does not have enough Agents, enough concentration of effort, nor enough money to insure foreknowledge of what is likely to follow in the next few years."[14]

When Division Five first singled out the Panthers for special attention in the fall of 1968, local San Francisco agents continued to downplay the menace, responding with minimal compliance to the flood of Panther directives pouring out of Division Five. They did what was required, but no more. They submitted bimonthly summaries on the Black Panther party, "recommendations as to the best method of creating opposition to the BPP on the part of the majority of the residents of the ghetto areas," and the names of "prominent Negroes" who would receive the anti-Panther mailings prepared by Division Five. Sullivan's men drafted dozens of "treatises," including one entitled "The Black Klan," for "referral to appropriate news media representatives."[15]

By the end of the year the Black Panther party had replaced the Student Nonviolent Coordinating Committee as the FBI's principal black threat. With Stokely Carmichael proposing an alliance with the Panthers, however, SNCC remained a problem. To keep the two groups apart, Division Five engaged in petty harassments, having a fictitious SNCC member calling the Panthers "pinheads" and so forth, while singling out Carmichael, whom Newton had "drafted" to serve as the party's East Coast field marshal, for special attention. Attributing the Panthers' growth during the late 1960s to the charismatic Carmichael, the FBI overlooked nothing. His sister's marriage "to a white man of Jewish background" provided fodder for a leak to "a cooperative news media source," and his mother received a telephone call warning of an alleged Panther assassination plot against her son. The Bureau made the whole thing up. No technique, no matter how ruthless, was rejected outright. Division Five even considered labeling Carmichael an informant for a government agency—the so-called "snitch jacket" technique used frequently in counterespionage investigations of Soviet-bloc spies and domestic intelligence investigations of CPUSA functionaries. "This is really nasty treatment from a country that is supposed to be free," complained Carmichael's wife, singer Miriam Makeba, a native of South Africa.[16]

George Moore, the chief of Division Five's racial intelligence squad, defended the use of the snitch jacket. "You have to be able to make decisions"—the decision here was to "tag" Carmichael with a "CIA label"—and "you'd want to make certain that it served a good purpose before you did it. . . . It's a serious thing. . . . As far as I am aware, in the black extremist area, by using that technique, no one was killed. I am sure of that." Was this the result of luck or careful planning? The snitch jacket, after all, had been used against Panther chapters in at least half a dozen cities. In Newark, for example, the FBI falsely implicated a Panther sister for a tip that led to the arrest of a fugitive. Division Five's anonymous letter writers asked the Newark Panthers, "How come the FBI pig fascists knew . . . ?" Another COINTELPRO supervisor admitted that the practice of labeling Panthers as informants may have led to injury or death. "You always have an element of doubt when you are dealing with individuals that I think most people would characterize as having a degree of instability."[17]

Despite this covert assault on the Black Panther party, the frontline FBI office in San Francisco remained reluctant to join the campaign. Things changed dramatically only in May 1969, after Charles Bates advised headquarters that the Panthers were not likely to "overthrow the Government by revolutionary means." That statement, if left unchallenged, would have undermined the entire internal security rationale for the Bureau's domestic intelligence network. "The Panthers right now are not many people and perhaps do not represent many people, as far as most of their actions are concerned," Bates explained. "However, they do represent an idea, or a voice in the ghetto, and are often called upon by Negro residents, to come quell a disturbance in a playground or talk to someone alleging police brutality." Counterintelligence activities, therefore, might "convey the impression that . . . the FBI is working against the aspirations of the Negro people." On this point, Bates of the FBI and Andrew Young of the SCLC were in agreement. The Panthers did not have any support, Young said, "until they became the victims of the persecution campaign of the FBI."[18]

Division Five did not agree. The Panthers' rhetoric alone justified their inclusion on the counterintelligence target list. If they downplayed the talk about guns and offing pigs in favor of social programs intended to overcome their isolation in the ghetto, Division Five reasoned, that would indicate their evolution into a more dangerous form and thus make them a more righteous COINTELPRO target. Sullivan's men lectured the San Francisco office on its responsibilities:

> Your reasoning is not in line with Bureau objectives. . . . You state that the Bureau . . . should not attack programs of community interest such as the BPP "Breakfast for Children." You state that this is because many prominent "humanitarians," both white and black, are interested in the program as well as churches which are actively supporting it. You have obviously missed the point. The BPP is not engaged in the "Breakfast for Children" program for humanitarian reasons, including their efforts to create an image of civility, assume community control of Negroes, and to fill adolescent children with their insidious poison.

Sullivan gave Bates two weeks to assign his best agents to the COINTELPRO desks and get on with the task at hand: "Eradicate [the Panthers'] 'serve the people' programs."[19]

The San Francisco office complied. "There was tremendous fear of Hoover out there," said agent Charles Gain. "It was almost all they could talk about. They were afraid of being sent to some awful post in Montana." So Gain, Cohendet, and the four other agents assigned to the BPP squad supervised the taps and bugs on Panther homes and offices; mailed a William F. Buckley, Jr., column on the Panthers to prominent citizens in the Bay area; tipped off *San Francisco Examiner* reporter Ed Montgomery to Huey Newton's posh Oakland apartment overlooking Lake Merritt; disrupted the breakfast-for-children program "in the notorious Haight-Ashbury District" and elsewhere by spreading a rumor "that various personnel in national headquarters of the BPP are infected with venereal disease"; tried to break up Panther marriages with letters to wives about affairs with teenage girls; and assisted with a plan to harass the Panthers' attorney, Charles Garry, after learning that Garry intended to represent Seale at the Chicago conspiracy trial. They carried out dozens of other counterintelligence operations as well.[20]

The attitude of FBI agents in other field offices balanced Charles Bates's lack of enthusiasm in San Francisco. The Chicago office focused on a proposed alliance between the Black Panther party and the Blackstone Rangers, a confederation of "violence-prone Negro street gangs" under a collective leadership known as the Main 21. The Panthers hoped to politicize the Rangers, to turn the black youths who flocked to the city's gangs away from street crime and toward constructive community action. The Rangers had in fact received some $1 million in Office of Economic Opportunity funding for a "high-risk" job-training program, but OEO terminated the grant in the midst of Senator McClellan's riot hearings. The Chicago Police Department's gang intelligence unit had linked the Rangers to extortion and gun and drug trafficking, and the principal Ranger leader, Jeff Fort, a seasoned felon who had been arrested twice for murder, had used OEO money to further the gang's criminal activities. City police had also linked the Rangers to several ritualistic murders of black teenagers in the course of intermittent warfare with the rival Gangster Disciples. In the FBI view, nonetheless, Ranger criminality was secondary. The "ever present danger," as one Chicago agent later put it, was that "this large Negro youth gang [might] develop black nationalism and align themselves [sic] with the black extremist BPP."[21]

The proposed Black Panther–Blackstone Ranger alliance had enough problems without the meddling of the FBI. On the evening of December 18, 1968, following the shooting of a Panther by a Ranger and the arrest of twelve Panthers and five known members of the Rangers, Jeff Fort met at the gang's headquarters with the two founders of the Panther's Chicago chapter, Fred Hampton, former youth leader of the NAACP branch in suburban Maywood, Illinois, and SNCC activist Bobby Rush.

Fort took the occasion to parade his firepower. According to an FBI informant report:

> Everyone went upstairs into a room which appeared to be a gymnasium, where Fort told Hampton and Rush that he had heard about the Panthers being in Ranger territory during the day, attempting to show their "power" and he wanted the Panthers to recognize the Rangers "power." . . . Fort then gave orders, via walkie-talkie, whereupon two men marched through the door carrying pump shotguns. Another order and two men appeared carrying sawed off carbines then eight more, each carrying a .45 caliber machine gun, clip type, operated from the shoulder or hip, then others came with over and under type weapons. . . . After this procession Fort had all Rangers present, approximately 100, display their side arms and about one half had .45 caliber revolvers. Source advised that all the above weapons appeared to be new.

Fort himself carried a .45 in a shoulder holster and a smaller caliber revolver in his belt. He gave the Panthers one of the machine guns to "try out," but "did not appear over anxious to join forces." A follow-up meeting on December 26, held at a southside bar, broke up when several of the Panthers and Rangers began arguing. Fort telephoned Hampton the next day to tell him the Panthers had twenty-four hours to join the Rangers or else. Hampton told Fort he had the same time to bring his people over to the Panthers and hung up. Later, when Chicago Panthers criticized Ranger leadership's "lack of commitment to black people generally," Fort said he would "'take care' of [the] individuals responsible for the verbal attacks."

Marlin Johnson, the special agent in charge of the FBI's Chicago office, saw in the "enmity and distrust" of these events an opportunity to end the proposed Panther-Ranger alliance once and for all. His office drafted the following letter to Fort and requested authority from Division Five to mail it:

Brother Jeff:

I've spent some time with some Panther friends on the west side lately and I know what's been going on. The brothers that run the Panthers blame you for blocking their thing and *there's supposed to be a hit out for you.* I'm not a Panther, or a Ranger, just black. From what I see these

Panthers are out for themselves not black people. I think you ought to know what they're up to, I know what I'd do if I was you. You might hear from me again [emphasis added].

(sgd.) *A black brother you don't know.*

Johnson thought the letter would work because the Rangers were "violence prone." "Consideration [had] been given to a similar letter to the BPP alleging a Ranger plot against the BPP leadership," he advised Division Five. "However, it is not felt this would be productive principally because the BPP at present is not believed as violence prone as the Rangers," for whom "violent type activity—shooting and the like—[was] second nature." An explicit suggestion of an assassination plot (a contract "hit"), Johnson continued, might "exact some form of retribution toward the leadership of the BPP." Fort, after all, had already threatened to blow Hampton's head off if he stepped onto Ranger turf. Division Five considered Johnson's proposal, and with Hoover's concurrence authorized the mailing on January 30.

In the months that followed, the Chicago field office used an informant to maintain the division between the Panthers and Rangers, and sent another anonymous letter to Hampton about "Brother Jeff." Yet another anonymous letter, mailed to a rival youth gang, the Mau Mau's, implied that two Panthers were gay. "They're sweethearts" and one of them "worked for the man," the letter writer added. "That's why he's not in Viet Nam." It was all part of a pattern of continually escalating political violence, a pattern that could be traced back to the first voter registration campaigns when FBI agents stood and took notes while the Klan or southern lawmen brutalized civil rights workers. Encouragement of violence through inaction had given way to incitement to violence.[22]

FBI men in southern California were even more calculating in their attempts to egg on a feud between the Black Panther party and US (as opposed to "THEM"), a black group headed by Maulana Karenga that challenged the Panthers' revolutionary political nationalism with its own cultural nationalism. "In the beginning the Panthers and US worked together," Karenga explained. "We used to do community patrol together." Amiri Baraka, who was caught up in the conflict, said Karenga's followers had "a kind of neo-African military quality," with their Karate training, armed security, and olive-drab, homeland garb. For their part,

the Black Panther party ridiculed Karenga's cultural nationalism, claiming US believed power flowed from the sleeve of a
Dashiki and not the barrel of a gun.[23]

FBI agents fueled the US-Panther feud in Los Angeles, San
Diego, and other California cities by mailing anonymous letters
and cartoons to the combatants. The goal was twofold: To in-
spire an "'US' and BPP vendetta" and to prevent that vendetta
from fizzling out. This was a reckless strategy. "Many of the
younger brothers in Karenga's organization were from eastside
youth gangs," wrote Earl Anthony, a former Black Panther functionary. "The young Panther cadre were from the same, or rival
gangs," and "both sides felt obligated to defend their respective
camps, regardless of whether there were orders to do so. By the
code of the street this was known as gang fighting and they had
been gang fighters long before they were nationalists." The FBI
wanted action, "shootings, beatings, and a high degree of unrest," and attained exactly that with an "imaginative and hard-
hitting" campaign that ran from November 1968 to May 1970.[24]

There is no evidence that the FBI inspired the initial violence
of the Panther-US feud. On November 5, 1968, Los Angeles
agents first noticed the "threats of murder and reprisals" and
informant reports about an US "assassination list" that supposedly included Cleaver's name. Initially, the Bureau saw this
merely as an opportunity to recruit informants and to feed the
Panther suspicion ("fecal material," Karenga said) that US members were cooperating with the CIA and the Los Angeles Police
Department. Things changed in January, at Campbell Hall on
the Westwood campus of the University of California at Los Angeles, where the two groups were competing for the right to advise administrators regarding the selection of a director for a
proposed Afro-American studies program. Four or five US members gunned down two Panthers then attending UCLA, Alpren-
tice ("Bunchy") Carter, on parole from an armed-robbery sentence, and John Huggins. One US member, Larry Stiner, was
wounded in the thirteen-shot, mostly one-sided firefight. Elaine
Brown and three other Panthers testified for the state at the subsequent murder trial, and Stiner, along with his brother, George,
received life sentences. The state sent a third member of Karenga's Simba Wachuka (Young Lions) to a prison for youthful offenders. Two others charged with the killings remained at large.

Baraka saw the roots of the conflict in macho fantasies and
personalities, especially "Cleaver's arrogance and shallow bohe-

mian anarchism which he passes off as Marxism, plus Karenga's Maulana complex." These delusions "sped up the tragic collision that finally saw Bunchy and Huggins dead." "From that point on," Baraka added, "the FBI escalated their 'intervention' into conflict."[25]

That conflict was most visible in San Diego, where the FBI inflamed the existing tensions between the two groups.[26] In early March local agents began mailing cartoons to the homes of Panther activists and the offices of two underground newspapers. These mailings included flyers that had US members gloating over the corpses of Huggins and Carter, and Panthers calling US a collection of "pork chop niggers." Bureau agents and informants tacked up additional copies of the cartoon flyers on walls and telephone poles. Mostly, the crude art work and even cruder captions ridiculed the Black Panther party, and were drawn and phrased to invite the inference of US origin. The Panthers, as expected, suspected Maulana Karenga and not J. Edgar Hoover. While all this was going on, the San Diego office placed anonymous telephone calls to Panther leaders naming other Panthers as police informants. FBI officials had no way of knowing exactly what would happen in the wake of these actions, but they could not have been surprised and were in no way disturbed when violence erupted once again. On March 16, after the Panthers fired into the home of an US member during a retaliatory raid, an US gunman wounded another Panther.[27]

Troubled by the specter of reconciliation in the aftermath (the two groups were actually trying "to talk out their differences"), the San Diego FBI office requested authority to mail a follow-up set of cartoons. The Bureau repeated the whole routine in May when an US activist named Tambuzio shot and killed yet another Panther, John Savage. In June, Division Five learned, US members began drilling with handguns and rifles and purchasing large quantities of ammunition. William Sullivan responded by approving the mailing of yet another inflammatory letter, forged under the signature of a Panther. Blood flowed again in August, when an US gunman shot three Panthers, including Sylvester Bell, who died. The Panthers responded by bombing US offices. In November, after learning that Karenga feared for his life, the San Diego field office mailed a letter asking why he had not retaliated. In January the FBI sent Panther leaders a third set of cartoons attributed to US. One cartoon labeled a Los Angeles Panther a brutalizer of black women and children, another accused the party of instigating a Los Angeles Police Department raid on US headquarters, and a third portrayed Karenga as a strongman who had "the BPP completely at his mercy."

Special agent in charge Robert Evans placed the name of a Panther attorney on the counterintelligence target list that same month—because the attorney had filed suit on behalf of two party members against the San Diego Police Department charging harassment. FBI agents not only encouraged this harassment; they held "racial briefing sessions" for police officers in order to increase their unwitting "contributi[on] to the over-all Counterintelligence Program." They also orchestrated a number of police raids. An especially successful raid, inspired by a Bureau tip about the alleged "sex orgies" occurring at the Panthers' San Diego headquarters, again resulted in violence. Evans considered the raid an outstanding success because, in the aftermath, "the brothers" beat up the woman who opened the front door of the Panther office at the command of the raiding party.

With merit incentives (cash) hanging in the balance for his men, Evans noted the violence "in the ghetto area of southeast San Diego" and tried to take the bows when describing the "tangible results" of his COINTELPRO efforts. "A substantial amount of the unrest is directly attributable to this program," he advised Division Five. "Feuding between representatives of [the Black Panther party and US] has in the past had a tendency to limit the effectiveness of both." Indeed, by March the Panther chapter in San Diego had disintegrated, a development that reduced Evans's men to watching a "former member . . . 'politicking' for the position of local leader if the group is ever reorganized." Division Five, nonetheless, authorized an anonymous mailing, to "selected individuals within the black community," identifying this person as a "police informant."[28]

Other FBI field offices helped out. In Los Angeles, where Karenga had held private meetings with police officials and even Governor Ronald Reagan in an effort to keep the city calm after Martin Luther King's assassination, FBI agents conducted a stringent interview program "in the hope that a state of distruct [sic] might remain among the members and add to the turmoil presently going on within the BPP." The SAC hoped to trigger "internecine struggle" by bringing the two organizations together and thus granting "nature the opportunity to take her course." "They'd shoot at one organization knowing that the other would get blamed, and ... retaliate in kind," Baraka charged, in an exaggerated if understandable participant's assessment of what was going on.[29] Even the faraway Newark office hyped the conflict with a fraudulent letter, allegedly from an SDS activist, to a Panther office in New Jersey. The letter went on about black racists and a "hankerchief head mama" before concluding with a warning ("watch out: Karenga's coming") and a scoreboard (bodycount?):

US - 6

Panthers - 0.[30]

"Our basic policy was to divide and conquer," one former Division Five executive said. "But I can guarantee that nobody was saying, 'Let's get these guys killing each other.'" The surviving combatants had a different perspective, obviously. "These motherfuckers intended to kill everyone of us," Elaine Brown charged.[31] Karenga said the FBI "interjected the violence into it," into the "normal rivalries of two groups struggling for leadership of the black movement. Hoover took his paranoia and imposed that as public policy. It was a violent time. Vietnam. Talk about power from the barrel of a gun. It was a time and context in which the gun was considered a political god, the ultimate arbiter of all conflicts. ... If somebody tried to do this now, we wouldn't be vulnerable in the same way. We're still recovering and rebuilding from that. We knew it wasn't going to be a tea party, but we didn't anticipate how violent the U.S. government would get. This is obviously an American problem, not an isolated campaign against rantin' and ravin' radicals."[32]

FBI attempts to incite violence ended, more or less, in the spring of 1970. In May the troublesome San Francisco field office asked Division Five if "we are ready to assume responsibility for the death of BPP members we 'set up' as FBI informants"? In fact, William Sullivan had lectured the same field office a few months earlier on this very point, after the SAC offered to drop some "dog eared" FBI paper in a Panther car recently used by Ray ("Masai") Hewitt, the party's Los Angeles–based minister of education. Division Five rejected the proposal on the grounds that "it could result in a Panther murder of one of their leaders."[33] There were two reasons for the Bureau's newfound caution. The first had to do with the torture-murder of New Haven Panther Alex Rackley, a suspected police informant,

and the second with the Bureau's involvement in an Illinois
State's Attorney's police raid on the Panthers in Chicago. Both
had to do with the specter of "embarassment to the Bureau."

The Panther who falsely accused Rackley of working for the
FBI went over to the government during the subsequent state
court murder trial. That after-the-fact informant, George W.
Sams, Jr., a seriously disturbed Panther security enforcer who
had spent two years in an institution for the mentally handi-
capped, had in fact engineered the events that resulted in
Rackley's death. Bobby Seale, who was indicted along with
Sams and twelve other Panthers, expelled him from the party in
the aftermath. Seale had launched a purge of "provocateur
agents, kooks, and avaricious fools" seeking to use the party as
a base for criminal activities, but Sams had slipped through.
Now here he sat as the principal prosecution witness, though
he pleaded guilty, along with two other Panthers, to charges of
second-degree murder and conspiracy to kidnap. The state dismissed its case against Seale when the jury reported itself hope-
lessly deadlocked. Sams, meanwhile, was pardoned after serving four years, given a new identity, and placed under the
federal witness protection program. He returned to prison many
years later, in 1977, following a series of arrests involving violent assaults.

Sams ended up in the witness protection program because he
was being groomed for services at a Black Panther party trial in
Chicago, a trial that had its roots in the State's Attorney's police
raid of December 1969 to seize illegal weapons at the party's
Monroe Street "crib," where the twenty-year-old Fred Hampton
stayed. The FBI had been involved in the raid during the planning stages, when one of its sixty-seven informants in the Black
Panther party, William O'Neal, helped his control agent, Roy
Mitchell, sketch out a floor plan of the apartment. A captain of
security in the Chicago chapter and for a time one of Hampton's
bodyguards, O'Neal worked with the Bureau to label innocent
Panthers as informants. He used a bull whip and a homemade
electric chair to coerce confessions from accused party members and thereby ease his spy hunting burdens, and pocketed
some $30,000 of Bureau money from 1969 to 1972 in salary and
perks (a car maintenance allowance). He was worth it, though
the Bureau knew he was unreliable. (A wiretap established his
involvement in a drug sale.) Neither O'Neal's actions nor his efforts to convince Hampton and the other decision makers to

move the Panthers into the world of bank robbery worried the FBI. No matter how unstable, no matter how unreliable, O'Neal was a prize informant, a man adept at "harassing and impelling the criminal activities of the Black Panther Party locally."[34]

The events leading to the charge that the Panthers kept illegal weapons at the Monroe Street apartment and the State's Attorney's police raid began in June—a time when Fred Hampton was in prison, having received a two- to five-year sentence for stealing $71 worth of ice cream bars. An FBI visit to the Panthers' Chicago office later that month led to eight arrests. Gun battles with city police followed in July and October. Another shootout on November 13 resulted in the deaths of two Chicago policemen and a former Panther, Jake Winters. Although Hampton had not even been released from prison on appeal bond until August and was out of town at the time of the November 13 tragedy, he received the blame—principally because he was the main Panther leader in Cook County, a charismatic and skilled organizer who formed a shaky alliance with SDS, organized a number of community welfare, medical, and educational programs, and somehow kept the rivalry with the Blackstone Rangers in check. The FBI placed his name on the Rabble Rouser Index on November 19, and sent William O'Neal's control agent, counterintelligence man Roy Mitchell, off to the State's Attorney's office with the sketch of the Panther apartment. Ironically, the Illinois Supreme Court had ordered Hampton back to prison by the first of the year, having denied his appeal.

Mitchell's sketch clearly marked the bed where Hampton normally slept with his eight-and-one-half month pregnant girl friend, Deborah Johnson—thereby making things easier for the fourteen Chicago policemen detailed to the Special Prosecutions Unit of the Cook County State's Attorney's Office who raided the apartment at 4:00 A.M. on December 4. They carried twenty-seven guns, including five shotguns and a submachine gun, and Sergeant James "Gloves" Davis, a black cop with a reputation for brutalizing black citizens, led them into combat. "Davis went in there with a grease gun," Civil Rights Division chief Jerris Leonard said, and his crew, poet James A. Emanuel wrote, came in

> behind guns cursin Black men
> makin gut noises
> wakin up the WORLD

They fired about ninety shots. The occupants of the apartment fired one shot. With a large dose of secobarbital in his system (there are claims that he was drugged), Hampton never woke up, never made it out of bed. He died in a one-way firefight, in his sleep, along with Mark Clark, a member of the Panthers' Peoria chapter.[35]

Shot through the heart at the moment Davis broke open the front door, Clark fired the only Panther round—into the floor, as he fell down dead. Four other Panthers, all teenagers, received serious wounds. Davis's crew directed a pattern of cross-fire, mostly from an M-1 carbine and a Thompson submachine gun, from the front room through the rear bedroom wall, at the location where the floorplan showed the head of Hampton's bed. At least one bullet from the M-1 hit Hampton, though the fatal shots apparently came from a handgun. Circumstantial evidence indicates that one of the officers fired two .45 caliber rounds, perhaps downward at close range, into Hampton's right forehead and right temple. The officer then dragged the body out into the dining room. The two bullets exited below Hampton's left ear and through his left throat, and were never found.

In the aftermath, O'Neal went out to Maywood, to pay his respects to Hampton's mother and father, and to circulate rumors that one of the other Panthers in the apartment that morning was a police informant. A few days later, he picked up a special $300 bonus from the FBI.[36] Over the next two years, he reported to the Bureau on such things as the strategies of the lawyers for the Hampton and Clark families. While O'Neal continued his services, State's Attorney Edward V. Hanrahan said the police "exercised good judgment" and "considerable restraint," a Cook County grand jury indicted the surviving Panthers for murder and attempted murder, and Emanuel wrote these lines about the *Panther Man*, Fred Hampton:

> Wouldn't think
> t look at m
> he was so dam bad
> they had to sneak up on m,
> shoot m in his head
> in his bed
> sleepin
> Afroed up 3 inches
> smilin gunpowder[37]

"Hampton and Clark were not good citizens," Jerris Leonard conceded. "On the other hand, no one had a right to summarily execute them. The Hampton-Clark killing was a perfect example of how a local police department, using bad judgment in dealing with a very serious situation, simply did not execute their attempt to arrest those people properly. The FBI was faced with similar situations, but they had real expertise, and they should have been used in the Hampton-Clark situation."[38] Leonard had it wrong. The FBI had mobilized, and had in fact "used" the State's Attorney's police. Under pressure from the press and public opinion generally, Leonard's Civil Rights Division opened a civil rights case. As always, the FBI did the investigating, and the agent assigned to the case worked under the close supervision of SAC Marlin Johnson. No Division executive recognized the irony in that or said anything when a federal grand jury convened in the winter of 1970 and the FBI withheld information regarding the roles of O'Neal and Mitchell. Leonard, who also served as the prosecutor in charge of the grand jury, said "O'Neal had nothing to do with the investigation we conducted."

In Leonard's view, the FBI conducted an exemplary civil rights investigation. "The Monroe Street apartment was a mess when I arrived there," he remembered. "Frozen pillars of water came down from the ceiling. There was water frozen on the floors and in the bathrooms. The FBI knew that the targets of our investigation were Chicago police officers, who were assigned to the State's Attorney's Office"—including "the chief of police himself. But the Bureau did its job. It did a tremendous mock-up of the apartment showing where every bullet hole had been fired. Bureau agents were on their hands and knees looking for shell casings and bullet fragments. If Clark or Hampton hadn't fired the first shot from inside the apartment, I have no doubt that the Chicago police who were involved, including the higher-ups, would have been indicted."[39]

When the grand jury finished its preliminary report, Leonard told Marlin Johnson there would be "no indictments of police officers."[40] In return, Hanrahan remained silent regarding the FBI role in setting up the raid. Because any sort of prosecution might compromise the Bureau, Hanrahan also agreed to the dismissal of indictments against the surviving Panthers. Not surprisingly, given the total corruption of the investigative process, the details of the Bureau's involvement surfaced only in the mid- and late 1970s. The families of the victims and the survivors of the raid filed a civil suit in 1970, and nearly a decade later a federal court of appeals held that the government had obstructed the judicial process by withholding information. "I thought that our Justice Department team had done a superb job in surfacing what actually happened at the Monroe Street apartment," Leonard said. "I was frankly never able to understand why the Hampton and Clark families filed their suit against us. I thought it was a harassment type case. But the Bureau got into trouble because they didn't cough up the evidence that they had on the informant. And the federal judge out there . . . got very angry about it." The FBI held onto the administrative memo indicating O'Neal's $300 bonus until the end, submitting the document in the very last volume of files surrendered in response to the court's order.[41]

Special agent in charge Johnson had no more luck when he claimed that the FBI had done nothing wrong. The information acquired by O'Neal and disseminated to the police was routine and strictly a matter of local interest, he said. "What they did with the information was none of our concern." The documents, however, were included in the counterintelligence file and bore such captions as "Operations Being Effected and Tangible Results Obtained." They showed that Johnson's office had tried to persuade the Chicago Police Department to conduct the raid before State's Attorney Hanrahan finally agreed to do it. Roy Mitchell, furthermore, had met with Hanrahan's representatives in a series of preraid, off-the-record conferences. And when arguing for the informant's bonus, the Racial Matters squad supervisor, Robert Piper, claimed that O'Neal's information provided "the only source of the raid."

O'Neal's last preraid report stated that there were no illegal weapons on the premises. All the guns were legally purchased and registered. The State's Attorney, nonetheless, had based the probable-cause evidence during the warrant-application process on information supplied by an unidentified informant (O'Neal). The ostensible purpose of the raid was to seize contraband that O'Neal said did not exist. Because Cook County authorities based their request for a warrant on hearsay (O'Neal told Mitchell and Mitchell told the police and the police went to the judge), the warrant itself was invalid. A valid affidavit, under Illinois law, would have required the signature of the informant's contact—the signature of the FBI's counterintelligence man, Roy Mitchell.

The raiding party chief, Sergeant Daniel Groth, helped cover up the FBI's role by claiming that the "probable cause" evidence in his original affidavit for the search warrant came not from O'Neal but from another informant in the Panthers' Chicago chapter. This claim presented a problem for the Bureau on another level, because the weapons referred to in Groth's affidavit, a sawed-off shotgun and a stolen police riot gun, were in violation of federal law. The normal FBI procedure would have been to notify the Alcohol, Firearms and Tobacco Division of the Treasury Department about these weapons. Because Bureau agents failed to do this, and because they avoided any reference to the shotgun or the riot gun in their summaries of the information O'Neal supplied, the survivors of the raid concluded that Groth invented the informant to validate the warrant and conceal the arrangement between the FBI and the Cook County State's Attorney's Office. Perhaps it was just another example of what one police official described to Hoover, a year before Hampton and Clark died, as "the wonderful, wonderful cooperation and rapport that exists between . . . [the] Chicago [FBI] Office, SAC Marlin C. Johnson, and the Chicago Police Department." "I was glad to hear that," the director replied. "We want to work hand in hand with them."[42]

In November 1982, thirteen years after Gloves Davis and the others entered the Monroe Street apartment, the Hampton and Clark families and the survivors agreed to a $1.85 million settlement that their attorney, G. Flint Taylor, Jr., described as "an admission of the conspiracy that existed between the F.B.I. and Hanrahan's men to murder Fred Hampton." Robert Gruenberg, the assistant U.S. attorney who handled the case, said the federal government settled merely to avoid another costly trial. That multimillion dollar cost included $36,000 paid to O'Neal for his services as a witness. Hampton's relatives used their money to endow their family project, the Fred Hampton Scholarship Fund, for "young blacks who want to become lawyers," brother William said.[43]

Initially, the deaths of Fred Hampton and Mark Clark caused few problems for the FBI. First, a number of counterintelligence proposals had to be scrubbed, as one Division Five executive noted, "in view of the fact that Hampton was recently shot and killed." Second, the killings had "triggered an avalanche of publicity favorable to the BPP," a development which inspired an FBI campaign to "portray the BPP in its true light as an aggregate of violence-prone individuals who initiate violence rather than persecuted victims of unprovoked police brutality."[44] By the spring of 1970, however, the Bureau anticipated criticism of its handling of the Panther investigations and its role in the events that led to the Monroe Street tragedy.

FBI officials confined their newfound caution to areas where they could conceivably be held legally responsible for inciting violence or even murder. Counterintelligence, the preferred option before Chicago, remained just that in the aftermath. The entire program continued on a similar if more subdued track. In San Diego, local agents supplemented their efforts to keep the Panther-US conflict simmering with several operations designed to drive the Panther breakfast-for-children program out of the basement of a Catholic church. Division Five ordered the field office to "keep the pressure on the Catholic hierarchy," and eventually it worked. The archdiocese transferred the priest who helped the Panthers, Frank Curran, to "somewhere in the State of New Mexico." "Completely neutralized," the Bureau said. New York agents tried to "deter individuals from joining" the Black Panther party by contacting anyone who showed an interest. They even interviewed the parents of grade-school children who had spoken to Panther organizers.[45]

Counterintelligence assaults occurred in every area of the country. In Detroit, the special agent in charge submitted a proposal involving forged letters to black businessmen demanding financial support for the Panthers or else. Agents assigned to the Jackson, Mississippi, office drafted a letter about "some colored boys" hanging around Senator Eastland's Sunflower County "with hair like Stokely Carmichael" and "jackets with the initials BPP on the back," and apparently sent it to several state and county government officials. They wanted to know why the Panthers had not been "run . . . out of Mississippi." The FBI sent another bogus letter, from an "irate [black] parent," to a Rochester, New York, school board official about a high school history teacher who ordered twenty subscriptions to the Panther newspaper for use in his class. When confronted, the teacher canceled the subscriptions. Sponsors of the breakfast-for-children program also received letters, along with copies of the outrageous Panther coloring book. Party leaders had rejected the coloring book and Bobby Seale ordered it destroyed, but that did not stop the FBI from adding violent captions and sending it around.[46]

One of the FBI's favorite tactics was to accuse the Panthers and other black nationalists of anti-Semitism, a tactic designed to destroy the movement's image "among liberal and naive elements." Bureau interest in anti-Semitism grew during the summer of 1967 at the National Convention for New Politics, when SNCC's James Forman and Rap Brown led a floor fight for a resolution condemning Zionist expansionism. The convention's black caucus introduced the resolution and SNCC emerged as the first black group to take a public stand against Israel in the Mid-East conflict.[47] Brown went on to become well known for his burn-baby-burn and violence-is-as-American-as-cherry-pie quotes, and he was only slightly less well known for another. "If America chooses to play Nazis, black folks ain't going to play Jews." In the FBI view, the black caucus resolution and Brown's rhetoric indicated an anti-Semitic attitude within the black movement as a whole. Division Five responded by directing the field "to compile all evidence of anti-Semitic activity by militant black nationalist extremists and their sympathizers," with a particular emphasis on the Black Panther party.[48]

The issue of anti-Semitism was an old one for FBI officials, so it is surprising that they did not react in a more timely manner. During the 1950s Division Five mailed literature detailing the extent of anti-Semitism in the Soviet Union to Jewish communists in the United States and disseminated a lengthy monograph entitled "Communism Versus the Jewish People" on a more selective basis to a number of prominent Americans, inside the government and out, including former President Herbert Hoover. And Crime Records chief Louis Nichols kept in touch with Hearst columnist George Sokolsky on the fact that so many of the persons exposed by the McCarthy-era committees had "names . . . of Jewish origin." Sokolsky was "a great American. A great Jew, too," Nichols said. The FBI assistant director also kept in touch with Herman Edelsberg, director of the Anti-Defamation League (ADL), who briefed Nichols on the ADL's arrangement with the House Committee on Un-American Activities on "the handling of witnesses." HUAC agreed to check ADL files before subpoenaing leftist Jews—"to insure that such witnesses didn't climb all over the Committee."[49]

When attempting to publicize the "anti-Semitic and unchristian posture" of the Panthers more than a decade later, Hoover's agents employed many of the same tactics that they had used to document the anti-Semitism of the Soviet state. The New York office enlisted one of its veteran and completely fictitious creations—"a disgruntled Jewish member of the Communist party" named "Irving." Division Five tried to disrupt the Panthers by manipulating Rabbi Meir Kahane and the "vigilante-type" Jewish Defense League (JDL), leaking information to college administrators and sources in the Anti-Defamation League, and working with newspaper columnists. The FBI compared Panther ideology with "the traditional anti-Semitism of organizations like the American Nazi Party" and the even more traditional anti-Semitism of the late Adolf Hitler. In the case of the JDL, the FBI did not limit itself to "the furnishing of factual information" because Kahane's group could not "be motivated to act" unless "the information . . . concerning anti-Semitism and other matters were furnished . . . [with] some embellishment."[50]

Another of the FBI's favorite counterintelligence tactics—the attempt to create dissension and factionalism within the Black Panther party—also continued unabated. The most dramatic episode involved the split between the West Coast followers of Huey Newton and the mostly East Coast followers of Eldridge Cleaver. When the FBI launched this campaign in March 1970, Newton sat in a California prison and Cleaver sat in Algiers in self-imposed exile. The Cleaver faction revolved around the so-called Panther 21—twenty-one Black Panthers indicted in New York City on April 2, 1969, on conspiracy charges to commit murder and arson. New York police officers and FBI agents gathered most of the evidence for the prosecution, presented by New York County District Attorney Frank Hogan and Assistant District Attorney Joseph A. Phillips. Complications arose within the party itself in February 1971, when Newton expelled the Panther 21, a purge that prompted rumors of kidnap plots and fratricide. Finally, on March 13, with the jury deliberating less than an hour, thirteen of the Panthers on trial won their freedom. Other Panthers were acquitted in absentia.[51]

The first COINTELPRO operation occurred in April 1970, when the FBI sent an anonymous letter to Cleaver in Algiers accusing Panther leaders in California of plotting against him. After Cleaver expelled three of the party's international representatives, Hoover gave "incentive awards" to the agents who sent the letter.[52] A follow-up letter to David Hilliard, the Panther chief of staff in Oakland, suggested that Cleaver had "tripped out." When FBI wiretaps on the Panthers' national office confirmed the effectiveness of this particular letter, the stage was set for more bogus letters. Following Newton's release from prison on August 13, an FBI informant distributed a "directive" to rank and file Panthers, with a copy to the national office in Oakland, questioning Newton's competence. Thereafter, the FBI mailed "a barrage of anonymous letters" to Newton and Cleaver and their respective followers. A letter of January 1971, drafted to appear as if it had been written by Newton's personal secretary, Connie Matthews, was typical:

> Things around headquarters are dreadfully disorganized with the comrade commander [Newton] not making proper decisions. The newspaper is in a shambles. No one knows who is in charge. The foreign department gets no support. . . . I fear there is a rebellion working just beneath the surface. . . . We must either get rid of the Supreme Commander or get rid of the disloyal members.

Division Five again noted the results of "our counterintelligence projects": Newton was prepared "to respond violently to any question of his actions or policies."[53]

In February, twenty-nine FBI field offices extended the campaign by promoting factionalism between Panther chapters and the national office. Another barrage of anonymous letters followed, including one to Newton's brother, Melvin, warning him that the Cleaver faction planned to assassinate him, and one to Cleaver warning about the possibility of violence directed against his wife, Kathleen. Newton believed an informant had infiltrated Panther headquarters, and his secretary went into hiding. FBI officials tried to take credit for everything, including Cleaver's expulsion from the party. But they were not prepared to rest on their laurels. They sent out more bogus letters, under the signatures of Newton and Hilliard, describing Cleaver as "a murderer and a punk without genitals." This last insult seemed particularly appropriate, since the Panthers sometimes talked about "pussy power" being good for the revolution.

"We absolutely felt Cleaver was a danger," San Francisco Panther squad agent William Cohendet explained. "Matter of fact, the party should be thankful for whatever help they got [from the Bureau]. Getting rid of Cleaver was a big thing; he took all those hoodlums with him. And so Huey didn't have any problems anymore. . . . Read the language in those letters. Would you think that was written by a bunch of white men? When you listen to them everyday for a couple of years you get to know their vocabulary. . . . Don't you think it was a pretty good operation, if you had to give a candid opinion of it?" [54]

The FBI campaign to split the Black Panther party finally stopped at the end of March, a few weeks after a gunman shot Cleaver-faction member Robert Webb while Webb was selling the party newspaper in Harlem. The Bureau concluded that "the differences between Newton and Cleaver . . . [were now] irreconciable." A few days later in Queens, another gunman shot and killed Samuel Lee Napier, the circulation manager of the Newton-faction newspaper.[55]

The Panther compaigns had unintended consequences. They corrupted the criminal justice system in the Hampton-Clark killings and the Cleaver-Newton conflict, and in every case where a black activist faced indictment under a criminal statute. In 1970 the president of Yale University, Kingman Brewster, Jr., questioned "the ability of black revolutionaries to achieve a fair trial anywhere in the United States." The experience of Elmer ("Geronimo") Pratt provides an example of Brewster's point.[56] In 1968 Pratt was a Vietnam war hero, "a sergeant in the 82nd Airborne . . . with a chest full of medals, including two Purple Hearts." Upon returning home, he enrolled at UCLA and joined the Black Panther party. The FBI placed him on the counterintelligence target list in 1969, and a Los Angeles County grand jury indicted him in 1970 on various counts of murder, assault, and robbery. On top of everything else, Huey Newton expelled Pratt after Melvin ("Cotton") Smith called Pratt a police agent. Another ex-Panther and sometime FBI probationary racial informant, Julius Butler, then wrote a letter to the Bureau identifying Pratt as the culprit in the $18 robbery and murder of a twenty-seven year old white woman back in December 1968.

Convicted on the murder and robbery charges, Pratt received a life sentence and claimed Hoover's FBI framed him—a claim based on a number of revelations about the Bureau's conduct that began to surface three years later, including the fact that the FBI sent "COINTELPRO informants" off to infiltrate the defense. Pratt's lawyers raised other points regarding Butler's "extensive contacts with the FBI" and a "lost" wiretap log that might have confirmed their client's presence in North Carolina at the time of the murder. None of it mattered. After Pratt had served eight years in San Quentin, including five years in solitary confinement, the court of appeals rejected his contentions in a majority decision that conceded his main point. "There is no dispute that FBI informants . . . were in the defense camp." But the court contended that the informants had "as much effect on whether or not defendant Pratt was afforded a fair trial conducted in California's superior court as did the furniture in the areas where the [attorney-client] discussions were conducted."[57]

An equally troubling case in New York involved another COINTELPRO target, R. Dhoruba Moore. A codefendant in the Panther 21 case who believed Newton had ordered his assassination, Moore jumped bail, fled the country, and was acquitted in absentia in March 1971. Police officers arrested him three months later at an after-hours club in the Bronx, booking him as a John Doe. The officers also confiscated a .45 caliber machine gun at the club. When they uncovered Moore's identity, they charged him with the attempted murder of two patrolmen who had been assigned to guard the Riverside Drive home of Panther 21 prosecutor Frank Hogan. Moore was indicted, tried, and convicted, with the court handing down a sentence of twenty-five years to life. The question that went to the heart of the criminal justice system had less to do with Dhoruba Moore's guilt or innocence than whether he had received a fair trial.

After the Black Liberation Army claimed responsibility for the Riverside Drive shooting, and as well the murder of two other patrolmen at a Harlem housing project, Richard Nixon ordered Hoover to conduct a "no punches pulled" investigation. The president did not want the FBI in "on a case by case basis," only those police killing cases where the director had "the scent and smell of a national conspiracy . . . like the Black Panthers." Hoover immediately launched a NEWKILL (New York police killings) investigation, and he had the New York FBI office send "a Panther expert to brief the police."[58] His aides also used these crimes to open more domestic intelligence files. "The Newkill case and other terrorist acts have demonstrated that in many instances those involved in these acts are individuals who cannot be identified as members of an extremist group," one executive concluded. "They are frequently supporters, community workers, or people who hang around the headquarters of the extremist group or associate with members of the group." Division Five ordered the field to round up Cleaver-faction Panthers and members of other visible black groups, and to list "supporters and affiliates of these groups with your file numbers on each, if you have a file. If you have no file, open files."[59]

FBI officials did not let up even after the Black Panther party's collapse and Hoover's own death, and even with President Nixon, in the midst of the Watergate muck, barely hanging on to his Oval Office desk. In May 1973, following a firefight on the New Jersey turnpike between three black radicals and state troopers that left one black man and one trooper dead, the Bureau opened its CHESROB file. Named after one of the badly wounded radicals on the turnpike that day, the CHESROB investigation attempted to hook former New York Panther Joanne Chesimard (Assata Shakur) to virtually every bank robbery or other violent crime involving a black woman on the East Coast. This "queen of the Black Liberation Army," as the press liked to call her, was subsequently indicted for robbery (twice) and armed robbery, the kidnapping and murder of a drug dealer, and the attempted murder of a policeman. The courts dismissed three indictments and juries acquitted on two other charges after three separate trials. A seventh indictment led to a mistrial when the court learned of Chesimard's pregnancy—a development that reportedly prompted the FBI "to conduct an investigation to determine how [she] got pregnant." Finally convicted on the seventh indictment at a new trial in March 1977, she received a life sentence for her role in the turnpike incident. Chesimard lives in exile today, having escaped in November 1979 from New Jersey's Clinton Correctional Institute. She surfaced in Cuba eight years later, to promote her autobiography.[60]

The post-Hoover FBI followed Panthers and other black radicals into the prisons with its PRISACTS program. Inspired by the terrorism of the Symbionese Liberation Army and an investigation by HUAC's successor, the House Committee on Internal Security, PRISACTS countered "extremist, revolutionary, terrorist, and subversive activities in penal institutions." Bureau officials launched the program in February 1974 "with the primary goals of promoting liaison and cooperation between the FBI and prison administrators nationwide relative to above elements, and to generally provide for two-way exchange of information."[61]

Most of the black radicals tried and jailed for murder and other violent crimes knew what they were doing. Some of them no doubt believed they were making a statement, spilling a little pig blood, to use the crude words of the day, for the people. Others came to recognize nihilistic terror for what it was. More than anything else, the notion that those black nationalists who went to war with the state and shot police officers in the back are somehow martyrs is a legacy of the FBI's counterintelligence program against the Panthers. To a lesser degree, another legacy of this Bureau program was the continuing harassment of imprisoned Panthers and others under such open-ended investigations as NEWKILL and CHESROB. In San Diego and Los Angeles, the FBI fed the bloody rivalry between the Black Panther party and US, and then helped local police and state prosecutors build murder and conspiracy cases against the survivors. The FBI targeted Geronimo Pratt and Dhoruba Moore under the counterintelligence program, and then helped prosecutors in California and New York put them behind bars. The FBI assisted prosecutors in the New Haven and Panther 21 conspiracy cases against other COINTELPRO targets, and in Chicago two more targets, Fred Hampton and Mark Clark, ended up dead.

A reasonable person could read the files pertaining to two operations (at least), the letter to Blackstone Ranger leader Jeff Fort and the raid on the Panthers' Monroe Street apartment, and conclude that the FBI responded to off-the-pig rhetoric with crazed schemes to off Panthers. The FBI did not plan Fred Hampton's death, but the FBI has had to spend considerable time since the morning of December 4, 1969, explaining that his corpse was not, in bureauspeak, the "tangible result" of a year-long campaign to "otherwise neutralize" one of the Black Panther party's most effective community organizers. The FBI once told Tom Charles Huston, Nixon's man and the principal author of the president's blueprint for a police state, that Hampton was responsible for the deaths of two Chicago police officers. That claim was absurd. Fred Hampton, by most accounts, is a legitimate movement martyr. But were people like Pratt and Moore martyrs or monsters? Cold-blooded killers or victims of Hoover's operatives in Division Five?

Amnesty International, an organization more accustomed to the torture and death squads that roam the jackboot world of military dictators, apartheid governments, and religious and political fanatics, studied the Pratt case and concluded that justice in the United States during those times had neither the appearance nor the reality of fairness. The FBI's counterintelligence program interfered "with the judicial process as selective enforcement of the law. Undoubtedly there is a clear distinction between framing an individual"—Pratt's claim—"and selective enforcement of the law; but both measures stem from an official willingness to abuse the criminal justice system. . . . The effect of COINTELPRO has been to destroy confidence in the *bona fides* of the FBI."[62]

Geronimo Pratt and Dhoruba Moore remain incarcerated, and, perhaps, they deserve to be.* A reasonable person might also conclude that their words and deeds deserved whatever FBI response they provoked. The record of FBI conduct, nonetheless, is there for Amnesty International to write reports about and for everyone to see. "The chief investigative branch of the Federal Government, which was charged by law with investigating crimes and preventing criminal conduct, itself engaged in lawless tactics and responded to deep-seated social problems by fomenting violence and unrest."[63] Physical violence, as opposed to violent rhetoric, was never more than a peripheral part of the black struggle for equality. Political violence, in contrast, was a central part of the FBI response to that struggle—something located within the mainstream of government policy toward blacks.

---

*New York State Supreme Court Justice Peter J. McQuillan reversed Moore's conviction in March 1990 and ordered a new trial—on the ground that the prosecution had failed to disclose evidence to the defense.

10

Citizens and Radicals

Hoover, Nixon, and the Surveillance State

The FBI's Panther campaigns were part of a larger strategy of intelligence and counterintelligence that expanded and grew bloodier and finally came to an end during the Richard M. Nixon years. The Watergate president sometimes tried to force the FBI to do things J. Edgar Hoover would not accept, and when the director resisted the president tried to fire him.[1] Eventually, in the midst of the events that drove him out of office, the president's recklessness would contribute, in an ironic and fortuitous way, to the dismantling of the FBI's "Racial Matters" surveillance apparatus. This took place after Hoover's death in 1972, when the Watergate scandal and its repercussions made it clear that the civil liberties of all Americans were at stake. When Nixon took the oath of office in 1969, however, it appeared to the director that the FBI's community surveillance and counterintelligence programs would flourish under the new administration. For a time, they did so.

Nixon's ties to the FBI dated from late 1947, when he worked closely with FBI Assistant Director Louis Nichols and cracked the Alger Hiss case, as Hoover often said, "almost single-handedly."[2] In the 1950s he vacationed with Hoover in Miami, attended an occasional Washington Senators baseball game with him, and met with him in the White House from time to time. In 1960 the director reportedly did a bit of covert campaigning for his friend. Nichols, though retired from the Bureau by then, helped too, and in 1968 he got Nixon his first electronic surveillance expert for the campaign, former FBI agent John J. Ragan. Nixon once compared the FBI favorably to the Central Intelligence Agency with its "muscle-bound bureaucracy which has completely paralyzed its brain," advising White House chief of staff H. R. Haldeman that CIA "personnel, just like the personnel in State, is primarily Ivy League and the Georgetown set rather than the type of people that we get into the services and the FBI." The president and the director assumed they would work well together.[3]

Nixon's policies confirmed that Hoover had more in common with this man than any of the other seven chief executives he had served. Nixon had his White House enemies list, while Hoover had a Not to Contact list of liberals and others. "The Nixon White House got the idea of the Enemies List from us," said William Sullivan. Hoover's list included all representatives of the CBS and NBC television networks and such newspapers as the *Washington Post*, the *New York Times*, the *Baltimore Sun*, and the *Los Angeles Times*. They were all "left-wing and trying to downgrade law enforcement," the director concluded. In the case of the *Los Angeles Times* ("a melting pot of garbage"), national editor Edwin Guthman, Robert Kennedy's former special assistant for public relations and a practicing member of "the Kennedy clique," directed the "smear gathering." The so-called liberal media ("jackals of the press") also made one of Nixon's enemy lists. "No one from AP. on social for 3 mos," Haldeman wrote on a notepad during a White House meeting. "No one Time, Newsweek, Post, Times." "Shaft . . . one by one." "Chop their heads—Screw them."[4]

When it came to biased use of the FBI name-check process, the Nixon White House rivaled the Johnson White House. Hundreds of requests filtered down from then counsel to the president John Ehrlichman and deputy assistant to the president Alexander P. Butterfield, white (Billy Graham, David Lawrence, Mr. and Mrs. Pat Boone) as well as black (Roy Wilkins, Joe Louis, Mr. and Mrs. Lionel Hampton).[5] The administration also solicited Hoover's opinion on a discussion draft of a presidential message on crime (the draft neglected campus and ghetto violence, the director said), and enlisted the FBI indirectly in its crude appeals to the George Wallace constituency. Bureau officials kept such ardent segregationists as Senators James Eastland and Strom Thurmond up-to-date, advising both men of the vague plans of SCLC activist Hosea Williams to organize demonstrations on Eastland's Mississippi plantation and Thurmond's South Carolina farm. Meanwhile, the president offered black America the "delusion" (Bayard Rustin's word) of black capitalism, refused to meet with black leaders, and nominated a segregationist, Clement F. Haynsworth, Jr., of South Carolina, for a seat on the U.S. Supreme Court. When Haynsworth's nomination collapsed, Nixon sent up the name of another segregationist, G. Harrold Carswell of Florida.[6]

Hoover described Haynsworth as "very conservative," "definitely in favor of law and order," a man with "a slight lisp but . . . a brilliant mind." A background check uncovered "no derogatory information" (other than the lisp?). Nor did the background check on Carswell—"a good man," Hoover thought—reveal any hint of a segregationist past. The FBI simply catered to the Nixon administration. Bureau agents routinely collected information regarding the attitudes of southern congressmen, judges, and other politicians toward integration, and Bureau officials routinely kept this information out of the reports they sent to the White House or the attorney general or Senator Eastland's Judiciary Committee. Eastland's own file, in the words of one Crime Records Division agent, "reflects that he is a strong advocate of 'White Supremacy.'"[7]

The FBI had been keeping information regarding segregationist sympathies to itself at least since the Kennedy years. Whenever John Kennedy considered nominating a liberal for a seat on the federal bench, in contrast, Hoover cited the most minute details concerning "subversive" affiliations. While President Kennedy mulled over the possible Supreme Court nomination of William Henry Hastie, a black circuit court of appeals judge, the director sent a memo to Robert Kennedy connecting the judge to ten groups on the attorney general's list of subversive organizations or other lists compiled by such bodies as the House Committee on Un-American Activities. Later, when Lyndon Johnson sent up Thurgood Marshall's name, the FBI extended such services to the press. "When I wrote an editorial telling . . . Eastland to cut the hijinks and get on with the nomination," recalled Patrick Buchanan, then a *St. Louis Globe-Democrat* reporter, publisher Richard H. Amberg "came by to let me know I had made a mistake. . . . A great admirer of J. Edgar Hoover, the publisher was in regular contact with the FBI." The director pursued these policies in the face of opposition from the Kennedys and LBJ, but with the support of Richard Nixon.[8]

"Hoover was more than a source of information" for the administration, John Ehrlichman wrote. "He was a political advisor to whom Nixon listened." The president and the director discussed the black and antiwar movements generally, and the need for more law-and-order judges on the Supreme Court. "[We need] a real man" on the court, Hoover told Nixon.[9] They also discussed the "thing at Cornell," where 250 well-armed black undergraduate and graduate students had occupied the student union building. Cornell President James A. Perkins's capitulation to their demands prompted Nixon to remark, "Basically the faculty does not have any guts." Hoover said "the Presidents [of other schools under siege] don't either," with the exception of S. I. Hayakawa of San Francisco State, who "brought order out of chaos by firing a number of the faculty who had been sparking the demonstrations."[10] Hoping to exploit these types of situations for political advantage, the White House expected the FBI to help make the case. "We simply have got to keep the label of radical sympathizers on the Democrats," Charles Colson noted. "We've got to show that their rhetoric over recent years has encouraged the kind of attitude of permissiveness that has allowed the revolutionaries to hold sway among the moderate students."[11]

National Security Adviser Henry Kissinger, Attorney General John Mitchell, and Vice President Spiro Agnew also used the director as a sounding board. The names of these three men graced the FBI's dissemination list for the weekly "Racial Digest," and as well the INLET (Intelligence Letter) Program, a service launched in late 1969 and intended to channel "items with an unusual twist or concerning prominent personalities." The Bureau scanned all racial matters intelligence, among other items, on a daily basis in search of items suitable for INLET.[12]

Hoover had his agents sweep Kissinger's home and office for taps and bugs, and forwarded information on topics ranging from the late Martin Luther King to Pentagon "employees who are still McNamara people and express a very definite Kennedy philosophy."[13] Hoover rated Mitchell as the best attorney general ever. Patricia Collins, a Justice Department lawyer who worked under fourteen attorneys general, said the director and the new attorney general "were the same kind actually. Hoover was a Republican from beginning to end." The director had his men check Mitchell's telephone for wiretaps and "the locks on the windows and doors" of his apartment at the Watergate.[14] With the campaign to declare Dr. King's birthday a national holiday gathering momentum, Hoover sent Agnew information on the civil rights leader's "highly immoral personal behavior." The vice president wanted "to be thoroughly conversant with all of that because if the crisis comes where we need to throw it, he will." Agnew, as Garry Wills once noted, was Nixon's Nixon—a baiter of blacks and kids. Hoover understood ("the President can't say some of the things the Vice President can"), and he admired Agnew "largely because he spoke out and named names." When Agnew's aide, Kent Crane, told the director "that 'you two' are birds of a feather," Hoover said he "was glad to be in that company."[15]

When Agnew asked for material on the Black Panther party and Ralph Abernathy of the Southern Christian Leadership Conference, the FBI dug into the files. "He wants to be able to let them have it," Hoover surmised. Agnew had expressed an interest in "especially graphic incidents that could be used as examples, which Governor Ronald Reagan has done a beautiful job with."[16] While the director briefed the vice president on the Panthers' financial contributors, especially "the entertainment industry people" and the whole "question of liberal support," the Los Angeles FBI office sent a letter from a fictitious person to Hollywood gossip columnist Army Archerd regarding Jane Fonda and her support for the party. "Jane and one of the Panthers," the letter read, had led the following refrain at a rally: "We will kill Richard Nixon, and any other M . . . F . . . who stands in our way."[17]

In April 1970, the same month that Agnew expressed his interest in "especially graphic incidents," FBI officials approved the mailing of a letter to another gossip columnist suggesting that actress Jean Seberg, star of *Paint Your Wagon* and *Airport* and a Black Panther supporter with a long history of psychiatric problems and suicide attempts, was pregnant by a party member. The Los Angeles office hoped to "cheapen her image," and gossip columnist Joyce Harber did publicize Seberg's pregnancy in the *Los Angeles Times*, without mentioning any names. Haber said "the FBI did not plant me directly because I don't know anyone in the FBI." The FBI claims that the original plan was canceled, an unconvincing denial of responsibility given the sequence of events and the director's close interest in the episode.

On the same day that the Haber column appeared, Hoover sent reports on Seberg to the White House. Even if the FBI's disclaimer is accepted at face value, it is clear that senior FBI officials felt no moral revulsion in any of the episode's outcomes.[18]

Seberg's problems only began with the *Los Angeles Times* piece. On June 8 the *Hollywood Reporter* identified her as the white actress carrying a Black Panther's child, and on August 7, nearly seven months pregnant, Seberg tried to kill herself by swallowing an overdose of sleeping pills. On August 23 she gave birth by Caesarian to a girl weighing less than four pounds. The August 24 edition of *Newsweek* said the father of her unborn child was not a former husband, the French novelist and World War II fighter pilot Romain Gary, but "a black activist she met in California"—presumably Los Angeles Panther Ray ("Masai") Hewitt. Based on information acquired through a wiretap, Hewitt emerged as the FBI's principal designated-father. The FBI also pursued an investigation of Seberg's prior relationship with sometime Panther Hakim Abdullan Jamal (Allen Donaldson), a cousin of Malcolm X. On August 25 Seberg's baby died, prompting a Division Five executive to advise his colleagues "of premature birth and death of child of" this "supporter of extremist Black Panther Party," this "alleged promiscuous and sex perverted white actress."

Four months later, on December 29, the FBI placed Seberg's name on the Security Index. One West Coast agent, in a reference to Seberg and Hewitt fraught with racist and sexual anxieties, reportedly said (according to *Jean Seberg Story* author David Richards), "I wonder how she'd like to gobble my dick while I shove my .38 up that black bastard's ass?" Seberg eventually sued *Newsweek* and two other publications which picked up the story, winning a modest award of $8,333. Gary, the real father of the dead baby, received $2,777. Not surprisingly, the FBI monitored the suit closely, from the day it was filed to the day of the court's final decision.

Jean Seberg's discovery, many years later, that she had been a COINTELPRO target fed her paranoia. She killed herself in Paris, in August 1979, by taking an overdose of barbiturates and alcohol. "Destroyed by the FBI," Romain Gary said, with some exaggeration. Seberg had been having trouble carrying the baby even before the *Newsweek* story broke. Gary committed suicide a year later, in his apartment on the Left Bank. By then, Hakim Jamal had been dead for seven years, murdered in Roxbury,

Massachusetts, by members of a black nationalist group called De Mau Mau, a crime that prompted the Boston FBI office to request approval from headquarters "to delete subject from the Extremist Photograph Album." Ray Hewitt left the Panthers and found work on a construction crew. "What a way to go down in history," he reflected, after the Seberg story spilled out. "The black man who went to bed with a white woman."[19]

On May 18, 1970, a month after the Seberg operation started, Spiro Agnew requested Hoover's assistance in a White House campaign to destroy Ralph Abernathy's credibility. This campaign began when the director and Attorney General Mitchell discussed the tragedy on the campus of predominantly black Jackson State College. A confrontation in front of a women's dormitory ended with city police and Mississippi troopers opening fire with rifles, shotguns, and carbines loaded with military ammunition, and a submachine gun. Some 400 bullets and pieces of buckshot, including armor piercing shells from two 30.06 rifles, struck the dormitory in a twenty-eight second fusillade, killing two black youths, Phillip Gibbs and James Earl Green, and wounding twelve. "[All] nigger gals . . . [and] nigger males," the police said. Hoover said there seemed "to be substantial proof . . . that there was sniper fire on the troops from the dormitory before the troops fired." The only provocations were words, chants ("Pigs! Pigs! Pigs!") and obscenities ("motherfucker!"). Mitchell planned to visit Jackson, and he asked Hoover to find out if there were any plans to picket him. The director advised him not to worry. Roy Moore had a new Cadillac and a chauffeur ready to drive him around, and a squad of agents standing by "in case any disturbance takes place."[20]

Agnew spoke to Hoover that same day, May 18, about Jackson State and Kent State as well. Hoover described the Kent State massacre (four dead white students and nine wounded—including an ROTC cadet) as "six of one and a half dozen of another, as you can't say it was proper to shoot, but we found . . . they were throwing 7 pound rocks at the soldiers and they hit one Guardsmen in the back and knocked him down. There is just so much a human being can stand." The Bureau opened a civil rights investigation (KENFOUR), but Hoover had already formed a conclusion. The students had "severely provoked" the guardsmen.[21]

Focusing on Jackson State, Agnew charged Abernathy with inciting the demonstrations there as well as rioting in Atlanta and

Augusta. Agreeing with this assessment of Abernathy ("I commented that he is one of the worst"), Hoover promised to do everything possible when Agnew asked for "information" for "executive use." The vice president wanted to document "the involvement of those people"—"whether fleeing from looting or what is going on." According to the director's account, Agnew "said he saw a picture about Augusta showing some of the Negroes jumping out of store windows with loot and booty and fleeing and you never hear anything about that." When Hoover again asked what the FBI could do to help, Agnew said he wanted anything "that can ameliorate some of the impact," anything that might assist in "destroying Abernathy's credibility." The director sent over a write-up the next day that included gossip about Abernathy's private life and connections with "suspect organizations."[22] A few months later, when an independent presidential commission condemned the Jackson State shootings as "an unreasonable, unjustified overreaction," Agnew dismissed the report as "pablum for the permissivists." He sided instead with the view of a Hinds County grand jury and a Kennedy judge. Students participating in civil disorders, Harold Cox said, "must expect to be injured or killed."[23]

The FBI continued its assault on Martin Luther King's memory while helping Agnew make his case against Abernathy. In fact, Hoover began this campaign even before Nixon assumed his duties as commander in chief. On Janury 17, 1969, Division Five executive George Moore recommended a memo detailing "the extensive communist influence on King" be sent to Nixon and Mitchell immediately after the inauguration. The director approved the plan, personally delivering additional documentation regarding King's "highly immoral behavior." "'His basic problem was he liked white girls,'" John Ehrlichman recalled the director saying. "Hoover went on at great length. . . . It was pretty obvious. He was trying to rewrite history. . . . In the great marketplace of ideas, Hoover was trying to establish a position on the civil rights issue by impugning the morality and rectitude of Martin Luther King."[24]

From there, Division Five placed the field on alert for "any efforts by city, county, or state governments to pass resolutions commemorating or honoring King." Hoover himself approved a briefing, after House Internal Security Committee member John Ashbrook (R., Ohio) approached the Crime Records Division, on behalf of two members of a subcommittee from the House Judiciary Committee. Crime Records felt the congressmen might be able to keep a bill regarding King's birthday bottled up in Committee if "they realize King was a scoundrel." Cartha DeLoach said it was "a delicate matter—but can be handled very cautiously." A few days later, on April 3, 1969, the Atlanta field office proposed a "counterintelligence action against Coretta Scott King and/or the continuous projection of the public image of Martin Luther King." This plan, like the House subcommittee briefing, was probably aborted. "The Bureau," as Division Five advised the Atlanta office, "does not desire counterintelligence action against Coretta King of the nature you suggest *at this time* [emphasis added]."[25]

Division Five was more receptive when DeLoach alerted "a friendly newspaper contact, on a strictly confidential basis," to the alleged plans of Mrs. King and Rev. Abernathy "to keep King's assassination in the news by pulling the ruse of maintaining that King's murder was definitely a conspiracy."[26] Crime Records also found the time "to choose a friendly, capable author, or the Reader's Digest, and proceed with a book" on the so-called MURKIN case—that is, a book on the FBI's civil rights investigation of King's murder.[27] DeLoach said there was a real need "to have a book . . . on college and high school library shelves so that the future would be protected." When Hoover approved the project, DeLoach tried to reach an agreement with *Reader's Digest* and a writer, Jim Bishop, with whom Crime Records had worked in the past. "Even though Bishop . . . [was] 'somewhat pompous and a little overbearing at times,'" DeLoach conceded, "he nonetheless has both the name and ability to produce a book on the King case which would give proper credit to the outstanding work done by the FBI."[28]

By early 1970 the FBI felt secure enough to back off a bit. When Congressman Peter Rodino, Jr. (D., N.J.), introduced yet another bill, the fifteenth since the assassination, to declare King's birthday a national holiday, Crime Records chief Thomas Bishop said no action was needed. Although passage of "such a bill would be a national calamity," Bishop argued that congressmen like Rodino were simply looking for black votes in their districts. The chances of any bill passing were "virtually nil," principally because Crime Records had already briefed the House leadership. In the Senate, Roman Hruska (R., Neb.), a member of the Judiciary Committee and a Bureau ally, chaired the Subcommittee on Federal Charters, Holidays, and Celebrations. Senator McClellan sat on the Subcommittee while Senator Eastland chaired the full Judiciary Committee. Bishop also said the FBI could count on the Senate minority leader, Hugh Scott (R., Penn.).[29] Hoover and Tolson agreed with Bishop's assessment, and the FBI did not mobilize in response to the Rodino bill. Bureau interest in such matters, nonetheless, remained high. When the Washington Committee for a Martin Luther King Holiday sponsored a program at Howard University, FBI agents and informers showed up to digest the speeches of Fannie Lou Hamer and Congressman John Conyers (D., Mich.). Division Five wrote everything up, and the director sent it on, once again, to the president, the vice president, and the attorney general.[30]

While Hoover worked on the King birthday case and handled special assignments for Nixon, Agnew, and Mitchell, FBI agents in the field and at headquarters tended to the community surveillance programs. At the time Lyndon Johnson left the White House, the Bureau operated some 3,300 "racial ghetto-type informants." That number jumped to nearly 7,500 by the end of Nixon's first term, with individual field offices engaged in crash programs to develop "Negro racial informants and Negro ghetto informants," even if their territory had no "militant black extremist organizations" in existence or "attempting to organize." For all practical purposes, the extent of black nationalism was irrelevant. FBI policy required every field office "to thoroughly saturate every level of activity in the ghetto."[31]

Other specialized FBI informant programs, including BLACPRO, also expanded during the Nixon years. Hoover approved the recruitment of eighteen-year-olds and a general escalation of "the scope and depth of the coverage provided by current racial . . . informants." Each field office submitted the names of informants with at least two of the following characteristics: "above average imagination and initiative"; "leadership ability"; "intelligence"; "unique knowledge or ability"; and "a willingness to expand his current affairs." Division Five hoped to create an elite informant squad and to send its members around the country and the world in pursuit of "domestic subversive, black militant, or New Left movements."[32] Information supplied by the informants led to the confiscation of explosives and the indictment of black radicals in Detroit, Richmond, and elsewhere on weapons and conspiracy charges. Most of the information provided, however, was far less dramatic, serving only as fodder for the files. The following report, filed on the

Black United Liberation Front (BULF) in Philadelphia, Pennsylvania, was typical:

> Informant advised . . . that the BULF is not going to buy a type setting machine. They are buying an electric typewriter. . . . Members are fighting and drinking more than ever. . . . There are only four persons staying at the BULF Headquarters now, SCHELL, RONNIE, CURTIS and PHIL. ROBIN stays there from 9 am until closing time but no longer sleeps there. She said SCHELL is 'fed up' and seems to be 'blowing his stack.' He is even talking about getting a job.[33]

Mundane information would not satisfy the Nixon White House. In June 1970, when the Ad Hoc Interagency Committee on Intelligence, the Huston Plan Committee that Hoover chaired, met to discuss the Panthers and the Muslims and especially "black student extremist influence," the director mentioned the events of the past school year: a total of 227 college disturbances and 530 secondary-school disturbances had "racial overtones." Demanding more informant coverage of "militant black student groups," along with more "live" informant coverage of "unaffiliated black militants," the Huston Plan Committee recommended recruitment among "former members of the Armed Forces presently attending college." The administration also needed additional nonhuman sources, including the "maximum use of communications interceptions," to determine the extent of foreign involvement in black student extremist matters.

The foreign angle was particularly important. Here again, the FBI, along with officials from other departments and agencies with internal security responsibilities, lumped everyone together—black students with white students, dissidents with spies and saboteurs, 1960s' militants in the United States with 1930s' popular fronters in Great Britain. Although Tom Charles Huston himself dismissed "old line Communist fronts" as "largely irrelevant to our current problem," the Huston Plan Committee pointed out that "H. A. R. (Kim) Philby, Guy Burgess, and Donald Maclean were all students at Cambridge during the depression period of the 1930's and were in the vanguard of what was then the New Left.[34]

Though Hoover eventually blocked the formal implementation of the Huston Plan Committee's reckless recommendations, he supported the escalation of surveillance aimed at black students. Nixon had been in office for a month when the FBI's four-year-old Columbia field office reported on its success in notifying the draft board of black student militants in 1-A status and developing black informants at South Carolina universities. The Norfolk field office plotted the dismissal of a faculty member at "the predominantly Negro Norfolk State College," while the Pittsburgh office contemplated counterintelligence plans to "neutralize" a person who had "been named coordinator of a drive to recruit black students for scholarships at the University of Pittsburgh." Even the Butte field office mobilized after discovering that a class at the University of Montana required a book entitled *The Student as Nigger.* The University had also hired a black man "to teach Afro-American classes at UM," the Bureau noted, "when the approximately twenty black students" complained they "had no one to relate to."[35] In California, the FBI assisted Governor Reagan's investigation into the use of public funds and facilities to further black extremist activities on the campuses.[36]

The scope of the dissemination and the general interest in black faculty and black student groups was routine. Black student unions (BSUs), quite common by the late 1960s, particularly after 1966 when Amiri Baraka formed one of the first at San Francisco State, were natural targets for the FBI. Investigative criteria—advocacy of "scholarships for black students, more black instructors on the faculty, and introduction of black and African courses in the curriculum"—had been established by the summer of 1968. But Hoover did not drop the minimum age of campus informants from twenty-one to eighteen until September 1970, on the grounds that the FBI needed to counter "violence-oriented youthful groups" and "fanatics . . . at large who are at war with the Government and the American people." Two months later, in November, Hoover approved the automatic investigation of "all BSUs and similar organizations organized to project the demands of black students." At that point, the FBI selected targets "regardless of their past or present involvement in disorders." The Inspection Division estimated a total new case load of 3,500 extending to 750 black student groups on 500 two- and four-year campuses.[37]

A number of black student unions and other student groups attracted the attention of FBI men assigned to the COINTELPRO desks. In Jackson, Mississippi, special agent Thomas Fitzpatrick offered the following rationale for placing a SNCC-affiliated Political Action Committee on the counterintelligence list: "The Tougaloo College PAC activities have, in the recent past, pertained to the sponsoring of on campus out-of-state militant Negro speakers, voter-registration drives, and African cultural seminars and lectures. Additionally, the group has vocally condemned various publicized injustices to the civil rights of Negroes in Mississippi."[38] Neither local FBI agents nor the executives in Washington saw anything wrong with these criteria. Tougaloo was as an "anything goes" campus, "a very liberal school," a "staging area for civil rights and militant Negro activities in Mississippi."[39] So Jackson agents shared informant reports with city and state police officials, and otherwise worked to intimidate the student body.[40] They even proposed to "neutralize" Tougaloo College itself, a suggestion that prompted Division Five to remind them about the Political Action Committee and its chairman, Howard Spencer, "since Tougaloo College, per se, is not a counterintelligence target."[41]

Division Five settled for a letter to the SNCC office in Atlanta implying that one or more Tougaloo PAC members were police informants; and a vague plan to label Jan Hillegas, a Southern Conference Educational Fund field worker who had recruited on the Tougaloo campus for "the Women's Liberation Movement in Mississippi," as an informer for the Mississippi Sovereignty Commission. Another action involved a rumor campaign against Tougaloo student and antipoverty worker Muhammad Kenyatta (then known as Donald Jackson). To drive him out of the state, the Bureau accused Kenyatta of various criminal activities, including the theft of a television set from the campus.[42] The most routine operations in Mississippi involved a series of leaks to *Jackson Daily News* columnist James ("Jackson Jimmy") Ward. The FBI eventually reached beyond the Tougaloo campus to black groups at other campuses, from area high schools to the University of Mississippi, Delta State College, and (of course) Jackson State. Bureau agents sometimes had city police and state troopers arrest "Negro Black Militants" from these schools on minor infractions. Nuisance arrests.[43]

The FBI continued to share the information gathered by its informants in the ghetto and on the campuses with the Central Intelligence Agency, the National Security Agency, state and local police, and various foreign intelligence agencies—though there is no hard evidence that the Bureau went as far as the

House Internal Security Committee. Chairman Richard Ichord (D., Mo.) ran file checks on the African National Congress and the Southwest Africa People's Organization for David Loewe of the South African embassy.[44] At the recommendation of CIA executive Richard Ober, the FBI submitted the names of black militants, Panthers and SNCC members, among others, to the agency for inclusion on its New York mail-opening "watch list." When requesting the assistance of the National Security Agency in "racial extremist matters," Hoover cast a net broad enough to encompass most every group interested in race and class, from the Panthers to the Society of Friends. The FBI submitted the names of "white and black racial extremists" ("natural allies of foreign enemies of the United States," Hoover said) directly to the NSA's so-called MINARET "watch list." The FBI also fed names to a computerized Secret Service list of 5,500 Black Nationalists that included the names of Jackie Robinson and Roy Wilkins.[45]

One of the FBI's own listings, the Agitator Index, included among its 1,191 names that of Jesse Jackson—the subject of a Racial Matters-Black Nationalists investigation. At least thirty-four human and other informants (taps, bugs, trash covers, and so forth) reported on Jackson's activities at any given time, and the FBI eventually opened parallel files on Operation Breadbasket and PUSH.[46] Hoover abolished the Agitator Index in the spring of 1971 and the more pervasive Security Index in the fall, following congressional repeal of the emergency detention provision (Title II) of the Internal Security Act of 1950, and replaced them with an Administrative Index (ADEX). Since FBI officials deemed subversives an "even greater" threat "than before repeal of the Act, since they no doubt [felt] safer . . . to conspire in the destruction of the country," they continued "the essence of the Security Index," and the Agitator Index as well, "under Presidential powers." John Mitchell approved the name change, and the new ADEX included "four categories representing degrees of dangerousness."[47]

Black activists were well represented on the ADEX. Category I listed the names of "national leaders of black extremist separatist organizations," and Category II the names of "secondary leadership," along with "active participants"—that is, people who furthered "the aims and purposes of the revolutionary or black extremist separatist organization with which affiliated." Category III listed "rank-and-file membership," along with the name of any "individual who, although not a member of or participant in activities of revolutionary organizations or considered an activist in affiliated fronts, has exhibited a revolutionary ideology." Category IV listed *"individuals whose activities do not meet criteria of Categories I, II, or III* [emphasis added]." All four categories were purposefully elastic, allowing the inclusion of "the new breed of subversive," the free-lance black radical who had "a seething hatred of the white establishment" and might at any time "assassinate, explode, or otherwise destroy white America." A parallel Reserve Index incorporated into ADEX the names of persons who did not engage in subversive activities ("teachers, writers, lawyers, etc."), but "were nonetheless influential in espousing their respective philosophies."[48]

If skin color attracted a casual interest, a politics of any stripe attracted the more serious interest of the Division Five COINTELPRO agents.[49] The Key Black Extremist (KBE) Program, the most refined Nixon-era list and the last of the targeting mechanisms for the counterintelligence program, had its roots in an October 1970 FBI racial conference. Noting the need for "intensified coverage on a group of black extremists who are either key leaders or activists and are particularly extreme, agitative, anti-Government, and vocal in their calls for terrorism and violence," the racial conference demanded the systematic identification and neutralization of such persons. "Certain elements" were simply "more likely to resort to or order terrorism as a tactic," and these types required "particular attention."[50]

Headquarters solicited nominations from the field, stressed the need for "initiative and imagination," and issued the inevitable guidelines for cataloguing Key Black Extremists and selecting candidates for timely counterintelligence action. Division Five listed the names of all KBEs in the ADEX (Priority I) and pasted their pictures in the Black Nationalist Photograph Album; monitored all bank accounts, safe-deposit boxes, investments, and other financial assets, as well as all travel and "financial arrangements for such travel"; obtained handwriting specimens and tape recordings of inflammatory statements and kept them in "the national security file" at the FBI laboratory; "vigorously investigated" all "possible" violations of federal law; processed individual reports every ninety days; and checked federal income tax records annually. On this last point, when the FBI requested the tax returns of seventy-two Key Black Extremists, the IRS honored every request, without asking any questions.[51]

With regard to the monitoring of financial assets, the FBI overlooked no bank account, even an account in the low two figures. A spot check at a Chester, Pennsylvania, bank revealed a grand total of $44.32 in the name of the National Black Economic Development Conference. The Invaders' bank account in Memphis totaled $33. The FBI obtained this sort of information routinely, through sources at the banks that held the accounts. Such sources were ubiquitous, in banks and other private-sector institutions, and they made things easier for field agents. It made no difference whether the Bureau wanted information from a source in a bank or the help of a source in "the membership section of the National Rifle Association" to purge a black militant member. The FBI mobilized all its resources.[52]

Division Five executives also tried to make things easier for field agents by expanding the Racial Calendar once again in late 1970, and by February 1971 they included "telephone numbers of black, New Left, and other ethnic extremists" in the Computerized Telephone Number File (CTNF)—an investigative tool originally confined to interstate gambling cases. They "entered into the CTNF" the names of all "black extremist groups, black extremist Security Index [ADEX] subjects, and individuals included in the Black Nationalist Photograph Album." The Photo Album alone contained the names of 484 activists.[53]

An even more valuable investigative technique, electronic surveillance, supplemented the "extremely valuable" CTNF. Though FBI wiremen pulled the plug on the Stanley Levison tap during the Nixon years, they installed new taps and bugs in other places. As of March 1971 the Bureau had a microphone hidden in Huey Newton's San Francisco home, and operated at least thirteen telephone surveillances. Six of these were on Black Panther offices (in San Francisco, Oakland, Los Angeles, Chicago, New Haven, and the Bronx), and another was on Newton's phone.[54] Mostly, the information uncovered by the Panther wiretaps had to do with pregnancies, transportation and telephone problems, the lack of heat in offices, calls home to mom. Hoover justified his request to Mitchell for a continuation of the tap on the Panthers' Chicago office on the grounds that it provided valuable information on such topics as Panther attempts "to organize the black workers employed by the Chicago Transit Authority."[55]

This justification contrasts with Hoover's argument when originally requesting authority to tap Panther offices in San

Francisco and Chicago. One Panther leader, the director wrote in April 1969, "has been involved in the direction of racial disturbances, has attempted to obtain dynamite to blow up public buildings, and has stated that if contact could be made with Negroes on the White House staff a plan might be formulated to poison people attending functions there." Party members, the director added, "possess guns" and "use the telephone extensively." That last point was perhaps the one that mattered most. On the whole, the wiretap transcripts "show how far removed the Panther reality was from its bloody guerrilla mystique." "Some of the things we used to hear on the wiretaps were funny," said William Cohendet, the FBI agent assigned to the Panther squad in San Francisco. "It reminded me of *Amos and Andy*. Fundamentally, I think, black people are jovial, happy and fun loving."[56]

The other six FBI wiretaps in place as of March 1971 were on the telephones of two nonwhite "racial extremist groups" (one of which was the Tampa-based Junta of Military Organizations), two "militant black extremist group members" (including a SNCC activist), yet another black extremist group functionary, and a member of a "racial group." Of these unidentified taps, one was on the telephone of the Jewish Defense League in New York, and another was on the telephone of an SDS affiliate in Chicago, the Worker Student Alliance. This modest number of taps and the equally modest number of bugs must be balanced against FBI access to the transcripts based on the hundreds of electronic surveillances installed by state and local police. In New Haven alone the wiring extended beyond the Panthers to include antiwar activists, Yale faculty, journalists, lawyers, housewives, and professional gamblers.[57]

Bureau agents used electronic surveillance less frequently during the Nixon years than they had during the Kennedy years or the early Johnson years. Between 1960 and 1966 they planted 738 "microphone sources" and an unknown number of wiretaps, informing the Justice Department of only 158 of the mikes.[58] "The risk potential," as Mark Felt put it in 1971, in reference to another illegal technique, "specialized mail coverage," was simply too high "in today's world of civil libertarians and 'blabbermouths'" to continue such extensive surveillances.[59] Hoover had first cut electronic surveillances in response to "hearings on bugging" by the Senate Subcommittee on Administrative Practice and Procedure, and the willingness of "hostile Department attorneys" like Ramsey Clark to send the Subcommittee "electronic surveillance memoranda dating back to 1925."[60] The controversy over who authorized the King wiretaps, Robert Kennedy or J. Edgar Hoover, compounded the FBI's problems. After documents produced in the Selective Service Act case against Muhammad Ali revealed that the ex-champ was overheard on one of the King taps, Hoover sent letters defending the FBI's position to Nixon, Agnew, and Mitchell.[61] He also sent letters of thanks to North Carolina television executive and future United States Senator Jesse Helms and anyone else who took the Bureau's side. When Congressman Robert L. Leggett (D., Cal.) asked for a briefing on the controversy, in contrast, the FBI ran his name through the files, noted his vote against HUAC's appropriation back in 1965, and then declined to help him. For Hoover, this was a standard test for distinguishing friends from enemies.[62]

A more restrained use of electronic surveillance and other questionable investigative techniques, including mail openings and break-ins, had no effect on the quantity of intelligence collected. The Nixon administration faced the same problem the Johnson administration faced: the need to organize and evaluate all the racial matters items the FBI kept sending over. Attorney General Mitchell and his deputy, Richard Kleindienst, planned to refine the intelligence apparatus. They wanted more "computer power," more control over the Interdivisional Intelligence Unit (IDIU) and the other Great Society things they had inherited. They ended up with an absolute mishmash of bureaucratic reform.

As a first step, in March and April 1969, Mitchell and Kleindienst, with the help of Secretary of Defense Melvin Laird, developed an Interdepartmental Action Plan for Civil Disturbances. The three men designated the attorney general ("the logical choice") as "the chief civilian officer in charge of coordinating all Federal Government activities relating to civil disturbances," including the accumulation of "raw intelligence data." Three months later, in July 1969, Mitchell created an ad hoc Intelligence Evaluation Committee (IEC), selecting Cartha DeLoach to chair it. Membership included the heads of the Justice Department's Civil Rights, Internal Security, and Criminal Divisions, and the Community Relations Service; and representatives from the IDIU, the Secret Service, and Army Intelligence. In late 1970, in the aftermath of the Huston Plan, Mitchell secretly resconstituted the IEC as a permanent body, expanding its membership to include representatives from the CIA and the National Security Agency. The new Committee held its first meeting on December 3 in John Dean's office, with Division Five executive George Moore representing a skeptical Hoover. The Committee met sporadically until 1974, when it was finally abolished and its functions absorbed by yet another new bureaucracy—the Civil Disturbance Unit, formerly the IDIU.[63]

Intelligence Evaluation Committee staff, together with staff from the old IDIU, processed some 42,000 incoming intelligence reports per annum in the years before the Civil Disturbance Unit organized. The FBI sent over most of the data.[64] Field agents read "all appropriate black extremist publications" in search of names to index, and their annual "subversive" and "extremist" case loads increased during Nixon's first term from 30,000 to 45,000 and from 17,000 to 25,000 respectively. Many of the individual reports forwarded to the IDIU and the IEC, moreover, were quite detailed. A strike organized by "blind black workers" at an Industries of the Blind plant in North Carolina rated sixteen pages. Division Five sent another copy of the report on this strike, based on information supplied by a state police intelligence unit, to the Civil Rights Division.[65]

While forwarding information to John Mitchell's new bureaucracy, Hoover embraced at least one of the attorney general's other priorities—namely, the emphasis on "computer power." To keep track of black and antiwar activists "against whom warrants are not outstanding," in February 1970 the director approved a "Stop Index" program for the computer in the FBI National Crime Information Center. Launched in January 1967, the Crime Information Center provided computerized searches for criminal histories, and was used most often by state and local police officers when making routine stops of motorists who had committed moving-code or vehicular-safety violations. By inserting a "Stop Index" for black and antiwar dissidents, Hoover had politicized the Crime Information Center and its law-enforcement mission.[66]

FBI files provided much of the information for yet another surveillance bureaucracy, the Special Service Staff (SSS) of the Internal Revenue Service. IRS officials set up the SSS in the summer of 1969 after IRS Commissioner Randolph W. Thrower, a former FBI agent, met with Tom Charles Huston and Arthur Burns, Nixon's economic counselor and later chairman of the

Federal Reserve Board. When Paul Wright, the IRS executive selected to run the Special Service Staff, told Hoover that Senator McClellan's PERM had asked for files on twenty-two groups, the director agreed to put the new bureaucracy on his dissemination list. He hoped to "deal a blow to dissident elements." In all, Bureau executives sent over COINTELPRO and other racial matters files (11,818 separate reports), principally because SSS staff did not feel competent to define an "ideological organization." Relying on the FBI for direction, IRS agents processed the reports in the basement of the Internal Revenue Service building under "red seal" security.[67]

The Nixon-era Special Service Staff institutionalized something the IRS and the FBI had dabbled in since the Franklin D. Roosevelt years.[68] Moving beyond Senator McClellan's 22 mostly left-wing groups to 77 organizations by the end of 1969, SSS files exploded thereafter. By August 1973, when IRS Commissioner Donald Alexander abolished the SSS just as it was preparing to put everything on the computer, the listings included 2,873 organizations and 8,585 individuals. The FBI contributed a list of more than 2,300 groups and more than 80 percent of the individual names in five basic categories: "liberal establishment," "New Left," "antiwar," "white right-wing extremist and racist," and "black and ethnic."[69] In all, SSS held files on fifty chapters of the National Urban League; the U.S. Civil Rights Commission; the Head Start program; the Ford Foundation; a black congressman from Detroit, Charles Diggs (and presumably all other black elected officials); and even "persons associated with or 'disassociated' with various racially oriented groups." None of this satisfied the White House however. "Dominated by Democrats," in the Nixon administration view, the IRS was unwilling to go as far as the president intended.[70]

While monitoring black activists with the help of the Special Service Staff and other surveillance appendages, the FBI pursued its other assigned "racial matters" task, the investigation of alleged violations of federal civil rights law, in the usual manner. Civil Rights Division chief Jerris Leonard, who was himself considered by a few of his own attorneys to be in "no way committed to civil rights" ("clearly in the McCarthy mold," "kind of a vile guy"), said the "Division had big problems with the FBI," particularly on police brutality matters, in the beginning. "We had to prod the Bureau at times in order to get them to respond to our requests. It might take three memoranda to them instead of one or two." But the Bureau came around, Leonard continued. "The fact of the matter is, they did the tough interviews in civil rights cases. . . . By the time I left the Civil Rights Division, the earlier problems had generally gone away."[71] Leonard's words could have been spoken by Harold Tyler or Burke Marshall or John Doar, three predecessors who also considered the FBI's performance terrible "in the beginning" but nonetheless believed that the FBI eventually came around. In a sense, the box memo of the Kennedy-era Civil Rights Division had given way to the three-memo cajoling of the Nixon-era Civil Rights Division.

Hoover told Egil Krogh at the White House that 2,301 agents were working in the "civil rights . . . area alone, and it has almost paralyzed us." He did not tell Krogh that most of those agents had racial intelligence responsibilities, not Civil Rights enforcement responsibilities. The Justice Department continued to request numerous "limited or preliminary" investigations of civil rights complaints. "They have been dumping them on us by the hundreds," Hoover said. But as Assistant Director Alex Rosen noted in July 1970, a time when the surveillance programs were flourishing, the FBI did "not have any full investigations in civil rights matters pending at this time."[72]

Eight months after Rosen wrote those words, on the evening of March 1, Hoover and his constant companion for the last forty years, Clyde Tolson, saw a "negro girl . . . in the 9th Street elevator" as they left their offices and headed home. The young woman, a file clerk assigned to the main FBI headquarters building, "had an extremely large hairdo which Mr. Tolson felt was a wig," prompting both the director and the associate director to ask who she was. The FBI executive who received the identification assignment located a likely candidate ("we feel [name deleted] may be empl Mr. Tolson referring to"), noting that "many of our female empls wear wigs of different types in accordance with current fashion and we have not objected to this practice." Upon hearing this, Tolson wrote: "Transfer to Ident Bldg. T." By scribbling a simple "Yes. H." next to his friend's words, Hoover banished the "negro girl" with the Afro wig to the Identification Building. The director acted here as he always did, in opposition to any visible form of protest, whether real or imagined.[73]

All in all, the year 1971 was a trying one for Hoover. He had to terminate the counterintelligence programs, for "security reasons," following the burglary of an FBI resident agency in Media, Pennsylvania, by an antiwar group, the Citizens' Commission to Investigate the FBI, on March 8, the night of the first Ali-Frazier fight. The director also endured a broadside of criticism from House Democratic majority leader Hale Boggs of Louisiana and two Democratic contenders for the presidency, Senators George McGovern of South Dakota and Edmund Muskie of Maine. Then, the surfacing of an FBI memo recording surveillance of Muskie and others attending the nationwide Earth Day environmental rallies further embarrassed the Bureau, despite White House press secretary Ron Ziegler's attempt to dismiss the resultant publicity as "blatantly political." In a sense, Ziegler was right. A Nixon aide had specifically requested an FBI report on Earth Day. All this paled in the face of the Media burglary. The Citizens' Commission liberated approximately 1,000 pieces of Bureau paper, sending a steady stream of samples to the press and members of Congress throughout the months of March and April.

In addition to the counterintelligence programs, the pilfered FBI documents compromised the Ghetto Informant Program and several other community surveillance programs aimed at black America. For Hoover, it was a public relations nightmare. The documents revealed surveillance of black student groups, the names of racial matters informants, the Black Panther party wiretaps, and miscellaneous pieces of surveillance paraphernalia. "Informant loss" was "moderate," Division Five said. "Most of the sources compromised could possibly be replaced within [a] reasonable period of time." The most "potentially . . . damaging item," one of William Sullivan's men concluded, "involved our interest in various Black Student Union groups. . . . Unfriendly critics could seek to portray our investigations as invasion of academic freedom or racially inspired investigations."[74]

Hoover had already given John Mitchell a more alarmist "damage assessment." With regard to one of the black organizations identified in the Media papers, James Forman's National Black Economic Development Conference, the director said the informants named in the Media papers were "in serious personal jeopardy." "Even death is a possibility," he predicted, mentioning the Panthers and Angela Davis's sister, a student at Swarthmore College and best childhood friend of Carole Robertson, one of the victims of Birmingham's Sixteenth Street Baptist

Church bombing, as extremists who might kill someone. Fania Davis was capable of "fatal violence," Hoover told Mitchell. She "intended to foment revolutions after she graduated," and had led a black student sit-in at the Swarthmore admissions office. That sit-in ended, the director added, only when the College president dropped dead of a heart attack.[75]

Attorney General Mitchell wanted the FBI to issue a press release urging the media not to print the purloined documents. He intended to appeal to patriotism, to emphasize the harm to the national security. Hoover would not do it. Instead, he urged the Justice Department, in the words of FBI legal counsel Dwight J. Dalbey, to "sponsor enactment of legislation similar to The Official Secrets Act which is a part of English law." "If we had such an act at this time," Dalbey reasoned, "it could be used against any person or organization, including the new media, which misused the data or failed to return upon demand." In the interim, the FBI looked for the Media burglars. But the director's agents never found them; the MEDBURG case never closed.[76]

Hoover's problems compounded. Under the sponsorship of the Committee for Public Justice (CPJ) and the Woodrow Wilson School of Public and International Affairs, a group of academics, journalists, celebrities, and former Justice Department lawyers met in October 1971 for an investigating-the-FBI conference at Princeton University. Their agenda included the Bureau's civil rights investigations as well as its domestic intelligence investigations. Arthur Schlesinger, Ramsey Clark, John Doar, and Roger Wilkins attended, and Burke Marshall, then deputy dean of the Yale Law School, chaired the conference. D. Robert Owen, the former Civil Rights Division attorney who had presented the grand jury case against the persons indicted in Neshoba County for denying Schwerner, Chaney, and Goodman their civil rights, and Victor Navasky, author of *Kennedy Justice*, were there, too. The FBI described Marshall as "no friend of the Bureau," Doar as "obnoxious," and Navasky "as a Kennedy apologist."[77] Intending to "handle" this "group of anti-FBI bigots," Hoover had his Crime Records agents brief at least fifteen of the FBI's "good friends in the news media" and "on the Hill."[78]

Hoover was still troubled by the Media burglary and the Princeton Conference on May Day 1972. In most every way it was an uneventful day in his life—nine hours at the office, dinner with Tolson, a late evening phone call to retired special agent/chauffeur and then all-around handyman James Crawford. Hoover wanted Crawford to come by the next morning, to help decide where to plant some new rose bushes just delivered by a nursery. After speaking with Crawford, Hoover went to bed. "Another May Day had passed," as his biographer noted, "without the Revolution he had predicted for a May Day in 1920, fifty-two years before. He had been twenty-five years old then; now he was seventy-seven."[79]

Hoover died alone in his room on the morning of May 2, with his three black servants, all in their proper place, waiting for him to come down for breakfast. When he did not come out of his room on time, they crept up the stairs to find out what was wrong. Annie Fields, the live-in housekeeper, wearing her gray maid's outfit, led the way, followed by Crawford and his brother-in-law, special agent Tom Moton, the director's driver for the past three years. They found Hoover's naked body sprawled on the floor. Following a state funeral with full military honors, a hearse carried the thousand-pound casket containing the director's remains to Congressional Cemetery. As the chaplain of the United States Senate, Edward L. R. Elson, sprinkled a handful of dirt across the casket, "black children from the neighborhood hung on nearby gravestones." Elson had barely finished before the kids began "to snatch away the big cottonball mums from the outlying flower baskets," even before the men from the funeral home began to lower the casket into the earth.[80] Afterward, James Crawford went to work as a handyman for Tolson and to wait for his inheritance. He received $2,000 and half of Hoover's clothes. Sam Noisette, the director's black office retainer, received the other half. Annie Fields received $3,000. Hoover left the great bulk of his estate to Tolson.

The Media burglary, the Princeton conference, and even the director's death were only a prelude to the collapse of the FBI domestic intelligence apparatus. "One of the things people forget," as Nicholas Katzenbach said, "is that J. Edgar Hoover was just about as powerful as anyone in the United States of America. Congressmen were scared to death of him. They got very brave after he died." Indeed, a month after Hoover passed away, the Congressional Black Caucus held hearings on government lawlessness, and one of the witnesses, investigative columnist Jack Anderson, brought along dozens of files on black activists provided by a source in the FBI.[81] Though the media largely ignored the Black Caucus's closed-door hearings, with the director gone and the Watergate scandal unraveling, the issue was no longer whether the FBI could avoid a substantive congressional investigation of its domestic intelligence activities but whether the inevitable investigation could be properly managed.

The House Subcommittee on Civil and Constitutional Rights posed the most immediate threat. Chaired by a former FBI agent, Don Edwards (D., Cal.), "the Democratic members of this Subcommittee," in the FBI view, were "extreme liberals." Edwards's proposed hearings "on COINTELPRO could be most troublesome." Bureau officials knew they would fare better by working with the "far friendlier" James Eastland, chairman of the Senate Committee on the Judiciary, and chairman as well of a hastily created appendage to that Committee—the FBI Oversight Subcommittee. Eastland brought in John McClellan and Strom Thurmond to sit on the Oversight Subcommittee, and informed Hugh Clegg, the former Bureau executive and Mississippi native, "that if he received any complaints concerning the FBI he would pitch them into the wastepaper basket and not bother to call together the Committee." He later "indicated his willingness to initiate hearings at any time at [the FBI's] request," agreeing that any report "should not be made public."[82]

In the House, the FBI worked with another sweetheart committee, Richard Ichord's Internal Security Committee. The Committee launched its own investigation of FBI domestic intelligence operations in 1973, part of a more general campaign "to insure that the FBI," in its time of trouble, "is given full Congressional support." Ichord told Clarence Kelley, the Nixon appointee who replaced the hapless L. Patrick Gray III, the acting director who managed to embroil himself and the Bureau in the Watergate cover-up, that the FBI's surveillance responsibilities represented "the backbone of all the Government security programs." Committee staff director Robert M. Horner told Ichord the investigation was timely. "If we don't do it other committees will but probably with a restrictive purpose in mind." With FBI agents helping Horner's staff behind the scenes and senior FBI officials agreeing to testify in public session, HISC finally held its hearings in 1974. But no one paid much attention. The media had no interest in the "'chilling' effect" all the revelations of surveillance abuses had on the FBI. By the end of the year the hearings ended the way they had begun, in obscurity.[83]

Clarence Kelley presided over the FBI during its time of trouble, working with Ichord and other friends in the Congress to defend the Hoover-era record.[84] At best, his success was mixed. When the Edwards Subcommittee finally held its hearings on COINTELPRO, the new director's testimony did not go well. He seemed "to be at his inarticulate worst," as Sanford Ungar observed. When attempting to limit the Bureau's domestic intelligence activities, moreover, Kelley met resistance from the Justice Department. On one occasion, in August 1974, he requested guidance from the Department regarding Bureau responsibilities for gathering and reporting data on civil disturbances. He wanted to limit FBI coverage "to those particular situations which are of such a serious nature that Federal military personnel may be called upon for assistance." Henry E. Petersen, the chief of the Criminal Division, rejected the proposal on the grounds that it was "not practical."[85]

Kelley wanted to extract the FBI from its traditional surveillance role *and* from a looming civil rights quagmire. At the time, the most pressing concern of the Justice Department's Civil Disturbance Unit was the busing issue and attendant violence. In October 1974, the same month that Petersen issued his directive, the Department ordered the Bureau to maintain "a constant oversight monitoring of troubled areas" and "school desegregation disturbances" in South Boston. The White House also monitored FBI activities in South Boston regularly until mid-December 1974, a time when it became clear that the Bureau's surveillance network would collapse.[86]

Newspaper stories about such things as FBI spying on Robert Kennedy and civil rights leaders at the 1964 Democratic National Convention were followed by the death of the Bureau's last hope for a friendly congressional investigation. On January 14, 1975, the House abolished its Committee on Internal Security, the Red-hunting Committee that traced its roots back to Martin Dies. The Senate established a Select Committee to Study Governmental Operations with Respect to Intelligence Activities (the Church Committee) thirteen days later, and the House created it own Select Committee (the Pike Committee) on February 19.[87] Inheriting most of this Watergate fallout, the Gerald Ford administration suspected the FBI would be the least cooperative of all the intelligence community bureaucracies. In that respect, the FBI might prove to be the least troublesome. The administration knew it would have "little control over the intelligence investigation," but proposed to do the best it could. That meant stonewalling.[88]

As the administration suspected, it did not work. Watergate had damaged the national security mystique. Intelligence community files, including the FBI's records, opened to an unprecedented degree. Even Ichord asked to see his file. "Requests for such files are not new," as one White House adviser noted. "What is new is that people—particularly in Congress—no longer give up when they are told no." With the "band wagon" effect of the investigating committees becoming "increasingly partisan" and impossible to control, the White House worried about Congresswoman Bella Abzug (D., N.Y.) and Senator Walter Mondale (D., Minn.), and wondered "how long it will be before we hear from [Ronald] Reagan." Secretary of State Kissinger, among others, thought a series of executive orders restricting "all intelligence agencies except the FBI" would be the best way to contain the committees, to limit the dangers posed to the national security and the Republican party's political prospects.[89]

Amendments to the Freedom of Information Act (FOIA) in 1974 and the sweeping investigations of the intelligence community in 1975–1976 posed no threat to the national security. The Church and Pike Committees and a functioning FOIA threatened only an unrestrained and unaccountable domestic intelligence mission. No one was surprised when the committees zeroed in on the FBI and the racial matters investigations. Bureau surveillance of blacks had never been a well-kept secret, and the earlier revelations, everything from the Martin Luther King wiretaps to the Media papers, gave the investigators a hint of what they would find. There was plenty of fodder for the conspiracy theorists who actually believed that the Bureau "neutralized" Dr. King by killing him. More rational people, like Harris Wofford, John Kennedy's civil rights adviser, merely charged "Hoover and the FBI" with helping to "create the climate that invited King's assassination."[90]

Church Committee members and staff did the most thorough job of all the congressional investigating committees, preparing reports on the FBI campaigns against King and the Black Panther party and questioning many of the principals. They asked Cartha DeLoach about the Atlantic City operation and the activities of the Crime Records Division, while grilling William Sullivan and his former Division Five deputy, George Moore, about the COINTELPROs.[91] "When things blow up," another former Division Five executive said, "they turn their backs on you." The Church Committee brought in Gary Rowe to discuss the Klan wars, and several Great Society reformers, notably former Attorneys General Katzenbach and Clark, to testify regarding the community surveillance programs—and what they knew or did not know about the counterintelligence programs. John Doar, having just completed a yearlong assignment with the House Judiciary Committee as special counsel during the impeachment inquiry, contributed a report on the Bureau and the voting litigation campaign.[92]

The FBI rode it all out. In the House, when the Pike Committee's staff director asked W. Raymond Wannall, one of Kelley's aides and a die-hard Hoover loyalist, a question about the Bureau's political philosophy, he replied: "I don't think the FBI [has] a political philosophy." Another Hoover loyalist, James B. Adams, thought the whole thing much ado about nothing. The civil liberties issue, the racism issue, and the abuse of power issue were all irrelevant. "Is the public afraid of us," Adams asked, "or the fact that they can't walk the streets at night?" The full House never debated that question. But with visions of political pendulums swinging back, the House voted to suppress the Pike Committee's final report following the unauthorized disclosure of information from that report to the *Village Voice*.[93]

In the aftermath, the only reforms were administrative. Congress made no law restricting the use and abuse of the FBI's domestic intelligence resources. The chief executive offered directives and guidelines that could be repealed with the stroke of one future president's pen. The courts called no Bureau official to account for the King or Panther campaigns, but President Jimmy Carter's Justice Department did pursue three top executives for the handling of one other investigation: the Department obtained indictments against L. Patrick Gray, Edward S. Miller, and W. Mark Felt in April 1978, charging them with conspiracy to violate the civil rights of friends and relatives of the Weather Underground—specifically, for authorizing burglaries of their homes in a "hard hitting" and "innovative" search for the antiwar group's fugitive bombers.

There is an irony in those indictments and subsequent convictions of Felt and Miller. (The government dropped its charges against Gray.) All three indictments came under the old Reconstruction Era statute, Section 241 (as revised in the Civil Rights Act of 1968), and the case began in the Civil Rights Division before the attorney general moved it out to the Criminal Division. When Hoover was alive he constantly complained about the inadequacy of the statute, about how "the colored elements" kept bothering him with requests to enforce an unenforceable law. Section 241 was good enough to convict two FBI men, even if President Ronald Reagan pardoned them in March 1981, without even bothering to read the trial transcript, on the basis of their good-faith attempt to safeguard the national security.

Hoover would never have appreciated the irony, though he would have appreciated President Reagan's deference to the FBI's historic mission. The director spent the last fifty-three years of his life protecting the national security, always guarding the republic from the terrible and timeless communists, and in the 1960s guarding the republic against the new enemies of middle America. He opposed the nihilists on the fringes of the black nationalist movement at the end of the decade just as he had opposed the men and women in the mainstream of the civil rights movement at the beginning of the decade. Hoover will always be remembered for standing against the Red menace, for fueling the periodic hysterias of the Red scare. He should also be remembered for standing against justice for blacks, for fueling the fears of a black scare in the time of Kennedy, Johnson, and Nixon.

CONCLUSION

<hr>

Racial Matters,
Racial Justice

J Edgar Hoover had always been a racist. He once referred to
Martin Luther King as a "burr head," if William Sullivan is
to be believed, and he marked hundreds of FBI documents, only
recently released under the Freedom of Information Act, with a
blue-ink scribble that reveals a racism that was casual when not
primitive. Hoover's FBI, moreover, had always had a racist com-
ponent in its organizational culture. The director and the men
around him had a private preference for segregation within
their own bureaucracy, and an institutional interest in letting it
alone in those areas of the country where separate-but-equal
ruled. The racism that infected the director and his FBI, however, cannot by itself explain the decision to stand against black
America. A final, absolute commitment to bring the weight of
Bureau resources against the black struggle for equality was not
made until the late summer of 1963, in the thirty-ninth year of
Hoover's directorship.

After intermittent conflict and constant preparedness over the
course of four decades (1919–1960), and then three years (1960–
1963) of continuous skirmishing over voting rights responsibilities and Freedom Ride failures, Hoover made his decision to destroy the civil rights movement in the wake of the March on
Washington. Only then did the director reconcile himself to the
fact that the movement would not go away, that the nation was
"in the midst of a social revolution with the racial movement at
its core," that his own bureaucracy was destined to play "an
integral part [in] this revolution." Hoover's decision came at a
time when he had the unqualified support of the segregationists,
who pestered him for documentation that all integrationists

355

were Reds, and the qualified support of the Kennedys, who approved his request to wiretap the telephone of the civil rights movement's most visible leader. In the years after 1963 the gathering white backlash offered Hoover a chance to move away from the segregationists and to form new alliances, and he did so without losing sight of his original enemies. The director developed a political agenda flexible enough to accommodate the destruction of Jim Crow America and even a sideshow war on the Ku Klux Klan, but not the promise and vision of the largest democratic mass movement of the twentieth century.

Responsibility for the FBI record does not stop with Hoover himself or his fellow internal security bureaucrats. In the forefront were elected officials and the men they brought with them to Washington, men who solicited "racial matters" intelligence from the FBI even as they pursued racial justice through the Civil Rights Act of 1964 and the Voting Rights Act of 1965. Bureau officials came to the movement with a contradictory mandate from the chief executive requiring them to protect black rights and to control black people, and they acted freely on that mandate according to their own priorities. No one in the Kennedy or Johnson administrations challenged their autonomy. No one questioned their pervasive intelligence gathering activities. The man who resisted the most, Ramsey Clark, presided over the birth of community surveillance. Bureau officials fought against the struggle for black equality for so long and with so much firepower because responsible government officials allowed them, and encouraged them, to do so.

During the March on Washington, SNCC Chairman John Lewis wanted to know which side the federal government was on. In 1979, fifteen years after Freedom Summer, a group of movement veterans gathered in Jackson, Mississippi, to reconsider those times and to try to answer Lewis's question. When one of them railed against "the subversion" of the movement by "the self-styled 'pragmatism' of those splendid scoundrels residing in the Camelot on the Potomac," he received "a cheering, standing ovation." One of the persons in the audience, *New York Times* columnist Anthony Lewis, said he came expecting a celebration of amazing change but instead found bitterness directed not at "the old segregationists of Mississippi but Northern liberals and, especially, the Kennedy and Johnson Administrations."[1] Neither the attempt of the Jackson radicals to tie the Kennedys "to Jim Eastland" nor Anthony Lewis's observation sufficiently illuminates the complexities of those times. The conduct of the FBI from Kennedy to Nixon has much to tell us about the way we governed ourselves. No better gauge of the moral state of United States' domestic policy exists than the history of the federal government's relationship with its most disadvantaged citizens; and that history cannot be understood without confronting the government's tolerance of the assaults Hoover's bureaucracy launched against blacks. The FBI's conduct and the executive leadership that tolerated it constitutes as much a legacy of the 1960s as the Civil Rights Act of 1964 or the Voting Rights Act of 1965. "Racial matters" dossiers remain as much a part of John Kennedy's New Frontier and Lyndon Johnson's Great Society, let alone Richard Nixon's surveillance state, as anything else they accomplished. When the FBI stood against black people, so did the government.

Hoover explained his willingness to spy on blacks by reference to national security responsibilities; and he explained his avoidance of civil rights enforcement responsibilities by reference to the constraints imposed by public opinion, federal law, and the United States Constitution. Looked at in isolation, Hoover's defense of FBI behavior to the public and to the men in the Justice Department and the White House seems reasonable. But the totality of the FBI response to the black struggle shows that Hoover viewed it as a threat to his way of life, his bureaucracy, and his vision of a white, Christian, and harmonious America. The nation's number-one law enforcement officer violated black people's civil liberties under the guise of Red hunting, and avoided civil rights enforcement under the guise of a commitment to the Constitution. Ultimately, his public justifications collapse under the weight of his unbecoming secret deeds.

While spying on civil rights workers, Hoover refused to make a commitment to protect them from anti–civil rights violence. A commitment would have placed his bureaucracy in a vulnerable position between states' rights advocates and civil rights activists calling for federal intervention. He offered federalism as a defense against the movement's cultural and political challenges as he offered federal surveillance to contain those challenges. Unwilling to establish a national criminal police force to investigate segregationist terror and other violations of civil rights law, he established a national political police force to investigate the personal lives of civil rights workers. If Hoover's agents had devoted the same amount of time and energy to civil rights enforcement as they devoted to dossier collecting and petty harassment, the controversy over the protection issue would have been far less pervasive and far less debilitating.

Because of its antagonistic attitudes and positions, the FBI adversely affected the course of black history in the time of Kennedy, Johnson, and Nixon. The FBI fed the internal tensions and rivalries among the myriad of groups that made up the mass-based civil rights movement, making it harder for the movement to present a united front during the years of urban riots and white backlash. By leaking derogatory information on activists to the media, the FBI dissuaded others from joining movement groups, from giving money, from otherwise supporting the black struggle. The FBI also limited the movement's potential by disseminating derogatory information to federal officials in the executive, legislative, and judicial branches of government—a practice that led, perhaps, to a lessened commitment to protect civil rights workers, and contributed, certainly, to John Kennedy's assessment of SNCC ("they're sons of bitches") and Lyndon Johnson's desperate search for subversives. During the last of the Johnson years and the first of the Nixon years, specific COINTELPRO actions against the Black Panther party and many of the lesser-known groups that made up the semisecret, hierarchical, and radical wing of the black movement provoked conflict and violence which might otherwise have been avoided. In some cases, individuals suffered psychological and physical harm.

From the director on down, the executives who ran the FBI constituted a disciplined, resourceful, and highly motivated political elite. Neither racism nor Red-hunting zealotry alone explain FBI officials' actions. The director and his closest aides were idealists who had long-term goals and tried to shape their political and social environment as well as their bureaucratic environment. They had their own dream of what America could and should be, no less than Martin Luther King, and in their America "racial matters" took precedence over racial justice. The FBI developed its own ideas and its own politics about matters of race, and the director worked tirelessly to insure that the Bureau's values would help shape the federal government's relations with its nonwhite citizens. Though Hoover contributed, in his own way, to the destruction of the Ku Klux Klan and its violent methods, he contributed to the rise of a more sophisticated and perhaps more damaging racism as an intractable force in national politics. He helped make the Republican party a white man's party, as Dr. King had feared, acting not so much on behalf of a hopeless cause (the salvation of Jim Crow America), but on behalf of the new law-and-order politics of race.

That Hoover experienced some success in accomplishing what he set out to do is no more important than the fact that he met such feeble resistance from within the White House and the Justice Department. Because so many Kennedy and Johnson administration officials accepted FBI actions, and because the FBI, no matter how autonomous it seemed, was part of a larger structure, the federal government's executive branch, the history of the FBI abroad in black America is nothing less than the history of a government at war with its own citizens. Don Whitehead celebrated the FBI by calling its record "the story of America itself."[2] Black America's FBI story is also America's story, but it evokes a sense of shame, not celebration.

Though Hoover cared very much for posterity, he left only a legacy of misfortune. It was the particular misfortune of those blacks who were tapped, bugged, or harassed that the director stood at the center of the struggle for racial justice, where he could do so much damage. It was the particular misfortune of the Kennedy and Johnson administration officials who accommodated themselves to the director's location that he did so much damage to their efforts to promote consensus and achieve racial and economic justice. It was the particular misfortune of those FBI agents who did brave work on civil rights cases whenever they were given the chance to have been soldiers in an army whose general did so much damage to the democratic promise of the civil rights movement itself. In the end, it was the particular misfortune of the nation that Hoover's obsession with "racial matters" did so much damage to the civil rights and civil liberties of all Americans.

Acknowledgments

==========◇◇◇==========

There was something odd about sitting up here in Alaska, especially during the winter months of four-hour sunshine days and ten or whatever below, and writing about Freedom Summer in Philadelphia, Mississippi, or Bloody Sunday in Selma, Alabama. For some reason it was nice to see the *National Geographic* come one day, with a slick picture of Robert Kennedy all bundled up and standing, back in 1967, on top of 13,905-foot Mt. Kennedy in the Yukon, less than ten miles from our state line. The picture went up on the wall of my office, next to the other pictures of Robert Kennedy. There are advantages to living and writing in Alaska, but there are disadvantages as well. It is especially difficult to conduct research from such a faraway place. If it were not for the help offered by a great many people and institutions, it would have been far more difficult. What follows here is a modest and no doubt inadequate attempt to express my gratitude. I have no idea how to thank everyone, and a few people have requested anonymity.

Colleagues and students at the University of Alaska Anchorage, particularly Sean Murphy, Cynthia Weinzetl, Joe Davies, Kathleen Rapp, Stephen Haycox, and Will Jacobs, were a constant source of inspiration. My University offered travel aid and other funding during the early stages of research. The National Endowment for the Humanities, the American Philosophical Society, and the Gerald R. Ford Library provided additional financial assistance. I should also mention Don W. Wilson, then director of the Ford Library and now Archivist of the United States, who answered my questions about the grant-application process forthrightly. Project '87, a joint venture sponsored by the American Historical Association and the American Political Science Association, awarded a grant to attend a summer seminar, on "Bureaucracy, Positive Government, and Politicization: The Twentieth Century Challenge to Constitutionalism," chaired by Herman Belz. I tested many of the ideas developed more fully in this book at the seminar, particularly in conversations with Paul Rosen. I also tested my ideas in journal articles. Portions of Chapters 3 and 7 appeared in slightly different form in the *Journal of Southern History* and the *Journal of American History* respectively, and a very small portion of Chapter 1 appeared in *Phylon*. I am grateful to the editors of these journals for permission to draw upon this work. The articles themselves are cited in the bibliography.

Nell Irvin Painter and J. Jeffrey Mayhook read the manuscript, and August Meier read part of it. My gratitude for their respective critiques is immense. At the Free Press, I am in debt to production supervisor Celia Knight and copyeditor Jack Rummel. My editor, Joyce Seltzer, prodded me through each successive draft, and in a sense her talents—and endurance—are largely responsible for whatever merit the reader may find in this final draft.

Among the archivists who always pointed me in the proper directions were: William H. McNitt of the Gerald R. Ford Library; Bob Tissing, Linda Hanson, David Humphrey, and especially Tina Houston of the Lyndon B. Johnson Library; Martin M. Teasley and John E. Wickman of the Dwight D. Eisenhower Library; Joan Howard, Bonnie Baldwin, Cynthia Fox and John W. Roberts of the National Archives; Michael Desmond, Jane E. Ward, and Ronald Whealan of the John F. Kennedy Library; Elinor DesVerney Sinnette of the Moorland-Spingarn Research Center at Howard Univeristy; Menzi Behrnd-Klodt and Joanne Hohler of the State Historical Society of Wisconsin; Dovie T. Patrick of the Robert W. Woodruff Library at the Atlanta University Center; Richard Shrader of the Wilson Library at the University of North Carolina at Chapel Hill; Marvin Y. Whiting and Thomas C. Haslett, Jr., of the Birmingham Public Library; Sheryl B. Vogt of the Richard B. Russell Memorial Library on the campus of the University of Georgia; Eileen Boyle of the San Diego Public Library; Tamara Silver of the Center for National Security Studies; D. Louise Cook of the Martin Luther King, Jr., Center for Nonviolent Social Change; Hank Holmes and William Hanna of the Mississippi Department of Archives and History; Kathleen McIntyre of the State Historical Society of Missouri Manuscripts; and Mary Ann Bamberger of the University of Illinois at Chicago Library.

Helen Near and Susan Rosenfeld Falb of the FBI, along with the FBI Office of Congressional and Public Affairs, solved some of the access problems that inevitably accompany a study of this nature. Others who helped me locate files released under the Freedom of Information Act (FOIA) or otherwise include Tony Freyer, Douglass Cassel, Jr., Michael Krinsky, Ann Mari Buitrago, Jack Novik, Anne Pilsbury, William Goodman, Joan Washington, Ron Kuby, Alan McSurely, Karl Evanzz, James Forman, John R. Salter, Jr., Edwin King, Clyde R. Appleton, Robert F. Williams, and Robert J. Boyle. For their courtesy and prompt replies to my questions about FOIA releases and other matters, I should also mention Katherine Taylor, Richard Smyser, Frances Keller, Ernest Holsendolph, Lennox Hinds, Louis Martin, Walter Naegle, Diane McWhorter, Frank Sikora, Robert Zangrando, Hugh Davis Graham, Nancy J. Weiss, Rick Blake, John Ricks, Pablo Eisenberg, David Burnham, Sanford J. Ungar, Flint Taylor, Juan Williams, Edith Tiger, Richard Gid Powers, Clayborne Carson, Howard Zinn, Arthur M. Schlesinger, Jr., Athan Theoharis, Mary Gail Gerebenics, Dan E. Moldea, David Garrow, and Theodore Kornweibel.

The great majority of the information contained in the pages of this book comes directly from over 150 of the FBI's only recently declassified files. I supplemented archival spelunking by interviewing former FBI executives and field agents, Justice Department and Civil Rights Commission attorneys, White House advisors and staff, newspaper reporters, movement activists, and members of the resistance. A good number of people took the time to talk to me, whether in person or on the telephone, and I thank them for doing so. Most of their names are listed in the bibliography.

While traveling Outside, as we say here in Alaska, a number of people fed me or housed me or did things for me that were quite inconvenient for them. Special thanks are offered to Elizabeth Moore, Robert Zeidel, Alan McSurely and his family, Rachel Rosen-DeGolia and Peter DeGolia, Susan and Michael Cooney (and all the other Cooneys as well), and the Gibbons people at Catholic. My parents allowed me to use their home in

Atlanta as a base of sorts during my research trips, and my sister, Mary Ann, loaned me her car. Finally, there is the matter of Maureen O'Reilly and our children, who put up with all those trips Outside and always took me back. For that, the great number of plenary indulgences to come will be well earned.

Notes

========XXX========

INTRODUCTION

1. Guyot, Johnson interviews; DeMuth, "'Tired,'" 548–51; Watters and Cleghorn, *Climbing*, 136–37, 146 n20, 363–75; Cagin and Dray, *We Are Not Afraid*, 23–24, 86–88; Zinn, *SNCC*, 93–96; Hamer Oral History; Hamer, *Praise*, 11–12; Misseduc Foundation, *Mississippi*, 19–24.
2. One of the last references to Hamer in the FBI's files, dated Jan. 12, 1970, no. 3697, FBI–King File (100-106670), concerns the D.C. Committee for the Martin Luther King Holiday. When Hamer died of cancer seven years later, Andrew Young delivered the eulogy at the funeral service in Ruleville. In 1963 it was Young who finally obtained the release of Hamer and the others from the Winona jail, on the same day a sniper shot and killed Mississippi NAACP leader Medgar Evers.
3. Grant, ed., *Black Protest*, 376; Lewis interview.
4. Evans, *Personal Politics*, 91.
5. In the timeless and contentious debate among jurists, Hoover unknowingly sided with "legal positivists."
6. "Civil Rights and Domestic Violence," March 15, 1947, Civil Rights and Domestic Violence Folder, FBI–Hoover O&C Files: Walter White to J. Edgar Hoover, Oct. 20, 1951, no. 601, FBI–NAACP File (61-3176).
7. "They were gonna' prosecute," Lawrence Guyot said. "The Bureau was interested." The Justice Department filed misdemeanor brutality charges in Oxford, but a jury acquitted the defendants after a brief trial.
8. Whitehead, *FBI Story*, vii, 396, 403.

CHAPTER 1.
The Negro Question

1. Memo, re Authority of the United States to Protect Negroes . . . , March 31, 1910, no. OG 3057, Bureau of Investigation (BI) Files.
2. Powers, *Secrecy and Power*, 9–10, 27, 36–41, 324.
3. Kluger, *Simple Justice*, 111; Woodward, *Strange Career*, 69, 81.
4. Kluger, *Simple Justice*, 104–5; Woodward, *Strange Career*, 93–96, 102–5.
5. Kornweibel, "FBI and Black America," 6.
6. Dept. of Justice, *Investigation Activities*, 162, 187. See also *Federal Surveil-*

lance of Afro-Americans, reels 17–18 (microfilm). A few Bureau agents submitted reports listing "NEGROES" and "IRISH MOVEMENT" under the same "Racial Activities" heading.

7. Henry G. Sebastian to A. B. Coxe, Aug. 9, 1919, Box 14, Glasser File, Dept. of Justice Files; William J. Neale to all SACs, Oct. 2, 1920, FBI–SAC File; James P. Rooney to William J. Burns, Sept. 20, 1921, no. BS 202600-1778-66, BI Files; Henry H. Stroud to Rooney, Sept. 19, 1921, no. BS 202600-1778-66, ibid.

8. John Edgar Hoover, Memo upon the work of the Radical Division, Oct. 18, 1919, no. OG 374217, BI Files; Dept. of Justice, *Investigation Activities*, 13, 162–67.

9. Hoover to Ridgely, Oct. 11, 1919, in *Marcus Garvey . . . Papers*, ed. Hill, vol. 2, p. 72; Hoover to George F. Ruch, June 8, 1920, ibid., vol. 2, p. 345; Hoover to Anthony Caminetti, Feb. 24, 1921, ibid., vol. 3, p. 235; Hoover to John B. Cunningham, Aug. 10, 1922, ibid., vol. 4, p. 841; Stein, *World*, 189–90.

10. Kornweibel, "F.B.I. and White American Hegemony," 7–26; Dept. of Justice, *Investigation Activities*, 163–64, 166; Stein, *World*, 186–208; Hill, "Foremost," 229.

11. Dept. of Justice, *Investigation Activities*, 162–63, 187; Kornweibel, "FBI and Black America," 17.

12. Whitehead, *FBI Story*, 73.

13. Lewis J. Baley to Director, July 18, 1922, no. 50-0-5, BI Files; Section 17, *FBI Manual of Instruction* (1936 ed.). Daniel, *Shadow*, touches briefly on the FBI role.

14. Whitehead, *FBI Story*, 69–73; Hoover, "Off-the-Record Remarks."

15. Mason, *Stone*, 151; Powers, *Secrecy and Power*, 520 n8.

16. Hoover failed to undertake a parallel purge of hard-core racists. He disciplined one such agent, but only because the agent accused him of trying to "whitewash" the patronage case against Perry Howard, the black Republican National Committeeman from Mississippi. The director, in fact, called the Howard case "bigger than Teapot Dome." See case file 70-40-1, Dept. of Justice Files; McMillen, "Howard," 212.

17. Director to Clyde Tolson, July 15, 1931, no. 142, FBI–Tolson Personnel File (67-9524); Demaris, *Director*, 33–34.

18. Hoover to Attorney General, Nov. 5, 1924, FBI–SAC File; Hoover to all SACs, Nov. 5, 1924, ibid.; Hoover to Charles P. Sisson, April 19, 1930, Colored Question, Pres. Papers, Herbert Hoover Papers; Hoover to Attorney General, Sept. 12, 1931, Moorhead, He., PSF, ibid.; Rhea Whitley to Director, Sept. 12, 1931, no. 1, FBI–Moorish Science File (62-25889).

19. Senate Select Committee to Study . . . Intelligence Activities (hereafter Church Committee), *Book II*, 25.

20. The Justice Department filed sedition charges in 1942 against eighty blacks, including Elijah Muhammad of the Nation of Islam, chiefly on the grounds that they had a "pan-colored" identification with the Japanese.

21. Hoover to Marvin McIntyre, May 7, 1942, OF 4952, Roosevelt Papers; Hoover to Edwin P. Watson, June 19, 1941, no. 835, June 26, 1942, no. 2194, OF 10-B, ibid.; Hoover to Harry Hopkins, Sept. 4, 1942, no. 2248-B, Feb. 1, 1943, no. 2304-A, July 3, 1943, no. 2355-C, July 6, 1943, no. 2356-A and -B, July 8, 1943, no. 2357-A, Sept. 15, 1943, no. 2346-A, OF 10-B, ibid.; Edward A. Tamm to P. E. Foxworth, June 24, 1941, no. 18X1, FBI–NAACP File (61-3176); D. Milton Ladd to Director, April 25, 1944, no. 9, FBI–CORE File (100-225892).

22. E. G. Fitch to Ladd, March 11, 1942, no. 220, FBI–National Negro Congress

File (61-6728); Klehr, *Heyday*, 460 n54; Hoover to SAC Philadelphia, n.d. [ca. Dec. 18, 1943], no. 178, FBI–NAACP File; Hoover to Tolson, Tamm, and Ladd, Sept. 30, 1942, no. 56, ibid.; Chicago Field Office Rept., Nov. 6, 1943, no. 2, FBI–CORE File; "Survey of Racial Conditions in the United States," n.d. [ca. Sept. 1943], in CF, Justice Dept. (5–6), Truman Papers.

23. Ladd to Director, Sept. 11, 1942, FBI File 62-116758; Ladd to Tamm, Oct. 21, 1942, ibid.; Richmond Field Office Rept., Jan. 26, 1943, no. 9, FBI–Moorish Science File; Hoover to SAC Louisville, Aug. 5, 1943, no. 12, FBI–Civil Rights Policy File (66-6200-44).

24. Richmond Field Office Rept., Jan. 26, 1943, no. 9, FBI–Moorish Science File; Ladd to Director, Sept. 30, 1943, no. 156, FBI–Detroit Riot File (44-802); Robert C. Hendon to Tolson, June 24, 1943, no. 55, ibid.; Hoover to McIntyre, June 23, 1943, no. 8, ibid.; Hoover to Attorney General, June 25, 1943, no. 14, ibid.

25. William Neale to all SACs, Oct. 2, 1920, FBI–SAC File; Birmingham Field Office Rept., Jan. 11, 1945, no. 20, FBI–Hudson File (100-24548).

26. Millspaugh, *Crime Control.*

27. Rosenman, ed., *Public Papers*, vol. 3, pp. 12–13, 242–45.

28. The White House press secretary's description. Stephen Early to the President, July 12, 1940, PPF 2993, Roosevelt Papers; Early to Lowell Mellett, July 30, 1940, OF 880, ibid.

29. H. L. Mencken to Fulton Oursler, May 15, 1939, no. 51, FBI–Oursler File (94-4-692).

30. Rable, "South," 201–20. Howe is quoted in Manchester, *Glory*, 107.

31. White, "U.S. Department of (White) Justice," 310.

32. Hoover to Walter Winchell, May 19, 1936, no. 42, July 6, 1938, no. 99, FBI–Winchell File; [name deleted] to Winchell, June 16, 1938, no. 99, ibid. FDR is quoted in Weiss, *Farewell*, 109; Wilkins in *Standing*, 132.

33. Fine, *Frank Murphy*, vol. 3, pp. 79, 82.

34. Schweinhaut's comments are paraphrased in W. Cleon Skousen to [File], Feb. 22, 1940, no. 2, FBI–Civil Rights File.

35. Sections 51 and 52, during the Roosevelt years; Congress recodified both provisions in 1948 and they are referred to throughout the text as Sections 241 and 242.

36. Section 242 penalties were of course less severe—a maximum fine of $1,000 and a maximum prison sentence of one year.

37. Dept. of Justice Circular no. 3356, April 4, 1942, no. illegible, FBI–Civil Rights File. See also Carr, *Federal Protection.*

38. Elliff, "Aspects," 609–18.

39. Ibid., 610–13.

40. Ibid., 617–18; Marcus B. Calhoun to Hoover, June 12, 1944, no. 17, FBI–Civil Rights File; SAC Dallas to Director, Aug. 31, 1949, no. 98, ibid.; Leland V. Boardman to Alex Rosen, Jan. 23, 1957, no. 487, ibid.; Hoover, "Protecting Our Freedom," n.d. [ca. March 1947], in Civil Rights and Domestic Violence Folder, FBI–Hoover O&C Files. The Supreme Court read a specific-intent requirement into the color-of-law statute in 1945, in *Screws v. United States* (325 U.S. 91).

41. There were exceptions. Capeci, "Lynching," 859–87.

42. Louis B. Nichols to Tolson, Oct. 13, 1939, no. 525, FBI–Cooper File (94-3-4-20); Courtney Ryley Cooper to Nichols, Oct. 21, 1939, no. 526X, ibid.; Hoover to Cooper, Nov. 3, 1939, no. 527X1, ibid.

43. SAC Letter, Feb. 19, 1946, FBI–SAC File; J. C. Strickland to Ladd, July 15,

1946, no. illegible, FBI–Civil Rights File; Hoover to Tolson, Tamm, and Ladd, July 17, 1946, no. illegible, ibid.; Ladd to Director, Aug. 29, 1946, no. illegible, ibid.

44. Ladd to Director, March 10, 1947, no. 10, Civil Rights and Domestic Violence Folder, FBI–Hoover O&C Files; Ladd to Director, Dec. 13, 1946, no. 40X, FBI–Civil Rights File. See also the Ernst Folder, FBI–Nichols O&C Files.

45. Ladd to Director, March 10, 1947, no. 10, Civil Rights and Domestic Violence Folder, FBI–Hoover O&C Files.

46. Rauh interview. Hoover's position on states' rights is set out in "Civil Rights and Domestic Violence," March 15, 1947, Civil Rights and Domestic Violence Folder, FBI–Hoover O&C Files; "Protecting Our Freedom," n.d. [ca. March 15, 1947], no. 6, ibid.

47. Director to Attorney General, Sept. 12, 1946, no. illegible, Sept. 17, 1947, no. illegible, FBI–Civil Rights File. For Sinatra and Welles, see Guy Hottel to Director, Sept. 18, 1946, no. 569, FBI–National Negro Congress File.

48. Attorney General to Director, Sept. 24, 1946, no. 35, FBI–Civil Rights File; Director to Attorney General, Sept. 12, 1946, no. illegible, Sept. 17, 1947, no. illegible, ibid.

49. "Civil Rights and Domestic Violence," March 15, 1947, Civil Rights and Domestic Violence Folder, FBI–Hoover O&C Files; Tamm to Director, Dec. 12, 1941, Dies Folder, ibid.; SAC San Francisco to Director, Dec. 3, 1946, no. 49, FBI–Robeson File (100-12304); [deleted] to Nichols, July 20, 1942, no. 65, FBI–NAACP File.

50. Leinbaugh interview; Whitehead, *FBI Story*, 15–16.

51. Hoover to Tolson, Tamm, Hugh H. Clegg, and Ladd, March 22, 1947, Civil Rights and Domestic Violence Folder, FBI–Hoover O&C Files.

52. "FBI Agents," 9–13; Nichols to Tolson, June 29, 1949, no. 148, FBI–Oursler File; Hoover to Oursler, Jan. 12, 1951, no. 176, ibid.; clipping, Jan. 7, 1951, no. 176, ibid.; Director to E. J. Brennan, Jan. 18, 1922, FBI–Amos File; Hoover to James E. Amos, Oct. 30, 1935, ibid; Amos to Hoover, Sept. 21, 1953, ibid.; Amos, *Theodore Roosevelt.*

53. Sullivan, *Bureau*, 123–24; Demaris, *Director*, 38–39; Walter White to Hoover, June 17, 1941, FBI, Group II, Series A, Box 268, NAACP Papers; Hoover to White, July 14, 1941, ibid.; C. Herbert Marshall to White, Dec. 13, 1941, ibid.; White to Marshall, Dec. 17, 1941, ibid.

54. Thurgood Marshall to White, Jan. 23, 1947, FBI, Group II, Series A, Box 268, NAACP Papers; White to Robert Carter, Aug. 21 and 27, 1946, ibid.; Carter to White, Aug. 26, 1946, ibid.; Marshall to Tom Clark, Dec. 27, 1946, exhibit 26, Civil Rights and Domestic Violence Folder, FBI–Hoover O&C Files; Clark to Marshall, Jan. 13, 1947, ibid.; Hoover to White, Jan. 13, 1947, no. 367, FBI–NAACP File; note, Hoover, n.d. [ca. April 10, 1947], no. 308, ibid.; Arthur B. Spingarn to Hoover, Sept. 15, 1943, no. 150, ibid.; T. J. Starke to Nichols, Sept. 23, 1943, no. X1, FBI–White File (100-382824); SAC Letter, Aug. 26, 1946, FBI–SAC File.

55. "Civil Rights and Domestic Violence," March 15, 1947, Civil Rights and Domestic Violence Folder, FBI–Hoover O&C Files; "General Problems," n.d. [ca. March 15, 1947], no. 5, ibid.

56. See the documents cited in the previous note.

57. President's Committee, *To Secure These Rights*, 124; McGowan interview; and the documents cited in note 55.

58. President's Committee, *To Secure These Rights*, 123; Robert K. Carr to

Hoover, March 21, 1947, in Civil Rights and Domestic Violence Folder, FBI–Hoover O&C Files.

59. Hoover to Tolson, Tamm, Clegg, and Ladd, March 22, 1947, Civil Rights and Domestic Violence Folder, FBI–Hoover O&C Files.

60. "FBI Agents," 9–13. See also the documents from Oursler's FBI File cited in note 52.

61. White and other NAACP leaders exerted constant pressure on the FBI to change its "'lily white' hiring policy." Leslie S. Perry to White, Sept. 17, 1947, FBI, Group II, Series A, Box 268, NAACP Papers; Perry to White, Sept. 18, 1947, ibid.; White to Hoover, Aug. 21, 1946, no. 349, FBI–NAACP File; W. R. Glavin to Director, Aug. [14?], 1947, no. 395, ibid.

62. Elliff, "Aspects," 628–29.

63. Attorney General to Director, April 22, 1947, no. 49, FBI–Civil Rights File; Director to Attorney General, April 16, 1947, no. 48, ibid.

64. Executives' Conference to Director, May 2, 1947, no. illegible, ibid.; Bureau Bulletin no. 26, May 14, 1947, FBI–Bureau Bulletin File.

65. Attorney General to Director, Oct. 10, 1952, no. illegible, FBI–Civil Rights File; Attorney General to Director, Dec. 19 and 21, 1951, no. not recorded, ibid.; Executives' Conference to Director, Jan. 2, 1952, no. not recorded, ibid.; SAC Letter, Jan. 5, 1952, FBI–SAC File.

66. Bureau officials proceeded with great care. Because the Department "has given us blanket authority to conduct preliminary inquiries in Civil Rights cases," Alex Rosen cautioned, it would not be "advisable to abrogate or abridge that rule by any communication over the Director's signature." Rosen to Boardman, Jan. 27, 1956, no. 395, FBI–Civil Rights File.

67. Rosen to Boardman, April 16, 1958, no. illegible, May 26, 1958, no. illegible, ibid.; Rosen to Alan H. Belmont, Dec. 5, 1961, no. 902, ibid.; Director to SACs Albany et al., April 16, 1958, no. 552, ibid.; SAC Letters, June 24 and July 22, 1958, FBI–SAC File.

68. Commission on Civil Rights, *Report–Book*, 5, 218 n138.

69. Between January 1, 1948, and June 30, 1955, the FBI investigated 9,340 police officers, an effort that led to 189 indictments under Section 242 and 35 convictions.

70. Director to Attorney General, Aug. 5, 1953, no. 216, Aug. 25, 1953, no. illegible, FBI–Civil Rights File; "Certain Governors' Comments," Nov. 20, 1953, no. 286, ibid.

71. Director to Attorney General, Aug. 25, 1953, no. illegible, ibid.; Nichols to Tolson, July 10, 1953, no. 180, Oct. 22, 1953, no. 203, Nov. 20, 1953, no. 207, FBI–Pegler File (62-36434); Rosen to Ladd, Aug. 26, 1953, no. 195, ibid. For the New York police, see House Committee on the Judiciary, *Hearings . . . Department of Justice;* Nichols to Tolson, Feb. 11, 1953, James M. McInerney Folder, FBI–Nichols O&C Files. McInerney, a former Bureau agent who went on to head the Department's Criminal Division, established the policy on his own initiative.

72. Quoted in SAC Los Angeles to Director, Aug. 27, 1953, no. illegible, FBI–Civil Rights File. See also Hoover to Arthur Hayes Sulzberger, Aug. 13, 1953, no. illegible, ibid.

73. Director to Attorney General, Sept. 1, 1953, no. illegible, ibid.; Nichols to Tolson, Sept. 11, 1953, no. 202, FBI–Pegler File; Hoover to Raymond Moley, Sept. 17, 1953, no. not recorded, ibid.; Hoover to Tolson and Nichols, Sept. 22, 1953, no. 200, ibid.; Milton A. Jones to Nichols, Aug. 28, 1953, no. 40X3,

FBI–Rushmore File (100-13058); memo, re FBI's Jurisdiction, Aug. 28, 1953, no. 40X3, ibid.; Belmont to Ladd, Oct. 16, 1953, no. 39, Folder 14, FBI–Hoover O&C Files

74. SAC Letter, Oct. 13, 1953, FBI–SAC File.

75. "Integration in Public Schools," n.d. [ca. Sept. 15, 1958], no. 2673, FBI–Little Rock File (44-12284); Nichols to Tolson, Jan. 10, 1956, no. 1153, FBI–NAACP File.

76. Gordon A. Nease to Tolson, Jan. 22, 1958, no. 6, Directorship Folder, FBI–Hoover O&C Files; Nichols to Tolson, Feb. 26, 1957, no. 19, FBI–Eastland File (94-4-5130).

77. Nease to Tolson, Jan. 22, 1958, no. 6, Directorship Folder, FBI–Hoover O&C Files. The director scribbled his comments on this memo.

78. Jones to Nichols, Oct. 29, 1947, no. not recorded, FBI–Humphrey File (62-26225); memo, re Hubert H. Humphrey, n.d. [ca. Oct. 29, 1947], no. 906, ibid.

79. Tamm to Director, May 10, 1947, no. 71, FBI–Robeson File; note, Hoover, n.d. [ca. May 7, 1947], no. 79, ibid.; memo, re Paul Robeson, May 7, 1947, no. 79, ibid.; Belmont to Boardman, April 18, 1957, no. not recorded, ibid. For Davis, see Nichols to Tolson, Feb. 18, 1948, no. 1495, FBI–HUAC File (61-7582).

80. Kimball, "History," 410; memo, re Mary McLeod Bethune, Dec. 20, 1946, PSF, FBI–B, Truman Papers.

81. Hoover to George Allen, Sept. 25, 1946, PSF, FBI–Communist Data, Truman Papers; Hoover to Harry Vaughan, June 3, 1947, PSF, FBI–W, ibid.; *Des Moines Register*, Sept. 4, 1983.

82. Church Committee, *Book II*, 51, 180, 250–51 n151a, *Book III*, 450; Hoover to Dillon Anderson, Jan. 16 and 24, March 2, 6, and 7, 1956, FBI Series, FBI L–N, Office of the Special Assistant for National Security Affairs, Eisenhower Papers; memo, re Communist Infiltration of the NAACP, Jan. 16, 1956, ibid.; memo, re Communist Party–USA, Negro Matters, Jan. 23, 1956, ibid.

83. Church Committee, *Book III*, 450; F. L. Price to Rosen, Dec. 27, 1956, no. not recorded, FBI–Civil Rights File.

84. Memo, re Racial Tensions and Civil Rights, March 1, 1956, Whitman File, Cabinet Series, Eisenhower Papers. In the months after the cabinet briefing the director began to send reports to the White House on the Citizens Councils.

85. Belmont to Boardman, Oct. 27, 1955, no. not recorded, FBI–NAACP File; memo, re Racial Tensions, Eisenhower Papers.

86. Memo, re Racial Tensions, Eisenhower Papers. See also Director to Attorney General, Jan, 3, 1956, no. not recorded, FBI–NAACP File; Hoover to Anderson, Jan. 3, 1956, no. not recorded, ibid.

87. Church Committee, *Book III*, 452–54, *Hearings—FBI*, 37–39; Hoover to Attorney General, Dec. 31, 1956, no. 61, King Folder, FBI–Hoover O&C Files; Fred J. Baumgardner to William C. Sullivan, Sept. 8, 1961, no. 62, ibid.; New York Field Office Rept., Jan. 28, 1955, no. deleted, FBI–Malcolm X File (file no. also deleted); Lincoln, *Black Muslims*, 99; FBI monograph, "Nation of Islam," 1960, passim.

88. Jones to Cartha D. DeLoach, Feb. 1, 1960, no. 424, FBI–Lewis File (94-4-2189); Hoover to Fulton Lewis, Jr., Feb. 2, 1960, no. 423, ibid. For Mrs. Roosevelt, see Church Committee, *Book II*, 51–52. For the pilgrimage, see memo, Feb. 28, 1958, no. 2, FBI–Wilkins File (62-78270). Oxnam requested and received a report of his own from the FBI in 1951 on a black minister

in the Bronx, Edward D. McGowan—because he found McGowan's performance disappointing: "He has not been particularly effective as a Negro." G. Bromley Oxnam to Nichols, Jan. 9, 1951, Louis B. Nichols Folder, Oxnam Papers; letter, Nichols to Oxnam, Jan. 25, 1951, ibid.

89. Senator Eastland held the most ambitious congressional investigation in 1954 in New Orleans—a "Great Southern Commie Hunt"—and the FBI supplied blind memos on several "unfriendly witnesses." Among others, the Eastland Committee subpoenaed Aubrey Williams, former chief of the National Youth Administration, and Virginia Durr, the veteran of the fight against the poll tax and wife of another New Dealer, onetime FCC chief Clifford Durr. For Virginia Durr on Eastland ("a vicious little fat toad of a man"), see Barnard, ed., *Outside*, 171–72, 258, 261, 266.

90. May, "Genetics," 420–22; Richard Arens to James C. Davis, May 3, 1957, Criticisms: HUAC (75-1-21-3), Southern Regional Council Archives. The Stamler Papers contains a lengthy compilation of *Cong. Record* excerpts based on Committee files.

91. Executives' Conference to Tolson, Aug, 4, 1954, no. 2473, FBI–HUAC File; SAC Washington to Director, Oct. 12, 1955, no. 2835, ibid.; Nichols to Tolson, Oct. 12, 1955, no. 2836, ibid.; G. H. Scatterday to Belmont, April 14, 1959, no. 4121, ibid. For the sedition trial, see Braden, *Wall Between*. For Tolson's directive, see memo, Feb. 28, 1958, no. 2, FBI–Wilkins File.

92. See "Integration in Public Schools," n.d. [ca. Sept. 15, 1958], no. 2673, FBI–Little Rock File.

93. FBI monographs, "Communist Party and the Negro," 1953, pp. i, iii, iv, 79–83, and 1956, pp. ii, v, 53. For the Comintern subsidy, see Hoover, *Masters*, 233.

94. Jones to DeLoach, Jan. 27, 1960, no. 5, FBI–Wilkins File; "Communist Party and the Negro," 1953, p. 83.

95. The document cited in note 92 lists these numbers. For Wilkins and White, see Jones to DeLoach, Jan. 27, 1960, no. 5, FBI–Wilkins File; Nichols to Tolson, Dec. 11, 1950, no. 5095, FBI–White File (100-3-81); Nichols to Tolson, June 21, 1951, no. 596, FBI–NAACP File.

96. "Current Weaknesses of the Communist Party," Oct. 1956, no. 47, FBI–COINTEL (CPUSA) File (100-3-104); "Communist Party and the Negro," 1956, pp. 19–25; Jones to DeLoach, March 16, 1965, no. not recorded, FBI–Wilkins File.

97. McGowan interview.

98. Thompson, ed., *Kennedy*, 122–23. For the Montgomery bus boycott, see Garrow, *Bearing*, 11–82.

99. House Committee on Appropriations, *Hearings* (1961), 423. See also C. B. Stanberry to SAC Birmingham, Oct. 31, 1960, no. 137-00-165, FBI–Bergman Freedom Rider Files; "Communist Party, USA—Negro Question," Aug. 23, 1963, no. 253X, FBI–CIRM File (100-3-116).

CHAPTER 2.
Paper Chains

1. A major theme of Navasky, *Kennedy Justice*.

2. For JFK's sensitivity to civil rights, see his correspondence in Subject Files 1953–60 (Civil Rights), Box 9, Sorensen Papers. See also Louis B. Nichols to Clyde Tolson, Jan. 16, 1952, no. not recorded, FBI–Civil Rights File (44-00); Milton A. Jones to Cartha D. DeLoach, July 13, 1960, no. 16,

Kennedy Folder, FBI–Hoover O&C Files. O'Donnell is quoted in Demaris, *Director*, 186; RFK in Navasky, *Kennedy Justice*, 97.

3. DeLoach to John P. Mohr, Feb. 5, 1962, no. not recorded, FBI–Wilson File (94-42524); Eastland Oral History, 22.

4. Lee C. White to Jack Valenti, Dec. 4, 1964, WHCF, Ex HU2, Johnson Papers.

5. R. O. Kittelsen to Alex Rosen, April 27, 1945, no. illegible, FBI–Civil Rights File.

6. Barnard, ed., *Outside*, 188.

7. Dwight D. Eisenhower to James F. Byrnes, July 23, 1957, Whitman File, Diary Series, Box 14, Eisenhower Papers; Schlesinger, *Robert Kennedy*, 299.

8. Director to Attorney General, March 19, 1958, no. not recorded, FBI–SCLC File (100-438794).

9. John Doar and Dorothy Landsberg, "The Performance of the FBI in Investigating Violations of Federal Laws Protecting the Right to Vote, 1960–1967," in Senate Select Committee to Study ... Intelligence Activities (hereafter Church Committee), *Hearings—FBI*, 892–94.

10. Ibid., 160, 474–75, 912–21; Doar, Tyler interviews.

11. Doar, "Performance," 912–21.

12. Doar, Tyler interviews. "I got along with Hoover," Tyler said, "partly because he was taken, in a Platonic sense, with my mother-in-law, and partly, I like to believe, because he liked and trusted me." Tyler remembered one time, at a party, where his mother-in-law and the FBI chief talked for several hours. Hoover had left his Cadillac outside with the motor running, and his driver, James Crawford, had to come inside to use the phone, having run out of gas.

13. The FBI opened what ultimately matured into a 132,000-page dossier on Wilkinson in 1942, when the city of Los Angeles hired him to manage the first integrated housing project in Watts. Bureau agents routinely checked voting records in California to see if Wilkinson had registered as a communist, and in 1961 they followed his case "closely at the Supreme Court." See serials 106-9, FBI–Wilkinson File (100-112434).

14. Doar, "Performance," 894; Evans interview.

15. Seigenthaler Oral History, 14; McMillen, "Black Enfranchisement," 351–72.

16. Thompson, ed., *Kennedy*, 110; Doar, "Performance," 948.

17. J. Edgar Hoover to [deleted], March 27, 1961, no. 4938, FBI–HUAC File (61-7582); memo, re John Doar, n.d. [ca. Nov. 19, 1971], no. not recorded, FBI–CPJ File (62-113909).

18. Doar, "Performance," 893, 904.

19. McGowan interview.

20. Doar, "Performance," 901, 905–06.

21. Ibid., 975; Fleischer interview.

22. Guthman interview.

23. In June 1944 Bureau executives wrote this language into the *Manual of Instruction*.

24. Edward A. Tamm to Director, Oct. 16, 1947, no. 60, FBI–Civil Rights File; Executives' Conference to Director, Oct. 27, 1947, no. 61, ibid.; J. Patrick Coyne to D. Milton Ladd, Oct. 29, 1947, no. 65, ibid.; Bureau Bulletin No. 66, Nov. 5, 1947, FBI–Bureau Bulletin File.

25. House Select Committee on Assassinations, *Hearings—King,* vol. 6, 93; J. F. Buckley to Ladd, Aug. 19, 1944, no. 19, FBI–Civil Rights File; Rosen to Ladd, Aug. 21, 1953, no. illegible, Sept. 4, 1953, no. not recorded, ibid.; SAC Letter, Aug. 27, 1953, FBI–SAC File.

26. Clement L. McGowan, Jr., to Gebhardt, May 30, 1974, no. 1072, FBI–Civil Rights File. See also serials 761, 927, 951, 982–3, ibid.

27. Doar, "Performance," 895, 903; Barrett interview.

28. Hoover to Tolson, Tamm, Hugh H. Clegg, and Ladd, March 22, 1947, Civil Rights and Domestic Violence Folder, FBI–Hoover O&C Files; Rosen to Ladd, Aug. 19, 1949, no. illegible, FBI–Civil Rights File; Rosen to Belmont, Dec. 22, 1961, no. illegible, ibid.

29. Ungar, *FBI,* 419; Howell, "Interview," 16; Schlesinger, *Robert Kennedy,* 313; Elliff, "Aspects," 652; Navasky, *Kennedy Justice,* 103; Marshall, Trebach, Doar interviews. Until December 1962 the FBI issued a warning to the *victims* in civil rights cases that anything they said could be used against them in a court of law. If a complainant agreed to an interview and insisted on having an attorney present, moreover, the FBI's agents had to request special authority before proceeding. SAC Letters, Sept. 2 and 16, 1965, FBI–SAC File.

30. Doar, "Performance," 897–900; *New York Times,* Nov. 5, 1979.

31. McGowan interview; Navasky, *Kennedy Justice,* 115–16.

32. Norbert A. Schlei to White, Sept. 30, 1964, WHCF, FG135-6, Box 188, Johnson Papers; White to Nicholas deB. Katzenbach, Aug. 4, 1964, ibid. Criminal Division chief Warren Olney III ordered the FBI to make on-the-spot arrests during the Little Rock crisis, but when Hoover complained Herbert Brownell rescinded the order. F. L. Price to Rosen, Oct. 4, 1957, no. 531, FBI–Civil Rights File.

33. D. W. Griffith to Ivan Conrad, March 29, 1963, no. 16, FBI–Forman File (44-21661); Director to SAC Memphis, March 29, 1963, no. 12 and no. 48, ibid.; McGowan to Rosen, March 29, 1963, no. 41, ibid.

34. Quinn Tamm to Tolson, Sept. 25, 1957, no. 529, FBI–Civil Rights File; Joseph J. Casper to Mohr, June 6, 1966, no. illegible, ibid.

35. U.S. marshals dressed in jackets and ties or lightweight riot gear provided whatever protection the federal government offered movement people.

36. Katzenbach, Rauh interviews.

37. McGowan interview; Doar, "Performance," 942–45.

38. Schardt, "Civil Rights," 172, 178; Calvin Williams interview.

39. Katzenbach interview.

40. Robert F. Kennedy Oral History, 637; Evans interview.

41. Seigenthaler Oral History, 17; Navasky, *Kennedy Justice,* 126.

42. Marshall interview; Marshall Oral History, 6–10, Bunche Collection.

43. Wilkins, "Chester Bowles," 813.

44. Seigenthaler Oral History, 9; Navasky, *Kennedy Justice,* 162. Marshall's book, *Federalism and Civil Rights,* contains no reference to the FBI.

45. Kennedy Oral History, 578–80; Belknap, *Federal Law,* 73–74; Brauer, *John F. Kennedy,* 317.

46. Marshall interview; Marshall Oral History, 6–10, Bunche Collection.

47. In the end, SNCC received only a pittance—the result, Fleming said, of the tax-exemption policies of a skeptical Internal Revenue Service and the high-risk policies of SNCC itself.

48. Navasky, *Kennedy Justice*, 118–19.
49. Garrow, *Bearing the Cross*, 170.
50. Doar, "Performance," 921–27; Moses interview.
51. Moses interview; Warren, *Who Speaks*, 93; Misseduc Foundation, *Mississippi*, 30–37.
52. Church Committee, *Hearings—FBI*, 209.
53. Watters and Cleghorn, *Climbing*, 159; Misseduc Foundation, *Mississippi*, 8–9; Burns, "Federal Government," 251. The Ruleville gunmen fired into two houses, missing Fanny Lou Hamer but hitting two voter registration workers from Jackson State College.
54. *Jackson Daily News*, Aug. 4, 1966; Sullivan, *Bureau*, 72, 125–26; Maurice House and C. B. McDavid to Jamie Moore, June 29, 1966, Box 4.4, Hamilton Papers.
55. Schardt, "Civil Rights," 172–73; Warren, *Who Speaks*, 93n.
56. Nichols to Tolson, Feb. 26, 1957, no. 19, FBI–Eastland File (94-4-5130).
57. 71 Stat. 104 (1957).
58. Harris Wofford to the President, Feb. 27, 1961, Office Files—Civil Rights General, Box 97, John F. Kennedy Papers; Schlesinger, *Robert Kennedy*, 326.
59. Bernhard interview. Eastland insisted on seeing the full FBI report on Commission nominees, not just the summary sheet usually provided.
60. Civil Rights Commission, *Report—Justice*, 61–62, 200 n47, 213–16 n134, 217–18 n138, 219 n147, 221–22; Trebach, Bernhard interviews.
61. Griswold interview, Rafferty Papers.
62. Bernhard Oral History, 19; Dulles, *Civil Rights Commission*, 150.
63. Schlesinger, *Robert Kennedy*, 327; Wofford, *Kennedys and Kings*, 161; Bernhard interview.
64. Navasky, *Kennedy Justice*, 110; Bernhard interview.
65. Bernhard interview.
66. Ibid.; Trebach interview.
67. Wofford, *Kennedys and Kings*, 161–62; Bernhard interview, Oral History, 17–19; William Taylor interview.
68. DeLoach to Hoover, Jan. 15, 1964, no. 10, Johnson Folder, FBI–Hoover O&C Files.
69. Tolson to Director, Dec. 5, 1961, no. not recorded, FBI–Civil Rights File.
70. Schlesinger, *Robert Kennedy*, 305; Barrett interview.
71. Doar, "Performance," 890, 949–50; Marshall Oral History, 24, Johnson Library; Schlesinger, *Robert Kennedy*, 303; Church Committee, *Hearings—FBI*, 208.
72. Doar, Marshall interviews; Wofford, *Kennedys and Kings*, 220; DeLoach to Hoover, Feb. 18, 1964, no. 315, FBI–King File (100-106670); Rosen to Belmont, Feb. 25, 1964, no. 317, Feb. 26, 1964, no. 319, ibid.; memo, re Burke Marshall, Nov. 19, 1971, no. not recorded, FBI–CPJ File; Marshall to Attorney General, Feb. 20, 1964, Special Correspondence, Attorney General, Box 8, Marshall Papers.
73. Moses interview.
74. Coles, "Social Struggle," 305, 307–08; Rustin interview.
75. Wilkins, Lewis, Bernhard interviews.
76. William Taylor interview; Wofford, *Kennedys and Kings*, 420.

CHAPTER 3.
Unbecoming Deeds

1. Navasky, *Kennedy Justice*, 23.

2. Elliff, "Aspects," 648.

3. [Deleted] to Alex Rosen, Feb. 26, 1960, no. 25, FBI–Racial Matters Policy File (157-00); Senate Select Committee to Study . . . Intelligence Activities (hereafter Church Committee), *Book III*, 456.

4. Wilkins, *Standing*, 283; Meier and Rudwick, "First Freedom Ride," 213–22.

5. Chicago Field Office Rept., Aug. 10, 1943, no. 1, FBI–CORE File (100-225892).

6. Raines, *My Soul*, 109–10.

7. Wofford, *Kennedys and Kings*, 153; Guthman, *Band*, 167.

8. Cartha D. DeLoach to John P. Mohr, May 4, 1961, no. illegible, FBI–Alabama Freedom Rider Files; Director to SACs Atlanta et al., April 24, 1961, no. 178, FBI–CORE File.

9. Meier and Rudwick, *CORE*, 137–38.

10. Director to Attorney General, May 15, 1961, no. 144-1-554, FBI–Bergman Freedom Rider Files.

11. Raines, *My Soul*, 114.

12. For Peck's account, see *Freedom Ride*. For Rowe, see Barrett G. Kemp to SAC Birmingham, May 17, 1961, no. 149-16-62, FBI–Bergman Files.

13. Meier and Rudwick, *CORE*, 138.

14. Rosen to Parsons, May 17, 1961, no. 321, FBI–CORE File.

15. Clement L. McGowan, Jr., to Rosen, May 18, 1961, no. 268, FBI–CORE File; John Doar to SAC Montgomery, May 22, 1961, no. illegible, FBI–Bergman Files. For Hoover, see his handwritten comments on DeLoach to Mohr, May 22, 1961, no. 149-1684-41, FBI–Alabama Files; UPI ticker, May 14, 1961, no. not recorded, ibid.; Rosen to Parsons, May 15, 1961, no. 215, FBI–CORE File.

16. Rosen to Alan H. Belmont, n.d. [ca. Nov. 13, 1961], no. 149-1684-236, Nov. 16, 1961, no. 149-1684-246, FBI–Alabama Files.

17. McGowan to Rosen, Sept. 5, 1961, no. 149-1684-153X, ibid.; Director to Attorney General, Sept. 6, 1961, no. 149-1684-145, ibid.; SAC Birmingham to Director, June 6, 1961, no. 149-1684-70, ibid.

18. Eugene "Bull" Connor to Thomas H. Cook, Aug. 9, 1960, Box 5.24, Connor Papers; SAC Birmingham to Director, Sept. 30, 1960, no. 157-198-17, FBI–Bergman Files; SAC Birmingham to Director, April 19, 1961, no. 157-198-35, April 26, 1961, no. 157-198-33, ibid.

19. SAC Birmingham to Director, May 5, 1961, no. deleted, FBI–CORE File; SAC Birmingham to Director, April 19, 1961, no. 157-198-35, April 24, 1961, no. 157-198-27, April 26, 1961, no. 157-198-33, FBI–Bergman Files; informant rept., April 25, 1961, no. 170-9-SF-42, ibid.; Kemp to SAC Birmingham, May 18, 1961, no. 149-16-69, ibid.

20. SAC Birmingham to Director, April 19, 1961, no. 157-198-35, FBI–Bergman Files; Director to SAC Birmingham, May 3, 1961, no. 157-198-31, ibid.; Director to SAC Atlanta et al., May 4, 1961, no. 157-198-34, ibid.; SAC Birmingham to Director, May 5, 1961, no. deleted, ibid.; Director to Attorney General, May 9, 1961, no. 144-1-554, ibid.; Seigenthaler interview.

21. Confidential interviews with former FBI officials.

22. Letterhead memo, May 12, 1961, no. 144-1-554, FBI–Alabama Files.
23. Raby interview; McGowan to Rosen, May 12 and 13, 1961, no. illegible, FBI–Alabama Files; Kenneth N. Raby to SAC Birmingham, May 13, 1961, no. 157-48-29, FBI–Bergman Files.
24. Director to SACs Albany et al., July 11, 1961, no. 157-198-39, FBI–Bergman Files; Director to Attorney General, May 15, 1961, no. 144-1-554, ibid.; Navasky, *Kennedy Justice*, 14.
25. Director to Attorney General, May 15, 1961, no. 144-1-554, FBI–Bergman Files.
26. Confidential interviews with former Birmingham FBI agents.
27. Wofford, *Kennedys and Kings*, 153–54; Lewis interview.
28. Schlesinger, *Robert Kennedy*, 309; Lewis interview and Oral History, 83.
29. Seigenthaler interview and Oral History, 41; Navasky, *Kennedy Justice*, 22; Rosen to Parsons, May 17, 1961, no. 321, FBI–CORE File.
30. Seigenthaler interview and Oral History, 41; Navasky, *Kennedy Justice*, 22; Civil Rights Commission, *Law Enforcement*, 166n; *New York Times*, May 8 and 19, 1976, Aug. 25, 1977. Seigenthaler learned about the FBI's file from his desk at the *Nashville Tennessean*, after he fired a copy editor, Jacqe Srouji, who also happened to be an FBI informant and a minor figure in the Karen Silkwood case. Ungar, "Piranhas," 19–27.
31. Robert Kennedy to Governor of Albama, n.d. [ca. May 20, 1961], General Correspondence, Civil Rights/Alabama, Attorney General's Files, Box 10, Robert Kennedy Papers.
32. Schlesinger, *Robert Kennedy*, 309–11; Lewis interview.
33. Yarbrough, *Judge Frank Johnson*, 83; Director to Attorney General, June 8, 1961, no. 157-387-306, June 10, 1961, no. 157-387-180, FBI–Bergman Files.
34. Milton A. Jones to DeLoach, Dec. 2, 1964, no. 126, FBI–Whitehead File (77-68662); J. Edgar Hoover to Clyde Tolson, Mohr, and DeLoach, Dec. 8, 1964, no. 127, FBI–Lawrence File (94-4-3169); Director to Attorney General, May 24, 1961, no. 144-1-554, FBI–Bergman Files.
35. New Orleans Field Office Rept., July 26, 1961, no. 157-387-793, FBI–Bergman Files.
36. George H. Scatterday to Rosen, May 22, 1961, in Dept. of Justice, *King Task Force*, 162–64; Garrow, *FBI and Martin Luther King*, 22, 24, 84.
37. Director to Attorney General, July 18, 1961, no. not recorded, FBI–COINTEL (CPUSA) File (100-3-104); Fred J. Baumgardner to William C. Sullivan, July 12, 1961, no. 2962, ibid.
38. Director to SAC San Francisco, Sept. 19, 1961, no. 2904, ibid.; SAC San Francisco to Director, Sept. 12, 1961, no. 2904, Sept. 22, 1961, no. 2903, ibid.; Baumgardner to Sullivan, Sept. 18, 1961, no. 2905, Oct. 3, 1961, no. 2964, ibid.; press release, Sept. 22, 1961, no. 2964, ibid.; *Cong. Record*, 87 Cong., 1 sess., Sept. 26, 1961, p. 21,329.
39. Confidential interview with former FBI agent.
40. Director to Attorney General, June 1, 1961, no. 157-387-57, June 6, 1961, no. 144-1-554, FBI–Bergman Files; Director to Marshall, June 16, 1961, no. 157-387-249, ibid.; Meier and Rudwick, *CORE*, 140–42.
41. For Williams's story, see *Negroes With Guns*.
42. Forman, *Making*, 158–63.
43. Memo, Susan Stankrauff, Aug. 28, 1961, General Correspondence, Civil Rights, Attorney General's Files, Box 9, Robert Kennedy Papers.

44. Blackstock, *COINTELPRO*, 67–89, 93–104, 152, 163–66; Forman, *Making*, 206; SAC Chicago to Director, Oct. 30, 1961, no. X3, FBI–Forman File (100-443566); Director to SACs New York et al., Oct. 12, 1961, in Church Committee, *Hearings—FBI*, 377. Williams served a self-imposed exile in Cuba, China, North Vietnam, and Tanzania until 1969, when he returned to the United States, clad in a Mao uniform. The FBI men he dreamed about met his plane, followed his "day-to-day activities," and compiled a thirty-two volume file. In March 1970 he testified before the Senate Internal Security Subcommittee and there were charges that he had made a deal with the CIA. FBI agents followed Mallory around, too, and she claimed "[they] got me kicked out of nursing school." Mallory Oral History, 18, 23; Williams Oral History, n.p.

45. Research Division Rept., Republican National Committee, Aug. 1963, in Cong. Papers, Civil Rights (B Series), Ford Papers.

46. Navasky, *Kennedy Justice*, 23.

47. Seigenthaler interview; Thompson, *Kennedy*, 124.

48. Rosen to Belmont, Dec. 22, 1961, no. illegible, FBI–Civil Rights Policy File (44-00); Marshall to Director, Dec. 29, 1961, no. illegible, ibid.; Marshall interview; Marshall to Attorney General, May 14, 1962, Civil Rights Div.—Mon. & Wed. Repts., Box 16, Marshall Papers.

49. Guthman interview. Kennedy's lawyer corps was just as white as Hoover's agent corps.

50. "Michigan's Cool Hand Luke," 32.

51. Schlesinger, *Robert Kennedy*, 304–5; Ollestad, *Inside*, 129.

52. Sullivan, *Bureau*, 125; Guthman, Seigenthaler interviews; Demaris, *Director*, 35, 37; Turner, *Hoover's F.B.I.*, 93; Brauer, *John F. Kennedy*, 83; Schlesinger, *Robert Kennedy*, 304–5; Church Committee, *Hearings—FBI*, 33.

53. Demaris, *Director*, 192.

54. Heim interview.

55. Leinbaugh interview.

56. Hoover to Tolson, DeLoach, James H. Gale, Rosen, and Thomas E. Bishop, April 14, 1969, no. not recorded, FBI–Tolson Memo File (67-9524); House Select Committee on Intelligence, *Hearings*, pt. 3, p. 1070; Fleischer interview; Ungar, *FBI*, 419–20; S. R. Burns to Walsh, Dec. 10, 1975, no. 62, FBI File 157-6160. In 1975 the FBI employed 103 black agents, 113 Hispanics, 14 Native Americans, 21 Asian-Americans, and 37 women—and over 8,300 white male agents.

57. *Ebony*, Oct. 1947, pp. 9–13, July 1958, pp. 46–47, Sept. 1962, pp. 29–34.

58. Heim interview.

59. Katzenbach Oral History, vol. 1, p. 12; Katzenbach interview.

60. FBI agents also investigated Major General Edwin A. Walker, the retired Army officer who commanded the paratroopers sent into Little Rock five years earlier. In Oxford, Walker stood on the other side, and the Bureau's reports provided the basis for a Justice Department attempt to have him committed for mental observation.

61. Director to Attorney General, Jan. 30, 1963, Mississippi File, Box 19, Marshall Papers; FBI letterhead memos, Feb. 13, 1961, Sept. 29 and 30, 1962, ibid.; Lord, *Past*, 199. Clegg was a veteran of the raid in 1934 on the Little Bohemia Lodge in Wisconsin, where John Dillinger and Baby Face Nelson escaped in a shootout that left one FBI agent dead.

62. Memo, re University of Alabama, n.d. [ca. June 11, 1963], General Corre-

spondence, Civil Rights (Univ. of Alabama), Attorney General's Files, Box 10, Robert Kennedy Papers; Director to Assistant Attorney General, Dec. 5, 1962, Alabama File, FBI Repts., Box 18, Marshall Papers; Church Committee, *Book II*, 82.

63. Employee suggestion of March 9, 1964, no. 67, FBI–Racial Matters File; Church Committee, *Book II*, 82; Edwin Guthman to Attorney General, Oct. 2, 1963, Demonstrations, Chronology, Box 32, Marshall Papers; David Marlin to Marshall, Aug. 22, 1963, July—Aug. 1963 Demonstrations, Box 32, ibid.

64. Director to SACs Atlanta et al., May 27, 1963, no. not recorded, FBI–Racial Matters File; Church Committee, *Book II*, 83.

65. *New York Post*, May 28, 1963; Navasky, *Kennedy Justice*, 112–15; Schlesinger, *Robert Kennedy*, 344–48; Wofford, *Kennedys and Kings*, 224.

66. Barrett interview; Navasky, *Kennedy Justice*, 16, 115.

67. Marshall, Barrett, Doar interviews.

68. Schlesinger, *Thousand Days*, 697, *Robert Kennedy*, 110. See also the documents on UAW organizers, officers, members, and attorneys in Box 701(3), Mundt Papers.

69. John and Robert Kennedy knew Hoover had accumulated information on the president's adventures with a string of girlfriends—from a World War II–era encounter with Inga Arvad, a one-time Miss Denmark and suspected Nazi agent, to a White House fling with Judith Campbell, a friend of mobsters Sam Giancana and John Rosselli, who had been introduced to JFK by Frank Sinatra. The FBI bugged Arvad's room in the Fort Sumter Hotel in Charleston, and Hoover had the tapes of her bed-top conversations with young Jack. Hoover also had an item on file regarding a party in New York attended by Kennedy, Sinatra, and "two mulatto prostitutes." The FBI even went to Robert once to alert him to a rumor being spread by gangster Meyer Lansky about an affair with a woman in El Paso, Texas. The attorney general said he had never been to El Paso. Courtney A. Evans to Belmont, Aug. 20, 1962, Folder 9, FBI–Hoover O&C Files; Theoharis and Cox, *Boss*, 334–35, 336.

70. James F. Bland to Sullivan, April 10, 1962, no. 94, Kennedy Folder, FBI–Hoover O&C Files; Hoover to P. Kenneth O'Donnell, Feb. 3, 1961, no. 720, FBI–National Negro Congress File (61-6782); Mitgang, "Annals," 55–56; Horne, *Communist*, 82.

71. Felt, *FBI Pyramid*, 62.

72. O'Reilly, "Herbert Hoover," 50–51.

73. George S. Mitchell to Files, Aug. 2, 1956, Criticisms: HUAC, 75-1-21-3, Southern Regional Council Archives.

74. Government Red-hunters accommodated blacks with a double-standard. Only rarely requiring black witnesses to name names, HUAC usually settled for a denunciation of Paul Robeson. Navasky, *Naming Names*, 192–94.

75. Wilkins to White, July 21, 1950, Communism 1950, Box 22, Wilkins Papers.

76. Director to SAC New York et al., March 31, 1960, no. 1577, FBI–COINTEL (CPUSA) File; Baumgardner to Sullivan, Oct. 27, 1965, no. illegible, ibid.

77. SAC St. Louis to Director, Oct. 11, 1963, no. 42–43, ibid.; Director to SAC St. Louis, Oct. 24, 1963, no. 42–43, ibid. For Randolph, see Baumgardner to Belmont, Nov. 30, 1960, no. 2109, Dec. 27, 1960, no. 2170, ibid.; Director to SAC Pittsburgh, Dec, 7, 1962, no. 39–32, ibid. For the NAACP, see

memo, Feb. 28, 1958, no. 2, FBI–Wilkins File (62-78270); Director to SAC New York, Dec. 4, 1959, no. illegible, FBI–COINTEL (CPUSA) File; Baumgardner to Belmont, June 7, 1960, no. 1727, ibid.; Baumgardner to Sullivan, Feb. 15, 1965, no. 31-312, March 5, 1965, no. 31-319, ibid.; Director to SAC Detroit, Feb. 19, 1965, no. 15-153, ibid.; Director to SAC New York, March 5, 1965, no. 31-320, March 17, 1965, no. 15-illegible, ibid.; Director to SAC Newark, May 6, 1965, no. 331, ibid. For the SRC, see Dunbar interview.

78. When asked at a press conference about methods SCLC used to screen people, Abernathy made a startling claim. "If we have a person coming to our staff . . . we will check with FBI men. . . . We don't want anything that is pink much less anything that is 'red.'" Hoover responded: "If I find anyone furnishing information to SCLC he will be dismissed." DeLoach to Mohr, July 1, 1965, no. 391, FBI–SCLC File (100-438794); Baumgardner to Sullivan, July 1, 1965, no. 392, July 1, 1965, no. 408, July 6, 1985, no. 521, ibid.

79. Rosen to Belmont, May 22, 1963, no. illegible, FBI–Civil Rights File; Director to Attorney General, May 23, 1963, no. 54, FBI–Racial Matters File.

80. Seigenthaler Oral History, 41; Farmer Oral History, 30; Farmer, *Lay Bare*, 270–71; DeLoach to Mohr, Nov. 20, 1963, no. 3882, Nov. 27, 1963, no. 3882, FBI–COINTEL (CPUSA) File.

81. Heim interview; Jones to DeLoach, March 16, 1965, no. not recorded, FBI–Wilkins File (62-78270).

82. SAC New York to Director, July 19, 1963, no. 51, FBI–National Urban League File (100-23219); DeLoach to Tolson, Oct. 11, 1967, no. not recorded, FBI–Young File (161-3130).

83. *Atlanta Daily World*, June 20, 1978.

84. Brown testified again years later, against a bill to declare King's birthday a national holiday. Senate Committee on the Judiciary and House Committee on Post Office, *Joint Hearings*, 43.

85. George C. Moore to Sullivan, April 18, 1969, no. 13, FBI–Hobson File (157-3707); Baumgardner to Sullivan, Aug. 24, 1964, no. X1, ibid.; Hobson interview; SAC Washington to Director, Sept. 24, 1969, no. 132, Oct. 1, 1969, no. illegible, FBI–COINTEL (Black Nationalist) File (100-448006).

86. House Select Committee on Assassinations, *Hearings—King*, vol. 6, p. 98.

87. McKissick interview; Director to Attorney General, June 6, 1961, no. 144-1-554, FBI–Bergman Files; Lewis Oral History, 172; Young Oral History, 25; A. Philip Randolph to Hoover, Aug. 7, 1964, J. Edgar Hoover Folder, Box 14, Brotherhood of Sleeping Car Porters Records. Even Malcolm X demanded an FBI investigation after police rousted a mosque in Buffalo. And Elijah Muhammad sent Hoover a threatening letter he had received from J. B. Stoner.

88. Farmer, *Lay Bare*, 285. On occasion, the FBI responded when movement activists needed protection. Following Farmer's near lynching in Plaquemines Parish, Louisiana, DeLoach dropped by the CORE office in New York and listened to Val Coleman explain that Farmer had been smuggled out of a church in a hearse to escape a mob and was planning to go back into the Parish the next day. "You guys have got to protect him," Coleman said. When Farmer showed up at the Plaquemines courthouse the following morning, five or six FBI agents were waiting for him on the steps.

89. Howell, "Interview," 14–16, 19–20; Young Oral History, 23; House Select Committee on Assassinations, *Hearings—King*, vol. 6, p. 4; Raines, *My Soul*, 430; Brown, *Die*, 61.

90. King, *Freedom Song*, 229; Rustin interview; DeLoach to Mohr, Dec. 2, 1964, no. 634, FBI–King File (100-106670); Howell, "Interview," 14–16, 19–20; Young Oral History, 23; House Select Committee on Asssassinations, *Hearings—King*, vol. 6, p. 4; Raines, *My Soul*, 430.

91. Forman, *Making*, 353; Forman interview.

92. Overstreet, *FBI in Our Open Society*, 167–68.

93. Even Jim Forman admitted that the FBI agents who worked the case did a good job, but he said "a lot of this is 'the horse is running wild and we caught the horse after the horse is out of the gate.' I mean, who opened the gate?"

94. Frank E. Smith to Robert Kennedy, June 26, 1963, General Correspondence, Civil Rights, Attorney General's Files, Box 9, Robert Kennedy Papers. A former agent claimed that the FBI arranged for one "Julio," a Mafia-connected fellow who was facing prosecution, to kidnap a segregationist who knew the identity of the person who pulled the trigger. Taken to a "safe house" in the Louisiana bayou, the man provided enough information, after "Julio" put a .38 in his mouth, to enable the FBI to reach out for Byron De La Beckwith. Villano, *Brick Agent*, 90–94.

95. SAC New Orleans to Director, June 19, 1963, no. 168, FBI–Desegregation . . . Jackson File (157-896); letterhead memo, re [deleted], June 19, 1963, no. 168, ibid.

96. Evers Oral History, 14; Schlesinger, *Robert Kennedy*, 358; Lewis, *Portrait*, 227–29.

97. After Salter left Mississippi to work in North Carolina for the Southern Conference Educational Fund, the FBI briefed Congressman L. H. Fountain (D., N.C.) on Salter's background.

98. Overstreet, *FBI in Our Open Society*, 167–68 (quotation). The Birmingham Police Department's surveillance apparatus rivaled the Jackson Police Department's. Birmingham wiremen recorded King's telephone call home from the city jail, and squads of detectives followed civil rights activists from one Baptist church to the next throughout the 1960s. They listened to preaching about "the movement" and "how good God has been," and filed uncomprehending reports on "the singing and praying . . . all going on at the same time. Seems as if anyone wanted to sing a different song from everyone else he just goes ahead. There are four different songs being sung at one time plus one Negro man praying." A. J. Cornelius and E. T. Coleman to Jamie Moore, March 13, 1967, Box 3.28, Hamilton Papers.

99. M. H. House to Moore, April 30, 1963, Box 13.4, Connor Papers.

100. Rustin interview.

101. Belmont to Tolson (addendum by DeLoach), Sept. 17, 1963, no. 211, FBI–BAPBOMB File (157-1025).

102. Birmingham police officers assigned to the Baptist Church bombing worked hard to solve the case. But the officers assigned to the "subversive squad" were scarcely more sympathetic than the person who sent in the green stamps. During the burial service for one of the girls at Grace Hill Cemetery, the police ran license-plate checks on the cars of those "few White people standing among the Negroes." Detective M. A. Jones then followed one of the cars, driven by a white man and carrying four girls, two white and two black, back into town, where he forced the driver to stop. When Jones tried to take pictures, "the White girls put their heads down between their knees. The Negro girls just giggled."

Jones kept trying to snap his shots until "a Cadillac loaded with Negroes [pulled up]. " Personal notes, M. A. Jones, Sept. 23, 1963, Box 3.40, Hamilton Papers.

103. Belmont to Tolson, Sept. 17, 1963, no. 211, FBI–BAPBOMB File. In the normal bombing case the FBI's principal goal was to prevent local police officers and politicians from shifting "the burden of their responsibility to us." Rosen to Belmont, April 11, 1964, no. not recorded, FBI–Civil Rights File.

104. DeLoach to Mohr, Sept. 20, 1963, no. 144, FBI–BAPBOMB File; Rosen to Belmont, Sept. 27, 1963, no. 308, ibid.

105. See serials 144, 308, 334, 335, 392, 463, ibid.; Raines, "Birmingham Bombing," 12ff; *New York Times*, Feb. 17 and 18, 1980.

106. Rosen to Belmont, Sept. 16, 1963, no. 28, FBI–BAPBOMB File; Hoover to the President, April 10, 1964, WHCF–CF, HU2/St1, Box 56, Johnson Papers; Lyndon B. Johnson to Edgar [Hoover], April 8, 1964, ibid.

107. Rosen to Belmont, Oct. 14, 1963, no. 485, FBI–BAPBOMB File; SAC Birmingham to Director, Dec. 13, 1966, no. 769, FBI–Liuzzo File (44-28601); Gale to DeLoach, May 27, 1966, no. 2, Microphone Surveillances Folder, FBI–Hoover O&C Files. The Bureau informed Kennedy of only one of its mike sources.

108. DeLoach to Mohr, Sept. 20, 1963, no. 63, FBI–BAPBOMB File; Evans to Belmont, Sept. 16, 1963, no. 67, ibid.; and the articles cited in note 105.

109. Hoover to Attorney General, Sept. 30, 1963, no. 333, FBI–BAPBOMB File.

110. Rosen to Belmont, Sept. 30, 1963, no. 283 and 284, ibid.

111. Hoover to Attorney General, Sept. 30, 1963, no. 333, ibid.; Evans to Belmont, Sept. 30, 1964, no. 337, ibid.

112. *New York Times*, Feb. 18, 1980; Eddy interview. Chambliss, sentenced to life imprisonment, died in the fall of 1985.

113. Rosen to Belmont, April 11, 1964, no. not recorded, FBI–Civil Rights File.

114. Schlesinger, *Robert Kennedy*, 345.

115. Newfield, *Robert Kennedy*, 23.

116. The FBI cannot be blamed for the Kennedy administration's early tendency to appoint segregationists to the federal bench.

117. Newfield, *Robert Kennedy*, 23. Newfield gradually changed his mind, believing Kennedy had been transformed into an "existential hero." Hoover himself described Kennedy as "a kind of Messiah for the generation gap."

118. Cheek interview; Laurie Pritchett to Asa Kelley, Oct. 19, 1962, City Manager's Office, Albany Movement Records.

119. Pritchett to S. A. Roos, Oct. 30 and Nov. 10, 1962, Police Dept., Mayor's Office, Albany Movement Records; memos, re statements from Chief Pritchett et al., July 23 and 24, 1962, ibid.; Pritchett interview; C. B. King Oral History, 1; *New York Times*, Dec. 14, 1961.

120. Rosen to Belmont, July 24, 1962, no. not recorded, FBI–King File.

121. Pritchett, Sitton interviews. Hansen is quoted in Carson, *In Struggle*, 61, 84. In the South as a whole, Sitton added, the conduct of the FBI "depended on the individual agents—some were very good, some were terrible ... extremely cooperative with the local police. Albany especially."

122. C. B. King Oral History, 18, 21.

123. Cheek interview.

124. Ibid.

125. Ibid.; C. B. King, Thomas interviews; Robert Kennedy to Martin Luther King, Jr., Dec. 4, 1963, King Papers. Jack Miller's Criminal Division brought the action, not Burke Marshall's Civil Rights Division.

126. DeLoach to Mohr, Jan. 15, 1963, no. not recorded, FBI–King File; R. W. Smith to Sullivan, Oct. 15, 1964, no. not recorded, FBI–SCLC File; C. B. King Oral History, 18; Barkan, *Protestors*, 69; Zinn, *Southern*, 212.

127. Zinn, *Southern*, 211, *Albany*, 31; Navasky, *Kennedy Justice*, 121–22; C. B. King interview.

128. This surveillance was on Rabinowitz's law office, not C. B. King's.

129. Slater King Oral History, 26.

130. Cheek, C. B. King, Sherrod interviews. Holtzman had criticized the FBI performance in Albany. *Harvard Law Record*, Oct. 3, Nov. 14, and Dec. 5, 1963.

131. Schlesinger, *Robert Kennedy*, 298; Wilkins, *Man's Life*, 173–74.

132. Brauer, *John F. Kennedy*, 319.

133. Wilkins, Trebach interviews.

CHAPTER **4.**
Black Dream, Red Menace

1. Schlesinger, *Robert Kennedy*, 365–66; White, Forman, Lewis interviews; Garrow, *Bearing*, 282–83.

2. Schlesinger, *Robert Kennedy*, 366–67; Louis B. Nichols to Clyde Tolson, July 23, 1953, Misc. A–Z Folder, FBI–Nichols O&C Files.

3. In preparation for the expected southern influx of Soviet-directed agents, FBI officials advised field agents to recruit informants by waving "the flag" and using their own "sons and daughters" at the high schools and colleges. C. B. Stanbery to SAC Birmingham, Oct. 31, 1960, no. 137-00-165, FBI–Bergman Freedom Rider Files.

4. House Committee on Appropriations, *Hearings* (1962), 343–44; SAC Birmingham to Director, April 12, 1963, no. 199, FBI–Levison File (100-392452).

5. William C. Sullivan to Alan H. Belmont, Aug. 30, 1963, in Dept. of Justice, *King Task Force*, 166; Director to SACs Atlanta et al., July 18, 1963, no. not recorded, FBI–CIRM File (100-3-116).

6. Milton A. Jones to Cartha D. DeLoach, March 16, 1965, no. not recorded, FBI–Wilkins File (62-78270); Director to SAC New York, Aug. 13, 1964, no. 856, FBI–COINTEL (CPUSA) File (100-3-104); SAC New York to Director, Aug. 24, 1964, no. 867, ibid.

7. David Marlin to Burke Marshall, Aug. 22, 1963, Aug. 1963 Demonstrations, Box 32, Marshall Papers; "Communist Party, USA—Negro Question," Aug. 23, 1963, no. 253X, FBI–CIRM File.

8. "Communist Party, USA—Negro Question."

9. Ibid.

10. Ibid. See also the cover memo, Fred J. Baumgardner to Sullivan, Aug. 23, 1963.

11. Baumgardner to Sullivan, Aug. 23, 1963, no. 253X, FBI–CIRM File.

12. Baumgardner to Sullivan, Aug. 23, 1963, no. 253X, Aug. 28, 1963, no. 230 and no. not recorded, ibid.; Senate Select Committee to Study . . . Intelligence Activities (hereafter Church Committee), *Book III*, 107.

13. Ungar, *FBI*, 295–314; Theoharis and Cox, *Boss*, 105.
14. Sullivan to Belmont, Aug. 30, 1963, no. 253X, Sept. 16, 1963, no. 367, Sept. 25, 1963, no. illegible, FBI–CIRM File; J. Edgar Hoover to all SACs, Sept. 24, 1963, no. not recorded, Oct. 1, 1963, no. illegible, ibid.; Tolson to Director, Sept. 18, 1963, no. 253X, ibid.; Dept. of Justice, *King Task Force*, 165–74.
15. Church Committee, *Book III*, 107–11. The Church Committee concluded that "preconceptions" and "bureaucratic squabbles" led to the intensification of surveillance after the March on Washington—and not "genuine concerns based on hard evidence that communists might be influencing the civil rights movement." The FBI position is that the initial decision to investigate King was fully justified and the excesses that followed resulted from Sullivan's recklessness. Sullivan himself testified before the Church Committee, but he was hardly an objective witness, having left the Bureau in 1971 under fire.
16. Ibid., 106, 108.
17. Internal debates over surveillance policies were common—as Hoover's comments about Castro suggest. The same type of debate occurred on the question of organized crime and would occur again during the height of the anti–Vietnam war demonstrations, when Division Five argued that "knowledgeable sources and confidential informants have failed to substantiate claims by the CP of substantial influence within the new Left movement." R. L. Shackelford to Charles D. Brennan, Dec. 31, 1970, no. 68, FBI–Kirk File (134-14771).
18. Rustin interview.
19. Sullivan to Belmont, Oct. 9, 1956, no. 47, FBI–COINTEL (CPUSA) File; "Weaknesses of the Communist Party, USA," Oct. 1956, no. 47, ibid.; FBI Monographs, "Communist Party and the Negro," 1953 and 1956. See also Hoover, *Masters*, 236.
20. Church Committee, *Book III*, 139; Sullivan, *Bureau*, 137–38.
21. Memo, re Martin Luther King, n.d. [ca. June 1963], King Folder, FBI–Hoover O&C Files.
22. Director to SAC New York, April 22, 1959, no. not recorded, FBI–Levison File; Baumgardner to Belmont, April 22, 1959, no. not recorded, ibid.; Garrow, *FBI and Martin Luther King*, 21–77; Director to SAC Atlanta, Sept. 20, 1957, no. X1, FBI–SCLC File (100-438794); Director to SACs New York et al., Dec. 1, 1964, no. 2108, FBI–COINTEL (CPUSA) File.
23. D. E. Roney to SAC New York, March 9, 1964, no. 1391, FBI–Levison File (New York Field Office File) (100-111180); Dept. of Justice, *King Task Force*, 141; note, April 30, 1962, no. not recorded, FBI–King File (100-106670).
24. Memo, re Stanley David Levison, June 3, 1963, no. 128, FBI–King File; SAC New York to Director, March 30, 1966, no. 2425, ibid.; note, March 30, 1966, no. 2425, ibid.; memo, re CIRM and Stanley Levison, Dec. 9, 1963, no. not recorded, ibid.
25. Schlesinger, *Robert Kennedy*, 372; Hoover to Tolson, Belmont, DeLoach, Alex Rosen, and Sullivan, June 17, 1963, no. 150, FBI–King File.
26. Garrow, *FBI and Martin Luther King*, 47–48. Division Five objected to the SISS subpoena.
27. Baumgardner to Sullivan, Oct. 8, 1962, no. 34-306, FBI–COINTEL (CPUSA) File; SAC New York to Director, Sept. 28, 1962, no. 34-295, ibid.; *Augusta Chronicle*, Oct. 25, 1962; *Birmingham News*, Oct. 26, 1962.
28. Director to SAC New York, April 24, 1964, in Church Committee, *Hearings—FBI*, 695–96; idem, *Book III*, 139.

29. Lewis interview.

30. Quoted in the SNCC monograph, Aug. 1967, no. 1386, FBI–SNCC File (100-439190).

31. House Select Committee on Assassinations, *Hearings—King*, 351.

32. Hoover to all SACs, Oct. 1, 1963, in Church Committee, *Book III*, 110–11.

33. Sullivan to Belmont, Dec. 24, 1963, no. not recorded, FBI–King File; memo, re Questions to be Explored, Dec. 23, 1963, no. 684, FBI–CIRM File; Church Committee, *Book III*, 133, 135; Sullivan to Belmont, Jan. 27, 1964, no. 15, King Folder, FBI–Hoover O&C Files.

34. Raines, *My Soul*, 430.

35. SAC Chicago to Director, Aug. 25, 1965, no. 9-531, FBI–COINTEL (CPUSA) File; SAC Los Angeles to Director, Oct. 28, 1963, no. 26-103, ibid. The most aggressive action launched against Lightfoot occurred in 1966, after he inherited a row house from his mother, when the FBI arranged publicity portraying him as a "slum lord." Division Five timed this action to coincide with an SCLC slum clearance campaign, hoping to divert attention from King's work in Chicago. Berlet, "Journalists."

36. The FBI campaign to destroy King has been meticulously chronicled in Garrow, *FBI and Martin Luther King* and *Bearing*.

37. Church Committee, *Book III*, 145.

38. DeLoach to Tolson, Oct. 25, 1966, no. 2756, Oct. 26, 1966, no. 2754, FBI–King File; Baumgardner to Sullivan, Nov. 3, 1966, no. 2782, ibid.

39. *Time*, Feb. 14, 1964; SAC New York to Director, Feb. 11, 1964, no. 34-565, Feb. 14, 1964, no. 34-582, FBI–COINTEL (CPUSA) File; Senate Select Committee On Intelligence, *Hearings on National Intelligence Reorganization*, 484–86.

40. Baumgardner to Sullivan, Sept. 17, 1963, no. 9-214, FBI–COINTEL (CPUSA) File.

41. Church Committee, *Book II*, 66, *Book III*, 430, 438–39.

42. Church Committee, *Book III*, 135, 139, 479; Baumgardner to Sullivan, Oct. 1, 1964, idem, *Hearings—FBI*, 609–11.

43. Church Committee, *Book III*, 139, 481–83.

44. Director to SACs Atlanta et al., July 14, 1964, no. illegible, FBI–Civil Rights Policy File (44-00); SAC Chicago to Director, May 26, 1966, no. 1442, FBI–SCLC File.

45. James F. Bland to Sullivan, Feb. 3, 1962, no. 135, FBI–Levison File.

46. Director to Assistant Attorney General, Dec. 18, 1975, no. X65, FBI File 62-117166; Director to Attorney General, Oct. 1, 1969, no. 353, FBI–Levison File.

47. Heim interview; Bishop, *Days of Martin Luther King*, 83.

48. SAC New York to Director, Oct. 14, 1963, no. 34-502, FBI–COINTEL (CPUSA) File; Navasky, "FBI's Wildest Dream," 716–18; Leinbaugh interview.

49. Statement, re J. Edgar Hoover, Nov. 19, 1964, Box 27.41, SCLC Papers; Church Committee, *Hearings—FBI*, 173; Garrow, *FBI and Martin Luther King*, 122–23; "FBI and Civil Rights," 56–58.

50. Garrow, *FBI and Martin Luther King*, 54–55; Zinn, *Albany*. King had been on record as a critic since February 4, 1961.

51. Hoover had monitored the percentage of southern-born agents assigned to civil rights cases since the mid-1950s.

52. DeLoach to John P. Mohr, Nov. 19, 1964, no. not recorded, FBI–King File; Navasky, *Kennedy Justice*, 122.

53. Cheek interview; House Select Committee on Intelligence, *Hearings*, pt. 3, p. 1047; House Select Committee on Assassinations, *Hearings—King*, vol. 6, pp. 92–96; Rustin interview.

54. Garrow, *FBI and Martin Luther King*, 125–26, 133–34, *Bearing*, 373–74.

55. Church Committee, *Book III*, 162; Garrow, *FBI and Martin Luther King*, 127.

56. DeLoach to Mohr, No. 27, 1964, no. 16, FBI–Wilkins File; Hoover to the President, Nov. 30, 1964, no. 15, ibid.; Church Committee, *Book III*, 162–63, *Hearings—FBI*, 172; Garrow, *Bearing*, 687–88n, *FBI and Martin Luther King*, 271 n41.

57. Guthman interview; Ungar, *FBI*, 281; Baumgardner to Sullivan, Feb. 15, 1965, no. 312, and March 5, 1965, no. 319, FBI–COINTEL (CPUSA) File.

58. Ungar, *FBI*, 279–95; Theoharis and Cox, *Boss*, 105n.

59. Church Committee, *Book III*, 168–71; Farmer, *Lay Bare*, 269–70.

60. Howell, "Interview," 16; Kennedy Oral History, 636; Hoover to Tolson, Belmont, Mohr, DeLoach, and Rosen, Dec. 1, 1964, no. 563, FBI–King File; DeLoach to Hoover, Dec. 2, 1964, no. 634, ibid.

61. Joseph A. Sizzo to Sullivan, Dec. 1, 1964, no. 3, King Folder, FBI–Hoover O&C Files. Rowan and Bunche, nonetheless, received derogatory information on King from time to time.

62. Stone interview; Garrow, *FBI and Martin Luther King*, 125–26, 133–34, *Bearing*, 373–74. The King flap continued to occupy a good deal of the FBI's time. On March 30, after Edwin C. Berry of the Urban League in Chicago criticized the director, SAC Marlin Johnson gave him a ninety-minute going over in the chambers of federal judge James B. Parsons, a Bureau ally. Another Chicago resident, Rev. Archibald Carey, met with DeLoach in May in a futile attempt to end the King-Hoover feud. Afterward, Hoover gave DeLoach the ultimate accolade ("Well handled. H."), though in this case it was a bit gratuitous. Carey had once named the director, along with the entire "Jewish community," as one of the ten living whites who had done the most to help black America. D. C. Morrell to DeLoach, March 31, 1965, no. not recorded, FBI–National Urban League File (100-23219); Archibald J. Carey, Jr., to [deleted], March 3, 1964, no. 27, FBI–Carey File (161-2040); DeLoach to Mohr, May 19, 1965, no. 30, ibid.

63. Hoover to Tolson, Mohr, and DeLoach, Dec. 8, 1964, no. 127, FBI–Lawrence File (94-4-3169); Roberts, *Papa Jack*, 144–84; *Chicago Defender*, Aug. 11 and 15, 1970.

64. Hoover's prurient interests extended beyond blacks. His old General Intelligence Division held a file on birth-control crusader Margaret Sanger; in the late 1930s his agents investigated several condom manufacturers on the grounds that their products were "often found in the possession of high school students"; and throughout his forty-eight year tenure his senior staff remained on alert for "sex deviates" among the faculty and staff of his alma mater, George Washington University.

65. "Communist Party and the Negro," 1953, p. 10.

66. Sexism within the movement should not be exaggerated, but it did exist—as evidenced by Stokely Carmichael's casual remark: "The only position for women in SNCC is prone."

67. Director to SAC New York, May 11, 1960, no. 1649, FBI–COINTEL (CPUSA) File; Director to SAC Atlanta, Aug. 19, 1964, no. not recorded, ibid.; Na-

vasky, *Kennedy Justice*, 16; Hoover to Tolson, Mohr, and DeLoach, Dec. 8, 1964, no. 127, FBI–Lawrence File; Director to SAC New York, Aug. 25, 1966, no. not recorded, FBI–Levison File; Director to SAC New York, Sept. 14, 1966, no. 1964, ibid. (New York Field Office File); House Committee on Appropriations, *Hearings* (1966), 296; Wilkins interview; SAC Chicago to Director, April 16, 1968, no. 2116, FBI–SCLC File; Dept. of Justice, *King Task Force*, 136.

68. Stone interview; Bishop, *Confessions*, 432.

69. Leinbaugh interview; Baumgardner to Sullivan, March 4, 1964, no. 312, Aug. 31, 1964, no. 450, Sept. 17, 1964, no. 479, FBI–King File; UPI ticker, Nov. 9, 1963, no. 264, ibid.; Hoover to Tolson, June 2, 1967, no. not recorded, FBI–Tolson Memo File (67-9524); Garrow, *FBI and Martin Luther King*, 121.

70. Leinbaugh interview.

71. Serials 59, 66, FBI–COINTEL (Black Nationalist) File (100-448006).

72. Evers, *Evers*, 112.

73. Church Committee, *Book III*, 52–53; SAC St. Louis to Director, Oct. 11, 1968, no. illegible, FBI–COINTEL (Black) File.

74. Director to SAC Philadelphia, June 17, 1965, no. 37-6, FBI—COINTEL (White Hate) File (157-9).

75. Press release, July 13, 1963, in Box 27.25, SCLC Papers; Courtney A. Evans to Belmont, July 16, 1963, no. 166, FBI–King File; Jones to DeLoach, July 16, 1963, no. 164, ibid.

76. Belmont to D. Milton Ladd, Aug. 25, 1953, no. not recorded, FBI–Highlander File (61-7511); Nichols to Tolson, Aug. 30, 1957, no. 198, ibid.; Director to SAC Savannah, April 29, 1959, no. not recorded, ibid.; Baumgardner to Sullivan, July 26, 1963, no. 286, ibid.; Director to SAC Knoxville, July 29, 1963, not recorded, ibid.; Jones to DeLoach, July 27, 1964, no. 299, ibid.; Director to SACs Atlanta and Knoxville, April 6, 1965, no. 1154, FBI–King File.

77. Church Committee, *Book III*, 98–100.

78. Russell was the man who laundered "the CIA budget in the Defense budget," said Secretary of State Dean Rusk. Rusk himself "never saw a budget for the CIA." Rusk Oral History, n.p.

79. Robert Kennedy to Russell, Nov. 1, 1963, Civil Rights Series, Civil Rights General, Special Correspondence, Box 4, Russell Papers; Kennedy Oral History, 683; Belmont to Tolson, Nov. 1, 1963, no. not recorded, FBI–King File; Evans to Belmont, Nov. 1, 1963, no. not recorded, ibid.

80. WHJ to File, Oct. 23, 1965, Intra Office Communications Series, Box 15, Russell Papers; Schlesinger, *Robert Kennedy*, 379.

81. Belmont to Tolson, Oct. 17, 1963, in Dept. of Justice, *King Task Force*, 176.

82. Hoover to Tolson, Belmont, Rosen, Sullivan, DeLoach, and Evans, Feb. 5, 1964, no. 297, FBI–King File; Hoover to Tolson, Belmont, Mohr, DeLoach, Rosen, and Sullivan, Oct. 25, 1963, no. 10, King Folder, FBI–Hoover O&C Files; Director to Attorney General, Oct. 25, 1963, no. 11, ibid.; "Communism and the Negro Movement—A Current Analysis," Oct. 16, 1963, no. 416, FBI–CIRM File; Evans to Belmont, Oct. 25, 1963, no. not recorded, FBI–Robert Kennedy File (77-51387).

83. Hoover to Tolson, Belmont, Rosen, Sullivan, DeLoach, and Evans, Feb. 5, 1964, no. 297, FBI–King File; DeLoach to Mohr, March 16, 1964, no. 320, ibid.

84. Baumgardner to Sullivan, April 17, 1964, no. 34-713, FBI–COINTEL (CPUSA) File.

85. House Committee on Appropriations, *Hearings* (1964), 308–09.

86. Church Committee, *Book III*, 155; Garrow, *Bearing*, 322; *New York Times*, April 22, 1964. Lewis is quoted in Carson, *In Struggle*, 107.

87. Rustin interview.

88. Leinbaugh interview.

CHAPTER 5.

Mississippi Burning

1. Belfrage, *Freedom Summer*, 55; Raines, *My Soul*, 287; Guyot, Moses interviews; J. Edgar Hoover to Clyde Tolson, Alan H. Belmont, Cartha D. De-Loach, and William C. Sullivan, Jan. 28, 1965, no. not recorded, FBI–Tolson Memo File. Senator Paul Douglas (D., Ill.) once asked the FBI, when compiling arrest records, to indicate if arrests had been made during nonviolent racial demonstrations. "Innocent" college students, he felt, should not be burdened by the stigma of a police record. Hoover refused the request—and not only because of the expected clerical burden. In 1960, when San Francisco municipal judge Albert Axelrod warned sixty-three students and others who had been arrested at a demonstration against HUAC about matters "which would be on their record for the rest of their lives," Hoover dismissed Axelrod as "another 'bleeding heart.'" SAC San Francisco to Director, May 28, 1960, no. 4508, FBI–HUAC File (61-7582); Navasky, *Kennedy Justice*, 10–11.

2. Barry Oral History, n.p.; Moses interview.

3. Belknap, *Federal Law*, 141; Aaron Henry, Robert Moses, and David Dennis to President Johnson, May 25, 1964, White House Aides' Files—Lee C. White, Miss. Summer Project, Box 6, Johnson Papers; Miller, ed., "Mississippi," 290.

4. Atlanta Field Office Rept., Sept. 28, 1964, no. illegible, FBI–SNCC File; Guyot interview; Whitehead, *Attack*, 4, 9.

5. During the Bureau's probe of the Mack Charles Parker lynching in 1959, a candidate for sheriff of Pearl River County invariably reminded his audiences that the FBI "talked to me like I was a nigger, or a dog." Tully, *F.B.I.'s Most Famous Cases*, 217.

6. Navasky, *Kennedy Justice*, 125.

7. See the SNCC monograph, Aug. 1967, no. 1386, FBI–SNCC File (100-439190).

8. John Doar and Dorothy Landsberg, "The Performance of the FBI in Investigating Violations of Federal Laws Protecting the Right to Vote, 1960–1967," in Senate Select Committee to Study ... Intelligence Activities (hereafter Church Committee), *Hearings—FBI*, 929–30; Burke Marshall to Attorney General, June 5, 1964, Alphabetical File, Box 3, Marshall Papers.

9. Marshall interview; Doar, "Performance," 931–32, 936; Navasky, *Kennedy Justice*, 105–06, 437–38; DeLoach to Tolson, Jan. 9, 1967, no. 1911, FBI–Robert Kennedy File (77-51387).

10. Robert F. Kennedy to the President, June 5, 1964, WHCF, Ex HU2/St24, Box 26, Johnson Papers; Marshall to Attorney General, June 5, 1964, Alphabetical File, Box 3, Marshall Papers.

11. Brown, *Strain*, 294–95.

12. Kennedy Oral History, 639, 655–56, 666; DeLoach to Hoover, Jan. 15, 1964, no. 10, March 6, 1964, no. 31, March 9, 1964, no. 26, Johnson Folder, FBI–Hoover O&C Files; DeLoach to Tolson, June 17, 1965, no. 34, ibid.; Hoover to Marvin Watson, June 29, 1965, no. 36, ibid.

13. DeLoach to Hoover, March 6, 1964, no. 31, Johnson Folder, FBI–Hoover O&C Files; Kennedy Oral History, 639, 655–56, 666.

14. Meier and Rudwick, *Core*, 276.

15. "Prosecutive Summary," Dec. 19, 1964, no. 1613, FBI–MIBURN File (44-25706); Cagin and Dray, *We Are Not Afraid*; Whitehead, *Attack*.

16. Henry Oral History, n.p; King, *Freedom Song*, 378–85; "Chronology of Contacts," June 21–22, 1964, in WATS/Neshoba, SNCC Papers.

17. Lee C. White to File, June 23, 1964, White House Aides' Files—Lee C. White, Miss. Summer Project Voter Registration, Box 6, Johnson Papers; Cagin and Dray, *We Are Not Afraid*, 324–25.

18. Moses to Parents of all Mississippi Summer Volunteers, n.d. [ca. June 22, 1964], White House Aides' Files—Lee C. White, Miss. Summer Project Voter Registration, Box 6, Johnson Papers; Alex Rosen to Alan H. Belmont, July 8, 1964, no. not recorded, FBI–Racial Matters Policy File (157-00).

19. White interview; White to File, June 23, 1964, White House Aides' Files—Lee C. White, Miss. Summer Project Voter Registration, Box 6, Johnson Papers.

20. Memo, re telephone call, Rita Schwerner to the White House, June 23, 1964, White House Aides' Files—Lee C. White, Miss. Summer Project Voter Registration, Box 6, Johnson Papers.

21. Memo, re telephone call, Rita Schwerner to Mary King, June 25, 1964, WATS Repts., Box 37, SNCC Papers; Misseduc Foundation, *Mississippi*, 62–63.

22. Memo, re telephone call, Rita Schwerner to Mary King, June 25, 1964, WATS Repts., Box 37, SNCC Papers; Raines, *My Soul*, 289.

23. Transcript, CBS News, June 25, 1964.

24. Clark Oral History, 30; Marshall Oral History, 24, 30, Johnson Library; House Select Committee on Assassinations, *Hearings—King*, vol. 7, p. 142; Milton A. Jones to DeLoach, Dec. 2, 1964, no. 126, FBI–Whitehead File (77-68662).

25. Ungar, *FBI*, 413–14. For Moore's career, see Tully, *F.B.I.'s Most Famous Cases*, 191–201; Subject File—Roy K. Moore, Mississippi Dept. of Archives and History, Jackson.

26. Jones to Thomas E. Bishop, Aug. 14, 1970, no. 18, FBI–Whitehead File (94-64866); Von Hoffman, *Mississippi*, 38; Sutherland, ed., *Letters*, 118.

27. Hoover to Walter Jenkins, July 13, 1964, WHCF, Ex HU2/St24, Box 26, Johnson Papers; Jones to Bishop, Aug. 14, 1970, no. 18, FBI–Whitehead File (94-64866).

28. Welch, *Inside*, 102, 106–7; Navasky, *Kennedy Justice*, 107; letterhead memo, July 1, 1964, WHCF, FG135-6, Box 188, Johnson Papers. In addition to the fingerprint service, SNCC's Lawrence Guyot remembered an FBI agent who "said, 'Look, Guyot, we want to . . . identify any scars on your body. . . . If anything happens to you we want to know how to be able to identify you.'" "They were as much a part of the fear apparatus as anything else," Guyot concluded.

29. Evers interview; and Hoover's letter to Jenkins, cited in note 27.

30. Johnson to Edgar [Hoover], July 13, 1964, WHCF, FG135-6, Box 188, John-

son Papers; Hoover to the President, July 16, 1964, WHCF, Ex HU2/St24, Box 26, ibid.; Hoover to Tolson, Belmont, Rosen, William C. Sullivan, and DeLoach, July 21, 1964, no. not recorded, FBI–King File (100-106670).

31. Hoover to Tolson, Belmont, Rosen, Sullivan, and DeLoach, July 21, 1964, no. not recorded, FBI–King File.

32. D. C. Morrell to DeLoach, Aug. 4, 1964, no. 422, ibid.; Lawrence A. Rainey to Hoover, July 28, 1964, no. 425, ibid.; Belfrage, *Freedom Summer*, 155, 164.

33. Memo, re telephone call, Freddy Lee Watson to Mary King, June 24, 1964, WATS Repts., Box 37, SNCC Papers; Clement L. McGowan, Jr., to Rosen, July 22, 1964, no. 405, FBI–King; "Mississippi Eyewitness," 38–39.

34. Moore interview; Welch, *Inside*, 100; *Jackson Daily News*, July 12, 1964; Warren, *Who Speaks*, 125n; Ungar, *FBI*, 415; Von Hoffman, *Mississippi*, 39, 54; Doar, "Performance," 941; Moody, *Coming*, 338.

35. Nicholas deB. Katzenbach to the President, Sept. 28, 1964, WHCF, Ex HU2/St24, Box 27, Johnson Papers; Director to Attorney General, Dec. 19, 1967, in Church Committee, *Hearings—FBI*, 526. For Hoover on Wallace, see DeLoach to Mohr, Dec. 2, 1964, no. 634, FBI–King File.

36. Doar, "Performance," 936-37; Ungar, *FBI*, 414–15.

37. As relayed by the director to his senior staff. He offered no evidence. Hoover to Tolson, Belmont, Rosen, Sullivan, and DeLoach, July 16, 1964, no. not recorded, FBI–Penn File (44-25873). For the statistics and the other quotes, see House Committee on Appropriations, *Hearings* (1965), 285; Doar, "Performance," 937; Demaris, *Director*, 207.

38. McGowan, Sullivan interviews; Mars, *Witness*.

39. Sullivan, *Bureau*, 74–77.

40. DeLoach to Mohr, Aug. 5, 1964, no. not recorded, FBI–Penn File; Prosecutive Summary, Dec. 19, 1964, no. 1613, and the Supplemental Summary, March 5, 1965, no. 1822, FBI–MIBURN File.

41. Katzenbach to the President, Sept. 4, 1964, White House Aides' Files—Lee C. White, Law Enforcement (Riots), Box 5, Johnson Papers. See also the prosecutive summaries cited in the previous note.

42. Cagin and Dray, *We Are Not Afraid*, 435, 452.

43. McGowan, Doar, Fleischer interviews; Hoover to Jenkins, Aug. 11, 1964, WHCF, FG135-6, Johnson Papers. King, Young, and Wilkins are quoted in *Whose FBI?*, ed. Wright, 381; Sullivan in Whitehead, *Attack*, 142.

44. Suggested statement re Katzenbach, Jan. 2, [1967?], Dept. of Justice, Box 58, SNCC Papers; Carson, *In Struggle*, 115.

45. Bernhard interview.

46. Aschenbrenner interview; deposition of James O. Ingram, Oct. 10, 1978, p. 7, *Muhammad Kenyatta v. Roy Moore et al.*, no. J77-0298(R) (N.D., Miss., 1985). Kenyatta's suit failed.

47. Hoover to Tolson, Mohr, and DeLoach, Dec. 8, 1964, no. 127, FBI–Lawrence File (94-4-3169); *Jackson Daily News*, Nov. 22, 1964. After a gentle nudge from Lawrence, Hoover qualified this characterization. "I thought it more appropriate to say state obligations than rights."

48. SAC Charlotte to Director, April 24, 1964, no. deleted, FBI–Lowenstein File (file no. also deleted).

49. Director to SACs Albany et al., June 12, 1964, no. 73, FBI–Racial Matters File. By this time the FBI had begun to experiment with "counterintelligence education" on the campuses of the schools that sent students into

the South. "Certainly," the head of the Milwaukee office wrote, in a clear statement of this ambitious campaign, "we should educate our students in Democracy" by supplying "information" to "reliable, dedicated, loyal college faculty," by developing "an outstanding student leader on each campus," and by disseminating data to "established sources of all college newspapers." SAC Milwaukee to Director, May 31, 1963, no. 34-47, FBI–COINTEL (CPUSA) File (100-3-104).

50. Moore interview; Ungar, *FBI*, 415–16; Harris, *Dreams*, 87.

51. DeLoach to Mohr, July 2, 1964, no. 44-25790-5, FBI–NLG Files; Hoover to Tolson, Belmont, Rosen, Sullivan, and DeLoach, July 21, 1964, no. not recorded, FBI–King File.

52. SAC Seattle to Director, Dec. 4, 1964, no. 50-157, FBI–COINTEL (CPUSA) File; Director to SAC Seattle, Nov. 30, 1964, no. 50-156, ibid.; Church Committee, *Book III*, 56.

53. SAC Jackson to Director, Sept. 16, 1969, no. 54-14, FBI–COINTEL (New Left) File (100-449698); Smead, *Blood*, 147–48. See also Subject File—State Sovereignty Commission, Mississippi Archives.

54. Karl E. Mundt to Joe Floyd, Feb. 23, 1962, Box 165(3), Mundt Papers. A few weeks after discussing Schwarz with Mundt, DeLoach recommended that Dwight Eisenhower not allow his name to be "used to lend prestige to such individuals." DeLoach to Mohr, June 27, 1962, Eisenhower Folder, FBI–Nichols O&C Files.

55. Director to SAC Atlanta, July 2, 1970, no. 2-16, FBI–COINTEL (New Left) File; SAC New Orleans to Director, July 31, 1970, no. illegible, FBI–COINTEL (Black Nationalist) File (100-448006).

56. Louis B. Nichols to Tolson, Feb. 26, 1954, no. not recorded, FBI–NAACP File (61-3176); "Plaintiff's Principal Factual Papers . . . ," Sept. 26, 1984, pp. 220–22, in NLG Papers; *National Lawyers Guild v. Attorney General et al.*, 77 Civ. 999 (S.D.N.Y.); Belmont to Leland V. Boardman, April 4, 1958, no. not recorded, May 15, 1958, no. not recorded, FBI–COINTEL (CPUSA) File; Director to SACs Baltimore et al., April 11, 1958, no. not recorded, ibid.

57. Goodman, "NLG," 1–7; Holt, *Summer*, 88–94.

58. The FBI described Dombrowski as "a preacher at heart who has gone 'nuts' on the brotherhood of man."

59. Baumgardner to Sullivan, Oct. 9, 1963, no. illegible, Feb. 26, 1964, no. 1065, FBI–McSurely Files (100-10355); Rosen to Belmont, Oct. 8, 1963, no. 1040, Feb. 20, 1964, no. 1066, ibid.; DeLoach to Mohr, March 4, 1964, no. 1067, ibid.; SAC Washington to Director, March 19, 1964, no. 1068, ibid.; McGowan to Rosen, Oct. 17, 1963, no. not recorded, ibid.; Marshall to Martin Luther King, Jr., Oct. 16, 1963, King Papers.

60. DeLoach to Mohr, July 2, 1964, no. 44-25790-5, FBI–NLG Files; *Cong. Record*, 88 Cong., 2 sess., July 22, 1964, pp. 16593-97.

61. Barkan, *Protestors*, 41–46; Greenberg interview. From the Inc. Fund's perspective, the problem was with SNCC. "Initially, we represented them very readily," Greenberg said. "As time went on they probably didn't want us."

62. Conversations recorded in DeLoach to Mohr, June 10, 1964, no. 100-7321-not recorded, FBI–NLG Files.

63. "Plantiff's Principal Factual Papers," 320–24; Church Committee, *Book III*, 59; *Atlanta Constitution*, Dec. 28, 1979. Crockett won election to the Recorder's Court and eventually won a seat in the U.S. House of Represen-

tatives. Hundreds of FBI informants reported on NLG members over the years, and a few of them sat on the executive boards of the major chapters. As late as September 1979 the FBI forwarded some four hundred pages of documents on the Guild to Senator Strom Thurmond in connection with a nomination for a federal judgeship. Thurmond specifically requested data on the executive board of the Detroit chapter for the years 1960–1965. "Plantiff's Principal Factual Papers," 390–92.

64. James F. Bland to Sullivan, June 24, 1964, no. 105-1913-362, FBI–NLG Files; UPI ticker, June 23, 1964, no. 105-1913-362, ibid.; Director to Attorney General, June 25, 1964, no. 105-1913-360, ibid.; memo, re Martin Popper, June 24, 1964, no. 105-1913-360, ibid.; Hoover to Jenkins, June 25, 1964, no. 105-1913-361, ibid.
65. SAC New York to Director, Aug. 10, 1964, no. not recorded, FBI–CIRM File (100-3-116).
66. Courtney A. Evans to Belmont, July 3, 1964, no. 44-25706-473, FBI–NLG Files. Hoover scribbled his comments on this memo.
67. Kennedy to Johnson, May 21, 1964, WHCF, Ex HU2, Box 2, Johnson Papers.
68. Forman, *Making*, 381–82.
69. Ibid.
70. Ibid.; Arthur M. Schlesinger, Jr., to author, June 11, 1986.
71. For the Bingham family, see Miller, *Fathers and Sons*.
72. The FBI, nonetheless, considered Schlesinger a parlor revolutionary. Belmont to Boardman, April 4, 1958, no. 1060, FBI–Winchell File (62-31615).
73. Forman interview.
74. Clifford Oral History, 39–41; Hoover to Tolson et al., Sept. 2, 1965, no. 1792X, FBI–Robert Kennedy File. Hoover began collecting information on Kennedy's campaign team as early as August 25, but there is no evidence that he interfered with Kennedy's Senate bid.
75. H. N. Bassett to Nicholas P. Callahan, Jan. 29, 1975, in Church Committee, *Hearings—FBI*, 503.
76. Schlesinger, *Robert Kennedy*, 692.
77. Evans to Belmont, Aug. 25, 1964, no. 1648, FBI–Robert Kennedy File. For DeLoach, see Ungar, *FBI*, 279–80, 287–89, 291–92; the documents in WHCF, Name File (Cartha DeLoach), Johnson Papers; Roche, McPherson interviews.
78. E. T. Turner to W. A. Branigan, Aug. 23, 1964, no. 440, FBI–King File; DeLoach to Mohr, Aug. 29, 1964, in Church Committee, *Hearings—FBI*, 495–502; DeLoach to Jenkins, Aug. 25, 1964, ibid., 715–16. See also ibid., 20–21, 175–78; idem, *Book III*, 335, *Book II*, 117 n575; Wise, *American Police State*, 288–91.
79. Wise, *American Police State*, 288.
80. See the sources cited in note 78.
81. Lee C. White to the President, Aug. 13, 1964, WHCF, PL1/St24, Box 81, Johnson Papers; Moyers to the President, Aug. 19, 1964, WHCF, Ex HU2/St24, Box 27, Johnson Papers.
82. Rauh Oral History, 15; Rauh interview.
83. White to the President, Aug. 19, 1964, WHCF, PL1/St24, Box 81, Johnson Papers; DeLoach to Jenkins, Aug. 25, 1964, in Church Committee, *Hearings—FBI*, 717; DeLoach to Mohr, Aug. 29, 1964, ibid., 498–99; Bassett to

Callahan, Jan. 29, 1975, ibid., 505–6; idem, *Book II*, 118–19, *Book III*, 347–49.

84. DeLoach to Jenkins, Aug. 25, 1964, in Church Committee, *Hearings—FBI*, 714–16; DeLoach to Mohr, Aug. 29, 1964, ibid., 495.

85. Bassett to Callahan, Jan. 29, 1975, ibid., 503–7; DeLoach to Mohr, Aug. 29, 1964, ibid., 496–97. See also ibid., 175, 178.

86. Bassett to Callahan, Jan. 29, 1975, ibid., 508–9 (for Jenkins's phone call); DeLoach to Mohr, Aug. 29, 1964, ibid., 502 (for Hoover's comment); DeLoach to Moyers, Sept. 10, 1964, WHCF, Name File (Cartha DeLoach), Box 117, Johnson Papers.

87. Katzenbach to the President, Feb. 14, 1966, WHCF, Ex HU2/St24, Box 27, Johnson Papers; MFDP Fact Sheet, n.d., [ca. Oct. 30, 1964], in WHCF, Name File (Miss. F-K), ibid.; Guyot interview. Forman, Lewis, Hamer, and seven other SNCC staffers traveled to Africa before returning to Mississippi.

88. Wilkins, *Standing*, 306; "Mississippi Freedom Democratic Party," 46 (for Edwin King); Rauh Oral History, 11; White, *Making of the President 1960*, 133.

89. SAC Jackson to Director and SAC Chicago, Sept. 5, 1968, no. 54-5, FBI–COINTEL (New Left) File; Hoover to Tolson, DeLoach, Bishop, and Sullivan, Aug. 16, 1968, no. not recorded, FBI–Humphrey File (62-77485); Church Committee, *Hearings–FBI*, 732–37, 756–59; Sullivan, *Bureau*, 159. Only one delegate, Kenneth Dean, then director of the Mississippi Council on Human Relations, has admitted to having a relationship with the FBI. He reported on convention activities under the code name "Mr. Magnolia," but denies that he was an informant.

90. Raines, *My Soul*, 265, 267.

91. Jones to DeLoach, March 22, 1965, no. X16, FBI–Forman File (100-443566); Jones to DeLoach, March 16, 1965, no. not recorded, FBI–Wilkins File (62-78270).

92. Church Committee, *Book III*, 334; Katzenbach to Harry C. McPherson, Jr., Sept. 17, 1966, Civil Rights(2), Box 22, White House Aides' Files—Harry McPherson, Johnson Papers.

93. Rosen to Belmont, June 7, 1965, no. deleted, June 17, 1965, no. deleted, FBI–Bronstein File (File no. also deleted); John de J. Pemberton, Jr., to Katzenbach, June 10, 1965, no. deleted, ibid.; Director to Attorney General, June 18, 1965, no. deleted, ibid.

94. Fleischer interview.

95. Marshall, *Federalism and Civil Rights*, 81.

96. Berry, *Amazing Grace*, 322–23.

CHAPTER 6.
Klan Wars

1. "The emphasis on all the intelligence investigations is to hit the left hard," former FBI agent Arthur Murtagh charged. "The only time they investigated the Klan was when there was actual murder." House Select Committee on Intelligence, *Hearings*, pt. 3, p. 1,067.

2. Cartha D. DeLoach to John P. Mohr, Dec. 2, 1964, no. 634, FBI–King File (100-106670); Hoover, "Off-the-Record Remarks."

3. James H. Gale to Alan H. Belmont, March 17, 1965, no. X14, FBI–Forman File (100-443566) (for Katzenbach); Young Oral History, 26.

4. Garrow, *Protest at Selma.*

5. The director's conversations with the attorney general are summarized in J. Edgar Hoover to Clyde Tolson, Belmont, DeLoach, and Alex Rosen, March 23, 1965, no. not recorded, FBI–Tolson Memo File (67-9524); Hoover to Tolson, Belmont, DeLoach, Gale, Rosen, and William C. Sullivan, March 12, 1965, no. not recorded, ibid.; Hoover to Tolson, Belmont, Rosen, Sullivan, and DeLoach, Feb. 19, 1965, no. not recorded, ibid.

6. Hoover to Tolson, Belmont, DeLoach, and Rosen, March 26, 1965, no. 15 and 16, FBI–Liuzzo File (44-2860) (for the director's conversations with the attorney general and the president); Belmont to Director, March 26, 1965, no. 33, ibid.

7. Marshall Oral History, 35–37, Bunche Collection.

8. Leinbaugh interview; Hoover, "Off-the-Record Remarks."

9. For the COINTELPROs, see Senate Select Committee to Study . . . Intelligence Activities (hereafter Church Committee), *Book III*, 3–77.

10. Gale to Tolson, July 30, 1964, no. 3, FBI–COINTEL (White) File; Whitehead, *Attack*, 91; Sullivan, *Bureau*, 127.

11. Gale to Tolson, July 30, 1964, no. 3, FBI–COINTEL (White).

12. SAC Chicago to Director, June 4, 1965, no. 5756, FBI–HUAC File (61-7582); Church Committee, *Book III*, 334.

13. Fred J. Baumgardner to Sullivan, Aug. 27, 1964, no. 2, Dec. 16, 1965, no. 21, FBI–COINTEL (White) File; Director to SACs Atlanta et al., Sept. 2, 1964, no. 1, ibid.; Gale to Tolson, July 30, 1964, no. 3, ibid.; Director to SACs Los Angeles et al., Dec. 17, 1965, no. 20, ibid.; Sullivan, *Bureau*, 127–28.

14. Donner, *Age*, 207; DeLoach to Mohr, Dec. 2, 1964, no. 634, FBI–King File.

15. Burke Marshall to Attorney General, Nov. 13, 1963, Special Correspondence, Attorney General, Box 3, Marshall Papers.

16. Katzenbach interview; Church Committee, *Hearings—FBI*, 213; Director to Attorney General, Sept. 2, 1965, Dec. 19, 1967, ibid., 513–14, 519; Nicholas deB. Katzenbach to Hoover, Sept. 3, 1965, ibid., 515; Hoover to Tolson, Belmont, DeLoach, Gale, Rosen and Sullivan, March 12, 1965, no. not recorded, FBI–Tolson Memo File.

17. DeLoach to Mohr, Dec. 2, 1964, no. 634, FBI–King File; Welch, *Inside*, 105; Ungar, *FBI*, 415; Director to SAC Jackson, Sept. 6, 1966, no. 54-38, FBI–COINTEL (White) File.

18. Charles D. Brennan to Sullivan, March 31, 1967, no. 8-83, FBI–COINTEL (White) File; SAC Charlotte to Director, Oct. 14, 1966, no. 8-61, Nov. 1, 1966, no. 8-66, ibid.; Director to SAC Charlotte, Oct. 19, 1966, no. 8-61, ibid.

19. Baumgardner to Sullivan, March 10, 1966, no. 24, April 20, 1966, no. 31, Aug. 9, 1966, no. 10-15, ibid.; Director to SACs Dallas et al., May 12, 1966, no. 28, ibid.; George C. Moore to Sullivan, Sept. 24, 1968, no. illegible, ibid.; Director to SAC Birmingham, Aug. 26, 1970, no. 4-162, ibid.; Hoover to Office of Management and Evaluation, Nov. 9, 1964, no. 2-11X, ibid.

20. Director to SAC Birmingham, Feb. 4, 1966, no. 4-40, ibid.; SAC Jackson to Director, April 14, 1965, no. 54-4, April 21, 1966, no. 54-25, Jan. 28, 1965, no. 6, Oct. 20, 1965, no. 54-14, ibid.; Baumgardner to Sullivan, May 19, 1965, no. illegible, ibid.

21. Baumgardner to Sullivan, April 23, 1965, no. 318, FBI–SCLC File (100-438794); Cobb interview.

22. DeLoach to Mohr, March 12, 1965, no. 5656, March 22, 1965, no. 5649, June

17, 1965, no. 5762, FBI–HUAC File; Baumgardner to Sullivan, March 12, 1965, no. 5657, June 25, 1965, no. 5763 ("digging" quote), June 25, 1965, no. 5657, ibid.; "The Klan Today," March 12, 1965, no. 5657, ibid.; Director to SAC Atlanta, July 14, 1965, no. 5784, ibid.

23. Rosen to Belmont, March 5, 1965, no. 378, FBI–Penn File (44-25873); Tully, *FBI's Most Famous Cases*, 205–11. See also Shipp, *Murder*.

24. The FBI also opened a file on the Deacons for Defense and Justice, one of the first black self-defense groups that had been formed in Bogalusa and environs in February 1965, and sent reports on this "gun-carrying black vigilante group" to "appropriate . . . authorities in the state of Louisiana." See serials 5, 12, 23, 111, FBI–Deacons for Defense and Justice File (157-2466).

25. Director to Attorney General, Dec. 19, 1967, and the accompanying memo, re Ku Klux Klan Investigations, Dec. 19, 1967, in Church Committee, *Hearings—FBI*, 516–27.

26. Schlesinger, *Robert Kennedy*, 266.

27. Franklin L. Dodge to Thomas J. Walsh, Feb. 2, 1927, Investigations, Dept. of Justice (1), Box 278, Walsh Papers; Edward J. Brennan to Dodge, Nov. 22, 1920, ibid; memo, re Facts Furnished, Jan. 21, 1927, ibid. See also Joseph E. Bayliss to Carl Mapes, March 26, 1929, Cabinet Offices, Justice, FBI (1929), Pres. Papers, Herbert Hoover Papers.

28. Louis B. Nichols to Tolson, Oct. 4, 1940, no. 676, FBI–Cooper File (94-3-4-20); William Allen White to Hoover, Dec. 11, 1940, Correspondence, J. Edgar Hoover, Series C, Box 343, White Papers; and the voluminous, if mostly perfunctory, correspondence in Box 29, Barton Papers.

29. Church Committee, *Hearings—FBI*, 88.

30. Buchanan, *Right*, 283; SAC Letter, July 16, 1963, FBI–SAC File; Attorney General to the President, Jan. 9, 1962, President's Office Files, Depts. and Agencies–Justice, Box 80, John Kennedy Papers. The president mentioned the FBI, but only in connection with "organized crime, racketeering, and youth delinquency."

31. DeLoach to Mohr, Feb. 4, 1964, no. 94-8-350-129, FBI–McSurely Files.

32. Stone interview.

33. DeLoach to Mohr, Dec. 8, 1964, no. 126, FBI–Lawrence File (94-4-3169); Hoover to Tolson, Mohr, and DeLoach, Dec. 8, 1964, no. 127, ibid.; Thomas E. Bishop to DeLoach, Sept. 6, 1967, no. 136, ibid.; Milton A. Jones to DeLoach, June 2, 1964, no. 1194, FBI–Winchell File (62-31613); John [Hoover] to Walter Winchell, Oct. 15, 1964, no. 1222, ibid.

34. Hoover to Tolson, Belmont, Rosen, and DeLoach, Nov. 24, 1965, no. 635, FBI–Liuzzo File; Belmont to Tolson, Aug. 31, 1965, no. not recorded, FBI–COINTEL (White) File; Hoover to Karl E. Mundt, Jan. 17, 1966, Box 167(6), Mundt Papers; Barron, "FBI's Secret War," 87–92.

35. Tully, *FBI's Most Famous Cases*, 205–30; Hoover, "Resurgent Klan," 617–20; Overstreet, *FBI in Our Open Society*; Sentner, *How the FBI Gets Its Man*; Adler, *Kids' Letters*.

36. DeLoach to Walter Trohan, June 9, 1961, Correspondence, Cartha DeLoach, Trohan Papers; Nichols to Mrs. Fulton Oursler, Aug. 3, 1955, no. 227, FBI–Oursler File (94-4-692); Grace Oursler to Nichols, Aug. 5, 1955, no. 228, ibid.; Heim interview.

37. DeLoach to Mohr, Nov. 3, 1964, no. not recorded, FBI–Lewis File (94-4-2189).

38. Heim interview; Sullivan, *Bureau*, 93; Jones to DeLoach, Feb. 9, 1965, no. not recorded, FBI–King File.

39. Rauh interview; *Washington Post*, Nov. 26, 1950; *Cong. Record*, 81 Cong., 2 sess., Nov. 30, 1950, pp. A7,342–50.

40. Thomas J. Jenkins to Richard Baker, March 5, 1973, no. not recorded, FBI–Civil Rights Policy File (44-00).

41. Martin Luther King, Jr., to DeLoach, Dec. 6, 1965, King Papers; Bishop, *Confessions*, 402; Guthman, Rauh interviews; Young Oral History, 26.

42. Sherrill, "Selling," 18–19.

43. Jones to DeLoach, Sept. 8, 1961, no. 37, FBI–Wilson File (94-42524); Executive Vice President, Warner Brothers, to DeLoach, Dec. 11, 1964, no. 1, FBI Television Series Agreement Folder, FBI–Hoover O&C Files.

44. The star, Efrem Zimbalist, Jr. ("Inspector Erskine"), presented the image of a "housebroken G-man." ABC wanted "a more adult approach," including "bigger and longer action sequences in which Inspector Erskine does not always get his man with one shot." Quinn Martin also asked the FBI to liberalize its name-check activities. The "derogatory information" the Bureau uncovered on "actors, actresses, writers, and directors" had led to a mini-blacklist of "a number of name personalities who could help the show." Assistant Director in Charge Los Angeles to Acting Director, Feb. 1, 1973, no. 4, FBI Television Series Agreement Folder, FBI–Hoover O&C Files; Brownfield to Jenkins, Feb. 6, 1973, no. 4, ibid.

45. DeLoach and Hoover are quoted in Jones to DeLoach, Nov. 19, 1964, no. 124, Dec. 1, 1964, no. 125, Dec. 2, 1964, no. 126, FBI–Whitehead File (77-68662).

46. Jones to Bishop, April 23, 1968, no. X, Aug. 26, 1969, no. not recorded, Sept. 17, 1969, no. 3, April 14, 1970, no. 8, May 21, 1970, no. 9, June 25, 1970, no. 11, July 20, 1970, no. 94, Aug. 25, 1970, no. 20, Jan. 31, 1972, no. 23, ibid. (94-64866); SAC Letter, Sept. 1, 1970, no. not recorded, ibid. (94-64866).

47. *New York Times*, Feb. 20 and 22, 1975; J. H. Campbell to George C. Moore, Sept. 12, 1975, no. not recorded, FBI–Whitehead File (94-64866); Schwerner, "Mississippi," 15.

48. Radio broadcast of April 7, noted in Jones to DeLoach, April 7, 1965, no. 518, FBI–Lewis File.

49. Wechsler, "FBI's Failure," 20–23; Clark Oral History, 29. For King's comments, see DeLoach to Mohr, March 28, 1965, no. not recorded, FBI–Liuzzo File; Schlesinger, *Robert Kennedy*, 669.

50. Doar interview, in Rafferty Papers; Leinbaugh interview; C. B. Stanberry to SAC Birmingham, Oct. 31, 1960, no. 137-00-165, FBI–Bergman Freedom Rider Files (for Baumgardner). The Laurel agent is quoted in Whitehead, *Attack*, 23.

51. Paraphrased in Stanberry to SAC Birmingham, Oct. 31, 1960, no. 137-00-165, FBI–Bergman Files. For Rowe's account of his life and times, see *My Undercover Years;* his deposition of Oct. 17, 1975, before the Church Committee; Church Committee, *Hearings—FBI*, 115–31.

52. SAC Birmingham to Director, Nov. 5, 1960, no. 170-9-64, FBI–Alabama Freedom Rider Files; SAC Birmingham to Director and SAC Mobile, May 14, 1961, no. 149-1684-2, ibid.; Barrett G. Kemp to SAC Birmingham, May 17, 1961, no. 149-16-62, FBI–Bergman Files; Rowe deposition, 10.

53. *New York Times*, Feb. 17 and 18, 1980; Church Committee, *Book II*, 13. See also the informant reports in FBI–Alabama Files.

54. Katzenbach to Hoover, Sept. 3, 1965, no. 16, FBI–COINTEL (White) File; Director to Attorney General, Sept. 2, 1965, no. 15, ibid.; Hoover to Marvin Watson, Sept. 2, 1965, no. not recorded, ibid.; Church Committee, *Hearings—FBI*, 18; *New York Times*, July 9, 11, and 14, 1978.

55. Church Committee, *Book III*, 252; McIlhany, *Klandestine*, 60–61.

56. L. E. Rogers to Robert F. Kennedy, Dec. 14, 1966, Legislative Series, Un-American (1965), Box U1, Russell Papers.

57. Hoover to Tolson, Belmont, DeLoach, and Rosen, March 26, 1965, no. 15, and 16, FBI–Liuzzo File.

58. White interview.

59. Director to Attorney General, March 26, 1965, no. 1, FBI–Liuzzo File; Rosen to Belmont, April 5, 1965, no. 162, ibid.; Detroit Field Office Rept., April 1, 1965, no. not recorded, ibid.; Mobile Field Office Rept., April 1, 1965, no. not recorded, ibid.

60. Letterhead memos, March 29, 1965, no. 48, Jan. 17, 1966, no. 684, ibid.; Rosen to Belmont, June 28, 1965, no. 407, ibid.

61. Quoted in Jones to DeLoach, April 1, 1965, no. not recorded, FBI–King File.

62. SAC Detroit to Director, May 12, 1965, no. 354, May 17, 1965, no. 351, FBI–Liuzzo File; DeLoach to Mohr, March 28, 1965, no. not recorded, ibid.

63. SAC Mobile to Director, May 4, 1965, no. 277, ibid.; Director to Attorney General, April 2, 1965, no. 110, ibid.

64. The director's assessment, as recorded in Hoover to Tolson, Belmont, De-Loach, Rosen, and Sullivan, May 7, 1965, no. 302, ibid.

65. Clement L. McGowan, Jr., to Rosen, March 27, 1965, no. 23, ibid.; SAC Mobile to Director and SAC Birmingham, March 27, 1965, no. 108, ibid.

66. McGowan to Rosen, May 8, 1965, no. illegible, ibid.; Morgan, *One Man*, 37.

67. Hanes interview; Hoover to Tolson, DeLoach, Rosen, Bishop, and Sullivan, June 20, 1968, no. 44-38861-4660, in House Select Committee on Assassinations, *Hearings—King*, vol. 7, p. 88; Rosen to Belmont, Oct. 13, 1965, no. 497, FBI–Liuzzo File; note, CDC, no. 444, ibid.; Jones to DeLoach, Aug. 24, 1965, no. 441, ibid.

68. Hoover to Tolson, Belmont, DeLoach, and Rosen, March 26, 1965, no. 16, Nov. 24, 1965, no. 635, FBI–Liuzzo File; Rosen to Belmont, March 30, 1965, no. 158, ibid.; Hoover to Tolson, Belmont, DeLoach, Rosen, and Robert E. Wick, Dec. 3, 1965, no. 617, ibid.

69. SAC Birmingham to Director, Dec. 13, 1966, no. 769, ibid.; Rosen to De-Loach, Dec. 22, 1966, no. 774, ibid.; DeLoach to John Doar, Dec. 23, 1966, no. 774, ibid.

70. The court of appeals upheld the conviction of the surviving defendants on April 27, 1967.

71. Director to Attorney General, Dec. 27, 1965, no. 676, FBI–Liuzzo File.

72. Katzenbach to Joseph A. Califano, Jr., Dec. 13, 1965, Civil Rights 1965 (1), White House Aides' Files—Harry McPherson, Johnson Papers.

73. Conversations summarized in Hoover to Tolson, Belmont, DeLoach, Rosen, and Wick, Dec. 3, 1965, no. 617, Nov. 24, 1965, no. 635, FBI–Liuzzo File.

74. Church Committee, *Book III*, 474.

75. Moore interview; Hoover to Tolson et al., March 25, 1966, no. not recorded, FBI–Tolson Memo File.

76. SAC Letters, April 30, 1968, Nov. 10, 1969, FBI–SAC File. See also Church Committee, *Hearings—FBI*, 679–80, *Book III*, 474–75.

77. Hoover, "Off-the-Record Remarks."

78. Sullivan interview.

79. A number of other embarrassing, tragic incidents followed. The most notable occurred in 1968, when the FBI and police officers in Meridian, Mississippi, paid $36,500 to two Klansmen as part of a plot to entice two other Klansmen to bomb the home of a Jewish businessman. One of the suspects showed up, unexpectedly accompanied by a woman—Kathy Ainsworth. A shoot-out followed, leaving the man wounded and Ainsworth dead. Hoover responded, in part, by gathering intelligence on Jack Nelson and other reporters who criticized the Bureau's judgment.

80. Morgan, *One Man*, 37–38.

81. *Conspiracy*, ed. Raines, 157–58; Marshall interview.

82. This is not to minimize more recent racist violence. In 1985 alone the FBI devoted "52 agent-years of attention" to the Aryan Nation investigation. Ungar, "F.B.I. On the Defensive," 78.

83. One FBI agent said the victims of Klan violence should have sued the city of Birmingham and its police department and not the FBI.

84. Greene, "Did the FBI Kill Viola Liuzzo?," 100ff.

85. Rowe deposition, 8.

CHAPTER 7.
White Backlash

1. McPherson, *Political Education*, 377.

2. Goodwin, "War Within," 42, *Remembering America*, 392–416.

3. Clark Oral History, 22; Milton A. Jones to Cartha D. DeLoach, March 16, 1965, no. not recorded, FBI–Wilkins File. In May 1964, Princeton historian Eric F. Goldman, one of the White House advisers who did think of civil rights in the North, pondered "the breakaway from the established organizations of the more irresponsible Negroes"—warning LBJ of the need for the administration to "re-establish control and keep the movement going in its legitimate direction." Otherwise, cities in the North would burn, a development which would "present a weapon to the Republicans in the election." Eric F. Goldman to the President, May 4, 1964, WHCF, Ex LE/HU2, Box 65, Johnson Papers.

4. The riots also had foreign policy implications. Dean Rusk to All Diplomatic and Consular Posts, July 18, 1964, Civil Rights (vol. 1), National Security File—Subject File, Johnson Papers.

5. "'Violence in our streets,'" political commentator Richard Rovere wrote, was Goldwater's "number-two issue. It came hard on the heels of 'the wall of shame in Berlin, [and] the sands of shame at the Bay of Pigs, [and] the slow death of freedom in Laos.'" *Goldwater Caper*, 85.

6. Wills, *Reagan's America*, 290; Greenfield, "Senator Goldwater," 27; "'Backlash' Issue," 24; *New York Times*, July 17, 18, 21, and 25, 1964; White, *Making of the President 1964*, 332–33n.

7. Task Force, *Prevention of Violence*, 224–25; Horowitz, "Alienation," 173–200; de Toledano, "Negro Minority," 814–15; Croce, "Backlash in New York?," 816–17; Wheeler, "Backlash in California?," 817; Wills, "Who Will Overcome?," 818–20.

8. King is quoted in Fred J. Baumgardner to William C. Sullivan, May 11, 1964, no. not recorded, FBI–King File (100-106670); White in *Making of the President 1960*, 203; Young in Andrew Young to Martin Luther King, Jr., Oct. 21, 1963, Box. 35:15, King Papers.

9. Schlesinger, *Robert Kennedy*, 657; DeLoach to J. Edgar Hoover, Sept. 9, 1964, no. 42, Riots Summer 1964 Folder, FBI–Hoover O&C Files.

10. DeLoach to Hoover, Sept. 9, 1964, no. 42, Riots Summer 1964 Folder, FBI–Hoover O&C Files.

11. The Bureau also sent over intelligence on two "white kids" riots that occurred over the Labor Day weekend in Seaside, Oregon, and Hampton, New Hampshire. "The President felt free to move in strongly," Dewey reasoned, according to Hoover's account, "because he had a couple of white riots to deal with." Hoover to Clyde Tolson, Alan H. Belmont, Alex Rosen, Sullivan, and DeLoach, Sept. 10, 1964, no. 54, Riots Summer 1964 Folder, FBI–Hoover O&C Files.

12. Goldwater had enough problems with disaffected Republicans operating in the sunshine. Goldwater, *With No Apologies*, 179.

13. Hoover to Tolson, Belmont, Rosen, Sullivan, and DeLoach, July 22, 1964, no. not recorded, FBI–King File; Hoover to Tolson, Belmont, Rosen, Sullivan, and DeLoach, Sept. 16, 1964, no. 52, Riots Summer 1964 Folder, FBI–Hoover O&C Files; Dick Nelson to Walter Jenkins, July 13, 1964, WHCF, Name File (Thomas E. Dewey), Box 161, Johnson Papers; Katzenbach interview.

14. Hoover to Tolson and Louis B. Nichols, April 27, 1948, no. 1 and 2, FBI–Nichols O&C Files; Sullivan, *Bureau*, 41, 44.

15. Conversations summarized in Hoover to Tolson, Belmont, Rosen, Sullivan, and DeLoach, Sept. 10, 1964, no. 22, Sept. 15, 1964, no. 54, Riots Summer 1964 Folder, FBI–Hoover O&C Files. See also Hoover to Thomas E. Dewey, Sept. 10, 1964, no. 9, and the accompanying blind memo, ibid.

16. Hoover to Tolson, Belmont, Rosen, Sullivan, and DeLoach, Sept. 15, 1964, no. 54, ibid.

17. In Philadelphia, Pennsylvania, for instance, city police arrested two SNCC workers and one CORE worker who had been at the boardwalk demonstrations in Atlantic City and were then on their way to Mississippi. The FBI ran name checks and consulted records at the University of Chicago (where one of the movement people was a student), the New York, Philadelphia, and Jackson police departments, and the House Committee on Un-American Activities. Philadelphia Field Office Rept., Sept. 9, 1964, no. 6, ibid.

18. Memo, re Communist Involvement in Racial Disturbances, Sept. 14, 1964, no. not recorded, ibid.; James F. Bland to Sullivan, Sept. 10, 1964, no. 4, ibid.; Hoover to Tolson, Mohr, and DeLoach, Dec. 8, 1964, no. 127, FBI–Lawrence File (94-9-3169).

19. Hoover to Tolson, Belmont, Rosen, Sullivan, and DeLoach, July 21, 1964, no. not recorded, FBI–King File.

20. White House staff and the president himself had only a few "nit-picking" objections to the report. "They took exception particularly to page four," Hoover advised his aides, "wherein the word 'Negro' is used three times and they felt that was overdoing it." Ironically, the FBI had once tried to discredit the Communist party by publicizing its frequent use of the word "Negro" as opposed to "Afro-American." SAC New York to Director,

March 24, 1961, no. 2439, FBI–COINTEL (CPUSA) File (100-3-104); Director to SAC New York, April 4, 1961, no. 2439, ibid.

21. "F.B.I. Report," 119; Wilkins, *Standing*, 304; *New York Times*, Sept 27, 1964 (for the report itself); *National Review*, Oct. 13, 1964, p. 1.

22. *New York Times*, Sept. 27, 1964; Senate Select Committee to Study . . . Intelligence Activities (hereafter Church Committee), *Book III*, 475. Johnson sought Hoover's endorsement from the beginning, asking him to comment on the proposed war-on-poverty speech. DeLoach to Mohr, March 10, 1964, no. 29, Johnson Folder, FBI–Hoover O&C Files.

23. *New York Times*, Sept. 27, 1964; Church Committee, *Book III*, 475.

24. Church Committee, *Book III*, 475–76; Director to SACs Albany et al., Aug. 20, 1964, no. 76, Sept. 8, 1964, no. 77, FBI–Racial Matters Policy File (157-00).

25. In March 1965 Johnson administration recruiters proposed another mission for Dewey. "How about asking him to come see you now," Bill Moyers suggested, "to discuss the crime problem. It might [also] help what with Nixon running around the way he is to have Dewey briefed on foreign policy." This time, Dewey declined. Dewey to the President, May 20, 1965, WHCF, Name File (Thomas E. Dewey), Box 161, Johnson Papers; William D. Moyers to the President, March 5, 1965, ibid.

26. Hoover to Jenkins, Oct. 1, 1964, WHCF, FG135-6, Box 188, Johnson Papers; "Prevention and Control of Riots," 70–76.

27. Hoover, "From Herbert Hoover," 144; Kearns, *Lyndon Johnson*, 305.

28. Wilkins, *Man's Life*, 166; Jacobs, *Prelude*, 13–60.

29. Katzenbach to the President, Aug. 17, 1965, WHCF, FG135-6, Box 188, Johnson Papers; Church Committee, *Book II*, 83, *Book III*, 490.

30. Conversations recorded in DeLoach to Mohr, Nov. 10, 1965, no. not recorded, FBI–King File.

31. Louis Martin to Marvin Watson, May 20, 1966, Civil Rights, Negroes (2), Box 18, White House Aides' Files—Marvin Watson, Johnson Papers; Baumgardner to Sullivan, Nov. 8, 1965, no. not recorded, FBI–SCLC File.

32. Hoover to Tolson, DeLoach, Sullivan, and Robert E. Wick, April 27, 1967, no. not recorded, FBI–King File.

33. Douglass Cater to the President, July 26, 1967, WHCF, Ex HU2, Box 5, Johnson Papers; Joseph J. Casper to Mohr, Sept. 7, 1967, no. 15-2145, FBI–Detroit Riot File (157-6); Hoover to Tolson, DeLoach, Sullivan, and Wick, July 27, 1967, no. 961, ibid.; Director to Attorney General, July 28, 1967, no. 967, ibid.; Hoover to Mildred Stegall, July 28, 1967, no. 988, ibid.

34. Hoover to Tolson, DeLoach, Sullivan, and Wick, July 26, 1967, no. 971, FBI–Detroit Riot File.

35. A January 1966 SNCC statement, signed by John Lewis and calling upon all young American men "to seek work in the civil rights movement as a 'valid alternative to the draft,'" threw the White House into a panic. Lewis suspected that the FBI responded by instigating a change in his own draft classification as a conscientious objector. When Burke Marshall intervened, Lewis received a 4-F deferment. "They said I was morally unfit," he recalled, because of a long civil rights arrest record. Another SNCC veteran, Robert Moses, who withdrew from an active role in the organization in 1965, also received a 1-A classification. Like Lewis, he suspected the FBI had visited his draft board.

36. Williams, *Empire*, 201.
37. An OEO official briefed the FBI on the episode. D. J. Brennan, Jr., to Sullivan, March 30, 1967, no. 180, FBI–McSurely Files (62-109683).
38. The secretary to the cabinet conceded that the administration's methods were similar to the methods of the late Senator Joseph R. McCarthy. Robert E. Kintner to the President, May 18, 1967, WHCF—CF, HU4, Box 57, Johnson Papers.
39. Lovin, "Lyndon B. Johnson," 567.
40. Hoover to Tolson, DeLoach, and Sullivan, July 25, 1967, No. 958 and 959, FBI–Detroit Riot File.
41. Ibid.; Hoover to Stegall, July 26, 1967, no. 2X, FBI–Hobson File (157-3707).
42. Director to Attorney General, July 26, 1967, no. 965, and the attached report, FBI–Detroit Riot File.
43. When Johnson pushed the FBI to find communist conspirators at the roots of the urban riots, Hoover resisted—largely because he agreed with the law-and-order advocates that liberal permissivists were the real culprits. On the issue of communist infiltration of the antiwar movement, Hoover needed no pushing.
44. Baumgardner to Sullivan, July 7, 1965, no. 1555, Aug. 16, 1965, no. 1768, Sept. 15, 1965, no. 1858, FBI–King File; letterhead memos, Sept. 15, 1965, no. 1866, Sept. 16, 1965, no. 1858, ibid.; Hoover to Rusk, July 7, 1965, no. 1538, ibid.; Hoover to Tolson, Belmont, Sullivan, and DeLoach, July 6, 1965, no. 1551, ibid. King even attracted the benign attention of Henry Kissinger, who invited him to participate in the international seminar at Harvard. King declined. Henry Kissinger to King, June 3, 1965, Henry Kissinger Folder, Box 14.5, King Papers; King to Kissinger, June 16, 1965, ibid.
45. DeLoach to Mohr, Aug. 14, 1965, no. 1782, FBI–King File; Bland to Sullivan, Sept. 20, 1965, no. 257, FBI–Levison File (100-392452); Thomas J. Dodd to Robert F. Kennedy, n.d. [ca. Aug. 29, 1962], Albany Movement Aug. 1962, Box 1:27, King Papers; Dodd to King, Aug. 31, 1962, ibid.
46. See the notation on UPI ticker, Dec. 7, 1966, no. 2796, FBI–King File.
47. George C. Moore to Sullivan, Oct. 18, 1967, no. 3129, ibid.; Garrow, *Bearing*, 555; Lewis Oral History, 157.
48. Hoover to Stegall, June 18, 1968, no. 2198, FBI–SCLC File; Hoover to Stegall, April 19, 1967, no. 2893, FBI–King File; Marvin [Watson] to the President, May 16, 1967, WHCF—CF, HU4, Box 57, Johnson Papers; Fairclough, "Martin Luther King," 19; Lawson, *In Pursuit of Power*, 8.
49. Cone, "Martin Luther King," 462; Garrow, *Bearing*, 564, 581.
50. Wilkins, *Man's Life*, 230–31.
51. Hoover to Tolson and Sullivan, Aug. 2, 1967, no. 985, FBI–Detroit Riot File.
52. Richard Helms to Walt W. Rostow, Aug. 9, 1967, National Security File—Subject File, Civil Rights and Antiwar Personalities, Johnson Papers; Rostow to the President, July 27, 1967, ibid.; W. G. Bowdler to Rostow, Aug. 3, 1967, ibid.; Kintner to the President, May 18, 1967, WHCF—CF, HU4, Box 57, Johnson Papers; Kintner to Attorney General, May 19, 1967, ibid.
53. Note, TJS, Sept. 16, 1967, no. 15-2159, FBI–Detroit Riot File; Ramsey Clark to Director, Sept. 14, 1967, in Church Committee, *Hearings—FBI*, 528–30.
54. Joseph A. Sullivan to Director, Aug. 2, 1966, no. not recorded, FBI–Racial Matters File. Hoover scribbled his comment on this document.
55. SAC Letter, Aug. 15, 1967, FBI–SAC File.

56. Director to SAC Detroit, Sept. 6, 1967, no. not recorded, FBI–Detroit Riot File (157-6); Moore to Sullivan, July 25, 1967, no. 1937, FBI–SCLC File; R. W. Smith to Sullivan, Aug. 8, 1967, no. 1386, FBI–SNCC File (100-439190).

57. Baker, May interviews.

58. Ibid.; McKnight, "Harvest," 11.

59. May interview; Hoover to Tolson and Sullivan, Aug. 2, 1968, no. 985, FBI–Detroit Riot File; DeLoach to Tolson, Aug. 3, 1967, no. 15, ibid.; Hoover to Stegall, Aug. 17, 1967, no. 115, FBI–McSurely Files (62-109683); Bland to Sullivan, Aug. 17, 1967, no. 115, ibid.; Marvin [Watson] to the President, Aug. 12, 1967, WHCF, FG135-6, Box 188, Johnson Papers; Larry Levinson to Joseph Califano, April 11, 1968, WHCF, FG135-6, Box 188, ibid.; Sargent Shriver to the President, Aug. 14, 1967, WHCF—CF, HU4, ibid.

60. DeLoach to Tolson, Oct. 11, 1967, no. not recorded, FBI–Young File (161-3190); Baker interview.

61. Bookbinder interview. The FBI, the Manhattan district attorney's office, and OEO itself investigated Haryou for fiscal mismanagement.

62. See the outline of Hoover's testimony, Aug. 1, 1967, in Witness Outline Digest, Box 1, National Advisory Commission on Civil Disorders Records; and the brief Division Five prepared for his use, "Racial Disturbances," Aug. 1, 1967, no. 988, FBI–Detroit Riot File. See also Hoover to File, July 31, 1967, no. not recorded, FBI–Tolson Memo File.

63. It was all part of the way LBJ governed. "[He] appointed 28 presidential commissions and, by rough count, 134 secret task forces in a tour de force of presidential advisement." Graham, "Ambiguous Legacy," 20.

64. McPherson, *Political Education*, 376; Johnson, *Vantage Point*, 173.

65. Donner, *Age*, 283; National Advisory Commission on Civil Disorders, *Report*, 1, 201–2, 487.

66. Cook County Grand Jury, *Improper Police Intelligence Activities*, July 10, 1975; Church Committee, *Book II*, 77.

67. Hoover to Tolson, DeLoach, Rosen, Bishop, and Sullivan, June 20, 1968, no. 4660, FBI–King Assassination File (44-38861). The Kerner Commission itself fed "white racism," according to Harry McPherson, by provoking "the deepest resentment among white workers whose unions had helped to pass the laws of the Great Society. The charge against white racism was true—but so was the bitterness of white families . . . when they were told that they were responsible for the sacking of the cities. . . . The commission had weakened the liberal bloc by charging part of it with crimes against the other." *Political Education*, 376.

68. "Statement of J. Edgar Hoover . . . Before National Commission on the Causes and Prevention of Violence," Sept. 18, 1968, in Church Committee, *Hearings—FBI*, 870–82.

69. Task Force on Violent Aspects of Protest and Confrontation, *Politics of Protest*, 263, 280, 288; Navasky, *Kennedy Justice*, 36. For the Nashville operation, see David Orange to Melvin Bailey, Aug. 22, 1967, Box 30.26, Boutwell Papers.

70. SAC Houston to Director, March 15, 1968, no. 26, FBI–COINTEL (Black Nationalist) File (100-448006).

71. Conversations recorded in DeLoach to Tolson, July 27, 1967, no. 5926, FBI–HUAC File (61-7582); Bishop to DeLoach, Aug. 3, 1967, no. 5928, ibid.

72. Senate Permanent Subcommittee on Investigations, *Hearings on Riots . . .*, pts. 1–25.

73. The FBI filed a report on the prosecutor and someone at OEO leaked the information to the press. Joseph A. Sizoo to Sullivan, Sept. 1, 1967, no. illegible, FBI–McSurely Files (105-164714); D. J. Brennan, Jr., to Sullivan, Sept. 6, 1967, no. 28, ibid.

74. Hoover to Mildred Stegall, Aug. 17, 1967, no. 115, ibid. (62-109683); SAC Louisville to Director, Aug. 14, 1967, no. 14, ibid. (105-164714); Bland to Sullivan, Aug. 28, 1967, no. 16, ibid. (105-164714). For the McSurelys' ordeal, see Harris, *Freedom Spent*, 125–311.

75. James Gaither to Califano, Oct. 17, 1967, White House Aides' File—James Gaither, Pres. Task Forces—Subject File, Riot Control, Poor People's March(1), Box 36, Johnson Papers.

76. Hoover to Tolson, DeLoach, Bishop, and Sullivan, Sept. 19, 1967, no. 1112, FBI–McSurely Files (62-18810).

77. Richard D. Cotter to Sullivan, June 30, 1970, no. 1186, ibid.; Donald F. O'Donnell to Bishop, Nov. 8, 1967, no. 1123, and the attached blind memos, ibid.; SAC Milwaukee to Director, Oct. 3, 1967, no. 1118, ibid.

78. DeLoach to Tolson, Sept. 13, 1967, no. not recorded, ibid.

79. DeLoach to Tolson, Nov. 7, 1967, no. not recorded, ibid.; Bishop to DeLoach, Oct. 12, 1967, no. not recorded, ibid.

80. DeLoach to Tolson, Nov. 7, 1967, no. not recorded, ibid.

81. Graham, "Ambiguous Legacy," 20–21; Bishop to DeLoach, Nov. 22, 1967, no. not recorded, FBI–Robert Kennedy File (77-51387).

82. The FBI had an interest in a number of other sections of the Omnibus Act, especially Section 2511, which pertained to electronic surveillance.

83. SAC Pittsburgh to Director, Dec. 18, 1968, no. 540, FBI–COINTEL (Black) File. The FBI source at the Mellon Foundation furnished "information on a confidential basis relating to . . . requests for financial grants made by various civil rights and racial–type organizations." SAC Pittsburgh to Director, Sept. 24, 1968, no. 2, Oct. 9, 1968, no. 3, FBI–Young File (157-10774).

84. Fleischer interview. When Jack Bass and Jack Nelson were researching a book on the incident, the FBI opened files on both men—and as well those Civil Rights Division attorneys who granted them interviews. Memo, re David Robert Owen, n.d. [ca. Nov. 19, 1970], no. not recorded, FBI–CPJ File (62-113909).

85. Hoover to Tolson, DeLoach, and Wick, July 6, 1966, no. not recorded, FBI–Tolson Memo File (67-9524).

86. Sellers, *River*, 223, 226; Carson, *In Struggle*, 250; *New York Times*, Sept. 29, 1970.

87. Hoover to Tolson, DeLoach, Sullivan, and Wick, July 26, 1967, no. not recorded, FBI–Tolson Memo File; Clark interview. Ultimately, the courts found Brown guilty on a charge of carrying a rifle from New Orleans to New York while under indictment. Another charge had to do with "this ol' negro FBI agent" who "testified against me in court," Brown wrote. "I said to him, 'I hope your children don't grow up to be a Tom like you' . . . The judge charged me with threatening an FBI agent and set $50,000." *Die*, 133.

88. Phillips, *Emerging*, 468, 472; Wills, *Nixon*, 247.

89. See McPherson, *Political Education*, 377: "I was concerned that Johnson, having earned recognition as the country's preeminent civil libertarian, might be forced to become its chief of police."

90. Powers, *Secrecy and Power*, 434; Schell, *Time of Illusion*, 62.

91. Kearns, *Lyndon Johnson*, 305.
92. Nixon, *RN*, 238.
93. Leinbaugh interview.

CHAPTER 8.
Black Hate

1. Goodwin, "War Within," 42.
2. Johnson, *White House Diary*, 687.
3. "I realize that emergencies arise," Stegall complained, on the FBI's behalf, "but . . . you can't make me believe there isn't some way we could get our hands on the lists sooner." DeLoach had just called to tell her the FBI "had to keep over fifty people *all night* to check [a] list of around 400 names." Mildred Stegall to Marvin Watson, Oct. 1, 1965, WHCF, PE6, Johnson Papers.
4. "His sophistication in rating the importance of a person's having attended a John Reed Society meeting back in 1938," Harry McPherson remembered, "left a hell of a lot to be desired."
5. Transcript of telephone conversation, J. Edgar Hoover and Vincent Astor, July 5, 1941, Roosevelt Folder, FBI–Nichols O&C Files. For the desires and policies of the Johnson White House, see Cartha D. DeLoach to Clyde Tolson, March 1, 1966, Johnson Folder, FBI–Hoover O&C Files; William Moyers to White House Personnel, Dec. 3, 1964, WHCF, Ex PE6, Johnson Papers; Walter Jenkins to White House Staff, Oct. 7, 1964, ibid.; DeLoach to Tolson, July 10, 1967, no. not recorded, FBI–King File (100-106670). For the early Do Not File files, see Edward J. Brennan to Franklin L. Dodge, Jr., Nov. 22, 1920, Investigations, Dept. of Justice (1), Walsh Papers.
6. Hoover to Watson, Jan. 20, 1967, no. 53, FBI–NLG Files (100-367743); Hoover to [deleted], March 14, 1968, no. 27, FBI–Owens File (77-72778). The name checks did not focus exclusively on blacks. The FBI ran Vince Lombardi's name through the files at White House request, too.
7. According to an inventory prepared by Johnson Library staff.
8. Senate Select Committee to Study . . . Intelligence Activities (hereafter Church Committee), *Book II*, 79 n338, 83, *Book III*, 495, 498.
9. The Office of Economic Opportunity collected the sort of physical and social intelligence that Califano referred to, but the White House considered the community action centers to be part of the problem. OEO's inspector general, Edgar May, "had an extraordinary staff," Sargent Shriver said. "Very independent, very quick, very street oriented. . . . FBI didn't have any people in those poverty-stricken areas—to begin with, at all. . . . The OEO people were in there where the poor people lived—in there where the 'revolutionaries' were . . . almost as if we had 2,000 or 3,000 'spies' in there. They weren't spies at all, but I'm trying to say that those poverty-stricken areas were where our OEO people lived."
10. Church Committee, *Book II*, 79 n337.
11. Ibid., 79, 84, *Book III*, 495–97.
12. Fred M. Vinson, Jr., to Ramsey Clark, Sept. 15, and Oct. 20, 1967, White House Aides' Files—James Gaither, Pres. Task Forces, Subject File, Riots 1967, Box 36, Johnson Papers; Church Committee, *Book II*, 79–84; *Book III*, 495–97.
13. Clark to FBI Director, Sept. 14, 1967, in Church Committee, *Hearings—*

FBI, 528–30. "The Ramsey Clark of 1967," as one FBI executive put it in 1974, "not only directed the Bureau to be certain that every attempt was made to get all information but to 'take every step' to determine the plans for racial violence." T. J. Smith to W. Raymond Wannall, March 18, 1974, no. not recorded, FBI–COINTEL (White Hate) File (157-9).

14. Wilkins, *Man's Life*, 230–31; Church Committee, *Book II*, 280; J. Walter Yeagley to Richard Russell, Aug. 10, 1967, Legislative Series, Un-American (1967), Box U1, Russell Papers. The FBI added to its files on Carmichael in the years that followed—trying to find something from his high school days in the Bronx, when he "read Karl Marx" and palled around with Eugene Dennis, Jr., to his black power days, when he embarked on a SNCC purge of "Caucasians" and was diagnosed, the FBI said, by Selective Service psychologists as a schizophrenic with psychopathic, pseudoneurotic, and paranoid tendencies.

15. Doar, Roche interviews; Theoharis and Cox, *Boss*, 87.

16. Roche interview; DeLoach to Tolson, May 7, 1968, no. not recorded, FBI–McSurely Files (62-98810); Clark Oral History, 21.

17. [Deleted] to William C. Sullivan, June 28, 1967, no. not recorded, FBI–Racial Matters Policy File (157-00). See also the references to an Aug. 7, 1967, directive in New York Field Office Inspection Rept., Oct. 27, 1967, FBI–Moore Files.

18. See Felt's comments in the inspection report cited in the previous note. In an attempt to "increase the quantity and quality of coverage of racial matters," the FBI also considered mobilizing thousands of American Legion Contact Program and Plant Informant Program sources. SAC Letter, Feb. 23, 1965, in Church Committee, *Hearings—FBI*, 678.

19. SAC Letter, March 12, 1968, FBI–SAC File; New York Field Office Inspection Rept., n.d. [ca. May 1968], FBI–Moore Files. See also the inspection report of Oct. 27, 1967, ibid.; SAC Letter, March 12, 1968, FBI–SAC File; Church Committee, *Book III*, pp. 493–94.

20. Sullivan, *Bureau*, 133; Garrow, *FBI and Martin Luther King*, 173–203.

21. SAC El Paso to Director, April 17, 1968, no. 16-4, FBI–COINTEL (New Left) File (100-449698); SAC Minneapolis to Director, April 3, 1968, no. 59, FBI–COINTEL (Black Nationalist) File (100-448006).

22. SAC Letter, Oct. 17, 1967, FBI–SAC File; Church Committee, *Book II*, 75–76, *Book III*, 253, 494, *Hearings—FBI*, 17.

23. Baraka, *Autobiography*, 269; SAC Letters, March 12 and April 30, 1968, FBI–SAC File.

24. SAC Philadelphia to all Field Office Agents, Feb. 26, March 29, and Aug. 12, 1968, in "Complete Collection," 52–54; New York Field Office Inspection Rept., Oct. 27, 1968, FBI–Moore Files; George C. Moore to Sullivan, Sept. 3, 1968, no. not recorded, FBI–Racial Matters File; Church Committee, *Book II*, 75–76, *Book III*, 253, 494, *Hearings—FBI*, 17.

25. Clark to Kevin T. Maroney, Thomas J. McTiernan, Hugh Nugent, and James P. Turner, Nov. 9, 1967, in Church Committee, *Hearings—FBI*, 531–32; Attorney General to John Doar, Vinson, Roger Wilkins, and J. Walter Yeagley, Dec. 18, 1967, ibid., 533–34; idem, *Book II*, 79–80, 83–84, *Book III*, 493, 497–98, 500.

26. SAC Letters, March 26, May 7, and June 4, 1968, FBI–SAC File; Moore to Sullivan, May 1, 1968, no. 153, FBI–Racial Matters File; Church Committee, *Book III*, 517–18.

27. Church Committee, *Book III*, 517–18.

28. Joseph A. Califano, Jr., to the President, Jan. 18, 1968, WHCF, Ex HU2, Box 7, Johnson Papers; Church Committee, *Book II*, 84–85, 260; Roche interview.

29. Church Committee, *Book II*, 84–85, 260; Roche interview.

30. M. E. Triplett to W. A. Branigan, Aug. 24, 1966, in Church Committee, *Hearings—Mail Opening*, 245–48; Senate Select Committee on Intelligence, *Hearings on National Intelligence Reorganization*, 503; Howard J. Osborn to Deputy Director for Support, Dec. 11, 1967, CIA–Brown File; memo, re Information [deleted] on Cuban Comments on Contacts with U.S. Negro Militants, April 25, 1968, ibid.; memo, re West Coast Subversive Organizations and their Interaction and Proposed Goals, March 20, 1968, CIA RESISTANCE/Black Student Unions File; Guiterrez, "Chicanos," 29–58.

31. Church Committee, *Book III*, 520–21.

32. SAC Letter, March 12, 1968, in Church Committee, *Hearings—FBI*, 681.

33. McKnight, "Memphis Sanitation Strike," 138–56, "Harvest," 8.

34. R. W. Smith to Sullivan, March 6, 1968, no. 53-1284, FBI–Levison File (157-6); memo, re Outlook for Racial Violence in Washington, D.C., n.d. [ca. March 6, 1968], no. 53-1284, ibid.

35. Milton A. Jones to Thomas E. Bishop, Jan. 17, 1968, no. 3193, FBI–King File; Director to SACs Washington, Atlanta, Boston, and Philadelphia, June 18, 1968, no. not recorded, FBI–SCLC File (100-438794); DeLoach to Tolson, May 3, 1968, no. 2130, ibid.; Sullivan, *Bureau*, 133.

36. For the FBI's general interest in disrupting the Poor People's Campaign, see serials 63, 82, 131, and 203, FBI–COINTEL (Black) File.

37. Hoover to Stegall, April 23, 1968, no. not recorded, FBI–SCLC File; Hoover to Stegall, Aug. 12, 1968, no. 315, Aug. 19, 1968, no. 316, FBI–Levison File (100-392452); SAC New York to Director, June 5, 1968, no. 306, ibid.; letterhead memo, June 19, 1968, no. 306, ibid.; letterhead memo, Aug. 16, 1968, no. 4, ibid.—Detroit Subfile (100-35176).

38. Matthew Nimetz to Califano, May 16, 1968, White House Aides' Files—James Gaither, Pres. Task Forces, Subject File, Riot Control—Poor People's March (1), Box 36, Johnson Papers.

39. See the comments of Felt and other FBI supervisors and agents in New York Field Office Inspection Division Rept., Oct. 27, 1967, FBI–Moore Files.

40. Ibid. See also the other inspection reports in these files.

41. Director to SAC New Haven, April 9, 1951, no. 227, FBI–Robeson File (100-12304); Church Committee, *Book III*, 417–22, 436–42, 542–48.

42. [Deleted] to [deleted], March 19, 1969, no. 3919, June 26, 1961, no. 2930, Feb. 11, 1969, no. not recorded, FBI–Security Index File (100-358086); James F. Bland to Sullivan, June 6, 1961, no. illegible, ibid.; memo, re Subversive Control Section Programs and Accomplishments, Oct. 20, 1961, no. 2980, ibid.; [deleted] to Director, Jan. 10, 1952, no. deleted, ibid.; D. Milton Ladd to Director, Feb. 12, 1951, no. 56, FBI–Responsibilities Program File (62-93875); Louis B. Nichols to Tolson, Feb. 12, 1951, no. 4, ibid.

43. Church Committee, *Book II*, 92; Charles D. Brennan to Sullivan, Nov. 22, 1968, no. 4046, FBI–COINTEL (CPUSA) File; Executives' Conference to [deleted], Feb. 27, 1969, no. not recorded, FBI–Security Index File.

44. Church Committee, *Book III*, 491–92.

45. Director to SACs Albany et al., Jan. 17, 1969, no. 181, FBI–Black National-

ist Photograph Album File (157-8415); SAC Letters, Aug. 4, 1967, Jan. 16, 1968, FBI–SAC File; Moore to Sullivan, March 20, 1968, no. 229, FBI–Rabble Rouser Index File (157-7782); Director to SACs Albany et al., Dec. 6, 1968, no. 473, FBI–COINTEL (Black) File; Church Committee, *Book II*, 89–90, *Book III*, 510–12, 517–18.

46. P. L. Cox to Sullivan, Sept. 5, 1967, no. 67, FBI–Rabble Rouser File.

47. Director to SACs Albany et al., March 4, 1968, no. 19, FBI–COINTEL (Black) File.

48. SAC Kansas City to Director, March 18, 1968, no. 30 and 31, ibid. See also serials 44–45, 58, 62, 64–65, 75, 80, and 91, ibid.

49. *Jackson Capital Reporter*, June 22, 1978; Church Committee, *Book III*, 20–21 n90.

50. SAC Washington to Director, Oct. 27, 1967, no. 4, Dec. 18, 1967, no. 7, FBI–COINTEL (Black) File; Director to SAC Washington, Nov. 14, 1967, no. 4, ibid.

51. SAC Newark to Director, April 2, 1968, no. 61, ibid.; SAC Pittsburgh to Director, March 28, 1968, no. 42, ibid.; SAC New York to Director, April 4, 1968, no. 69, ibid.

52. SAC San Francisco to Director, April 3, 1968, no. 95, ibid.; SAC San Diego to Director, April 3, 1968, no. 78, ibid.; SAC Los Angeles to Director, April 2, 1968, no. 76, ibid. For the other field offices, see serials 52, 87, 102, ibid.

53. SAC Birmingham to Director, April 3, 1968, no. 51, ibid.; SAC Mobile to Director, March 27, 1968, no. 33, ibid. See also serials 38, 56, 70, and 73, ibid.

54. SAC Memphis to Director, May 22, 1968, no. illegible, Aug. 30, 1968, no. not recorded, ibid.; SAC Memphis to Director, April 19, 1967, no. 28-19, FBI–McSurely Files (100-439190); SAC Jacksonville to Director, July 2, 1968, no. 53-5, FBI–COINTEL (New Left) File.

55. Church Committee, *Book III*, 4.

56. Director to SACs Albany et al., Aug. 25, 1967, no. 1, FBI–COINTEL (Black) File.

57. Dept. of Justice, *King Task Force*, 141.

58. SAC New York to Director, Sept. 25, 1967, no. not recorded, FBI–COINTEL (Black) File; Fred J. Baumgardner to Sullivan, April 22, 1966, no. 11-5, FBI–COINTEL (White) File.

59. Director to SACs Albany et al., March 4, 1968, no. 19, FBI–COINTEL (Black) File.

60. Moore to Sullivan, Feb. 29, 1968, no. 19, ibid.; Church Committee, *Book III*, 6.

61. Director to SACs Albany et al., March 4, 1968, no. 19, FBI–COINTEL (Black) File.

62. Navasky, "FBI's Wildest Dream," 716–18.

63. SAC Charlotte to Director, April 4, 1968, no. 77, FBI–COINTEL (Black) File; SAC Chicago to Director, April 22, 1968, no. illegible, ibid.

64. Director to SACs Chicago et al., May 3, 1968, no. illegible, ibid.

65. Director to SACs Albany et al., Jan. 7, 1969, no. 580, ibid.; SAC San Francisco to Director, Aug. 7, 1968, no. 230, ibid.; *New York Times*, Oct. 19, 1980; Bishop to DeLoach, June 25, 1969, no. 155, King Folder, FBI–Hoover O&C Files; Hoover to Gerald Ford, Oct. 29, 1969, FBI, Cong. Papers, Box B140-19, Ford Papers; Moore to Sullivan, June 27, 1969, no. 3660, FBI–King File.

66. Moore to Sullivan, Nov. 1, 1968, no. illegible, FBI–COINTEL (Black) File; SAC San Diego to Director, May 31, 1968, no. illegible, ibid. The FBI gathered background data on Smith and Carlos; placed the principal organizer of a black athlete boycott/protest at the Olympic games, Harry Edwards, on the Rabble Rouser Index; and recruited a student in Edwards's sociology class at San Jose State as an informant. Edwards, *Struggle*, 181, 185, 193.

67. SAC Boston to Director, Feb. 1, 1968, no. 9, FBI–COINTEL (Black) File; Director to SAC Boston, Feb. 8, 1968, no. 9, ibid.

68. Moore to Sullivan, April 17, 1968, no. 96, ibid.

69. Director to SAC New York, July 10, 1968, no. 100-161140-illegible, FBI–Moore Files; Director to SAC Washington, April 2, 1968, no. 43, FBI–COINTEL (Black) File; SAC Houston to Director, March 14, 1968, no. 27, ibid.; SAC Charlotte to Director, July 9, 1968, no. illegible, ibid.

70. Church Committee, *Book III*, 25; Brennan to Sullivan, May 9, 1968, idem, *Hearings—FBI*, 393–94; Director to SACs Albany et al., July 7, 1968, ibid., 395–97.

71. Hayden, *Reunion*, 150; SAC Chicago to Director, Dec. 31, 1968, no. 9-29, FBI–COINTEL (New Left) File; Director to SAC Chicago, Dec. 23, 1968, no. 9-28, ibid.; SAC Baltimore to Director, June 7, 1968, no. 3-1, ibid.; Church Committee, *Book III*, 42.

72. DeLoach to Tolson, Aug. 22, 1966, no. 5888, FBI–HUAC File (61-7582).

73. Bishop to DeLoach, Aug. 3, 1967, no. 5928, ibid; DeLoach to Tolson, July 10, 1967, no. not recorded, FBI–King File. In addition to the suggested HUAC campaign, Johnson urged the Bureau to work with Drew Pearson. DeLoach "doubted Pearson would print derogatory information concerning these characters."

74. DeLoach to Tolson, July 10, 1967, no. not recorded, FBI–King File.

75. Ibid.; Walter Trohan to Comrade [DeLoach], Sept, 24, 1964, Correspondence, J. Edgar Hoover, Trohan Papers.

76. Larry Temple to the President, May 28 and June 19, 1968, White House Aides' Files—Larry Temple, SACB, Johnson Papers; Temple to the President, Jan. 19, 1968, WHCF—CF, FG285, ibid.; note, LBJ, Aug. 27, 1967, WHCF, Ex FG285, ibid.; Barefoot Sanders to the President, Feb. 29, 1968, WHCF, Ex FG411/U-Z, ibid.; Hoover to Tolson, DeLoach, and Sullivan, July 25, 1967, no. 959, FBI–Detroit Riot File (157-6); Lovin, "Lyndon B. Johnson," 94–112; Francis J. McNamara to Richard H. Ichord, June 1, 1966, Accredited Newsmen Covering War in Vietnam, Box 184, Ichord Papers; press release, re Du Bois Clubs, n.d. [ca. Oct. 1967], U.S. Dept. of Justice, Box 58, SNCC Papers. The Du Bois Clubs formed after Dr. Du Bois joined the Communist party in 1961, at the age of ninety-three. The FBI responded by leaking derogatory information through the U.S. Information Agency "in view of the esteem in which Du Bois is held in African nations." Bland to Sullivan, Nov. 21, 1961, no. 193, FBI–Du Bois File (100-99729).

77. Director to SACs New York et al., June 7, 1965, no. 3931, FBI–COINTEL (CPUSA) File; Baumgardner to Sullivan, Oct. 27, 1965, no. illegible, Nov. 16, 1965, no. not recorded, ibid.; Brennan to Sullivan, Oct. 13, 1967, no. not recorded, FBI–COINTEL (Black) File.

78. George Christian to the President, April 8, 1967, WHCF—Name File (Martin Luther King, Jr.), Box 144, Johnson Papers.

79. John P. Roche to the President, Sept. 1, 1967, WHCF—CF, Name File (Hon), Box 4, ibid.; Roche to the President, April 5, 1967, WHCF—CF, HU2, Box

56, ibid.; Roche to Watson, Dec. 22, 1967, WHCF—CF, PU1-2, ibid. The Carmichael rumor, Roche explained, "was a joke which grew out of a photo in the *Post* (I think) of Julian Bond, Andrew Young, and Stokely C. with a bunch of African nationalists at some conference (Lagos?). They looked like whites. My Irish irony always got me into jams, but I loved to work over Marvin who was a solemn Fundamentalist."

80. The Catholic War Veterans operations (see note 77) were carried out under the Communist party and black nationalist COINTELPROs.

81. The President lost his enthusiasm for counterintelligence action against his antiwar critics after Tet. Lovin, "Lyndon B. Johnson," 564.

82. Garrow, *FBI and Martin Luther King*, 207.

83. Aptheker interview; SAC Cincinnati to Director, March 28, 1966, no. not recorded, FBI–COINTEL (CPUSA) File; Hoover to Tolson, DeLoach, Sullivan, and Robert E. Wick, April 27, 1967, no. not recorded, FBI–King File.

84. Director to SAC New York, July 10, 1968, no. illegible, FBI–Moore Files.

85. Director to SACs New York et al., Oct. 12, 1961, in Church Committee, *Hearings—FBI*, 377; idem, *Book III*, 18.

86. Idem, *Book III*, 12–13 n54–55.

87. Hoover to Tolson, DeLoach, John P. Mohr, James H. Gale, Alex Rosen, and Sullivan, March 11, 1968, no. not recorded, FBI–Tolson Memo File (67-9524).

CHAPTER 9.
The Only Good Panther

1. Wolfe, *Radical Chic*, 8.

2. Davis, et al., *If They Come*, 21.

3. Rubin, *Do It!*, 142.

4. For Panther rhetoric, see the party newspaper, the *Black Panther*.

5. Seale, *Lonely Rage*, 134–36.

6. Sheehy, *Panthermania*, 6; John Ehrlichman to J. Edgar Hoover, Dec. 22, 1969, Black Panther Party, WHSF—John Ehrlichman, Box 15, Nixon Papers; Director to SACs Albany et al., Sept. 3, 1968, no. illegible, FBI–Hampton Files.

7. Watters and Gillers, eds., *Investigating*, 196, 214, 216.

8. The casualty counts in Black Panther mythology and police department lore are considerably higher. Epstein, "Panthers," 45–77.

9. Elliff, *Crime*, 130, 140; Leonard interview; Pinkney, *Red, Black*, 110; Harris, *Justice*, 236.

10. Director to SAC San Francisco et al., June 25, 1969, no. illegible, FBI–Hampton Files; Director to SACs Chicago et al., June 25, 1969, no. illegible, ibid.; Director to SAC New York, June 6, 1969, no. 999, FBI–COINTEL (Black Nationalist) File (100-448006).

11. Conversations recorded in Hoover to Clyde Tolson, Cartha D. DeLoach, James H. Gale, Alex Rosen, and William C. Sullivan, April 23, 1969, no. not recorded, FBI–Tolson Memo File (67-9524); Hoover to Tolson, DeLoach, Sullivan, and Thomas E. Bishop, July 14, 1969, no. not recorded, ibid.

12. Senate Committee to Study . . . Intelligence Activities (hereafter Church Committee), *Book III*, 10–11, 528–29. A federal grand jury indicted Seale and seven others under the antiriot provision of the 1968 Civil Rights Act, the so-called Rap Brown Law which made it a federal crime to cross a

state line with intent to incite riot. Verbal clashes between Seale and Judge Julius J. Hoffman marked the early stages of the trial, and the judge finally ordered the Panther publicist gagged and chained to his chair in the courtroom. When Seale persisted, Hoffman found him in contempt, sentenced him to four years in prison, severed his case from that of the others, declared an individual mistrial, and set a new trial date.

13. Bates interview; Ungar, *FBI*, 208.

14. Bates interview; SAC San Francisco to Director, April 3, 1968, no. illegible, April 3, 1968, no. illegible and 95, FBI–COINTEL (Black) File. A liberal cadre had not infiltrated this FBI office. San Francisco had more operatives (eighty-nine) assigned to domestic intelligence than any other field office, and their reports on the New Left were filled with musings about attacks on "the Establishment"—that is, "the organized, lawful society which the Bureau represents." SAC San Francisco to Director, Jan. 27, 1969, no. 47-44, FBI–COINTEL (New Left) (100-449698).

15. George C. Moore to Sullivan, Dec. 17, 1968, no. illegible, FBI–COINTEL (White Hate) File (157-9); Moore to Sullivan, Sept. 27, 1968, no. 306, Oct. 28, 1968, no. illegible, Oct. 10, 1968, no. illegible, FBI–COINTEL (Black) File; Director to SAC San Francisco et al., Sept. 30, 1968, no. 306, ibid.

16. Makeba, *Makeba*, 162; Church Committee, *Book III*, 9, 47, 199 n60; Director to SAC Washington, July 1, 1968, no. 113, FBI–COINTEL (Black) File; Moore to Sullivan, Nov. 8, 1968, no. 465, April 15, 1970, no. 1751, ibid. The FBI also placed anonymous calls to SNCC's James Forman, informing him that the Panthers intended to "get him," and sent threatening letters to the twenty-one person board of directors of the Black United Front. One of the recipients, Sumner Stone, remembered sitting "up half the night" with his wife. "I thought I was going to be assassinated."

17. Church Committee, *Book III*, 9, 40, 46–48.

18. SAC San Francisco to Director, May 14, 1969, no. 961, FBI–COINTEL (Black) File; Watters and Gillers, eds., *Investigating*, 196.

19. Director to SAC San Francisco, May 27, 1969, no. 964, FBI–COINTEL (Black) File. The reluctance of a particular field office to go along with Division Five was not unusual. When Detroit SAC Neil Welch balked at a directive to intensify surveillance of the League of Revolutionary Black Workers, a small group of UAW dissidents, suggesting that the matter be referred to the attorney general, Division Five told him that the attorney general's "authority is not necessary for our intelligence operations." Welch, *Inside*, 172-73.

20. See the San Francisco subfile, FBI–COINTEL (Black) File. Gain is quoted in Bergman and Weir, "Revolution," 47.

21. The discussion of the Ranger-Panther conflict in this and the next three paragraphs is based on serials 534, 591, 599, 606, 608, FBI–COINTEL (Black) File; Church Committee, *Book III*, 195–99.

22. See the sources cited in the previous note. The Rangers later changed their name to the Black P. Stone Nation. In the more recent past they have called themselves the El Rukn tribe of the Moorish Science Temple of America, and finally El Rukn, Sunni Muslims under their religious leader, Malik (Jeff Fort). In late 1987 a federal jury convicted Fort and four other members of conspiring to commit terrorist acts against the United States on behalf of Libya. El Rukn bought an antitank rocket from an undercover FBI agent, and the FBI implicated Fort as the mastermind of the entire terrorism-for-hire plot—even though he was incarcerated in Texas at the

time, serving a thirteen-year sentence. He received eighty years on the conspiracy charges.

23. Baraka, *Autobiography*, 254; Karenga interview; Karenga, *Roots of the US/Panther Conflict.*

24. Anthony, *Picking Up the Gun*, 75–76. The US-Panther vendetta can be traced in serials 466, 482, 541, 795-6, 813, 833, 1234, 1283, 1435, 1600, 1777, FBI–COINTEL (Black) File; Church Committee, *Book III*, 41, 43, 47–48, 189-95, 199, 213, 221–22.

25. Baraka, *Autobiography*, 279.

26. San Diego agents also launched a campaign against New Leftists that included the incitement of the paramilitary Secret Army Organization to acts of violence against Vietnam war protestors.

27. See the sources cited in note 24; and the following issues of the *San Diego Union* (all 1976), Jan. 4 and 15, March 11, May 6, 7, 19, and 20, June 11, 18, and 25.

28. Ibid. In 1972 Evans and another agent who helped egg on the feud received a nonpunitive transfer to Butte, Montana. The agent who headed up the counterintelligence program in San Diego, Robert L. Baker, left the Bureau in 1975 at the mandatory retirement age of fifty-five.

29. Baraka, *Autobiography*, 279; Church Committee, *Book III*, 194, 199; Karenga interview.

30. Director to SAC Newark, Sept. 16, 1969, no. illegible, FBI–COINTEL (New Left) File; SAC Newark to Director, Aug. 25, 1969, no. illegible, ibid.

31. Bergman and Weir, "Revolution," 49.

32. Karenga interview; Karenga, *Roots of the US/Panther Conflict*, 7. A year later, in June 1971, Karenga was sentenced to a year in prison for allegedly torturing two young black women.

33. SAC San Francisco to Director, May 11, 1970, no. 211, June 17, 1970, no. 221, FBI–COINTEL (Special Operations) File (105-174254); Director to SAC San Francisco, June 26, 1970, no. 221, ibid.; Church Committee, *Book III*, 208; SAC San Francisco to Director, Dec. 29, 1969, no. 1569, FBI–COINTEL (Black) File.

34. The discussion of the Hampton case is based on Flint Taylor interviews; Donner, *Age*, 226–30; the voluminous documents in FBI–Hampton Files; *Iberia Hampton et al. v. Edward V. Hanrahan et al.*, 600 F.2d 600 (1979); Commission of Inquiry, *Search and Destroy.*

35. Leonard interview; James A. Emanuel, "Panther Man" (c. 1970).

36. Director to SAC Chicago, Dec. 17, 1969, no. illegible, FBI–Hampton Files; SAC Chicago to Director, Feb. 11, 1970, no. illegible, ibid.

37. Emanuel, "Panther Man." Hanrahan is quoted in Commission of Inquiry, *Search and Destroy*, ix.

38. Leonard interview.

39. Ibid.

40. SAC Chicago to Director, April 8, 1970, no. illegible, FBI–Hampton Files.

41. Flint Taylor, Leonard interviews.

42. Flint Taylor interviews; Hoover to Tolson, DeLoach, Bishop, Rosen, and Sullivan, Sept. 19, 1968, no. not recorded, FBI–Tolson Memo File.

43. *New York Times*, Nov. 14, 1982.

44. Berlet, "Journalists," 22; Director to SAC Chicago, Dec. 10, 1969, no. 1448, FBI–COINTEL (Black) File.

45. This program began in late 1968 and by the spring of the following year
the FBI had conducted over 500 interviews. Director to SAC New York,
Nov. 14, 1968, no. 100-161993-illegible, FBI–Moore Files; SAC New York
to Director, April 8, 1969, no. 100-161993-illegible, ibid. For the "Catholic
hierarchy" quote, see Director to SAC San Diego, Sept. 11, 1969, no. 1269,
FBI–COINTEL (Black) File.

46. Church Committee, *Book III*, 208–12. The FBI proposed hundreds of
fraudulent letters; it is not always clear which ones were mailed out and
which ones were not. For the examples cited here, see serials 743, 1233,
1771, 1826, 1861, FBI–COINTEL (Black) File.

47. Carson, "Blacks and Jews," 126–27.

48. Director to SACs Albany et al., May 6, 1968, no. 32, FBI–Moore Files (157-
601).

49. Herman Edelsberg to Louis B. Nichols, July 7, 1953, no. not recorded,
FBI–HUAC File (61-7582); Hoover to Herbert Hoover, Feb. 20, 1957, J.
Edgar Hoover Folder, Post-Pres. Individual, Herbert Hoover Papers; Nichols to Tolson, March 9, 1955, no. not recorded, FBI–Sokolsky File (62-
89885).

50. Moore to Sullivan, Jan. 8, 1969, no. 586, Sept. 22, 1969, no. 1306, Nov. 21,
1969, no. 1444, FBI–COINTEL (Black) File; SAC New York to Director,
Sept. 10, 1969, no. 1306, ibid.; Director to SAC New York, April 10, 1969,
no. illegible, ibid.; SAC Boston to Director, Aug. 13, 1970, no. illegible,
ibid.; SAC San Francisco to Director, May 28, 1970, no. illegible, ibid.; Director to SAC Baltimore, Feb. 25, 1969, no. illegible, ibid.; Moore to
Charles D. Brennan, Aug. 20, 1970, no. not recorded, ibid.; Director to SAC
Boston, July 29, 1970, no. illegible, ibid.

51. The indictments included 150 counts involving plans to dynamite five mid-
town department stores, the Morrisania (Bronx) police station, and Penn
Central Railroad tracks above 148th Street.

52. Moore to Sullivan, May 14, 1970, no. 1820, FBI–COINTEL (Black) File. Division Five listed this as one of five COINTELPRO highlights, alongside syndicated columns on the Panthers by Robert S. Allen and John A. Gold-
smith; the collapse of a Panther chapter in Cleveland, Mississippi, in the
wake of a leak to James Ward of the *Jackson Daily News;* the eviction of
US from its San Diego headquarters; and a Miami television documentary
on the Nation of Islam.

53. Church Committee, *Book III*, 200–07.

54. Bergman and Weir, "Revolution," 47, 48.

55. Church Committee, *Book III*, 200–07.

56. *New York Times*, April 25, 1970.

57. Amnesty International, *Proposal*, 15–33; *Sixty Minutes* (CBS Television network), Nov. 29, 1987, pp. 6–10.

58. Director to SAC Newark, Aug. 13, 1971, no. 9X10, FBI–Moore Files (152-
22627); Hoover to Tolson, Sullivan, Brennan, Gale, Rosen, and Casper, May
26, 1971, no. not recorded, May 27, 1971, no. not recorded, FBI–Tolson
Memo File. Hoover had no intention of having the FBI "assume the responsibility for taking over the killing of all police officers." Nixon agreed,
because, among other reasons, Senator Harrison A. Williams, Jr. (D., N.J.),
had charged "the President of not backing up law and order, et cetera"—
specifically, by "blocking his attempt to let the FBI go into these police
killings." Raising the specter of "a national police force," once again, Hoover said "Williams wants to make a Lindbergh case where there is a pre-

sumption of Federal jurisdiction at the end of 24 hours and we would be in every case in the country," adding that "Williams is the last man who should be doing any talking as his background is so bad it ought to be looked into." Years later, the FBI targeted Williams under its ABSCAM sting operation. Hoover to Tolson, Sullivan, Bishop, Brennan, Joseph J. Casper, Gale, and Rosen, May 28, 1971, Folder 128, FBI–Hoover O&C Files.

59. Director to SAC Newark, Aug. 13, 1971, no. 9X10, FBI–Moore Files (152-22627); Hoover to Tolson, Sullivan, Brennan, Gale, Rosen, and Casper, May 26, 1971, no. not recorded, May 27, 1971, no. not recorded, FBI–Tolson Memo File.

60. Shakur, *Assata*, 123; National Conference of Black Lawyers, et al., *Human Rights*, 1–83 (Appendix VII).

61. SAC Letter, Feb. 19, 1974, FBI–SAC File; A. B. Fulton to W. Raymond Wannall, Feb. 7, 1974, no. 6162, FBI–HUAC File; Director to Attorney General, Feb. 8, 1974, no. 6162, ibid.; memo, re PRISACTS, July 15, 1975, no. 57, FBI–Moore Files (157-12065); House Committee on Internal Security, *Revolutionary Target*. See also the more recent report, Dept. of Justice, *Prison Gangs*. By 1975, if not earlier, the FBI had extended the PRISACTS dissemination program to include Ku Klux Klan literature entering the nation's prisons and Klan activity in general among inmates.

62. Amnesty International, *Proposal*, 32–33. Bureau counterintelligence actions also served as the foundation for a petition on human rights violations submitted in December 1978 to a United Nations commission by the National Conference of Black Lawyers and other groups. Hinds, *Illusions*.

63. Church Committee, *Book III*, 189.

CHAPTER 10.
Citizens and Radicals

1. When Hugh Sidey mentioned Nixon's plan in his *Life* magazine column, the FBI ran its mandatory file check. Milton A. Jones to Thomas E. Bishop, Oct. 18, 1971, no. not recorded, FBI–CPJ File (62-113909).

2. See the director's introduction of the vice president at the FBI National Academy graduation exercises, June 11, 1954, in Folder 8, FBI–Hoover O&C Files.

3. Richard Nixon to H. R. Haldeman, May 18, 1972, Pres. Memos, WHSF—H. R. Haldeman, Box 230, Nixon Papers.

4. Haldeman notes, May 31, 1970, WHSF—Haldeman, Box 41, ibid.; Cartha D. DeLoach to Clyde Tolson, Feb. 27, 1970, no. 5, Press Media Campaign Against Director Folder, FBI–Hoover O&C Files; newspaper clippings, May 18, 1971, no. 2049, May 27, 1971, no. 2051, FBI–Robert Kennedy File (77-51387); J. Edgar Hoover to Tolson, DeLoach, John P. Mohr, Bishop, Joseph J. Casper, and William C. Sullivan, May 1, 1970, no. not recorded, FBI–Tolson Memo File (67-9524); Tolson to Director, Aug. 26, 1971, in Senate Select Committee to Study . . . Intelligence Activities (hereafter Church Committee), *Hearings—FBI*, 443. Sullivan is quoted in Demaris, *Director*, 84.

5. Charles Colson to John Dean, April 28, 1972, Misc. Intelligence, WHSF—John Dean, Box 89, Nixon Papers; John Ehrlichman to Hoover, Dec. 17, 1971, Charles Evers, WHSF—John Ehrlichman, Box 18, ibid.; Hoover to Alexander P. Butterfield, March 16, 1970, no. not recorded, FBI–Lawrence File (95-54-3169); Hoover to Ehrlichman, July 2, 1969, no. 42, FBI–Wilkins File (62-78270).

6. Rustin, *Down the Line*, 260; notes, June 12, 1969, no. not recorded, June 14, 1964, no. not recorded, June 16, 1969, not recorded, FBI–SCLC File (100-438794); letterhead memo, July 18, 1969, no. not recorded, ibid.; George C. Moore to Sullivan, Jan. 22, 1969, no. not recorded, FBI–Eastland File (94-4-5130); Jones to DeLoach, July 14, 1965, no. 47, ibid.; Jones to Bishop, March 5, 1969, no. 2, Folder 131, FBI–Hoover O&C Files; Director to Deputy Attorney General, March 5, 1969, ibid.

7. Jones to Louis B. Nichols, Sept. 3, 1954, no. 12, FBI–Eastland File; Hoover to Tolson, DeLoach, and James H. Gale, July 1, 1969, no. 23, Mitchell Folder, FBI–Hoover O&C Files; Director to Attorney General, July 1, 1969, no. 24, ibid.; Hoover to Tolson, DeLoach, Gale, and Bishop, Jan. 19, 1970, no. not recorded, FBI–Tolson Memo File; Turner, *Hoover's F.B.I.*, 91–92.

8. Buchanan, *Right*, 282–83; Director to Attorney General, April 2, 1962, no. not recorded, FBI–Levison File (100-392452).

9. Hoover to Tolson, DeLoach, Gale, Alex Rosen, Sullivan, and Bishop, April 23, 1969, no. not recorded, FBI–Tolson Memo File; Powers, *Secrecy and Power*, 440.

10. Hoover to Tolson, DeLoach, Gale, Rosen, Sullivan, and Bishop, April 23, 1969, no. not recorded, FBI–Tolson Memo File.

11. Colson to Jim Keogh, Sept. 22, 1970, Campus Unrest, WHSF—Charles Colson, Box 44, Nixon Papers.

12. Director to SACs Albany et al., Nov. 26, 1969, in Church Committee, *Hearings—FBI*, 368–69; Richard D. Cotter to Charles D. Brennan, Nov. 3, 1970, no. 1X3, FBI–Racial Digest File (157-19573).

13. Hoover to Tolson, DeLoach, Sullivan, and Bishop, May 9, 1969, in House Committee on the Judiciary, *Statement of Information—Book VII*, pt. 1, p. 143; Hoover to Tolson, Sullivan, Mohr, Bishop, and Ivan W. Conrad, Feb. 4, 1971, no. not recorded, FBI–Tolson Memo File.

14. Hoover to Tolson, DeLoach, Nicholas P. Callahan, Rosen, and Bishop, March 19, 1969, no. not recorded, FBI–Tolson Memo File; Conrad to Mohr, March 14, 1969, no. 6, March 18, 1969, no. 1, March 27, 1969, no. 4 and 5, June 17, 1969, no. 17, June 18, 1969, no. 19, Mitchell Folder, FBI–Hoover O&C Files; Director to Attorney General, March 20, 1969, no. 8, March 28, 1969, no. 10, ibid.; Demaris, *Director*, 140.

15. Moore to Sullivan, June 18, 1969, no. 3602, FBI–King File (100-106670); Hoover to Spiro Agnew, June 19, 1969, no. 3602, ibid.; Hoover to Tolson, DeLoach, Rosen, Sullivan, and Bishop, May 14, 1970, no. not recorded, May 18, 1970, no. not recorded, FBI–Tolson Memo File; Hoover to Tolson, DeLoach, Sullivan, and Bishop, April 21, 1970, no. not recorded, ibid.; Hoover to Tolson, Sullivan, Bishop, and Brennan, Jan. 7, 1971, no. not recorded, ibid.

16. Egil Krogh, Jr., to Hoover, June 27, 1969, Black Panther Party, WHSF—Ehrlichman, Box 15, Nixon Papers; Krogh to Attorney General, Jan. 28, 1970, ibid.; Krogh to Haldeman, March 12, 1970, ibid.; Krogh to Brad Patterson, Jan. 14, 1970, ibid.; Ehrlichman to the President, May 8, 1970, OA #103, WHSF—Egil Krogh, Box 58, Nixon Papers; Hoover to Tolson, DeLoach, Sullivan, and Bishop, April 21, 1970, no. not recorded, FBI–Tolson Memo File; Hoover to Tolson, DeLoach, Rosen, Sullivan, and Bishop, May 14, 1970, no. not recorded, ibid.; Hoover to Tolson, Sullivan, Bishop, and Brennan, Jan. 7, 1971, no. not recorded, ibid.

17. House Committee on Appropriations, *Hearings* (1971), 743; Director to SAC Los Angeles, June 25, 1970, no. 1868, FBI–COINTEL (Black Nationalist)

File (100-448006); SAC Los Angeles to Director, June 17, 1970, no. 1868, ibid.; SAC New York to Director, March 6, 1969, no. 2085, FBI–Moore Files (100-161993).

18. The discussion of the Seberg case is based on Richards, *Played Out*, 220, 237–41, 245, 247, 253, 277, 325, 374, 378; Moore to Sullivan, April 14, 1970, no. 28, FBI–Seberg File (157-13876); Hoover to Ehrlichman, May 19, 1970, no. 30, ibid.; Hoover to Attorney General, May 19, 1970, no. 30, ibid.; Moore to Brennan, Aug. 28, 1970, no. 32, ibid.; Director to SACs Los Angeles et al., Sept. 11, 1970, no. 33, ibid.; Director to SAC Los Angeles, May 6, 1970, no. 1766, FBI–COINTEL (Black) File; SAC Los Angeles to Director, April 27, 1970, no. 1766, June 3, 1970, no. 1831 (Haber's column is filed under this serial), June 10, 1970, no. 1837, ibid.; SAC San Francisco to Director, April 23, 1970, no. 26-1137, FBI–Black Panther Party File (105-165706); SAC Boston to Director, May 4, 1973, no. 125, FBI–Jamal File (100-44622).

19. See the sources cited in the previous note.

20. Hoover to Tolson, DeLoach, Rosen, Sullivan, and Bishop, May 18, 1970, no. not recorded, FBI–Tolson Memo File; President's Commission, *Campus Unrest*, 436, 438–39. Moore disagreed with Hoover on Jackson State, saying "the trouble began with 'the street corner boys,' youngsters who dropped out of school" and "were on campus looking for trouble, spreading rumors—'Did you know Charlie Evers was shot?'" Moore interview.

21. Memo, Hoover to Tolson, DeLoach, Rosen, Sullivan, and Bishop, May 18, 1970, no. not recorded, FBI–Tolson Memo File. Field agents, in contrast, were critical of the guardsmen in Kent and the policemen in Jackson. When the *Washington Post* ran a story "to the effect that the FBI has said that the (National) Guards are to blame in the Kent State matter," Nixon called Hoover to complain. "The President said that from what he had seen . . . it looks like the Guard had a lot of provocation. I said I thought they definitely had. The President said he told his people he was going to have [the FBI report] 'shot down' as he was not going to have this student business erupting as, basically, what do you expect the Guards to do." Hoover to Tolson, Sullivan, Bishop, and Rosen, July 24, 1970, no. not recorded, ibid.; Hoover to Tolson, Sullivan, Bishop, Brennan, Gale, and Rosen, July 24, 1970, no. not recorded, ibid.; Leonard interview.

22. Director to SACs Atlanta and Philadelphia, May 19, 1970, no. 2932, FBI–SCLC File; Director to SAC Atlanta, May 19, 1970, no. 2929, ibid.; Moore to Sullivan, May 18, 1970, in Church Committee, *Hearings—FBI*, 493; Hoover to Agnew, May 19, 1970, ibid., 494; Hoover to Tolson, DeLoach, Rosen, Sullivan, and Bishop, May 18, 1970, no. not recorded, FBI–Tolson Memo File.

23. Graham, "On Riots," 22; President's Commission, *Campus Unrest*, 436, 450, 458–59.

24. Ehrlichman interview; Moore to Sullivan, Jan. 22, 1969, no. 3562, FBI–King File; Hoover to the President, Jan. 23, 1969, no. 3560, ibid.; Director to Deputy Attorney General, March 3, 1969, no. 3571, ibid.; Moore to Sullivan, Jan. 17, 1969, no. 127, King Folder, FBI–Hoover O&C Files.

25. Church Committee, *Book III*, 183; Director to SAC Atlanta, April 14, 1969, no. not recorded, FBI–SCLC File; Director to SACs Baltimore et al., March 27, 1969, no. 3581, FBI–King File; Jones to Bishop, March 18, 1969, no. 3586, ibid.

26. DeLoach to Tolson, March 11, 1969, no. 5654, FBI–King Assassination File (44-38861); Moore to Sullivan, March 5, 1969, no. 772, FBI–COINTEL (Black) File; Director to SAC Atlanta, March 13, 1969, no. 772, ibid.

27. When the FBI finally made an arrest in June, the director told the attorney

general that "the supporters of Dr. King will do everything in their power to kill [James Earl Ray]." Hoover to Tolson, DeLoach, Rosen, Bishop, and Sullivan, June 20, 1968, no. 4660, FBI–King Assassination File.

28. DeLoach to Tolson, March 11, 1969, no. 5654, FBI–King Assassination File; Jones to Bishop, March 20, 1969, no. 5655, ibid.; Rosen to DeLoach, Jan. 16, 1970, no. 5854, ibid. Bishop wrote his book, but it was not the type of book DeLoach wanted and it is not clear whether Crime Records provided much assistance.

29. Moore to Sullivan, Feb. 28, 1970 (addendum by Bishop), no. 3728, FBI–King File; Jones to Bishop, May 22, 1968, no. 149, King Folder, FBI–Hoover O&C Files.

30. Moore to Sullivan, Jan. 13, 1970, no. 3699, FBI–King File; SAC Washington to Director, Jan. 12, 1970, no. 3697, ibid; letterhead memos, Jan. 5, 1971, no. 3871, Dec. 31, 1970, no. 3867, ibid.; SAC Washington to Director, Jan. 11, 1971, no. 3689, ibid.

31. SAC Letter, May 27, 1969, in Church Committee, *Book III*, 518. See also ibid., 228, 252–55, *Book II*, 75, *Hearings—FBI*, 17; SAC Richmond to Director, May 14, 1969, no. 918, FBI–COINTEL (Black) File.

32. Director to SACs Baltimore et al., July 16, 1970, no. 230, FBI–COINTEL (Special Operations) File.

33. Richard E. Logan to SAC Philadelphia, Jan. 27, 1971, in "Complete Collection," 50; Church Committee, *Book III*, 246–50.

34. House Committee on the Judiciary, *Statement of Information—Book VII*, pt. 1, pp. 398–402; Tom Charles Huston to Haldeman, Aug. 25, 1970, HRH Security/FBI, WHSF—Haldeman, Box, 147, Nixon Papers.

35. SAC Columbia to Director, Feb. 28, 1969, no. illegible, May 28, 1970, no. illegible, FBI–COINTEL (Black) File; SAC Pittsburgh to Director, Sept. 4, 1969, no. 1257, ibid.; SAC Norfolk to Director, April 6, 1970, no. 932, FBI–COINTEL (New Left) File; SAC Butte to Director, Sept. 12, 1968, no. 7-6, March 12, 1969, no. 7-14, ibid.

36. SAC Sacramento to Director, April 1, 1970, no. 931, FBI–COINTEL (New Left) File; SAC Los Angeles to Director, July 31, 1968, no. 26-7, Sept. 30, 1968, no. 26-13, ibid.; Director to SAC San Diego, Sept. 18, 1969, no. 1284, FBI–COINTEL (Black) File; Director to SAC San Francisco, Feb. 27, 1969, no. illegible, ibid.; SAC San Diego to Director, Oct. 6, 1969, no. 1338, Nov. 10, 1969, no. illegible, Feb. 18, 1970, no illegible, ibid.

37. Note, re Domestic Intelligence Division Inspection, Jan. 12, 1971, in Church Committee, *Hearings—FBI*, 709; Director to SACs Albany et al., Nov. 4, 1970, ibid., 698-99; Executives' Conference to Tolson, Oct. 29, 1970, ibid., 701; SAC Letter, Sept. 15, 1970, FBI–SAC File. See also Director to SACs Albany et al., Jan. 31, 1969, no. 2, FBI–Black Student Groups on College Campuses File (157-12176).

38. SAC Jackson to Director, April 4, 1968, no. 73, Feb. 11, 1969, no. illegible, FBI–COINTEL (Black) File; deposition of Thomas Fitzpatrick, April 27, 1978, pp. 87–88, 208, *Muhammad Kenyatta v. Roy Moore, et al.*, no. J77-0298(R) (S.D. Miss., 1985).

39. SAC Jackson to Director, Feb. 26, 1969, no. illegible, March 7, 1970, no. illegible, FBI–COINTEL (Black) File.

40. Church Committee, *Book II*, 46; SAC Jackson to Director, March 7, 1970, no. illegible, FBI–COINTEL (Black) File.

41. SAC Jackson to Director, Feb. 26, 1969, no. illegible, FBI–COINTEL (Black) File; Director to SAC Jackson, March 3, 1969, no. illegible, ibid.

42. Aschenbrenner interview; SAC Jackson to Director, Sept. 16, 1969, no. 54-

14, Oct. 13, 1969, no. 54-15, FBI–COINTEL (New Left) File; Director to SAC Jackson, Oct. 1, 1969, no. 54-14, ibid. Bureau agents insist that Kenyatta did in fact steal the television in question.

43. *Jackson Capital Reporter*, June 22, 1978; SAC Jackson to Director, Oct. 13, 1969, no. 1348, FBI–COINTEL (Black) File; Director to SAC Jackson, Aug. 17, 1970, no. illegible, Feb. 8, 1971, no. 2195, ibid.; SAC Jackson to Director, July 21, 1970, no. 1893, Aug. 5, 1970, no. 1910, Aug. 4, 1970, no. 1914, Aug. 3, 1970, no. 1911, Feb. 1, 1971, no. 2195, ibid.; Moore to Brennan, Aug. 7, 1970, no. not recorded, ibid. Moore's agents also helped Ward write about the Republic of New Africa.

44. Richard H. Ichord to William H. Stapleton, July 2, 1974, Misc. Memoranda 1973-74, Box 175, Ichord Papers.

45. Bamford, *Puzzle Palace*, 322; Church Committee, *Book III*, 573, 624, 631, 751, *Book II*, 107; National Conference of Black Lawyers, et al., *Human Rights*, Appendix VI.

46. Letterhead memo, Jan. 29, 1971, no. 27, FBI–Jackson File (157-6760); Moore to Brennan, Aug. 14, 1970, no. 22, Aug. 17, 1970, no. 23, ibid.; Moore to Brennan, Aug. 18, 1970, no. 3834, FBI–King File; Director to SAC Chicago, Aug. 21, 1970, no. illegible, FBI–COINTEL (Black) File; Moore to Brennan, Aug. 18, 1970, no. 2981, FBI–SCLC File.

47. Cotter to Miller, Sept. 17, 1971, no. illegible, FBI–Security Index File (100-358086); Thomas J. Smith to Miller, Nov. 11, 1971, no. 4116, ibid.; Moore to Brennan, April 21, 1971, no. 294, FBI–Agitator Index File (157-7782).

48. Church Committee, *Book II*, 125–26, *Book III*, 546–47.

49. This also applied to people with red skin, with Division Five preparing a directive to the field requiring the counting of Indians! All reservation and nonreservation natives were to be tallied up and spied upon. "We are *outraged* by the conduct of these Indians," L. Patrick Gray III agreed, but Division Five "rhetoric" needed to be toned down. Gray aborted the directive in favor of a more moderate one requiring the surveillance of all American Indian Movement chapters. Moore to Edward S. Miller, Nov. 27, 1972, no. 73, FBI–AIM File (100-462483); Acting Director to SACs Albany et al., Nov. 28, 1972, no. 73, Dec. 29, 1972, no. 108, ibid.; note, F [Felt], n.d. [ca. Nov. 27, 1972], no. 73, ibid.; note, G [Gray], Nov. 29, 1972, no. 73, ibid.

50. Moore to Brennan, Oct. 29, 1970, no. 2053, Nov. 2, 1970, no. 2113, FBI–COINTEL (Black) File; Director to SACs Albany et al., Dec. 23, 1970, no. not recorded, ibid.; Church Committee, *Book II*, 91, *Book III*, 530–31.

51. See the sources cited in the previous note.

52. SAC Washington to Director, Feb. 17, 1969, no. 680, FBI–COINTEL (Black) File; [deleted] to SAC Philadelphia, June 18, 1970, in "Complete Collection," 49–50.

53. Church Committee, *Book III*, 534; Director to SACs Albany et al., Feb. 26, 1971, no. 227, FBI–Computerized Telephone Number File (62-3491). A year later, Division Five renamed the Black Nationalist Photograph Album the Extremist Album and added the names of about twenty-five or thirty Ku Klux Klansmen.

54. For a day in the life of a wiretap (PH 1209-R), see Ronald Butler to SAC Philadelphia, Feb. 4, 1971, no. illegible, in "Complete Collection," 26–28.

55. John Mitchell to Hoover, July 14, 1969, no. illegible, FBI–Hampton Files; Hoover to Attorney General, April 29, 1969, no. illegible, Oct. 19, 1970, no. illegible, ibid.

56. Koning, *Nineteen Sixty-Eight*, 52; Bergman and Weir, "Revolution," 46;

Hoover to Attorney General, April 29, 1969, no. illegible, Oct. 19, 1970, no. illegible, FBI–Hampton Files.

57. Houlding, "Wiring," 685. For the Levison tap, see SAC New York to Director, Sept. 24, 1969, no. 353, FBI–Levison File; Hoover to Attorney General, Oct. 1, 1969, no. 353, ibid. For the breakdown of electronic surveillances, see W. Raymond Wannall to Brennan, March 29, 1971, no. 3, Intelligence Coverage, Domestic and Foreign Folder, FBI–Hoover O&C Files.

58. Gale to DeLoach, May 27, 1966, no. 2, Microphone Surveillances Folder, FBI–Hoover O&C Files.

59. Felt to Tolson, July 7, 1971, no. 2, Folder 142, ibid.

60. Director to Attorney General, Sept. 14, 1965, no. 14, Microphone Surveillances Folder, ibid.; Ramsey Clark to the President, Vice President, Members of the Cabinet, and Robert E. Kintner, Jan. 6, 1967, WHCF—CF, FG100/RS, Box 102, Johnson Papers.

61. FBI surveillance of Muhammad Ali sucked in everyone around him, from Howard Cosell to Angelo Dundee and even Johnny Carson. Whenever Ali appeared on the *Tonight Show*, an agent stayed up to watch and record the telecast.

62. Moore to Sullivan, July 2, 1969, no. 3643, FBI–King File; Hoover to Jesse Helms, July 7, 1969, no. not recorded, ibid.; Hoover to Attorney General, June 10, 1969, no. 92, King Folder, FBI–Hoover O&C Files; Hoover to the President, June 16, 1969, no. 95, July 1, 1969, no. 156, ibid.; Hoover to Agnew, June 16, 1969, no. 97, ibid.

63. Leonard interview; Church Committee, *Book II*, 80–81, *Book III*, 500–04, 536; memo, for the President, April 1, 1969, Civil Rights, Busing(1), Box 3, Domestic Council—Geoffrey Shepard Files, Ford Papers.

64. The FBI compiled "estimates" on such topics as "The Interrelationships of Black Power Organizations in the Western Hemisphere."

65. Church Committee, *Book II*, 256–57, *Hearings—FBI*, 349–50; Director to SACs Albany et al., Nov. 6, 1969, no. 6049, FBI–Moore Files (100-161993).

66. Executives' Conference to Tolson, Feb. 12, 1970, no. 1, FBI–Stop Index/ National Crime Information Center File (62-115784); W. G. Campbell to Thomas J. Jenkins, Feb. 22, 1974, no. 71, ibid.

67. D. J. Brennan, Jr., to Sullivan, Aug. 15, 1969, no. 1000, FBI–McSurely Files (62-17909); Senate Committee on the Judiciary, *Political Intelligence in the IRS*, 17; Joint Committee on Internal Revenue Taxation, *Investigation of the Special Service Staff*, 23-27; John L. McClellan to Henry Fowler, Sept. 19, 1968, IRS-McSurely Files; D. O. Virdin to File, March 14 and May 28, 1969, ibid.

68. FDR's secretary of the treasury, Henry Morgenthau, Jr., had a Bureau of Internal Revenue intelligence unit compile a report, complete with thirty-seven exhibits, on Paul Robeson. At the time, the IRS rarely shared data with the FBI. Tolson and Edward A. Tamm to Director, Dec. 12, 1941, Dies Folder, FBI–Hoover O&C Files; Elmer Irey to the Secretary, Aug. 7, 1941, Confidential Repts. About People 1941, Morgenthau Papers; Internal Revenue Intelligence Unit Rept., July 31, 1941, ibid.

69. Joint Committee, *Investigation of the SSS*, 7–8, 13–14, 37, 101–10; Senate Committee on the Judiciary, *Political Intelligence in the IRS*, 39–40, 43–47; Church Committee, *Book II*, 95, *Book III*, 842. The IRS also had an informal name-check arrangement with the FBI. Memo, Sept. 19, 1966, no. 14X1, FBI–Forman File (100-443566).

70. Joint Committee, *Investigation of the SSS*, 7–8, 11, 37; Committee on the

Judiciary, *Political Intelligence in the IRS*, 39–40, 43–47; Church Committee, *Book II*, 95, *Book III*, 842.

71. Leonard, Fleischer interviews; Greenberg, "Revolt," 32–40.

72. Rosen to DeLoach, July 9, 1970, no. 1015, FBI–Civil Rights Policy File (44-00); Hoover to Tolson et al., Sept. 11, 1970, no. not recorded, Oct. 12, 1970, no. not recorded, FBI–Tolson Memo File.

73. W. S. Tavel to Mohr, March 2, 1971, Folder 83, FBI–Hoover O&C Files; Tavel to Mohr, March 2, 1971, ibid.

74. Brennan to Sullivan, March 15, 1971, no. 215, FBI–MEDBURG File (52-94527).

75. Director to Attorney General, March 5, 1971, no. 91, ibid. In 1969, when Forman presented his "Black Manifesto" calling for reparations from white churches, the Bureau opened a racketeering/extortion investigation of the Black Economic Development Conference.

76. Rosen to Sullivan, March 24, 1971, no. 264, ibid.; Dwight J. Dalbey to Tolson, March 24, 1971, no. 425, ibid.

77. For the conference, see Watters and Gillers, eds., *Investigating*. For the blind memos and other documents on conference participants, see FBI–CPJ File.

78. Director to Attorney General, April 30, 1971, no. 4, FBI–CPJ File; Rosen to Sullivan, Sept. 24, 1971, no. 10, ibid.; C. Bolz to Charles W. Bates, Oct. 13, 1971, no. 14, Oct. 19, 1971, no. 18, ibid.; Jones to Bishop, Oct. 1, 1971, no. 8, Oct. 27, 1971, no. 25, ibid.; *Cong. Rec.*, 92d Cong., 1st sess., 1971, Oct. 19, pp. 36,883–84, Oct. 28, pp. 38,091–92, Nov. 2, pp, 38,792–94, Nov. 9, pp. 40,073–79, Nov. 19, p. 42,222.

79. Powers, *Secrecy and Power*, 479–80.

80. Ibid., 478–85; *Washington Evening Star*, May 5, 1972, in U.S. Congress, *Memorial Tributes*, 229.

81. National Conference of Black Lawyers et al., *Human Rights*, Appendix V; Katzenbach interview.

82. R. R. Frank to Jenkins, March 21, 1974, no. not recorded, FBI–HUAC File (61-7582); Jenkins to Callahan, Nov. 15, 1973, no. not recorded, FBI–Eastland File.

83. Robert M. Horner to Ichord, Sept. 19, 1973, FBI (Oversight Hearings), Box 179, Ichord Papers; Ichord to Clarence M. Kelley, June 25, 1973, Justice Dept., Box 175, ibid.

84. A former FBI agent who headed the Birmingham office from 1957 to 1960, Kelley came to the directorship with the reputation of being an innovative law enforcement man. A single blemish marred his record as police chief of Kansas City—the charge that he was insensitive to minorities. Ungar, *FBI*, 582, 587–88.

85. Henry E. Petersen to Director, Oct. 22, 1974, in Church Committee, *Hearings—FBI*, 703–5; idem, *Book III*, 555–56.

86. Laurence H. Silberman to Donald Rumsfeld, Dec. 12, 1974, Civil Rights, Busing-Boston, Domestic Council—Geoffrey Shepard Files, Box 3, Ford Papers.

87. Chaired in the Senate by Frank Church (D., Ida.), and in the House by Lucien N. Nedzi (D., Mich.) and then Otis Pike (D., N.Y.).

88. Mike Duval to Jack Marsh, Oct. 23, 1975, Draft Plans for IGC, Box 11, Raoul-Duval Papers.

89. Henry A. Kissinger et al. to the President, Sept. 18, 1975, WHCF, ND6,

Ford Papers; Dudley Chapman to Buchen et al., Nov. 5, 1974, Counsel to the President, Exec. Priv., Gen. (1), Box 13, Edward C. Schmults Files, ibid.; Duval to Marsh, Oct. 23, 1974, Draft Plan for IGC, Raoul-Duval Papers; Ichord to Kelley, Oct. 23, 1975, Departmental: Justice–FBI, Box 139, Ichord Papers; Kelley to Ichord, Oct. 30, 1975, ibid.

90. Wofford, *Kennedys and Kings*, 206.
91. Sullivan died in a deer hunting accident in November 1977.
92. Katzenbach submitted Doar's report, originally prepared for the Princeton conference. *Hearings—FBI*, 888–991.
93. House Select Committee on Intelligence, *Hearings*, pt. 3, pp. 1,035, 1,042; Stone, "Schorr Case," 6–11; Freeman, "Investigating," 103–18.

CONCLUSION

1. *New York Times*, Nov. 5, 1979; Salter, "Reflections," 23–24.
2. Whitehead, *FBI Story*, 396.

Selected Bibliography

========≡≡≡≡≡≡≡≡========

Books and Pamphlets

ADLER, BILL. *Kid's Letters to the F.B.I.* Englewood Cliffs, N.J.: Prentice Hall, 1966.

Amnesty International. *Proposal for a Commission of Inquiry into the Effect of Domestic Intelligence Activities on Criminal Trials in the United States of America.* London: Amnesty International, 1981.

AMOS, JAMES E. *Theodore Roosevelt: Hero to His Valet.* New York: John Day, 1927.

ANTHONY, EARL. *Picking Up the Gun.* New York: Dial, 1970.

BAKER, WILLIAM J. *Jesse Owens: An American Life.* New York: Free Press, 1986.

BAMFORD, JAMES. *The Puzzle Palace.* New York: Penguin ed., 1983.

BARAKA, AMIRI. *The Autobiography of LeRoi Jones.* New York: Freundlich Books, 1984.

BARKAN, STEVEN E. *Protestors on Trial.* New Brunswick, N.J.: Rutgers University Press, 1985.

BARNARD, HOLLINGER F., ed. *Outside the Magic Circle: The Autobiography of Virginia Foster Durr.* University: University of Alabama Press, 1985.

BARNES, CATHERINE A. *Journey from Jim Crow.* New York: Columbia University Press, 1983.

BELFRAGE, SALLY. *Freedom Summer.* New York: Viking, 1965.

BELKNAP, MICHAL R. *Federal Law and Southern Order: Racial Violence and Constitutional Conflict in the Post-Brown South.* Athens: University of Georgia Press, 1987.

BELL, DERRICK A., JR. *Race, Racism and American Law.* Boston: Little, Brown, 1973.

BERMAN, WILLIAM C. *The Politics of Civil Rights in the Truman Administration.* Columbia: Ohio State University Press, 1970.

BERRY, JASON. *Amazing Grace: With Charles Evers in Mississippi.* New York: Saturday Review Press, 1973.

BISHOP, JIM. *A Bishop's Confessions.* Boston: Little, Brown, 1981.

——. *The Days of Martin Luther King, Jr.* New York: G. P. Putnam's Sons, 1971.

BLACKSTOCK, NELSON. *COINTELPRO: The FBI's Secret War on Political Freedom*. New York: Vintage, 1975.

BRADEN, ANNE. *The Wall Between*. New York: Monthly Review Press, 1958.

BRANCH, TAYLOR. *Parting the Waters: America in the King Years, 1954–1963*. New York: Simon and Schuster, 1988.

BRAUER, CARL M. *John F. Kennedy and the Second Reconstruction*. New York: Columbia University Press, 1977.

BROWN, H. RAP. *Die, Nigger, Die*. New York: Dial Press, 1969.

BROWN, JULIA. *I Testify: My Years as an F.B.I. Undercover Agent*. Belmont, Mass.: Western Islands, 1966.

BROWN, RICHARD M. *Strain of Violence*. New York: Oxford University Press, 1975.

BUCHANAN, PATRICK J. *Right From the Beginning*. Boston: Little, Brown, 1988.

BURK, ROBERT F. *The Eisenhower Administration and Black Civil Rights*. Knoxville: University of Tennessee Press, 1984.

CAGIN, SETH, and PHILIP DRAY. *We Are Not Afraid: The Story of Goodman, Schwerner, and Chaney and the Civil Rights Campaign in Mississippi*. New York: Macmillan, 1988.

CAMPBELL, CLARICE T., and OSCAR ALLAN ROGERS, JR. *Mississippi: The View from Tougaloo*. Jackson: University Press of Mississippi, 1979.

CARLSON, JODY. *George C. Wallace and the Politics of Powerlessness*. New Brunswick, N.J.: Transaction Books, 1981.

CARMICHAEL, STOKELY, and CHARLES V. HAMILTON. *Black Power: The Politics of Liberation in America*. New York: Random House, 1967.

CARR, ROBERT K. *Federal Protection of Civil Rights: Quest for a Sword*. Ithaca, N.Y.: Cornell University Press, 1947.

CARSON, CLAYBORNE. *In Struggle: SNCC and the Black Awakening of the 1960s*. Cambridge, Mass.: Harvard University Press, 1981.

CARTER, DAN T. *Scottsboro: A Tragedy of the American South*. Baton Rouge: Louisiana State University Press, 1969.

Chicago Commission on Race Relations. *The Negro in Chicago: A Study of Race Relations and a Race Riot*. Chicago: University of Chicago Press, 1922.

CLARK, RAMSEY. *Crime in America*. New York: Simon and Schuster, 1970.

CLEAVER, ELDRIDGE. *Soul On Ice*. New York: Random House, 1968.

COLBURN, DAVID R. *Racial Change and Community Crisis: St. Augustine, Florida, 1877–1980*. New York: Columbia University Press, 1985.

Commission of Inquiry Into the Black Panthers and the Police. *Search and Destroy*. New York: Metropolitan Applied Research Center, 1973.

CUMMINGS, RICHARD. *The Pied Piper: Allard K. Lowenstein and the American Dream*. New York: Grove, 1985.

DANIEL, PETE. *The Shadow of Slavery: Peonage in the South, 1901–1969*. Urbana: University of Illinois Press, 1972.

DAVIS, ANGELA. *Angela Davis: An Autobiography*. New York: Random House, 1974.

——, ET AL. *If They Come in the Morning*. New York: Signet, 1971.

DEMARIS, OVID. *The Director: An Oral Biography of J. Edgar Hoover*. New York: Harper's Magazine Press, 1975.

DE TOLEDANO, RALPH. *J. Edgar Hoover: The Man in His Time*. New Rochelle, N.Y.: Arlington House, 1973.

DONNER, FRANK J. *The Age of Surveillance.* New York: Knopf, 1980.

DULLES, FOSTER RHEA. *The Civil Rights Commission, 1957–1965.* East Lansing: Michigan State University Press, 1968.

EDWARDS, HARRY. *The Struggle That Must Be.* New York: Macmillan, 1980.

EHRLICHMAN, JOHN. *Witness to Power.* New York: Simon and Schuster, 1982.

ELLIFF, JOHN T. *Crime, Dissent, and the Attorney General.* Beverly Hills, Calif.: Sage Publications, 1971.

EVANS, SARA. *Personal Politics: The Roots of Women's Liberation in the Civil Rights Movement and the New Left.* New York: Knopf, 1979.

EVERS, CHARLES. *Evers.* New York: World, 1971.

FAIRCLOUGH, ADAM. *To Redeem the Soul of America: The Southern Christian Leadership Conference and Martin Luther King, Jr.* Athens: University of Georgia Press, 1987.

FARMER, JAMES. *Lay Bare the Heart.* New York: Arbor House, 1985.

FELT, W. MARK. *The FBI Pyramid from the Inside.* New York: G. P. Putnam's Sons, 1979.

FINE, SIDNEY. *Frank Murphy.* 3 vols. Ann Arbor: University of Michigan Press, 1975–1984.

FORMAN, JAMES. *The Making of Black Revolutionaries.* New York: Macmillan, 1972.

FRADY, MARSHALL. *Wallace.* New York: World, 1968.

FREYER, TONY. *The Little Rock Crisis.* Westport, Conn.: Greenwood, 1984.

FRIEDMAN, LEON, ed. *Southern Justice.* New York: Random House, 1965.

GARROW, DAVID J. *Bearing the Cross: Martin Luther King, Jr., and the Southern Christian Leadership Conference.* New York: Morrow, 1986.

——. *The FBI and Martin Luther King, Jr.: From "SOLO" to Memphis.* New York: Norton, 1981.

——. *Protest at Selma: Martin Luther King, Jr., and the Voting Rights Act of 1965.* New Haven, Conn.: Yale University Press, 1978.

GITLIN, TODD. *The Sixties: Years of Hope, Days of Rage.* New York: Bantam, 1987.

GOLDWATER, BARRY M. *With No Apologies.* New York: Morrow, 1979.

GOODWIN, RICHARD N. *Remembering America.* Boston: Little, Brown, 1988.

Governor's Commission on the Los Angeles Riots. *Violence in the City—An End or a Beginning.* Los Angeles: College Book Store, 1965.

GRANT, JOANNE, ed. *Black Protest.* Greenwich, Conn.: Fawcett, 1968.

GUTHMAN, EDWIN. *We Band of Brothers.* New York: Harper and Row, 1971.

HAMER, FANNIE LOU, ET AL. *To Praise Our Bridges.* Jackson, Miss.: KIPCO, 1967.

HARRIS, DAVID. *Dreams Die Hard.* New York: St. Martin's/Marek, 1982.

HARRIS, RICHARD. *Freedom Spent.* Boston: Little, Brown, 1976.

——. *Justice.* New York: Avon Books ed., 1970.

HAYDEN, TOM. *Reunion: A Memoir.* New York: Random House, 1988.

HILL, ROBERT A., ed. *The Marcus Garvey and Universal Negro Improvement Association Papers.* Los Angeles and Berkeley: University of California Press, 1983–.

HINDS, LENNOX S. *Illusions of Justice.* Iowa City: School of Social Work, University of Iowa, 1979.

HOLT, LEN. *The Summer That Didn't End.* New York: Morrow, 1965.

HOOVER, HERBERT. *Memoirs*. 3 vols. New York: Macmillan, 1951–1952.

HOOVER, J. EDGAR. *Masters of Deceit*. New York: Pocket Books ed., 1959.

HORNE, GERALD. *Black & Red: W. E. B. Du Bois and the Afro-American Response to the Cold War, 1944–1963*. Albany: State University of New York Press, 1986.

———. *Communist Front? The Civil Rights Congress, 1946–1956*. Rutherford, N.J.: Fairleigh Dickinson University Press, 1988.

JACOBS, PAUL. *Prelude to Riot*. New York: Vintage ed., 1967.

JOHNSON, LADY BIRD. *A White House Diary*. New York: Holt, Rinehart & Winston, 1970.

JOHNSON, LOCH K. *A Season of Inquiry: The Senate Intelligence Investigation*. Lexington: University of Kentucky Press, 1985.

JOHNSON, LYNDON B. *The Vantage Point*. New York: Holt, Rinehart & Winston, 1971.

KARENGA, M. *The Roots of the US/Panther Conflict*. San Diego: Kawaida Publications, 1976.

KEARNS, DORIS. *Lyndon Johnson and the American Dream*. New York: Harper and Row, 1976.

KELLEY, CLARENCE. *Kelley: The Story of An FBI Director*. Kansas City, Mo.: Andrews, McMeel and Parker, 1987.

KING, MARTIN LUTHER, JR. *Why We Can't Wait*. New York: New American Library, 1964.

KING, MARTIN LUTHER, SR., with CLAYTON RILEY. *Daddy King: An Autobiography*. New York: Morrow, 1980.

KING, MARY. *Freedom Song*. New York: Morrow, 1987.

KINOY, ARTHUR. *Rights on Trial*. Cambridge, Mass.: Harvard University Press, 1983.

KIRBY, JOHN B. *Black Americans in the Roosevelt Era*. Knoxville: University of Tennessee Press, 1980.

KLEHR, HARVEY. *The Heyday of American Communism*. New York: Basic Books, 1984.

KLUGER, RICHARD. *Simple Justice*. New York: Knopf, 1975.

KONING, HANS. *Nineteen Sixty-Eight*. New York: Norton, 1987.

KORNWEIBEL, THEODORE, JR. *No Crystal Stair: Black Life and the* Messenger, *1917–1928*. Westport, Conn.: Greenwood, 1975.

KRUEGER, THOMAS A. *And Promises to Keep: The Southern Conference for Human Welfare, 1938–1948*. Nashville: Vanderbilt University Press, 1967.

LAWSON, STEVEN F. *Black Ballots: Voting Rights in the South, 1944–1969*. New York: Columbia University Press, 1976.

———. *In Pursuit of Power: Southern Blacks and Electoral Politics, 1965–1982*. New York: Columbia University Press, 1985.

LEWIS, ANTHONY. *Portrait of a Decade*. New York: Random House, 1964.

LEWIS, DAVID L. *King: A Critical Biography*. New York: Praeger, 1970.

LINCOLN, C. ERIC. *The Black Muslims in America*. Rev. ed. Boston: Beacon, 1973.

LORD, WALTER. *The Past That Would Not Die*. New York: Harper and Row, 1965.

LOWENTHAL, MAX. *The Federal Bureau of Investigation*. New York: William Sloane, 1950.

MCADAM, DOUG. *Freedom Summer*. New York: Oxford University Press, 1988.

McCoy, Donald R., and Richard T. Reutten. *Quest and Response: Minority Rights and the Truman Administration*. Lawrence: University Press of Kansas, 1973.

McGovern, James R. *Anatomy of a Lynching: The Killing of Claude Neal*. Baton Rouge: Louisiana State University Press, 1982.

McIlhany, William H., II. *Klandestine: The Untold Story of Delmar Dennis and His Role in the FBI's War Against the Ku Klux Klan*. New Rochelle, N.Y.: Arlington House, 1975.

McMillen, Neil R. *The Citizens' Council: Organized Resistance to the Second Reconstruction, 1954–1964*. Urbana: University of Illinois Press, 1971.

McPherson, Harry C., Jr. *A Political Education*. Boston: Little, Brown, 1972.

Makeba, Miriam, with James Hall. *Makeba: My Story*. New York: New American Library, 1988.

Malcolm X. *The Autobiography of Malcolm X*. New York: Grove, 1965.

Manchester, William. *The Glory and the Dream*. New York: Bantam ed., 1975.

Marable, Manning. *Race, Reform and Rebellion: The Second Reconstruction in Black America, 1945–1982*. Jackson: University Press of Mississippi, 1984.

Mars, Florence. *Witness in Philadelphia*. Baton Rouge: Louisiana State University Press, 1977.

Marshall, Burke. *Federalism and Civil Rights*. Foreword by Robert F. Kennedy. New York: Columbia University Press, 1964.

Mason, Alpheus Thomas. *Harlan Fiske Stone: Pillar of the Law*. New York: Viking, 1954.

Matusow, Allen J. *The Unraveling of America*. New York: Harper and Row, 1984.

Mazón, Mauricio. *The Zoot-Suit Riots*. Austin: University of Texas Press, 1984.

Meier, August, and Elliott Rudwick. *Along the Color Line*. Urbana: University of Illinois Press, 1976.

———. *CORE: A Study in the Civil Rights Movement, 1942–1968*. New York: Oxford University Press, 1973.

Mendelsohn, Jack. *The Martyrs*. New York: Harper and Row, 1966.

Meredith, James. *Three Years in Mississippi*. Bloomington: Indiana University Press, 1966.

Miller, Char. *Fathers and Sons: The Bingham Family and the American Mission*. Philadelphia: Temple University Press, 1982.

Millspaugh, Arthur C. *Crime Control by the National Government*. Washington, D.C.: Brookings Institution, 1937.

Misseduc Foundation. *Mississippi Black Paper*. New York: Random House, 1965.

Mitgang, Herbert. *Dangerous Dossiers: Exposing the Secret War Against America's Greatest Authors*. New York: Donald I. Fine, 1988.

Moody, Anne. *Coming of Age in Mississippi*. New York: Dial Press, 1968.

Moore, Jesse T., Jr. *A Search for Equality: The National Urban League, 1910–1961*. University Park: Pennsylvania State University Press, 1981.

Morgan, Charles, Jr. *One Man, One Voice*. New York: Holt, Rinehart and Winston, 1979.

Morris, Aldon D. *The Origins of the Civil Rights Movement*. New York: Free Press, 1984.

MYRDAL, GUNNAR. *An American Dilemma.* New York: Harper and Row, 1944.

NAISON, MARK. *Communists in Harlem during the Depression.* Urbana: University of Illinois Press, 1983.

National Conference of Black Lawyers et al. *Human Rights Violations in the United States.* Petition to the United Nations Commission on Human Rights. December 1978.

NAVASKY, VICTOR. *Kennedy Justice.* New York: Atheneum, 1971.

———. *Naming Names.* New York: Viking, 1980.

NELSON, JACK, and JACK BASS. *The Orangeburg Massacre.* New York and Cleveland: World, 1970.

NEWFIELD, JACK. *Robert Kennedy: A Memoir.* New York: Dutton, 1969.

NIXON, RICHARD M. *RN: The Memoirs of Richard Nixon.* New York: Grosset and Dunlap, 1978.

NORRELL, ROBERT J. *Reaping the Whirlwind: The Civil Rights Movement in Tuskegee.* New York: Knopf, 1985.

OATES, STEPHEN B. *Let the Trumpet Sound.* New York: Harper and Row, 1982.

OLLESTAD, NORMAN. *Inside the F.B.I.* New York: Lyle Stuart, 1967.

O'REILLY, KENNETH. *Hoover and the Un-Americans.* Philadelphia: Temple University Press, 1983.

OVERSTREET, HARRY and BONARO. *The FBI in Our Open Society.* New York: Norton, 1969.

PAINTER, NELL IRVIN. *The Narrative of Hosea Hudson.* Cambridge, Mass.: Harvard University Press, 1979.

PECK, JAMES. *Freedom Ride.* New York: Simon and Schuster, 1962.

PHILLIPS, KEVIN P. *The Emerging Republican Majority.* New Rochelle, N.Y.: Arlington House, 1969.

PINKNEY, ALPHONSO. *Red, Black, and Green: Black Nationalism in the United States.* New York: Cambridge University Press, 1976.

POFFORD, TIM S. *Lynch Street: The May 1970 Slayings at Jackson State College.* Kent, Ohio: Kent State University Press, 1988.

POWELL, ADAM CLAYTON, JR. *Adam by Adam.* New York: Dial, 1971.

POWERS, RICHARD GID. *G-Men: Hoover's FBI in American Popular Culture.* Carbondale: Southern Illinois University Press, 1983.

———. *Secrecy and Power: The Life of J. Edgar Hoover.* New York: Free Press, 1987.

RAINES, HOWELL. *My Soul Is Rested: Movement Days in the Deep South Remembered.* New York: G. P. Putnam's Sons, 1977.

RAINES, JOHN C., ed. *Conspiracy.* New York: Harper and Row, 1975.

RECORD, WILSON, *The Negro and the Communist Party.* Chapel Hill: University of North Carolina Press, 1951.

———. *Race and Radicalism: The NAACP and the Communist Party in Conflict.* Ithaca, N.Y.: Cornell University Press, 1964.

RICHARDS, DAVID. *Played Out: The Jean Seberg Story.* New York: Random House, 1981.

ROBERTS, RANDY. *Papa Jack: Jack Johnson and the Era of White Hopes.* New York: Free Press, 1983.

ROBESON, PAUL. *Here I Stand.* New York: International Publishers, 1960.

ROSENMAN, SAMUEL, ed. *The Public Papers and Addresses of Franklin D. Roosevelt.* 13 vols. New York: Random House, 1938–1950.

ROTHSCHILD, MARY A. *A Case of Black and White: Northern Volunteers and the Southern Freedom Summers, 1964–1965.* Westport, Conn.: Greenwood, 1982.

ROVERE, RICHARD. *The Goldwater Caper.* New York: Harcourt, Brace and World, 1965.

ROWE, GARY THOMAS, JR. *My Undercover Years with the Ku Klux Klan.* New York: Bantam, 1976.

RUBIN, JERRY. *Do It!* New York: Simon and Schuster, 1970.

RUSTIN, BAYARD. *Down the Line.* Chicago: Quadrangle, 1971.

SALTER, JOHN R., JR. *Jackson, Mississippi.* Hicksville, N.Y.: Exposition Press, 1979.

SCHELL, JONATHAN. *The Time of Illusion.* New York: Knopf, 1976.

SCHLESINGER, ARTHUR M., JR. *Robert Kennedy and His Times.* Boston: Houghton Mifflin/Book Club ed., 1978.

———. *A Thousand Days.* Boston: Houghton Mifflin, 1965.

SEALE, BOBBY. *A Lonely Rage.* New York: Times Books, 1978.

SELLERS, CLEVELAND, with ROBERT TERRELL. *The River of No Return: The Autobiography of a Black Militant and the Life and Death of SNCC.* New York: Morrow, 1973.

SENTNER, DAVID. *How The FBI Gets Its Man.* New York: Avon Books, 1965.

SHAKUR, ASSATA. *Assata: An Autobiography.* Westport, Conn.: Lawrence Hill, 1987.

SHAPIRO, HERBERT. *White Violence and Black Response: From Reconstruction to Montgomery.* Amherst: University of Massachusetts Press, 1988.

SHEEHY, GAIL. *Panthermania.* New York: Harper and Row, 1971.

SHIPP, BILL. *Murder at Broad River Bridge.* Atlanta: Peachtree Publishers, 1981.

SILVER, JAMES W. *Mississippi: The Closed Society.* New York: Harcourt, Brace and World, 1963.

SIMS, PATSY. *The Klan.* New York: Stein and Day, 1978.

SITKOFF, HARVARD. *A New Deal for Blacks.* New York: Oxford University Press, 1978.

SMEAD, HOWARD. *Blood Justice: The Lynching of Mack Charles Parker.* New York: Oxford University Press, 1986.

STEIN, JUDITH. *The World of Marcus Garvey.* Baton Rouge: Louisiana State University Press, 1986.

SULLIVAN, WILLIAM C., with BILL BROWN. *The Bureau: My Thirty Years in Hoover's FBI.* New York: Norton, 1979.

SUTHERLAND, ELIZABETH, ed. *Letters from Mississippi.* New York: McGraw-Hill, 1965.

THEOHARIS, ATHAN. *The Boss: J. Edgar Hoover and the Great American Inquisition.* Philadelphia: Temple University Press, 1988.

———. *Spying on Americans.* Philadelphia: Temple University Press, 1978.

THOMPSON, KENNETH W., ed. *The Kennedy Presidency.* Lanham, Md.: University Press of America, 1985.

TULLY, ANDREW. *The FBI's Most Famous Cases.* New York: Morrow, 1965.

TURNER, WILLIAM W. *Hoover's F.B.I.* New York: Dell ed., 1971.

UNGAR, SANFORD J. *FBI.* Boston: Little, Brown, 1975.

VILLANO, ANTHONY, with GERALD ASTOR. *Brick Agent.* New York: Quadrangle/New York Times Book Co., 1977.

VON HOFFMAN, NICHOLAS. *Mississippi Notebook*. New York: David White, 1964.

WADE, WYN CRAIG. *The Fiery Cross*. New York: Simon and Schuster, 1987.

WARREN, ROBERT PENN. *Who Speaks for the Negro?* New York: Random House, 1965.

WASHBURN, PATRICK S. *A Question of Sedition: The Federal Government's Investigation of the Black Press during World War II*. New York: Oxford University Press, 1986.

WASHINGTON, JOSEPH R., JR., ed. *Jews in Black Perspectives*. Rutherford, N.J.: Fairleigh Dickinson University Press, 1984.

WASKOW, ARTHUR I. *From Race Riot to Sit-In: 1919 and the 1960s*. Garden City, N.Y: Doubleday, 1966.

WATTERS, PAT, and REESE CLEGHORN. *Climbing Jacob's Ladder*. New York: Harcourt, Brace and World, 1967.

———, and STEPHEN GILLERS, eds. *Investigating the FBI*. Garden City, N.Y.: Doubleday, 1973.

WEISS, NANCY. *Farewell to the Party of Lincoln: Black Politics in the Age of FDR*. Princeton: Princeton University Press, 1983.

———. *The National Urban League, 1910–1940*. New York: Oxford University Press, 1974.

WELCH, NEIL J., and DAVID W. MARSTON. *Inside Hoover's FBI*. Garden City, N.Y.: Doubleday, 1984.

WHEATON, ELIZABETH. *Codename GREENKILL: The 1979 Greensboro Killings*. Athens: University of Georgia Press, 1987.

WHITE, THEODORE H. *The Making of the President 1960*. New York: Atheneum, 1962.

———. *The Making of the President 1964*. New York: Atheneum, 1965.

WHITEHEAD, DON. *Attack on Terror*. New York: Funk and Wagnalls, 1970.

———. *The FBI Story*. New York: Pocket Books ed., 1958.

WHITFIELD, STEPHEN J. *A Death in the Delta: The Story of Emmett Till*. New York: Free Press, 1988.

WILKINS, ROGER. *A Man's Life*. New York: Simon and Schuster, 1982.

WILKINS, ROY, with TOM MATHEWS. *Standing Fast*. New York: Penguin Books ed., 1984.

WILLIAMS, ROBERT F. *Negroes With Guns*. Chicago: Third World Press ed., 1973.

WILLIAMS, WILLIAM APPLEMAN. *Empire as a Way of Life*. New York: Oxford University Press, 1982.

WILLS, GARRY. *The Kennedy Imprisonment*. Boston: Little, Brown, 1981.

———. *Nixon Agonistes*. New York: New American Library, 1971.

———. *Reagan's America: Innocents at Home*. Garden City, N.Y.: Doubleday, 1987.

WILSON, JAMES Q. *The Investigators*. New York: Basic Books, 1978.

WISE, DAVID. *The American Police State*. New York: Random House, 1976.

WOFFORD, HARRIS. *Of Kennedys and Kings*. New York: Farrar, Straus and Giroux, 1980.

WOLFE, TOM. *Radical Chic and Mau-mauing the Flak Catchers*. New York: Farrar, Straus and Giroux, 1970.

WOODWARD, C. VANN. *The Strange Career of Jim Crow*. 2d rev. ed. New York: Oxford University Press, 1966.

WRIGHT, RICHARD O., ed. *Whose FBI?* LaSalle, Ill.: Open Court, 1974.

YARBROUGH, TINSLEY E. *Judge Frank Johnson and Human Rights in Alabama.* University: University of Alabama Press, 1981.

ZANGRANDO, ROBERT L. *The NAACP Crusade Against Lynching, 1909–1950.* Philadelphia: Temple University Press, 1980.

ZAROULIS, NANCY, and GERALD SULLIVAN. *Who Spoke Up? American Protest Against the War in Vietnam, 1963–1975.* Garden City, N.Y.: Doubleday, 1984.

ZINN, HOWARD. *Albany.* Atlanta: Southern Regional Council, 1962.

——. *SNCC: The New Abolitionists.* Boston: Beacon, 1964.

——. *The Southern Mystique.* New York: Knopf, 1964.

Articles, Papers, Essays

BARRON, JOHN. "The FBI's Secret War Against the Ku Klux Klan." *Reader's Digest,* Jan. 1966, 87–92.

BELKNAP, MICHAL R. "The Vindication of Burke Marshall: The Southern Legal System and the Anti-Civil Rights Violence of the 1960s." *Emory Law Journal* 33(Winter 1984): 93–133.

BERGMAN, LOWELL, and DAVID WEIR. "Revolution on Ice: How the Black Panthers Lost the FBI's War of Dirty Tricks." *Rolling Stone,* Sept. 9, 1976, 41–49.

BERLET, CHIP. "Journalists and G-Men." *Chicago Reader,* June 12, 1978, 1, 8ff.

BILLINGTON, MONROE. "Lyndon B. Johnson and Blacks: The Early Years." *Journal of Negro History* 62(Jan. 1977): 26–42.

BOOKER, SIMEON. "J. Edgar Hoover—The Negro in the FBI." *Ebony,* Sept. 1962, 29–34.

BURNS, HAYWOOD. "The Federal Government and Civil Rights." In *Southern Justice,* ed. Leon Friedman, 228–54. New York: Random House, 1965.

CAPECI, DOMINIC J., JR. "The Lynching of Cleo Wright: Federal Protection of Constitutional Rights during World War II." *Journal of American History* 72(March 1986): 859–87.

CARSON, CLAYBORNE, JR. "Blacks and Jews in the Civil Rights Movement." In *Jews in Black Perspectives,* ed. Joseph R. Washington, Jr., 113–31. Rutherford, N.J.: Fairleigh Dickinson University Press, 1984. ·

COLES, ROBERT. "Social Struggle and Weariness." *Psychiatry,* 27(1964): 305–15.

COMMAGER, HENRY STEELE. "'To Form a Much Less Perfect Union.'" *New York Times Magazine,* July 14, 1963, 5ff.

CONE, JAMES H. "Martin Luther King, Jr., and the Third World." *Journal of American History* 74(Sept. 1987): 455–67.

CREWDSON, JOHN. "Seeing RED: An FBI 'Commie Hunter' Rebels at Illegal Tactics." *Chicago Tribune Magazine,* March 2, 1985, 8ff.

CROCE, ARLENE. "Backlash in New York?" *National Review,* Sept. 22, 1964, 816–17.

DEMUTH, JERRY. "'Tired of Being Sick and Tired' . . ." *The Nation,* June 1, 1964, 548–51.

DE TOLEDANO, RALPH. "A Negro Minority vs. a White Majority." *National Review,* Sept. 22, 1964, 814–15.

ELLIFF, JOHN T. "Aspects of Federal Civil Rights Enforcement: The Justice Department and the FBI, 1939–1964." *Perspectives in American History* 5(1971): 605–73.

EPSTEIN, EDWARD JAY. "The Panthers and the Police." *New Yorker*, Feb. 13, 1971, 45–77.

FAIRCLOUGH, ADAM. "Martin Luther King, Jr. and the War in Vietnam." *Phylon* 45(Spring 1984): 19–39.

FLEMING, HAROLD C. "The Federal Executive and Civil Rights: 1961–1965." *Daedalus* 94(Fall 1965): 921–48.

FREEMAN, J. LEIPER. "Investigating the Executive Intelligence." *Capitol Studies* 5 (Fall 1977): 103–18.

GLEN, JOHN M. "The Making of a Southern Radical: Myles Horton and the Highlander Folk School." *Southern Historian* 7(Spring 1986): 5–22.

GOODMAN, ERNEST. "The NLG, the FBI, and the Civil Rights Movement: 1964— A Year of Decision." *Guild Practitioner* 38(Winter 1981): 1–17.

GOODWIN, RICHARD N. "President Lyndon Johnson: The War Within." *New York Times Magazine*, Aug. 21, 1988, 35ff.

GRAHAM, HUGH DAVIS. "The Ambiguous Legacy of American Presidential Commissions." *Public Historian* 7(Spring 1985): 5–25.

———. "On Riots and Riot Commissions: Civil Disorders in the 1960s." *Public Historian* 2(Summer 1980): 7–27.

GREENBERG, GARY J. "Revolt at Justice." *Washington Monthly*, Dec. 1969, 32–40.

GREENE, JOHNNY. "Did the FBI Kill Viola Liuzzo?" *Playboy*, Oct. 1980, 100ff.

GREENFIELD, MEG. "Senator Goldwater and the Negro." *Reporter*, Oct. 8, 1964, 27–28.

GUTIÉRREZ, JOSE ANGEL. "Chicanos and Mexicans Under Surveillance: 1940–1980." *Renato Rosaldo Lecture Series Monograph* 2(Spring 1986): 29–58.

HACKER, ANDREW. "The States' Righters Still Wage War." *New York Times Magazine*, Oct. 21, 1962, 31ff.

HALISI, IMAMU CLYDE. "Maulana Ron Karenga: Black Leader in Captivity." *Black Scholar*, May 1972, 27–31.

HARRIS, LOUIS. "The 'Backlash' Issue." *Newsweek*, July 13, 1964, 24–27.

HART, JOHN. "Kennedy, Congress and Civil Rights." *Journal of American Studies* 13(Aug. 1979): 165–78.

HILL, ROBERT A. "'The Foremost Radical Among His Race': Marcus Garvey and the Black Scare, 1918–1921." *Prologue* 16(Winter 1984): 215–31.

HOOVER, HERBERT. "From Herbert Hoover on His 90th Birthday." *Reader's Digest*, Sept. 1964, 144.

HOOVER, J. EDGAR. "Off-the-Record Remarks." Informal Reception for Editors of Georgia and Michigan Newspapers, April 15, 1965, Washington, D.C.

———. "The Resurgent Klan." *American Bar Association Journal* 52 (July 1966): 617–20.

HOROWITZ, DAVID ALAN. "White Southerners' Alienation and Civil Rights: The Response to Corporate Liberalism." *Journal of Southern History* 54(May 1988): 173–200.

HOULDING, ANDREW. "The Wiring of New Haven." *The Nation*, June 7, 1980, 685–88.

HOWELL, LEON. "An Interview with Andrew Young." *Christianity and Crisis*, Feb. 16, 1976, 14–20.

KARENGA, M. "A Response to Muhammad Ahmad." *Black Scholar*, July–Aug. 1978, 55–57.

KIMBALL, PENN. "The History of *The Nation* According to the FBI." *The Nation,* March 22, 1986, 399–426.

KLIBANER, IRWIN. "The Travail of Southern Radicals: The Southern Conference Educational Fund, 1946–1976." *Journal of Southern History* 49(May 1983): 179–202.

KORNWEIBEL, THEODORE, JR. "Black on Black: The FBI's First Negro Agents and Informants and the Investigation of Black Radicalism during the Red Scare." Annual Meeting of the American Historical Association, Dec. 30, 1986, Chicago.

———. "The F.B.I. and White American Hegemony: The Campaign Against Marcus Garvey during the Red Scare." American Studies Convention, Nov. 2, 1985, San Diego.

———. "The FBI and Black America, 1917–1922." Annual Meeting of the Organization of American Historians, March 13, 1984, Los Angeles.

LICHTMAN, ALAN. "The Federal Assault Against Voting Discrimination." *Journal of Negro History* 54(Oct. 1969): 346–67.

LOVIN, HUGH T. "Lyndon B. Johnson, the Subversive Activities Control Board, and the Politics of Anti-Communism." *North Dakota Quarterly* 27(Winter 1986): 94–112.

———. "The Lyndon Johnson Administration and the Federal War on Subversion in the 1960s." *Presidential Studies Quarterly* 17(Summer 1987): 559–71.

McKNIGHT, GERALD D. "A Harvest of Hate: The FBI's War Against Black Youth—Domestic Intelligence in Memphis, Tennessee." *South Atlantic Quarterly* 86(Winter 1987): 1–21.

———. "The 1968 Memphis Sanitation Strike and the FBI: A Case Study in Urban Surveillance." *South Atlantic Quarterly* 83(Spring 1984): 138–56.

McMILLEN, NEIL R. "Black Enfranchisement in Mississippi: Federal Enforcement and Black Protest in the 1960s." *Journal of Southern History* 43(Aug. 1977): 351–72.

———. "Perry W. Howard, Boss of Black-and-Tan Republicanism in Mississippi, 1924–1960." *Journal of Southern History* 48(May 1982): 207–24.

MAY, RONALD R. "Genetics and Subversion." *The Nation,* May 16, 1960, 420–22.

MEIER, AUGUST, and ELLIOTT RUDWICK. "The First Freedom Ride." *Phylon* 30(Fall 1969): 213–22.

MILLER, CHAR, ed. "The Mississippi Summer Project Remembered: The Stephen Mitchell Bingham Letter." *Journal of Mississippi History* 47(Nov. 1985): 284–307.

MITGANG, HERBERT. "Annals of Government: Policing America's Writers." *New Yorker,* Oct. 5, 1987, 47ff.

NAVASKY, VICTOR. "The FBI's Wildest Dream." *The Nation,* June 17, 1978, 716–18.

O'REILLY, KENNETH. "The FBI and the Civil Rights Movement During the Kennedy Years: From the Freedom Rides to Albany." *Journal of Southern History* 54(May 1988): 201–32.

———. "The FBI and the Politics of the 1960s' Riots." *Journal of American History* 75(June 1988): 91–114.

———. "Herbert Hoover and the FBI." *Annals of Iowa* 47(Summer 1983): 46–63.

———. "A New Deal for the FBI: The Roosevelt Administration, Crime Control, and National Security." *Journal of American History* 69(Dec. 1982): 638–58.

————. "The Roosevelt Administration and Black America: Federal Surveillance Policy and Civil Rights During the New Deal and World War II Years." *Phylon* 48(March 1987): 12–25.

RABLE, GEORGE C. "The South and the Politics of Antilynching Legislation, 1920–1940." *Journal of Southern History* 51(May 1985): 201–20.

RAINES, HOWELL. "The Birmingham Bombing Twenty Years Later: The Case that Won't Close." *New York Times Magazine,* July 24, 1983, 12ff.

RICKS, JOHN A., III. "'De Lawd' Descends and Is Crucified: Martin Luther King, Jr., in Albany, Georgia." *Journal of Southwest Georgia History* 2(Fall 1984): 3–14.

ROWAN, CARL T. "Martin Luther King's Tragic Decision." *Reader's Digest,* Sept. 1967, 37–42.

SALISBURY, HARRISON E. "The Strange Correspondence of Morris Ernst and John Edgar Hoover, 1939–1964." *The Nation,* Dec. 1, 1984, 575–89.

SALTER, JOHN R., JR. "Reflections on Ralph Chaplin, the Wobblies, and Organizing in the Save the World Business—Then and Now." Unpublished paper. Dec. 1984.

SCHWERNER, NAT. "Mississippi: Whitewashing the FBI." *Rights,* April–May 1975, 15.

SHERRILL, ROBERT. "The Selling of the FBI." In *Investigating the FBI,* ed. Pat Watters and Stephen Gillers, 3–32. Garden City, N.Y.: Doubleday, 1973.

STONE, I. F. "The Schorr Case." *New York Review of Books,* April 1, 1976, 6–11.

TOLBERT, EMORY J. "Federal Surveillance of Marcus Garvey and the U.N.I.A." *Journal of Ethnic Studies* 14(Winter 1987): 25–47.

UNGAR, SANFORD J. "Among the Piranhas: A Journalist and the FBI." *Columbia Journalism Review,* Sept.–Oct. 1976, 19–27.

————. "The F.B.I. On the Defensive Again." *New York Times Magazine,* May 15, 1988, 46 ff.

WALL, ROBERT A. "Special Agent for the FBI." *New York Review of Books,* Jan. 27, 1972, 12–18.

WECHSLER, JAMES. "The FBI's Failure in the South." *Progressive,* Dec. 1963, 20–23.

WHEELER, RICHARD S. "Blacklash in California?" *National Review,* Sept. 22, 1964, 817.

WHITE, WALTER. "U.S. Department of (White) Justice." *Crisis,* Oct. 1935, 309–10.

WICKER, TOM. "What Have They Done Since They Shot Dillinger?" *New York Times Magazine,* Dec. 28, 1969, 4ff.

WILKINS, ROGER. "Chester Bowles." *The Nation,* June 14, 1986, 813.

WILLIAMS, DAVID. "The Bureau of Investigation and Its Critics, 1919–1921: The Origins of Federal Political Surveillance." *Journal of American History* 68(Dec. 1981): 560–79.

WILLS, GARRY. "Who Will Overcome?" *National Review,* Sept. 22, 1964, 818–20.

"The 'Backlash' Issue." *Newsweek,* July 13, 1964, 24.

"The Complete Collection of Political Documents Ripped-Off From the F.B.I. Office in Media, Pa." *WIN,* March 1972 (entire issue).

"Father and Son FBI Team." *Ebony,* July 1958, 46–47.

"FBI Agents in Action." *Ebony,* Oct. 1947, 9–13.

"The FBI and Civil Rights—J. Edgar Hoover Speaks Out." *U.S. News and World Report*, Nov. 30, 1964, 56–58.

"F.B.I. Report." *Commonweal*, Oct. 23, 1964, 119.

"Michigan's Cool Hand Luke." *National Review*, Nov. 7, 1986, 32.

"Mississippi Eyewitness." *Ramparts*, Summer 1964 (special issue).

"Mississippi Freedom Democratic Party and the Atlantic City Convention." Freedom Summer Reviewed Conference, Millsaps College, Nov. 2, 1979, Jackson.

"Opinion: 'Leave It to Experts.' " *Time*, Aug. 17, 1962, 18–19.

Government Documents

U.S. Commission on Civil Rights. *Law Enforcement: A Report on Equal Protection in the South.* Washington, D.C.: Government Printing Office, 1965.

———. *Report—Book 5, Justice.* Washington, D.C.: Government Printing Office, 1961.

U.S. Congress. Joint Committee on Internal Revenue Taxation. *Investigation of the Special Service Staff of the Internal Revenue Service.* 94th Cong., 1st sess., 1975.

U.S. Congress. Senate Committee on the Judiciary and House Committee on Post Office and Civil Service. *Joint Hearings on Martin Luther King, Jr., National Holiday, S.25.* 96th Cong., 1st sess., 1979.

U.S. Congress. House. Committee on Appropriations. Subcommittee on Departments of State and Justice, the Judiciary, and Related Agencies. *Hearings.* 87th Cong., 1st sess.-92d Cong., 1st sess., 1961–1971.

U.S. Congress. House. Committee on Internal Security. *Hearings on Domestic Intelligence Operations for Internal Security Purposes.* 93d Cong., 2d sess., 1974.

———. *Revolutionary Target: American Penal System.* H.Rept. 738. 93d Cong., 1st sess., 1973.

U.S. Congress. House. Committee on the Judiciary. *Hearings Before the Special Subcommittee to Investigate the Department of Justice.* 83d Cong., 1st sess., 1953.

———. *Statement of Information—Book VII, White House Surveillance and Campaign Activities.* 93d Cong., 2d sess., 1974.

U.S. Congress. House. Committee on Un-American Activities. *Communist Infiltration and Activities in Newark, N.J.* 85th Cong., 2d sess., 1958.

———. *Hearings on Bills to Make Punishable Assistance to Enemies of U.S. in Time of Undeclared War.* Pts. 1–2. 89th Cong., 2d sess., 1966.

U.S Congress. House. Select Committee on Assassinations. *Hearings on Investigation of the Assassination of Martin Luther King, Jr.* Vols. 1, 6–7. 95th Cong., 2d sess., 1978.

U.S. Congress. House. Select Committee on Intelligence. *Hearings on Domestic Intelligence Programs.* Pt. 3. 94th Cong., 1st sess., 1975.

U.S. Congress. Senate. *Memorial Tributes to J. Edgar Hoover in the Congress of the United States and Various Articles and Editorials Relating to His Life and Work.* 94th Cong., 2d sess., 1974.

U.S. Congress. Senate. Committee on Government Operations. Permanent Subcommittee on Investigations. *Hearings on Riots, Civil and Criminal Disorders.* Pts. 1–25. 90th Cong. 1st sess.-91st Cong., 2d sess, 1967–1970.

U.S. Congress. Senate. Committee on the Judiciary. Subcommittee on Constitutional Rights. *Hearings on FBI Counterintelligence Programs*. 93d Cong., 2d sess., 1974.

——. *Political Intelligence in the Internal Revenue Service*. 93d Cong., 2d sess., 1974.

U.S. Congress. Senate. Select Committee on Intelligence. *Hearings on National Intelligence Reorganization and Reform Act of 1978*. 95th Cong., 2d sess., 1978.

U.S. Congress. Senate. Select Committee to Study Governmental Operations with Respect to Intelligence Activities. *Final Report—Book II, Intelligence Activities and the Rights of Americans*. 94th Cong., 2d sess., 1976.

——. *Final Report—Book III, Supplementary Detailed Staff Reports on Intelligence Activities and the Rights of Americans*. 94th Cong., 2d sess., 1976.

——. *Hearings—Federal Bureau of Investigation*. Vol. 6. 94th Cong., 1st sess., 1975.

——. *Hearings—Mail Opening*. Vol. 4. 94th Cong., 1st sess., 1975.

U.S. Department of Justice. Investigation Activities of the Department of Justice. S. Doc. 153, 66th Cong., 1st sess., 1919.

——. *Prison Gangs: Their Extent, Nature, and Impact on Prisons*. Washington, D.C.: Government Printing Office, 1986.

——. *Report of the Department of Justice Task Force to Review the FBI Martin Luther King, Jr., Security and Assassination Investigations*. Washington, D.C.: Government Printing Office, 1977.

U.S. National Advisory Commission on Civil Disorders. *Report of the National Advisory Commission on Civil Disorders*. New York: Bantam ed., 1968.

U.S. National Advisory Commission on Selective Service. *In Pursuit of Equity*. Washington, D.C.: Government Printing Office, 1967.

U.S. National Commission on the Causes and Prevention of Violence. Task Force on Historical and Comparative Perspectives. *Violence in America*. Ed. Hugh Davis Graham and Ted Robert Gurr. New York: Signet ed., 1969.

——. Task Force on Violent Aspects of Protest and Confrontation. *The Politics of Protest*. Under the direction of Jerome H. Skolnick. New York: Simon and Schuster ed., 1969.

U.S. President's Commission on Campus Unrest. *The Report of the President's Commission on Campus Unrest*. Washington, D.C.: Government Printing Office, 1970.

U.S. President's Committee on Civil Rights. *To Secure These Rights*. New York: Simon and Schuster ed., 1947.

Other Government Documents and Records

Bureau of Investigation Files, 1908–1922. Record Group 65. National Archives. Washington, D.C.
  Bureau Section Files.
  Mexican Files.
  Miscellaneous Files.
  Old German Files.
Central Intelligence Agency Files.
  H. Rap Brown File.
  HTLINGUAL Files.
  RESISTANCE/Black Student Unions File.

Department of Justice Files. Record Group 60. National Archives.
　　Washington, D.C.
　　Numerical Files.
　　Abraham Glasser File.
　　Perry Howard File.
Department of State Files. Record Group 59. National Archives.
Federal Bureau of Investigation Files and Records (Freedom of Information
　　Act and other releases; including partial releases).
　　Agent's Handbook.
　　Agitator Index Files.
　　Alabama Freedom Rider Files.
　　American Civil Liberties Union (ACLU) File.
　　American Indian Movement (AIM) File.
　　James E. Amos Personnel File.
　　Walter and Frances Bergman Freedom Rider Files.
　　Birmingham Sixteenth Street Baptist Church Bombing (BAPBOMB) File.
　　Black Nationalist Photograph Album File.
　　Black Panther Party File.
　　Black Student Groups on College Campuses File.
　　Alvin J. Bronstein File.
　　Bureau Bulletin File.
　　Archibald J. Carey, Jr., File.
　　Civil Rights Policy File.
　　Clergy and Laity Concerned About Vietnam File.
　　Committee for Public Justice (CPJ) File.
　　Communist Influence Racial Matters (CIRM) File.
　　Communist Party of the United States of America—Negro Question File.
　　Computerized Telephone Number File.
　　Congress of Racial Equality (CORE) File.
　　Courtney Ryley Cooper File.
　　Counterintelligence Program (COINTEL) File.
　　　　Black Nationalist Subfile.
　　　　Communist Party, United States, Subfile.
　　　　New Left Subfile.
　　　　Puerto Rican Nationalists Subfile.
　　　　Special Operations Subfile.
　　　　White Hate Group Subfile.
　　Deacons for Defense and Justice File.
　　Desegregation of Jackson Business Establishments and Public Facili-
　　　　ties File.
　　Detroit Race Riot Files (1943 and 1967).
　　Dissemination of Information Policy File.
　　W. E. B. Du Bois File.
　　James O. Eastland File.
　　Wallace D. Fard File.
　　Filing and Records Procedures (microfilm; Scholarly Resources).
　　Five Percenters File.
　　James Forman File.
　　Fred Hampton Files.
　　Highlander Folk School File.
　　Julius Hobson File.
　　J. Edgar Hoover Official and Confidential Files.
　　　　Inga Arvad Folder.
　　　　Civil Rights and Domestic Violence Folder.
　　　　Martin Dies Folder.

FBI Directorship Folder.
FBI Television Series Agreement Folder.
Intelligence Coverage, Domestic and Foreign Folder.
Lyndon B. Johnson Folder.
John F. Kennedy Folder.
Martin Luther King, Jr., Folder.
George McGovern Folder.
Microphone Surveillances Folder.
John Mitchell Folder.
Press Media Campaign Against Director Folder.
Riots Summer 1964 Folder.
Adlai Stevenson Folder.
Other folders: 8, 9, 14, 76, 83, 96, 128, 131, 136, 142, 151, 161, and 163.
J. Edgar Hoover Personnel File.
House Committee on Un-American Activities (HUAC) File.
Hosea Hudson File.
Hubert H. Humphrey File.
Jesse Jackson File.
Hakim Abdullan Jamal File.
June Mail File.
Robert F. Kennedy File.
Kent State File.
Muhammad Kenyatta File.
Martin Luther King, Jr., File.
Martin Luther King, Jr., Assassination File.
Gerald Kirk File.
Law Enforcement Assistance Administration (LEAA) File.
David Lawrence File.
Stanley Levison File.
Fulton Lewis, Jr., File.
Little Rock, Arkansas, School Desegregation File.
Viola Liuzzo File.
Huey Long File.
Allard K. Lowenstein File.
Alan McSurely Files.
Malcolm X File.
Manual of Instruction (1927, 1936, 1941, and 1978 editions, microfilm; Scholarly Resources).
Media Burglary (MEDBURG) File.
Medical Committee for Human Rights File.
Mississippi Burning (MIBURN) File.
Montgomery Improvement Association (MIA) File.
R. Dhoruba Moore Files.
Moorish Science Temple of America File.
Elijah Muhammad File.
National Association for the Advancement of Colored People (NAACP) File.
National Black Economic Development Conference File.
National Lawyers Guild (NLG) Files.
National Negro Congress File.
National Urban League File.
Louis B. Nichols Official and Confidential Files.
American Youth Congress Folder.
Hugh H. Clegg Folder.
Thomas E. Dewey Folder.
Dwight D. Eisenhower Folder.

Morris L. Ernst Folder.
James M. McInerney Folder.
Misc. A-Z Folder.
Kermit Roosevelt Folder.
Operation Breadbasket File.
Fulton Oursler File.
Jesse Owens File.
Westbrook Pegler File.
Lemuel Penn File.
PUSH File.
Rabble Rouser Index File.
Racial Digest File.
Racial Matters Policy File.
Responsibilities Program File.
Revolutionary Union File.
Paul Robeson File.
Howard Rushmore File.
John R. Salter, Jr., File.
Jean Seberg File.
Security Index File.
Senate Internal Security Subcommittee (SISS) File.
Clarence 13X Smith File.
George Sokolsky File.
Southern Christian Leadership Conference (SCLC) File.
Southern Conference Educational Fund (SCEF) File.
Special Agent in Charge (SAC) Letter File.
Stop Index/National Crime Information Center File.
Student Nonviolent Coordinating Committee (SNCC) File.
Clyde Tolson Memo File.
Clyde Tolson Personnel File.
Walter White File.
Don Whitehead File.
Roy Wilkins File.
Frank Wilkinson File.
Lyle Wilson File.
Walter Winchell File.
Whitney Young File.
Misc. Files.
    62-116758.
    62-117166.
    157-6160.
Federal Bureau of Investigation Monographs and Reports.
    "Certain Governors' Comments on Civil Rights Investigations" (1953).
    "Civil Rights and Domestic Violence: A Summary" (1947).
    "Communism and the Negro Movement—A Current Analysis" (1963).
    "The Communist Party and the Negro" (1953 and 1956).
    "Communist Party, USA—Negro Question" (1963).
    "Integration in Public Schools, Little Rock" (1958).
    "The Nation of Islam" (1960 and 1965).
    "Prevention and Control of Riots" (1965).
    "Racial Disturbances" (1967).
    "Student Nonviolent Coordinating Committee" (1967).
    "Survey of Racial Conditions in the United States" (1943).
    "Weaknesses of the Communist Party, USA" (1956).
Federal Surveillance of Afro-Americans (1917–1925): The First World War, the

Red Scare, and the Garvey Movement (microfilm; University Publications of America).
Internal Revenue Service Files (Freedom of Information Act and other releases).
Alan McSurely Files.
Special Service Staff Files.
Military Intelligence Division Files. Record Group 165 (War Department). National Archives.

Manuscripts

Albany Movement Records. Martin Luther King, Jr., Center for Nonviolent Social Change. Atlanta.
Americans for Democratic Action Papers. State Historical Society of Wisconsin. Madison.
Bruce Barton Papers. State Historical Society of Wisconsin.
Randolph Battle Papers. King Center.
Berl Bernhard Papers. John Fitzgerald Kennedy Library. Boston.
Francis Biddle Papers. Franklin D. Roosevelt Library. Hyde Park, New York.
Albert Boutwell Papers. Birmingham Public Library. Alabama.
Carl and Anne Braden Papers. State Historical Society of Wisconsin.
Brotherhood of Sleeping Car Porters Records. Library of Congress. Washington, D.C.
Tom Clark Papers. Harry S. Truman Library. Independence, Missouri.
Congress of Racial Equality Papers. King Center.
Congress of Racial Equality Papers. State Historical Society of Wisconsin.
Eugene "Bull" Connor Papers. Birmingham Public Library.
Council of Federated Organizations Papers. State Historical Society of Wisconsin.
Dwight D. Eisenhower Papers. Dwight D. Eisenhower Library. Abilene, Kansas.
Office of the Special Assistant for National Security Affairs.
Ann Whitman File.
Gerald R. Ford Papers. Gerald R. Ford Library. Ann Arbor, Michigan.
Congressional Papers.
Office of Domestic Council.
 Geoffrey Shepard Files.
 Edward C. Schmults Files.
White House Central File.
William C. Hamilton Papers. Birmingham Public Library.
Arthur J. Hanes Papers. Birmingham Public Library.
Herbert Hoover Papers. Herbert Hoover Presidential Library. West Branch, Iowa.
Post-Presidential Papers.
Presidential Papers.
President's Secretary's File.
Hosea Hudson–Nell Irvin Painter Papers. Southern Oral History Collection.
Southern Historical Collection. University of North Carolina, Chapel Hill.
Richard H. Ichord Papers. Western Historical Manuscripts Collection/State Historical Society of Missouri Manuscripts. Columbia.
Lyndon B. Johnson Papers. Lyndon Johnson Library. Austin, Texas.
Administrative Histories.

Department of Justice.
Federal Bureau of Investigation.
National Security File.
White House Aides Files.
James Gaither.
Harry McPherson.
Mike Manatos.
William Moyers.
Larry Temple.
Marvin Watson.
Lee C. White.
White House Central File.
John F. Kennedy Papers. Kennedy Library.
Office Files.
White House Central File.
Robert F. Kennedy Papers. Kennedy Library.
C. B. King Papers. King Center.
Edwin King Papers. Tougaloo College. Tougaloo, Mississippi.
Martin Luther King, Jr., Papers. King Center.
Slater King Papers. King Center.
Burke Marshall Papers. Kennedy Library.
Mississippi Freedom Democratic Party Papers. King Center.
Henry Morgenthau, Jr., Papers. Roosevelt Library.
Karl E. Mundt Papers. Dakota State College. Madison, South Dakota.
National Advisory Commission on Civil Disorders Records. Johnson Library.
National Association for the Advancement of Colored People Papers. Library
of Congress.
National Lawyers Guild Papers. New York.
Richard M. Nixon Papers. Nixon Presidential Materials Project. National Ar-
chives. Washington, D.C.
White House Special Files.
Charles W. Colson.
John Dean.
John D. Ehrlichman.
H. R. Haldeman.
Egil Krogh.
White House Central File.
G. Bromley Oxnam Papers. Library of Congress.
Scott J. Rafferty Papers. Kennedy Library.
Michael Raoul-Duval Papers. Ford Library.
Franklin D. Roosevelt Papers. Roosevelt Library.
Official File.
President's Personal File.
Richard B. Russell Papers. Richard B. Russell Memorial Library. University
of Georgia. Athens.
John R. Salter, Jr., Papers. Mississippi Department of Archives and History.
Jackson.
Theodore Sorensen Papers. Kennedy Library.
Southern Christian Leadership Conference Papers. King Center.

Southern Regional Council Archives. Atlanta University Center.
Jeremiah Stamler Papers. State Historical Society of Wisconsin.
Student Nonviolent Coordinating Committee Papers. King Center.
Walter Trohan Papers. Hoover Library.
Harry S. Truman Papers. Truman Library.
  Confidential File.
  President's Secretary's File.
Thomas J. Walsh Papers. Library of Congress.
William Allen White Papers. Library of Congress.
Alexander Wiley Papers. State Historical Society of Wisconsin.
Roy Wilkins Papers. Library of Congress.

Interviews and Oral Histories

Aptheker, Herbert. Feb. 5, 1987 (phone), San Jose, Calif.
Aschenbrenner, Lawrence. Sept. 9, 1987, Anchorage.
Baker, Donald M. July 21, 1986, Washington, D.C.
Barrett, St. John. July 21, 1986, Washington, D.C.
Barry, Marion. By Katherine Shannon, Oct. 3, 1967. Marion Barry Oral History. Ralph J. Bunche Oral History Collection. Moorland-Spingarn Research Center. Howard University. Washington, D.C.
Bates, Charles W. Aug. 14, 1986 (phone).
Bernhard, Berl. July 23, 1986, Washington, D.C.
——. By John Stewart, June 17, 1968. Berl Bernhard Oral History. John F. Kennedy Library. Boston.
Bookbinder, Hyman. July 9, 1986, Washington, D.C.
Braden, Anne. Feb. 5, 1987 (phone), Louisville, Ky.
Branton, Wiley. July 20, 1987 (phone), Washington, D.C.
Cheek, Marion E. July 2, 1986 (phone).
Clark, Kenneth B. April 8, 1987 (phone), Hastings-on-Hudson, N.Y.
Clark, Ramsey. Oct. 26, 1987 (phone), New York.
——. By T. H. Baker, Oct. 30, 1968, Feb. 11, March 21, April 16, and June 3, 1969. Ramsey Clark Oral History. Lyndon B. Johnson Library. Austin, Tex.
Clifford, Clark. By Larry J. Hackman, Feb. 4, 1975. Clark Clifford Oral History. Kennedy Library.
Cobb, Charles. July 20, 1987, Washington, D.C.
Dean, Kenneth. Sept. 14, 1987 (phone).
Derian, Patt. July 14, 1987, Washington, D.C.
Doar, John. Jan. 14, 1987 (phone), New York.
——. By Scott J. Rafferty, Jan. 26, 1976. Scott J. Rafferty Papers. Kennedy Library.
Dunbar, Leslie. Sept. 2, 1986 (phone), Pelham, New York.
Durr, Virginia. Feb. 12, 1987 (phone), Montgomery, Ala.
Eastland, James O. By Joe B. Frantz, Feb. 19, 1971. James O. Eastland Oral History. Johnson Library.
Eddy, Bob. Jan. 26, 1987 (phone), Mobile, Ala.
Ehrlichman, John. Feb. 16, 1987 (phone), Santa Fe, N.M.

Evans, Courtney A. July 25, 1986 (phone), Washington, D.C.

Evers, Charles. Sept. 18, 1987 (phone), Fayette, Miss.

——. By John Jones, Feb. 10, 1981. Charles Evers Oral History. Mississippi Department of Archives and History. Jackson.

Farmer, James. By Paige Mulhollan, July 20, 1971. James Farmer Oral History. Johnson Library.

Fleischer, Hugh. Jan. 16, 1987, Anchorage.

Fleming, Harold. July 15, 1987, Washington, D.C.

Forman, James. July 24, 1986, Washington, D.C.

Greenberg, Jack. Sept. 10, 1987 (phone), New York.

Griswold, Erwin. July 9, 1987, Washington, D.C.

——. By Scott J. Rafferty, Oct. 29, 1975. Rafferty Papers.

Guthman, Edwin O. Jan. 14, 1987 (phone), Philadelphia, Penn.

Guyot, Lawrence. July 10, 1987, Washington, D.C.

Hamer, Fannie Lou. By Robert Wright, Aug. 9, 1968. Fanny Hamer Oral History. Bunche Collection.

Hanes, Arthur J. Feb. 4, 1987 (phone), Birmingham, Ala.

Heim, Lawrence J. July 23, 1986.

Henry, Aaron. By John Dittmer and John Jones, April 22, 1981. Aaron Henry Oral History. Mississippi Archives.

Hobson, Tina C. July 13, 1988, Washington, D.C.

Holtzman, Elizabeth. Aug. 19, 1988 (phone), Brooklyn.

Johnson, June. July 15, 1987, Washington, D.C.

Karenga, Maulana. Jan. 13, 1987 (phone), Los Angeles.

Katzenbach, Nicholas deB. Aug. 13, 1986 (phone), Morristown, N.J.

——. By Paige Mulhollan, Nov. 11 and 12, and Dec. 11, 1968. Nicholas deB. Katzenbach Oral History. Johnson Library.

Kennedy, Robert F., and Burke Marshall. By Anthony Lewis, Dec. 4, 6, and 22, 1964. Robert F. Kennedy and Burke Marshall Oral Histories. Kennedy Library.

King, C. B. Jan. 14, 1987 (phone), Albany, Ga.

——. By Stanley Smith, Aug. 1968. C. B. King Oral History. Bunche Collection.

King, Edwin. April 20, 1986 (phone), Jackson, Miss.

King, Slater. By Stanley Smith, Aug. 1968. Slater King Oral History. Bunche Collection.

Leinbaugh, Harold P. July 24, 1986.

Leonard, Jerris. July 10, 1986, Washington, D.C.

——. By Robert Wright, Feb. 11, 1970. Jerris Leonard Oral History. Bunche Collection.

Lewis, John. July 21, 1987, Washington, D.C.

——. By Katherine Shannon, Aug. 22, 1967. John Lewis Oral History. Bunche Collection.

McGowan, Clement L., Jr. July 9, 1986.

McKissick, Floyd. Sept. 22, 1987 (phone), Oxford, N.C.

McPherson, Harry C., Jr. July 21, 1987, Washington, D.C.

McSurely, Alan. July 23, 1984, Amherst, Mass.

Mallory, Mae. By Malaika Lumumba, Feb. 27, 1970. Mae Mallory Oral History. Bunche Collection.

Marshall, Burke. June 18, 1986 (phone), New Haven, Conn.

——. By T. H. Baker, Oct. 28, 1968. Burke Marshall Oral History. Johnson Library.

——. By Robert Wright, Feb. 27, 1970. Burke Marshall Oral History. Bunche Collection.

May, Edgar. Sept. 12, 1987 (phone), Springfield, Vt.

Moore, Roy K. Aug. 13, 1986 (phone).

Moses, Robert. Sept. 11, 1987 (phone), Boston.

Pritchett, Laurie. July 2, 1986 (phone), Southmont, N.C.

Raby, Kenneth N. July 3, 1986 (phone).

Rauh, Joseph L., Jr. July 10, 1986, Washington, D.C.

——. By Paige Mulhollan, July 30, and Aug. 1 and 8, 1969. Joseph L. Rauh, Jr., Oral History. Johnson Library.

Reedy, George. April 20, 1982, Milwaukee.

Roche, John P. Sept. 16, 1986 (phone), Boston.

Rusk, Dean. By Hugh Gordon Cates, Feb. 22, 1977. Dean Rusk Oral History. Richard B. Russell Memorial Library. University of Georgia. Athens.

Rustin, Bayard. Jan. 22, 1987 (phone), New York.

——. By T. H. Baker, June 17 and 30, 1969. Bayard Rustin Oral History. Johnson Library.

Sanders, Harold Barefoot. Oct. 27, 1987 (phone), Dallas.

Schwerner, Nathan. Sept. 2, 1986 (phone), Pelham, N.Y.

Seigenthaler, John. Jan. 16, 1987 (phone), Washington, D.C.

——. By Robert Campbell, July 10, 1968. John Seigenthaler Oral History. Bunche Collection.

Sherrod, Charles. Feb. 2, 1987 (phone), Albany, Ga.

Shriver, Sargent. July 25, 1986, Washington, D.C.

Sitton, Claude. Sept. 18, 1987 (phone), Raleigh, N.C.

Stone, C. Sumner, Jr. Aug. 29, 1986 (phone), Philadelphia, Pa.

Sullivan, Joseph A. Aug. 18, 1986 (phone).

Taylor, G. Flint. Sept. 16, and Oct. 16, 1987 (phone), Chicago.

Taylor, William L. July 18, 1986, Washington, D.C.

Thomas, Robert. Jan. 15, 1987 (phone), Albany, Ga.

Trebach, Arnold. July 12, 1988, Washington, D.C.

Tyler, Harold R., Jr. April 1, 1987 (phone), New York.

Watson, Marvin. Sept. 16, 1987 (phone), Dallas.

White, Lee C. July 9, 1987, Washington, D.C.

Wilkins, Roger. Aug. 8, 1986 (phone), Washington, D.C.

Wilkins, Roy. By T. H. Baker. April 1, 1969. Roy Wilkins Oral History. Johnson Library.

Wilkinson, Frank. Oct. 17, 1986, Anchorage.

Williams, Calvin. Feb. 7, 1987, Anchorage.

Williams, Robert F. By James Mosby, July 22, 1970. Robert F. Williams Oral History. Bunche Collection.

Wofford, Harris. By Larry J. Hackman, Feb. 3, 1969. Harris Wofford Oral History. Kennedy Library.

Young, Andrew. By T. H. Baker, June 18, 1970. Andrew Young Oral History. Johnson Library.

Index